Introducing
Human Resource Management

Visit the *Introducing Human Resource Management Fifth Edition* Companion Website at **www.pearsoned.co.uk/foothook** to find valuable **student** learning material including:

- A variety of tests for every chapter, including multiple-choice, fill in the blank, and true/false questions as well as crosswords and word puzzles

- Answers are provided to help you check your understanding

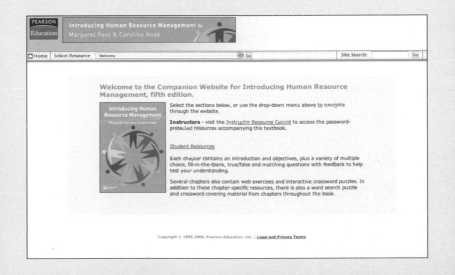

We work with leading authors to develop the strongest
educational materials in human resources, bringing
cutting-edge thinking and best learning practice to a
global market.

Under a range of well-known imprints, including
Financial Times Prentice Hall, we craft high quality print
and electronic publications which help readers to
understand and apply their content, whether studying
or at work.

To find out more about the complete range of our
publishing, please visit us on the World Wide Web at:
www.pearsoned.co.uk

Introducing
Human Resource
Management

Fifth Edition

Margaret Foot
Caroline Hook

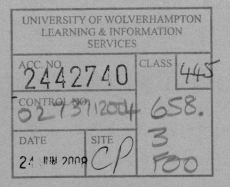

FT Prentice Hall
FINANCIAL TIMES

An imprint of **Pearson Education**
Harlow, England • London • New York • Boston • San Francisco • Toronto
Sydney • Tokyo • Singapore • Hong Kong • Seoul • Taipei • New Delhi
Cape Town • Madrid • Mexico City • Amsterdam • Munich • Paris • Milan

Pearson Education Limited

Edinburgh Gate
Harlow
Essex CM20 2JE
England

and Associated Companies throughout the world

Visit us on the World Wide Web at:
www.pearsoned.co.uk

_____

First published under the Longman Group Limited imprint 1996
Second edition published under the Addison Wesley Longman imprint 1999
Third edition published 2002
Fourth edition published 2005
Fifth edition published 2008

ISBN 978-0-273-71200-8

British Library Cataloguing-in-Publication Data
A catalogue record for this book is available from the British Library

Library of Congress Cataloging-in-Publication Data
Foot, Margaret, 1949–
   Introducing human resource management / Margaret Foot, Caroline
Hook.—5th ed.
      p. cm.
   Includes bibliographical references and index.
   ISBN-13: 978-0-273-71200-8 (alk. paper)
1. Personnel management. 2. Employee rights. I. Hook, Caroline, 1946– II. Title.
   HF5549.F5875 2008
   658.3—dc22

                                         2008003521

10 9 8 7 6 5 4 3 2 1
12 11 10 09 08

Typeset in 9.5/13 Giovanni by 73
Printed and bound by Rotolito Lombarda, Milan, Italy

The publisher's policy is to use paper manufactured from sustainable forests.

Brief contents

Contents

Supporting resources

Visit **www.pearsoned.co.uk/foothook** to find valuable online resources

Companion Website for students

- A variety of tests for every chapter, including multiple-choice, fill in the blank, and true/false questions as well as crosswords and word puzzles
- Answers are provided to help you check your understanding

For instructors

- Complete, downloadable Instructor's Manual including case study notes
- PowerPoint slides that can be downloaded and used for presentations

Also: The [regularly maintained] Companion Website provides the following features:

- Search tool to help locate specific items of content
- E-mail results and profile tools to send results of quizzes to instructors
- Online help and support to assist with website usage and troubleshooting

For more information please contact your local Pearson Education sales representative or visit **www.pearsoned.co.uk/foothook**

Quick guide to employment legislation and related documents

Preface

Managing people is an important part of all managers' jobs whether they are line managers or HR specialists. Successful management and leadership make a huge difference to the performance of teams and to the achievement of strategic objectives. We have written this book primarily as an introductory text for students who are working towards management positions and who have started their career strategy by studying for a degree such as a BA in HRM, Business Studies or Business Management. It is also suitable for students on a Higher National Diploma or a foundation degree programme in Management or Business Studies. Students on the Chartered Institute of Personnel and Development's professional courses will also find this text useful, especially for the Management and Leadership module or for the Certificate in Personnel Practice. The textbook has also proven its worth in the workplace. Students on business placements and graduates in their first jobs have reported back to us that they turn to the book for a quick and accessible review of a variety of people management concepts.

The content represents an introduction to the philosophical and legal framework of people management strategies aimed at achieving a high-performance workplace. The book further examines the basic operational areas and good practice associated with HRM. Chapter 1 provides an overview of current issues in the field of HR, which are taken up in more detail in the rest of the book. Chapters 2–5 review aspects of strategy and the philosophy and legal underpinnings of people management, including an exploration of employment relations issues such as the psychological contract and employee engagement. Together with in-depth coverage of equality and diversity, the discussion of these issues provides a background to the areas dealt with in Chapters 6–12. Here we focus on the functional areas that, if executed well, can add value for both employers and employees. We examine strategic and good practice issues in recruitment, selection, performance management, learning and development, reward systems, and health, safety and welfare. The final two chapters consider how to deal with situations where problems develop in the employer–employee relationship with an examination of discipline, grievance, dismissal, redundancy and outplacement. This new, fifth edition, also offers a regular review of cross-cultural or international aspects of HRM.

The book is divided into 14 chapters to provide a topic each week for a modular course, but if your tutor wishes to involve you in more skills development work, or to go into these areas in more detail, the subject matter in the chapters may be spread over two terms. Each chapter starts with a list of objectives. These are important as they list the concepts that you should know or the skills you should be able to apply by the time you have finished the chapter. When you have finished the chapter, look back at the objectives and ensure that you have achieved them.

We intend that you should become actively involved in your own learning as you progress through the book, and to this end, as well as the list of learning objectives, there are activities for you to undertake and opportunities to pause and think about issues raised in each chapter. We recommend that you have a pen and paper beside you as you read the book, so that you can complete the activities. Reflection is important, so resist any temptation to skip these exercises.

Discussion about specific points raised in the activities is often an integral part of the text, but we have also occasionally referred you to the companion website for our thoughts on these issues. This should encourage you to think things through on your own first, and using the website should provide some variety in your approaches to learning. There are short-answer or multiple-choice questions at the end of each chapter so that you can check your own understanding and go back, if necessary, to points that you may not be clear about. There are also review questions and activities designed to help you examine key learning points in more depth. As an innovation in this edition, we have included an article from the *Financial Times* in each chapter to provide some real-life scenarios and information relevant to the concepts introduced there, together with suggested questions to stimulate discussion. Your tutor should have a further set of activities and case studies to help with the main learning points in each chapter, and you can gain further practice by trying out the exercises on the companion website at **www.pearsoned.co.uk/foothook**. You can also take your studies to a higher level by trying out the 'What next?' exercise at the end of each chapter.

The Fabric Brothers, Recovery Insurance Group, Spartan Insurance Company, Shepley Computers and the Sheffley Company, which appear in activities and case studies in this text, are fictional organisations. The scenarios are based on real-life situations, but none of the people or organisations named in them actually exists. Details have been drawn together from a number of events to create totally fictional, although realistic, situations. Real organisations are, however, mentioned in the text, particularly where they serve as examples of good practice, and the *Financial Times* articles obviously describe real-life people, events and organisations.

Margaret Foot and Caroline Hook
March 2008

Publisher's acknowledgements

We are grateful to the Financial Times Limited for permission to reprint the following material:

Chapter 2 Jobs without borders, © *FT.com*, 25 October 2007; Chapter 3 It's better if they give a damn, © *FT.com*, 10 August 2006; Chapter 7 Call to raise job interview standards, © *Financial Times*, 4 October 2007; Chapter 12 Health and safety red tape, © *Financial Times*, 6 October 2007; Chapter 12 Union hits at labour safety stance, © *Financial Times*, 29 October 2007; Chapter 14 OECD warns of unfair dismissal lawsuits discouraging French job creation, © *Financial Times*, 31 March 2006;

We are grateful to the following for permission to use copyright material:

Chapter 4 No harm in asking for flexible working hours from *FT.com*, 18 February 2007, © Geoff Armstrong; Chapter 5 Gender equality: a solid business case at last from *FT.com*, 28 October 2007, © Lynda Gratton and Lamia Walker; Chapter 6 Computer says: You're hired from *FT.com*, 7 November 2007, © Jessica Twentyman; Chapter 9 Tools help staff see the effects of effort, *The Financial Times Limited*, 7 November 2007, © Sam Hiser; Chapter 10 Keeping managers sane and ahead of the game from *The Financial Times Limited*, 12 November 2007, © Rod Newing.

Guided tour

Introducing human resource management

Objectives

By the end of this chapter you will be able to:

● define what is meant by the term 'human resource management'
● outline the historical development of human resource management
● understand the roles of line managers and human resource managers in managing people
● outline the range of activities with which practitioners of human resource management are likely to be involved
● demonstrate how human resource management can make a difference by adding value to an organisation
● outline some of the current issues facing HR managers.

HRM? What's it all about?

This book is designed as an introductory text for students studying human resource management (HRM) either with a view to becoming HR specialists themselves, or for those who are starting or hoping to start a career in management. As you will discover, people management forms a large part of every manager's job, whether they work in a large multinational organisation, a not for profit organisation or a small charity. Organisations also increasingly aim for all employees to be engaged, so an understanding of the subject is important for everyone.

As stated in the preface, we intend that you should become actively involved in your own learning as you progress through the book. Even though you are just beginning this subject, you may already have ideas about some of the topics that you are about to study and you may even have a general idea of the role and functions of the human resource management or personnel department in an organisation. Your ideas may not all be right but, after all, that is why you are studying the subject. Many students talk of studying HRM because they would 'like to work with people' and they seem to think of human resource management as a cosy job that involves being nice to people at all times. While this view is not entirely accurate, it is certainly a career which provides a wealth of variety and great deal

1

Chapter objectives summarise what you will be able to do by the end of the chapter.

Chapter 7 Selection: shortlisting and interviews

Comment

Each of these questions could be answered by a simple response 'yes' or 'no'. If the interviewer is trying to elicit as much information as possible, these questions are not very useful. Closed questions can, however, be useful for checking the correctness of information. An example might be: 'Did you use Excel on the computer at XYZ Ltd?'

Pause for thought 7.5 Before you go on to read about leading questions and open questions, stop to rephrase the two closed questions in the example above as open questions. That is, how would you put these questions so that an interviewee would be encouraged to speak more freely?

Leading questions

● You do enjoy working with the computer, don't you?
● You have had sales experience, haven't you?

Comment

The phrasing of these questions implies that an affirmative response is expected of the candidate. At the very least this will destroy the confidence of a candidate who answers in the negative. It could also induce a nervous candidate to give false information on the spur of the moment. It is so easy just to answer 'yes' to questions like those above.

Open questions

● What experience have you had working with a computer?
● Tell me about your experience working with a computer.
● What did you like about working in sales?
● How did you decide to take up a career in personnel management?

Comment

None of these questions can be answered with a one-word answer, neither do they indicate what the questioner expects to hear. Open questions usually start with words like what, why or how. Alternatively, the interviewee can simply be asked to talk about something: 'Tell me about . . .'

It should be obvious that the majority of the questions in an interview should be phrased as open questions, with relatively few closed questions to check facts. Leading questions are not very useful and should be avoided.

Did you know?

According to the CIPD survey of recruitment and selection processes published in 2003, there was a marked increase in the number of employers using competency-based interviews to improve their selection decisions. The percentage of respondents using these rose from 25.8 per cent in 2002 to 58.7 per cent in 2003 (CIPD, 2003). More recently, the IRS (2007b) has reported that 69.7 per cent of employers are using competency-based questions in their employment interviews. This is good evidence that employers recognise the value of this type of questioning.

Situational and behavioural questions

It is a fairly straightforward task to gather information about qualifications and skills by careful questioning and listening and by using a variety of tests. Assessing attitudes and interpersonal skills is more difficult. Situational and behavioural questions are suitable for this purpose, as well as for assessing skills and how these would be translated into behaviour in the workplace. Research has long since indicated that the use of these two types of question improves both the reliability and the validity of selection interviews (Latham *et al.*, 1980; Weekley and Gier, 1987).

188

Did you know? and **Pause for thought** boxes provide a thought-provoking fact or question to keep you interested and keep you thinking.

Chapter 5 Equality and diversity

requirement discriminate against? Fewer women than men, for instance, are six feet tall. This requirement therefore discriminates indirectly against female applicants.

The European Union Directives on equality have brought about some changes in the definition of indirect discrimination, including replacing the phrase 'requirement or condition' with the phrase 'provision, criterion or practice'. As the IRS (2003) point out, this terminology broadens the sphere of potential indirect discrimination to include informal practices.

ACTIVITY 5.1

Can you think of any other instances of indirect discrimination and identify which groups might be affected by them?

Look through the records of cases heard by employment tribunals and you will find some examples. To find reports of such cases you can use several sources:

● A number of human resource management journals have a section that gives updates on the law and describes recent cases. Look, for instance, in *People Management* and *Personnel Today*.
● You can look in the subject index of the *Legal Journals Index*, for instance under the heading 'sex discrimination'. This will give a brief summary of the major points of the case, and refer to a journal in which you can read more about the case.
● There are also numerous cases reported in the *Equal Opportunities Review* and some issues of the *IRS Employment Review*.
● CIPD members have access to descriptions of numerous tribunal cases in the Employment Law at Work section of the CIPD website (www.cipd.co.uk).

You may wish to compare the instances you find with those found by others in your class.

Did you know?

In most cases an employee needs to have completed a one-year qualifying period of employment to take a complaint of unfair dismissal to an employment tribunal. This qualifying period does not apply if the complainant feels that the reasons for the unfair dismissal were connected to any of the types of discrimination covered by legislation. You can read more about this in the section on the burden of proof later in this chapter.

Victimisation occurs when someone is treated less favourably because that person has made a complaint or indicated an intention to make a complaint about sex or race discrimination. An example of this might be a woman who has complained to the Equality and Human Rights Commission about lack of promotion in comparison to similarly qualified men and who is subsequently dismissed unfairly.

The legislation also stipulates that this unfair treatment must be to the disadvantage of the person so treated. In the case of employment this includes the person being refused employment, promotion or training opportunities or being dismissed.

● **Harassment**

There is no specific definition of harassment in the original sex and race discrimination Acts, but harassment has been deemed to constitute discrimination under these Acts through case law. A specific definition of harassment is integrated into the RRA through the EU Race Directive and harassment is also addressed specifically in the

122

Activities get you applying what you're reading about to the real world.

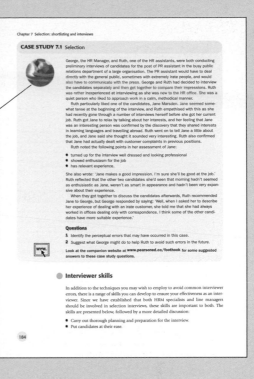

Case studies help you think about what you would do in certain scenarios.

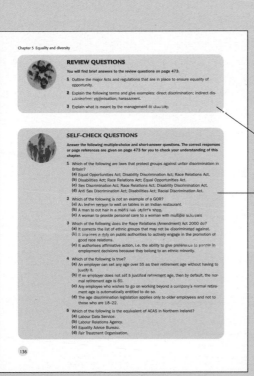
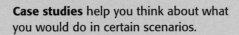

Review questions reinforce what you have learnt in the chapter and **Self-check questions** let you test your understanding. Answers are provided at the back of the book.

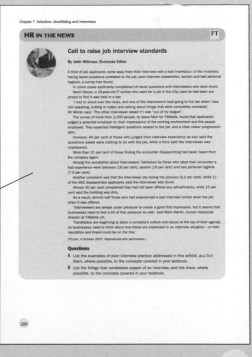

New **HR in the news** features contain articles from the *Financial Times* and promote discussion of real examples of HR in practice.

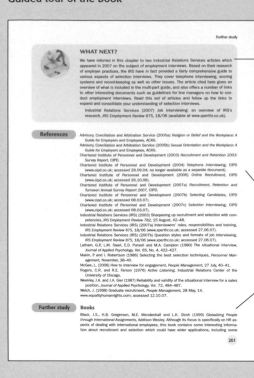

What next? features encourage you to find out more about a topic.

Comprehensive **References** and annotated **Further Study** boxes point you in the direction of wider reading.

A variety of resources such as **True or false** questions, **Match the phrase** questions and **Crossword puzzles** on the Companion Website at **www.pearsoned.co.uk/foothook** test your learning and monitor your progress.

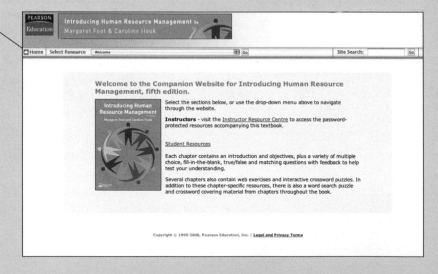

Introducing human resource management

Objectives

By the end of this chapter you will be able to:

- define what is meant by the term 'human resource management'
- outline the historical development of human resource management
- understand the roles of line managers and human resource managers in managing people
- outline the range of activities with which practitioners of human resource management are likely to be involved
- demonstrate how human resource management can make a difference by adding value to an organisation
- outline some of the current issues facing HR managers.

HRM? What's it all about?

This book is designed as an introductory text for students studying human resource management (HRM) either with a view to becoming HR specialists themselves, or for those who are starting or hoping to start a career in management. As you will discover, people management forms a large part of every manager's job, whether they work in a large multinational organisation, a not for profit organisation or a small charity. Organisations also increasingly aim for all employees to be engaged, so an understanding of the subject is important for everyone.

As stated in the preface, we intend that you should become actively involved in your own learning as you progress through the book. Even though you are just beginning this subject, you may already have ideas about some of the topics that you are about to study and you may even have a general idea of the role and functions of the human resource management or personnel department in an organisation. Your ideas may not all be right but, after all, that is why you are studying the subject. Many students talk of studying HRM because they would 'like to work with people,' and they seem to think of human resource management as a cosy job that involves being nice to people at all times. While this view is not entirely accurate, it is certainly a career which provides a wealth of variety and great deal of job satisfaction. It is also a career which is constantly changing as the role evolves in response to changing social, political, economic and demographic issues.

According to the Chartered Institute of Personnel and Development (2005) when HR managers were asked whether they would choose a career in HR if they had the opportunity to start again, 'the vast majority (81%) said "yes". The reasons people give for enjoying their HR careers related to variety, challenge and interest, and the view that HR is at the heart of the business and can make a difference.'

ACTIVITY 1.1

What do you think are the main areas in which a human resource manager is likely to be involved? Make a list of these areas. For each of the areas on the list, indicate the type of involvement of the human resource practitioner and whether other managers are also likely to have a role in handling this activity (use Table 1.1). We have completed the first row of Table 1.1 to start you off. Our suggestions for this Activity are given at the end of the chapter in Table 1.3.

Table 1.1   The main activities of human resource practitioners

Main areas of activity of human resource management specialist	Type of involvement of the human resource management specialists	Type of involvement of line manager
Recruitment and selection	Design of policies and procedure for fair recruitment and selection in order to contribute to the fulfilment of the organisation's corporate strategy. Carry out interviews or monitor and give advice on interview technique or on terms and conditions of employment.	Carry out interviews.
Learning and development		

We shall discuss in this book the variety of roles and tasks that modern HR professionals cover but it is important to note that it is not just the HR professionals who work in these areas: line managers are also involved. Therefore, this book is also written as an introduction to HRM for them.

Let us start with an activity opposite to help you focus on your ideas about human resource management. You can compare your answers with the answer that we give at the end of the chapter. Later in the chapter we shall also look at what researchers and HR practitioners say HR is about.

The main activities of human resource management

The areas that we would list are as follows:

- recruitment and selection
- learning and development
- human resource planning
- provision of contracts
- provision of fair treatment
- provision of equal opportunities
- managing diversity
- motivating workers to achieve improved performance
- employee counselling
- talent management
- employee welfare
- payment and reward of employees
- health and safety
- disciplining individuals
- dealing with grievances
- dismissal
- redundancy
- negotiation
- encouraging involvement and engagement
- adding value
- ethics and corporate responsibility
- knowledge management
- change management
- managing cross-cultural issues or international HRM.

You may have included some slightly different activities since human resource managers, as you can see from this list, do become involved in a wide range of issues and it is difficult to predict the exact nature of the job in any particular enterprise. We have selected the main topics with which we feel most human resource managers are likely to be involved, but this will vary from organisation to organisation and may also depend on the way the function itself is organised. The type of involvement of the HR specialists will also vary. Some HR specialists operating at a high level in the organisation will be concerned with the provision of clear strategic direction for HR and linking this to the strategic objectives of the organisation. Others will be concerned to provide specialist advice, while still others will focus on the provision of administration and support. All will be concerned in some way to ensure that HRM activities add value by helping the organisation achieve its strategic objectives. They will focus on ensuring that the overall HR policies and procedures support the strategic objectives and that there is consistency in approach and implementation across the organisation.

However, for each activity it is likely that other managers will also be involved to some extent. Line managers will be concerned with the actual implementation of the policies and procedures in so far as they affect their team, whereas the HR specialists will also be involved in the bigger picture, although the extent of the differences in role will vary between organisations.

The fact that aspects of managing the human resource are an element of every manager's or supervisor's job is an important point for you to keep in mind. Many of you will find that your career may take you from line management to human resource management and then back to line management, or vice versa. In a survey of HR managers carried out by the CIPD (2005) 'only about a quarter (26%) of respondents started out in HR' and at some point in their careers 'eighty-three percent of respondents have worked outside HR, the most frequently cited functions being sales, marketing and retail.'

Pause for thought 1.1 A line manager is a person who has direct responsibility for employees and their work. Since line managers seem to have such a large part to play in people management, to what extent do you think they need human resource managers at all?

Obviously, we consider that line managers do need to call on the services and expertise of human resource specialists. If you look at our discussion of Activity 1.1 in Table 1.3 at the end of this chapter, you will see that although a great deal of work can be devolved to line managers, there is also a role for a person skilled in human resource management to establish policies, standards and procedures, to integrate these with the organisation's objectives to ensure that they contribute to the organisation's strategic objectives, to provide expert advice and consistency, and to coordinate and provide training and development. Human resource practitioners will also often be involved in initiating company-wide programmes such as promoting employee engagement, communication and consultation. The exact nature of their involvement will vary from one organisation to another, as will the range of activities they cover. The human resource department may carry out some administrative work and maintain central records on people and may also provide advice and expertise for other managers to draw on. In some organisations the human resource department may carry out all the activities listed above, while in others many or most of these functions may be devolved to other managers. Increasingly more and more aspects of the HR function are being devolved to line managers and you will find as you work through the book that we emphasise the roles of line managers in HR activities.

Even among human resource managers there will be differences in the scope of their job, so it is also important to consider the ways in which HR jobs are organised as specialist or generalist roles. Does an organisation employ its own HR practitioners in-house, or is the HR department outsourced and provided by a form of shared services for other divisions of the same organisation or with other organisations? Are the individuals themselves consultants or business partners or do they have some other job title such as employee champion? Is their role dealing with issues just in one country or is it a multinational? We shall deal with some of these issues about the variety of roles in HRM and the ways in which HRM can be organised later in this chapter.

Cross-cultural issues will provide another dimension to be considered in relation to each of these tasks. Multinational organisations have to consider both expatriates and host-country nationals employed by them around the world as well as their home-country-based employees. Recently several of our students who have graduated from the BA Human Resource Management degree at the University of Huddersfield have taken up first jobs in HR which have involved them working at least for some of their time in other countries and this has meant that they needed an awareness of cultural issues in learning and development quite early in their careers. The expansion of the European Union with the entry of several Eastern European countries such as Poland has also meant an increase in workers from these countries coming to the UK to seek employment and so an awareness of cross-cultural issues is also of increasing importance to HR managers, even if they work exclusively in the UK.

Given the changes to the way organisations are operating in terms of their recruitment, you may find yourself working with migrant workers in this country, recruiting internationally or working in another country yourself in an international organisation. We shall therefore consider later in this chapter some of the cross-cultural or international issues in HRM and in some later chapters we shall also touch briefly on cross-cultural or global dimensions.

The historical background to human resource management

It may help you to understand the diversity of roles that are sometimes adopted by human resource managers if we look briefly at the development of the profession. A variety of names have been used to describe those who specialise in managing people. In this book we have chosen to use the terms *human resource manager* or *people manager* as these are increasingly the main terms used but you will also find other terms such as *personnel manager* or *employee champion* used and we shall discuss some of these other job titles later in this chapter.

The role of HR manager has changed in response to social, economic, political conditions and to changes in technology and it is still developing dynamically. The relative importance of many of the activities has changed as external circumstances have affected the needs of organisations and it is still a dynamic area where the roles and ways of organising the HR function continue to change and develop.

Industrial welfare

The earliest activity with which the HR practitioner was involved was welfare work. During the nineteenth century, conditions of work for men, women and children in the factories were generally appalling compared to today's accepted standards. In 1833 the Factories Act appointed the first (male) factory inspectors, and in 1878 legislation was passed to try to regulate hours of work and conditions at least for women and children, reducing their hours of work to 60 hours per week! The trade union movement was also developing during this period, as individuals realised the strength they could gain by joining together to negotiate with employers. Collective bargaining was developing and in 1868 the first Trades Union Conference was held. In 1885 eleven trade unionists were elected to the House of Commons and demanded improvements in wages and conditions of employment.

There were some enlightened employers who wanted to try to improve working conditions for their employees and adopted schemes to improve the lot of their workforce as part of their company policy. Among these were several Quaker organisations, and it is generally held that the first personnel officer, referred to at that time as an industrial welfare officer, was Miss Mary Wood who was appointed by Rowntree's in York in 1896. She was appointed to be a type of social worker for the factory, with responsibility for ensuring the well-being of women and children in the workforce and watching over their health and behaviour.

Although Mary's first day at work over 100 years ago is very different from the type of work that we associate with human resource managers of today, welfare and the well-being of the workforce is still an area in which some HR practitioners will be involved. Health, safety and welfare are also issues affected by legislation, and in many organisations the human resource manager will have a role in ensuring compliance. Levels of absenteeism are expensive, so modern organisations which have been proactive in encouraging a healthy workforce have also shown benefits in reduced levels of absence with consequent saving for the organisation.

Rowntree's, as we have seen, approached the issue of welfare by employing a specialist to deal with it. Cadbury's was another pioneering company at this time which developed a totally different approach, believing that the well-being of the workforce was the responsibility of each member of staff. Edward Cadbury spoke in 1900 of the need to 'develop the social and moral character of each worker,' stating that 'the supreme principle has been that business efficiency and the welfare of employees are but different sides of the same problem' (Niven, 1978, p. 23).

Although such a paternalistic approach is unlikely to be acceptable today, even in these early approaches you can see the start of the development of involvement in welfare activities for both the early people managers and other managers.

> ### Did you know?
>
> Mary Wood's first day at work at Rowntree's was rather different from the type of activity you would associate with human resource managers today.
>
> Her first morning was spent placing flowers in workrooms – perhaps not so ineffectual a beginning as might be thought when the drabness of factories and homes at the time is remembered – and in the afternoon she went to visit girls who were sick, ordering groceries for the most necessitous cases and seeing such slums that she had never dreamt existed. Her first opportunity for making headway came during the dinner hours, when the fact that there was no supervision meant that pandemonium broke out. By degrees she brought order and discipline and before long was arranging an occasional concert or talk during the last half hour of the break. She then turned to organising games as an outlet for the high spirits of the younger girls and as a means of strengthening their physique.
>
> (*Source*: Niven, 1978)

Recruitment and selection

The early industrial welfare workers met with great success, and Mary Wood and others were soon asked to start recruiting girls, which was the beginning of the development of the role of recruitment and selection. (Remember this was well before equal opportunities had been thought of!) During the First World War there was rapid development in many fields of personnel management, largely as a result of government initiatives to encourage the best possible use of people, and also because of legislation. In 1916 the Ministry of Munitions set up its own Industrial Welfare

Department with Seebohm Rowntree in charge, with responsibility for introducing new welfare and personnel policies by persuasion into the factories. It became compulsory to have a welfare worker in all explosives factories, and it was strongly encouraged in munitions factories. There was also a great deal of work done, mainly by the armed forces, during this period on how to test abilities and IQ, and research was undertaken into the human factors at work.

Acquisition of other people management activities

In 1921 the National Institute of Industrial Psychologists was established, and its members published results of studies on selection tests, interviewing techniques and training methods so providing an academic rationale for some aspects of people management.

During the Second World War the work spread from welfare, recruitment and selection to training, improving morale and motivation, discipline, health and safety, joint consultation and often wages policies. This expansion of duties required the establishment of an adequate personnel department with trained staff.

Industrial relations

Joint consultation between management and workforce spread during the Second World War, and personnel departments became responsible for its organisation and administration. There was an increased emphasis on health and safety and a need for specialists to deal with industrial relations, so that gradually the personnel manager became the usual spokesperson for the organisation in discussion with trade unions and shop stewards.

Industrial relations were also of great importance in the late 1970s. The heated political climate during that period reinforced the importance of this aspect of people management and saw the development of a specialist role in industrial relations negotiation. In many organisations the personnel manager had executive authority to negotiate deals about pay or other collective issues.

Legislation

During the 1970s the growth in the amount of employment legislation resulted in the personnel function often adopting the role of specialist adviser, ensuring that managers did not fall foul of the law and that cases did not end up at industrial tribunals, as they were then called. This is still an important role for people managers, particularly as a great many changes to legislation have either recently been introduced or are about to be introduced, and we have included some chapters in which we discuss their role in relation to particular aspects of law, such as employment contracts, dismissal, and health and safety.

Flexibility and diversity

In the 1990s there was a major trend for employers to seek increasingly flexible arrangements in the hours worked by employees, with a growth in the number of employees who worked part time or on temporary contracts, and an increase in distance working and working from home. This trend has continued in the early years of the twenty-first century. The workforce and patterns of work are becoming increasingly diverse; this will provide challenges to employers who cannot rely on their traditional recruitment practices and who will also need to develop policies in relation to managing diversity and the equal opportunities issues that managing an increasingly diverse workforce raises.

Human resource management

The concept of human resource management first appeared in the 1980s and the use of the term grew in the 1990s. Initially, writers in the field focused on trying to distinguish between personnel management and HRM, but according to Boxall and Purcell (2003) HRM has, in spite of the lack of clarity over definition, become the most popular term to refer to the activities of managers in relation to people management.

The major characteristics of the HRM approach to people management have been identified as follows:

- The importance of adopting a strategic approach is emphasised.
- Line managers play a predominant role.
- Organisational policies must be integrated and cohesive in order to better project and support the central organisational values and objectives. Along with this, communication plays a vital role.
- An underlying philosophy is adopted that emphasises the achievement of competitive advantage through the efforts of people. This can variously be interpreted into actions that are known as hard HRM or those that are known as soft HRM (see page 11).
- A unitarist rather than a pluralist approach prevails in the relationship between managers and employees.

Focus on strategy

Throughout the 1980s and 1990s business leaders came to accept more and more that competitive advantage could be achieved only through the efforts and creativity of the people employed by them. In companies that follow through with the logical conclusions to this statement rather than simply paying lip service to the rhetoric, developing strategies for their human resources will inevitably play a prominent role when they are formulating the corporate strategy, and senior managers will want to call on the expertise of a specialist to get the best input possible. Thus strategic activity becomes a major focus for specialists in HRM, but probably only those acting at the higher levels will be involved in board-level meetings where strategic alternatives are discussed. It should also be noted that in order to have effective input into the corporate strategy, the HRM specialist will require a high level of business acumen in addition to knowledge of people strategies and programmes. It is this recognition that people are a resource to be managed as efficiently and effectively as any other resource that has led to the term human resource management.

Role of the line manager

We have defined strategic involvement as being a key characteristic of HRM and noted that this means a focus on strategic activity for high level HRM practitioners. However, the HRM approach recognises the centrality of the human resource for all business activities, and therefore consideration of the people management aspects would be expected in the strategic planning input from managers in all business functions (e.g. production, marketing, etc.). Likewise, the importance of active management of people matters becomes more clearly an integral part of every line manager's job. Line managers must combine their commitment to the technical aspects of task completion with attention to people aspects and recognise the symbiotic nature of these two elements of the managerial role.

This means that some activities that might traditionally have been undertaken by specialist personnel management staff have now been devolved to line managers. Increased line involvement in training and recruitment and performance management can be cited as areas where this has occurred. There is still, however, a substantial role for human resource specialists, as you discovered when you completed Activity 1.1, in designing strategic HR solutions, advising and disseminating information about evolving people management programmes to line managers, in ensuring consistency in the treatment of employees company-wide and, in general, in being supportive partners to managers in their efforts to achieve company goals.

The pivotal role of the line manager is one of the most often cited characteristics of human resource management but line managers do not always see things this way. Finding ways of educating and encouraging line managers to take responsibility for the people management aspects of their job is in many organisations one of the key challenges that face HR specialists. (See Storey's table of the take-up of HRM techniques in Storey and Sisson, 1993.)

Integrated policies and effective communication

Proponents of HRM emphasise that policies across the whole HR spectrum (recruitment, selection, reward, employee relations) must be fully integrated and consistent with the organisation's culture. This is logically consistent with the strategic, forward planning nature of HRM. Effective communications are a pivotal aspect of this as they constitute a means of conveying senior management's values and commitment to their goals (Legge 1995, p. 75). It is also an important aspect of knowledge management.

Competitive advantage through people

The balanced scorecard

At this point it is appropriate to introduce the concept of the balanced scorecard (BSC). This concept emanates from work done on business strategy by Kaplan and Norton (1992, 1996) in the Harvard Business School in the early 1990s, but it emphasises the role of the human resource in the achievement of business strategy. The BSC has become a well-established technique used extensively not only in the

USA, but also worldwide, including some UK companies, for instance Tesco (see Industrial Relations Services 2000).

The essential idea behind the balanced scorecard is the notion that businesses must measure the success of their plans in order to validate their actions, identify and evaluate their successes, and build on them for the future. Traditionally businesses have focused mainly if not exclusively on financial results to evaluate the success of their strategy, but Kaplan and Norton propose that measuring success in only one area is inadequate for a number of reasons. One argument is that financial results are always a retrospective measure of past success and do not necessarily indicate that similar actions in the future will meet with similar achievements. Also, although financial gains may be the ultimate desired outcome, it is imperative to know exactly what factors contributed to this outcome and in what way they contributed.

A more satisfactory approach to formulating strategic initiatives, and subsequently evaluating their success, is to take a more balanced approach, which is represented by the balanced scorecard. The scorecard is a flexible tool, which can be adapted according to the nature of the business adopting it, but the original model proposes four elements that should be evaluated in order to achieve a balanced overview of what contributes to a company's success:

- financial results
- customer relations
- internal processes
- learning and development.

The examination of financial results is, of course, still a necessary part of evaluating business success but, according to Kaplan and Norton, this focus needs to be balanced out by taking the other criteria into consideration. Each of the three other criteria contributes to financial success, and purposively focusing on them helps to shift managerial awareness to the role each plays. Typically, the formulation of a corporate strategy would start with a goal to increase shareholder value, and a strategy that focuses on the customer's perspective is most likely to succeed in achieving this aim (Kaplan and Norton, 2000). A company must then examine its internal processes with regard to their fitness to achieve this customer strategy and adapt them where necessary. This in turn goes hand in hand with the development of the human resource that will deliver the strategy. An organisation's capacity for learning and development is regarded as being one of the key factors contributing to success in today's competitive environment.

Just as the balanced scorecard is used to formulate the overall corporate strategy and measure its success, it can also be used to plan for the component parts and measure their contribution to the achievement of company strategy. Thus, while the examination of internal processes must be carried out throughout the organisation and constitutes one component of the balanced scorecard used to measure the whole company's performance, the BSC can also be used to guide and evaluate each individual's performance. That is, the development of individuals becomes explicitly tied in to the key issues addressed in the BSC at corporate strategy level, and in appraising each individual, the question is asked to what extent the individual contributed to the financial success of the company, to customer relations, to the improvement of internal processes, and to learning and growth. The Halifax is one company in the UK that has used a balanced scorecard to evaluate its employees' performance.

The adoption of the balanced scorecard by Tesco also served to strengthen and redefine the role of the stores' personnel managers. The scorecard highlighted the importance of all employee contribution to the success of the company, and therefore the importance of people management issues. To complement this, personnel managers in Tesco stores are also expected to be fully involved in the day-to-day running of the stores, thus enhancing their business awareness and their credibility (IRS, 2000).

Hard and soft HRM

The basic requirement of HRM to serve the corporate strategy and achieve corporate aims by means of a high-performance workforce can be read in two ways:

- The primacy of business needs means that human resources will be acquired, deployed and dispensed with as corporate plans demand. Little regard is paid to the needs of those human resources and the emphasis is on quantitative aspects. This is known as hard HRM.
- In order to gain a competitive advantage through the workforce, regardless of whether they are full- or part-time, temporary or contract staff, all potential must be nurtured and developed, and programmes that pay due notice to knowledge about the behavioural aspects of people at work are developed. This is characterised as soft HRM.

The emphasis in our text lies mainly with soft HRM, but as Legge (1995, pp. 66–67) argues, the two are not mutually exclusive, and you will detect elements of hard HRM in the discussion of human resource planning.

Unitarist and pluralist approaches to management–employee relations

Human resource management is identified as being a unitarist rather than a pluralist approach (Legge, 1995, pp. 72–73). Briefly, the unitarist stance is characterised as a senior management assumption that all members of the organisation are dedicated to the achievement of a common goal with no conflict from personal interests. Pluralism, on the other hand, recognises that within a large group of people there are inevitably a variety of interests and that these have to be managed. The adoption of one or other of these two philosophies obviously has a major impact on the way that managers treat the workforce.

We explore the concepts of unitarism and pluralism in greater depth in Chapter 3 where we come to the conclusion from observing current rhetoric that we may now be witnessing a merging of the two stances in the development of the partnership theme. This promotes the idea that managers and employees can pursue common goals while still recognising that diverging interests exist. The common purpose of the unitarists is pursued in a pluralist framework.

We refer throughout the text to the key characteristics described here and their links with specific activities. In particular, we emphasise the role of the line manager in all of the activities we discuss, but in addition we focus on the theme of strategy in Chapter 2 where we examine the human resource planning activity, and the topics of employee involvement/engagement and communication as a part of high-performance working in Chapter 3.

Other views of HRM

Roles of HR specialists

Another way to try to establish what is meant by HRM is to look at research into possible roles that HR practitioners have. Ulrich and Brockbank (2005) have been very influential in trying to clarify the roles of HR specialists and some large organisations have restructured along the lines of the Ulrich model of HRM. He originally envisaged the HR function in large organisations as having four main streams in order to deliver value to the organisation. According to Arkin (2007) these were:

● transactional HR carrying out administrative work through service centres
● embedded HR working directly with business leaders
● centres of expertise providing specialist advice
● corporate HR, which oversees the whole function, implementing organisation-wide initiatives and working with the top business leaders.

Ulrich's earlier work listed four roles to go with these structures: the business partner, administrative expert, employee champion and change agent, and according to Arkin (2007) 'a growing number of CIPD members now describe themselves as "HR business partners", a title sometimes prefixed with the word "strategic".' A quick survey of the titles used in job advertisements in *People Management* in early 2007 reveals that the most popular titles advertised were for HR managers, HR directors, Heads of HR and then Business Partners but there were also smaller numbers of advertisements for HR advisers, coordinators and consultants and for a few HR administrators. It does appear that the title HR Business Partner is becoming more popular but it still has not overtaken the titles of HR Manager or Director in popularity at least in the editions of the magazine reviewed.

In 2005 Ulrich and Brockbank updated these HR roles for the twenty-first century saying that their new descriptions reflected the changing roles in the organisations in which they work. They said 'all HR professionals aspire to add value. But it is not always easy for the provider of a service to see what contribution they are making. To help our profession to get a better handle on this, we have tried to explain it in terms of the mastery of certain roles.' They list these as follows: employee advocate, functional expert, human capital developer, strategic partner and HR leader.

Did you know?

In 2003 the CIPD carried out a survey to test the reality of what was occurring in HRM in the UK and to find out what activities HR managers say take up most of their time and which were perceived by them to be the most important. Clear differences between the time spent on activities and their views as to the relative importance of these activities were found.

The top three activities that were viewed by the HR practitioners as being of most importance were:

1 developing HR strategy and policy
2 business strategy
3 the provision of specialist HR input to wider business issues.

However, when we compare this with the top three most time-consuming activities clear differences emerge. For those HR practitioners in the sample the most time-consuming activities were:

1 providing support for line managers
2 implementing HR policies
3 HR administration.

1 Employee advocate

This role focuses on the current needs of the workforce and on employee relations issues. Caring for, listening to employees and understanding their viewpoint is important in this role. However, the employee advocate also has to understand the points of view of other stakeholders and be able to communicate these to employees so they can in turn contribute to achieving value. Developing policies and procedures for fairness and diversity and rooting out discrimination are also key to this role. Keeping employees in touch with competitive realities and dealing with issues such as discipline or dismissal in a fair way are also important. According to Ulrich and Brockbank (2005) this role consumes about 19 per cent of the HR professional's time.

2 Functional expert

This role is one where the role holder concentrates on increasing the administrative efficiency of the HR department by using his or her expertise to design HR policies and procedures. The use of technology has been influential in changing this role from that of the administrative expert of the 1990s. Ulrich and Brockbank (2005) say that this role involves HR professionals in accessing a body of knowledge so that they act with insight and make well-informed and more effective decisions. They divide the role of the functional expert in two and say that it involves knowledge of both foundational and emerging HR practices.

Foundational HR practices are described as the practices for which HR departments have direct responsibility such as recruitment and selection, learning and development and reward, in fact many of the things that you will have associated with HR when you completed Activity 1.1 earlier in this chapter. They describe as emerging HR practices the types of things that will have a big impact on HRM but which may not be directly under the influence of the HR department. These are things such as process design, internal communications, sharing information and organisational design and restructuring. According to Ulrich and Brockbank (2005), 'By mastering the concepts and research of these foundational and emerging practices and ensuring their alignment with the key business priorities HR professionals will optimize their impact on business performance.' Certainly HR professionals should possess knowledge and expertise in HR areas but also need to be knowledgeable about other areas of the organisation in order to be able to see things from other managers' points of view and to be able to discuss their specific business needs with them. This role may also fit with the concept of knowledge management which we mentioned earlier.

3 Human capital developer

This role is about developing the workforce so that they are successful in the future. This could involve developing individual workers but also could involve the development of teams so the focus is on learning and development and on identifying approaches that can help people to learn appropriate skills, knowledge, behaviour and attitudes using approaches such as coaching.

4 Strategic partner

This role operates at a high level within the organisation and could involve several things such as being an expert in the business, thinking and planning strategically, or it could be someone who acts as a consultant or is a knowledge manager. Ulrich and Brockbank (2005) say that 'In their role as a strategic partner, HR professionals bring know-how about business, change, consulting and learning to their relationships with line managers.' They basically see the role as divided into three main areas: strategy formulators, strategy implementers and facilitators.

Ulrich and Brockbank (2005) see the sub-role of strategy formulator being divided into three areas also. First, HR strategic partners should act as devil's advocate and ask awkward questions about an organisation's strategy and about its ability to fulfil it. This, however, while important, is a purely reactive role.

Second, they should play a more proactive role in which they design the strategies based on their own knowledge of existing and future customer needs and ensure resources are aligned to those needs. Finally, according to Ulrich and Brockbank (2005), they should play a role in developing and improving the standards of strategic thinking among managers.

In terms of strategy implementers and change agents, they are involved in ensuring that all the HR systems and policies and procedures are aligned with the organisation's vision and goals so that they help these to be fulfilled. They plan for the future and make the future happen.

In the third variant of the role of strategic HR manager, they facilitate the work of managers and teams to help them achieve their aims and this also involves them in sharing knowledge and spreading it between people. Once again this links with the idea of knowledge management as explained earlier.

5 The HR leader

This involves all of the other four roles and also involves leading the HR function and working with other business functions in setting standards for strategic thinking and corporate governance. However, Ulrich and Brockbank (2005) envisage the leadership role as being so important that it needs to be a role in its own right. The effective HR leader will establish goals and will communicate these clearly to all; they will manage change and show results in relation to the added value for workers, shareholders, customers and the managers. Ulrich and Brockbank also emphasise the fact that it is not just those at the top of HR who should be leaders but that every HR manager should also exercise personal leadership.

Ulrich and Brockbank (2005) do emphasise the point that not everyone operates at a strategic level and that all the roles are important within an organisation, although it appears to have been the role of business partner or strategic business partner that has captured the imagination of HR practitioners. While all HR managers need to be aware of the need to think strategically and to align HR policies and procedures with the organisation's strategic objectives, many, particularly when starting out in their careers, are likely to act in roles such as employee advocate. As Ulrich and Brockbank (2005) say, 'Some argue that HR should move exclusively to strategic partnering, to help business leaders define and deliver financial and customer goals. We disagree. Employee advocacy is not merely window dressing: it contributes to building the human infrastructure from which everything else in the organisation flows.'

The people and performance model

A different approach was adopted by John Purcell and a team of researchers from the University of Bath who carried out studies sponsored by the CIPD over a three-year period to try to ascertain what aspects of HRM actually make a difference to performance within organisations (Purcell *et al.* 2003).

They found that on their own, good HR policies were not sufficient to create an effective organisation but excellent policies about recruiting, developing and retaining the people in the organisation were important. Purcell *et al.* (2003) referred to this as the 'human capital advantage'. Much of this book will address ways to achieve this type of human capital advantage. However, the other key factor that distinguished effective organisations from those that were less effective was the way they 'worked together to be productive and flexible enough to meet new challenges'. We also emphasise this approach throughout this book.

The researchers identified two vital ingredients in effective organisations. According to Purcell *et al.* (2003) these are:

● First, they had strong values and an inclusive culture.
● Second, they had enough line managers who were able to bring HR policies and practices to life.

Strong values and an inclusive culture

Purcell and his team of researchers found that organisations that developed a strong and inclusive culture usually had what they called a 'big idea'. This was always something that was clearly communicated to everyone in the workforce and that could be easily understood.

The big ideas the researchers identified were ideas such as the 'pursuit of quality' at Jaguar cars, 'living the values' at Tesco and the 'principles of mutuality' at Nationwide Building Society. Everyone shared and understood these ideas and they became the foundation for all the HR policies and procedures, enabling everyone to see why they were necessary.

Line managers who could bring the policies to life

We have already mentioned the importance of line managers in the HRM approach to the management of people and here we have recent research that substantiates this view. In the research by Purcell and his team (Purcell *et al.*, 2003) the line managers were found to be the other vital ingredient in making an effective organisation. The line managers had not only to see the relevance of the HR policies and procedures to themselves, but also to see how they could use them to contribute to an effective organisation.

Pause for thought 1.2 The researchers from Bath University said, 'It's better to ensure that HR policies are properly implemented than to try to develop new policies' (Purcell *et al.*, 2003). As you work through this book and learn more about HR policies and procedures, remember that the way they are introduced into an organisation is also very important and worker involvement and excellent communication are also crucial to the effectiveness of the organisation.

The ACAS model

Donaghy (2007) in the forward to the ACAS 2007 annual report says that 'Our experience tells us that the way you do something is just as important as what you do. Having the right policies and procedures is vital but they won't work properly unless they are introduced and used in the right spirit.' ACAS have developed a model to help organisations improve the effectiveness of their people management. This shows some similarities to the findings of Purcell *et al.* but is based on thirty years of experience on the part of ACAS in assisting organisations with people management issues. They list the following as key issues:

Formal procedures for dealing with disciplinary matters, grievances and disputes that managers know about and use fairly.

Ambitions, goals and plans that employees know about and understand.

Managers who genuinely listen to and consider their employees' views so everyone is actively involved in making important decisions.

A pay and reward system that is clear, fair and consistent.

A safe and healthy workplace.

People to feel valued so they can talk confidently about their work and learn from both successes and mistakes.

In the following chapters we examine many of the key HR policies, practices and procedures that can contribute towards an effective workplace and we have tried to emphasise the roles of both the specialists in HR and line managers in implementing these in ways which will benefit the organisation. We have already shown how the role of HR practitioners has evolved and the importance of the role of line managers in HRM issues.

The changing HR function

Reality does not always match the theories, as a two-year CIPD-sponsored research project led by Reilly (2007a) into *The changing HR function* showed. According to Reilly (2007b), 81 per cent of the 781 organisations that responded said that they had recently reorganised or restructured their HR departments but less than 20 per cent had adopted the Ulrich model in full. A quarter of the organisations surveyed had a single HR team, but the remainder had central teams with operational HR staff aligned to specific business units. In this sample shared service centres were only found in large organisations that employed more than 5,000 employees and in most instances these were not outsourced to other organisations, although they were sometimes in-sourced to separate parts of the organisation.

There was a widespread use of HR business partners but the survey found a wide variation in their roles. Some were solo operators, concentrating on strategic issues, while others were team members, focusing on operational work: some reported to HR directors while others reported to heads of business units.

Some organisations did form centres of HR expertise. The most common centres of expertise specialised in learning and development followed by those centres that focused on recruitment/resourcing, reward and employee relations/employment law. If there was no centre of expertise then the work was usually done within the business unit so it could reflect specific challenges to that unit, although sometimes the work was done in the corporate centre itself.

The research showed that many organisations are trying to make the HR function more strategic and in larger organisations many of the administrative functions are being consolidated and often routine functions are becoming automated. These changes bring their own problems and some organisations talk of fragmentation and lack of communication and problems with the IT systems. The greatest problem remains the issue of devolving more of the transactional aspects of HR to line managers. Reilly (2007b) concluded that organisations 'who choose a style to suit their organisation are carrying off restructuring rather well'.

The role and tasks are constantly changing and developing in response to economic, demographic, social and legal issues. The next section briefly addresses some of the key issues in HRM which are shaping current and future developments in people management and you will find that a number of these are taken up again in various chapters.

Current issues in HRM

Information technology

If you glance through any journal relating to human resource management nowadays, you will find countless advertisements relating to the various ways that information technology (IT) can assist those in the HR department to do their jobs. These include: systems for e-recruitment; online shortlisting of applicants; online performance management and appraisals; e-learning; online psychometric testing; as well as IT systems to help with payroll, employment data, recruitment administration, references and pre-employment checks. There are also some large organisations which use HR shared service centres where they bring many of the HR services together and use technology such as email, a company intranet or telephones to provide HR information in order to deal with HR queries and provide expert advice for people working at various sites, sometimes in different countries.

Pause for thought 1.3 How do you think the increased use of information technology will affect the job of the HR manager? Will it enable them to get rid of the routine jobs by delegating them to IT systems, or will it mean that more people end up in routine jobs working with computers?

The increasing use of information technology is already having both of these effects, at least to some extent. For many HR managers, using IT for routine tasks frees them from more mundane tasks, so they have more time to think strategically. Increasing use of IT has also ensured a much greater amount of information is available on which to base decisions and to plan for the future.

Teleconferencing and tele-working mean that people no longer have to be in the same place to hold a meeting or to work in the same building. E-learning means people are often able to learn at their desks or via their iPod. All such developments raise issues and pose different problems about the ways staff should be managed and these will be of concern to the HR manager.

Some people will be in high-value jobs, using their expertise to design these labour-saving IT systems. Others may find that, perhaps for part of their career, they are dealing with completion of basic tasks using computers; or, on the other hand, they may use their knowledge and expertise in people management to deal with HR queries from around the world, via computers or telephones in shared service centres.

Human capital

By the early 2000s several new areas were starting to be of concern to those involved in managing people. The term 'human capital' was being discussed and, in particular, ways to measure human capital was an area of concern to some employers. The government set up a strategy group to examine the concept of human capital and created the Accounting for People Task Force to investigate it.

Professor Scarborough and the CIPD Human Capital Task Force (2003) defined the term 'human capital' as 'the contribution of people [their skills and knowledge] in the production of goods and services.'

An article in *People Management* (2003) by Professor Scarborough discussed the TV series *Jamie's Kitchen* and said, 'we witnessed "human capital" in action, when a group of unemployed young people were transformed on TV into top-class chefs.' Jamie Oliver tried to pass on many of his culinary, business and professional skills to a group of unemployed 16 to 24-year-olds and used a variety of methods from coaching to hectoring and pleading to achieve this. He was successful with most members of the group and created within them a desire to perform at a high level, although in the TV series it often seemed to be harder than he had imagined it would be. However, according to Scarborough 'this blending of new skills and attitudes into high performance sums up exactly what human capital can be and why it is so important to business.'

The concept of human capital also encourages organisations to move beyond just training people to do their jobs, although doing the job they are employed to do is of course still important. It is about encouraging organisations to make use of the whole range of abilities that people bring to the organisation and, as such, it is also linked to ideas about performance management discussed in Chapter 9. Measuring human capital is an attempt to measure the difference that people make to the organisation.

Added value

Another related concept that has gained in popularity in recent years is that of 'added value'. This is also concerned with making a difference. This concept aims to show how the HRM function or other related functions make a difference to the organisation and how they can help to shape the organisation's business strategy. Once again one of the concerns is for measurement of the difference the people initiatives have made. According to Harrison (2002), in order to add value, HRM or human resource development (HRD) must 'achieve outcomes that significantly increase the organisation's capability to differentiate itself from other similar organisations, and thereby enhance its progress. It must also achieve these outcomes in ways that ensure, through time, that their value will more than offset the costs that they incurred.' So, they have to make a difference to the organisation but do so in a way that is also cost-effective.

Green (1999) had criticised HR professionals for not having sufficient awareness of the effects that new HR interventions would have on the organisation, and maintained that in order to provide added value, people professionals needed to provide three things:

- *alignment* – pointing people in the right direction
- *engagement* – developing belief and commitment to the organisation's purpose and direction
- *measurement* – providing the data that demonstrate the improved results achieved (Green, 1999).

We can also use the TV series *Jamie's Kitchen* as an example of added value. In this case it was not the HRM department that introduced initiatives to add value as the organisation was too small to have an HRM department. However, Jamie Oliver added value to the trainees themselves by using, perhaps without knowing, the series of techniques which Green (1999) referred to as alignment, engagement and measurement.

Alignment

Jamie tried to point the trainees in the right direction in several ways. These included conventional on-the-job training, off-the-job training and team-building exercises on outward-bound programmes. He also used many student-centred approaches such as coaching, mentoring, counselling and sometimes cajoling, hectoring or pleading, and he drew attention to the fact that the business aim was to create a top-class restaurant and that all the trainees needed to work effectively in order to achieve this.

Engagement

Jamie tried to develop belief in and commitment to the organisation's purpose and direction. He tried to instill in the unemployed youngsters some sense of purpose and the idea that they had responsibilities to themselves, the team and the organisation. He tried to point them in the right direction; in this case to become experts in culinary skills so the restaurant would be successful. A further aim of his efforts to engage the group was that they would work effectively together as a team to achieve the excellent standards required by what he hoped would be a top restaurant.

Measurement

In this case the measurement was partly undertaken by the TV programme itself as it provided a visual record of the developing skills of the trainees. The trainees and the viewing public could clearly see the extent to which some individuals changed, but many other measures such as restaurant reviews by food critics, numbers of bookings and repeat bookings, numbers of complaints and amount of praise also helped to quantify the added value. In a later TV series some of the original trainees even went on to set up and run their own restaurants which provided a further visible indicator of the skills that had been developed.

Jamie Oliver was successful in adding value to most of the young people he took into his kitchen. They developed from being unemployed youngsters who had very little sense of purpose into highly trained and skilled workers who were able to work together to achieve the level of cookery skills required by the organisation. In spite of the high-profile nature of the experiment there were still some youngsters who did not become motivated by any of the techniques used and preferred to drop out, showing that it can be difficult to always add value in all circumstances.

Knowledge workers

In the UK there has been a decline in traditional manufacturing industry and a growth in areas of work such as the service sector or knowledge economy, where the workers are sometimes referred to as knowledge workers. The management guru

Peter Drucker (1999) identified the growth and management of knowledge workers as being one of the key issues for the twenty-first century. The way organisations share and manage knowledge and motivate their knowledge workers may be a critical factor in determining the success of organisations in the twenty-first century and this is likely to be an issue for many involved in managing people. However, as we said earlier, all workers are vital for an organisation if it is to be successful and all workers should be managed in ways that will motivate them and help them to contribute to the achievement of their organisation's objectives.

There are varying views about the importance of knowledge workers and how they should be managed. Nolan (2001) says that 'the shift to a knowledge intensive economy won't necessarily diminish the importance of sectors producing tangible goods and services.' He claims that the new economy will only account for a tiny percentage of workers and visualises an hourglass-shaped economy where there is a growth in the numbers of knowledge workers but also a growth in unglamorous jobs as support staff.

Talent management

The term 'talent management' is now widely used as in economies such as that of the UK where there is currently a low level of unemployment and where organisations complain of being unable to fill their vacancies, the idea of attracting and keeping talented workers is very important. The concern of employers is illustrated by the quarterly survey report for winter 2006–7 where 'Forty-six percent of employers surveyed anticipate recruitment difficulties this quarter, a higher proportion than the autumn figures (44%)' (CIPD, 2007a). In this sort of economic environment it is important not only to attract but to develop and retain talented workers and the war for talent and talent management affects all aspects of HR from recruitment and selection to reward and motivation and learning and development.

The term talent management does nowadays seem to have a variety of meanings. According to Clake and Winkler (2006), there is broad agreement that 'talent management is not just about upward career moves. Horizontal career moves that broaden an individual's experience are also an integral part of many processes. For many, detailing a talent management strategy has seen a deliberate increase in the "sharing" of talent within an organisation.' According to Clake and Winkler (2006), the most common reasons for becoming involved in talent management are 'developing high-potential individuals (67%), growing future senior managers (62%) and enabling the achievement of strategic goals (42%).' They also found that some organisations (28 per cent) do have a more inclusive view of talent management and use it to develop the 'whole workforce' while 38 per cent of organisations use it to meet future anticipated skills requirements and 36 per cent use it as a means of attracting and recruiting key staff and 33 per cent as a means of retaining key staff.

According to Clake and Winkler, in-house development programmes are the most popular method of talent management with 63 per cent of their sample using this approach. Other approaches such as succession planning and coaching, mentoring and buddying are also popular and graduate training schemes and sponsored MBAs are also used in some organisations as forms of talent management. The topic of talent management is obviously very important in the current economic climate and it will be referred to at various points within this book, particularly in the chapters on recruitment and selection, strategic planning, reward and learning and development.

Knowledge management

Another related area of concern nowadays is in knowledge management. All workers possess a great deal of knowledge which can be easily lost to the organisation when systems change or when there is a reorganisation and of course when people leave an organisation. HR specialists today also therefore have a role to play in trying to ensure that knowledge is shared and retained since this knowledge is a great source of competitive advantage. This presents issues about the best ways of communicating and sharing knowledge but also issues about retention of workers.

Cross-cultural issues in HRM

Some organisations are multinational and produce and sell their goods or services in other countries. Others may use overseas workers in call centres to deal with queries in the UK or in other parts of the world. For many organisations this is a question of minimising the costs of labour while for others the tendency is due to labour and skill shortages and the expansion of the EU. Because there is a tight labour market with nearly full employment in the UK, many organisations who may not have previously regarded themselves as international have been recruiting numbers of migrant workers. Several have been changing their recruitment strategies and have even been targeting these groups for recruitment purposes in their country of origin. Evidence of the extent to which some parts of the UK are now multicultural was provided on 7 July 2005 when terrorists in London killed 52 people who were in the main just on their way to or from work and who happened to be using the London transport system. Those killed came from 13 different countries including the UK. While not all areas of the UK can claim to have as culturally diverse a population as London, it is increasingly the case that many areas are becoming increasingly culturally diverse, so issues around cross-cultural management are important. In the twenty-first century, managing people who come from a culture different to their own is likely to be a part of every manager's job even if they do not consider themselves to be working in an international organisation. According to French (2007), 'it is now possible to present a strong case that all managers should possess cross-cultural sensitivity at the level of managing people at work.'

There is no one theory of cross-cultural management that covers all issues but certain approaches have been very influential. Professor Gert Hofstede's (1980, 1997) research has been instrumental in helping organisations and individuals to understand cultural differences and, according to him, 'For those who work in international business, it is sometimes amazing how different people in other countries behave. We tend to have a basic human instinct that "deep inside" all people are the same – but they are not. Therefore, if we go into another country and make decisions based upon how we operate in our own country – the chances are we'll make some very bad decisions.'

Hofstede conducted a study of values in the workplace and how these are influenced by culture. He used the following dimensions: power distance index, individualism versus collectivism, masculinity versus femininity, uncertainty avoidance and, later, long-term orientation versus short-term orientation. All of these have some effect on how people behave in organisations and will impact on the ways HR managers need to manage people.

Table 1.2 Hofstede's cultural characteristics

Power distance	Uncertainty avoidance	Individualism/Collectivism	Masculinity/Femininity	Long-term orientation/short-term orientation
The extent to which people accept authority structures, i.e. acceptance that it is right for some to make decisions and for others to follow their lead.	Tolerance of ambiguity. The extent to which people desire certainty about what to do in various circumstances or about future events. People with high uncertainty avoidance would welcome rules and regulations.	The extent to which people's actions are determined with reference to their own individual benefit or benefit of the community.	The importance that is placed on material outcomes (masculinity) versus the quality of relationships (femininity).	This relates to values associated with a long-term orientation such as thrift and perseverance as opposed to values more frequently associated with a short-term orientation such as respect for tradition, fulfilling social obligations and protecting one's 'face.'

High power distance	Low power distance	High uncertainty avoidance	Low uncertainty avoidance	High individualism	High collectivism	High masculinity	High femininity	High long-term orientation	Low long-term orientation
Malaysia	USA	Greece	India	USA	Japan	Japan	Sweden	China	UK
Philippines	Great Britain	Portugal	Malaysia	Great Britain	Greece	Great Britain	Portugal	India	USA
Mexico	Sweden	Japan	Great Britain	Sweden	Malaysia	USA	France		
India		Germany	Sweden	France	Pakistan	India			
France				Germany					
Japan									

These categories are listed and described in Table 1.2, together with some examples of which countries tended towards high or low scores on the various values.

Hofstede's work is not to be applied as a model which will solve all problems that stem from intercultural differences, but it does serve to highlight various issues which may affect work relationships. At the very least, an awareness of these differences as potential sources of misunderstanding or conflict provides a basis from which to work towards more effective relationships. For instance, Western approaches towards performance management rest heavily on managers and subordinates being very open with each other in analysing plans for the future and possible weaknesses on the employee's part. Indeed, upward and 360 degree appraisal require constructive criticism of managers by their subordinates. A person from a high power distance country would probably experience extreme discomfort if asked to do this.

In a multicultural society like that in the UK, one is likely to encounter elements of different ethnic cultures even in the domestic workplace, and the influx of migrant workers with the expansion of the EU has added to this cultural diversity.

Cross-cultural issues are becoming increasingly important not just in multinational organisations but also in organisations that recruit to fill skills gaps from workers in the expanded EU and elsewhere. Other issues relating to the treatment of migrant workers in the UK and of workers in third world countries are equally important. In the UK we have become used to comparatively cheap clothes and food but this also has implications for the way in which we pay and treat workers both within the UK and the third world (Lawrence, 2007; McVeigh, 2007). The issue of pay and conditions for migrant workers in the UK and also for suppliers of products from third world countries has been raised in national newspapers and will be discussed in more detail in later chapters. There is clearly a strong moral and ethical issue here which links with the next topic of corporate social responsibility.

Corporate social responsibility (CSR)

This is an area that is becoming of increasing interest and importance to organisations and to the people in them. Frequently the interest has been generated by public scandals and mismanagement, or by the great disparity in salaries of directors in some organisations who get hefty rewards even though their organisation has not done well under their leadership. It also includes issues about fairness and ethics as well as environmental concerns about the threat of global warming and about ways organisations can help to minimise their carbon footprint. According to the CIPD (2007b), 'CSR covers all aspects of company governance. It is about how companies conduct their business in an ethical way, taking account of their impact economically, socially, environmentally and in terms of human rights.'

As such it affects everyone and not just those who are the core stakeholders in the business: the shareholders, the workforce, suppliers and customers. There are other stakeholders such as local communities who may be affected by the action or inaction of businesses and their impact on the community or its environment. If some of its goods are produced in another country the organisation may have global responsibilities towards the workforce in terms of their fair treatment as well as to its suppliers and the local communities. An organisation's actions can even affect future generations.

The CIPD (2007b) has worked with the Department of Trade and Industry (now the Department for Business Enterprise and Regulatory Reform) to develop a competency framework which identifies six competencies that underpin CSR. These are:

1 Understanding society – understanding the role of each player in society, including government, business, trade union, non-governmental organisations and civil society.
2 Building capacity – external partnerships and creating strategic networks and alliances.
3 Questioning 'business as usual' – openness to new ideas, challenging others to adopt new ways of thinking and questioning business as usual ideas.
4 Stakeholder relations – identifying stakeholders, building relations externally and internally, engaging in consultation and balancing demands.
5 Strategic view – taking a strategic view of the business environment.
6 Harnessing diversity – respecting diversity and adjusting the approach to different situations.

As you can see from this list, there are a great many areas in which HR can become involved, although clearly others will also need to be involved in any form of organisational culture change such as this. HR can play an important part in initiating and coordinating ideas or by providing a forum for discussion as many of the best ideas will come from the workforce. HR can also contribute through training, communication and support and by setting objectives for change. For CSR ideas to be acted upon, they also need to make business sense and many simple ideas, for example switching off lights in offices or installing time controls on water coolers to switch them off at night, help the environment and also save organisations' money.

CSR is increasingly of importance to people when choosing which organisation they want to work for and for some of you this may be a strong guiding factor in your choice. According to the CIPD (2007b), 'The way a company treats its employees contributes directly to it being seen as willing to accept its wider responsibilities.

Building credibility and trusting their employer are being increasingly seen as important by employees when they choose who to work for. People, especially generation X and younger, don't want to work where there is a clash with their personal values. Present and future employees are placing increasing value on the credibility of an organisation's brand. Employers are using the positive aspects of their brand in recruiting, motivating and retaining highly skilled people.'

Clarke (2006) goes further and suggests that 'there is evidence that tapping into this interest and engaging staff is also likely to benefit the company brand and reputation. The recent Carbon Trust survey showed that more than three quarters of employees considered it important to work for a company that had an active policy to reduce its carbon emissions.' As organisations increasingly incorporate their ideas about CSR into their company brand image, using it in effect as a marketing tool, it is important that HR professionals utilise the benefits too in all aspects of people management. However, it is not sufficient just to have policies about the environment and corporate social responsibility if they are not implemented. According to Emmott (2005), 'Companies that want to build or protect their brand also need to think about their employer brand, and there is evidence that more and more people want to work for organisations that they respect. No company competing in the "war for talent" can afford to ignore this advice.'

Conclusion

In this chapter we have discussed the historical background to HRM and introduced some of the areas in which HR managers are currently working, and to discussions and debates about the ever-changing roles of HR specialists. We have chosen to focus on current thinking and research about HRM and the extent to which various HRM strategies contribute to the organisation being effective. We have also emphasised the fact that line managers should play important roles nowadays in many aspects of managing people.

In reality, HR roles are very diverse and no one model explains them completely. In small or medium-sized organisations there will be HR practitioners who will deal with all aspects of HRM and who will regard themselves as generalists. In larger organisations there may be a much greater degree of specialisation and some will use business partners and may adopt a shared services approach alongside this. The survey *The Changing HR Function: Transforming HR?* led by Reilly (2007a) showed the wide variety of roles being adopted as HR departments adapted to meet new demands and continued to search for ways to add value to their organisations and contribute to their strategic objectives.

In the next chapter we focus on some of the issues relating to strategy. Since each organisation will have different strategic objectives, it is actually not surprising that they do not just adopt one approach to the way they organise their HR departments, and rather than looking to one model of 'best practice' we should be considering different approaches to 'good practice' depending on what works for specific organisations in the context in which they operate. We shall continue in the next chapters to explain the key aspects of areas of HRM and will take into account when doing so other important issues in the way these topics are handled, such as cross-cultural issues and issues relating to ethics and corporate social responsibility.

REVIEW QUESTIONS

1 We include here a pictorial representation of this chapter in the form of a mind map (Figure 1.1). Use the key words we have included to refresh your memory of what we have covered in this chapter. Add your own key words or drawings to this mind map to reinforce your learning.

2 Identify at least three issues that currently engage the attention of people managers. Explain why each of these is important.

3 Examine three job advertisements for HR specialists. Compare these with the roles listed by Ulrich and Brockbank (2005) of employee advocate, functional expert, human capital developer, strategic partner and HR leader. To what extent do the job advertisements relate to Ulrich and Brockbank's roles?

4 Interview a human resource specialist about his or her job and main duties. Does this person think of themselves as a business partner to the organisation? How do the results from your interview compare with the roles and main duties we described in this chapter?

Figure 1.1 Mind map of Chapter 1

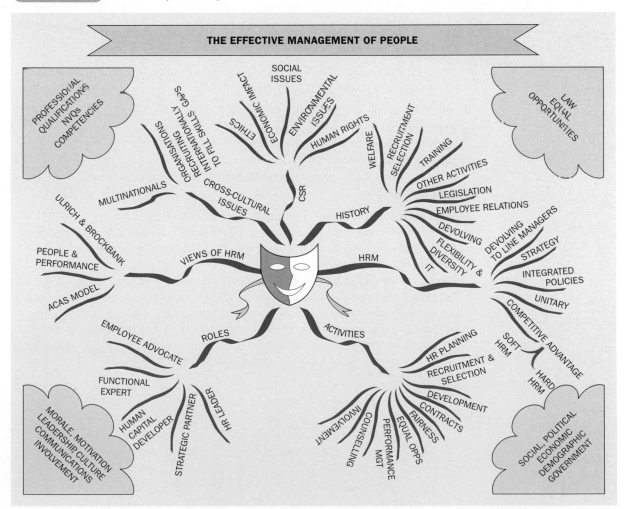

SELF-CHECK QUESTIONS

Answer the following multiple-choice questions. The correct responses are given on page 470 for you to check your understanding of this chapter.

1 To which of the following do the letters CIPD refer?
   (a) The Chartered Institute of Professional Development.
   (b) The Constitutional Institution for the Progress of Devolvement.
   (c) The Chartered Institute of Personnel and Development.
   (d) The Community Institute of Personal Development.

2 Which of the following is not identified in this chapter as a current issue of major importance in the field of people management?
   (a) The need to attract and retain good employees.
   (b) The need to demonstrate how people management activities add value.
   (c) The need to apply advances in IT to improve people management.
   (d) The need to keep wages low to improve competitive advantage.

3 Which of the following statements best sums up the role of the human resource manager in managing people?
   (a) The human resource manager is the sole person who should be involved in all people management activities.
   (b) Both the human resource manager and line manager are likely to be involved in differing ways in managing people.
   (c) The line manager always acts alone in all organisations in dealing with people management activities.
   (d) The human resource manager is only concerned with people management at the day-to-day level.

4 Which of the following statements would be true of the human resource management approach to managing people at work?
   (a) It tackles issues in a piecemeal way.
   (b) It relies on traditional forms of communication.
   (c) There is not much involvement of the workforce in decision making.
   (d) It is strategic.

5 Which of the following sums up an underlying theme in the philosophy of HRM?
   (a) People are important whether they are full-time or part-time employees, permanent or temporary, or contract workers who are actually employed by another company.
   (b) People are important only if they are full-time, permanent employees.
   (c) People are important whether they are full-time or part-time employees so long as they are permanent and are employed by your company.
   (d) People are important whether they are full-time or part-time, permanent or temporary so long as they are employed by your company.

HR IN THE NEWS

Letters to the editor:
Vital link between people management and performance

From Duncan Brown

Sir, Stefan Stern wonders what would happen if you took away the human resources department ('Human resources departments are unloved but not unnecessary', April 18), repeating criticisms made more tellingly over 50 years ago by Peter Drucker. He concludes that there might be a few 'hiccups' around recruitment, pay and employment law – presumably like the recent walkout of more than 1m public-sector workers at proposed changes to their pension arrangements, and the serious oil production problems caused by staff shortages, which the FT recently reported.

Recruitment shortages, skill deficiencies and the growth in employment legislation contributed to the numbers in the UK engaged in HR and training occupations increasing by 15 per cent between 2001 and 2004, hardly indicative of a profession 'at crisis point'. A Chartered Institute of Personnel and Development survey of over 1,000 members found the vast majority implementing a version of Dave Ulrich's 'pathway to salvation' model which Mr Stern describes, and more than four in five feeling fulfilled and increasingly influential in their work – a figure I suspect few other professions could match.

Another research study on organisational changes carried out for CIPD by Said Business School found that effective people management was critical to success, and that chief executives valued the input of HR professionals on change management issues more highly than that of any other function.

The outdated cliché that HR is just about 'tea and sympathy' misses the key area of concern, which is the link between people management and performance in our knowledge and service-based UK economy. There is a wealth of research – from the CIPD, McKinsey, the Work Foundation and many others – demonstrating the direct link between a high standard of HR management practice and organisation performance, be that profitability and productivity in the private sector, or mortality rates in the National Health Service.

Of course line managers actually manage their staff. But the fact that the McKinsey/LSE international comparative research showed UK companies were, on average, the worst managed and least productive in the study, demonstrates that quite a few will need the expert strategic input, skills, support and advice of HR professionals for some time to come, if we are ever to close the productivity gap.

Duncan Brown,
Assistant Director General,
Chartered Institute of Personnel and Development,
London SW19 1JQ

(*Financial Times*, 20 April 2006. Reproduced with permission.)

Questions

1 What arguments would you use to counter the cliché that HR is just about 'tea and sympathy'?

2 What evidence was provided in this letter to demonstrate the value of the role of HR managers?

3 How do the views expressed here about the role of HR compare with the ideas expressed in Chapter 1?

WHAT NEXT ?

Now that you have read the first chapter and completed the exercises, you may want to go further and test your understanding.

1 There are exercises that will help you to do this on our website at **www.pearsoned. co.uk/foothook**.

2 Listen to the following podcast to gain a further understanding of the social, political and ethical issues that face HR managers as they try to build capacity and competence in a global economy. Go to **www.timesonline.co.uk/mbapodcasts** and listen to Sandra Dawson speaking about management, leadership and the global economy. What do you think are the key issues mentioned in this facing HR managers nowadays?

3 Go to **www.acas.org** and examine in more detail the ACAS Model Workplace mentioned earlier in this chapter. Use the model as a checklist. Think of an organisation you know well and compare the way they manage people with the ACAS checklist.

Table 1.3 The main activities of human resource practitioners (Activity 1.1 answer)

Main areas of activity human resource/people management specialist	Type of involvement of the human resource/people management specialist	Type of involvement of line manager
Recruitment and selection	Design of policies and procedure for fair recruitment and selection in order to contribute to the fulfilment of the organisation's corporate strategy. Commission online recruitment activities. Carry out interviews or monitor and give advice on interview technique or on terms and conditions of employment.	Carry out interviews.
Learning and development	Involved in planning learning and development opportunities for the whole organisation, to meet the needs of the organisation as expressed in its strategic plan and to meet the needs of individuals. These could be formal training courses, online materials or less formal approaches such as coaching or mentoring. May design and organise training courses for groups and sometimes run them. May keep training records centrally and request information from line managers as part of planning exercise or to monitor success of training and development.	May also be involved in planning and provision of training and development opportunities to meet the needs of individuals and their departmental needs linked to the organisation's strategic plan, primarily for employees in his or her own department. May provide training and may also keep records of training and provide information to central HRM department.
Human resource planning	Depending on the level of appointment he or she is likely to be involved to various degrees in contributing to the strategic plan. Collection and analysis of data, monitoring targets for the whole organisation. Providing information to managers. Conducting exit interviews and analysing reasons for leaving.	Collect information on leavers and provide information on anticipated requirements for employees for his or her department.
Provision of contracts	Provide written statement of particulars for new employees and issue them to these employees, having checked that the detail is correct. Keep copies of all documentation relating to the employee and advise on any alterations to the contract.	Possibly issue documents and get signature of new employee.

Table 1.3 Continued

Main areas of activity human resource/people management specialist	Type of involvement of the human resource/people management specialist	Type of involvement of line manager
Provision of fair treatment	Involvement in design of policies and procedures for the whole organisation to encourage fair treatment at work. Inform and train people in these policies and procedures. Monitor the success of these policies.	Responsible for fair treatment of people in his or her department to ensure all treat others in a fair way. Listen and respond to grievances as an initial stage in the grievance procedure or informally before someone gets into the grievance procedure. May contribute suggestions about design of policies.
Equal opportunities	Involvement in design of policies to encourage equal opportunities. Train and inform managers and all employees throughout the organisation in these. Monitor the effectiveness of the equal opportunities policies by collecting and analysing information.	May also be involved in, and contribute to, the design of policies. Will be responsible for ensuring that all employees for whom he or she is responsible do not suffer from any form of unfair discrimination while at work.
Managing diversity	Developing policies about diversity and promoting and ensuring a diverse workforce so that the organisation can benefit from ideas generated by individuals from a range of different backgrounds.	Line managers need to actively and encourage diversity to be valued within their own team or department.
Motivating workers to achieve improved performance	Involvement in design and implementation of techniques to assess effectively performance of employees in a way that links clearly with the organisation's strategic plan. Review all HR policies to ensure strategic integration with the strategic plan. Train, inform and involve people in performance management techniques and encourage line managers to work towards a high-performance workplace. Monitor the effectiveness of the procedures. May maintain central records about performance of individual employees.	Contribute to achievement of a high-performance workplace by taking an active role in people management and performance management of his or her own department. Assess performance of those in own department. Involve teams and individuals in setting and agreeing targets and monitoring performance. Monitor their success and give feedback.
Employee counselling	Establish appropriate system, either in-house or by external consultants, for employee counselling or for employee assistance programmes. May be involved in counselling employees with problems or may have to refer them to specialised counselling service.	May be involved in the initial counselling of employees in his or her own section, or may need to suggest alternative sources of counselling if he or she does not feel qualified to deal with the situation.
Employee welfare	Establish appropriate systems for employee welfare in accordance with the objectives of the organisation. Monitor the cost and effectiveness of this provision.	Ensure the well-being of employees in his or her department and draw their attention to, and encourage use of, any provisions designed by the organisation to improve their welfare.
Payment and reward of employees	Establish appropriate payment and reward systems for all employees in order to support achievement of aspects of the organisation's strategic plan. Monitor the success of these. Collect comparative data for other organisations in area or nationally. Deal with individual problems about pay. May be involved in negotiation about payment or reward systems. Tell individuals of their level of pay when they join the organisation or change jobs. May deal with individual problems or complaints about pay.	May be involved in, and contribute views about, appropriate systems of payment or reward to be used in the organisation. May be involved in negotiation to some extent over issues relating to own department. May deal with problems concerning pay raised by employees in his or her department in the first instance.

→

Table 1.3 Continued

Main areas of activity human resource/people management specialist	Type of involvement of the human resource/people management specialist	Type of involvement of line manager
Health and safety	Involvement in design and implementation of the organisation's health and safety policy in order to contribute to the organisation's strategic plan and ensure policies are integrated with other HR policies. Monitor the effectiveness of this. May sit on safety committee or may have line management responsibilities for safety officer or organisation's nurse. Involvement in promotion of health and safety and encouraging the involvement of others throughout the organisation.	Responsible for health and safety of employees working in his or her department. Encourage the involvement of individuals and teams in health or safety promotion activities. Monitor activities of own staff. Carry out regular safety inspections in own department. May take initial disciplinary action against those who infringe health and safety rules.
Disciplining individuals	Design of disciplinary procedure. Monitor the effectiveness of the procedure. Give advice to line managers on disciplinary problems. Organise training for line managers and employees about disciplinary issues to ensure they comply with organisation's policy and with the law. In some organisations he or she may still issue warnings in later stages of disciplinary procedure. Maintain central records of disciplinary action taken.	Conduct informal disciplinary interviews with own staff if necessary. Issue formal warnings as outlined in disciplinary procedure. Maintain records of warnings issued. Ensure compliance both with the organisation's policy and with the statutory discipline, dismissal and grievance procedures.
Dealing with grievances	Participate in the design of grievance procedure and encourage the involvement of others in this. Inform and train people in grievance handling and in the requirements of the statutory procedure. Monitor the effectiveness of the grievance procedure. May deal with some stages in the grievance procedure or appeals.	Deal initially with grievances raised by employees in his or her department. This may be handled informally at first or as part of the formal grievance procedure. Deal with grievances within specified time limits and ensure that these are dealt with in accordance with the organisation's policy and the statutory procedures.
Dismissal	Review procedures for dismissal to ensure that they comply with legislation. Provide advice and guidance on fair dismissal procedure. Provide training for all who may be involved in the dismissal process. May dismiss employee.	In many organisations the actual dismissal will be handled by someone from the HR department with the manager being present. However, nowadays managers in many organisations will also be fully trained to take full responsibility for dismissing an employee in their section in a fair way.
Redundancy	Is likely to be involved in consultation with appropriate people with regard to redundancy. Is likely to be involved in selection of those to be made redundant. May inform employee of redundancy and amount of pay and rights. May organise provision of more generous redundancy payment if this is in line with organisation's policy. May organise provision of outplacement facilities either in-house or by consultants.	Is likely to be involved in selection of those to be made redundant from his or her department. May be involved in telling them of the decision to make them redundant.
Negotiation	Is likely to be involved in negotiation on a wide range of organisation-wide issues.	Is likely to be involved in negotiation on a wide range of issues that affect employees in his or her department.

Table 1.3 Continued

Main areas of activity human resource/people management specialist	Type of involvement of the human resource/people management specialist	Type of involvement of line manager
Encouraging involvement and engagement	Will have an extremely important role in creating a culture within the organisation in which employees are encouraged to be involved in decision making and engaged in working towards the organisation's objectives. Will be involved in designing policy and procedures to encourage employee involvement in line with strategic plan. Will also provide training to encourage employee involvement.	Will contribute to organisation's policies and will encourage involvement of employees in his or her department.
Adding value	Ensuring that all HR activities help to add value to the organisation by helping it achieve its objectives and become a high-performance workplace.	Ensuring that all HR activities help to add value to their department or section by ensuring they contribute to its objectives.
Ethics and corporate responsibility	HR managers are concerned with all issues relating to fairness whether or not this is covered by legislation. Increasingly they are becoming involved in design of policies and procedures which take account of the impact of their business economically, socially, environmentally and in terms of human rights. They may challenge the way things have been done to draw attention to the corporate and social responsibility issues. They are likely to play an important role in support of environmental issues.	Ensure that all activities in their own section comply with the organisation's policies on corporate and social responsibility and that they always act in a way consistent with these.
Knowledge management and talent management	HR specialists are likely to be involved in devising polices and strategies to encourage the sharing of knowledge within the organisation and to try to ensure that the organisation keeps its knowledge workers and has communications systems that facilitate the sharing of knowledge so it is not lost to the organisation if someone leaves. They will also be concerned to identify and develop talent.	Line managers will need to manage knowledge workers in sensitive ways to ensure they stay with the organisation. They should encourage the sharing of knowledge within their team. They will also play a key role in identifying talent and nurturing it within their team.
Change management	HR specialists will deal with the people aspects of change and will have a role to design policies and procedures to support change. They will also ensure that there is clear communication, consultation, involvement and engagement with the workforce with any changes that are planned. They are likely to be involved in designing learning and development initiatives to support the changes.	The line manager will be involved in implementing the changes but will also play an important part in communicating issues relating to the changes to their team and in communicating concerns about the changes upwards to senior management. They will run learning and development activities to support the changes.
Managing cross-cultural issues or international HRM	The HR specialist may be involved in recruitment drives in other countries or in managing cross-cultural issues within this country as workers from many differing ethnic origins are employed. Policies and procedures will need to take account of cross-cultural issues and if working in a multinational organisation there will also need to be decisions made about the way HR policies are implemented within each country. They are likely to have involvement in learning and development initiatives to support this.	The line manager will deal with day-to-day issues arising form cross-cultural issues in the workplace, whether he or she is working in his or her home country or working in another country with host country nationals and expatriate workers.

References

Advisory, Conciliation and Arbitration Service (2007) *The ACAS Model Workplace,* ACAS.

Arkin, A. (2007) Street smart, *People Management,* 5 April, Vol. 13, No. 7.

Atkinson, J. (1984) Manpower strategies for flexible organisations, *Personnel Management,* August, 28–31.

Atkinson, J. (1989) Four stages of adjustment to the demographic downturn, *Personnel Management,* August, 20–24.

Boxall, P. and J. Purcell (2003) *Strategy and human resource management,* Houndsmills: Palgrave McMillan.

Chartered Institute of Personnel and Development (2005) *Survey report 2005. HR: Where is your career heading?* CIPD (www.cipd.co.uk; accessed 6.4.07).

Chartered Institute of Personnel and Development (2006a) *CIPD Annual Report 2006,* CIPD (www.cipd.co.uk; accessed 25.7.07).

Chartered Institute of Personnel and Development (2006b) *Reflections on the learning and development,* CIPD (www.cipd.co.uk; accessed 9.4.07).

Chartered Institute of Personnel and Development (2007a) *Overview of CIPD surveys. A barometer of HR trends and prospects 2007,* CIPD (www.cipd.co.uk; accessed 6.4.07).

Chartered Institute of Personnel and Development (2007b) *Corporate Social Responsibility,* CIPD.

Clake, R. and V. Winkler (2006) *The Change Agenda: Reflections on talent management,* CIPD (www.cipd.co.uk; accessed 9.4.07).

Clarke, E. (2006) Power brokers, *People Management,* 18 May, Vol. 12, No. 10.

Crail, M. (2007) *HR Prospects 2007: HR priorities and the factors that shape them,* IRS Employment Review, Issue 876, 18.6.07.

Donaghy, R. (2007) Forward to *ACAS Model Workplace,* ACAS.

Drucker, P. (1999) *Management Challenges for the Twenty-first Century,* Harper Business.

Emmott, M. (2005) CSR laid bare, *People Management,* Vol. 11, No. 16, 11 August, 38–40.

French, R. (2007) *Cross-cultural management in work organisations,* CIPD.

Green, K. (1999) Offensive thinking, *People Management,* Vol. 5, No. 8, 27.

Guest, D. (1987) Human resource management and industrial relations, *Journal of Management Studies,* Vol. 24, 503–521.

Hall, L. and D. Torrington (1998) *The Human Resource Function: The Dynamics of Change and Development,* Financial Times Pitman Publishing.

Harrison, R. (2002) *Learning and Development,* CIPD.

Hayes, C. (2005) The world has moved on but the Ulrich model hasn't, *People Management,* 14 July, Vol. 11, No. 14, 4.

Hofstede, G. (1980) *Culture's Consequences: International Differences in Work Related Values,* McGraw-Hill.

Hofstede, G. (1997) *Cultures and Organisations: Software of the Mind,* revised edition, McGraw-Hill.

Hoque, K. and M. Noon (2001) Counting angels: a comparison of personnel and HR specialists, *Human Resource Management Journal,* Vol. 11, No. 3, 5–22.

Industrial Relations Services (IRS) (2000) In-store personnel managers balance Tesco's scorecard, *IRS Employment Trends,* May, 13–16.

Industrial Relations Services (IRS) (2001) HR in 2001: the IRS audit, *IRS Employment Trends,* 728, May, 4–10.

Kaplan, R.S. and D.P. Norton (1992) The balanced scorecard – measures that drive performance, *Harvard Business Review,* January–February, 71–79.

Kaplan, R.S. and D.P. Norton (1996) *The Balanced Scorecard: Translating Strategy into Action,* Harvard Business School Press.

Kaplan, R.S. and D.P. Norton (2000) Having trouble with your strategy? Then map it, *Harvard Business Review,* September–October, 167–176.

Lawrence, F. (2007) The miracle of cheap fresh food depends on illegality, *The Guardian,* Comment and Debate, Thursday 17 July.

Legge, K. (1995) *Human Resource Management: Rhetorics and Realities,* Macmillan Business.

McVeigh, K. (2007) Asda, Primark and Tesco accused over clothing factories, *The Guardian,* Monday 16 July.

Niven, M. (1978) *Personnel Management 1913–63,* IPM.

Nolan, P. (2001) Shaping things to come, *People Management,* Vol. 7, No. 25, 30–31.

Office for National Statistics (2003) Labour Force Survey, *Part time working by sex,* Spring (www.statistics.gov.uk; accessed 16.09.04).

Purcell, J., N. Rinnie, S. Hutchinson (2003) Open minded, *People Management,* Vol. 9, No. 10, 31–33.

Reilly, P. (2007a) *The changing HR function: Transforming HR?* CIPD.

Reilly, P. (2007b) HR transformation: Facing up to facts, *People Management,* Vol. 13, No. 19.

Scarborough, H. (2003) Recipe for success, *People Management,* Vol. 9, No. 2, 32–35.

Scarborough, H. and the CIPD Human Capital Task Force (2003) Human capital: external reporting framework, *The change agenda,* CIPD (www.cipd.co.uk; accessed 16.9.04).

Scott, A. (2007) Is HR still admin-focused? *People Management,* Vol. 13, No. 14, 13.

Sparrow, P. and M. Marchington (1998) *Human Resource Management: The New Agenda,* Financial Times Pitman Publishing.

Storey, J. and K. Sisson (1993) *Managing Human Resources and Industrial Relations,* Open University Press.

Tyson, S. (ed.) (1995) *Strategic Prospects for HRM,* CIPD.

Ulrich, D. and W. Brockbank (2005) Role call, *People Management,* 16 June, Vol. 11, No. 12, 24–28.

Further study

Books

Advisory, Conciliation and Arbitration Service (2007) *The ACAS Model Workplace,* ACAS. This can be used as a checklist or point of reference to compare effectiveness of people management issues within any organisation. It can be obtained free from ACAS or downloaded from www.acas.org.uk.

Journals

Advisory, Conciliation and Arbitration Service (2007) *Employment Relations Matters,* ACAS. This is a series of quarterly journals covering various employment relations issues which you can either request be sent to you or which you can download free from www.acas.org.com. It includes an annual workplace relations survey which highlights various trends.

Human Resource Management Journal. Quarterly, contains articles on a wide range of HRM issues of interest to practitioners and academics alike.

People Management. Twice-monthly journal produced on behalf of the CIPD with topical articles relating to personnel management issues.

Personnel Review. Journal produced six times per year with in-depth articles on personnel topics.

Personnel Today. Contains topical articles on personnel management.

Internet

There are numerous useful sources of information from around the world relating to human resource management. We have found the following to be particularly useful:

The Advisory, Conciliation and Arbitration Service   **www.acas.org.uk**
Useful articles, news and lists of ACAS publications.

The American Society for Human Resource Management   **www.shrm.org**
The website for a US body that represents HRM managers. This includes topical people-related issues in America and video clips and podcasts.

The Australian Human Resource Institute   **www.ahri.com.au**
Many articles relating to human resource management in Australia.

Chartered Institute of Personnel and Development   **www.cipd.co.uk**

The website for the professional body that represents personnel and development professionals in the UK. This includes a wide range of information, including podcasts, but some of the information is only accessible to CIPD members.

Department for Business, Enterprise and Regulatory Reform   **www.berr.gov.uk**

Many useful publications, discussion documents and booklets can be found on this site, particularly in the 'Employment Matters' section.

The Government   **www.direct.gov.uk**

Useful information site covering a wide range of employment-related topics such as holiday entitlements, disability issues etc.

Incomes Data Services Limited   **www.incomesdata.co.uk**

Some very useful articles on a range of HRM topics, including a section on management pay and remuneration, plus lists of contents for IDS publications.

People Management   **www.peoplemanagement.co.uk**

Journal produced on behalf of the CIPD with topical articles relating to personnel management issues.

Trades Union Congress   **www.tuc.org.uk**

This gives the TUC's views on many current HRM issues and new legislation in Britain.

Workforce online (US)   **www.hrhq.com**

Another American site that provides useful information about HRM in the USA.

Xpert HR   **www.xperthr.co.uk**

This is the source for IRS publications such as the *IRS Employment Review*.

CHAPTER 2

Human resource strategy and planning

Objectives

When you have studied this chapter you will be able to:

- describe the three basic levels of strategic planning
- explain the concept of strategy formulation
- explain the need for human resource strategies in work organisations
- describe the stages involved in human resource planning
- identify and describe the issues that have an impact on supply and demand forecasts
- use basic mathematical techniques to produce forecast supply figures
- describe the skills shortages encountered by employers, their causes and possible solutions
- comment on the use of IT systems in strategic HRM.

The chapter introducing human resource management (HRM) established that a key characteristic of the HRM approach is the involvement of the people management function at a strategic level. We will now look briefly at the different levels at which strategy can be formulated and the generic types of strategy that are encountered, and comment on the links between the formulation of business strategy and consideration of human resource issues. You must remember that we shall be looking at the ideal situation or models of how corporate/business strategy and HR considerations could interact. What we describe as an ideal is not always found in reality, or, indeed, the specific circumstances in which a business is operating might call for a different approach. You will find that occasionally throughout the text we refer to contingency approaches, which means that there is no one right way to manage human resources in an organisation.

Following an overview of corporate/business and human resource strategies, we examine the activities that underpin the development of HR strategies, namely the techniques involved in human resource planning and the factors which have a major impact on planning decisions. This chapter ends with a discussion of the role of IT in supporting strategic human resource management (SHRM) endeavours, and a brief overview of some relevant aspects of people management in the international sphere.

Strategy

Strategy can be defined as a plan of action for the future, answering the questions, first, of *what* to do, then, of *how* to do it. The three commonplace questions used to give a simple explanation of the strategic process are: Where are we now? Where do we want to be? How do we get there? A strategic plan should have a long-term focus, business plans usually being developed around a five-year perspective. The aim of designing and following a strategic plan is to create a competitive advantage, and all efforts in the formulation and implementation processes will be directed towards this. As far as work organisations are concerned, strategy can be formulated and implemented at different levels, and there are recognised generic forms of strategy that organisations or sub-divisions of organisations might adopt.

Levels of strategy

The levels at which strategy is formulated and implemented are most frequently identified as corporate, business and functional or operational (see, for example, Anthony *et al.* 1996; Boxall and Purcell, 2003; Greer, 2001; Lynch, 2003; Marchington and Wilkinson, 2005).

Corporate and business strategies

Corporate strategy is concerned with the overall direction that an organisation will follow. For large corporations, this is a question of which lines of business they will choose to be engaged in. These organisations would then develop separate business level strategies for their divisions, each of which might be engaged in producing very different products or services. As Anthony *et al.* (1996) point out, corporate and business strategy would be one and the same thing for a small organisation dealing only with one line of products or services, and it follows that you will sometimes find writers using the terms interchangeably when they are discussing these two levels of strategy.

Functional strategy

The functions represented in an organisation depend on the type of business, its size and structure, but may include production, marketing, sales, finance, research and development, and human resources. Each of these functional areas needs to be following strategic plans that are consonant with the corporate and business plans adopted by their organisations. The strategic plans adopted by all these functional departments must be integrated, however, to ensure the success of the organisation; they are interdependent and cannot be formulated in ignorance of each other. Indeed, it can be stated incontrovertibly that the human resource is an integral part of every one of the above-named functions.

The strategy formulation process

You will find throughout the discussion of the strategic planning process that there is a great deal of emphasis on gathering information as a basis for decision making.

There is a need to focus on relevant information, but it is also imperative to be comprehensive so you do not miss something that could have an impact. Since planning implies forecasting future actions, there is always the potential for developments that you may not have foreseen. This means that planning becomes a rolling process, and that a five-year plan developed in 2008 cannot be followed slavishly until the year 2013, but will probably need to be adjusted on an ongoing basis to account for unforeseen developments.

Pause for thought 2.1 What kinds of information might senior managers in a company manufacturing and distributing consumer goods need to consider in order to formulate strategic plans?

You may have considered a variety of factors and kept in mind the types of changes that businesses in general are facing. Your list may include some of the following:

- **Product life cycle:** Is the product or service a new one with room for development and an expanding potential market? Is the product something that is bought once or do customers replace it? Is the product mature and not likely to attract more customers? Are customers likely to look for an alternative to the product or service?
- **Changing consumer tastes and requirements:** How are these likely to affect the demand for the product? Are there changes in customer expectations that organisations need to respond to?
- **Expansion of business into other countries:** Are there opportunities to sell your product or service abroad?
- **Competition:** What are the threats from competitors and the opportunities to compete? What will be the impact of new issues such as the growth of global competition, for instance increasing competition from countries like China?
- **Technological developments:** Will new technology affect the design of products, work processes and costs?
- **Legislation:** What regulations are in the pipeline and what are the associated implications for costs, work processes and product standards?

These are just some of the factors that affect business planning, and you may be able to identify even more. Information about all of these factors will influence what managers see as threats and opportunities and will therefore affect the strategic choices made and formulation of the strategic plan.

Keeping an eye on all of these issues is referred to as environmental scanning, and the acronym PEST or its alternative forms of PESTEL, PESTLE or EPISTLE are commonly used as a reminder of the issues that businesses need to take into consideration when formulating their strategies. The initials in PEST stand for political, economic, social and technological issues. The E and L in variations of the basic acronym variously stand for European, environmental and legislative issues.

ACTIVITY 2.1

Think of some current examples in these categories which may be of particular import to business strategists. Go to the companion website at **www.pearsoned.co.uk/foothook** to compare your suggestions with ours.

In summary, then, a strategic approach implies a *long-term view*, encompassing *global information* from *all relevant perspectives*, and focusing on an *ultimate goal of corporate success* through achieving and exploiting a position of *competitive advantage*. Furthermore, a strategic approach requires the *integration* of *activities and processes* throughout an organisation, all *aligned* to the *organisation's goals*.

Generic types of corporate and business strategy

There are a number of recognised generic types of strategies that companies may choose to follow. The overarching corporate strategies are generally cited as being growth, stability and retrenchment (Millmore *et al.*, 2007), but there are a number of ways of pursuing each of these. Growth can be achieved, for instance, through the development of new products, by acquiring a larger share of the market for existing products, through mergers and acquisitions. Glaister (1995) also lists internationalisation as a possible generic strategy that organisations might wish to follow. These strategic directions (i.e. growth, stability and retrenchment) are normally associated with the life cycle stages of products and markets (Johnson *et al.*, 2006) and the idea behind the BCG matrix put forward by the Boston Consulting Group in the 1970s is that large corporations would aim to have a balanced portfolio of businesses encompassing a range of these (see Lynch, 2003).

The work of Michael Porter (1980) is frequently cited in discussions of business-level strategies. The generic concepts he developed are cost leadership, differentiation and focus. One or a combination of these can be adopted in order to achieve the chosen corporate strategy. In adopting a strategy based on cost, companies will attempt to improve efficiency by reducing staffing and production costs. A strategy of differentiation means emphasising the distinctiveness of one's products or services, for example by being known for consistent high quality. A market or niche focus approach entails concentrating on a particular segment rather than the whole industry. As Glaister comments, this strategy can be pursued in combination with either cost leadership or differentiation. Innovation as a strategic direction can also provide a major focus (see, for instance, Johnson and Johnson's website at **www.jnj.com**) and Guest *et al.* (1997) make the point that all business strategies need an element of innovation.

Human resource strategies

Human resource strategies arise from the adoption of a strategic approach to people management which is aligned with the business strategy and which is reflected in a set of HR policy initiatives specifically designed to achieve the strategic goals of the business. This implies that an appropriate HR strategy is being 'read off' the corporate strategy to provide the 'best fit' between the two levels of strategy (discussed in detail by Marchington and Wilkinson, 2005, pp. 106–113). Ideally, however, human resource considerations should inform the corporate strategy and affect what is included in it (CIPD, 2006b). The costs of the HR strategies and the probability of their success should have been a factor in the decision to pursue the particular business strategic goal in the first place.

HR strategies reflect the philosophy of senior management with regard to the treatment of human resources and address the various activities related to their management. The underlying premise of this is that the HR function supports corporate goals by developing and implementing people management practices which engage employees and encourage them to direct their efforts towards the achievement of organisational goals (CIPD, 2005). The most tangible aspect of strategic HRM is, therefore, the set of HR policies and processes in existence in an organisation, and these would normally address the various aspects of people management such as recruitment, diversity management, development, reward and employee relations. In other words, rather than being able to identify *the* human resource strategy of an organisation, one will encounter an organisation's recruitment strategy or its diversity strategy or its reward strategy, either explicitly addressed as a strategy or reflected in the organisation's policies and processes. For many organisations, the main focus of their HR strategies is to acquire, develop and maintain a high-performance workforce, and this is dealt with in Chapter 3.

As environmental factors change, different issues may assume critical strategic importance. One example of this which is examined later in this chapter (see the discussion of skills shortages) and in other parts of the book is the issue of the war for talent. Because of increased competition for skilled employees in a wide variety of positions, many organisations across the globe have developed a talent management strategy or talent management processes (CIPD, 2007c; Ready and Conger, 2007; Wooldridge, 2006). The strategic approach to the various aspects of people management is covered in the relevant chapter throughout this text.

Because there are so many important aspects of people management strategy, it becomes essential that these various strategies are coherent and supportive of each other as well as being aligned with the overall business strategy. Other crucial aspects of successful strategic HRM are effective communication and change management (CIPD, 2005). In order to be motivated to achieve an organisation's goals, its people need to understand what is expected of them and how their efforts contribute to their organisation's success; hence the need for excellent communication systems. Also, of necessity, operating in a strategic fashion means dealing with change since the definition of a strategic approach involves planning for the future and adjusting to a turbulent business environment. The CIPD (2005, p. 3) poses a number of questions for HR strategists to consider when embarking on the strategy formulation, development and implementation processes. Some examples of these questions are: Will line managers support strategy initiatives and do they have the skills to implement them? How are staff generally likely to react to the strategy? Can any difficulties be anticipated, and if so, how can they be dealt with? These questions help the practitioner to focus on more general aspects of project and change management processes as well as developing the HR strategies *per se*.

The discussion of strategic HRM and HR strategies so far has emphasised the role of the HR practitioner as a business partner, one of the roles in HR described by Ulrich (CIPD, 2006b). The devolution of people management responsibilities to line managers at all levels in an organisation is, however, recognised as a basic element of the HRM approach (Storey, 2007), so line involvement in the development and implementation of HR strategies is essential. Hutchinson and Purcell (2003) emphasised that front-line managers, defined as line managers with no managerial staff reporting to them, play a crucial role in ensuring that HR strategies are carried out effectively. Strategic HR practitioners, therefore, need to incorporate line management views into the HR strategy planning process, nurture the relationship between the HR function and line managers, and ensure that line managers are actively engaged with the people management strategy. Unfortunately, the achievement of this goal of mutual understanding between HR strategists and line managers has been identified as problematic (Smethurst, 2005). This is obviously another instance where improvements in communication and change management are required.

Human resource planning

Whatever the strategy adopted by an organisation, it is recognised that an unrelenting and increasing rate of change is an unavoidable phenomenon of today's workplace. The implication is that tomorrow's workplace will not be the same as today's. Employment patterns are changing, as we discuss in more detail in Chapter 4 on the employment relationship, and changing work methods, arising, for instance, from technological advances, give rise to requirements for different and new skills and for flexibility from existing employees to acquire these new skills or adapt to new methods of working. This highlights the need for human resource planning which responds to this situation by taking a long-term view and works towards preparing an organisation to cope with its future requirements and achieve its strategic objectives. The information acquired through the process of human resource planning provides the foundation for the development of human resource strategies.

The next few sections of this chapter examine the stages involved in the human resource planning process, the types of issues and information that need to be considered, and techniques for processing that information.

Estimating the demand for human resources

Whatever the goals of the corporate/business plan are, they can be achieved only by the application of human skill and effort. One of the primary stages in the human resource planning process is therefore to estimate what will be required in terms of skills and numbers of people to achieve the corporate goals, i.e. the demand for human resource inputs. Let us take some examples of corporate goals so that we can envisage what this exercise might entail.

ACTIVITY 2.2

Examine the following two scenarios, and evaluate what will be required in terms of human resources in order to achieve the goals stated in each case. What factors would have to be considered in making forecasts of requirements?

1 A UK distributor of women's clothing wishes to expand its customer base into Germany, France and Spain. It intends to open a warehouse and distribution depot in France.
2 A regional building society and a national bank are set to merge.

Discussion of Activity 2.2

In order to assess the requirements for human resources in the above scenarios, you would have to envisage:

- what tasks need to be done
- the skills required to complete these tasks
- how the tasks could be grouped together to form jobs, taking the skills requirements into consideration
- how many people would be required to complete the volume of work.

First, then, there is a matter of the identification of discrete work tasks, followed by the organisation of those work tasks into jobs (i.e. a collection of tasks that somehow belong together and could reasonably be carried out by one individual), and a qualitative analysis of the skill base required to perform those jobs and achieve the organisation's goals. The records that document tasks and skills in an organisation are the job descriptions (JDs) and person specifications, and the information contained in these documents is collected and organised through the processes of job analysis and job design, which are discussed more fully in Chapter 6, which deals with recruitment. Alternatively, an organisation might use a competency framework to describe the skills and attributes required and create job profiles based on this (see pages 153–155). Second, there is the task of quantifying the numbers of people required.

In scenario 1 you will have identified the need for the staff to run the warehousing and distribution processes in the new depot in France. This will include a manager, picking and packing staff, administrative staff and drivers. You may further have considered the need for language skills among some of these staff to cope with communications with the customers in Spain and Germany and with the home base in the UK. The expansion of business into these countries might also mean adding new tasks and skill requirements to existing posts in the home base, or it may mean recruiting a new manager and/or administrative staff who have the requisite language skills and knowledge of marketing and business processes in those countries. At the very least, the expansion of business into new countries implies a need for someone to coordinate the activities with headquarters. You would need additional information about the expected volume of business to be able to calculate how many people will be required in each category of employee.

Scenario 2 requires an examination of where skills and functions overlap within the two types of business, which might imply that some duties can be merged and not all of the existing posts will be needed. Alternatively, because the new, merged organisation will cover a wider range of tasks than either of the separate organisations had, there may be a new requirement for people who can combine skills and manage tasks in both areas.

Quantitative aspects of estimating demand

Having worked out what is required in terms of tasks to be done and skills needed to complete those tasks, an analysis is required of how many people are needed for the volume of work.

Pause for thought 2.2 Imagine you are a manufacturer who is going to export clothes to mainland Europe. You have estimated that you will require sewing machine operators to produce an additional 10,000 blouses in the first year. What methods could you use to estimate how many people you would need for this task?

If you have no previous measures of how much work is produced by your employees, you can engage in work study techniques. This involves determining how the task can be performed most efficiently and timing the operation. You would then calculate how many blouses can be sewn at this rate in one year by one operator and divide your production target of 10,000 by this number to get the number of employees required.

If prior data do exist, you can use past production figures and calculate the ratio of operatives to the number of blouses produced by taking the total figure of blouses produced divided by the total number of operatives engaged in this or similar work. You might also apply managerial judgement by basing your calculations on a task that is similar to producing a blouse.

Another historical figure employers might use is the ratio of various categories of personnel to the volume of sales or the number of customers. For instance, if a distribution company has one invoice clerk for every 10,000 customers, and it intends to increase its customer base by 10,000, the historical ratio indicates a need for one additional invoice clerk.

You would need to take account of the fact that new employees might not work at full capacity until fully trained, or you might envisage savings from economies of scale or from changing work methods or the technology used. In other words, even when statistical methods are used to calculate the demand for human resources, managerial judgement will also be a factor.

Estimating the internal supply of human resources

As with estimating the demand for human resources, organisations need to combine qualitative data based on managerial judgement with quantitative data to assess whether the requisite resources will be available.

A properly designed human resource information system (HRIS) will provide data on the numbers of existing employees in various categories of posts (the internal supply of human resources), and personal data that may have an impact on how long they are likely to be with the organisation. There are some simple statistical techniques that enable employers to forecast fluctuations in their workforce numbers. The basic figure that most employers calculate is the labour turnover rate, sometimes referred to as the wastage rate or the separation rate, which represents the proportion of employees who leave in a given period of time, usually a year or a quarter. This figure is calculated as a percentage by dividing the number of leavers by the total complement of staff and multiplying this figure by 100. If the requirements for staff vary during the time period, the total complement can be calculated as an average of the number required at the beginning of the period and the number required at the end. This would give an overall turnover rate for an organisation, but it is usually more useful to calculate the rate for specific categories of staff such as secretarial staff, systems analysts, employees in specified production areas, etc.

For example, if a company requires 50 machinists throughout the year, and 5 of these have left in one year, then the turnover rate is $(5/50) \times 100 = 10$ per cent. The average turnover rate experienced over a period of time can be used as a trend to forecast requirements for the future. For instance, if the turnover rate for machinists in our example company has been fairly stable at about 10 per cent over the past three years, then this employer knows that it is likely to be necessary to recruit five machinists next year to maintain his or her supply. If the demand forecast implies that additional machinists will be needed over the next few years, the 10 per cent turnover rate should be factored into the recruitment calculation.

ACTIVITY 2.3

At the end of 2008, the employer in question decides that she will require 10 additional machinists in each of the next three years. The additional machinists are to be recruited at the beginning of each year. How many machinists will she have to recruit during each year to maintain the workforce?

Discussion of Activity 2.3

These figures are best calculated by tracking the base figure required each year, the increase in personnel required, and an adjustment for the expected turnover. As you can see, the manufacturer needs not only to recruit the additional 10 employees each year, but also to cover the turnover on the new base figure. With a typical labour turnover rate of 10 per cent, in 2009, five of the original employees may leave, and perhaps one of the new employees. The figures are presented in Table 2.1.

Table 2.1 Estimated recruitment figures adjusted for labour turnover

	Number of machinists required	Increase over previous year	Projected turnover during year	Number to recruit during the year
End of 2008	50			
2009	60	10	6	16
2010	70	10	7	17
2011	80	10	8	18

Another calculation that can be made is known as the stability index. This also gives an indication of turnover, but provides information additional to the base turnover figure and is calculated as follows: (Number of people currently employed with one year or more of service/number of people employed one year ago) × 100.

ACTIVITY 2.4

This is a simple activity that will help you to focus on the information that can be gleaned by analysing the same data in different ways.

1 You are asked to perform a simple calculation for each of three situations.
   (a) Your organisation has 20 drivers. In one year, 5 of these drivers leave and have to be replaced. Calculate the turnover rate.
   (b) Your organisation has 20 drivers. At the end of one year, you still have 19 of those drivers with you, but you have had to recruit 5 times to keep your staff complement up to 20. Calculate the turnover rate and the stability index.

(c) Your organisation has 20 drivers. In one year, 5 drivers leave. Each of them had 2–5 years of service. You have had to replace each of them and your new recruits are still with you. Calculate the turnover rate and the stability index.

2 What do these turnover and stability index figures tell you?

Discussion of Activity 2.4

You should have calculated a turnover figure of 25 per cent for each of these circumstances. On its own, the turnover figure reveals nothing about the underlying causes of turnover, and this is emphasised by the fact that you have the same figure for the two very different circumstances described as (b) and (c) above. The turnover rate on its own becomes meaningful only if you can compare it with rates experienced by your organisation in the past or by other organisations in your industry for similar categories of staff. Then you can deduce whether you are performing in a competitive way in terms of retaining staff, or whether there are problems you need to investigate.

> **Did you know?**
>
> The CIPD (2007b) report that the average labour turnover figure in the 905 organisations they surveyed was 18.1 per cent in 2006. Private sector organisations suffered the highest wastage rates with an average of 22.6 per cent.

The stability index figures, 95 per cent in scenario (b) and 75 per cent in scenario (c), are much more revealing. The similarity among all three scenarios in the exercise is that there have been five recruitment actions in each case; the stability index, however, reveals that the situations are different and the reasons for the vacancies differed. The higher figure, which means that the turnover is not occurring among the longer-serving employees, indicates that there is a problem with retaining new recruits. The lower figure indicates that the problem lies with the retention of longer serving employees. Each problem requires different action to remedy it, and this will be very important when you arrive at the stage of formulating human resource management action plans.

> **Pause for thought 2.3** In the discussion of Activity 2.4, we mentioned that comparing your turnover to that experienced by your competitors might prompt you to analyse retention problems. If your turnover rate was unfavourable in such a comparison, what might some of the problems and remedies be?

Some of the problems and remedies associated with excessive turnover are represented in Table 2.2.

There are some other factors that have an impact on the turnover rate. Some of these might be reflected in long-term trends and others may cause occasional fluctuations. One such factor is the age of employees. Retirement may account for a certain percentage of leavers on an ongoing basis, but it also sometimes happens that an organisation has a large number of people due to retire at the same time, which will temporarily increase the turnover rate. This continues to be a consideration even if one pays due attention to the changing regulations with regard to the

Table 2.2 Labour turnover: causes and remedies

Cause	Remedy
Poor handling of new recruits	Design and implement induction process
Unfavourable salary/terms and conditions of employment	Revise reward strategies
Job dissatisfaction	Improve job design
Low morale	Organisational culture change Employee involvement and engagement practices Employee opinion surveys
Recruits not equipped for work demands	Improve recruitment and selection practices Improve training

Did you know?

In 2007 a report was produced highlighting the difficulties schools, in particular primary and special schools, were facing in recruiting head teachers. The problem was exacerbated by the numbers of senior staff reaching retirement age, with the peak of retirements forecast to occur in 2008.

(*Source*: Howson, J. (2007) *22nd Annual Survey of Senior Staff Appointments in Schools in England and Wales*, Education Data Surveys)

normal retirement age discussed in Chapter 5, 'Equality and diversity'. Factors such as this need to be taken into consideration in forecasting the supply of human resources and when adjusting the estimates to reflect the effects of labour turnover. To achieve successful strategic planning, the HRIS should be set up so that it can provide this information.

In addition to information about numbers, the analysis of various aspects of the workforce can highlight a range of problems or issues that deserve consideration. Some of the analyses that could be obtained are:

- the male/female distribution of personnel across the whole workforce or in each category of employee
- the distribution across the workforce or by employee category of members of specified ethnic minority groups
- age profiles
- length of service for each of the above.

These analyses could help managers to see where new approaches or policies are needed to help the organisation reach its goals.

A further factor that may have an impact on future internal supply is the fact that people often have skills that their employer may not have required them to use in their current post. These could include facility in foreign languages, computer knowledge, training skills and interpersonal skills. In order to have a full picture of skills available from the current workforce the organisation needs to develop a skills inventory, with each individual's competencies recorded on his or her personal record, which will form part of the organisation's HRIS. The skills inventory should list skills that are available but not being used in addition to those that are being used.

Assessing the external supply of human resources

At the same time as analysing their internal supply of human resources, employers need to be aware of the availability of potential employees externally in case the internal supply falls short of what is required. If the internal supply of employees cannot meet the demand, managers must know whether there are problems with the availability of workers from outside the organisation. Indeed, the Industrial Relations Services (2001) reported that competition for new recruits was likely to be a major problem for employers throughout the first decade of the twenty-first century. The ongoing problems with skills shortages, reported later in this chapter, indicate that this has in fact proven to be the case.

The labour force is defined as the number of people aged 16 and over, and who are either in employment or available for work. As such, those members of the labour force who are not currently employed by a particular employer constitute that employer's external labour market. Sometimes separate figures are given for people of working age, but since some people continue working past the state retirement age, figures for persons in their late sixties and seventies are included in estimates of the total labour force. Current debate about the state retirement age also suggests that it is likely to be raised before 2010.

Pause for thought 2.4   There are many factors that have an impact on:

- the size of the labour force in general
- the availability of employees from the labour force to any particular employer.

Before you go on to read about these factors, make a list of as many of them as you can think of. You may also wish to consider what employers might have to do to counteract any problems you identify.

Size and composition of the labour force

British labour force projections for the years 2006–2020, as reported in *Labour Market Trends* (Madouros, 2006), included the following data:

- Between 2006 and 2020 the labour force is set to increase, but the rate of increase will decline over that period. The labour force is projected to consist of 32.1 million economically active people in 2020.
- The working age is defined here as 16–64 years old, but a growing number of people *above* the age of 64 are expected to continue to be economically active.
- The proportion of people in the labour force aged under 50 will fall to 69 per cent by 2020. By comparison, it was 75 per cent in 2005.
- 50 to 54-year-olds will constitute the largest economically active group in 2020.
- The activity rates of women will increase over this period, partly because, by 2020, women will have to work until the age of 65 before they can claim the state pension.
- The proportion of women in the labour force increased noticeably in comparison to the proportion of men in the 1970s and 1980s. These relative proportions are now stabilising: 54.2 per cent male and 45.8 per cent female in 2005, expected to be 53.3 per cent male and 46.7 per cent female in 2020. So female participation in the labour force is still expected to increase but at a slower rate than previously.

Changes in the numbers of people in the labour force are caused by a combination of population effects and activity rate effects. The largest population effect is the variation in the number of births. There was a peak birth rate around 1964 which accounts for some of the increase in the 45 and over age group in the projection period, and the birth rate was particularly low in the years 1973–1979 (Armitage and Scott, 1998). Further demographic changes which affect the projections of the labour force are increased life expectancy and migration. Salt and Millar (2006, p. 353) conclude that: 'As far as we may ascertain, 2005 saw the largest ever entry to the UK of foreign workers.'

Economic activity rates also affect the size and composition of the labour force. Increasing numbers of young people are choosing to study full time which, together with birth rate effects, account for the lower numbers of people in the lower age groups available for work. However, this may be offset by an increase in the numbers of students who work on a part-time basis. The ageing of the labour force is a noticeable phenomenon, and there is an expectation that more older people will wish to extend their participation in the workforce until a later age, many of them for financial reasons such as poor pension provision. The important issue from the point of view of analysing the external labour market is the extent to which employers are noting this shift and adjusting their recruitment strategies in response. As will be seen later, skills shortages are a continuing challenge for employers, and if the people available in the labour market belong increasingly to an older age group, this may call for different strategies in attracting them, a different approach to training may be required, and older employees may have different requirements with regard to flexibility in their working arrangements.

The growing proportion of women in the labour force is attributed in part to socio-economic influences such as the greater availability of part-time work and the social acceptability of women in employment as well as the raising of the state pension age for women. All of the factors discussed in this section have implications particularly for employers who have a traditional view of whom they might employ, for instance in positions thought of as being suitable for school leavers. The changing demographic structure of the external labour market may oblige employers to adopt more open approaches to recruitment and to consider the necessity of providing training.

The figures provided by surveys of the national labour force are important in providing a broad indication of factors to be considered in human resource planning. There are, however, some limitations on their usefulness. The statistics are only estimates, projections of the numbers of people expected to be economically active in the future. As such, they have to be predicated on some basic assumptions linked with patterns of economic activity observed at the time the analysis is performed. Obviously, unexpected events can occur which may have a sizeable impact on the validity of the projected figures. The IDS study, *The Future Workforce* (1996), provides some useful guidelines on how to interpret statistical data culled from workforce surveys, and the CIPD (2007e) provides some insight into the complexity of broader economic factors.

Tight and slack labour markets

As the CIPD (2007e) explains, the interplay of many factors in the economy may result in a tight labour market or one that has more slack in it. Examples of these factors are the demand for goods and services, employers' recruitment intentions, how much employers have to pay to attract people. Also, as we have already indicated, the number of migrants who choose to come here to look for work has an impact on the number of people who are economically active in the UK.

Rates of unemployment and the prevalence of redundancies have an obvious impact on the numbers of people looking for work. This does not necessarily mean, however, that meeting one's requirements for human resources is automatically easier in times of high unemployment. Redundant jobseekers may have a range of skills, but not necessarily in the areas required by other employers. There is also resistance among newly redundant people to accepting a large immediate drop in earnings. The existence of large numbers of unemployed or newly redundant people, therefore, does not equate directly with a ready supply of human resources.

The existence of competitors that also need people with the same skills will obviously influence the availability of human resources. This may have a direct impact on recruitment and pay strategies as employers try to attract the best people in direct competition with other companies. For the purposes of human resource planning, it will be important to be informed about existing competitors and to assess the likelihood of new competitors arriving on the scene.

If the labour market is tight, this means that employers experience difficulties in recruiting and the term 'skills shortages' is used to describe this. A slacker labour market means that there are plenty of appropriate human resources on the market and employers can fill their vacancies more easily. Skills shortages can arise for a variety of reasons and this term does not necessarily imply that the required skills are actually in shortage. They may not be available to employers for other reasons which we shall explore later.

Skills shortages

The issue of skills shortages fluctuates over time. They were regarded as a serious and widespread issue in the early years of the twenty-first century, but, as the CIPD (2007a) has reported, fewer employers reported these difficulties in 2005, probably because of the large influx of migrants after the enlargement of the EU in 2004 and because this was a difficult year in terms of economic growth so demand was suppressed to some extent. Problems with recruitment increased again in 2006 with a stronger economy, and with 84 per cent of employers reporting recruitment difficulties in 2006, it obviously continues to be an issue of some concern.

It is vital that organisations take steps to counteract skills shortages as they have a detrimental impact on operational effectiveness. The IRS (2000) reports that one major result of recruitment difficulties, together with the problem of skill gaps identified in internal staff, is a poorer level of customer service. Lost business and an inability to develop new products as planned are also identified as consequences of skills shortages and skill gaps. Employees can suffer too, as HR specialists and line managers might have to neglect 'other areas such as training and development, coaching and general employee welfare issues' (Sloane, 2007) to spend more time on difficult recruitment campaigns. These business repercussions highlight the effect of skills shortages on strategy formulation both at the corporate and the functional HR level.

Examples of skills shortages reported

The CIPD (2007b, p. 2) states that employers surveyed about their recruitment experiences report skills shortages in the 'necessary specialist skills' and a lack of sufficient experience, but they also reported a problem with 'higher pay expectations'. All sectors reported some level of recruitment difficulty (manufacturing and production; voluntary, community and not-for-profit; private sector services; public sector), and the types of jobs that were difficult to fill included managers and professionals, senior managers, administrative, secretarial and technical positions, services (including customer and sales services) and, to a lesser extent, manual and craft workers (CIPD, 2007b, p. 6).

It is possible to glean information about skills shortages from a wide range of other sources too. HR Zone (2007) reported on a wide range of problems, including sales representatives, engineers and electricians. Mediaplanet (2007) publicised a shortfall in the numbers of business consultants needed. Sometimes the problem can be worse in a particular region, as indicated by *People Management*'s report on the difficulties in finding employees in 'the property, professional services and transport sectors' (North, 2007, p. 31) in London. Some skills shortages are even commented on in BBC Radio 4 programmes, such as a news broadcast in July 2007, reporting that ageing agricultural workers were not being replaced and that the National Farmers Union was therefore launching a recruitment campaign to attract more people into this kind of work.

A more general problem is that employers for some years have reported that school leavers do not possess the competencies they are looking for. The CIPD (2007b, p. 6) cites the specific problems of a lack of 'ability to communicate or to work collaboratively'. Other areas in which employers are looking for improvements in this group are more acceptable attitudes towards work (work ethic) and listening skills.

Reasons for skills shortages

As indicated previously, there can be a variety of factors that contribute to any one employer's recruitment problems. It might be that there is an actual lack of specific skills available in the labour market. It might be that the terms and conditions, pay and benefits offered by the employer are less attractive that those offered by a competitor. The organisation's reputation in general might attract some and not others. Public perceptions of what a job entails will make occupations seem more attractive or less so. Recruitment difficulties might be a regional issue connected to the cost of living and travel in different parts of the country. With so many potential causes for skills shortages, it is self-evident that there could be a variety of solutions, and an appropriate solution or mix of responses will be necessary to address the problem.

Solutions to skills shortages

Provide training

If employers recognise that the required skills actually are not available, one solution is to recruit people who can be trained up. Organisations may also look to their own current employees (their internal supply of human resources) for skills they do not have. This is known as a 'skills gap', and again, provision of training can be the answer. The CIPD's survey (2007b) indicates that the provision of training is the preferred response to skills shortages, with 70 per cent of respondents providing training for new recruits and 89 per cent training up their current employees. This approach is seen as leading to improved retention of existing staff, in which case employers would have less need for recruitment activities in the first place.

A case study of Gordon Ramsay Holdings (CIPD, 2007c) reveals that the well-known chef prefers to focus on the development of his staff so they can take on more senior roles in the future. This is true, even if it means letting them go to competitors for a while to hone their skills, in the knowledge that they will come back at some time.

Some organisations have even gone to the extent of setting up their own educational establishment and qualifications to ensure a supply of skills at the appropriate level. Arcadia Group founded a Fashion Academy in 2006, and the BBC founded a College of Journalism to raise the level of skills and knowledge in its reporters and newsreaders in areas such as politics and the law (Sherwin, 2007).

Recruiting overseas/targeting migrant workers/offshoring

Subject to immigration laws, it is possible for employers to go to other countries and recruit people there to come and work in the UK: 75 per cent of employers surveyed by the CIPD (2007b) felt this approach was beneficial, although only 11 per cent engaged in it. Equally useful but actually used slightly more (14 per cent) was targeting migrant workers from the extended EU. For example, the transport company First was reported to have recruited a number of Polish nationals as bus drivers (Campling, 2004), and Tesco has also taken on employees from Poland (Czerny, 2005). Although often undertaken for reasons of costs, skills shortages could also be addressed by relocating jobs to countries such as India and China where resources are in plentiful supply. The CIPD (2007a, p. 19) reports the following countries as attracting the highest levels of offshoring from the UK: India (favoured by 53 per cent of the survey respondents), China (27 per cent) and Poland (18 per cent).

> **Did you know?**
>
> An interesting by-product of the influx of Polish workers into the UK was the demand for Polish priests to provide religious services to their communities here.

Diversity and the labour market

The problem of skills shortages can be alleviated by eliminating entrenched stereotypical ideas about who might be suitable for particular types of jobs. In spite of legal obligations to provide equality of opportunity in the workplace, there are still some occupations where barriers need to be broken down to facilitate access for particular groups of people, and sometimes individuals too have stereotyped ideas about the suitability of certain occupations. A BBC Radio 4 (2007) section of *Woman's Hour* examined the persistence of the stereotyping of some occupations as men's jobs (construction; engineering) and others as women's jobs (hairdressing; nursing; caring). The programme highlighted the need for improved standards in careers advice and training for careers advisers, while acknowledging the role of attitudes and cultural influences on career choice. The consensus was that steps need to be taken to ensure that women are better equipped to make informed decisions about career choices.

Employers can engage in targeted recruitment to encourage applications from groups who do not normally apply for certain jobs. In recent years, some metropolitan police forces have had recruitment campaigns encouraging Asians to apply to join the police, and B&Q was a well-known example of making a point of recruiting older employees long before age discrimination regulations were in force (IDS, 2004). It is also advisable to re-visit the person specification for jobs to confirm that all the requirements listed there for qualifications and experience are really necessary.

Further examples of innovative approaches to easing recruitment difficulties through the promotion of diversity come from the judiciary and the utilities sector. *The Times* reported that Judge Geoffrey Kamil was one of 45 circuit judges visiting their local community groups to speak to them about how the judicial system works, which might even result in increased interest in working in the system (Gibb, 2007). *Personnel Today* (2007) reported on steps taken by the water companies, including going out to schools and offering a qualification as part of the GCSE course, targeting people leaving the Armed Forces, and focusing on training for ex-offenders.

Employer branding

Among other things, being known as an employer that is committed to diversity is very much a part of creating an employer brand which will attract applicants. Being an employer of first choice would also entail things such as good pay and working conditions, but equally important are the less tangible aspects of the workplace such as ensuring that employees have a voice and that they are fully engaged. Employers must obviously treat employees appropriately on an ongoing basis to deserve and maintain their employer brand, but it is important to communicate this, partly through advertising, to attract prospective employees. 85 per cent of employers identify their mission, culture and values as being the essence of their employer brand (CIPD, 2007b), but many also recognise the significance of other aspects of their organisation for their reputation as an employer of first choice. These include the quality of the career and development opportunities and the reward packages they offer, their commitment to supporting work–life balance and diversity, and their stance on corporate social responsibility.

Although it is only one of a list of the attributes of an employer brand, it is worth highlighting the importance of the work–life balance issue, which we also address in more detail in Chapter 4 on the employment relationship. We have addressed diversity in the workforce here and in Chapter 5, and diversity of necessity brings about a requirement for greater flexibility in working arrangements to respond to the varying needs of people from different cultures and at differing stages in their lives. If employers wish to obtain the benefits offered by diversity, they must make reasonable efforts to accommodate their employees' needs and help them to achieve an acceptable balance between their work and their non-work lives.

● Summary

All the factors that affect the labour force are important to employers. Similar to the need for environmental scanning that was described regarding the formulation of corporate or business strategy, up-to-date information is the key to effective human resource planning. Managers need to be aware of local, regional, national and global trends and be able to integrate this knowledge into their strategic plans. Knowledge of the key issues will enable organisations to assess the threats and opportunities in their environment, and to evaluate their ability to respond with their existing and available resources.

Comparing demand and supply forecasts

A comparison of your expected demand for human resources and your expected supply will identify what you need to accomplish in your human resource plans in order to achieve your corporate goals, or, as already mentioned, there may be an indication that the corporate/business plan needs some adjustment. You can be faced with a number of situations:

- internal supply = demand
- internal supply > demand
- internal supply < demand
- internal plus external supply < demand.

Since there are so many changes affecting organisations, as we have already discussed, and since this is likely to continue for the foreseeable future, internal supply is not likely to equal demand. This is more likely to occur in very stable conditions. If internal supply is greater than demand, human resource plans will need to focus on eliminating the surplus through redeployment or redundancy or through other adjustments to working arrangements. When internal supply is less than demand, an organisation will be involved in recruitment or other methods of acquiring the necessary skills. In the final instance, where internal supply plus external supply is inadequate to meet demand, the solutions we have just described with regard to combating skills shortages come into play, or organisational goals must be revisited and adjusted to reflect the resourcing problems.

Developing and implementing human resource strategies

In Chapter 1 we presented a long list of the major people management activities, and these can be categorised into four broad areas: resourcing, development, reward and relations. It is useful to refer to these categories to identify the areas in which it is necessary to develop human resource strategies and action plans.

Resourcing

If demand exceeds supply, the organisation will have to develop plans to acquire the additional skills it needs. This may involve recruitment activities, but there may also be a need for career and succession planning for existing employees, and the organisation may consider subcontracting work. If internal supply exceeds demand, the organisation may have to release staff, but consideration should first be given to redeployment and to providing the training that this might entail.

Development

If skills gaps exist, meaning that the competencies the organisation needs are not present in its current workforce, managers should make plans to develop those skills through training, team and individual development, and performance management. The provision of opportunities for development is identified by the CIPD (2007b) as one of the major retention initiatives undertaken by employers.

Reward

A review and restructuring of the reward system might enable an organisation to attract and retain the required complement of human resources. The organisation should examine its pay levels and the attractiveness of its benefits packages and terms and conditions compared with those of competitors. Action plans should also address the issue of linking rewards properly to the achievement of corporate goals.

Employment relations

Improvements in the contribution that employees make to their employing organisation can often be achieved through developing better employment relations. Areas to consider include consultation, communications, employee involvement and engagement, and the development of a partnership approach.

All of the functional areas mentioned briefly above are discussed in greater depth in the chapters that follow. The major aspects of the strategic human resource planning process are captured in the model presented as Figure 2.1. You should be able to track the elements of this model back to the discussion contained in this chapter.

Information technology systems and HR

Some comment about HR uses of computerised information systems is apropos at this juncture. We have established the need for a broad spectrum of information to manage HR activities in a strategic fashion and to make the business case, but still observers of HR in practice are reporting that a majority of HR experts are unable to pull the requisite figures together with an acceptable level of speed and accuracy (Twentyman, 2006). As mentioned in Chapter 1, HR specialists are increasing their use of IT systems for many operational activities such as recruitment and development, and this is reflected in much of the published material about how organisations are using IT in the context of people management (CIPD, 2006a; IRS, 2006; Twentyman, 2007).

The use of IT is seen as being instrumental in the successful delivery of a number of people management strategies once these have been formulated, e.g. facilitating the level of communication needed to support employee voice and engagement (CIPD, 2006a). This is still, however, an operational use of IT. There are also suggestions that these transactional uses of IT free HR experts up to engage in more activities at a strategic level (CIPD, 2006a; CIPD, 2007d). Where they need to make greater strides, however, is in the provision of HR metrics to inform and support strategic decision making.

Twentyman (2006) gives some examples of strategic analyses using business intelligence tools. She reports on Rotherham Metropolitan Borough Council and how it has used its HRIS to compile its best value performance indicators with regard to the achievement of strategic diversity objectives. Other potential and real applications reported are a breakdown of the workforce by strategically important variables such as availability of specified skills, employers' use of information to benchmark themselves against other organisations, analyses based on 'what if' scenarios, modelling

Figure 2.1 Model of the human resource planning process

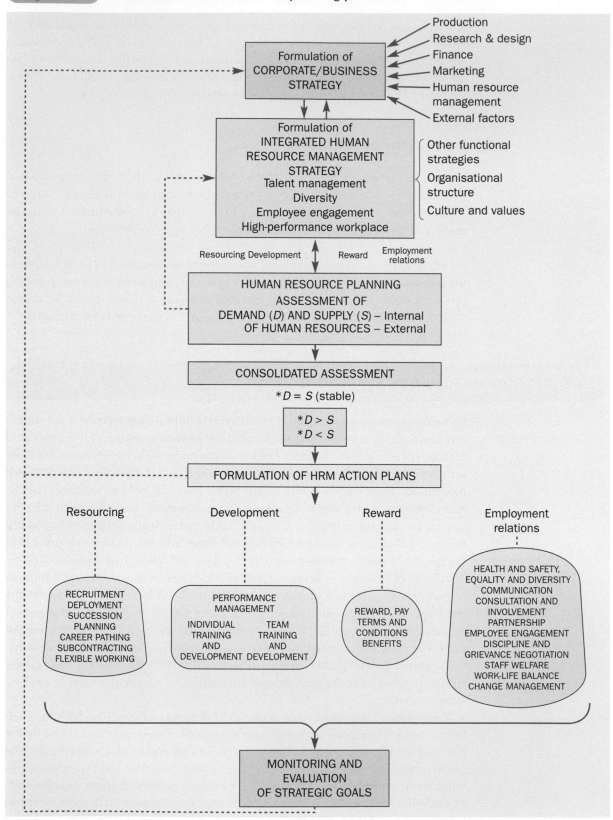

the impact of proposed changes. There are some indicators elsewhere that HR may be making such use of IT, but the evidence is not strong. The CIPD (2006a), for instance, mainly addresses operational uses of IT, but it does also allude to HR undertaking 'more strategic work as business partners . . . by providing the managers with quantifiable data to drive this strategy' (p. 11). They further state that 'HR can also play an important role in the formulation of strategy by making explicit the human capital resources required to support various strategies and strategic initiatives' (p. 12).

The CIPD (2006a) comes to the conclusion that the technology-driven changes in HR roles 'will undoubtedly lead to a change in the skills needed as their role shifts towards more strategic issues' (p. 12). This statement implies that the HR profession still has some way to go before it is fully effective at the strategic level, and that the potential of IT systems is yet to be fully exploited.

International issues

Skills shortages

Offshoring and recruiting overseas have been mentioned above as potential solutions for skills shortages and the level of migration has been identified as a factor which has an impact on the size of the labour force. It should be noted that this applies to migration out of the UK as well as migration into the country. All of these eventualities raise issues in terms of the management of language and communication competencies, cultural differences and diversity.

Looking at things on a global scale, employers must also be aware that their solution to skills shortages might well be someone else's problem and that this might lead to further developments which will have to be managed. The ethics of recruiting nurses from less developed countries to come to the UK was raised as an issue in the early years of the twenty-first century, and the NHS, which was suffering from a shortage of nurses and other medical professionals at that time, pledged not to recruit from those countries. Economic issues other than corporate social responsibility can also arise. The emigration of Polish workers into the UK and other parts of Europe has meant that Poland itself is facing skills shortages, particularly in terms of resourcing the European Football Championships to be held there in 2012. Berry (2007) reports that Poland will need to attract 200,000 workers to return to Poland from the UK and Ireland to get ready for this event. Not an inconsiderable number of people!

There are other examples of skills shortages being reported around the world. For example, *The Times* (Macartney, 2007, p. 53) reports that 'China's new middle classes have Tesco and Ikea, Chivas Regal and Starbucks; but they are having trouble getting what they really want – a maid'. *The Times* also reports that foreign investors in China are increasingly having trouble finding human resources with the appropriate level of talent for their high-end jobs, and that wages are rising so that the source of low-cost labour has moved to Vietnam and Indonesia (Lewis, 2007; Mortished, 2007). China and India are also expected to create a large demand for airline pilots over the next two decades. Jameson (2007), again in *The Times*, reports that China will have difficulty in attracting qualified people from the West unless there are big improvements in pay and conditions. She also reports that China's current overseas sources of pilots include South America and Eastern Europe.

Did you know?

The Adlon. The Kempinski. The Dorint. Three luxury hotels in Berlin, and where do they get their laundry done? In Poland, according to an article in a German TV magazine in 2006. Even with the time and cost needed for transport between the two locations, the service provided in Poland is superior and personnel with the required skills are more readily available.

(*Source*: Ernst, F. (2006) Waschtag in Polen, *HÖRZU*, Nr 11, 10.03, 18–19)

Wooldridge (2006) produced a special report for *The Economist* with a subheading 'Talent has become the world's most sought after commodity' (p. 3), emphasising that the war for talent is a worldwide issue. These news stories are all evidence of the fact that labour supply can be a truly global issue, that labour markets are dynamic and subject to change, and that organisations have constantly to acquire information to stay ahead of the game.

● An ageing workforce

The increasing proportion of the population represented by older people is not just occurring in the UK. In 2007, the 6th Munich Economic Summit focused on the demographic challenge that business faces in Europe, i.e. the ageing of the workforce. Among others involved were the CEOs of BMW and Siemens as well as EU politicians. The summit was attended by representatives from 22 countries including Germany, France, Italy and The Netherlands. The issues discussed there echoed some of the problems we have highlighted in this chapter, especially the impact of what those attending the summit referred to as the 'double aging of Europe', i.e. low birth rates combined with greater life expectancy. The business representatives, however, saw some positive angles to this. Both Siemens and BMW forecast an increased demand for their products, and in terms of people management, the representative from BMW stated that using their 'programme "Today for Tomorrow", the company keeps up the productivity of its employees. The programme includes health prevention measures, ergonomic work spaces and a good age balance among working teams, which makes it possible for older employees to pass on their wealth of experience to younger employees, thus enabling life-long learning' (**www.munich-economic-summit.com**).

Did you know?

The ageing of the workforce is a phenomenon that is not restricted to the UK or Europe. The IRS (2003) reports that employers in the USA are also facing similar developments. The Society for Human Resource Management there expressed concerns that US employers were not preparing adequately for this demographic shift.

REVIEW QUESTIONS

You will find brief answers to these review questions on pages 470–471.

1 Describe the different levels of strategy found in organisations, and comment on their interconnecting nature.

2 Outline the major stages of the human resource planning process, and comment on the major considerations at each stage.

3 'Information is crucial as a basis for decision making in the human resource planning process.' Comment on this statement, and describe the sources of information available to management.

4 Explain what is meant by the terms 'skills shortages' and 'skills gaps'. Why do they arise and what can employers do about them?

SELF-CHECK QUESTIONS

Answer the following multiple-choice and short-answer questions. The correct responses are given on page 471 for you to check your understanding of this chapter.

1 Name the three major generic strategies available at the corporate level.

2 Name the three business level strategies described by Porter.

3 A local supermarket employs 50 sales assistants on a part-time basis. Over the past year the personnel department has had to recruit 25 new employees to keep the establishment full. Of the assistants who were hired over a year ago, 40 are still working with the supermarket in the same positions. Calculate the turnover rate.

4 Calculate the stability index for the situation in question 3.

5 What does the stability index indicate?

6 Which stage has been left out of the following brief description of the human resource planning process?
   ● development of corporate strategy
   ● estimation of the demand for human resources
   ● formulation of human resource management plans.

7 How are IT systems predominantly used in HR: for strategic or for operational purposes?

8 Which countries are facing issues to do with an ageing workforce?

HR IN THE NEWS

FT

Jobs without borders: Nordic nations want Baltic immigrants

By Robert Anderson

Ginta Yermava remembers bursting into tears when she spread the cash from her first Swedish pay on her bed in the flat she shares with three other Latvian cleaners. 'In one week I earned as much as I did in one month as a teacher in Latvia,' she says.

The company Ms Yermava works for, Rent Hos Dig ('clean at your place'), is able to undercut rival cleaning companies by more than half by bringing Latvian women to Stockholm for six-month stints.

Throughout the Nordic region, migrant workers such as Ms Yermava are filling vacancies and providing services. The inflow from the new European Union member states, particularly Poland and the Baltic states, is the largest since the 1970s, when governments shut the door to southern European migrant workers.

Some 75,000 migrants are working legally in Norway – making up 3 per cent of the labour force. Denmark, the second most popular destination, granted 20,000 new work permits last year. Employers – from big companies to the individuals who are Ms Yermava's customers – welcome them. That is because, across the region, there are labour shortages caused by robust economic growth, ageing populations and labour market rigidities.

That has severe consequences for many companies. 'Almost in every sector we have problems now, especially in finding skilled manual workers and engineers,' says Jussi Järventaus,

→

57

managing director of the Federation of Finnish Enterprises. In Sweden, 'large new investments are not being made as firms find it difficult to attract workers to work there quickly enough', says Stefan Fölster, chief economist of Svenskt Näringsliv, that country's enterprise confederation.

The labour shortages mean any slowing in economic growth will make it more difficult to finance the region's generous welfare systems. Workers in the care and health sectors are also needed to look after the fast-ageing populations. Tobias Billstrom, Sweden's migration minister, says hospitals in southern Sweden would have to close over the summer if it were not for migrant workers.

In Finland, where the demographic problem looms earliest, the number of employed workers to each welfare benefit recipient will drop from 1.7 now to 1.0 by 2030, according to the Organisation for Economic Co-operation and Development. Labour migrants – by filling vacancies, keeping wages competitive, paying taxes and spending their salaries, while drawing few state benefits – could boost economic growth and stave off the need to make fundamental reforms to welfare systems.

'We have been able to keep the wheels running at high speed because we have taken workers from elsewhere in Europe,' says Sigrun Vageng, executive director of NHO, the Norwegian enterprise confederation.

Denmark – whose minority government has relied on the backing of the nationalist People's party – has tried to tighten asylum procedures while relaxing labour permit rules to allow highly qualified people from outside the EU to seek work. But it restricts jobseekers from the new EU member states and imposes tough skill and salary requirements on those from outside the EU.

Nevertheless, this month the centre-right government announced plans both to launch a publicity campaign to attract migrant workers and to reform the work permit system to make it easier for them to enter. With a snap general election called on Wednesday, if it wins a majority it may move further in this direction. Every Nordic government is now rethinking its migration policies to try to attract more legal workers, targeted at the right sectors.

There are already sizeable flows of workers within the region, with oil-rich Norway drawing some 20,000 migrant Nordic workers. There is also significant migration as well as commuting between southern Sweden and Copenhagen, made easier by the new Oresund bridge. But the real battle is on for cheaper workers from the new member states and highly skilled experts from all over the world.

Unlike the rest of the EU, Sweden and Finland have imposed no restrictions on workers from the new member states. Norway (not an EU member) and Denmark have controls, although in effect they allow migrants to enter to find work but make it difficult for them to claim social benefits.

The Nordic region is not the first choice for migrants from the new EU members, because of its high costs and taxes. Moreover, wages in their home countries are rising so fast – at more than 30 per cent in the last year in Latvia – that migration may soon slow. Highly skilled workers find that salaries at the top end are not competitive in the Nordic region, because income differentials are less than in the rest of western Europe. In fact, all the Nordic nations are losing young workers to countries such as the UK, where real remuneration can be higher. Swedes joke that London is fast becoming the biggest Swedish city after Stockholm because of the number of young workers who have moved there.

Consequently, every Nordic country has recently announced its intention to revamp policies to attract foreign workers. The Swedish government proposed in August to allow companies to seek workers from anywhere without first consulting state agencies and trade unions on whether there was a need. Migrants with special skills would also be allowed to enter on three-month visas to seek work and would be granted 24-month visas once they found a job, with a chance to win an indefinite stay after four years.

Compared with the UK, for example, there is less fear of an immigration wave and more concern that the region's high taxes will deter migrants. 'My worst nightmare is not that we have 300,000 wanting to come in but that we will make all these changes and we still will not be able to attract enough people,' says Mr Billstrom.

'We are opening up,' says Kim Graugaard, deputy director general of Dansk Industri, the Danish industry confederation. 'But it's one thing to open your borders and another thing to attract people to cross them.'

Norway is also beginning to rethink its policy towards workers from outside the EU. Although it has taken in more than half the labour migrants who have gone to the region from the EU's new member states, last year it handed out only 2,000 of a possible 5,000 permits to workers from outside the EU.

Finland, traditionally a country of emigration rather than immigration, wants to attract workers from the former Soviet Union, where it thinks it stands the best chance. Finland already has some 47,000 Russian-speaking immigrants – about one-third of the total – who have been attracted by the similar climate and the short distance home. 'In immigration we are looking eastwards,' says Tarja Cronberg, labour minister.

Yet luring migrant workers could also pose a challenge to the traditional Scandinavian policies of providing refuge for asylum seekers and regulating labour markets. Left-wing parties, which have traditionally dominated the region but are now out of power except in Norway, fear that opening the door to migrant workers could end up closing it for refugees.

Sweden and Norway in particular have a proud asylum record but often refugees have failed to find jobs and have added to the costs of financing the welfare system. Consequently, nationalist parties in Denmark, Norway and Sweden have put pressure on governments to restrict refugee flows.

Some fear the new focus on labour migration could worsen the marginalisation of unemployed refugees and increase popular resentment against them. 'We think it is important to have a generous asylum system,' says Erland Olauson, first vice-president of the Swedish trade union confederation. 'If you mix it [with labour migration] and there are problems, people will say – like in Denmark – "Don't bring them in, leave them outside".'

Sweden's government sees no conflict in having generous asylum and labour migration policies. Indeed, it argues that the two should be complementary. 'When Swedes are critical of immigration, they refer to the issue of people not working,' says Mr Billstrom. 'Labour migration could drive the integration process of those people who are already here.'

Unions are worried, however, by the threat labour migration poses to wage levels and employment rules. This threat was demonstrated in 2004 when a Latvian company brought in its workers to build a school in the Stockholm suburb of Vaxholm and refused to sign a collective wage agreement.

The company abandoned the contract after unions picketed the site. The enterprise confederation took the case to the European Court of Justice, which this year ruled in a preliminary judgment that under Sweden's accession treaty with the EU the company should have signed the agreement. 'When workers come they should be treated like all the others,' says Mr Olauson. 'We don't accept an apartheid labour market.'

Norway's Labour government has taken the toughest stand against low-wage migration, with tight checks on employers, subcontractors and recruitment agencies. Even the centre-right Swedish government defended the unions in the Vaxholm case.

Reconciling the need for imported workers with Scandinavia's labour arrangements is likely to remain the biggest difficulty. Hindering migration flows could undermine welfare financing but too relaxed a regime could hurt popular backing for inward migration.

(FT.com, 24 October 2007. Reproduced with permission.)

Questions

1 What are the causes of skills shortages in Norway, Sweden, Denmark and Finland?

2 Which sectors and occupations are drawing on migrant labour in these countries?

3 Which parallels can you draw between these countries and the situation in the UK as described in your textbook and drawing on any current information you have accessed?

4 List some of the economic and political factors that have an impact on or are in turn affected by patterns of migration and changes in the labour force.

WHAT NEXT?

In this chapter we have looked at the factors that affect the external labour market and the impact this can have on employers in resourcing their strategic plans. One aspect that should be evident is that the supply of labour can fluctuate from year to year, bringing ever-changing opportunities and threats to employers. It is important to keep up to date on developments, and regular perusal of the following publications can assist you in doing this.

Economic and Labour Market Review, a monthly journal published by the Office for National Statistics, formerly published as *Labour Market Trends*.

Labour Market Outlook, a quarterly review published by the CIPD together with KPMG.

We have referred a number of times to the CIPD annual survey of recruitment, retention and turnover. The survey report provides a good statistical overview of employers' experience of labour turnover, skills shortages, retention etc., but it also gives informed comment on and explanations of the major issues. The most recent report available at the time of writing was the 2007 edition, reporting on experiences from 2006. Soon after this text is published, the 2008 report should be available to download on the CIPD website. Go to **www.cipd.co.uk/surveys** to find and read the most recent report available. It will help you to stay in the know about labour market issues.

References

Anthony, W.P., P.L. Perrewe and K.M. Kacmar (1996) *Strategic Human Resource Management*, 2nd edition, Harcourt Brace.

Armitage, B. and M. Scott (1998) British labour force projections: 1998–2011, *Labour Market Trends*, June, 281–291.

BBC Radio 4 (2007) *Woman's Hour News: Career Advice*, 27/08 (podcast downloaded at www.bbc.co.uk; accessed 27.08.07).

Berry, M. (2007) Poland needs to lure 200,000 workers back home to get facilities ready for 2012 European Football Championships, *Personnel Today*, 17 May (available at www.personneltoday.com; accessed 17.05.07).

Boxall, P. and J. Purcell (2003) *Strategy and Human Resource Management*, Palgrave Macmillan.

Campling, K. (2004) Why our new bus drivers will have extra Polish, *Huddersfield Daily Examiner*, 11 August, 3.

Chartered Institute of Personnel and Development (2005) *HR Strategy: Creating the Framework for Successful People Management*, CIPD (CIPD tool available at www.cipd.co.uk; accessed 31.03.05).

Chartered Institute of Personnel and Development (2006a) *HR and Technology: Beyond Delivery*, CIPD. (Change Agenda available at www.cipd.co.uk; accessed 17.08.07.)

Chartered Institute of Personnel and Development (2006b) *HR Business Partnering*, CIPD. (Factsheet available at www.cipd.co.uk; accessed 02.11.06.)

Chartered Institute of Personnel and Development (2007a) *A Barometer of HR Trends and Prospects 2007. Overview of CIPD Surveys*, CIPD.

Chartered Institute of Personnel and Development (2007b) *Recruitment, Retention and Turnover. Annual Survey Report 2007*, CIPD.

Chartered Institute of Personnel and Development (2007c) *Research Insight: Talent Management*, CIPD.

Chartered Institute of Personnel and Development (2007d) *Technology in HR: How to Get the Most out of Technology in People Management*, CIPD. (HR tool available to members at www.cipd.co.uk; accessed 17.08.07.)

Chartered Institute of Personnel and Development (2007e) *Understanding the Economy and Labour Market,* CIPD. (Factsheet available at www.cipd.co.uk; accessed 06.03.07.)

Czerny, A (2005) Tesco to take on more Polish workers, *People Management,* 29 September, 10.

Gibb, F. (2007) Out of the ivory towers and into mosques, *The Times* (*Law* section), 26 June.

Glaister, K. (1995) Introduction to the strategic management process, in C. Clarke-Hill and K. Glaister (eds) *Cases in Strategic Management,* 2nd edition, Pitman Publishing.

Greer, C.R. (2001) *Strategic Human Resource Management: A General Managerial Approach,* 2nd edition, Prentice Hall.

Guest, D., J. Storey and W. Tate (1997) *Innovation: Opportunity through People. Consultative Document,* Institute of Personnel and Development, June.

Howson, J. (2007) *22nd Annual Survey of Senior Staff Appointments in Schools in England and Wales,* Education Data Surveys.

HR Zone (2007) Employers struggle to find skilled staff, *HR Zone,* 28 March (available at www.hrzone.co.uk; accessed 03.04.07).

Hutchinson, S. and J. Purcell (2003) *Bringing Policies to Life: the Vital Role of Front Line Managers in People Management,* CIPD.

Incomes Data Services (1996) *IDS Focus: The Future Workforce,* No. 80, December, IDS.

Incomes Data Services (2004) Cultural diversity at B&Q, *IDS Diversity at Work,* No. 5, November, 7–10.

Industrial Relations Services (IRS) (2000) Responding to the challenge of skills shortages, *Employee Development Bulletin 130,* October, 4–9.

Industrial Relations Services (IRS) (2001) Be prepared: forecasts for recruiters' needs to 2020, *Employee Development Bulletin 139,* July, 5–7.

Industrial Relations Service (IRS) (2003) US employers face old age question, *IRS Employment Review 782,* 15 August, 16.

Industrial Relations Service (IRS) (2006) HR management systems move online as the web matures, *IRS Employment Review 855,* 22/9 (available at www.xperthr.co.uk; accessed 20.07.07).

Industrial Relations Service (IRS) (2007) Aligning HR with the business: two steps forward, one step back, *IRS Employment Review 866,* 20/3 (available at www.xperthr; accessed 20.07.07).

Jameson, A. (2007) China and India lure pilots from West to plug gaps, *The Times,* August 5, 48.

Johnson, G., K. Scholes and R. Whittington (2006) *Exploring Corporate Strategy,* 7th edition, Financial Times Prentice Hall.

Lewis, L. (2007) Japan leads a corporate shift to Vietnam in its hunt for cheaper labour, *The Times,* 24 August, 56.

Lynch, R. (2003) *Corporate Strategy,* 3rd edition, Financial Times Prentice Hall.

Macartney, J. (2007) Maids clean up as busy middle classes run out of helpers, *The Times,* 23 June, 53.

Madouros, V. (2006) Projections of the UK labour force, 2006–2020, *Labour Market Trends,* January, 13–27.

Marchington, M. and A. Wilkinson (2005) *Human Resource Management at Work: People Management and Development,* 3rd edition, CIPD.

Mediaplanet (2007) *Business Excellence: Your Guide to the Business of Consulting,* 5 July (supplement distributed in *The Times*).

Millmore, M., P. Lewis, M. Saunders, A. Thornhill and T. Morrow (2007) *Strategic Human Resource Management: Contemporary Issues,* Financial Times Prentice Hall.

Mortished, C. (2007) China boom under threat by loss of cheap labour, *The Times,* 23 June, 67.

North, S. (2007) Regional overview, *The Guide to Recruitment Consultancies,* April, 31–32 (supplement distributed with *People Management*).

Personnel Today (2007) Water companies consider radical recruitment drive to avoid looming skills crisis, *Personnel Today,* 27 February (available at www.xperthr.co.uk; accessed 03.04.07).

Porter, M.E. (1980) *Competitive Strategy,* Free Press.

Ready, D.A. and J.A. Conger (2007) Make your company a talent factory, *Harvard Business Review,* June, 68–77.

Salt, J. and J. Millar (2006) Foreign labour in the United Kingdom: current patterns and trends, *Labour Market Trends,* October, 335–355.

Sherwin, A. (2007) Paxman and Co are going back to school, *The Times,* 16 January, 28.

Sloane, W. (2007) We put in an infrastructure more efficiently ourselves, *The Sunday Times,* 14 January (available at www.timesonline.co.uk; accessed 22.01.07).

Smethurst, S. (2005) HR roles: the long and winding road, *People Management,* 28 July, 25–29.

Storey, J. (2007) *Human Resource Management: A Critical Text,* 3rd edition, Thomson.

Twentyman, J. (2006) Show me the numbers, *Personnel Today,* 5 December (available at www.xperthr.co.uk; accessed 20.07.07).

Twentyman, J. (2007) Expanding HR: How forward planning and investing in technology can help, *Personnel Today,* 20 February (available at www.xperthr.co.uk; accessed 20.07.07).

Wooldridge, A. (2006) A survey of talent, *The Economist,* 7 October, 3–20.

www.jnj.com; accessed 20.07.07.

www.munich-economic-summit.com; accessed 15.08.07.

Further study

Books

Advisory, Conciliation and Arbitration Service (2006) *Managing Attendance and Employee Turnover,* ACAS (available at www.acas.org.uk; accessed 05.10.07).

Chartered Institute of Personnel and Development (2007) *HR and Technology: Impact and Advantages,* CIPD. The most recent research report produced for the CIPD by a team of researchers at Cranfield School of Management. The report includes a number of interesting case studies.

Incomes Data Services (IDS) (2004) *IDS HR Studies 765: Improving Staff Retention,* IDS. Looks at various methods of calculating labour turnover, what the implications of the resulting figures might be and ways of improving retention, and provides case studies of six organisations.

Joseph Rowntree Foundation (2006) *Findings: Central and East European Migrants in Low Wage Employment in the UK,* Joseph Rowntree Foundation. Examines the experiences of migrant workers and the views of their employers both before EU enlargement in 2004 and afterwards. The findings and the full report can be downloaded at www.jrf.org.uk where you will also find other reports of research on social issues.

Articles

Cornish, A. (2003) How to form a resourcing strategy, *People Management,* 4 December, 44–45. One of *People Management*'s 'How to …' series: concise overviews of topical issues.

Economic and Labour Market Review. A monthly journal produced by the Office for National Statistics. Contains statistical analyses of various aspects of the workforce, and articles and news items about issues of current interest. Essential reading for keeping up to date.

Industrial Relations Service (IRS) (2003) Effective retention strategies, *IRS Employment Review* 773, 4 April, 32–38. Two reports on retention strategies used by a variety of employers.

Industrial Relations Services (IRS) (2007) Labour turnover trends, rates and sources 2007/2008, *IRS Employment Review 870,* 10/4. Provides links to a set of articles which constitute the IRS guide to labour turnover for 2007/2008. Separate articles address how to collect and use labour turnover information, the costs of labour turnover, the latest trends and an overview of what is happening on a national scale. Available at www.xperthr.co.uk; accessed 20.07.07.

Morrow, P. and J. McElroy (2007) Efficiency as a mediator in turnover-organizational performance relations, *Human Relations*, Vol. 60(6), 827–849. An American research article examining how labour turnover affects organisational efficiency in the banking sector.

People Management. Produced for the Chartered Institute of Personnel and Development, this magazine is aimed at keeping HR practitioners informed, and frequently contains articles on HR strategy. A good source of case studies.

Internet

Chartered Institute of Personnel and Development   **www.cipd.co.uk**

The CIPD site provides a wide range of useful information on HR strategy and uses of technology. The tool on technology in HR, available to members, includes a number of interesting case studies of organisations, including Cancer Research UK and BSkyB.

CHAPTER 3

High-performance working: employee engagement through involvement and participation

Objectives

When you have studied this chapter you will be able to:

- explain what is meant by the terms 'unitarism' and 'pluralism'

- describe the concepts of partnership, participation, employee involvement, engagement and high-performance working

- describe developments in EU legislation relating to employee rights to information and consultation

- appreciate the importance of communication and consultation in the employment relations arena

- name and describe the techniques that can be used to enhance employee involvement

- describe the concepts of commitment and employee engagement, and explain how they are connected to employee involvement and high-performance working.

Chapter 1 established that the HRM approach to managing employees entails developing strategies and using techniques that result in employees giving their best efforts for the success of the organisation and reaching their full potential. This approach to management recognises that the contribution of an organisation's people is critical to the creation of a competitive advantage. Employers acknowledge that their organisations will flourish if they can engage their employees, meaning that they will be fully motivated to give of their very best to their employer, and indeed many adopt a strategy of employee engagement in order to achieve the high-performance workforce that will give them this edge. Sisson (2007, p. 21) even goes so far as to say that 'employee engagement can make or break a business.'

Later chapters will examine specific functions that can be performed in such a way as to acquire such employees (HR planning, recruitment and selection), retain them (payment systems), and develop them (performance management, training), HR practices which, if carried out with strategic forethought, ought to result in the desired high-performance workplace (EEF/CIPD, 2003). The willingness of employees to contribute their best efforts, however, can be affected pervasively by the way they are treated on a day-to-day basis, by their relationships with managers and by the attitude they perceive management in general to have towards them. This is a matter of organisational culture which develops in part from the philosophical stance of senior managers and the owners of enterprises as to the role they expect employees throughout the organisation to play in the life of the organisation.

This chapter reviews major concepts from the field of employment relations that have developed over several decades, ending with a review of the current discussion of employee engagement. We examine the basic stances that managers can adopt towards the workforce, looking at the concepts of unitarism and pluralism, which provide a framework for an examination of partnership, participation and employee involvement (EI). The techniques of participation and employee involvement are believed to enhance the willingness and ability of employees to contribute to the achievement of their organisation's goals, and the levels of commitment and engagement that are expected to arise from these approaches are fundamental in the creation of the high-performance workplace.

Pause for thought 3.1	Given that the aim of human resource management is to use the potential of employees, how would you expect this to be achieved in terms of general management attitude towards employees and their place in the decision-making process?

In keeping with basic concepts of motivation theory, you have probably stated that employees are more likely to produce greater effort if they have a sense of responsibility and a feeling of achievement from their work. According to Herzberg *et al.* (1959) and later work by Hackman and Oldham (1980), one of the ways to achieve this is by job enrichment. One method of enriching jobs is to shift responsibility for making some decisions from supervisors to more junior employees. This is known as a vertical job loading factor, designed to improve motivation. Employee empowerment became a business buzzword in the 1990s, and this too involves devolving the responsibility for decision making through all levels in the organisation.

The fact that we can talk about the *devolution* of decision making implies that it lay elsewhere before it was devolved. Traditionally owners and managers have regarded the right to make decisions as being theirs, an attitude reflected in the ideas of Frederick Winslow Taylor (1911). In Taylor's concept of scientific management, managers were to plan and control the work and give orders, while other employees were meant simply to carry out these orders. Taylor's ideas were underpinned by a view that workmen (at that time Taylor's work was primarily involved with men rather than men and women together in the workplace) were motivated only by money and the possibility of gaining financial incentives for producing more work.

Later theories of motivation, such as those of Herzberg, moved away from this concept of money being the only motivating factor for employees, but in spite of a growing acceptance of the fact that people look for responsibility, achievement and a sense of autonomy at work, the debate over the managerial prerogative to make decisions has continued. The ability or willingness of managers to share their decision-making powers with employees at a lower level in the organisation's hierarchical structure will be very much influenced by those managers' general attitude towards management–workforce relationships. The two major philosophical stances have been described as unitarism and pluralism, and another important concept, i.e. partnership, became the focus of debate in the late 1990s. Recent and ongoing legislative developments emanating from the EU have also meant that there is a heightened need to address employees' rights to information and consultation about what is happening in their workplace.

The unitary and pluralist perspectives

The type of relationship that will develop between employer (as represented by managers) and employee, and the techniques that are utilised to regulate this relationship, are influenced by the beliefs of the employer. You will see that a unitary stance is likely to result in a workplace culture that is different from what you would expect to find in an organisation headed by pluralists. These concepts were developed in the work of Fox (1974).

The unitary perspective

Unitarists believe that all members of an organisation have the same interests, that they will all accept the organisation's goals and direct all their efforts towards the achievement of these goals. This implies that there is no conflict in such organisations; if conflict were to arise, it would be attributed to some misunderstanding of what the goals are or to deliberate trouble-making on the part of some individual. The unitarist stance also implies that the person or persons leading the organisation have decided what the goals are, and there is an expectation that everyone who joins the organisation will internalise those goals. Unitarist organisations, therefore, depend on strong leadership from the top and are likely to recruit purposefully like-minded members. The signature of this philosophy is the belief that there is a common goal and that everyone is directing his or her efforts towards the achievement of this goal.

The pluralist perspective

Pluralists, on the other hand, believe that in any organisation a range of interests are likely to be represented among the members. One example of this is that employees are likely to be interested in increasing the pay they receive for a unit of work, whereas managers and owners will be concerned to increase profits. This is a clear example of differing objectives or a plurality of interests in the workplace. The existence of different interests means that conflicts are likely to arise as the various parties pursue their interests, and pluralists accept that this is natural and needs to be managed. These conflicts should be managed in such a way that they do not disrupt the running of the organisation, or even so that they potentially contribute to its success.

Pause for thought 3.2   Considering what you have just read about the unitary and pluralist approaches to employee relations, which would you consider to be more likely to accept unionisation of the workforce and which more likely to resist it? Give reasons for your choice.

Unitary employers are more likely to resist unionisation; pluralist employers are likely to accept unionisation more readily. Unionisation implies the existence of different sets of interests and the will to set up mechanisms for resolving these differences. Pluralists accept the existence of these differences and the need to work towards their resolution, whereas unitarists expect everyone to have the same goals. According to unitarists there should be no conflict, and therefore no need to have mechanisms for representing differing points of view and resolving conflict. Pluralists recognise from the outset that differing interests in the workplace will have an impact on the achievement of organisational goals, and therefore need to be incorporated into the decision-making process. This is an important point to bear in mind when you read about the methods employers can adopt for involving employees in decisions.

Partnership, participation and employee involvement

As well as the effects that involvement in decision making has on employee motivation, as discussed earlier, there is also a broader philosophical debate about the role of owners, managers and employees as players in the employment relations scene. Are owners and managers the only participants in the workplace with the right to make decisions? Are the providers of capital the only ones with a vested interest in the success of an enterprise? The concept of stakeholders suggests that the success of an organisation does not affect only those who have a financial stake in it, but that a range of people have a direct interest in what an organisation does. Everyone who is affected in any way by the actions and decisions of an enterprise is a stakeholder, including:

- employees, who depend on their organisation for their livelihood and for the pleasantness or otherwise of their work life
- customers, who have their own requirements of the organisation and who expect organisations to take their concerns into consideration
- suppliers, who depend for their own livelihood on the success of client organisations
- the community, which depends on organisations to protect the environment.

This raises again the question of managerial prerogative in deciding what should happen in the workplace versus the right or the desire of employees to have their interests represented. Arguments for maximising employees' input include their democratic right to have a say in any decisions that will affect them directly, their vested interest in the success of the organisation and, on another level, the fact that it makes sense to use the expertise that is available throughout the organisation.

The preceding discussion touches on major political and ethical questions to which there are no easy answers, and certainly no one answer that everyone will accept. In the discussion of the role that employees should play in an enterprise there is often perceived to be a tension between economic and social imperatives (McGlynn, 1995). Improvements in employee consultation, especially if they are legislated and therefore compulsory, are frequently seen as essentially social measures that impose unnecessary costs on businesses. But it is congruent with HRM thinking to see these improvements as measures leading to economic success; that is, you can attain a competitive edge by maximising the contribution of your employees, and the contribution of employees is greater the more they are consulted on, and therefore involved and engaged in, what is happening in the organisation. These arguments lead us into a discussion of the concept of partnership and the Labour Government's support for it.

Partnership

Coupar and Stevens (1998) make some interesting comments about the long-established pedigree of partnership, but the partnership concept in modern times emerged more clearly as part of the employee relations agenda in 1997, and the terminology appeared with increasing frequency throughout 1998, although an IPA (Involvement and Participation Association) paper on the benefits of partnership had already appeared earlier, in 1992. A clear link can be seen between a strategic goal of innovation and partnership as a method of engaging the full commitment of employees (Allen, 1998), and the Labour Government, first elected in 1997, quickly aligned itself with the idea of partnership (*Fairness at Work 1998*, Chapters 1 and 2), presenting it as one of the 'three pillars' which supported its 'strategy for achieving competitiveness' (s1.3). So, obviously, partnership was placed well and truly on the employee relations agenda for the foreseeable future.

As with HRM, partnership is an evolving concept and several commentators in the late 1990s observed that there was at that time no accepted definition of what partnership was and what it encompassed (Beardwell, 1998; Marchington, 1998). As the Government pointed out in its *Fairness at Work* paper, businesses should be free to adopt a contingency approach and develop whatever programmes suit their particular circumstances and, indeed, the IRS (2004) assert that companies tend to adopt their own definition of partnership. It may be, then, that the search for an authoritative definition of partnership is not a productive exercise.

We have gathered a number of descriptions of partnership from several publications, and present them here, followed by a comment on the similarities that emerge.

Employers and employees working together jointly to solve problems.
(ACAS, 1997, p. 13)

Key components might include high degrees of communication, personal development, employment security and an emphasis on ethical people management.
(Beardwell, 1998, p. 36)

Individual representation; consultation and communication; values; and understanding and promoting the business.
(Allen, 1998, p. 41, describing the partnership deal agreed between Tesco and Usdaw)

- Employment security and new working practices.
- Giving employees a voice in how the company is run.
- Fair financial rewards.
- Investment in training.
(Monks, 1998, p. 176)

1 A commitment to working together to make a business more successful.
2 Understanding the employee security conundrum and trying to do something about it.

3 Building relationships at the workplace which maximise employee influence through total communication and a robust and effective employee voice.

(Coupar and Stevens, 1998, p. 157)

- Commitment to the success of the enterprise.
- Building trust.
- Recognising legitimate roles and interests.
- Employment security.
- Information and consultation.
- Sharing success.
- Training and development.

(Industrial Relations Services, 2003a, p. 9 and 2004, p. 15)

- Commitment to the success of the enterprise.
- Recognizing the existence of different interests.
- Employment security.
- Quality of working life.
- Genuine sharing of information and consultation.
- Added value from both partners.

(Gennard and Judge, 2005, p. 224–5)

Common themes that emerge among these definitions are the importance of security, the common aim of business success and the concept of employee voice.

Of these three components, the one which is probably the most contentious is security, implying, as it seems to, that employees are promised their jobs will be safe no matter what happens. The numbers of redundancies declared in the early years of this century are an indicator of how difficult it has been for many organisations to comply with such a promise (ACAS, 2001), and the threat of redundancy continues at least for some workers, with the CIPD (2007b) reporting that 25 per cent of employers surveyed were considering redundancies in the Spring 2007 *Labour Market Outlook Survey*. On the other hand, as John Monks points out: 'Security in exchange for positive work flexibility is at the heart of the partnership approach' (1998, p. 176). You will note, however, that Monks and Beardwell, as cited above, both refer to *employment* security rather than *job* security, and this distinction is important to the concept of partnership and the modern psychological contract. Employment security implies that employees will be developed in such a way that, should an employer ultimately have to declare redundancies, the employees affected will be highly skilled and therefore their chances of employment elsewhere will be enhanced. Nonetheless, redundancies can still pose a problem for the effectiveness of the partnership approach, a fact that we shall return to in our concluding comments on partnership.

Did you know?

A search of the Times Online website revealed a number of redundancies or threatened redundancies declared in 2006 and 2007. Organisations reported on include the BBC, *The Times* and *The Sunday Times*, Remploy, and Weetabix.

(*Source*: www.timesonline.co.uk)

The combination of a 'common aim of business success' and the concept of 'employee voice' is interesting, given our previous discussion of unitarism and pluralism. Working in partnership calls for the recognition of a mutually desirable goal (business success), but seems to imply at the same time that employees may have different opinions from management and that therefore some mechanism is needed to facilitate 'employee voice'. We shall return to this point after our initial overview of participation and involvement.

Some further interesting points to note about partnership before investigating ways in which it can be achieved are as follows:

- The Government emphasises the development of a satisfactory work–life balance for employees as being another key feature of effective partnership.
- Partnership can be achieved in both a unionised and non-unionised environment. There is nothing to stop a non-unionised organisation from making arrangements with its employees to consult with elected representatives on a wide range of issues and indeed, as described in more detail later in this chapter, the scope of all employees' statutory rights to information and consultation is increasing. On the other hand, the Government obviously feels that if the majority of employees in an organisation wish to be represented by a union, employers should not be obstructive. The Employment Relations Act 1999 introduced new regulations to facilitate union recognition where an appropriate majority of the workforce desire it.
- The Government also stated its intention to examine ways in which ACAS can expand the good work it already does in this area of endeavour in its periodic review of the service.

There is a definitive link between partnership and employee participation which can be the channel for employee voice, and between partnership and employee involvement initiatives in that these can represent the way to achieve partnership. Coupar and Stevens (1998, p. 157) state that 'the IPA sees partnership as a unique combination of employee involvement processes which has the potential to maximise the benefits to the company and to employees in the process of change'. They also comment (1998, p. 151) on the previously mentioned phenomenon, that 'companies typically use a very wide range of differing activities to develop the mix needed to gain staff commitment and achieve success in the marketplace.'

We shall now provide an overview of the difference in approach implied by the terms employee involvement and participation, sometimes referred to together as EIP (Marchington and Cox, 2007) although commentators at the same time make a distinction between the two. We shall also comment again on the concept of partnership in that context before continuing with a more detailed exploration of EIP.

Employee involvement and participation (EIP)

The main purpose of EIP is to make workers feel like active participants in what happens in the workplace. There are numerous practices aiming to achieve this, and these have been categorised as *representative* methods and *direct* methods. Representative methods mean that workers are not involved in communications and decision making directly and individually, but through elected representatives who will put forward the workers' views. This sort of representation is often referred to as workers having a *voice*, and practices involving employee representatives are typically categorised as *participation*. Often, such participation is supported by legal structures as in the case of European Works Councils (EWCs), addressed by the Transnational Information and Consultation of Employees Regulations 1999, and the national councils formed under the Information and Consultation of Employees (ICE) Regulations 2004.

Direct methods are those typically described as constituting *employee involvement*, and they include communications targeted straight at employees (i.e. not cascaded by representatives) and other techniques that involve individuals or groups of workers. Employee involvement practices focus on the agenda set by management and attempt to get employees to understand the importance of organisational goals and commit to them.

Pause for thought 3.3	Consider the descriptions of employee involvement and employee participation. Which one is a unitary employer likely to adopt? Which one is a pluralist employer likely to adopt?

Employee participation recognises that groups within an organisation will have different points of view, and allows for input on those differences, giving employees a voice during the decision-making process at higher levels. In accepting the validity of the existence of differing interests, employee participation is pluralist in nature. Employee involvement calls for commitment to decisions managers have made and the organisational goals they have set, so it is essentially unitary in nature.

Commentators on the employment relations scene in the UK state that a combination of direct and representative approaches is likely to work best (Sisson, 2007; Earls, 2007; Coupar, 2007), although they also indicate that direct practices are likely to predominate (Coupar, 2007; Marchington and Cox, 2007). As the ICE Regulations become more embedded in the UK employment relations scene, we may witness a strengthening of representative participation for workers, but that remains to be seen.

It is certainly true of a partnership approach, however, as we have described it, that it comprises both employee involvement and participation. It can be said, then, that partnership exemplifies a blend of some aspects of unitarism with some aspects of pluralism: we can have the pursuit of the unitarist common goal within a pluralist framework. Appealing as this may be, some critics question the viability of partnership agreements, pointing to the imbalance of power between management and worker representatives so that the management agenda is likely to prevail (Smith, 2006; IRS, 2006b).

We shall now review in more detail the concept of worker participation, developments with regard to regulatory information and consultation rights, and a variety of employee involvement practices that have been identified in a number of companies.

EU rights to information and consultation

European Works Councils

Participative structures have been a subject of debate for many years among the member states of the European Union, and a number of directives were proposed but subsequently failed to be adopted. These include the Vredeling Directive and the Fifth Company Law Directive, which each contained broad proposals on consultation and information. On 22 September 1994 a Directive of more limited scope was adopted, and this is the European Council Directive on the establishment of a European

Works Council or other procedure in Community-scale undertakings or Community-scale groups of undertakings for the purposes of informing and consulting employees. The main background details of the Directive and features of the works councils are described in the following paragraphs, and a fuller outline of events that preceded the adoption of the Directive and of the development of European thought on employee consultation and information can be found in Gold and Hall (1994) and Mill (1991).

The key issues in the Directive are that employees should be properly informed and consulted about major issues that will have an impact on them. The Directive refers to transnational undertakings where decisions could be made in one country that would affect employees in another country. In such circumstances, it seemed essential to most member states in the European Union that proper mechanisms should be in place in order to ensure that employees in the different countries of a transnational operation receive equal treatment with regard to information and consultation. This is the objective of the European Works Council Directive.

When the Maastricht Treaty on European Union was ratified in 1993, the UK Government opted out of the agreements on social policy, but the Protocol on Social Policy and Agreement on Social Policy, which are annexed to the treaty, allowed the other member states to adopt social policy measures without having to consult or gain agreement from the UK. This was the background against which the Directive on European Works Councils was developed.

Approximately 100 UK-owned undertakings were affected by the Directive because they have establishments in other member states that meet the threshold requirements. They were obliged to adhere to the Directive for employees located in other member states, but this obligation did not extend to employees located in the UK. That is, they did not have to establish works councils in relevant UK establishments, but they could do so if they chose to. Two UK-owned multinationals that quickly decided to establish works councils in their undertakings in the UK were BP Europe and United Biscuits (see *Industrial Relations Review and Report*, December 1994, cited in the further study section, for more details).

The date set for the implementation of the Directive was 22 September 1996. If companies established a transnational agreement on information and consultation covering the whole workforce before this date, the Directive would not apply; i.e. companies that made an agreement by then would not be constrained by the terms of the Directive. This is, in fact, what companies such as BP Europe and United Biscuits opted to do.

By the end of 1997, this scenario had changed, when the Labour Government ended the UK's opt-out from the Social Chapter by signing the Treaty of Amsterdam. This meant that the Directive on European Works Councils now applied fully to relevant companies in the UK. The Directive was implemented in the UK as the Transnational Information and Consultation of Employees Regulations 1999.

The essential characteristics of the regulations and the prescribed process for developing and implementing a European Works Council (EWC) are listed below.

Characteristics

- The threshold at which employers come under the terms of the regulations is that they have at least 1,000 employees within the member states and at least 150 employees in each of any two member states.

- The terms of the regulations come into effect either when management initiates action or when a written request is made by at least 100 employees or their representatives in at least two undertakings in at least two member states.

Process

- Management and labour meet each other in order to establish a procedure for consultation about the issue of an EWC.
- There are four possible outcomes of this consultation process:

  - the parties establish an EWC
  - if they decide against an EWC, they may establish an alternative procedure for information and consultation on transnational issues
  - the parties agree not to have a specific procedure relating to transnational issues
  - the parties fail to reach agreement.

- The regulations establish a framework for handling confidential information.
- If the parties fail to reach agreement, there are minimum standards that will be applied: an EWC will be established and will meet management once a year, or more often if necessary, to be informed and consulted on any matters that will significantly affect the employees. Matters that the EWC will consider include the structure of the undertaking, its financial situation and the future development of the business. These issues set down in the minimum standards are a good indicator of the kinds of issues the ministers from the member states felt employees should be consulted on.

Information and Consultation of Employees: Works Councils and Employee Forums

The EU Directive on Information and Consultation of Employees was finally adopted and came into force on 23 March 2002 after many years of discussion about its content and wording. The Department of Trade and Industry (as it was called at that time) engaged in extensive consultation to establish the context of communication and consultation that already existed in the UK in order to provide a suitable framework for the national regulations. These came into force on 6 April 2005 as the Information and Consultation of Employees (ICE) Regulations 2004.

A phased introduction of the regulations is taking effect as follows:

- 2005 – establishments with 150 or more employees
- 2007 – establishments with 100 or more employees
- 2008 – establishments with 50 or more employees.

The establishment of these regulations introduces employee rights to consultation on matters likely to affect the economic status of their employer, and any proposed changes that might affect their employment status. Among the probable issues for information and consultation, the CIPD (2006c) lists information about profit and loss, sales performance and strategic plans, proposed changes to working time and working practices, restructuring and reorganisation. Consultation should include the provision of timely and accurate information to employees from management, opportunities for employees to put forward their views, a managerial response to these views together with reasons for their response, and an attempt to reach agreement on decisions. A request from 10 per cent of the workforce will trigger the obligation for management to set some formal mechanism for the provision of information and consultation. The mechanisms have been variously referred to as national works councils (IRS, 2001; IDS, 2002a), consultation committees, company councils (IDS, 2002b), forums and staff councils (IDS, 2004b), works councils, and employee forums (IRS, 2006a).

The IRS (2006a) reports that only 19 per cent of employers surveyed said that they had made changes to their information and consultation processes as a direct result of the ICE Regulations, but 31 per cent had introduced changes since their implementation anyway. Luckhurst (2007) points out that it can be difficult to get workers to take on the role of employee representative and to ensure that discussions are properly focused. His suggestions for these two problems are that the agenda in meetings must be management driven and focused on important strategic issues so that the meetings do not dissolve into discussions of 'tea and toilets' issues (p. 1). He further gives guidance that full explanations of decision-making processes should be given, exploring, for instance, what the alternatives were, so that employees fully understand why certain decisions have been made, leading to greater trust and more willingness to participate as representatives of the workforce. The CIPD (2006c) sees the involvement of employees in information and consultation as a key part of achieving greater motivation, commitment and engagement.

Employee involvement (EI) and high-performance working (HPW)

As described previously, direct methods of employee involvement are widely used to achieve employee commitment and engagement, leading to the high-performance workplace which is necessary to maintain and improve levels of productivity. Our focus in the rest of this chapter is firstly on a detailed overview of employee involvement practices, followed by an explanation and comment on the concepts of commitment and engagement.

Pause for thought 3.4 Make a list of at least three techniques that could be used to promote the involvement of employees in decisions relating directly to their work or in general to make employees feel more that they are an equal partner in the workplace whose contribution is sought after and valued. As you read through the next section you can check your list against the practices that are discussed here.

In 1994, the Department of Employment (DoE), as it was then called, used six categories, each with a range of initiatives, to describe employee involvement and they are still useful as a basis for a structured examination of EI practices. These are summarised in Table 3.1, but updated to include more recent developments, and discussed in more detail below. The practices listed by the DoE remain representative of the bundles of HRM practices described by later commentators such as the EEF and the CIPD (2003), Incomes Data Services (2004a, 2004b and 2007) and the Involvement and Participation Association (2007). We shall refer to these and other sources as we review the various practices identified by the DoE. The Department of Employment's categorisation is not an all-inclusive definition, i.e. you do not have to be involved in all the listed activities at the same time to say you are practising employee involvement.

| Table 3.1 | Employee involvement categories and practices |

Category	EI practices
Sharing information	Team briefing Employer and employee publications Company videos Company website, intranet and email Roadshows
Consultation	Employee suggestion schemes Employee opinion surveys Works committees Health and safety committees
Financial participation	Profit-related pay Employee share schemes Share incentive plans
Commitment to quality	Continuous improvement Teamwork Total quality management Quality circles Self-managed project groups Employee award schemes
Developing the individual	Performance management Appraisal schemes Employee development programmes Investors in People A qualified workforce
Beyond the workplace	The community The environment

Different combinations of practices will be suitable for different businesses, and Edwards (2007) draws attention to the fact that it may be difficult, for example, to adapt HPW practices for small businesses which are so important to the UK economy. Marchington and Cox (2007) also allude to the fact that EI practices work well in combination with each other, depending on the circumstances, and that often one practice will support the effectiveness of another.

It must be stressed again that various combinations of these measures are taken up by organisations at different times (IRS, 2003b). Research conducted by Marchington *et al.* (1993) revealed that individual managers tended to adopt their preferred measures, which might well be dropped when they moved on. This is an unfortunate aspect of the voluntary and flexible nature of involvement arrangements. As you will see in the discussion of the initiatives, a longer-term commitment on the part of managers is needed if the techniques are to work to best effect. Formal partnership deals agreed between managers and employees may introduce an element of continuity into this scenario.

Sharing information

- team briefing
- employer and employee publications
- company videos
- company website, intranet and email
- roadshows.

Keeping people informed is often described as one of the cornerstones of employee involvement, and in fact provides the foundation on which many of the individual techniques can be built. Without information it is impossible for people to develop and contribute their own ideas. A commitment to sharing information is an essential component of involvement and engagement, and the list of associated practices gives an indication of some of the vehicles that can be used to get information to employees: face to face in small, regular meetings (team briefing), materials that could use the written word, graphics or electronic systems such as a company's intranet (company and staff newsletters, notices, posters), and videos. The IDS (2003) give Safeway (now part of the Morrisons group) as an example where senior managers often go on the road to ensure that information about major changes is disseminated effectively. Careful consideration should be given to choosing the form of communication most appropriate to the type of message.

Marchington and Cox (2007) report on research that shows that team briefings and mass meetings with the workforce are by far the most popular methods chosen by organisations to involve their employees: 91 per cent of organisations surveyed in 2004 used this method, up from 85 per cent in 1998. So, not only is this the most used method, but its use is also on the increase. With more legal pressures to inform and consult employees, for instance because of the ICE Regulations, we can expect to see even more attention being paid to this area of employment relations.

● Consultation

- employee suggestion schemes
- employee opinion surveys
- works committees
- health and safety committees.

Along with sharing information, consultation is a key concept in developing good employee relations, and much of the ongoing debate about the development of mechanisms to improve the employer–employee relationship centres on the employee's right to information and consultation. Of the information-sharing techniques we have discussed in the preceding section, briefing sessions allow for some immediate feedback from employees, but most of the other vehicles encourage only one-way communication. ACAS (2005a) emphasises that effective communication requires a two-way flow of information and ideas. The consultation mechanisms named in this section essentially provide a route for employees to feed ideas back to their employers. These vehicles only represent true consultation, however, if there is an honest willingness to consider the ideas proffered and to incorporate reasonable suggestions into the decision-making process. As the regulations on information and consultation bed in, the use of those of the consultation mechanisms described here which are voluntary will be further supported by regulatory measures.

Most staff suggestion schemes are linked with a reward for successful suggestions, especially those where a cost saving for the organisation or other improvements in productivity can be identified. The reward does not, however, have to be financial for people to feel encouraged to contribute their ideas. Often people wish merely to see their expertise recognised, gaining a sense of achievement from this, and they need only to be encouraged by the introduction of a recognised scheme. The reward for successful suggestions could be linked to information vehicles from the first category, i.e. a mention in the company or staff newsletter.

Employee opinion surveys are an excellent method of collecting honest feedback from employees about what they see as the important issues, and what aspects of the workplace affect their levels of commitment and engagement both positively and negatively. The surveys obviously need to be constructed properly, addressing relevant issues, and employees need to see that their feedback is taken seriously and leads to identifiable action, otherwise the system of obtaining employee feedback will fall into disrepute and cease to be taken seriously by the employees. A further important aspect of employee opinion surveys is that not everyone is motivated by the same things (Gratton, 2007), and analysing employee feedback can enable management to tailor their EI practices to the needs of different groups of employees.

Works committees to promote information and consultation involve meetings of management and employee representatives who may be elected directly or nominated through the trade unions. Their terms of reference can be tailored to the requirements of individual organisations, and may vary widely from one organisation to another. In its work with companies, ACAS very often establishes joint working committees to solve a variety of problems. Works councils may have been established in some organisations on a voluntary basis, but the Information and Consultation of Employees (ICE) Regulations now also provide a framework for the constitution and remit of such councils. Employers who have already established information-sharing and consultation committees in their organisation may apply to the Central Arbitration Committee to have them recognised as valid arrangements under the ICE Regulations. One caveat, however, is that such arrangements must apply to all employees (Pickard, 2004). You will find information about health and safety committees in Chapter 12.

All of the methods in this category of EI practices involve upward communication, a chance for employees to put forward their point of view and ideas, an opportunity to be heard. We have already noted that this is referred to as *employee voice*, an important concept in modern employment relations. Several commentators emphasise the crucial nature of employee voice in achieving successful employee involvement leading to engagement (IDS, 2007; Purcell, 2006). The CIPD (2006b, p. 14) goes so far as to say that: 'Allowing people the opportunity to feed their views and opinions upwards is the single most important driver of engagement.'

Financial participation

- profit-related pay
- employee share schemes
- share incentive plans.

Although mentioned less frequently than other EI practices, a number of share schemes, often with tax relief approved by HM Revenue and Customs, exist to provide employees with financial participation in their organisations. The schemes include group or individual bonuses (which *are* subject to income tax) linked to the company's profit performance, and ownership of shares.

Again, various schemes exist in relation to share ownership. In some schemes, shares may be bought by a trust for employees, usually at no direct cost to them, and are later distributed to them; other schemes give employees the opportunity to buy shares directly. A variety of arrangements exist regarding the percentage of shares that employees can hold, what happens to the shares when an employee leaves the company, and, very importantly, whether the shares are voting or non-voting shares. If ownership of the shares gives employees a voice at shareholders' meetings, this is essentially a form of employee participation as it has been defined in this chapter. The Incomes Data Services study on all-employee share schemes (2001) contains excellent information on the types of plan brought in by the Finance Act 2000, and XpertHR (2007) reports that 'one of the most popular types of approved scheme is "share save", also known as Save As You Earn (SAYE).'

As intimated above, financial participation is certainly recognised as an EI practice, but it is not used as frequently as other methods. Lloyd and Payne (2007) mention profit sharing in passing, and O'Connell *et al.* (2007) point out that foreign-owned companies operating in Ireland are more likely to use performance-related financial incentives. That recognition and reward in general have a place in EI is mentioned by several observers (Brown *et al.*, 2007; CIPD, 2007a), but the 2004 Workplace Employment Relations Survey (Kersley *et al.*, 2005) reports that only 21 per cent of private sector workplaces have an employee share scheme in place as part of the reward package.

> ### Did you know?
>
> *People Management* reported on the return enjoyed by staff at Tesco who had participated in the supermarket's employee share scheme. Staff members who had been in the scheme since it started in 2002 were due to receive upwards of £7,000 each, which represented a 120 per cent return on investment.
>
> (*Source*: Tesco staff enjoy share windfall (2007) *People Management*, 22 February, p. 11)

Commitment to quality

- continuous improvement
- teamwork
- total quality management
- quality circles
- self-managed project groups
- employee award schemes.

The human resource management approach and modern ideas about employee motivation go hand-in-hand with an emphasis on the social aspects of work. Human beings on the whole work better in groups, they respond to the stimulation of feedback on their achievements, and there are synergies in terms of improved ideas and methods of working to be gained from having people work in teams rather than as isolated individuals. All these factors are reflected in the techniques listed above.

The idea that benefits can be gained from the formation of teams and self-managed groups is addressed in the work done by Trist and Murray at the Tavistock Institute (1993). You may have encountered their concept of sociotechnical systems in your course on organisational behaviour. Basically this theory says that organisations must pay attention to the social systems in the workplace as well as the technical systems when designing jobs. ACAS (2005b) also addresses the value of teamwork as a motivational tool.

Total quality management emphasises the responsibility of each individual for ensuring the quality of his or her work and de-emphasises the role of supervision or inspection. This puts responsibility firmly with each individual employee. If this is combined with employee award schemes, it heightens an individual's awareness of the contribution he or she can make to the organisation and of the extent to which this is valued. The term 'quality circles' is linked with an approach adopted by Japanese companies, but the method stems from the work and thinking of an American, Dr W. Edward Deming. Essentially, quality circles involve having a group of people, usually from one work area, meet away from the shop floor to discuss improvements that could be made in the work systems. The group analyses data and sets up proposals which are presented to senior managers who consider the new ideas and report back to the quality circle, either accepting the proposal or explaining why it is rejected. Since this requires a greater level of analytical skill than the employees may need for their jobs, quality circles often have a facilitator who provides assistance in the presentational aspects but does not contribute ideas as far as content is concerned.

Continuous improvement is an umbrella term for any programme that focuses on identifying and solving problems or exploring opportunities to improve the organisation's performance. These programmes often focus on an improved response to customer requirements or a reduced rate of errors which can be targeted by a combination of initiatives such as teamwork, quality management and problem-solving groups.

Developing the individual

- performance management
- appraisal schemes
- employee development programmes
- Investors in People
- a qualified workforce

All the employee involvement techniques that we have discussed contribute to the development of employees: better communication means that people are well informed; encouragement to share ideas through consultation equates with encouragement to develop ideas rather than accept the status quo; financial participation increases awareness and knowledge of the economic performance of the organisation. Employee development extends the boundaries of knowledge, interest and understanding and enables each employee to feel more involved and more able to participate in decisions. Chapters 9 and 10 explore in detail all the practices listed above related to developing people and the contribution that these practices make to the organisation.

Beyond the workplace

- the community
- the environment.

The Department of Employment (1994) proposed that attempts to make employees feel more committed should not be limited to activities at work. We have stated in other contexts, for instance with regard to human resource planning, that employers need to be aware of the community within which they operate, and this can mean the global community as well as the local community. A number of employers have empowered their staff to become involved in community initiatives such as working with schools or with disabled persons. This has the effect of increasing the loyalty of employees and strengthening the organisation's public image.

A similar argument is extended to environmental issues. If employers show concern for the environment and enlist employees in methods of protecting the environment, this is likely to gain loyalty and make employees proud to be associated with the organisation.

Additional influences

In addition to the practices described above, the CIPD (2006a and b) comment on the importance of providing flexibility for employees, and state that employees who achieve a good work–life balance are more likely to be engaged. Flexible working arrangements and work–life balance are addressed in more detail in the next chapter.

Commitment

As intimated previously, the reason for pursuing a programme of employee involvement is the expectation that improvements in productivity levels will follow, leading to a high-performance workplace. By informing and consulting with employees and using other techniques to make them feel more involved in the workplace, workers will be enabled and feel empowered to add more value to their organisations. An important concept in terms of the expected motivational outcomes of EI is employee commitment. The direct effect of involvement in the organisation is expected to be an increase in the individual employee's commitment to colleagues, the workplace or the job, which will be reflected in increased productivity, lower labour turnover and reduced absenteeism.

The human resource management approach is intent on maximising the contribution of employees as a critical success factor, and increasing employee commitment through involvement is seen as a way to do this. There may, however, be some problems with the contention that involvement arrangements result in increased commitment. Commitment is an attitude, and the connection between attitudes and behaviour is not a straightforward one. Behaviour depends on a variety of influencing factors, including values and beliefs and what each individual sees as motivating factors, so attitudes are not always reflected in behaviour. For instance, if a person has a positive emotional reaction to a management innovation, we could say that that person may feel greater commitment to the job or the organisation. If, however, that person is influenced by co-workers who are not like minded, and the person values his or her relationship with those co-workers, then the positive attitude may not be reflected in subsequent behaviour. In fact, the person may attempt to rationalise the positive feelings away. EI could therefore engender a positive attitude in some people and not in others, and even where it does result in positive attitudes, it is only one feature of the workplace and other influences could result in this positive attitude not being reflected in the behaviour managers are hoping for. You will find a fuller explanation of these concepts in Cascio (1998).

This discussion of attitudes and behaviour is included just to sound a cautionary note that increases in commitment and productivity are not a foregone conclusion. In general, however, the introduction of EI initiatives is welcomed by the workforce and results in a positive response. Some reactions will depend on the culture and relations that have traditionally existed either in the organisation or in a particular industry. If employees do not trust management, they will greet management initiatives with scepticism. If employers wish to encourage change in these circumstances, they will have to build trust, which can only be achieved in the long term.

Engagement

Employee engagement is recognised as being the stage beyond commitment. Employees may feel committed to their colleagues, clients, work or employer, and yet not expend the sought after discretionary effort expressed in those well-known HRM phrases such as 'going the extra mile' and 'working beyond contract'. It is when employees display these behaviours that they can be said to be engaged (Coupar, 2007). The IDS (2007) uses phrases such as 'passionate about their job' (p. 2) and a firm's 'ability to ignite enthusiasm' (p. 3) as indicators of engagement.

All of the practices we have described as participation and involvement can contribute to the creation of commitment. As Woodruffe (2006, p. 9) states: 'Engagement has become something of a vogue word, eclipsing commitment and motivation in the management literature.' Edwards (2007, p. 55) expresses a similar idea with regard to the related concept of the high-performance work system: 'The HPWS is not new. It is that employees need to be given the ability to contribute to the performance of the firm together with the means and the incentive to do so. This principle can be found in the Quality of Working Life movement of the 1960s, and indeed earlier.'

In spite of the long-established pedigree of EI practices and the much vaunted recognition of the crucial importance of engagement to business, surveys of the level of engagement in the UK report poor results. The CIPD (2006a, p. 3) reports that 'three in ten employees are engaged in their work' and that 'levels of engagement among the under-35s are significantly lower than those in older age groups'. The PeopleIndex (2007) reports a more favourable level at 52 per cent, yet calls this an alarming figure. These statistics raise questions about why EI practices are not more effective, and indeed the current focus of debate on these issues revolves around the question about what are the crucial elements that drive employees from commitment to engagement. Observers of employment relations repeatedly emphasise the prime importance of communication and leadership, and the CIPD (2007a) confirms this view by identifying the psychological contract and relationships as being the key issues with regard to achieving a high-performance workplace.

We have already established that various forms of communication, and in particular employee voice, are major and essential components of EI. Beyond actually communicating, organisations need to demonstrate that they are fully committed to the processes involved and provide evidence that employee voice is being taken seriously.

Among a number of writers on EI, Marchington and Cox (2007) emphasise the importance of line managers in creating engagement. Managers may make choices about the extent to which they wish to subscribe to and encourage EI practices, which will obviously have an impact on the effectiveness of EI programmes within an organisation. Marchington and Cox allude to 'informal EIP' (p. 189), and link this with management style. Other commentators also draw attention to the importance of adopting an appropriate management style to encourage involvement, commitment and engagement (Earls, 2007), and to the need to ensure that managers have the appropriate skills to be able to provide leadership in this area (Gratton, 2007).

CASE STUDY 3.1 Employee engagement through involvement and participation

You are the head of HR at the headquarters of a national chain of supermarkets. The stores have always operated with a very hierarchical structure and a set of rigid rules. Major decisions about the business are made centrally by a board of senior executives in Birmingham, and only information that is deemed necessary is passed down the line to the next level of staff who then cascade information further down the line as they see fit. The normal chain of command consists of a regional manager, a store manager, department managers and unit supervisors. Personnel at each level deal only with the level above them. Shop assistants expect explicit instructions from their supervisors, and will refer all matters to a supervisor if a question arises on which they have not been briefed. The extent of each person's authority is strictly defined, e.g. shop assistants cannot deal with returned items; unit supervisors are responsible for deciding when displays will change, what to display, and for maintaining the general tidiness of their area. All employees know their role and their limits, and managers and supervisors do not ask for opinions from their subordinates. This is accepted by all staff members, and everyone who has been with the company for any length of time is used to the way things are done.

A new chief executive has recently joined the company, and she is not pleased with the current way of running things. She asks you to investigate ways of changing the culture to improve the contribution from every employee, and to prepare a confidential report for her.

Questions

1 Draw up a list of the changes that could be made and how these changes would be implemented.

2 List the benefits to be gained if you try to implement your suggested changes, and the problems that may be encountered.

Conclusion

We have discussed a range of management approaches to the workforce, and the implications that different philosophies have for the ways in which, and the extent to which, employees might be encouraged to participate in the decisions made in the workplace. The development of employee involvement initiatives and partnership deals and a focus on engagement are likely to be found in organisations that espouse the tenets of human resource management. Through the use of involvement and partnership practices, these organisations will attempt to maximise their employees' contribution to the achievement of organisational goals and their ability to add value through high-performance working while also directly benefiting the employees themselves.

REVIEW QUESTIONS

Brief answers to these review questions are provided on page 471.

1 Describe the two main philosophical approaches underlying management—employee relations, and comment on the likelihood of each of these espousing worker participation or employee involvement initiatives.

2 Explain the connections between employee involvement, employee commitment, engagement and high-performance working.

3 Describe the history of initiatives to improve employee consultation and information in the European Union.

4 Name the major components of partnership, and comment on its aims.

SELF-CHECK QUESTIONS

Answer the following multiple-choice and short-answer questions. The answers are provided on page 472 for you to check your understanding of this chapter.

1 Which of the following statements best describes the unitary perspective?
   (a) Managers expect all employees to espouse the organisation's goals. There are occasional conflicts of interest which managers settle by negotiation.
   (b) Managers espouse the organisation's goals and recognise that employees are likely to have their own set of interests. Differences in interests are regulated by negotiated agreements.
   (c) Managers expect all employees to espouse the organisation's goals. There are no conflicts of interest.

2 Participation is the method that you are most likely to find in unitarist organisations. TRUE or FALSE?

3 What is the threshold number of employees at which the Transnational Information and Consultation of Employees Regulations 1999 obliges a community-scale company to establish a European Works Council?

4 Which of the following statements are NOT true?
   (a) The Labour Government actively promotes partnership deals in the workplace.
   (b) Partnership deals can only be made when the workforce is not unionised.
   (c) Partnership deals can be made in both unionised and non-unionised companies.
   (d) Partnership deals can only be made in a unionised environment.

5 Which of the following was NOT named specifically by the Department of Employment as a technique for promoting employee involvement?
   (a) quality circles
   (b) peer appraisal
   (c) team briefing
   (d) financial participation.

→

6 Managers can confidently expect that employee commitment to work will be a direct result of employee involvement initiatives and will lead to improved motivation and productivity. TRUE or FALSE?

7 What does the acronym SAYE stand for?

8 Which techniques are listed in your textbook as being part of sharing information?

9 Which of the following has NOT specifically been identified as a standard component of partnership agreements.
   (a) improvements in employment security
   (b) fair wages for employees
   (c) consultation on matters affecting employees
   (d) provision of flexible benefits.

10 Name two elements that have been identified as crucial for the creation of employee engagement.

HR IN THE NEWS

FT

It's better if they give a damn

By Alison Maitland

Do you have a best friend at work? If you have never been asked, you might think it an odd question for your employer to include in an employee survey. Why do they want to know, you might wonder. What business is it of theirs? Standard Life, the life assurer that demutualised and floated on the London Stock Exchange last month after a painful restructuring, found the question was very much 'its business'.

Two years ago it experienced a huge drop in 'employee engagement', as measured by a regular survey designed to identify whether staff felt part of the business, understood its goals, and were willing and able to contribute their best to achieving these.

It was the biggest fall that Gallup, which administers the 12-question survey, has ever seen in a company. The worst scores were on employees' understanding of what the organisation stood for and what it expected of them. Stephen McCafferty, human resources director, says this demonstrated how badly their trust had been damaged by hefty job cuts and the group's decision to shed its longstanding mutual status.

'Employees were saying: "We're not sure we trust the business any more. We thought this was a stable business – we don't understand why things have changed",' he says. 'You get pulled up sharply by these scores. It's a bit of a shock, but in some regards it's a good thing.'

Among the dire results was something more positive: responses to the item stating 'I have a best friend at work' were less badly affected. Relationships within teams and between individuals remained good, despite the departure of long-serving colleagues and loss of faith in the company.

'So this question is very much the company's business – it has huge value in sustaining a level of engagement through very tough times,' says Mr McCafferty. 'When you come to rebuilding, you are rebuilding from a sound base.'

Identifying where the worst scores were helped the insurer to understand what action was needed most urgently. As a result, senior managers changed the way they developed strategy, asking for employees' input before setting it in stone.

It reviewed the appraisal process to make individuals' objectives clearer and overhauled the handling of customer inquiries and the measurement of team performance.

Since then, engagement scores have almost recovered to 2003 levels, but still lag behind the global average. 'One of my team put it that we were swimming along quite nicely in the middle of the pool and suddenly hit the bottom,' says Mr McCafferty. 'We managed to get half-way back up [by the 2005 employee survey] and we are now back on the surface.'

Standard Life's use of employee surveys to measure engagement demonstrates the growing attention that companies are paying to the concept. Having an 'engaged' workforce – a step beyond employee satisfaction or commitment – has been shown to improve the bottom line. Gallup's research, for example, has found a correlation between increased engagement and higher earnings per share. ISR, a rival employee research and consulting firm, found an average 19 per cent rise in operating income over 12 months for companies with a 'highly engaged' workforce, compared with a fall of 33 per cent for companies with low engagement scores.

International surveys also show companies have their work cut out if they want to have a fully engaged workforce. Globally, 24 per cent of employees are 'disengaged' and only 14 per cent are 'highly engaged', according to one such survey by Towers Perrin, the professional services firm.

Towers Perrin says that engagement is affected by significant change, whether positive or negative, Given the dramatic reshaping of the business environment from Asia to North America, 'it is hardly surprising that so many employees exhibit a sense of dislocation and frustration at what they see as an ever-changing employment "deal" with their employers.'

Gauging employee opinion is, of course, only the first step. Acting on the findings is much harder. 'There is a tendency with surveys to think: we've done that, and to put it to one side,' says Sue Hayday, a research fellow at the UK's Institute for Employment Studies. 'Organisations like to have a figure for engagement so they can say they are better or worse than others. But just knowing the figure doesn't really help.'

The numbers are particularly useful in identifying and addressing different levels of engagement within an organisation, she says.

For example, the institute's research in the National Health Service has found that engagement generally declines with age and length of service, But once employees hit 60, they suddenly become highly engaged – an intriguing finding given impending UK legislation to outlaw age discrimination.

Ms Hayday says that employee engagement, unlike satisfaction or commitment, involves a two-way relationship. 'It's not just about the employee going the extra mile. The employer has to give something back.'

This is echoed in Gallup's research into the subject, which has sought to identify the elements of engagement that team managers can influence. Immediate supervisors and colleagues are crucial in determining an individual's engagement level, says Peter Flade, managing partner at Gallup in the UK. 'Graduates might join a great company, but they tend to leave a lousy manager.'

He says Gallup's 12 questions are also closely linked to productivity and staff retention.

For example, it has found the item about having a best friend at work to be the single biggest predictor of 'shrinkage' – or theft – in the retail industry. 'A high level of trust in the team dissuades people from leaving the warehouse door open,' he says.

Standard Life has used its survey findings to pinpoint teams with better than average scores for engagement. It found staff turnover in these teams was about half that of poorly scoring teams, and absenteeism was 30 per cent lower. Team leaders were asked what they did and the information shared online.

'They are straightforward things,' says Mr McCafferty. 'These managers actively involve people in agreeing their individual targets. They differentiate clearly between "must haves" and "desirables". Members of the team quickly flag when anything is unclear, regular checks are made on progress, and progress meetings take a variety of forms to suit team members and business needs.'

Team leaders also play a more important part in internal communications than in the past, he says. As a mutual, the group used to take the approach of 'management knows best', even to the extent of drawing up questions it thought employees would ask and providing the answers.

→

'Now we give people information and have a dialogue. In the past, it was parent-to-child communication. Now it's adult-to-adult.'

Take your staff's pulse

As a business services firm, BDO Stoy Hayward depends entirely on the quality of its 2,900 people. As part of its efforts to keep them engaged, it takes their pulse each year in a survey covering a wide range of issues, from the firm's strategy and leadership to how they feel about their careers.

The findings are split by business unit, service stream (audit, tax, corporate finance), gender, grade and seniority. 'If a particular group of people has got an issue in a particular area, we can quickly see what it is and tackle it at that level,' says Tony Perkins, head of the firm's London operation, which employs 1,100 staff.

In one case, the survey revealed that recently qualified, twenty-something employees were unhappy with their appraisal forms, finding them cumbersome to complete and inadequate at conveying their objectives. The procedure was duly improved.

Staff in each office meet to discuss the survey results – administered by ISR, the employee research and consulting firm – and to work out what action needs to be taken. 'Each group monitors these actions over time, so every member of staff can see that the comments they have made are followed up,' says Mr Perkins.

(FT.com, 10 August 2006. Reproduced with permission.)

Questions

1 What does Maitland identify as indicators of employee engagement?
2 Why had levels of employee engagement fallen at Standard Life?
3 What practices can an organisation adopt to address employee engagement?
4 What other factors affect employee engagement?
5 Why is employee engagement regarded as being important?

WHAT NEXT?

The major message in this chapter has been about the important role that communication and consultation and other HRM practices play in the development of good employment relations with a focus on the UK. Questions of communication, involvement and participation and their effects are, of course, also of interest in other countries. We have found three research articles investigating these issues: one is a comparative study of Britain and Denmark; the second reports research involving 49 countries, not named but analysed according to certain characteristics; the third is based in Asia Pacific. These three articles will give you an idea of international aspects of communication, participation and commitment.

Croucher, R., P. Gooderham and E. Parry (2006) The influences on direct communication in British and Danish firms: country, 'strategic HRM' or unionization? *European Journal of Industrial Relations,* Volume 12, Number 3, 267–86.

Gelade, G.A., P. Dobson and P. Gilbert (2006) National differences in organizational commitment. Effect of economy, product of personality, or consequence of culture? *Journal of Cross-Cultural Psychology,* Volume 37, Number 5, September, 542–56.

Markey, R. (2006) The internationalization of representative employee participation and its impact in the Asia Pacific, *Asia Pacific Journal of Human Resources,* Volume 44, 342–63.

References

Advisory, Conciliation and Arbitration Service (1997 and 2001) *Annual Report,* ACAS.

Advisory, Conciliation and Arbitration Service (2005a) *Employee Communications and Consultation,* ACAS (available at www.acas.org.uk; accessed 13.10.07).

Advisory, Conciliation and Arbitration Service (2005b) *Teamwork: Success through People,* ACAS (available at www.acas.org.uk; accessed 13.10.07).

Allen, M. (1998) All-inclusive, *People Management,* 11 June, 36–42.

Beardwell, I. (1998) Voices on, *People Management,* 28 May, 32–36.

Brown, A., M. Roddan, S. Jordan and L. Nilsson (2007) The time of your life, *People Management,* 26 July, 40–43.

Cascio, W.F. (1998) *Applied Psychology in Personnel Management,* 5th edition, Prentice Hall.

Chartered Institute of Personnel and Development (2006a) *Change Agenda: Reflections on Employee Engagement,* CIPD.

Chartered Institute of Personnel and Development (2006b) *How Engaged are British Employees? Annual Survey Report 2006,* CIPD.

Chartered Institute of Personnel and Development (2006c) *Information and Consultation of Employees Regulations,* CIPD (factsheet available at www.cipd.co.uk; accessed 15.06.06).

Chartered Institute of Personnel and Development (2007a) *Employee Engagement,* CIPD (podcast available at www.cipd.co.uk; accessed 12.10.07).

Chartered Institute of Personnel and Development (2007b) *Labour Market Outlook. Quarterly Survey Report,* Spring 2007, CIPD.

Coupar, W. (2007) Employee Involvement and High Performance, in Involvement and Participation Association, *High Performance Working,* IPA.

Coupar, W. and B. Stevens (1998) Towards a new model of industrial partnership: Beyond the 'HRM versus industrial relations' argument, in P. Sparrow and M. Marchington (eds) *Human Resource Management: The New Agenda,* Financial Times Pitman.

Department of Employment (1994) *The Competitive Edge: Employee Involvement in Britain,* Department of Employment.

Earls, J. (2007) Good work: an agenda for trade unions and employers, in Involvement and Participation Association, *High Performance Working,* IPA.

Edwards, P. (2007) The High Performance Work System and the small firm, in Involvement and Participation Association, *High Performance Working,* IPA.

EEF/CIPD (2003) *Maximising Employee Potential and Business Performance: the Role of High Performance Working,* EEF/CIPD.

Fairness at Work, Government White Paper, May 1998 (paper available at www.berr.gov.uk; accessed 13.10.07).

Fox, A. (1974) *Beyond Contract: Work Power and Trust Relations,* Faber and Faber.

Gennard, J. and G. Judge (2005) *Employee Relations,* 4th edition, CIPD.

Gold, M. and M. Hall (1994) Statutory European Works Councils: The final countdown? *Industrial Relations Journal,* Vol. 5, No. 3, September, 177–186.

Gratton, L. (2007) *Why Some Companies Buzz with Energy and Others Don't* (MBA Podcast available at www.timesonline.co.uk; accessed 13.07.07).

Hackman, J.R. and G.R. Oldham (1980) *Work Redesign,* Addison Wesley.

Herzberg, F., B. Mausner and B. Snyderman (1959) *The Motivation to Work,* Wiley.

Incomes Data Services (2001) *IDS Study 712: All-Employee Share Schemes,* IDS.

Incomes Data Services (2002a) *IDS Studies 722: European Works Councils,* IDS.

Incomes Data Services (2002b) *IDS Studies 730: Company Councils,* IDS.

Incomes Data Services (2003) *IDS Studies 741: Internal Communications,* IDS.

Incomes Data Services (2004a) *IDS HR Studies Plus 777: Employee Attitude Surveys + Guide to Suppliers,* IDS.

Incomes Data Services (2004b) Information and consultation: nine months to go,*IDS HR Studies Update* 776, June, 1–9.

Incomes Data Services (2007) Employee engagement, *IDS HR Studies Update 846,* May.

Industrial Relations Services (2001) Common position reached on national works councils text, *European Industrial Relations Review 330,* July, 13–15.

Industrial Relations Services (2003a) An open relationship, *IRS Employment Review 779,* 4 July, 8–21.

Industrial Relations Services (2003b) Raising productivity: policy and practice, *IRS Employment Review 776,* 23 May, 10–15.

Industrial Relations Services (2004) We're all in this together – partnership at work, *IRS Employment Review 801,* 4 June, 15–17.

Industrial Relations Services (2006a) A two-way process: informing and consulting employees, *IRS Employment Review 859,* 17/11 (available at www.xperthr.co.uk; accessed 20.07.07).

Industrial Relations Services (2006b) Unions in search of a new role in employee engagement, *IRS Employment Review 860,* 1/12 (available at www.xperthr.co.uk; accessed 03.04.07).

Involvement and Participation Association (2007) *High Performance Working,* IPA.

Kersley, B., C. Alpin, J. Forth, A. Bryson, H. Bewley, G. Dix and S. Oxenbridge (2005) *Inside the Workplace: First Findings from the 2004 Workplace Employment Relations Survey,* DTI.

Lloyd, C. and J. Payne (2007) High performance work organisation – a driver for the high skills vision, in Involvement and Participation Association, *High Performance Working,* IPA.

Luckhurst, D. (2007) The five key steps to engagement, *IPA Bulletin,* Number 67, July, 1 and 4 (available by email via www.ipa-involve.com; accessed 02.10.07).

Marchington, M. (1998) Partnership in context: towards a European model? in P. Sparrow and M. Marchington (eds) *Human Resource Management: The New Agenda,* Financial Times Pitman.

Marchington, M., A. Wilkinson and P. Ackers (1993) Waving or drowning in participation? *Personnel Management,* March, 46–50.

Marchington, M. and A. Cox (2007) Employee involvement and participation: structures, processes and outcomes, in J. Storey, *Human Resource Management: A Critical Text,* 3rd edition, Thomson.

McGlynn, C. (1995) European Works Councils: towards industrial democracy? *Industrial Law Journal,* Vol. 24, No. 1, March, 78–84.

Mill, C. (1991) The long road to employee involvement, *Personnel Management,* February, 26–27.

Monks, J. (1998) Trade unions, enterprise and the future, in P. Sparrow and M. Marchington (eds) *Human Resource Management: The New Agenda,* Financial Times Pitman.

O'Connell, L., W. Liu and P. Flood (2007) Ireland's National Workplace Strategy: High performance through partnership: An examination of the evidence, in Involvement and Participation Association, *High Performance Working,* IPA.

PeopleIndex (2007) *Employee Engagement Benchmark* (www.yougov.com; accessed 28.08.07).

Pickard, J. (2004) Informed decision, *People Management,* 16 September, 31–34.

Purcell, J. (2006) Building better organisations, in CIPD, *Change Agenda: Reflections on Employee Engagement,* CIPD.

Sisson, K. (2007) Right challenge – wrong conclusion, in Involvement and Participation Association, *High Performance Working,* IPA.

Smith, A. (2006) 'Partnership' at work? *Work, Employment and Society,* Volume 20(4), 811–817.

Taylor, F.W. (1911) *The Principles of Scientific Management,* Harper.

Trist, E. and H. Murray (eds) (1993) *The Social Engagement of Social Science: A Tavistock Anthology,* Vol. II: The Socio-Technical Perspective, University of Pennsylvania Press.

Woodruffe, C. (2006) From 'Whatever' to 'My pleasure': how can employers increase engagement? in CIPD, *Change Agenda: Reflections on Employee Engagement,* CIPD.

XpertHR (2007) Employee share schemes and employee share ownership plans, *Employment Law Reference Manual* (available at www.xperthr.co.uk; accessed 23.10.07).

Further study

Books

Advisory, Conciliation and Arbitration Service (2005) *Employee Communications and Consultation,* ACAS (available at www.acas.org.uk; accessed 13.10.07). Gives detailed coverage of the uses, benefits and methods of communication and consultation in the workplace.

Advisory, Conciliation and Arbitration Service (2005) *Representation at work,* ACAS (available at www.acas.org.uk; accessed 13.10.07). Covers the various ways in which workers may be supported or involved through the use of employee representatives.

Incomes Data Services (2001) *IDS Study 704: Secondments and Volunteering*, IDS, February. Outlines the benefits to be gained from company support of employee secondments or volunteering, including fulfilling expectations of social responsibility, enhancement of employee competencies, and provides some case studies of existing programmes.

Incomes Data Services (2001) *IDS Study 705: Bonus Schemes,* IDS, March.

Incomes Data Services (2002) *IDS Studies 752: Suggestion Schemes,* IDS. Practical advice on how to run an effective suggestion scheme, with case studies of seven organisations.

Incomes Data Services (2004) *IDS HR Studies Plus 777: Employee Attitude Surveys + Guide to Suppliers,* IDS. Practical advice on how to design, conduct, analyse and use employee attitude surveys, with case studies of six organisations and a guide to suppliers.

Incomes Data Services (2006) *IDS HR Study 824: European Works Councils*, IDS. Gives an overview of the legislation, the operation of an EWC, and case studies of six organisations.

Johnson, M. (2004) *The New Rules of Engagement: Life–Work Balance and Employee Commitment*, CIPD. Based on conversations with a number of people, and written in a lighter tone than standard academic publications, this book provides a readable overview of aspects of employee engagement and some insights most readers will identify with. There are some trenchant messages for managers here.

Sparrow, P. and M. Marchington (eds) (1998) *Human Resource Management: The New Agenda*, Financial Times Pitman Publishing. Part 2 of this book, 'Developing partnership and employee voice', contains six excellent chapters giving different perspectives on partnership.

Articles

First British European Works Councils established (1994) *Industrial Relations Review and Report*, No. 574, December, 4–7. A description of the EWCs set up by BP Oil Europe and United Biscuits, involving UK employees even before the directive was adopted by the UK.

Industrial Relations Services (2000) Buy in or sell out? *IRS Employment Trends 716,* November, 6–11. A review of what happens after union–management partnership agreements. Provides references to 12 IRS case studies.

Industrial Relations Services (2000) Towards commercial consciousness raising, *IRS Employment Trends 718,* December, 12–16. HR specialists' views on the link between enhanced communication with employees and improved performance.

Industrial Relations Services (2003) Raising productivity: policy and practice, *IRS Employment Review 776,* 23 May, 10–15. An overview of what various companies have done to improve productivity, with profiles of 12 organisations.

Industrial Relations Services (2003) Sharing the spoils: profit share and bonus schemes, *IRS Employment Review 784,* 19 September, 28–32.

Internet

Advisory, Conciliation and Arbitration Service   **www.acas.org.uk**
Provides good practice advice on how to implement the ICE Regulations. Also has a downloadable advisory booklet on communications in the workplace and an e-learning course on informing and consulting.

Chartered Institute of Personnel and Development   **www.cipd.co.uk**
Information on consultation and information, employee voice and high performance working. The website also has a downloadable podcast on employee engagement.

Department for Business, Enterprise and Regulatory Reform   **www.berr.gov.uk**
Provides masses of information on employment matters.

Involvement and Participation Association   **www.ipa-involve.com**
A rich source of information on partnership, employee involvement, high-performance working, information and consultation.

CHAPTER ⬤4

The employment relationship

Objectives

When you have read this chapter you will be able to:

- understand and describe the rights and obligations of both parties to the employment relationship
- understand the basis of the contract of employment and describe the terms that should constitute a basic contract of employment
- describe the main employment rights provided by legal statute
- describe a variety of flexible working arrangements and assess their usefulness and impact for both employers and employees
- describe the issues to be considered when an employee leaves an organisation.

The relationship between employers and their employees can be described in many ways. To get a clear picture of what this might entail, think first of any relationship between people, including personal relationships between friends, life partners and relatives; that is, think about relationships, but not necessarily in the context of employment. Any relationship is formed within a context of rights, expectations and obligations on the part of each party to the relationship. These rights etc. may be individualised for each pair of individuals as in marital relationships, or it may be that a group of people see themselves as forming one party to a relationship and that they therefore have shared interests that they wish to see represented on a collective basis. Some of these rights, expectations and obligations are unspoken: you assume that your close friends will not purposely do anything to harm you, but you do not feel that this needs to be said explicitly. In other things, you may need to negotiate and reach agreement: in spite of the much heralded concept of the 'new man', the division of labour in the household can still be a contentious area in heterosexual relationships. Beyond what individuals agree among themselves, both implicitly and explicitly, there is a legal framework that imposes obligations and guarantees rights, such as the division of possessions when a marital relationship fails. Relationships are also affected by cultural norms, custom and practice, views on what is and is not acceptable and the balance of power. These influences may be relatively stable for long periods of time, but the twentieth century was recognised as a period of great and rapid change, a phenomenon which will no doubt continue in the twenty-first century.

Pause for thought 4.1	Stop to consider the last two sentences in the preceding paragraph. Can you identify examples of these issues either in your own life or in those of people you know? What are the determinants of power in personal relationships? What changes in these areas can you identify? Discuss this with a group of fellow students, and you will probably identify a surprising number of influences and changes.

If you accept that this complex framework applies to personal relationships, it should not come as any surprise that the employment relationship is governed by a complex mix of individual and collective agreements, implicit and explicit under-standings, and rights and obligations enshrined in legal statutes, and that other in-fluences such as culture and the balance of power apply to it too. This chapter will attempt to give an overview of the many threads that weave together to create the can-vas of the employment relationship, and will also look at how trends within it can be monitored. In particular we shall examine the legal aspects of the employment rela-tionship, together with some cultural and psychological factors and the concept of flexibility in working arrangements. We shall also look briefly at what happens on the termination of the employment relationship.

Rights and obligations of the two parties

Balance of power

The extent to which one party in a relationship has rights and the extent to which that party has obligations depend in some measure on the balance of power between the two parties.

Pause for thought 4.2	Put aside for the moment the notion that as a proponent of the HRM approach you would be seeking to develop a workforce that shared a common purpose with management and with which there was therefore little conflict. If you regard an individual employee or a group of employees as having some areas of conflict with a manager, who would you judge to have more power than the other? List your reasons. What are the implications of this balance of power for the relationship between workforce and managers?

In spite of legislation that protects a range of employee rights, the general feeling in the industrial relations arena in the 1990s was that the balance of power lay with the employer. These sentiments had been fuelled by legislation throughout the 1980s and early 1990s which progressively curtailed the powers of the trade unions, and by high levels of unemployment and frequent redundancies which undermined many employees' sense of job security. There was also a large number of redundancies in the early years of the twenty-first century, many attributed to the global effects of the slowdown in the American economy at that time.

The implications of this for the relationship between employees and their managers lie in the areas of trust, openness, willingness to cooperate and amenability to different points of view. Where there is an imbalance of power, these areas of a relationship can suffer or at least they can be difficult to maintain. In the workplace this means that managers will have to find ways of reassuring employees that they will be treated as equal partners in the relationship. Managers will attempt to do this of their own volition if they believe that an employee relationship based on partnership is in fact a contributory factor in the success of their organisation. We have already explored this belief more fully in our examination of employee involvement and engagement in Chapter 3.

The Labour Government, first elected in 1997, produced a programme of employment measures emphasising the development of fairness at work and a partnership approach to the relationship between employer and employee. Some of its original proposals have subsequently been enshrined in the Employment Relations Act 1999 and other regulations. These include improved regulations on union recognition, enhanced rights to time off work, and rights to request serious consideration of flexible working arrangements to support people in combining their family life commitments with work. As the new rights become established, they will no doubt affect the nature of employment relations. The implementation of EU legislation on consultation and information is also shifting the focus more firmly towards employees' rights. We have discussed some of these issues in Chapter 3 in our detailed discussion of partnership, participation and employee involvement. This chapter attempts to build up a fuller picture by addressing more of the elements that combine to create our employment relations climate.

Expectations of the two parties: the psychological contract

The concept of the psychological contract aroused much interest among observers of HRM in the late 1990s, and interest in the concept and its impact on the employment relationship continues (CIPD, 2005). Attributed initially to Argyris (1960), the concept was further developed by Schein (1978), among others. It concerns the expectations that each party holds with regard to the other, and is recognised as having an impact on the way people behave in the workplace. The psychological contract is akin to the implied terms in a legal contract, i.e. much of it will be assumed and unspoken, but whereas implied terms in a contract would be fairly standard across organisations, the psychological contract is more likely to vary. It includes factors that result in feelings such as loyalty and perceptions of fair treatment, and many intrinsic factors that affect motivation. Much of the debate in the 1990s was about expectations of job security as an element of the psychological contract and the extent to which organisations could or could not continue to offer reassurance with regard to job security. Guest and Conway (1997) refer to the *new* psychological contract where the focus has shifted to employment security or employability rather than job security. This means that if employees can no longer expect their employer to guarantee them a job for life, they might instead expect their employer to support their development to make them more employable.

The nature of the psychological contract and the motivation of the individual can be influenced by the culture of an organisation and its predominant management style, and can be seen as coercive, calculative or cooperative (Handy, 1985). Coercion, where people are motivated to expend effort in order to avoid punishment, is generally regarded as unproductive and inappropriate for today's work organisations. A calculative contract will come into being where the connection between effort and reward is explicit, and each employee can calculate the value to him or herself of expending extra energy on the organisation's behalf. The cooperative contract arises when individuals identify with the goals of their organisation. The latter is the kind of psychological contract one would expect to find in an organisation that espouses the human resource management approach towards maximising the contribution of its employees through the use of practices that involve and engage them.

The cooperative contract implies a more participative style of management and greater employee involvement in decisions in the workplace. Individuals differ, however, in what they perceive as motivating, as Handy points out, and he goes on to say that managers may sometimes be disappointed at a lack of response when they try to change from, say, a calculative contract to a cooperative contract. However, if an organisation is run on participative lines, it is likely to engender positive attitudes in new employees, and perseverance with new techniques may help to alter attitudes among existing staff. The renewed emphasis of the late 1990s on fairness at work and partnership between employers and employees tied in well with this concept of a cooperative contract, and the work by Guest and Conway (1997) also highlights the link between a climate of employee involvement, as described in the preceding chapter, and a positive psychological contract.

More recently, reflective analysis from the CIPD (2005) has highlighted important aspects of the psychological contract. The paper as a whole strongly emphasises the importance of the role of line managers in establishing a positive psychological contract, the effects of stress and well-being, and developments in attitudes towards career expectations. The CIPD (2007b) in its factsheet on the psychological contract makes the point that most workers in large organisations identify their line manager as the employer as this is the person with whom they have contact on a day-to-day basis. As such, line managers and their management style therefore have the most immediate impact on perceptions of the psychological contract.

Both Woodruffe (2005) in the set of reflections and the CIPD (2007b) point out that different employees may be motivated by different things. Woodruffe writes of graduates as being 'the talent pool from which the future senior management of an organisation will be drawn' (p. 8) and suggests that their need for independence will need to be carefully managed in order to retain them. The CIPD (2007a) state that: 'Younger people – the so-called "generation X" – want excitement, a sense of community and a life outside work.'

This brings us to a final point, which is that work–life balance is identified as an important issue in general for the development of a positive psychological contract (CIPD, 2007b). This is an issue which we shall revisit later in the chapter in our examination of flexible working practices.

The legal framework

Contract and common law

Contract and common law, the latter being law established by judges' decisions rather than by statute, are important components of the legal framework that delineates the employment relationship. The first question that arises is whether or not a person is regarded in the eyes of the law as being an employee in the first place, and this has implications for a person's ability to claim the right to the protections provided by statutory employment law.

As with many legal questions, there are instances where there is no straightforward answer to the question of whether two parties have the relationship of employer and employee, and it is up to the courts to interpret the law and come to a decision. There is also no single definitive test that will give a conclusive answer, but some combination of the following factors can be considered in order to conclude whether a person is rendering services as an employee or on a self-employed basis. In deciding on the relationship between two parties, the courts will subject the relationship to a number of tests, including whether:

- the employer is entitled to exercise control over what the employee does and how he or she does it
- the employee is integrated into the structure of the organisation
- there is a mutual obligation to supply and accept work.

A person who is performing work for someone on a self-employed basis is not entitled to the rights enshrined in statutes such as the Employment Rights Act 1996 since such a person is not an employee in the eyes of the law.

The situation is further complicated, however, by the use of another term, i.e. 'worker'. Willey (2003) explains that a worker may be under some sort of contract, but may fail on one or more of the tests applied to determine whether the person can be classed as an employee. In a table showing the entitlements of employees and workers, Willey (2003, p. 89) indicates that both workers and employees would be covered by certain pieces of legislation (for example the Working Time Regulations and the statutory minimum wage), but that workers would not have all of the statutory rights that can be claimed by those classed as employees (such as basic maternity leave and the right to return to work). Willey further indicates that the law is developing in such a way as to provide a fuller range of rights to 'workers'.

The contract of employment

It is a common misapprehension that the letter offering employment or the written documentation supplied by an employer to an employee constitutes the contract of employment. A contract is basically an agreement, and despite the saying that 'an oral contract is as good as the paper it is written on,' if a person offers you employment over a cup of coffee in a restaurant and you accept the offer, you have a contract with each other. The written statement is evidence or proof that a contract exists, but it is not a contract *per se*; it is a statement of what has been agreed.

Implied and express terms

Contracts are made up of express terms and implied terms. As the phrases indicate, an express term is something that is regarded as important enough to be dealt with specifically and agreed on. Some terms may be assumed and not stated explicitly. For example, it may be stated how much notice an employee is to give if he or she wishes to terminate the contract of employment, but if it is not explicitly stated, the implied term would be whatever is customary in that particular industry or line of work. There is a statutory minimum as far as the amount of notice that an employer should give is concerned, so if there is no explicit mention of this in the contract, the statutory minimum will be the implied term.

On the whole it is best for employers to be explicit about any terms they require, for example with regard to mobility. If you are likely to require an employee to work at various locations, particularly if you already have establishments in various geographically dispersed locations, it is advisable to include this requirement as an express term in the contract. Even then, the enforcement of such contract terms is not without difficulties; you have to be able to show that the term is justified. In a case involving a British Council requirement of its employees to work anywhere in the UK on promotion to a certain grade, *Meade-Hill* v. *British Council*, it was held that this could amount to indirect sex discrimination unless the broadly stated requirement could be justified. Such a clause could be seen as indirect discrimination because fewer women would be able to comply with it than men. Implied terms include:

- on the part of the employer
  – the duty to maintain mutual trust and confidence
- on the part of the employee
  – the duty to obey lawful and reasonable orders
  – the duty of fidelity
  – the duty to work with due diligence and care.

The duty of fidelity can be explained as the obligation to act in good faith in dealings with an employer or on behalf of an employer. For example, submitting a tender for a contract that your employer is pursuing could be construed as breaching the implied duty to give faithful service. The employee also has an implied duty not to disclose confidential information, and a duty to cooperate with the employer, i.e. not to deliberately cause disruptions.

Variation of the terms of a contract

An employer must give written notice to an employee of any intended changes in the terms of the contract. The employer does not, however, have the right to vary unilaterally the terms of the contract, but must consult with employees and if possible obtain their agreement to the changes. If an employer tries to enforce a change without the agreement of an employee, this may be taken as a fundamental breach of contract which has the effect of repudiating the contract. In these circumstances, the employee may, after following the internal grievance procedure, resign, claiming constructive dismissal, and pursue compensation at an employment tribunal. An example of a variation of terms would be insisting that a person who had been contracted to work an evening shift should start working the day shift.

Employment law

A variety of employee rights are protected by legal statute, but it is beyond the scope of this text to provide a comprehensive description of employment law. We shall give a brief explanation of how European Union law affects UK legislation, and then focus on some of the issues that have been of recent interest and that you are likely to be asked about as either a line manager or a human resource practitioner. Remember that the law can be very complex and its interpretation most difficult. To assist employers to understand and keep up to date with legislation, a number of professional journals, such as *People Management*, publish regular briefings which help employers to interpret the law, especially in the light of new decisions on tribunal or court cases. Professional and government websites also provide guidance on various aspects of the law, and some even provide interactive tools which take the user through questions addressing individual cases. Web pages showing FAQs are also often particularly useful. Several of these sites are listed at the end of this chapter. We shall be looking at some aspects of employment law in greater detail, but remember that if you are in any doubt about an employee's or worker's rights, it is best to consult a solicitor.

You should also keep in mind the fact that the law usually states the minimum entitlement of an employee, and in most circumstances employers can decide to enhance the legal entitlement with more generous contractual provision. Enhancing entitlements may be a way of attracting and retaining employees with superior abilities, and so may be a consideration in pursuing the corporate strategy, particularly one of growth or innovation. All employees and workers should ensure that they are aware of their contractual provisions, but as a line manager or HR practitioner, you are likely to be asked for explanations.

We have dealt with certain employee rights in other chapters, so we shall not repeat that information here. You will find a discussion of the equality legislation in Chapter 5, certain aspects of the right to consultation and information in Chapter 3, dismissal and redundancy rights in Chapter 14 and health and safety regulations in Chapter 12. Our discussion here will focus on:

- the statement of particulars of employment
- notice of termination of employment
- employee rights to time off work
- guaranteed payments
- the written statement of reasons for dismissal
- maternity and other parental rights
- the rights of part-time staff
- working hours
- protection of employee data.

In addition to the issues we have chosen to address, readers should be aware of the Transfer of Undertakings (Protection of Employment) Regulations 2006 (TUPE 2006). The regulations protect the terms and conditions of employees in cases of a transfer of ownership of a trade or business, and state that dismissal because of the transfer is unfair. The original 1989 regulations were updated in 2006 to incorporate the many developments that had occurred over the intervening years. This is a very complex area of legislation which is beyond the scope of this introductory textbook.

The European Union (EU) and UK employment law

EU law takes effect in a number of ways, the most important being regulations that have direct effect in member states (i.e. they override domestic law) and directives that have to be implemented through national legislation. Some directives, for example those that encourage improvements related to health and safety, can be adopted by qualified majority voting, which means that they must be enacted by all member states, including the minority that voted against them. An example of this is the European Working Time Directive which was adopted in 1993 with dissension from the then Conservative Government of the UK. As the directive was considered to be a health and safety measure, the UK was obliged to accept and implement it. This contrasts with directives concerning the social rights and interests of employees, which require unanimity and from which individual member states can opt out. For example, the Conservative Government in the UK opted out of several social measures that were adopted by the rest of the EC at the time of the Treaty on European Union 1992 (the Maastricht Treaty). Since then, however, the Labour Government has signed up to the Social Chapter which is now integrated into agreements made in the Treaty of Amsterdam 1997.

Employees in the public service sector can rely upon the direct effect of directives, i.e. if the directive has not been implemented, this group of employees can take their case to the European Court. National courts also take account of the purpose of directives when interpreting national legislation. This gave rise, for example, to the House of Lords finding in 1994 that the two-year threshold, in force at that time, to be able to claim a range of employment protection rights should apply to all employees irrespective of the number of hours worked, in spite of the fact that this was not stated explicitly in UK law at the time of the finding. (See the later section in this chapter on part-time employees for more detail, and note that this two-year threshold was itself later reduced to a one-year qualifying period.)

Written statement of particulars of employment

Although the documentation referred to in this section does not constitute a contract as such, an employer is bound by law to issue a statement of terms and conditions to most employees, and the content of these documents serves as proof of the existence of a contract and evidence of the terms that were agreed. The legislation covering this statement is to be found in part I of the Employment Rights Act 1996. This Act consolidates various individual employment rights which had previously been enshrined in a number of pieces of legislation, including the Employment Protection Consolidation Act 1978, the Employment Protection (Part-Time Employees) Regulations 1995 (both of these now completely replaced by the Employment Rights Act 1996), and parts of the Trade Union Reform and Employment Rights Act 1993 (TURERA).

The Employment Rights Act sets out what kinds of information employees are entitled to receive about their contract with their employer, and the time frame within which this should be issued, i.e. within two months of the commencement of employment. This entitlement includes all employees contracted to work for one month or more irrespective of the number of hours worked. Parts of the documentation may be given in instalments within that two-month period.

The information to be included in a statement of particulars of employment is indicated in the Employment Rights Act 1996. What would you expect to be included in this list?

The statement should contain certain details and at least refer to other documents so that employees are aware of their existence and know where they may examine them. The details to be made explicit in the statement are:

- the names of the parties to the contract
- date of commencement of employment
- date of commencement of period of continuous employment
- hours of work
- location of the workplace and an indication if there could be a requirement to work elsewhere
- details about pay – rate of pay or how it is calculated; frequency of payments (weekly, monthly, etc.)
- job title or a brief description of the duties
- holiday entitlements
- arrangements about sick pay and sick leave
- details about any company pension plan
- entitlement to receive notice of termination of employment and obligation to give notice
- date employment ends if the contract is for a fixed term
- any terms of a collective agreement that affect working conditions.

Did you know?

The Department for Business, Enterprise and Regulatory Reform (DBERR) is seeking to simplify employment law and reduce the burden of costs employers suffer in adhering to it. The production of the statement of employment particulars is recognised as being complex and costly. DBERR has provided an interactive tool on **www.businesslink.gov.uk** to assist employers in drawing up these statements, and it is looking at further enhancement or simplification of the process.

(*Source*: www.berr.gov.uk)

Employees are entitled to be notified in writing of any changes to be made to any of these terms.

Details about sick pay, notice periods and pension arrangements may be given to employees by referring them to other documents, but again any subsequent changes in these documents must be notified directly to individual employees. Employees should also be referred to documents outlining the disciplinary rules, procedure, named person or position of person to whom appeals against decisions can be made, grievance procedures and name or position of person to whom a grievance should be referred in the first instance.

Notice of termination of employment

Employers may have their own schedule of the notice they require from employees and are prepared to give to employees, but the statutory rights of employees as stated in part IX of the Employment Rights Act are:

- 1 week's notice after 1 month and up to 2 years' service
- 2 weeks' notice after 2 years and up to 3 years' service, continuing to increase by one week for every completed year of service to a maximum of 12 weeks' notice.

Employee rights to time off work

The Employment Rights Act provides for employees to have a right to time off work in various circumstances. This may be unpaid or paid, depending on the circumstances, and includes time off for:

- union officials, in a union recognised by the employer, to complete certain duties such as taking part in negotiations with the employer (paid)
- members of a recognised union to participate in certain activities (unpaid)
- public duties such as acting as a justice of the peace (unpaid)
- employees selected for redundancy to look for work or make arrangements for training (paid; 2 years' service required)
- antenatal care (paid).

This is not a comprehensive list, but gives you some idea of existing entitlements to time off. The phrase that is applied to the entitlement to time off is that it should not be unreasonably refused, and in some circumstances, for example those related to the performance of public duties, employers are entitled to give consideration to business needs in assessing what a reasonable amount of time off work would be.

The Employment Relations Act 1999 also introduced rights to time off which had been addressed in the *Fairness at Work* White Paper (1998): revised maternity rights and rights to paternity leave (both dealt with later in this chapter), and entitlement for all to time off for dependants, i.e. unpaid leave in cases of emergency to arrange for care for any person who is dependent on the employee to do so. In its guidance booklet, the DTI (2000), now renamed as the DBERR, includes an elderly neighbour in its definition of dependants as well as family members, but explicitly excludes tenants or boarders.

Guaranteed pay

Under the Employment Rights Act, employees are entitled to five days' pay within any three-month period for workless days if the employer cannot provide work as contracted.

Written statement of reasons for dismissal

Employees with one year of service are entitled to receive a written statement of reasons for dismissal on request. As noted in the following section, however, different rules apply to anyone dismissed during pregnancy or maternity leave.

Maternity and other family support rights

Support for family life whilst enabling people to continue working is an issue that is evidently of continuing importance to the Government, so HR professionals need to ensure they are aware of the latest developments. The following sections give an overview of parental and other family support rights as they stand at the time of writing (October 2007), but since this is an area of continuing change, any practitioner responsible for interpreting related rules and policies will need to study this area in more depth and check for the latest status of the regulations.

Beginning with the Maternity and Parental Leave etc. Regulations 1999, a number of enhancements in maternity and other parental rights have come into effect in the years since 1999. The major piece of recent legislation in this area is the Work and Families Act 2006 which brought in key changes with regard to maternity, paternity, and some other family relationships. A crucial consideration with regard to the employment rights of pregnant employees is that it is a complex area and one in which there will be many individual circumstances to take into account. Note that we have simplified matters by using the terminology relating to birth parents. The rights we describe apply to same-sex relationships too, and a broadly similar range of rights to leave and pay (standard rate as described below) apply to adoptive parents. The Department of Business, Enterprise and Regulatory Reform website pages on maternity and parental rights are a good starting point for more detailed information (**www.berr.gov.uk**; accessed 13.10.07). The key points are as follows.

Antenatal care

As mentioned earlier, pregnant employees have a right not to be unreasonably refused paid time off work for antenatal care, regardless of length of service and hours worked.

Dismissal or selection for redundancy

Dismissal for a matter related to pregnancy or childbirth is automatically unfair. There is no qualifying period of employment or threshold of hours worked attached to this right. It is also unlawful to select a woman for redundancy on grounds of pregnancy or childbirth.

Written statement of reasons for dismissal

An employee dismissed during pregnancy or maternity leave is entitled to receive a written statement explaining the reasons for the dismissal. The employee does not have to request the statement in these circumstances, and again there is no qualifying length of service or number of hours worked.

Maternity leave

All pregnant employees are entitled to 9 months/39 weeks of maternity leave, regardless of length of service or hours worked: 26 weeks of this leave is called *ordinary* maternity leave, and the rest is *additional* maternity leave. Further additional maternity leave is available to all pregnant women, taking the leave period up to 52 weeks. These entitlements have applied to all pregnant employees whose expected date of childbirth was on or after 1 April 2007. The Government intends to extend ordinary maternity leave to 1 year by the end of 2009.

Women who have been on maternity leave are also entitled to return to work at the end of this leave period. The DTI (2007) booklet *Pregnancy at Work*, written for employees, explains that women have the right to return to their job after ordinary maternity leave on the same pay and conditions as they would have received if they had been at work during that period. However, if the employer cannot reasonably accommodate a return to the same job after the longer period of absence involved in additional maternity leave, then the employee must be given a similar job without any detriment with regard to terms and conditions.

Keeping in touch days

The Work and Families Act 2006 has introduced the concept of keeping in touch days. During their maternity leave, employees can go back into the workplace without affecting their entitlement to maternity leave and pay. The purpose of these days might be for training, to do a day's work or to be kept informed about developments. The keeping in touch days should not exceed 10 days in total and the employee is not obliged to undertake them.

Maternity pay and conditions

An employee on ordinary maternity leave continues to benefit from all the terms and conditions of her contract except for remuneration. This means, for example, that she continues to accrue holiday entitlement, payments into the pension scheme should continue, and the maternity leave period counts as continuous service. The legal contract of employment continues during additional maternity leave, but some issues, such as paid holidays and contributions to pension, may depend on the individual organisation's contractual agreements (IDS, 2007; TUC, 2007).

All qualifying pregnant employees are entitled to 9 months/39 weeks of statutory maternity pay (SMP). The qualifications are that they have worked for their employer for at least 26 weeks by the qualifying week (i.e. the fifteenth week before the week of expected childbirth) and their average weekly earnings are relevant for national insurance contributions. With regard to the qualifying period of employment, the DTI (2007, p. 3) puts this more simply as 'you already worked for your employer before you became pregnant'.

SMP is 90 per cent of the employee's average weekly earnings during the first six weeks of the maternity leave, and the remaining weeks are paid at the standard rate, which was £112.75 from April 2007 (or 90 per cent of the employee's weekly earnings if this is a smaller amount). Additional maternity leave beyond the 39 weeks is unpaid but, as noted earlier, the Government is considering extending ordinary maternity leave to 1 year, and SMP would then cover this period too.

Employers can recoup 92 per cent of the SMP they have paid out, and small employers can recoup 104.5 per cent if they qualify for Small Employer's Relief. More information on this is available from the employers' information pages on the website of HM Customs and Revenue (**www.hmcr.gov.uk**; accessed 13.10.07). Pregnant employees who do not qualify for SMP may be eligible for the maternity allowance paid by Jobcentre Plus.

Did you know?

According to the CIPD (2007a), fewer than half of the fathers approached in a survey said that they would take paternity leave at the current level of statutory paternity pay. However, 80 per cent would take it if the pay were raised to 90 per cent of full pay. The IDS (2007) note that take-up of the proposed opportunity to transfer unused maternity leave and pay to partners is unlikely to be high because of the low income involved.

Paternity leave

The spouse or partner of a new mother has an entitlement to 2 weeks of paternity leave, paid at the SMP rate, during the 2 months following the birth of a child. This entitlement applies to unmarried as well as married partners, and to same-sex as well as opposite-sex partners. ACAS (2005b) suggests that it might be better to think of 'paternity leave' as 'maternity support leave.' Organisations might consider using such non-discriminatory terminology in their policies. An additional criterion applied to employees requesting this type of leave is that they must, alongside the mother's responsibilities, have the main responsibility for the upbringing of the child.

When ordinary maternity leave is extended to one year, as the Government intends, there will be a facility to transfer up to 26 weeks of the mother's (unused) maternity leave and statutory maternity pay to her partner. Details about how this would be administered are yet to be published.

Parental leave

Parents of children under the age of 5 are entitled to 13 weeks of unpaid parental leave or 18 weeks for disabled children under the age of 18. This leave may be taken up until the 5th, or respectively 18th, birthday of the child, but there is a qualifying period of 1 year of service for this entitlement. The leave can be taken in blocks of 1 week up to a maximum of 4 weeks per year or in blocks of 1 day in the case of a disabled child, and the leave must be for the purpose of taking care of the child.

Right to request flexible working arrangements

Parents of children under the age of 6 (or 18 for a disabled child) have the right to request flexible working arrangements so they can give adequate attention to their family responsibilities while continuing to work. Qualifying employees with at least 26 weeks of service are entitled to request a change in the hours they work or in their place of work. Employers must give such requests serious consideration, but they are entitled to deny a request if there is a valid business reason for doing so, including the cost involved, the impact on the organisation's ability to meet its customers' needs, structural issues such as the potential for redistributing the employee's work to others or the availability of recruits with the appropriate skills and knowledge. These rights and obligations were introduced in the Employment Act 2002, supplemented by the Flexible Working (Procedural Requirements) Regulations 2002 and the Flexible Working (Eligibility, Complaints and Remedies) Regulations 2002.

The IRS (2004) give a detailed overview of this legislation and its implications, explanations of how to put it into practice, and what issues need to be considered.

ACTIVITY 4.1

The IRS article cited above lists other relevant pieces of legislation for employers to keep in mind when applications for flexible working are made under these regulations and responses are delivered, and maybe when changes to the employee's contract are initiated. Think about the processes involved and which other pieces of legislation might be relevant and require some action or thought, and compare your ideas to those listed in the article.

The right to request flexible working arrangements has been extended by the Work and Families Act 2006 to cover employees who are carers of certain adults. The caregiving relationships specified are spouse, partner, civil partner and close relative. Macpherson (2007) states that 'employees who care for an adult living at their home address will also have the right to make a request'.

Contractual enhancements

Maternity and paternity leave and pay, similar arrangements with regard to adoption, and considering requests for flexible work arrangements are all areas where employers may choose to adopt family-friendly policies which are more generous than the minimum requirements of the law. The IDS (2007) review 26 organisations which offer enhancements on various aspects of these regulations, such as giving full pay for some or all of the maternity leave. Macpherson (2007) also suggests that employers might consider extending the right to request flexible working arrangements to groups of employees not covered by the legislation in order to promote good working relationships and a sense of fairness in the workplace.

Part-time employees

The treatment accorded to part-time employees in the UK was traditionally inferior to that given to full-time employees. However, as employers came to depend more on employees to be flexible, and to recognise the benefits organisations can gain from employing people on non-standard contracts, they also had to recognise the necessity of addressing the needs of these employees and treating them fairly. The statutory rights of part-time employees were strengthened in the mid-1990s by a ruling from the House of Lords, and subsequent legislative developments have also bolstered their position.

Prior to 1994, part-time employees had to work for considerably longer than full-time employees to acquire the employment protection rights then enshrined in the Employment Protection Consolidation Act 1978. In March 1994 the House of Lords held that the UK had been in breach of Article 119 of the Treaty of Rome and the Equal Pay and Equal Treatment Directives. The existence of differing thresholds to obtain a variety of employment protection rights amounted to indirect sex discrimination since the majority of part-time employees are women. The right of part-time employees to claim statutory protection against unfair dismissal and redundancy should be the same as that of full-time workers, i.e. a two-year qualifying period at that time. In response to this judgment, the Government implemented the Employment Protection (Part-Time Employees) Regulations 1995 (now incorporated into the Employment Rights Act 1996) which created equality between full- and part-timers in terms of statutory employment rights. The qualifying period with regard to unfair dismissal was subsequently reduced to one year.

Part-time staff also have rights to membership of pension schemes as outlined in the Pensions Act 1995 ss 62–66 and the Occupational Pension Schemes (Equal Treatment) Regulations 1995. Their rights have been strengthened more recently by the adoption of the EU Part-Time Work Directive which was implemented on 1 July 2000. The Part-Time Workers (Prevention of Less Favourable Treatment) Regulations 2000 give part-timers equal rights to the full array of contractual terms, including rights to staff discounts, and access to training and promotion opportunities. A major aspect of the regulations is that it is unlawful to discriminate against a person because of his or her part-time status; cases of discrimination against part-time employees will no longer have to be presented as sex discrimination, though the IRS (2000) argue that it may still be expedient to do so.

Working time

The Working Time Regulations 1998 came into force in October 1998. The key features are described here in brief.

Working hours

Essentially the regulations provide for a maximum of 48 weekly working hours averaged over a period of 17 weeks. It should be noted that there are provisions in the regulations for employers to reach agreement with employees to work longer hours while the legislation protects employees from being obliged to work longer hours. The IRS (2001a, p. 2) reported that 'a significant minority of workers are opting out of the maximum 48-hour working week'. This provision has been the subject of much debate at EU level, and some observers expected that it would be rescinded in a subsequent review of the regulations. At the time of writing, however, the opt-out is still in effect in the UK though it continues to be the subject of debate at EU level (**www.berr.gov.uk**, checked on 13.10.07). Jameson (2004) reported on an amendment of the Working Time Regulations introducing a proviso that a recognised union could veto an individual's agreement to work longer hours. Arrowsmith (2004) points out that basic working hours in the countries that joined the EU in 2004 were in general longer than the European average, resulting in a sudden change to the overall picture, which may have accounted for the less decisive approach of the European Commission to this issue at that time.

ACTIVITY 4.2

Check the employment pages on the DBERR's website to find out whether there have been any developments with regard to the UK opt-out or any other aspect of the Working Time Regulations.

Rest breaks

Employees should have 11 consecutive hours of rest in any 24-hour period, and a 24-hour rest in every seven days. There is also an entitlement to a 20-minute break if the work day exceeds 6 hours.

Annual leave

Until the advent of this legislation there was no legal obligation for employers to provide paid annual leave for their employees, other than arrangements for statutory holidays. Of course, the vast majority of employers did make such provision, and annual leave has often been part of collective bargaining agreements between employers and trade unions. Even now, many employers will provide more than the basic entitlement, but at least this legislation guarantees a basic entitlement, which was three weeks in the first year that the legislation was introduced and four weeks after November 1999.

The Work and Families Act (2006) gave the Government power to extend the entitlement to annual leave because the Government was concerned to make it clear that the entitlement to four weeks did not include statutory bank holidays. The enhancement of annual leave is taking effect on a phased basis, with an entitlement to 4.8 weeks (24 days) from 1 October 2007, rising to 5.6 weeks (28 days) from 1 April 2009. Part-timers will have this entitlement on a pro rata basis.

Derogations and subsequent amendments

There were some groups of workers who were not originally covered by these regulations, including workers involved in air, sea and road transport, junior hospital doctors and people who have autonomous decision-making powers, such as senior managers. In 2003, this opt-out was rescinded with reference to 'all non mobile workers in road, sea, inland waterways and lake transport, all workers in the railway and offshore sectors, and to all workers in aviation who are not covered by the sectoral Aviation Directive' so that workers in these areas were included in the terms of the regulations with effect from 1 August 2003 (**www.berr.gov.uk**; accessed 13.10.07). Regulations limiting the working hours of junior hospital doctors were also put into effect, but not until 1 August 2004.

The CIPD (2007c) points out that amendments have been made to the Working Time Directive almost every year since it first came into effect.

> **Did you know?**
>
> A long hours working partnership project was set up by the Department for Trade and Industry (DTI) in conjunction with the Confederation of British Industry (CBI) and the Trades Union Congress (TUC). The aim was to investigate best practice in companies that have successfully tackled the long hours culture in the UK, and master classes were offered to companies that wanted to improve in this area. The case studies have been presented in a report entitled *Managing Change – Practical Ways to Reduce Long Hours and Reform Working Practices*, which is available from the DBERR website.
>
> (*Source*: www.berr.gov.uk; accessed 13.10.07)

Data protection

Employers gather and keep a wide range of personal information about employees, and employees have a right to expect that those data will be kept confidential and that a high standard of accuracy will be maintained. The Data Protection Act 1984 provided for some assurances with regard to computerised information, and since 1 March 2000, when the Data Protection Act 1998 came into effect, information relating to individuals which is kept on paper, or in any other format, is also covered. Whistleblowers have also gained some protection via the Public Interest Disclosure Act of 1998, while the Human Rights Act 1998 applies to aspects of an individual's privacy. The Freedom of Information Act 2000 provides a statutory right of access to 'recorded' information held by public authorities and this Act came fully into force from January 2005. The Information Commissioner has responsibilities for providing an integrated role relating to both the Freedom of Information Act 2000 and to the Data Protection Act 1998.

The Data Protection Act 1998

The Data Protection Act 1998 covers all the stages involved in gathering data, from collection, safe storage, use and disclosure to destruction. The Act applies to personal information used in the workplace, including recruitment and selection, employment records, monitoring at work and information about workers' health. The legislation applies to any filing systems kept by managers as well as to centralised HR record systems.

The Information Commissioner's Office (2005) has produced a code related to employment practices, covering the handling of personal data in the areas noted above. The purpose of the code is to enable employers to understand better their obligations under the Data Protection Act 1998.

The provisions of the Data Protection Act 1998 were originally applied in stages, but since 24 October 2001 they have applied to all manually stored records that have been collected since 24 October 1998, and also to all computerised record systems. The Act includes eight principles:

- Data must be handled and processed in a fair and lawful manner.
- The reasons for obtaining these data must be legal and have been clearly specified. The data must only be used for the reasons specified.
- Data collected must be sufficient and relevant for the specified purpose. There should be no excessive collection of data.
- Any data collected must be accurate and be updated regularly.
- It should not be kept for any longer than is necessary, so data need to be regularly reviewed so that out-of-date information is removed.
- Data should be processed in accordance with the rights of individuals.
- The data must be kept secure.
- Data may only be transferred to countries that have adequate data protection.

We said earlier that this applies to personal data held by all managers, not just HR managers, and consequently most organisations need to complete an audit to establish exactly what data is kept and by whom. Lots of managers maintain their own filing systems and may store out-of-date personal data. Someone in the organisation, possibly from within the HR department, has to take on the role of data controller and ensure that everyone who keeps personal data also complies with the eight data protection principles. Personal data means information which identifies an individual. Information which, for instance, reviews salary structures for a whole workforce or for particular groups of staff is not likely to be deemed personal information.

Data subjects have the right to know what information is kept about them and can ask to see the data. Employers can charge a fee for this, but must supply the information within 40 days. The person identified as data controller may be liable if there are breaches in the security of information, or if losses occur as a result of such a breach.

Statutory rights: a concluding statement

As well as understanding the rights and obligations of both employers and employees already established in law, it is essential to be aware that this is an area where issues develop and change very rapidly. These changes can arise, as we explained earlier, from formal consideration of statutes in Parliament, perhaps following on from discussions at EU level, or because new understanding of various circumstances arises when judgments are handed down on cases in the courts. In 1995 the *Walker* case, among others, focused attention on employer obligations with regard to the mental health of employees. Lobbying on behalf of disabled people engendered changes in the mid-1990s in statutory law regarding their rights to equal opportunity in employment. One way of staying informed about developments in employment law is to read the legal update articles that appear in journals such as *People Management*, *Personnel Today*, *Equal Opportunities Review* and *Industrial Law Journal*.

It is essential to review and update policies and practices to reflect the law as new requirements come into effect. The willingness of employers to offer employees more than the minimum that is required by the law might also contribute to improved employment relations and so enhance the contribution that employees are willing to make.

ACTIVITY 4.3

The Employment Law at Work section on the CIPD website, a resource for CIPD members, has links to frequently asked questions on a wide range of topics such as family-friendly working, maternity, paternity and adoption leave and pay, and working time regulations. Look at some of the FAQs and formulate your own response before checking out what the CIPD says. Go to www.cipd.co.uk and follow the links to the Employment Law at Work and FAQs pages (accessed 13.10.2007).

Flexible working arrangements

Many people still have an image of traditional working patterns that involve spending Monday to Friday in a workplace with contractual provisions for a 36 to 40-hour working week and something like four weeks' holiday. There are, however, many new patterns evolving to suit both the changing requirements of businesses, some of them due to increasing pressures to provide goods and services on a 24/7 basis, and employees' needs to balance their family and personal life commitments with their availability for work. Supermarkets now open on Sundays, and the once restrictive Sunday licensing hours for public houses have also been relaxed. Some people are working fewer hours to provide flexibility, and some are working more to cope with the pressures of work. The new working patterns include numerous variations on shift work, part-time employment, contracting-out of work, arrangements for flexitime, and contracts based on annual or even zero hours. All this variety and change suggests that for some part of your working life you are as likely to be working under flexible conditions as in a supposedly traditional arrangement.

The mix of working arrangements can mean that employers have the flexibility to call on people's services only when they need them. The emphasis in this case is on developing arrangements to increase flexibility in the availability of human resources and the organisation's ability to respond rapidly and well to changing requirements. Meeting the needs of business can, however, be synonymous with meeting employee needs if an organisation wishes to use flexibility as a strategy to attract and retain valuable workers. Since the late 1990s there has been growing recognition of the importance of achieving a good balance between work and private commitments. A good work–life balance can meet both employer and employee needs in terms of stress management, health, productivity and, of course, employers must respond to the right of eligible parents and carers to request flexible working arrangements as described earlier. We shall review some of the important developments in flexible working, looking specifically at annual hours contracts, job sharing, fixed-term contracts and teleworking.

Annual hours

Instead of contracting employees to work, say, a 40-hour week regularly throughout the year, which might entail periods of under-employment and periods of overtime for which the employer pays at an enhanced rate (usually one and a half times or double the normal rate), the employer estimates the number of hours he or she will need an employee over the period of a year, and contracts the employee to work those hours at the standard rate but according to an agreed, irregular pattern that corresponds better to fluctuating business needs. This means that, subject to agreed arrangements, the employer can call on the services of employees when they are needed, and most importantly does not pay employees for their presence at times when they are not needed. Employees are guaranteed payment for the hours that they have been contracted for, and normally the salary would be paid in equal amounts spread over the year.

Terms that would usually need to be imposed on this arrangement would be agreements on things such as the maximum number of hours an employee could be expected to work in a given number of days, entitlement to a consecutive number of days off, notice of a call in to work. The arrangements should be such that employers are able to cover both scheduled and unscheduled requirements. The IDS (2006) reports that reserve hours are often factored into annual hours schemes to allow for emergencies, and these hours may or may not be worked, but they will be paid for.

A number of organisations have found that annualised hours work to their advantage, but the IDS (2006) cautions that care needs to be taken when introducing such a scheme and organisations must ensure that workers understand the advantages that they too will enjoy. Annual hours schemes should reduce the need for overtime work and payment significantly, but effective rostering of hours should mean that workers have longer periods of time away from work.

The IDS (2006) report that annualised hours are used mostly in manufacturing in terms of numbers of workers employed on such schemes, but the utilities companies (electricity, gas and water) have the greatest proportion of their workers on annual hours.

Job share

The concept of having two people share the tasks designated as constituting one post probably grew out of the recognition that some women did not wish to return to full-time work after maternity leave but would prefer to continue in their careers, working a reduced number of hours. Some employers developed job-sharing schemes partly to accommodate this desire, but also because they recognised that this was one way of retaining scarce talent and benefiting from the investment they had made in employees who no longer wished to work full time. As we explained in the section on parental rights, it has also become increasingly clear that there is an obligation on all employers to at least consider the viability of flexible arrangements such as this.

Job sharing requires additional arrangements to ensure coordination between partners, which has implications for the managers of job-share partners, but there are numerous benefits: it can bring additional flexibility in terms of availability of staff when required for extra work; it shows that the employer is willing to consider new arrangements that accommodate staff needs; the talents and ideas of two people are applied to one job; and it is good for morale. In fact, it is an arrangement that can clearly bring mutual benefit. Also, although we stated earlier that the arrangement probably grew out of the wishes of women returning from maternity leave, job share is not just of benefit to women. Men can also have responsibilities as the primary care givers in their families and welcome the opportunity to work part time, and job share is also attractive to people who wish to combine a steady income with consultancy activities.

Fixed-term contracts

Fixed-term contracts are addressed specifically in part XIII, s 197 of the Employment Rights Act 1996, but other sections of the Act also apply, such as the need to issue a written statement of employment particulars to anyone hired for longer than one month. Fixed-term contracts obviously offer some flexibility to employers in terms of adjusting the numbers of employees at different times to suit fluctuating business needs. There has been some concern about the rights of employees on fixed-term contracts, however, and the European Directive on Fixed Term Work required the member states to address these issues. The Fixed-term Employees (Prevention of Less Favourable Treatment) Regulations 2002 came into effect on 1 October 2002 and provided extra protection for employees on such contracts. The issue of consecutive fixed-term contracts to an employee is now limited to a period of 4 years, after which the position must be made permanent. Employers are also not entitled to include a redundancy waiver in the terms of a fixed-term contract.

The major features of fixed-term contracts are as follows:

- They state the maximum period of the contract, giving the date on which the contract will end.
- Non-renewal at the end of a fixed-term contract is a dismissal.
- A contract for a specific purpose is now included in the definition of a fixed-term contract.
- Service over a series of fixed-term contracts can be aggregated to constitute continuity of service.

Teleworking/homeworking

The work arrangements we are referring to as teleworking are not to be confused with the kind of low-paid piece work that involves activities such as stuffing envelopes. Teleworking has evolved with the rapid developments in information technology and telecommunications. With the advent of fax and email, people do not need to be in the same building to transmit written documents and reports instantaneously. Distance working is also used as a term for employees who no longer need to go into an office to do their work, 'tele' being the Greek root meaning 'far'. In other words, the term can be used for people who mainly use technology to produce reports, but also for people out on the road seeing customers. Orders can be relayed using information technology, and often it is more sensible for such employees to use their home as their base rather than an office in a town centre. Jobs are no longer equated with a desk in the office.

Pause for thought 4.4 Make a list of what you think the advantages and disadvantages of teleworking are. For every disadvantage you identify, suggest a solution.

Advantages

- A wider range of people can be gainfully employed, for instance those who have care duties and cannot leave home for prolonged periods of time but who can organise their time at home to include periods of work.
- Flexibility in working hours: some people like to work at three in the morning while others sleep, and teleworking gives them the opportunity to do so.
- Working at home cuts down on travelling time and on costs of office accommodation and furniture.

Disadvantages

- Social factors may be the source of disadvantages, but that simply means that the social system needs to be managed properly. Teleworkers may suffer from isolation and a feeling of not being part of an organisation. An antidote for this is to arrange training sessions and regular briefing sessions when employees can get together and review common problems, and to use communication channels to keep people in touch. If some isolation cannot be avoided, recruiters should attempt to select people who will be suited to the type of work.
- Some managers, particularly those who adopt a control style, may be uncomfortable supervising teleworkers. It is possible to institute regular reporting mechanisms and control the volume of work done in a period of time, but on the whole the development of teleworking calls for a different style of management and a higher level of trust. The emphasis is definitely on the fact that the work gets done rather than on imposing controls on when and where it is done.

Employers who develop teleworking arrangements should be aware of their duties with regard to the health and safety of employees. They will need to conduct a risk audit of the employee's home-based workplace – information about this is readily available from the Health and Safety Executive (see Chapter 12 for information about access to HSE information).

ACTIVITY 4.4

Your class will conduct a survey to establish what kinds of working patterns are in existence and whether these meet the needs of the employees concerned. You should decide who your target population will be. For example, you may wish to survey only local businesses and residents, or to include the friends and relatives of students to extend your geographical coverage. You may wish to target a particular industry, for example, the manufacturing sector or retail outlets. You should probably exclude full-time students from your survey, as they have an obvious need to work only part time.

1 Work out in class what you want to find out and what questions you need to ask to gather this information. You will want to include some of the following issues. Establish what basis each person is employed on: part time, permanent, temporary, etc. Establish whether they are satisfied with this or would prefer some other arrangement. What are the main reasons for their levels of satisfaction or dissatisfaction?
2 Each student will conduct a survey of 5 to 10 people who have some sort of employment and make an analysis of this small sample. Compare your findings with those of others in your class.
3 Work in groups of five and compile an analysis of your pooled information. Report your results to the class and compare your results with those of the other groups in your class.
4 Establish which patterns of employment and employee attitudes have emerged.
5 Discuss how this information might be used by employers to improve their human resource management practices.

The concept of flexible working arrangements is directly connected with the HRM approach in that these innovations lead to empowerment (as must be the case with teleworkers), and the flexibility that is necessary to become a high-performance organisation.

Termination of employment

Employees leave their organisations in a variety of ways and a number of circumstances, and for a number of reasons. Stop for a moment and make a list of as many of these circumstances as you can think of.

In making your list you may have categorised the reasons for employee exit into those that signify voluntary exit and those that are involuntary. Voluntary reasons include:

- to take up another post
- retirement or voluntary early retirement (although not everyone welcomes retirement at the normal retirement age and some may request to go on working past the age of 65, as described in Chapter 5)
- voluntary non-employment, often due to a change in circumstances including parenting or studying.

The involuntary reasons you have listed may include:

- redundancy
- dismissal, including dismissal due to ill-health.

For each of these reasons for exit, there is a range of circumstances that apply, except perhaps for retirement, which usually occurs at the organisation's normal retirement age (but note the caveat about requests to continue working beyond this age). People taking up another post, for example, may be doing so for a number of reasons, such as:

- personal reasons for moving to another geographical area
- because they have been offered more pay or better conditions for doing the same work with another employer
- opportunities for promotion
- to escape from uncongenial managers or colleagues
- a desire for a change of career.

If you have read the chapter on human resource strategy and planning (Chapter 2), you will realise that it is essential for employers to understand why people leave their organisations so that appropriate recruitment and retention plans can be devised as part of the talent management strategy. For this reason, many employers gather information from staff who are leaving for voluntary reasons by conducting an exit interview with them.

Exit interviews and employee opinion surveys

It is important to gather data on any problems connected with aspects of the employment relationship so that employers can take action to remedy any arrangement that might potentially cause more valuable employees to leave. The areas usually covered in an exit interview include:

- the reason for leaving, particularly if the person is going to another job – is it for pay/opportunity/some other benefit?
- relationships with supervisors and co-workers
- working conditions in general and specific ones that might be problematic, such as shift work.

With the expansion of equality legislation, ACAS (2005a, 2005b and 2006) suggest the inclusion of questions about whether a person has ever felt harassed in the workplace with regard to any of the types of harassment covered in the regulations.

Exit interviews are usually conducted by someone in the human resource management department since employees, even when they are leaving an organisation, may be more willing to talk about problems with a person who does not work directly with them. The interviewer should ensure confidentiality and explain that information gained from exit interviews is normally used to identify trends rather than to act on information from any individual. These reassurances can make people open up. It should be noted, however, that any references to bullying or harassment do need to be followed up as it would not be acceptable to ignore reports of unlawful harassment.

A good process will include a form that the employee can complete in advance of the interview, and the interview can then be used to clarify details. You will find a similar process recommended for appraisal interviews in Chapter 10.

ACTIVITY 4.5

Design an exit interview form and process, either generic or for an organisation of your choice. Refer to Chapter 7 to read about interview questioning techniques and apply some of the techniques you learn about there in formulating your questions, particularly open and closed questions in this case. You can also get some excellent guidance on the design of questionnaires and types of questions from an IRS (2001b) article on separation questionnaires.

Rather than waiting to gather information from employees who have decided to leave, employee opinion surveys can be used to assess the levels of satisfaction within an existing workforce in a variety of work conditions. It is well recognised that management must demonstrate a willingness to take action on the issues raised, or at least respond to these issues in some way, if they wish to retain the trust of their employees and have employees take any subsequent surveys seriously.

Retirement

One of the benefits that employers can offer their employees is preparation for retirement through some kind of formal pre-retirement programme. Moving from working life to retirement requires a big adjustment, and can be achieved more successfully with careful planning, in terms of coping with a changed financial situation as well as increased leisure time. Financial advice on pensions is a complex subject beyond the scope of this text. It is sufficient to note that this is another area that can be affected by changing legislation.

Employers can further consider programmes for keeping in touch with people who have retired from employment with them. It can be a low-cost benefit to arrange occasional social gatherings for past and present employees and to send the organisation's newsletter to past employees, and the returns in terms of morale and commitment from current employees who witness this evidence of their employer's concern for employee welfare may well repay these costs many times over.

Of course, the issue of what should be regarded as the normal retirement age continues to be a matter for debate. It remains to be seen how this will be affected by Government policy in the future. Remember too that there is a formal process for dealing with retirements and this will be addressed in Chapter 5.

Conclusion

We have seen that the relationship between employer and employee consists of rights and obligations on both sides, and that these are determined by law and various other agreements. Innovations in terms, conditions and working arrangements are a sign of the times as organisations attempt to respond to increasing competitive challenges and to social changes such as increasing expectations of an acceptable work–life balance. The expectation of further developments in legislation also guarantees that this will continue to be an area of change in the future.

REVIEW QUESTIONS

You will find brief answers to the review questions on page 472.

1 Peruse the 'Law at work' sections in *People Management* or the court cases listed in the Industrial Cases Reports for the last three months or so. Select the articles or cases that are concerned with contractual issues and review them. Summarise the major hot topics of the day. Have these issues arisen because of any changes in legislation?

2 We mentioned that employment legislation usually sets out minimum provisions for employee rights. Can you identify a number of areas where some employers are known to provide more than the minimum?

3 Explain what the purposes of making flexible working arrangements are. Describe at least two forms of flexible working arrangement, and comment on the benefits of each for both the employer and the employee.

SELF-CHECK QUESTIONS

Answer the following multiple-choice and short-answer questions. The correct responses are given on page 472 for you to check your understanding of this chapter.

1 Which of the statements below best describes the psychological contract?
   (a) Managers will do nothing to destroy the relationship of trust they have with their subordinates.
   (b) Employers will do all they can to promote the mental well-being of employees, for instance by providing facilities for counselling on personal problems.
   (c) The expectations that managers and employees have of each other can lead to a relationship based on coercion, a calculation of reward for effort, or cooperation.

2 Explain the difference between implied and express terms in a contract.

→

3 Name the terms that are implied in an employment contract on the part of an employee.

4 Joe Biggins has worked for Actwell Company for nine years. There is nothing in his contract about how much notice he should get if his job is terminated. The company is now moving to another location and, following appropriate consultation, has had to dismiss all its employees. How much notice should Joe receive?

5 Annie Creston has been with Actwell for only two months. How much notice should the company give her?

6 Which piece of legislation contains the duty of an employer to supply employees with a written statement of their particulars of employment?

7 How many weeks constitute ordinary maternity leave?

8 A woman needs to have two years of service before the expected birth in order to qualify for additional maternity leave. TRUE or FALSE?

9 An annual hours contract means that employees are not allowed to work overtime. TRUE or FALSE?

10 What major problems were identified related to teleworking?

HR IN THE NEWS

FT

No harm in asking for flexible working hours

By Geoff Armstrong

There appears to be an almost universal assumption that business will oppose extending the right to request flexible working hours to all workers, which was floated last week by Beverley Hughes, the children's minister. But talk to most employers and things look very different.

In spite of talk of a 'long hours culture', the UK already has a flexible pattern of working time that is the envy of most of our continental cousins – and employers have been leading the way. Our tight labour market has created intense competition for talented and motivated people.

Many employers are willing to help staff balance work and non-working lives. Those employers find they can attract staff from a wider pool of talent. The people they recruit are more likely to be motivated, to stay and to contribute to the full extent of their ability. Enlightened management of people makes a huge contribution to business performance.

But the adoption of flexible working must be a two-way street, which is why some employers seem cautious about ministerial prescription. Meeting an employee's understandable desire for a better work–life balance has to go hand in hand with an appreciation of the employer's need for flexibility too. The 'deal' has to engage both parties.

The reality is that some people have to be at a particular place at a particular time – carers when their services are needed, for example, or baggage handlers when planes are taking off and landing – so there can be no automatic and unilateral right to change working patterns. Yet many employers in the service industries are finding that flexible working patterns can help them meet the demands of our increasingly 24-hour service culture.

Britain's generally light-touch regulations, which encourage rather than decree, are the best way to drive cultural change. This is in contrast to offering workers strict minimum rights, which leads to a box-ticking approach that achieves little more than those minimum standards. Encouragingly, Ms Hughes seems to be advocating just such a light-touch approach to work–life balance.

There is no right to demand flexible working – and Ms Hughes is not suggesting that there should be – just an extension of the right to ask for it and for that request to be considered. Evidence suggests that most employers grant the majority of such requests from those staff, such as parents of young children, who already have the right. Our research shows that two out of five employers extend flexible working practices further than the legislation requires.

Yes, there are management challenges associated with flexible working arrangements. But if managers are equipped to meet these challenges, the business can be the winner.

An employer might find that by accommodating a job-sharing arrangement, it gets two willing workers who can come up with different solutions to the same challenges. Equally, allowing experienced team members to adjust their hours can ensure they stay with the company and continue to contribute fully. This safeguards the investment the employer has made in the development of that employee.

A failure to extend the right to request flexibility also poses potential challenges for employers and government. There is a danger that, by assuming that only parents and carers should be able to work flexibly, we create a divided workforce.

Our latest research shows that employees who are allowed to work flexibly are more committed to the company and more motivated in their work. Why would employers limit these performance and productivity benefits to parents and carers?

There are greater threats to the future success of British business than an extension of the right to request flexible working. The European Agency Workers Directive, for example, could, if adopted, undermine the benefits that UK employers gain from a flexible labour market. This proposal seeks to match the pay and conditions of permanent and temporary workers, but fails to reflect the benefits to both parties of the way agency workers are employed in the UK. Employers are right to oppose that.

But turning down an opportunity to engage constructively with employees on the basis of 'something for something' is short-sighted and self-defeating. The extension of the right to request flexible working could be a sensible, light-touch effort to extend the benefits of a flexible labour force.

The writer is the director-general of the Chartered Institute of Personnel and Development.

(FT.com, 18 February 2007, © Geoff Armstrong. Reproduced with permission.)

Questions

1 List the benefits this article associates with the provision of flexible working arrangements.

2 What are the major factors identified with regard to how flexible working arrangements should be/are being dealt with in work organisations?

WHAT NEXT?

Relax and listen to the CIPD's podcast on employment law which reviews a range of issues, including family-friendly legislation, employee status and discrimination law.

CIPD Employment Law–one of the CIPD series of podcasts available at www.cipd.co.uk.

If you would like to read more about flexible working, we can recommend two excellent sources. The IDS booklet reviews the range and take-up of flexible working practices, and provides a number of organisational case studies. ACAS also reviews the range of possible arrangements and addresses the advantages and disadvantages of each one.

Advisory, Conciliation and Arbitration Service (2007) *Flexible Working and Work-Life Balance,* ACAS.

Incomes Data Services (2006) *IDS HR Studies Update 834: Flexible Working,* November, IDS.

References

Advisory, Conciliation and Arbitration Service (2005a) *Religion or Belief and the Workplace: A Guide for Employers and Employees,* ACAS.

Advisory, Conciliation and Arbitration Service (2005b) *Sexual Orientation and the Workplace: A Guide for Employers and Employees,* ACAS.

Advisory, Conciliation and Arbitration Service (2006) *Age and the Workplace: Putting the Employment Equality (Age) Regulations 2006 into Practice,* ACAS.

Argyris, C. (1960) *Understanding Organisational Behaviour,* Dorsey Press.

Arrowsmith, J. (2004) Counting the hours, *People Management,* 16 September, 37–41.

Chartered Institute of Personnel and Development (2005) *The State of the Employment Relationship. Reflections on Employee Well-Being and the Psychological Contract,* CIPD.

Chartered Institute of Personnel and Development (2007a) *Maternity, Paternity and Adoption Rights,* CIPD (factsheet available from www.cipd.co.uk; accessed 18.10.07).

Chartered Institute of Personnel and Development (2007b) *The Psychological Contract,* CIPD (factsheet available from www.cipd.co.uk; accessed 06.02.07).

Chartered Institute of Personnel and Development (2007c) *Working Hours in the UK,* CIPD (factsheet available from www.cipd.co.uk; accessed 12.07.07).

Department of Trade and Industry (2000) *Time off for Dependants: A Guide for Employers and Employees,* DTI (available at www.berr.gov.uk; accessed 13.10.07).

Department of Trade and Industry (2007) *Pregnancy and Work: What You Need to Know as an Employee,* DTI (available at www.berr.gov.uk; accessed 19.10.07).

Fairness at Work (1998) Government White Paper, HMSO, May (the Paper can be viewed on the Internet at www.berr.gov.uk; accessed 13.10.07).

Guest, D. and N. Conway (1997) *Issues in People Management No 21: Employee Motivation and the Psychological Contract,* IPD.

Handy, C. (1985) *Understanding Organizations,* 3rd edition, Penguin.

Incomes Data Services (2006) *IDS HR Study 815: Annual Hours,* IDS.

Incomes Data Services (2007) *IDS HR Study 851: Maternity and Parental Leave,* IDS.

Industrial Relations Services (IRS) (2000) The Part-time Workers (Prevention of Less Favourable Treatment) Regulations 2000, *Industrial Relations Law Bulletin 646,* August, 2–8.

Industrial Relations Services (2001a) Changing working time patterns prompt smarter ways of working, *IRS Employment Trends 729,* June, 2.

Industrial Relations Services (IRS) (2001b) Separating retention fact from fiction, *Employee Development Bulletin 136,* April, 3–7.

Industrial Relations Services (IRS) (2004) Flexible working – avoiding the legal pitfalls, *IRS Employment Review 801,* 4 June, 51–60.

Information Commissioner's Office (2005) Data Protection: *The Employment Practices Code,* ICO (available at www.ico.gov.uk; accessed 02.10.07).

Jameson, A. (2004) Industry to challenge EU over working hours, *The Times,* September 23, 50.

Macpherson, K. (2007) Flexible working for carers, *HR Zone,* 5 July (available at www.hrzone.co.uk; accessed 12.07.07).

Schein, E.H. (1978) *Career Dynamics: Matching Individual and Organisational Needs,* Addison Wesley.

Trades Union Congress (2007) *Worksmart: Know Your Rights. Maternity Leave and Pay,* TUC.

Willey, B. (2003) *Employment Law in Context: An Introduction for HR Professionals,* 2nd edition, Financial Times/Prentice Hall.

Woodruffe, C. (2005) Commitment and satisfaction: the true state of the psychological contract, in Chartered Institute of Personnel and Development, *The State of the Employment Relationship. Reflections on Employee Well-Being and the Psychological Contract,* CIPD.

www.berr.gov.uk; accessed 13.10.07.

www.hmcr.gov.uk; accessed 13.10.07.

Further study

Books

Advisory, Conciliation and Arbitration Service (2005) *Personnel Data and Record Keeping,* ACAS. An advisory booklet, this reviews the types of information an employer may need to obtain from employees, and explores ways of storing the data.

Incomes Data Services (2002) *IDS Studies 729: Teleworking,* IDS. A review of the types and prevalence of teleworking with case studies from four organisations.

Lewis, D. and M. Sargeant *Essentials of Employment Law,* CIPD.

Selwyn, N. *Law of Employments,* Butterworths. Two excellent sources of information on employment law. Make sure you refer to the latest edition available.

Articles

Adams, M. (2004) How to tackle the long hours culture, *People Management,* 30 September, 56–57.

Gartshore, A. (2004) How to introduce homeworking, *People Management*, 2 September, 44–45.

Industrial Relations Services (2003) Home comforts, *IRS Employment Review 779,* 4 July, 22–23.

Industrial Relations Services (2003) Not just another day at the office, *IRS Employment Review 780,* 18 July, 8–15. Two of a number of articles on teleworking provided by the IRS. The second one provides an overview of a number of employers using teleworking and what they regard as the advantages and disadvantages.

Industrial Relations Services (2007) The right to request flexible working, *IRS Employment Review 869,* 21/3 (available at www.xperthr.co.uk; accessed 03.04.07). A good, concise overview of the various rights and how requests should be handled.

'Law at work' is a regular feature in *People Management*. The authors offer readable interpretations of employment laws and regulations, addressing specific issues that are of current concern to HR practitioners and line managers.

McCartney, C. (2004) How to make flexible working work, *Personnel Today*, 7 September, 33–35. Provides some brief case studies of organisations that have benefited from improved flexibility, with tips on how to implement them.

Internet

There are many Internet sites that can give you access to legal information. We have listed only a selection here for you to try. Most of them have numerous linked sites that you can click on to get more specific information.

Advisory, Conciliation and Arbitration Service **www.acas.org.uk**
In addition to advisory booklets, the website has e-learning courses on working parents and contracts and written statements.

Business Link **www.businesslink.gov.uk**
A government-sponsored website with lots of employment-related information for employers. There is also an interactive tool to guide employers through queries specific to an individual employee's circumstances with regard to issues such as maternity leave and pay, annual leave entitlement etc.

Chartered Institute of Personnel and Development **www.cipd.co.uk**
A number of legislation-related factsheets are available to all visitors to the CIPD website as is the employment law podcast which covers a range of issues. The Employment Law at Work subject area, for members of the CIPD, links to many interesting and informative pages. The CIPD provides a succinct summary of how UK law is made, including an explanation of statutory instruments (SIs), how to find the most recent court decisions and how to cite case law. There are also lists of forthcoming employment statutes and regulations, SIs in force etc., and a list of law-related factsheets and surveys. The pages on records also address which ones have to be kept to fulfil statutory obligations and for how long.

Department for Business, Enterprise and Regulatory Reform   **www.berr.gov.uk**

A fount of information on employment matters with links to other sites. Extensive guidelines for both employers and employees on maternity and other parental rights, including a 120-page guide to maternity rights which can be downloaded at the site.

HM Revenue and Customs   **www.hmrc.gov.uk**

Here you will find the Employers' Helpbook: *Pay and Time off Work for Parents,* which contains a lot of useful information.

HR Zone   **www.hrzone.co.uk**

A wide assortment of articles on various aspects of HR, including legal issues. An article by Annie Hayes, *HR Zone's Maternity Law Briefing 2007: Where next?* appeared on the site on 24 May 2007. It gives a good overview of current issues with some interesting comments about business and employee reaction to developments.

Trades Union Congress   **www.tuc.org.uk**

Several downloadable publications under the heading of Worksmart: Know Your Rights, including *Maternity Leave and Pay,* April 2007 edition; *Adoption Leave and Pay*, April 2007 edition; *Flexible Working for Parents and Carers*, April 2007 edition; and *Working in the UK: Your Rights*, written for migrants to the UK from member states which joined the enlarged EU in 2004. All of these booklets are written in plain, easily understandable language.

CHAPTER 5

Equality and diversity

Objectives

When you have studied this chapter you will be able to:

- understand the issues relating to equality of opportunity in the workplace
- describe the legislation that addresses equality
- explain the practical implications of the equality legislation with regard to recruitment and selection
- explain the concept of workforce diversity and how to manage it successfully.

Equality and diversity

Equality and diversity are major issues that affect everyone in the workplace. All employees, current and potential, have a right not to be discriminated against unfairly and blocked in their careers for reasons that have nothing to do with their abilities in relation to their work. Legislation exists to protect the interests of groups of people who may have historically been discriminated against in terms of employment and services, and employers have a duty to ensure that this legislation is upheld in their organisations. Beyond the need for compliance with legislation, however, there are also business arguments for equality and diversity.

The distinction between equality of opportunity and the management of diversity has often been described in terms of equal opportunity being driven by legislation and applying to specified groups whereas diversity refers to all differences among people (e.g. Kandola and Fullerton, 1998). This way of making a distinction between the two terms is becoming more and more tenuous as the equality legislation expands to encompass ever more segments of society. It is still useful, however, to examine the equality legislation and then to look at broader issues of diversity and its implications for management in workplace organisations.

Readers should note that there have been many developments in equality legislation during the first few years of the twenty-first century and activity in this area continues apace. One issue under consideration at the time of writing this text (October 2007) is the consolidation of the many strands of discrimination law into a single equality bill. Part of this process is the establishment of a single equality commission, the Equality and Human Rights Commission, to have oversight of all equality issues. The new commission took up its full mandate in October 2007, and the separate commissions relating to gender, race and disability were all subsumed under this one body. However, the publications of the individual commissions are still available on the new consolidated website, so each commission has been described and cited in later sections of this text. Their documents can still be found at **www.equalityhumanrights.com**.

Equal opportunities: the legislative framework

As already stated, legislation exists in the UK to protect the interests of groups of people that have historically been discriminated against in terms of employment and services. The Acts and Regulations that provide protection against unfair discrimination, together with just a selection of subsequent amendments, and the areas they cover are summarised in Table 5.1.

Table 5.1 Anti-discriminatory legislation

Act	Areas covered
Sex Discrimination Act 1975	Sex and marital status (the latter referring specifically to persons who are married)
Sex Discrimination (Gender Reassignment) Regulations 1999	Persons who intend to undertake a sex change, are currently in the process of doing so or have completed treatment
Race Relations Act 1976	Race, colour, nationality, national or ethnic origins
Race Relations (Amendment) Act 2000	The duty of public authorities to take positive action to promote good race relations
Disability Discrimination Act 1995	Persons with a disability as defined by the Act
Disability Discrimination Act 2005	People with cancer and HIV covered *from the point of diagnosis*
	Mental health problems do not need to be clinically well recognised
	The disability equality duty of public authorities
Employment Equality (Sexual Orientation) Regulations 2003	Orientation towards persons of the same sex, of the opposite sex, of both the same sex and the opposite sex
Employment Equality (Religion or Belief) Regulations 2003	Religion or belief
Employment Equality (Age) Regulations 2006	Both younger and older persons; a default retirement age of 65
Equality Act 2006	Created the Equality and Human Rights Commission
	The gender equality duty of public authorities
Equal Pay Act 1970	Male and female pay for like work, work rated as equivalent, and work of equal value
Rehabilitation of Offenders Act 1974	Persons with spent convictions
Human Rights Act 1998	Prohibition of forced labour and slavery; right to respect for private and family life (*inter alia*)

Because of historical developments in Northern Ireland, certain statutes apply there that differ from the rest of the UK. These are outlined in a separate section later in this chapter.

The Sex Discrimination Act 1975 and the Race Relations Act 1976

In spite of the existence of legislation providing protection against sex and race discrimination for more than 30 years, both types of discrimination are still rife in the UK and continue to make headline news. For example, Sir William Macpherson, investigating the handling of the Stephen Lawrence murder case, found evidence of institutional racism in the police force and in his report of the inquiry in 1999 made 70 recommendations on action to break down institutionalised racism. Naaz Coker (2001) of the King's Fund reported on racism found in the NHS, and racial tensions in the community resulted in violent outbursts in Oldham and Bradford in 2001. These occurrences highlight why it is still essential to actively promote equality, and in fact as a result of the Macpherson inquiry report, new legislation was promulgated to strengthen the Race Relations Act 1976 in the form of the Race Relations (Amendment) Act 2000.

The Sex Discrimination Act (SDA) makes it unlawful to treat people unfavourably because of their sex or marital status, the latter meaning specifically because a person is married. Civil partners have also been covered by this since the implementation of the Civil Partnership Act 2004. A European Court ruling in 1996 specified that sex discrimination laws also apply to transsexuals, and this protection has been further strengthened by the Sex Discrimination (Gender Reassignment) Regulations 1999. This means that employees are protected if they suffer less favourable treatment than other employees because they have undergone, are undergoing or intend to undergo a change in gender.

The Race Relations Act (RRA) prohibits less favourable treatment of people on racial grounds. These include race, colour, nationality, and ethnic or national origins.

The SDA and the RRA address unfair discrimination in similar ways. Both referred originally to three kinds of discrimination:

- direct discrimination
- indirect discrimination
- victimisation.

Direct discrimination occurs when someone is treated less favourably for a reason directly to do with his or her sex, marital status (i.e. being married), race or racial origin, etc. Examples of this would be to refuse a woman a job as a truck driver simply because she is a woman, and to refuse a Chinese person a job in a school kitchen simply because all the other employees are white European and the employer fears that a person from a different racial background will not 'fit in'.

Indirect discrimination occurs when someone is treated unfairly because of some requirement or condition that would disproportionately exclude the particular group that person belongs to, and when the requirement cannot be objectively justified. For example, if you wished to hire someone to clean the windows in your building, and you stipulated that applicants must be six feet tall, could this requirement be justified in terms of the skills and abilities required to do the job? Which groups might such a requirement discriminate against? Fewer women than men, for instance, are six feet tall. This requirement therefore discriminates indirectly against female applicants.

The European Union Directives on equality have brought about some changes in the definition of indirect discrimination, including replacing the phrase 'requirement or condition' with the phrase 'provision, criterion or practice'. As the IRS (2003) point out, this terminology broadens the sphere of potential indirect discrimination to include informal practices.

ACTIVITY 5.1

Can you think of any other instances of indirect discrimination and identify which groups might be affected by them?

Look through the records of cases heard by employment tribunals and you will find some examples. To find reports of such cases you can use several sources:

- A number of human resource management journals have a section that gives updates on the law and describes recent cases. Look, for instance, in *People Management* and *Personnel Today*.
- You can look in the subject index of the *Legal Journals Index*, for instance under the heading 'sex discrimination'. This will give a brief summary of the major points of the case, and refer to a journal in which you can read more about the case.
- There are also numerous cases reported in the *Equal Opportunities Review* and some issues of the *IRS Employment Review*.
- CIPD members have access to descriptions of numerous tribunal cases in the Employment Law at Work section of the CIPD website (**www.cipd.co.uk**).

You may wish to compare the instances you find with those found by others in your class.

Did you know?

In most cases an employee needs to have completed a one-year qualifying period of employment to take a complaint of unfair dismissal to an employment tribunal. This qualifying period does not apply if the complainant feels that the reasons for the unfair dismissal were connected to any of the types of discrimination covered by legislation. You can read more about this in the section on the burden of proof later in this chapter.

Victimisation occurs when someone is treated less favourably because that person has made a complaint or indicated an intention to make a complaint about sex or race discrimination. An example of this might be a woman who has complained to the Equality and Human Rights Commission about lack of promotion in comparison to similarly qualified men and who is subsequently dismissed unfairly.

The legislation also stipulates that this unfair treatment must be to the disadvantage of the person so treated. In the case of employment this includes the person being refused employment, promotion or training opportunities or being dismissed.

Harassment

There is no specific definition of harassment in the original sex and race discrimination Acts, but harassment has been deemed to constitute discrimination under these Acts through case law. A specific definition of harassment is integrated into the RRA through the EU Race Directive and harassment is also addressed specifically in the sexual orientation, religion, belief and age discrimination regulations. The Employment Equality (Sex Discrimination) Regulations 2005 established harassment as a recognised unlawful form of discrimination with regard to gender.

Harassment is defined as unwanted conduct that intimidates or humiliates an individual, affecting their dignity or creating a hostile work environment. The behaviour in question can be verbal or physical, and it is important to note that the target individual's perception of the effect of the conduct can contribute to the behaviour being deemed to be harassment.

The Disability Discrimination Act 1995

The Disability Discrimination Act 1995 (DDA) updated and replaced previous legislation relating to disabled people. Disability is defined under the Act as a mental or physical impairment which has a substantial and long-term adverse effect on a person's ability to carry out normal day-to-day activities.

This definition is very broad and open to interpretation so that, although the Act provides further information on what is to be regarded as a disability, this question was also the focus of some of the early cases that were taken to employment tribunals (IRS 2000). Decisions on whether a person is disabled may hinge, for example, on judgements about the meaning and applicability of the terms 'substantial', 'long-term' and 'normal day-to-day activities'. A range of impairments may, depending on the circumstances, contribute to a person's being deemed disabled: severe disfigurement, sight or hearing impairments, cancer, multiple sclerosis, muscular dystrophy and HIV infection. Some issues have also been clarified by further regulations such as the Disability Discrimination (Blind and Partially Sighted Persons) Regulations 2003 which specifically addressed the rights of people who are certified as blind or partially sighted under this legislation, and the Disability Discrimination Act 2005 further clarified that cancer and HIV are covered by the legislation from the point of diagnosis, i.e. before a person's abilities may begin to be impaired by his or her symptoms.

In relation to employment, job applicants should not be discriminated against because of a disability or be treated in a less favourable way than other applicants unless 'the treatment in question is justified'. However, the DDA also makes it clear that employers must 'make reasonable adjustments in any arrangements or to work premises' in order that disabled employees should not be disadvantaged. This may include a review of work allocation, consideration of flexible hours to accommodate the needs of a disabled person, or modifying equipment. The requirement to make reasonable adjustments in the DDA is the equivalent of dealing with indirect discrimination in the other pieces of equality legislation. Employers are compelled at least to consider these matters seriously and be prepared to justify their decisions with regard to their reasonableness. Anyone who feels that they have suffered discrimination because of a disability has the right to take their case to an employment tribunal.

The DDA not only applies to employment, but also affects any organisation which provides a service to the public. Under the Act, such an organisation must make reasonable adjustments to their premises or to the way in which they provide services in order to accommodate the needs of disabled people.

Employment Equality (Sexual Orientation) Regulations 2003

These regulations state that persons should not be treated unfavourably because of their sexual orientation, i.e. orientation towards persons of the same sex, of the opposite sex, of both the same sex and the opposite sex. Note that the legislation addresses sexual orientation and not sexual practices, where existing law continues to apply. Sexual orientation refers to gay and lesbian preferences, heterosexuality and bisexuality. Issues such as consensual versus non-consensual sex, paedophilia, etc. are not covered by the equality regulations. The regulations apply to recruitment and selection and to treatment in the workplace, such as opportunities for training and promotion.

> **Did you know?**
>
> The RAF's first recruitment drive to be specifically targeted at gays and lesbians was widely reported in the news media in August 2004 when the RAF recruited at a gay pride festival.

As with the SDA and the RRA, employers need to guard against direct and indirect discrimination, harassment and victimisation. It is worth noting that remarks about a person's family members or friends with regard to their sexual orientation can also constitute harassment.

Employment Equality (Religion or Belief) Regulations 2003

The Employment Equality (Religion or Belief) Regulations 2003 outlaw discrimination based on religion and originally referred to *similar* philosophical beliefs. The latter was subsequently amended by the Equality Act 2006 to expand the meaning of belief rather than restricting it to belief similar to a religion. Whether a set of beliefs is recognised under these regulations will be for employment tribunals to decide. For example, in the terms of the original regulations, it was clear that humanism would be recognised, but the amended definition of belief raises questions about what might be covered, for example political beliefs. The IRS (2006b) point out that the 2006 Act also clarified that those with no religion, e.g. agnostics, are included in the legislation.

> **Did you know?**
>
> ACAS (2007) reports that cases of discrimination based on sexual orientation and religion or belief are more likely to be brought by men than by women, as represented by two-thirds of both types of case.

The regulations work in a similar way to the sexual orientation regulations in terms of types of discrimination (direct, etc.). With regard to harassment, it is necessary to make it clear to all employees that so-called banter can be regarded as offensive by individuals and should be avoided. Communications with employees and the creation of a culture of tolerance and acceptance of diversity have become even more important in the twenty-first century with the broadening of equality laws such as this.

Employment Equality (Age) Regulations 2006

The Employment Equality (Age) Regulations 2006 protect people against discrimination at both the younger and the older ends of the age spectrum. This legislation has emphasised for employers the need to focus on competencies when making selection decisions and the need to avoid making stereotypical judgements about people's capabilities according to their age. Although these regulations affect all aspects of the employment relationship like any other aspect of equality, their immediate impact has been in the area of recruitment and selection. Much guidance has been offered to organisations in terms of redesigning their application forms and other parts of the recruitment and selection processes to comply with the legislation (see, for instance the Employers Forum on Age at www.efa.org.uk; the Government website at www.agepositive.gov.uk; ACAS, 2006). The implications of these regulations will therefore be examined in more detail in the next chapter, which looks at recruitment.

In spite of the fact that it is now unlawful to discriminate against older employees, the regulations do allow for a default retirement age of 65. An employer can only require employees to retire at an earlier age if this can be objectively justified, and even with normal retirement at 65, the employer must inform employees at least 6 months but not more than 1 year before their retirement date that their retirement is imminent. Employees have the right to request to continue working beyond 65, and employers must give serious consideration to such requests, but they are not obliged to agree to them.

Genuine occupational qualifications/requirements

In exceptional circumstances there may be a requirement for an employee to be of a particular sex, racial background, religion, sexual orientation or age. These are known as genuine occupational qualifications (GOQs) or genuine occupational requirements (GORs). GOQ is still the term used with reference to the SDA; the 2003 and 2006 regulations refer to GORs; the RRA refers to GOQ with reference to colour and nationality and to GOR with regard to race and ethnic or national origins. The adoption of the GOR terminology coincides with the amendments to legislation that have occurred since 2003 to bring UK legislation into line with the relevant EU Directives. Since the race Directive refers only to race and ethnic or national origins, and not specifically to colour or nationality, this accounts for the difference in the terminology used in the UK in different instances of racial discrimination.

Such requirements and qualifications are acceptable in instances where authenticity is required, say in entertainment, modelling (for instance male or female fashion clothes) or serving food in ethnic restaurants to create a specific ambience, and where privacy and decency in the provision of personal services are concerned. An example of a genuine occupational qualification would be to advertise for a female care attendant to provide personal services to a female stroke victim. A further example might be an organisation that offers support and advice on relationships to bisexual persons and which may wish to recruit bisexual counsellors who may be more able to empathise with their clients.

Note that the word 'genuine' is used. It is a term that is meant to be narrowly defined and not regarded as a loophole to avoid compliance with the legislation. Employers must carefully evaluate whether a position merits a GOR or GOQ. If anyone interested in such a post feels that they have been unfairly excluded on this basis, they can challenge the GOR or GOQ at an employment tribunal, which is the ultimate arbiter of the acceptability of such requirements.

Employers are not the only participants in the recruitment process who are bound by the terms of the equality legislation. Publishers of advertisements also have a duty to ensure there is no unlawful discrimination in the advertisements they print. If a person of a particular sex etc. is required, the publisher must also ensure that a reference to the relevant section of the legislation is included. For example, an advertisement for a female project leader to provide personal support to young homeless women might carry the statement 'section 7(2)(E) of the Sex Discrimination Act applies'.

Note that the presence of a GOR/GOQ means not only that persons from the specified group are being invited to apply, but also that only such a person will be selected. This is often confused by less informed job-seekers with encouragement for members of under-represented groups to apply for vacancies so they can be considered along with all other qualified applicants in the selection process. You can read more about the recruitment of under-represented groups in Chapter 6, under the heading 'Targeted recruitment'.

The equality commissions

As stated earlier in this chapter, the Equality and Human Rights Commission took up its full mandate in October 2007, with a view to providing oversight over all equality issues. The former commissions have ceased to exist and have been subsumed into this one commission. The aim is to create a higher level of simplicity so that organisations can understand the framework of equality legislation better. In this transitional time, however, it is advisable to know about the original commissions and what their remit was, keeping in mind that all of this has been transferred to the Equality and Human Rights Commission.

The Sex Discrimination Act 1975 established the Equal Opportunities Commission (EOC) and the Race Relations Act 1976 established the Commission for Racial Equality (CRE) to promote and monitor equality of opportunity. As part of that duty, the EOC produced a code of practice in 1985 and the CRE produced a code of practice in 1984. As recently as 2006, both the EOC and CRE published an updated version of their codes, and these are still available on the new website at **www.equalityhumanrights.com**.

The codes provide guidelines to employers and employees on the meaning of the relevant legislation, on practical measures that can be taken to eliminate discrimination and on techniques that can be used to promote equality of opportunity. These guidelines refer to all phases of employment, including the recruitment and selection stages. The Equality and Human Rights Commission also gives advice to employers as well as dealing with complaints from those who feel they have encountered discrimination, and it may assist those who decide to take a complaint to an employment tribunal.

The Commission can also issue a non-discrimination notice against employers if it investigates a complaint and finds that there is evidence of discrimination in an employer's actions, whether intentional or unintentional. A non-discrimination notice may oblige an employer to inform the Commission about changes it has initiated to bring its employment practices more in line with the codes of practice. Similar provisions exist, of course, in relation to all other aspects of unlawful discrimination. Many cases of disability discrimination centre on employers' failure to make reasonable adjustments to enable disabled people to either take up or remain in employment with them.

ACTIVITY 5.2

Check the website for the equality commission to get an overview of the extent of fascinating information provided there.

● Good practice in equal opportunities

Essentially, to operate within the spirit of the equality legislation, all actions and documents involved in HR processes must be free of any criteria that could be interpreted as being discriminatory within the terms of the legislation. As ACAS (2005a and 2005b) points out, the existence of an up-to-date equality policy signals an organisation's intention to follow good practice with regard to all discrimination issues covered by the law. A good policy establishes a framework that enables current employees to know how they are expected to behave with regard to these issues and that they themselves will be treated fairly. Prospective employees may also be attracted to an organisation that demonstrates its intentions to treat employees fairly. It must be noted, however, that the mere existence of an equality policy is not enough to signify that an employer is serious about equal opportunities. Communication of the policy and training of line managers in implementing it are crucial. The IRS (2007a) emphasise the benefits an employer can obtain from having a policy established in this way. Benefits include the recruitment and retention of excellent staff, leading to an enhanced ability to compete and avoidance of discrimination complaints.

The equality legislation has practical implications for all aspects of people management, and some of these are dealt with in other chapters. For instance, the role of flexible working was dealt with in Chapter 4 on the employment relationship; equal pay will be addressed in Chapter 11. To illustrate the practical implications of equality here, we shall take a look at some examples from the area of recruitment.

Did you know?

It is interesting to note that it is generally regarded as unacceptable to request an applicant to attach a photograph to a job application in the UK, whereas this is still common practice in France and Germany. Such a requirement would conflict with the spirit of the UK legislation, as a photograph can only provide information about sex, racial background and age and not about skills and knowledge. The use of such input can be seen as unfair discrimination.

Advertisements, job descriptions and person specifications, documents which are explained more fully in Chapter 6, must not include anything that could be construed as an intention to discriminate on an unlawful basis. Except in the case of a GOQ or GOR, as described earlier, advertisements should not include words that might indicate a preference for hiring females rather than males, or vice versa. For example, it is not lawful for a restaurant to advertise for waitresses as this would imply that men could not apply for these posts. This would be direct discrimination on the basis of sex. The same stricture applies to the other groups protected by legislation.

The advent of the age discrimination regulations brought with it a lot of discussion about words which might imply a preference for persons from a particular age group. To advertise for 'young people' would quite obviously be unlawful, but practitioners were also discussing the viability of other terms such as 'mature' (which might imply a preference for an older person) or energetic (which might imply that a younger person was being sought). Whether or not these and similar terms suggest that unlawful age discrimination is intended, the wording of an advertisement is certainly something which employers need to think about carefully. We shall return to further implications of the age discrimination legislation in the next chapter.

The existence of a good person specification can help an employer to avoid inadvertent sex, race or other unlawful discrimination when advertising for a post and carrying out the selection process. The design and use of person specifications is discussed more fully in Chapter 6 with specific reference to recruitment. Direct discrimination is rarely overtly expressed ('We really don't think a woman can do this job'). The intention to discriminate can be inferred from various events, and introducing new criteria after the person specification has been agreed is one such event. If a post involves a GOR or GOQ, this should be decided before the post is advertised and made clear to everyone through the person specification and the job advertisement.

Positive action is allowed under the discrimination legislation in terms of providing assistance to underprivileged groups to enable them to compete on a more level playing field. This might involve assistance with the completion of application forms or the provision of training for specified groups. Final hiring decisions must, however, be made on the basis of each individual's ability to do the job.

Organisations that wish to promote equality of opportunity can also introduce complaints procedures, so that applicants who feel they may have been discriminated against can appeal in the first instance to the organisation concerned. This would normally mean that at least one staff member would be designated as responsible for the promotion of equal opportunities, so that applicants felt they were approaching a disinterested person.

Monitoring of equality and the extent to which it is reflected in an organisation is also regarded as being crucial to the achievement of goals in this area (IRS, 2006a). Most organisations place an emphasis on monitoring during the recruitment and selection processes, but it can also be carried out with regard to training, appraisals, grievance, discipline and dismissal, promotions and resignations (IRS, 2006a). By monitoring their HR processes to measure any apparently adverse treatment of any particular group, organisations can identify any areas that require investigation and action.

The equality duty of public sector employers

As indicated in Table 5.1, the Race Relations (Amendment) Act 2000 strengthened the RRA by imposing a duty on public authorities actively to promote improvements in race relations. The disability equality duty was introduced by the Disability Discrimination Act 2005 and the gender equality duty in the Equality Act 2006. Public authorities include organisations such a local councils, the police and fire service, educational establishments and the NHS.

The equality duty of public sector employers goes further than simply prohibiting discrimination and responding to claims of discrimination. These organisations now have a duty to promote equality for the designated groups and are expected to take positive action in various ways to do this and to eliminate discrimination. The legislation refers to the provision of services as well as employment, but our focus here is naturally on employment.

Some local authorities have approached their race equality duty by forging relationships with community groups to examine what their problems and requirements are. Public sector employers must prepare a scheme showing which actions they intend to take to fulfil the equality duties. The groups concerned must be involved in the design of these schemes, and the authorities must review and assess the impact of the steps they have taken to promote equality.

Burden of proof in discrimination cases

From 2001, a number of regulatory amendments introduced a shift in the burden of proof into the equality legislation, meaning that the burden of proof is shared between the complainant and the respondent employer if anyone takes a case of discrimination to an employment tribunal. Once a tribunal is satisfied that an applicant has provided prima facie evidence of discrimination (that is, it considers that on the balance of probabilities, discrimination may have occurred), it is then up to the employer to provide positive evidence that it did not discriminate, and that its decisions and actions were not discriminatory. Taking the recruitment and selection processes as an example, such evidence could include copies of the documentation used throughout these processes, including equality policies, non-discriminatory job descriptions and person specifications, and evidence that only non-discriminatory questions were used during interviews. Further evidence to support an employer's claim to have acted in a non-discriminatory fashion might include notes made during interviews, the results of non-biased tests, analysis of data collected for monitoring purposes, evidence of how the position was advertised and a description of equality training that is provided to managers and others involved in the selection process.

As the European Commission (2003) points out, it is the managers making decisions who have the full information behind why a particular decision was made and who are therefore best placed to demonstrate that it was made on a non-discriminatory basis. Of course, claims of discrimination could also relate to issues such as harassment in the workplace; they are not necessarily restricted to events during recruitment and selection.

Updating the equality legislation

It is evident, even from this overview of discrimination legislation and its development, that any affected parties face an extremely complex array of laws and regulations, and that anomalies have arisen, for example with regard to the use of the GOR and GOQ terminology in the context of race issues. The Discrimination Law Review was set up in 2005 to review the existing laws and work towards a simplified framework which would help employers in achieving their obligations with regard to equality. The Equalities Review Panel, also set up in 2005, has published an extensive report on all aspects of equality, including health, educational and other social aspects, and has made recommendations to the Discrimination Law Review about possible changes in employment equality legislation. One such recommendation is to review and extend the potential to engage in positive action during recruitment in order to achieve a higher level of equality for disadvantaged groups (Equalities Review, 2007).

The IRS (2007b) proposes that the progress towards a Single Equality Act will not result in a major shift in the approach to employment discrimination already established, but will rather be a matter of consolidation and clarification. One change that they do foresee is the removal of the ban on discrimination against married people in the SDA since this clause now seems to be dated.

ACTIVITY 5.3

Check the website for the Equality and Human Rights Commission and the Equalities Review to find out what the most recent developments are with regard to discrimination legislation and the proposed Single Equality Act.

Equal Pay Act 1970

The Equal Pay Act and its subsequent amendments provide for members of one sex to claim equal pay with a member of the opposite sex who is doing like work, or work of a different nature which can be shown to be similar in terms of the requirements for skill and effort, i.e. work of equal value. The Equal Pay Act is dealt with in more detail in Chapter 11, which examines payment systems and the evaluation of jobs. The major point to be made here is that it would be unlawful to advertise different pay rates for men and women doing the same work, or to offer employees of one sex disadvantageous terms and conditions.

Rehabilitation of Offenders Act 1974

The Rehabilitation of Offenders Act 1974 stipulates a range of time periods after which convictions for various offences are regarded as being spent. This means that a past offender should not be expected to reveal his or her offence once the conviction is spent, and should not be denied employment because of this previous offence. An offence that attracts a sentence of life imprisonment or a sentence of more than 30 months' imprisonment is never spent. The time periods over which convictions do become spent vary, and include 7 years for imprisonment for less than 6 months, 10 years for a prison sentence of 6 to 30 months, 1 year for a probation order (longer if the order covers a longer period) and the period of a disqualification for a driving offence. A number of exceptions to these rules about spent convictions apply to people who in the course of their jobs have unsupervised access to minors or other groups of vulnerable people, meaning that for this category of employee certain convictions can never be regarded as spent. Issues relating to employer access to criminal records will be explored more fully in Chapter 8.

The Human Rights Act 1998

The Human Rights Act 1998 (HRA) implements the provisions of the European Convention on Human Rights, and came into force in October 2000. The Act has direct effect on public authorities (which are deemed to include employment tribunals), so employees of those organisations have direct recourse to the courts if they feel their rights have been infringed under the HRA. However, the courts are also bound to interpret other national law with reference to the meaning of the HRA, so in that way, all employers in the UK are affected by the HRA.

Some of the rights guaranteed under the HRA are covered well by existing legislation in the UK, such as the right to freedom from discrimination based on sex or race.

CASE STUDY 5.1 Discrimination

Mrs Meninder Patel applied for a post as a careers adviser with a local authority. The advertisement and person specification for the post had listed three years' experience in careers advice as one of the criteria being sought, and Mrs Patel had worked as a careers adviser in local schools for four years. The careers service received a number of good applications and the selection panel had difficulty in shortlisting a small number of applicants to call for interview. After some deliberation they decided that they would interview those candidates who had experience dealing with adults, because the careers service was going to expand into this area and the panel decided that this specific experience would be valuable. Mrs Patel was not one of the applicants called to interview. She felt that she was well qualified for the post according to the advertisement and the job description and person specification that had been sent to her. Mrs Patel felt that she must have been discriminated against unfairly and decided to pursue the matter.

Comment on the equal opportunities implications of this case. Why might Mrs Patel feel that she has been the victim of unlawful discrimination? What should the local authority do?

Discussion of case study

In times of high unemployment it is common to find large numbers of people applying for vacancies. It is difficult to achieve the correct balance between a tight person specification and one that excludes people unnecessarily. However, introducing criteria after applications have been submitted could be seen as an attempt to exclude people for covert reasons, for example to exclude women or certain racial groups. Depending on who was ultimately hired for this post, Mrs Patel could believe that she had been discriminated against because of her sex, marital status or ethnic origin.

Let us assume that there was no discriminatory intent on the part of the selection panel and that they were merely seeking a device to enable them to carry out the shortlisting exercise. The case points out the importance of developing a good person specification in the first place, and the equal opportunities implications that this can have.

The local authority should ensure that there is an adequate internal mechanism for dealing with Mrs Patel's query. The fact that an employer tries to address any problems of this nature in a sincere fashion would be recognised by the Equality and Human Rights Commission as part of good equal opportunities practice. Of course, local authorities are also subject to the duty to promote equality in terms of race, gender and disability, so this employer should also have the relevant action plans in place.

The employer should also ensure that training is provided to all employees involved in recruitment and selection to ensure that they understand the importance of each element of the process.

Fair employment in Northern Ireland

Although regulations relating to discrimination on the basis of religion or belief were only introduced to the rest of the UK in 2003, legislation banning religious discrimination in the workplace has existed in Northern Ireland since 1976. The special issue of sectarian discrimination between Protestants and Roman Catholics was originally addressed in the Fair Employment (Northern Ireland) Act 1976, updated in an Act of the same name in 1989 and updated again in 1998 by the Fair Employment and Treatment (Northern Ireland) Order 1998. These Acts also address political beliefs.

Like the rest of the UK, Northern Ireland is expected to comply with the European Union Race and Equality Directives so, in that regard, legislation is drafted in Northern Ireland which mirrors the regulations in the rest of the UK. Generally, the province has structures to deal with a range of discriminatory issues that are similar to those in the rest of the UK, but with different agencies and nomenclature. For instance, there was a Fair Employment Commission set up to deal with complaints under the relevant legislation named above, but this has now been replaced by an Equality Commission which also deals with complaints lodged under the whole range of equality legislation. It is notable that race discrimination legislation was only introduced into Northern Ireland in 1997. The Labour Relations Agency in Northern Ireland undertakes functions similar to those of ACAS.

Unlike in the rest of the UK, monitoring of the composition of the workforce and of job applicants with regard to religious belief is compulsory in Northern Ireland. Employers are required to review a wide range of their practices with regard to fair employment opportunity, including recruitment and selection, provision of training, promotion, and redundancy (**www.equalityni.org**). A further example of the difference in approach engendered by the circumstances in Northern Ireland is provided in a *People Management* article (Johnson, 2003) about the Police Service of Northern Ireland (PSNI, formerly the Royal Ulster Constabulary or RUC). In order to redress the imbalance of Catholic and Protestant police officers in the force, the responsible authorities had to apply a quota system during recruitment, for which they needed special dispensation from the European Union. They called this 50–50 recruitment (Johnson, 2003, p. 32), which meant that from every pool of qualified applicants, an equal number of Protestants and Catholics would be selected. The need for such drastic measures is perhaps understandable when one considers that 92 per cent of the staff in the RUC were Protestant (Johnson, 2003, p. 31). It must be remembered, however, that this recruitment action is an exceptional case and the pursuit of quotas is not a normal aspect of the fair employment initiatives in Northern Ireland.

As with the equality laws in the rest of the UK, there are many amendments to update the legislation in Northern Ireland. With due regard to subsequent amendments then, the main pieces of legislation in Northern Ireland include:

- Equal Pay Act (Northern Ireland) 1970
- Sex Discrimination (Northern Ireland) Order 1976
- Disability Discrimination Act 1995
- Race Relations (Northern Ireland) Order 1997

- Fair Employment and Treatment (Northern Ireland) Order 1998
- Northern Ireland Act 1998
- Equality (Disability, etc.) (Northern Ireland) Order 2000
- Employment Equality (Sexual Orientation) Regulations (Northern Ireland) 2003
- Employment Equality (Age) Regulations (Northern Ireland) 2006.

Did you know?

'The Irish Traveller community is specifically identified in the Race Relations (Northern Ireland) Order as a racial group which is protected against unlawful racial discrimination.'

(*Source*: www.equalityni.org)

The Equality Commission for Northern Ireland is also concerned about the difficulties employers may encounter in dealing with so many separate pieces of equality legislation. It gives guidance on its website to employers about creating employment equality plans to integrate their approaches to all equality issues, and is working on producing guidance which consolidates advice on all of these matters. The development of a Single Equality Bill is also under consideration.

ACTIVITY 5.4

Check the website for the Equality Commission for Northern Ireland (**www.equalityni .org**) to find out what the most recent developments are with regard to producing a unified employment equality guide.

Managing diversity in the workplace

As stated previously, equality and diversity are so intimately interwoven, it can be difficult to make a distinction between the two concepts. Traditionally, equality has been thought of in terms of the discrimination legislation, referring to designated groups that are protected against being treated less favourably than other groups. This leads to notions of compliance with the law and treating everyone the same so that no one is favoured unlawfully over someone else for reasons not to do with actual competence. Legislation deals with designated groups, diversity deals with all differences (Kandola and Fullerton, 1998). This distinction is becoming more difficult to make, however, with the broadening of the equality legislation, but the CIPD in its publications (2006a and b; 2007a) and in its equality podcast (2007b) still differentiates between equality and diversity.

One way of coming to grips with the two terms is to reflect that, logically, compliance with the equality laws will inevitably lead to a diverse workforce, and the CIPD (2006a) strengthens this notion with the neat phrase 'diversity takes equality forward'. If we accept that compliance with equality legislation leads to a diverse workforce, this raises several questions: is compliance with the law enough as a driver of diversity and does managing a diverse workforce raise further issues for employers? We also still do not have a definition for diversity, so let us deal with that first.

Definitions of diversity

When describing diversity, the CIPD (2006a and b, and 2007a) frequently emphasises that each one of us is different from the next person in some way, and that these differences should be valued and celebrated. It is through recognising, responding to and managing these differences, drawing out each individual's unique potential, that diversity can thrive and make a contribution to organisations. Wolff (2007) reinforces some of this terminology when describing Arriva's approach to diversity: '. . . diversity is about valuing differences in staff and customers in terms of all aspects of difference. This includes not only colour, religion, birthplace, gender, sexual orientation and age, but also which school people have been to, what they like and do not like, what they believe in and what is important to them.'

Drivers of diversity

Compliance with discrimination legislation is not enough to respond to the political social agenda as evidenced by the equality duties imposed on public authorities. They have a duty to promote equality and not just to comply with the laws prohibiting discrimination. It is notable, however, that these equality duties do not extend to private sector organisations, so is compliance with the law enough for them? The CIPD (2007a) reports that the law is still the major driving force behind diversity initiatives, particularly in the private sector. Some private sector organisations, however, such as those profiled by the IDS (2006), have demonstrated a real commitment to diversity for business reasons.

The words from the article by Wolff (2007) cited above give a clue to at least one business argument for diversity: customers. A workforce which reflects the diversity of an organisation's customers should enable the organisation to understand and better respond to its customers' needs and wishes. Combined with this, organisations can expect greater creativity and access to a wider range of ideas from a diverse workforce. This has been known to result in product and marketing innovations (see, for example, the account of B&Q's experiences in IDS, 2004).

Further business case arguments are reflected in the major reasons cited for pursuing diversity initiatives by respondents to a CIPD survey (2006b). The following drivers were each identified by 60–68 per cent of respondents: legal pressures, better recruitment and selection, corporate social responsibility (CSR) goals, being seen as an employer of choice, it makes business sense and it is morally right. This confirms our previous statement that complying with the law is still the major driving force behind diversity initiatives, but as the CIPD also points out, at least four of the drivers identified here are to do with business objectives. Skills shortages, due in part to population change, were examined in Chapter 2 along with the resulting focus of organisations on talent management. Aiming for a diverse workforce means that organisations are recruiting from a wider pool of applicants and are more likely to gain access to the talent they require. Being seen as an employer that believes in and promotes equality is likely to contribute to the organisation's image, thus bringing the business benefits of diversity that relate to CSR and being recognised as an employer of choice.

Management of diversity

We now turn to the question about initiatives employers may need to engage in specifically to achieve their diversity objectives. As with the other people management issues we address in this book, line managers play a front-line role in the delivery and achievement of objectives. Senior management commitment to and their objectives re diversity need to be communicated to line managers. Godwin (2005) suggests that line managers' performance objectives and reward should be linked to diversity to underline the organisation's commitment. Line managers need to be trained further in understanding what the organisation aims to gain from diversity, and in managing people in such a way that they can achieve their full potential.

Of course line managers are not the only people involved in making diversity work; everyone is. Bentley (2006) suggests that providing diversity training to everyone might be too costly, but recommends that organisations should lay out their expectations to all employees, for instance as part of an induction programme.

A further issue for employers to consider is the need to offer flexible working arrangements to accommodate the inevitable differing needs of a diverse workforce. Various employees will require leave at different times for religious observances, some employees will need to adapt their working hours to fit in with child care or care of elderly or infirm dependants, and yet others may wish to take extended study leave. Offering such flexibility can itself engender further benefits for employers, as reported in *Personnel Today* (2007) referring to a survey on work-life balance: 'Increased retention was perceived to be the greatest factor in favour of offering flexible working (cited by 87% of respondents), followed by workers being happier in their jobs (82%) and increased productivity (65%).' A variety of flexible working arrangements are dealt with in detail in Chapter 4.

International issues

One of the main concerns for international organisations with regard to equality is that laws may differ in other countries. International HR specialists would need to be familiar with the legislation in force in other countries and ensure that they abide by the appropriate regulations. They also need to consider their commitment to diversity initiatives and decide how far these can be carried out in overseas locations, taking cultural differences into consideration. In terms of selecting employees for overseas assignments too, Brewster *et al.* (2007) highlight the issue of the levels of participation of women in foreign assignments, and state that it is necessary to improve on the current situation if the benefits of diversity are to be obtained.

The International Labour Organization (ILO) conducts research on equality standards on a global basis. They find that improvements are still needed in many countries, and state that: 'Despite advances, in particular the considerable progress in women's educational attainments, women continue to earn less than men everywhere, and the unequal burden of family responsibilities places them at a disadvantage in finding full-time employment' (ILO, 2007, ix). To combat this and other persistent types of discrimination, the ILO promotes the development of 'active labour market policies' (xi) including training and job creation programmes.

REVIEW QUESTIONS

You will find brief answers to the review questions on page 473.

1 Outline the major Acts and regulations that are in place to ensure equality of opportunity.

2 Explain the following terms and give examples: direct discrimination; indirect discrimination; victimisation; harassment.

3 Explain what is meant by the management of diversity.

SELF-CHECK QUESTIONS

Answer the following multiple-choice and short-answer questions. The correct responses or page references are given on page 473 for you to check your understanding of this chapter.

1 Which of the following are laws that protect groups against unfair discrimination in Britain?
   (a) Equal Opportunities Act; Disability Discrimination Act; Race Relations Act.
   (b) Disabilities Act; Race Relations Act; Equal Opportunities Act.
   (c) Sex Discrimination Act; Race Relations Act; Disability Discrimination Act.
   (d) Anti Sex Discrimination Act; Disabilities Act; Racial Discrimination Act.

2 Which of the following is not an example of a GOR?
   (a) An Indian person to wait on tables in an Indian restaurant.
   (b) A man to cut hair in a men's hair stylist's shop.
   (c) A woman to provide personal care to a woman with multiple sclerosis.

3 Which of the following does the Race Relations (Amendment) Act 2000 do?
   (a) It corrects the list of ethnic groups that may not be discriminated against.
   (b) It imposes a duty on public authorities to actively engage in the promotion of good race relations.
   (c) It authorises affirmative action, i.e. the ability to give preference to people in employment decisions because they belong to an ethnic minority.

4 Which of the following is true?
   (a) An employer can set any age over 55 as their retirement age without having to justify it.
   (b) If an employer does not set a justified retirement age, then by default, the normal retirement age is 65.
   (c) Any employee who wishes to go on working beyond a company's normal retirement age is automatically entitled to do so.
   (d) The age discrimination legislation applies only to older employees and not to those who are 18–22.

5 Which of the following is the equivalent of ACAS in Northern Ireland?
   (a) Labour Data Service.
   (b) Labour Relations Agency.
   (c) Equality Advice Bureau.
   (d) Fair Treatment Organisation.

Gender equality: a solid business case at last

By Lynda Gratton and Lamia Walker

Gender parity at work is one of those topics guaranteed to polarise opinion, whether at the dinner table or around the executive boardroom table. Most emotive, perhaps, is the fact that, despite policies to ensure equal opportunity, widely reported disparities persist.

Proposals for new interventions to address this issue are usually met with the challenge: 'Show me the business case.' The topic has been debated for decades with little change in the number of women achieving senior office. In fact, the number of women on the boards of UK publicly listed companies is reported to be falling in the FTSE 100, 250 and 350 (according to Cranfield's Female FTSE report of 2007 and PwC research, also in 2007).

Two questions emerge that must be addressed. How can we better understand and therefore value the relative contribution of men and women in professional teams? And what is the business case today for ensuring that more women achieve senior corporate office?

Over the past six months at the Lehman Brothers Centre for Women in Business, at London Business School, we have been studying how men and women work in teams that are critical to the business. An important feature of the research is that the 100 knowledge-based teams studied, from 21 global companies, were chosen from a variety of disciplines on the basis of the male-to-female ratio.

Key findings will be published this week in our report, Innovative Potential. Team members of both sexes identify that working groups with 50 per cent men and 50 per cent women deliver optimal performance in most areas that drive innovation. Gender imbalances create a significant deterioration in knowledge-based work with regard to experimentation, knowledge transfer, the capacity to work across functional or business boundaries, and general efficiency. These results were consistent, regardless of the sex of the team leader.

What is clear from this is the crucial role that gender balance plays when knowledge-based teams are working on business-critical innovative tasks.

Our research supports a number of recent studies that show the positive effect of gender parity in business. This year alone, three studies found consistent evidence for the business case. McKinsey reports that better-than-average financial performance is experienced by European companies with the highest proportion of women in leadership roles. Research at the University of Helsinki finds that companies with female chief executives or board directors achieve a 10 per cent higher return on capital, regardless of the company or sector, while Catalyst reports that Fortune 500 companies with the highest proportion of female directors are more profitable and efficient, on average, than those with the lowest.

So to every chief executive we ask: why, given the evidence that to do so results in suboptimal performance, do you persevere in recruiting disproportionate numbers of men to senior ranks? Across most industrial sectors, while 50 per cent of graduates recruited are women, only 30 per cent of managers are women and about 15 per cent of senior executives are women.

Clearly, there is a leak in the pipeline that filters out many women en route to the corporate suite. Many reasons for this leak have been explored. Women fail to see role models at the top and leave to find a better working situation or create one of their own. They might also leave because they feel forced to choose between work and home. Only 48 per cent of female team leaders we surveyed have children, while 96 per cent of their male colleagues are fathers. A worrying trend is that more women are leaving. Without swift action, the 50:30:15 ratios will continue to be a drain on talent and a negative pull on performance.

The executives who continue to ask for a business case should now turn their analytical skills to the management of their own employee base. They should put in place clear measures of progress; create and champion family-friendly working policies; encourage role models; and ensure that half of the people on leadership track projects (overseas assignments, leading business-critical projects) are women.

→

With such a mass of data pointing to the business case for gender parity, every chief executive should now see that these actions are a crucial part of their vision of good business.

Lynda Gratton is professor of management practice and co-director of the Lehman Brothers Centre for Women in Business at London Business School. Lamia Walker is co-director of the Centre.

(FT.com, 28 October 2007, © Lynda Gratton and Lamia Walker. Reproduced with permission.)

Questions

1 What are the main factors in the business case for gender equality?
2 Name some of the possible causes of the gap in gender equality.
3 What can companies do to improve gender equality?

WHAT NEXT?

ACAS published a policy discussion paper about the service's experiences with equality in the workplace in November 2006. It is entitled *Back to Basics,* and can be downloaded at the ACAS website (**www.acas.org.uk**). ACAS is approached for help and guidance by employers and employees alike, which provides them with a unique take on attitudes towards equality issues. This discussion paper provides an interesting overview of equality issues as they are experienced in practice.

Alternatively, you may wish to examine developments in equality from a more global perspective. In 2007, the International Labour Organization published an in-depth report about equality developments in the workplace on a global basis. The report is entitled *Equality at Work: Tackling the Challenges.* Reading this will give you a wider perspective on equality issues in countries as diverse as the member states of the EU, Mexico, Brazil and New Zealand, among others.

References

Advisory, Conciliation and Arbitration Service (2005a) *Religion or Belief and the Workplace: A Guide for Employers and Employees,* ACAS.

Advisory, Conciliation and Arbitration Service (2005b) *Sexual Orientation and the Workplace: A Guide for Employers and Employees,* ACAS.

Advisory, Conciliation and Arbitration Service (2006) *Age and the Workplace: Putting the Employment Equality (Age) Regulations 2006 into Practice,* ACAS.

Advisory, Conciliation and Arbitration Service (2007) Exploring the impact of the 2003 equality regulations on sexual orientation and religion or belief, *Employment Relations Matters,* Issue 8, Spring, 1–3.

Bentley, R. (2006) Diversity training: Different strokes for different folks, *Training & Coaching Today,* 1 February (available at www.xperthr.co.uk; accessed 03.04.07).

Brewster, C., P. Sparrow and G. Vernon (2007) *International Human Resource Management,* 2nd edition, CIPD.

Chartered Institute of Personnel and Development (2006a) *Diversity: An Overview* (factsheet available from www.cipd.co.uk; accessed 12.07.06).

Chartered Institute of Personnel and Development (2006b) *Diversity in Business: How Much Progress Have Employers Made? First Findings,* CIPD.

Chartered Institute of Personnel and Development (2007a) *Diversity in Business: A Focus for Progress. Survey Report March 2007,* CIPD.

Chartered Institute of Personnel and Development (2007b) *Diversity Podcast,* CIPD (available at www.cipd.co.uk; accessed 12.07.07).

Coker, N. (ed) (2001) *Racism in Medicine: An Agenda for Change,* King's Fund.

Commission for Racial Equality (2006) *Statutory Code of Practice on Racial Equality in Employment,* CRE.

Equal Opportunities Commission (2006) *Code of Practice – Sex Discrimination,* EOC.

Equalities Review (2007) *Fairness and Freedom: The Final Report of the Equalities Review,* Crown Copyright.

European Commission (2003) *Annual Report on Equality and Non-Discrimination 2003: Towards Diversity,* Office for Official Publications of the European Communities.

Godwin, K. (2005) Promoting diversity – the role of line managers, *Equal Opportunities Review,* Issue 147, 1/11 (available at www.xperthr.co.uk; accessed 03.04.07).

Incomes Data Services (2004) Cultural diversity at B&Q, *IDS Diversity at Work,* No. 5, November, 7–10.

Incomes Data Services (2006) *IDS HR Study 825: Promoting Race Equality,* July, IDS.

Industrial Relations Services (IRS) (2000) Disability discrimination: the current state of play, *Industrial Relations Law Bulletin 649,* September, 2–12.

Industrial Relations Services (IRS) (2001) DRC puts carrots before sticks, *IRS Employment Trends 729,* June, 6–10.

Industrial Relations Services (IRS) (2003) Unlawful discrimination – a new era, *IRS Employment Review 781,* 1 August, 50–64.

Industrial Relations Services (IRS) (2006a) Equality structures: an EOR survey, *Equal Opportunities Review,* Issue 157, 1/10 (www.xperthr.co.uk; accessed 20.07.07).

Industrial Relations Services (IRS) (2006b) Philosophical beliefs, *IRS Employment Review 845,* 21/4 (www.xperthr.co.uk; accessed 20.07.07).

Industrial Relations Services (IRS) (2007a) Avoiding discrimination – policies and monitoring, *Employment Law Reference Manual,* 4/7 (www.xperthr.co.uk; accessed 15.08.07).

Industrial Relations Services (IRS) (2007b) Proposals for a single equality Bill, *IRS Employment Review 876,* 18/7 (www.xperthr.co.uk; accessed 15.08.07).

International Labour Organization (2007) *Equality at Work: Tackling the Challenges,* ILO.

Johnson, R. (2003) Bill of rights, *People Management,* 9 October, 28–35.

Kandola, R. and J. Fullerton (1998) *Diversity in Action: Managing the Mosaic,* 2nd edition, IPD.

Macpherson, W. (1999) *The Stephen Lawrence Inquiry: Report of an Inquiry by Sir William Macpherson,* HMSO.

Personnel Today (2007) The Work and Families Act: What are employers doing in practice about flexible working? *Personnel Today,* 27 March (available at www.personneltoday.com; accessed 28.03.07).

Wolff, C. (2007) Arriva: dramatic results on diversity, *Equal Opportunities Review,* Issue 160, 1/1 (available at www.xperthr.co.uk; accessed 03.04.07).

www.acas.org.uk (accessed 16.09.07).

www.agepositive.gov.uk (accessed 16.09.07).

www.crflaw.co.uk (accessed 17.09.07).

www.efa.org.uk (accessed 16.09.07).

www.equalityni.org (accessed 16.09.07).

Further study   Books

Commission for Racial Equality (2006) *Code of Practice on Racial Equality in Employment,* CRE. This replaces the code produced in 1984. The code provides a wealth of practical information and definitions of terms such as harassment which are relevant to other equality issues. Available at www.equalityhumanrights.com; accessed 12.10.07.

Disability Rights Commission (2006) *The Disability Equality Duty and Employment – A Straightforward Guide,* DRC. Provides explanations about the legislation and guidance on how to proceed.

Equal Opportunities Commission (2006) *Code of Practice – Sex Discrimination*, EOC.

Incomes Data Services (2006) *IDS HR Study 825: Promoting Race Equality,* July. A good overview of race equality and several case studies of employers who have approached the issues in positive ways, including Arriva and Tesco.

Industrial Relations Services (2000) *Managing Disability. IRS Management Review 18,* IRS. Various chapters deal with the position of disabled people as part of the workforce, recruitment and retention, the Disability Discrimination Act 1995, employer case studies, and resources for employers and employees.

Selwyn, N. (latest edition) *Law of Employment,* Butterworths. This is an excellent reference book on employment law. The book is updated fairly frequently, so you should always make sure you are working with the latest edition.

Articles

Cooper, C. (2003) Minority support, *People Management,* 4 December, 25–27. Cooper provides an interesting overview of the state of play in a number of organisations in the week that the new regulations on religious discrimination were introduced. There are a number of interesting articles on this and the sexual orientation regulations in this issue of *People Management.*

Fredman, S. (2001) Equality: a new generation? *Industrial Law Journal,* Vol. 3, No. 2, June, 145–168. A very readable overview of the then current and planned status of equality legislation in the EU and its implications for the UK. Still valuable as an interesting discussion of the values underpinning attitudes towards equality though subsequent changes in the law should be kept in mind when reading this article.

How to develop a dyslexia-friendly workplace (2004) *People Management,* 16 September, 50–51.

Industrial Relations Services (IRS) (2007) Determining the needs of the job, *Employment Law Reference Manual,* 31/3. Provides examples of genuine occupational qualifications and requirements.

Ingham, J. (2003) How to implement a diversity policy, *People Management,* 24 July, 44–45. The 'How to . . .' series provides very useful summaries of the major considerations in a range of human resource management activities.

International Labour Review (2003/04) Vol. 142, No. 4. Entire special issue on equality at work.

Wolff, C. (2007) Arriva: dramatic results on diversity, *Equal Opportunities Review,* Issue 160, 1/1 (available at www.xperthr.co.uk; accessed 03.04.07). Provides a very interesting case study of how Arriva approaches the management of diversity and what it sees as the benefits.

Internet

Advisory, Conciliation and Arbitration Service **www.acas.org.uk**
ACAS offers e-learning courses on the sexual orientation, religion or belief, and age discrimination regulations.

Age Posi+ive **www.agepositive.gov.uk**
A website dedicated to 'tackling age discrimination and promoting age diversity in employment'.

Chartered Institute of Personnel and Development **www.cipd.co.uk**
The CIPD website contains a wealth of information on various aspects of equality and the law. The website provides a podcast on equality and the podcast on employment law also contains relevant sections on parental rights and age.

Communities and Local Government **www.communities.gov.uk**
A government department with a remit to 'reduce inequalities and build community cohesion . . . taking the lead with other key departments in promoting equality and the aim of social justice and sustainable, economically viable communities.'

Employers' Forum on Disability **www.efd.org.uk**
A fount of information for employers, including guidelines and factsheets, information on events and awards, and links to many more sites.

Equality and Human Rights Commission   **www.equalityhumanrights.com**
The Equality and Human Rights Commission has been established to deal with all equality issues.

Race issues in Britain   **www.guardian.co.uk/race**
Provides links to *Guardian* news items, other reports and the scripts of TV news reports.

Northern Ireland sites

Department for Employment and Learning   **www.delni.gov.uk**
Supplies information about employment rights in NI.

Equality Commission   **www.equalityni.org**
Provides a good overview of the equality legislation in NI.

Labour Relations Agency   **www.lra.org.uk**
Provides advice and guidance to promote good employment relations in NI.

CHAPTER 6

Recruitment

Objectives

When you have read this chapter you will be able to:

- explain the aims of recruitment and describe how specified policies and procedures contribute to these aims
- understand the role of human resource managers and line managers in the recruitment process
- describe and design support documentation for the recruitment process – job description, person specification, job advertisement, application form, letters to applicants
- evaluate and draft recruitment policies and procedures
- identify a range of recruitment methods.

Organisations recognise the crucial part their people play in achieving and sustaining a competitive edge, and they are therefore aware of the need to attract people of the right calibre. Because of skills shortages and the resultant 'war for talent', as described in Chapter 2, talent management has become well established as an HR priority and is recognised to be of strategic importance to business organisations (CIPD, 2007b). Talent management focuses largely on the development and retention of employees, but to achieve these goals, an organisation has to attract and hire people with the appropriate competencies in the first place. This confirms the strategic importance of recruitment, and in fact in a CIPD survey (2007c, p. 2) about the future of HR, published in September 2007, 'when asked about the main objectives of the HR function, recruitment and retention was given as the highest priority'. Competition for scarce resources also means that organisations have to be innovative in their recruitment methods, and examples of some recent innovations will be presented in this chapter.

The processes of recruitment and selection are closely linked. Both activities are directed towards obtaining employees with the requisite competencies and attitudes, and recruitment activities lay the groundwork for the selection process by providing the pool of applicants from whom the selectors may choose. However, although the two activities are closely connected, each requires a separate range of skills and expertise, and may in practice be carried out by different individuals. The recruitment activity, but not normally the selection decision, may be outsourced to an agency. It makes sense, therefore, to treat each activity separately. This chapter will deal with recruitment processes, actions, policies and procedures which, of course, should be designed to meet the strategic objectives of the organisation.

Recruitment can be defined as:

- all activities directed towards locating potential employees
- attracting applications from suitable candidates.

The aims of recruitment

Organisations do not operate in a vacuum, and recruitment drives are one of the times when an organisation has direct contact with the outside world. Other factors affecting recruitment are the framework imposed by legislation and the fact that no organisation will want to spend money on unnecessary activities. In light of this and the definition of recruitment given above, the aims of recruitment are:

- to obtain a pool of suitable candidates for vacant posts
- to use a fair process and be able to demonstrate that the process was fair
- to ensure that all recruitment activities contribute to organisational goals and a desirable organisational image
- to conduct recruitment activities in an efficient and cost-effective manner.

These statements intimate that a number of judgements have to be made about how recruitment is carried out. What is meant by a 'suitable candidate', and who decides this? Does the organisation have a process for evaluating the need to fill a post? What is a fair recruitment process and in what terms can fairness be evaluated or demonstrated? What recruitment actions can contribute to, or damage, an organisation's image? What are the costs involved in recruitment and how can they be managed to maximise the efficiency of the process? Acting as an umbrella to all of these considerations is also the need to tailor recruitment action to the corporate strategic plan, which itself should have incorporated factors in the environment such as skills shortages, technological advances, etc. Figure 6.1 is a mind map of some of the factors that need to be considered in a systematic recruitment process.

Most human resource management issues can be analysed in terms of legal, moral and business considerations. With reference to the stated aims of recruitment, these considerations could be said to be:

- *legal* – to comply with anti-discrimination legislation
- *moral* – to avoid unfair discrimination for moral reasons as well as legal reasons
- *business* – to ensure that all efforts are directed towards achieving corporate goals.

To achieve all these aims, and because recruitment is likely to involve a wide range of people within an organisation, it is important to have a systematic approach so that all steps of the recruitment and selection process are conducted in line with:

- the organisation's human resource strategy
- equality goals.

The first step towards ensuring that the recruitment process achieves these aims in a coordinated manner is to develop and implement appropriate policies and procedures.

Figure 6.1 Mind map of recruitment considerations

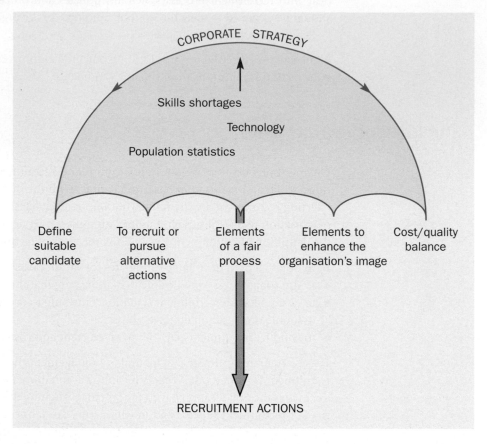

Recruitment policies

A policy is simply a statement of intent on the part of an organisation; it outlines the approach everyone is expected to adopt and the standards they should achieve in carrying out an organisation's business. A recruitment policy enables all employees involved in the process to direct their efforts towards achieving the organisation's goals and to know that they are acting in the spirit intended by the organisation.

A basic recruitment policy should at the very least include statements about the organisation's stance on:

● the overall goal of recruitment
● equality of opportunity.

To show that they value their employees, wish to retain them and want to provide them with every opportunity to develop, organisations may also adopt a policy of giving preference to suitably qualified internal applicants over external applicants, and this too would need to be stated explicitly in the organisation's recruitment policy. Such a policy would have implications for the way that recruitment procedures are developed.

One argument that is sometimes raised against internal recruitment policies is that they may lead to entrenching any equality problems that exist. That is, if the organisation has not previously hired from a particular ethnic group, for example, then it will not improve its record by hiring from within. A counter-argument to this is that if current employees are moved to new positions, presumably they eventually leave a vacancy that must be filled by external candidates. Organisations following good equality policies would be able to address any problems at this stage.

Organisations that wish to take the human resource management approach to enhancing the contribution and commitment of their employees should certainly consider adopting a policy on internal recruitment.

Pause for thought 6.1 Imagine you are in a company that has decided to formulate a recruitment policy which reflects its commitment to equality of opportunity along with an intention to give preference to internal candidates. Before you read on, consider what might be included in a recruitment policy for this company.

The following is an example of how such a policy might be worded:

This company aims to employ the person best suited for each post without regard to sex, marital status, racial origin, disability, sexual preference, religion, age or any other factor that cannot reasonably be construed as being related to a person's ability to do the job.

The company values the contribution of its employees and so will seek wherever possible to help employees develop new skills so that they may be considered for promotion opportunities. The company will advertise vacancies externally only if there are no suitably qualified internal candidates for transfers or promotions.

Recruitment procedures

The first step in the recruitment process is to assess the need for additional human resources and decide whether or not you have a vacancy you wish to fill. The vacancy may be a new post that has been identified through the development of the corporate strategic plan, or it may have arisen because an employee has resigned, retired or been dismissed. The latter are sometimes referred to as replacement posts to distinguish them from new posts. You may also decide to recruit a job-share partner for an established employee who no longer wishes to work full time.

Filling vacancies which arise because an employee has decided to leave or creating new posts should be part of a careful planning process, scrutinised in terms of how the action contributes to the organisation's strategic goals. When a jobholder leaves, HR and line managers should take the opportunity to examine the work done and consider whether it can be covered in another fashion. Here are some of the factors that could be considered:

- Are all the tasks necessary?
- Can some tasks be incorporated into another post?
- Should the job be redesigned to include more interesting and challenging work?
- Can some tasks be completed in other ways, e.g. by machine, by computer?
- Can the work be done on a part-time, flexitime or job-share basis?
- Is there a permanent need for the output of the post or should it be filled on a temporary basis or even contracted out?

A systematic approach to recruitment as recommended by the CIPD (2006c) includes:

- preparation of all supporting documents such as job descriptions and person specifications or competency profiles
- guidelines on actions to be taken such as writing and placing advertisements, and administrative procedures related to contacting prospective candidates.

Job descriptions and person specifications/competency profiles

In organisations that engage fully in human resource planning there will be on-going work dedicated to producing and maintaining job descriptions and person specifications/competency profiles, since these documents contain much of the information required for the planning process. Job analysis is the name of the process which is followed to produce these documents. However, even in organisations that do not engage fully in human resource planning, it is essential to produce job descriptions and person specifications/competency profiles for all existing posts as a basic framework for recruitment and, later, selection activities. These documents contain the information around which the job advertisement and the assessment of candidates will be structured and they can also be used to provide evidence of a fair process.

Job analysis

Job analysis is a process of gathering together all data about an existing job, which activities are performed and what skills are needed. Some decisions, as described in the next section, need to be made about who will carry out the job analysis most effectively. The collected data are then structured to create job descriptions and person specifications or a job profile related to a competency framework. A similar process can be carried out to create this documentation for new posts though this would inevitably rely more on managerial knowledge and judgement.

The following aspects of job analysis need to be considered:

- What techniques can be used for gathering the information required?
- Who can best provide the information?
- Who can best gather the information?
- Who should write the job description and person specification?

What techniques can be used for gathering the information?

A range of techniques are available for performing job analysis, including observation, critical incident analysis and the use of questionnaires and interviews.

Observation involves shadowing employees and observing what they actually do. Obviously this can be very time-consuming and could stretch over a long period if, for instance, some tasks were performed infrequently. This technique is therefore most appropriate in the case of routine jobs with a narrow range of repetitive tasks.

Critical incident analysis involves getting a number of jobholders and their supervisors to describe events that showed successful behaviour on the job and events that showed unsuccessful behaviour. The analyst collects a large number of such anecdotes and condenses out of them a list of dimensions that represent the job. The advantage of this is seen as being that it focuses on behaviours, i.e. what people actually do, but the process is very time-consuming and may miss some of the more routine aspects of the job.

A sound approach for gathering information would involve written questionnaires and face-to-face interviews. A structured questionnaire can be used to gather initial information from the jobholder, supplemented with details from the line manager. The job analyst can then interview both and obtain clarification on the details outlined in the questionnaire. The draft job description should then be submitted to the jobholder and line manager for further comment. A structured questionnaire will guide people into giving relevant and adequate information.

Pause for thought 6.2	If you were asked to design a form in order to conduct a job analysis, what questions would you include?

The questions on a job analysis form might be dictated to some extent by the type of company you are working in. For instance, if you worked in a bank which is closed in the evening, you would not include questions about night shift work, whereas if you worked in a chemical plant with a 24-hour process, you obviously would ask questions about shift patterns. If we ignore such differences between organisations, however, there are some basic data that you would want to include in any job analysis. These would include such details as:

● a description of the duties performed
● the most important or responsible duties
● time spent on each duty
● how often each duty is performed (daily/weekly/monthly/annually)
● levels of supervision/independence
● the skills and skill levels needed to perform each task
● any special conditions related to the performance of these tasks.

The questionnaire and interview should be designed so that information needed for each section of the job description will be obtained. If employees and their managers are asked to describe ways in which they think their jobs will change, this adds information to the job analysis beyond what is already observable about the job. Pearn and Kandola (1993) provide a detailed description and evaluation of a wide variety of job analysis methods.

Although many people are happy to talk about their job, some people do not respond well to questioning or they may lack good powers of expression. The person performing the job analysis needs to develop good interviewing techniques to extract all the relevant information. Interviewing skills are an essential part of many aspects of human resource management and you will find more information about relevant techniques and skills development in Chapter 7 on selection.

Who can best provide the information?

Before you read on, stop and ask yourself: 'Who knows most about any particular job?' Most people would probably respond by saying: 'The person who actually does the job'. The postholder is, therefore, a good source of information about any post. But is the postholder the best source, or the only source? The direct line manager will also know the job requirements intimately, and will probably have a better perspective on how the job fits into the wider context of the company. Gathering information from both of these individuals will create a better picture of the post than gathering information from only one of them.

HR specialists too are often in a position to develop detailed knowledge of the tasks performed throughout the company, and in fact must do so particularly if they are involved in the human resource planning process, so they can bring an even wider perspective to the description of an individual post. To that extent they can also provide input to the job description, but their major role as far as job descriptions are concerned is about structuring, standardising and maintaining them rather than providing content-based information.

ACTIVITY 6.1

Information given by any person will be influenced by his or her perceptions and self-interest. Consider the pros and cons of involving the postholder and the line manager in the production of job descriptions and make a list of these before you continue reading.

Your list might include the following points:

1 *The postholder*:
   - knows the job in detail
   - may wish to inflate the importance of certain duties as a matter of status or self-image
   - may represent preferred duties as more important duties
   - may have incorrect perceptions of the level of authority he or she can exercise
   - may not have the specialised skills needed to gather information and compose job descriptions
   - may be reluctant to spend the time necessary to develop a good job description.

2 *The line manager*:
   - knows the job well, but may not know every step the jobholder takes to complete the job
   - can give information about how the job fits in with other functions performed in the company
   - may sometimes be reluctant to define which tasks his or her subordinates have full authority for
   - may not have the specialised skills needed to gather information and compose job descriptions
   - may be reluctant to spend the time necessary to develop a good job description.

Who can best gather the information?

A human resource specialist is probably in the best position to fulfil this role. Although line managers may often put job descriptions to good use, most of them would not consider the production of JDs to be part of their duties, and there is no reason to assume that line managers in a wide range of functions would necessarily have the skills needed in order to produce a good job description. The human resource management function would normally provide this as a service to line management, and of course people with the requisite skills would be recruited and selected to perform this duty. It is rare to see an HR position totally devoted to job analysis, but depending on the structure of the HRM division, the task could be allocated to a recruitment specialist or an HR generalist.

Who should write the job description?

Again the HR specialist can probably best perform this task because of the writing skills required and the opportunity to become familiar with jobs throughout the organisation. This means that all job descriptions will be written in a uniform manner, providing an excellent database of all tasks performed within the organisation, thus facilitating a range of HR tasks such as the human resource planning activities described in Chapter 2. The various uses of JDs are examined later in this chapter.

How to write a job description

Structure and content

Since a collection of job descriptions can serve as a database of all tasks performed within an organisation, it makes sense to adopt a standard format for all job descriptions. This will ensure that the same types of information are gathered for each post, and will make the information more accessible to the reader and facilitate coding if the data are to be entered onto a computerised information system. The following elements are commonly found in job descriptions:

- job title
- reporting structure:
  - reports to
  - responsible for
- purpose of job
- major duties.

These are the essential elements of a job description, but you will find an assortment of other dimensions included in some job descriptions, for example: contacts, working conditions, salary grade, performance standards. Each organisation must decide what factors should be included in a job description, and this will depend on the nature of the business. For instance, some local authorities include a description of the contacts their employees are expected to deal with because they have complex internal structures, and contact with the public is an important part of their operation. The four elements listed above, however, are the basic information you would expect to find in any job description. Figure 6.2 shows a sample job description.

Most JDs contain a summary description of the post or, as we have called it, an outline of the purpose of the post. This is a brief paragraph encapsulating what the job is all about – what the jobholder contributes to the organisation. The major part of any JD is the list of major duties, itemising in detail the activities the jobholder undertakes and what he or she is meant to achieve.

Torrington *et al.* (2005) demonstrate the inclusion of performance standards in job descriptions. This can certainly enhance a job description by giving more information about what is expected from the jobholder. For instance, the second duty in our sample JD might read: 'Answer phone queries within three rings.'

Figure 6.2 Sample job description

JOB DESCRIPTION

Job title: Receptionist

Reports to: Office Services Manager

Responsible for: Assistant receptionists (2)

Purpose of post: To ensure that visitors to the company are received in a welcoming fashion, to answer routine queries and to ensure that all other queries are handled expeditiously by the appropriate staff member. To ensure that all telephone queries are handled in the same manner.

                         As the first point of contact for the company, the receptionist must maintain high standards of customer care.

Contacts: All customers and other visitors to deal with initial and routine queries. All members of staff to pass on queries as appropriate.

Major duties:
- Greet walk-in visitors and ascertain purpose of their visit. Handle or redirect queries as appropriate.
- Answer phone queries as above.
- Answer all initial queries about receipt of payments using the online payment receipts system.
- Open and sort incoming post by department. Organise delivery of post by assistant receptionists.
- Perform clerical tasks assigned by departments in agreement with the Office Services Manager.
- Supervise assistant receptionists and delegate work as appropriate.
- Perform other duties as assigned by the Office Services Manager or other authorised manager.

Writing style

One important pointer when you are writing a job description is to use verbs to describe what a person is doing. For instance, the phrase 'responsible for letters' does not indicate what this employee would actually be doing. It is much better to employ a verb and say: 'writes letters'; 'sorts and distributes letters'; 'replies to letters'.

You should also, where possible, avoid the temptation to use the phrase 'assists with', as again this does not give a clear picture of what an individual employee is actually doing. Take, for example, the phrase: 'assists the manager with invoices'. It must be possible to get a clearer idea of which duties have been delegated to the employee and what activities are retained by the manager. 'Sorts the invoices by date'; 'processes invoices and forwards them to appropriate departments'; 'checks that invoices have been processed and payment made': each of these indicates a different activity

Did you know?

An IRS (2003b) survey of 250 organisations identified that 71 per cent of employers use job descriptions for all of their posts, 3 per cent use them for most posts, and a further 9 per cent use them for some posts.

and a different level of responsibility, and each is certainly more meaningful than 'assists the manager with invoices'.

Uses of the job description

It has been mentioned previously that job descriptions can be used for a number of purposes. These will be dealt with more extensively in other chapters, but it is worth pausing here to reflect briefly on what the applications of job descriptions are and whether they have any implications for how job descriptions are compiled and written. The major uses of job descriptions are as follows:

- human resource planning
- recruitment and selection
- day-to-day performance management
- long-term performance management/performance appraisal
- identification of training needs
- job evaluation.

Can one description provide all the information needed for the whole range of these activities? Some HR managers may argue that different input is needed, for example, for the job evaluation process. More detailed information may be needed about the amount of freedom that employees have to make decisions independently, the impact their actions have on other colleagues, or the financial implications of their work. The question arises of whether a different job description is needed for the purposes of job evaluation. You can form a better opinion on this when you read about these other activities and the uses of job descriptions to support them.

ACTIVITY 6.2

1 Design a generic questionnaire that could be used to solicit adequate information from an employee to draft a job description. (It might help you if you have one or two posts in mind while you design the questionnaire: what sorts of question would you need to ask in order to elicit all the relevant information? You may also wish to work with a group of fellow students to pool your ideas about the questionnaire design.)
2 Test your questionnaire on a friend, relative or other willing volunteer, and follow up with an interview to fill in the gaps.
3 Analyse this process and make recommendations for improvement.
4 Draft the job description from the information you have gathered.

Person specifications

The person specification is a document that outlines the skills and qualities a person would need to have in order to be able to do the tasks on the job description. Drawing up a person specification requires a fair amount of judgement in assessing what level of skill is necessary. To ensure equality of opportunity, care must be taken *not* to inflate these requirements, especially with regard to academic qualifications and length of experience. The requirements detailed in a person specification should be the minimum standards required for a person to be able to perform the job. There should be an expectation that any person will improve performance while doing a job, and the fact that training could be provided should also be considered.

How to write a person specification

Several models of person specifications are available, those designed by Alec Rodger in 1952 and John Munro Fraser in 1978 being the most widely known. We shall briefly describe the criteria set out in these two models, with some indication of how you might interpret the recommended dimensions in modern circumstances, and then we shall apply a simplified model to our sample job description.

Rodger developed the seven-point plan which described people in terms of:

- *Physical make-up*: any particular physical requirements of the job, such as visual acuity
- *Attainments*: education and training
- *General intelligence*: it is difficult to make a meaningful statement about intelligence unless you intend to test for it
- *Special aptitudes*: verbal, numerical and diagrammatical abilities related to the job
- *Interests*: current wisdom is that private interests are not good indicators of job performance
- *Disposition*: job-related behaviours such as persuasiveness
- *Circumstances*: only job-related circumstances such as availability for shift work

The criteria suggested by Fraser are known as the five-fold framework:

- *Impact on others*: similar to Rodger's physical make-up and disposition
- *Qualifications and experience*: education, training and skills developed through work experience
- *Innate abilities*: similar to intelligence in Rodger's plan
- *Motivation*: difficult to apply for recruitment and selection purposes since differing motivational structures can lead to equally good performance
- *Emotional adjustment*: Relevant personality factors such as the ability to cope with the demands of the job

In essence, the person specification should cover three areas of requirements:

- knowledge
- skills
- personal attributes or qualities.

These three dimensions have long been used to create person specifications in North America where they are referred to as KSAs.

The person specification can be drawn up by examining each task in the job description and determining:

1 what each task requires in terms of knowledge, skills and personal qualities
2 how these skills, knowledge and personal qualities might be acquired.

As mentioned earlier, a high level of judgement is needed to decide on relevant criteria, and one person's judgement may differ from another's. You must be able to justify any requirement you make and be ready to explain why it is reasonable, particularly when the specification is to be used later in recruitment and selection. You should also take care to avoid meaningless clichés like 'a sense of humour', when what is really required is the ability to deal calmly with challenging situations.

Once you have a list of the criteria you are looking for, they must be arranged in a logical and understandable fashion:

● Similar criteria, e.g. all skills and knowledge involving numeracy, should be grouped.
● Criteria can be designated as essential for the post or merely desirable.

The sample person specification in Table 6.1 relates to the sample job description in Figure 6.2.

Table 6.1 Sample person specification

Person specification		
Post: Receptionist		
Attributes	Essential	Desirable
Knowledge	Knowledge of clerical systems	Knowledge of the company
Skills	Experience of clerical work Experience in handling queries in person and over the telephone	Supervisory experience
Personal qualities	Polite manner Ability to work under pressure	

Pause for thought 6.3 One of the major requirements for the job described in Figure 6.2 has been missed out of the model person specification in Table 6.1. Can you identify it? What can you add to the person specification to cover this requirement?

The job description mentions use of an online system to answer queries about receipt of payment, yet there is no requirement for computer skills in the person specification. Obviously a low level of skill is required. It would not, for instance, be appropriate to ask for programming skills, but it would be reasonable to require the 'ability to extract information from a computerised database'.

ACTIVITY 6.3

Draft a person specification for the job description in Figure 6.2 using the models provided by Alec Rodger and John Munro Fraser. Compare your drafts with those of other students and incorporate the best ideas into a final version.

Competency frameworks

Competencies are work-related behaviours that have been identified as necessary for successful performance at work. Rather than designing a person specification for each post, perhaps using new vocabulary each time to describe the skills, knowledge and personal attributes required, it may be possible to design a schematic or framework of competencies that can be applied to all jobs performed in a particular company. At least it should be possible to identify a set of core competencies required of all employees, with more specialised competencies attached to the job descriptions of particular posts. With the broadening of equality legislation, the focus in setting requirements during recruitment and selection is shifting firmly towards the use of competencies. Assessments of candidates must centre on their abilities, not on aspects of their background, such as length of work experience or non-essential academic qualifications, that may tie in with their sex, race, age etc. Requirements for particular qualifications or a number of years of work experience can take attention away from an evaluation of actual competencies.

Setting up a competency framework is a complex endeavour, and organisations that wish to introduce one into their HRM systems would normally call on the services of a firm of occupational psychologists to assist in the design and implementation processes. Competency frameworks come in many shapes and sizes, and the issues that would typically need to be addressed in designing a system include the following:

- Should we adopt a framework geared towards particular categories of employee (e.g. managers) or design one that can be applied to all employees in the organisation?
- What are the competencies relevant to our enterprise? How many should we include to build a comprehensive but manageable representation of the skills, knowledge and personal qualities required in the organisation?
- Which competencies can be grouped together as clusters, how many performance levels should there be for each competency and how will these levels be described?
- How do these competency clusters, individual competencies and levels of competency relate to individual jobs in the organisation?

An example of a competency cluster, individual competency and levels of competency should help you to recognise the significance of these issues and appreciate the potential usefulness of a competency framework. Typical competencies that are required by organisations include things like communication skills, analytical abilities, ability to work in a team, leadership, and ability to plan work.

Let us take the employees in a supermarket as an example. Most of these employees would at some time come into contact with the public, so 'working with people' might well be a major area of competence which would subsume a cluster of related competencies. 'Working with people' therefore becomes a competency cluster, and the competencies included under this designation might include communication, customer service and teamwork. These competencies might be applied to all jobs in the supermarket, including managerial, supervisory, office and shop-floor employees. Obviously, different levels of these competencies would be expected from employees working in different functions and at different levels in the organisation. Thus a description of the level of competence in teamworking required of a manager would probably allude to the ability to devise and implement new structures that enhance productivity, whereas the level of competence expected of a shelf stacker would probably involve statements such as 'assists other team members when own work is completed' or 'helps other team members solve queries'.

Whiddett and Hollyforde (1999) provide a more detailed sample competency framework, the Incomes Data Services (IDS, 2001) review examples of the frameworks used in a number of organisations, and the IRS (2006) give a general overview of the use of competencies at various stages in the recruitment and selection processes, along with two organisational case studies.

ACTIVITY 6.4

The competencies we have just outlined in our supermarket example are presented in a grid in Figure 6.3. Provide descriptions of the levels of competency left blank for all the competencies, and indicate which jobs these would apply to.

Figure 6.3   Competency framework exercise

	LEVEL 1	LEVEL 2	LEVEL 3	LEVEL 4	LEVEL 5
WORKING WITH THE TEAM	• Demonstrates willingness to help other members of the team complete their work • Uses knowledge to help other team members solve problems			• Designs and implements new team work structures to improve efficiency and effectiveness	
CUSTOMER SERVICE					
COMMUNICATION SKILLS					

The job description in the recruitment context

The four basic elements of the job description are: the job title; the reporting structure, i.e. the job title of the person to whom the postholder reports and the number and categories of the people the postholder is responsible for; a statement of the purpose of the post; and a description of the major duties. Taken together, they should provide a job applicant with a good idea of what the job entails.

The job title, such as sales assistant, warehouse supervisor, marketing department manager or nurse, already contains a lot of information about the position. In choosing a job title you should be careful not to inflate the level of the job, for instance by the inappropriate use of words such as executive or director, and you should avoid any potentially biased language such as waitress and foreman.

The information given in the sections on reporting structure enables applicants to see where the job fits into the organisation's structure and whether the post has any supervisory responsibilities. If there are particularly pertinent details about terms and conditions, such as shift work or a requirement to work on Sundays, they should also be included since this will enable candidates to judge whether they are willing to take on such responsibilities.

The person specification/competency profile in the recruitment context

The very fact that an employer draws up a person specification/competency profile demonstrates an attempt to introduce some objectivity into what can otherwise be a very subjective process. Rather than relying on instinctive personal judgements about the knowledge, skills and qualities the successful candidate should possess, the employer with a person specification/profile is following a much more methodical and reasoned process. It is also a much more open process, since the specification is a written record of what the employer is basing his or her selection decision on. These written records can be requested by employment tribunals should anyone complain of unfair treatment, but many employers now share this information openly with applicants for posts, so applicants also know in detail what the employer is looking for in a candidate.

Care should therefore be taken that no one is unfairly excluded from being considered for a position because the requirements were set unnecessarily high. This could constitute indirect discrimination, as certain disadvantaged groups may have more difficulty in acquiring some qualifications or competency levels. Care should also be taken that none of the criteria set are directly unlawfully discriminatory.

The information about skills, knowledge and personal qualities should be summarised and included in advertisements for the post.

As mentioned above, the person specification/competency profile can be included with the information sent to candidates to give them more details about requirements. It is an excellent practice to design and send to candidates a form showing each requirement and how it will be assessed, for example from information included on the application form, at the interview or from references. Table 6.2 shows an example of this, based on the person specification for a receptionist which was given earlier in this chapter (Table 6.1).

Table 6.2 Assessment of person specification criteria

Post: Receptionist

Attributes	Criteria	How assessed
Knowledge	Knowledge of clerical systems	Application form Interview Work sample test
	Knowledge of the company	Interview
Skills	Experience of clerical work	Application form Interview Work sample test
	Experience of handling queries in person and on the telephone	Application form Interview
	Ability to extract information from a computerised database	Application form Interview
	Supervisory experience	Application form Interview
Personal qualities	Polite manner	Interview
	Ability to work under pressure	Interview

Job advertisements

Once you know you have a vacancy to fill, you must decide what is the best way to let people know about it. The following are some methods of advertising the existence of vacancies:

- on-site noticeboards
- local/national newspapers
- professional journals
- minority group newspapers and magazines
- recruitment agencies
- university/college/school careers centres
- job centres
- radio/television (including text pages)/cinema
- Internet sites
- set up a stall at a recruitment fair or exhibition.

Deciding where to place an advertisement

You will need to assess the available advertising methods in terms of their appropriateness for a particular vacancy. Considerations will include: the likelihood of finding people with particular skills in a particular geographical location; the type of qualifications you are seeking and which publications people with those qualifications are likely to read; salary level and whether you are likely to be able to attract someone to move to your area for the salary you are offering. Obviously some judgement is required to make these decisions, but one should always be wary of making assumptions about what people will do given their personal circumstances, and one should strive to keep recruitment open and fair. It may be unfair, for example, to restrict applications to your geographical area as there may be good candidates who would be willing to move to your area for the sake of the job. That should remain the personal decision of the prospective candidate.

The costs of advertising are also a factor. You may be more willing to spend a large portion of your advertising budget on a senior post than on a junior one. However, you may have a relatively junior post that requires skills not readily available in your locality, or you may have a large number of low-paid posts and the need to fill these posts may call for the willingness to spend more on advertising.

Word-of-mouth advertising is often listed in textbooks as a possible method of recruitment, and it is used to varying extents in some organisations. It is mentioned here for clarification but excluded from the recommended list because of its potentially discriminatory effects. Organisations that recruit heavily by word of mouth run the risk of perpetuating the gender and ethnic make-up of their workforce. In general, employees tend to recommend people like themselves from among their family and friends. For example, in general, if an organisation's workforce were all white Europeans, word-of-mouth recruitment would tend to bring in more white Europeans. A commitment to equality of opportunity means that this cycle has to be broken, and one way of doing this is to advertise in the ethnic press.

Designing recruitment advertisements

First consider what the objectives of a job advertisement are, and what techniques might be used to achieve those objectives. The overall aim of the advertisement is to secure sufficient applications from suitably qualified persons with the end result that the employer will find 'the best person for the job'. Note that advertisers wish to obtain a reasonable number of applications, but not an overwhelming number. The first principle of writing job advertisements is therefore to *give sufficient information about the post so that suitable candidates will apply but also so that unsuitable candidates will be discouraged from applying.*

What will attract good applicants to a post? Consider these factors and also consider how they should be incorporated into an advertisement to achieve maximum impact. For example, is salary a major selling point for your organisation? Should salary figures be included or excluded? Should they be displayed at the top of the advertisement, in the body of the text or at the end? A job advertisement is an opportunity to tell people what you can offer as well as what you require. The following are some suggestions of the kind of factors you may wish to include in a job advertisement:

- organisation name and information
- job title and major duties
- competencies required
- opportunities and challenges
- salary and benefits
- statement of policy on important issues such as equality of opportunity
- how to apply.

Did you know?

One way of promoting one's employer brand would be to achieve a 3-star listing as a 'best company' to work for. Factors that can get you into the list include offering a fair deal, recognition, good leadership and management, good communication and providing opportunities for development. Companies that made it into the list in 2007 include Robert Half International (a recruitment consultancy), Camelot, and JJ Group (a marketing agency). You can find out more at **www.bestcompanies.co.uk**.

(*Source*: Brockett, J. (2007) Search for a star, *People Management*, 8 February, 16)

Organisation name and information

Obviously people need to know which organisation they are applying to. Information about the organisation's prospects and what it can offer as an employer can be a selling point: 80 per cent of respondents to a CIPD survey (2007, p. 22) stated that they invested in their employer brand in order to 'attract the people they wanted to recruit'.

Job title and major duties

The job title should be the one used in the job description, and the main duties should be summarised for the advertisement to give potential applicants a good idea of what the job entails.

Competencies required

The person specification/competency profile will provide a good basis for summarising the abilities you are looking for.

Opportunities and challenges

The tasks in a job can be described as requirements, but it is much more appealing to most people if you emphasise the opportunities a job will offer them to use their skills and feel a sense of achievement, and the challenges that will provide them with a chance to develop.

Salary and benefits

Every organisation will have records of the salary ranges and benefits that are attached to each job. An organisation might have a particularly attractive range of benefits that could be the deciding factor for someone deliberating on whether or not to apply for a position. You can read more about salaries and benefits in Chapter 11.

How to apply

A range of possibilities exist, and the most appropriate will depend on the particular post being filled, the volume of applications expected or desired, and the systems and capabilities of the department receiving the applications. You may request interested applicants to do any of the following:

- call in person
- attend an open day interview event
- phone/leave a message on a 24-hour answer machine requesting an application form
- write a letter applying for the post
- contact a particular person
- request and return an application form
- request further information
- send a curriculum vitae (CV) and covering letter
- send a CV or acquire and return an application form online
- apply by a certain date.

Style of writing

The style of writing that is appropriate for a job advertisement depends on the nature of the position. Traditionally, advertisements were written in a very formal style, using phrases like: 'The successful candidate will possess a university degree and two years of directly related work experience.' In recent years, most advertisements have been written in a less formal and more direct style, using 'you' as if the recruiter were speaking directly to the prospective applicant.

Other techniques that have been used to attract the reader's attention are the use of questions and bold or controversial statements such as:

Are you looking for your next challenge and an opportunity to develop your project management skills?

or

You'd have to be crazy to take on this job!

or

We can offer you long hours and tiring days . . . but plenty of rewards too.

These are acceptable techniques for producing job advertisements, but care should be taken that they are not overused, thereby losing their freshness and impact. A list of questions at the start of an advert can become tedious. Once you have caught your reader's attention, you should proceed swiftly to giving information. You should also avoid using hackneyed phrases, clichés or essentially meaningless phrases. Most employers would like to employ enthusiastic, intelligent, well-motivated and outgoing people. However, since practically no one is likely to admit to not being any of these, it seems pointless to include them as criteria in a job advertisement as they help neither qualified persons to identify themselves nor unsuitable persons to screen themselves out.

Use of colour and graphics

Organisations often use colour and graphics to draw attention to their advertisement. A company logo may be part of promoting the employer brand, and photographs can convey an impression of an organisation's culture or maybe its commitment to diversity.

Job advertisements: whose responsibility?

Depending on its particular circumstances, every organisation needs to decide who should be responsible for producing job advertisements.

There are several contingencies to consider. For instance, is the post of a routine nature, with simple duties or a job description that has not changed much? Does a previous advert exist that can be used without much change? A junior member of the HRM department could handle this or the administrative staff in any unit where this activity has been devolved to line management.

If the post is new or has changed considerably, the line manager should be more involved in deciding the content, and more expertise in composing advertisements will be needed so someone with more experience in this area and well-developed writing skills should take on the task.

If the post is difficult to recruit for (maybe due to a local skills shortage), you may consider using the specialised skills of a recruitment advertising agency. The additional cost of this would be a factor to weigh against the cost of unsuccessful recruitment attempts. Some organisations save costs by maintaining a list of preferred suppliers and negotiating special deals with them in return for putting more work their way. The general consensus about using recruitment agencies, however, seems to be that the major benefits come from a faster recruitment and selection process as these agencies may handle applications and carry out the initial sifting process, and the process may be more efficient and effective since the agencies have specialist knowledge of recruitment such as where to tap into supplies of scarce skills (CIPD, 2007a; IRS, 2007b).

If you have any doubts about your writing ability, get help! Advertisements are very expensive and very public, and can contribute to the public image of your organisation. If the requisite skill is not available within your organisation, you may have to consider using the services of an advertising agency.

Recruitment technology

As the twenty-first century progresses, the use of the Internet to advertise posts and deal with recruitment processes is becoming ever more well established, and developments in Web 2.0 technology are opening up more opportunities for innovative approaches. Vacancies for a wide range of posts are listed by some organisations on their own website, in other cases by recruitment agencies, on job boards such as Fish4Jobs and on the jobs pages of newspapers and journals. The CIPD (2006d and 2007c) reports increasing usage of e-recruitment. The 2006 CIPD report comments specifically

Did you know?

Some of the companies reported as using online recruitment successfully include Flybe, an airline based in Exeter; the Yellow Pages company, Yell UK; the insurance company Legal and General; and Loop, a contact centre operator.

(*Source: The Sunday Times*, 2007)

on various aspects of online recruitment such as the reasons for using it, and assessments of its potential. The survey report in 2007 (CIPD, 2007a, p. 12) merely makes the point that online advertising on companies' own websites had grown to equal their respondents' usage of local newspaper advertising.

One of the major reasons for using the Internet for recruitment is that it provides access to an increasingly large pool of applicants. The numbers of job-seekers online reportedly continues to grow apace. Between 2000 and 2001, the numbers grew from 4 million to 5.4 million. Both Tulip (2003) and Smethurst (2004) reported some 11 million online job-seekers in the UK in 2003/04. More recently, commentators are highlighting the impact of the spread of Broadband and the accompanying growth in the use of the Internet (CIPD, 2006b). The increased access to a large pool of applicants is not, however, unproblematic: 47 per cent of organisations reported that e-recruitment led to an increase in the numbers of unsuitable applications (CIPD, 2006d). Henkes (2007) emphasises the importance of the design and content of web-based advertising if organisations hope to make their recruitment process more effective and efficient. The CIPD (2006b) and HR Zone (2007) both raise the issue of diversity, pointing out that some potential applicants may be excluded if recruitment is limited to those who have a preference for Internet access to jobs.

Further expected advantages from e-recruitment processes are reductions in the cost of advertising and speed in completing the recruitment and selection processes.

Did you know?

A case study of Cancer Research UK (CIPD, 2006a) lists the business objectives this organisation had in adopting an online recruitment system. These included 'reduction of costs, faster and more efficient recruitment, reduction in paper-based administration, increased reach to international job seekers, efficient management of speculative applications, and maintenance of the organisation's "cutting edge" image' (p. 4). Cancer Research UK also found that 'as the candidate data is now entered directly by the candidate, there are fewer errors in the information, therefore making the process significantly more accurate' (p. 8).

The Sunday Times (2007) distributed a special supplement on uses of technology for recruitment which reviewed a number of recent innovations including: company presence on social networking sites such as Facebook and My Space; the production of podcasts offering careers advice; employee video blogs included in company websites; virtual tours of a company's premises so people can see what the physical environment looks like. Other commentators have reported on further technological advances in recruitment processes such as using text messages to inform potential applicants of vacancies (*People Management*, 2006) and candidates' use of video CVs to present themselves (HR Zone, 2007).

Did you know?

'Even visitors to video website YouTube will encounter three-minute blasts of underground creativity by guerrilla teams of workers from Ernst and Young and Price Waterhouse Coopers. Their aim? To get across the idea that accountants can get crazy, too.'

(*Source: The Sunday Times,* 2007, p. 4)

Human resource managers need to be aware of these issues and developments to maximise the effectiveness of their organisation's recruitment process.

ACTIVITY 6.5

One advantage of using a website for recruitment purposes is that organisations can provide easy access to a lot of information for prospective candidates. You can easily find some current job advertisements in the print media that include an Internet address, or you can locate companies with job vacancies via a search engine. Visit a selection of these websites to see for yourself how employers are using the World Wide Web for recruitment.

Targeted recruitment

The equality Acts and regulations described in Chapter 5 are designed to protect specified groups against unfair discrimination in employment. What they do not prescribe is affirmative action such as deliberately hiring a quota of members of any specific group to redress any imbalances. Targeted recruitment is a method of encouraging previously disadvantaged groups to apply for vacancies but, in keeping with the intention of equality legislation, any subsequent selection must be based on merit only.

Targeted recruitment can be drawn to potential applicants' attention in job advertisements in several ways:

- A statement that encourages under-represented groups to apply for a post, for example: 'We welcome applications from people with disabilities, women, and members of black and ethnic minority groups as they are under-represented in the company in positions at this level.'
- A statement not targeted at any particular specified group, but emphasising that diversity is valued and that all candidates will be assessed on merit without reference to sex, race, age, etc.
- Photographs and text that show people in non-traditional roles, thus emphasising an employer's desire to receive applications from groups that do not traditionally apply for particular posts.
- An assurance that qualified candidates with a disability will be invited to interview.
- Photographs showing a mix of men, women and members of various racial groups, ages, etc.

Employers who engage in targeted recruitment have recognised that good, able people have become discouraged from even applying for certain jobs because of a history or perception of discrimination. A number of such companies were profiled in a seminal *Personnel Management* article (Paddison, 1990). The experience of these companies was that targeted recruitment attracted a much greater pool of suitable candidates, and not only from the specified groups. There was an overall improvement in the quality of applications. Targeted recruitment, then, speaks loudly about an organisation's level of commitment to equality, and may help the organisation address equality issues *per se*, but a side-effect is that it also attracts applications from better candidates in general.

ACTIVITY 6.6

Review a number of job advertisements from a variety of sources, and comment on what you regard as poor and good factors with regard to the elements described in this chapter. For example:

- What caught your eye?
- How complete is the information about tasks, skills requirements, salary, etc.?
- Does the advert appropriately assist the reader in self-selection?
- Are important aspects of organisational culture presented, such as equality and diversity policies?

You may wish to discuss your findings with others in your class in small groups, and present your combined findings to the whole class.

Application forms

Once you have provided people with information about your vacancy, you must decide on the best way for interested candidates to present information about themselves. The major choices are:

- application form
- curriculum vitae (CV) } submitted on paper or electronically
- letter of application
- handwritten/typed submission
- personal call.

Many organisations prefer to use their own application form because of the advantages this can offer. Application forms can be designed to elicit information specific to the types of work done in your organisation. The information can be arranged so that very important information is seen first, for example, academic qualifications or membership of professional bodies which are regarded as being essential for particular posts. One advantage of application forms over CVs is that the organisation controls the information that is given, not the applicant. In this way the organisation can ensure that the same types of information are gathered from all applicants, the information is relevant to the work the organisation can offer, and information that could potentially lead to unlawful discrimination is excluded.

The application form is a bridge between the recruitment process and the selection process. Once a completed form has been received, it can be used as a basis for the initial selection exercise, but until this occurs, it is part of the recruitment process and its design should be subject to recruitment considerations. A poorly designed form – one, for example, that requests inappropriate information – could alienate potential applicants and discourage some from applying.

The design of the content and layout of an application form must also take several other factors into consideration. We have mentioned the avoidance of unlawful discrimination above, but the age discrimination regulations further sharpened the focus on the need to redesign application forms so that they would be age neutral. Forms should also address issues such as making arrangements to assist people with disabilities, monitoring for equality and diversity purposes, data protection issues, and other legalities.

Questions regarding disabilities

According to the IRS (2007a), it is permissible to ask questions on the application form about an applicant's disability, with an emphasis on what arrangements might be necessary to facilitate the application process and enable the candidate to perform the work in question.

It is also regarded as good practice to offer alternative ways of applying to accommodate disabilities. The IRS (2007a) give the following examples: application forms in Braille, on audio tape, electronic submission of applicant details.

Age neutral application forms

The age discrimination regulations have renewed the focus on competencies in the recruitment and selection process instead of concentrating on qualifications and experience. These two latter factors continue to be important, but HR and employers are being encouraged to shift their attention more simply to an assessment of a person's capabilities rather than depending, for instance, on length of experience as a yardstick. The Employers Forum on Age (EFA) (2006) has interesting information on its website about eliminating dates from the application process so that employers will focus on competencies rather than making judgements based on information that is linked to age.

Equality and diversity monitoring

Many application forms now contain an equality monitoring section so that employers can evaluate their success in attracting applications from qualified members of designated groups, and also monitor the handling of these applications at all stages of the selection process. The information on this form should be used only to provide feedback to the organisation that it is operating in a non-discriminatory fashion, and should not be used as part of the selection process. It is essential that candidates are informed about why the information is being requested and how it will be used. They should also be informed that it is not compulsory to provide this information and that this will not be detrimental to their application.

It is best if the monitoring form can be detached from the application form so that it is clear to applicants that the monitoring and selection processes are completely separate. Monitoring forms usually request information about factors which are directly addressed in the legislation on discrimination. ACAS (2005a and 2005b) recommends that employers give a great deal of thought to whether and how they introduce new categories of information into their monitoring forms as many people may feel sensitive about issues such as sexual orientation and religious belief and regard any queries about these as an invasion of privacy. It is also regarded as good practice to invite applicants to specify any special requirements that may need to be met to enable them to attend an interview (e.g. avoidance of a clash with timing of a religious festival or time of religious observance).

Data protection and other legal issues

Employers inevitably gather a lot of personal information about their candidates, so the design and handling of application forms is subject to the Data Protection Act 1998. The principles of data protection are described in more detail in Chapter 4 on the employment relationship, but the principles that obviously apply here are that the information collected should be appropriate for its intended use, it should be used only for the purpose for which it was collected and it should be handled in a secure fashion. Application forms should contain a statement to this effect and indicate that applicants should sign indicating acceptance of the organisation's stated use of their data. A sample data protection statement can be seen on the EFA website, and the issue is also addressed by the IRS (2007a). There is also detailed guidance available from the Information Commissioner's Office (2005).

All employers need to be sure that potential employees have the right to work in the UK, so application forms must request confirmation of this. This is dealt with in more detail in Chapter 8.

ACTIVITY 6.7

1 Choose an employer and design an application form that could be used for all posts within that organisation. Check that your form elicits all relevant information from applicants. Consider the design and layout of your application form: is it easy to complete; is it easy for selectors to locate relevant information?

2 Compare your application form with the sample form given on the website of the Employers Forum on Age at **www.efa.org.uk** (accessed 17.07.07).

Equality implications

In order to promote access to jobs, employers may wish to assist those with poor language skills in completing application forms. There are many posts where the duties to be performed do not require the levels of reading, writing and language ability that are necessary for a person to be able to complete an application form. Positive measures to ensure that such people are not unfairly excluded from such posts would be an example of good practice and could lead to an organisation acquiring committed employees who might otherwise have been excluded. Employers who are genuinely interested in equality and diversity would also naturally include a statement on their application forms to this effect as part of their employer branding efforts.

CVs

Although we have presented the advantages of using an application form, there are some advantages to using CVs too. If an advertisement required all applicants to submit a CV, the organisation would have eliminated the steps, and therefore the cost, of designing, producing and sending out application forms. It must be remembered, however, that preparing a CV requires a fairly good standard of writing skills, so it would not be appropriate to require this for all positions. Many advertisements for managerial posts request interested candidates to apply by sending in a CV.

Administrative procedures

The final aspect of the recruitment process we need to consider is how you are going to handle applications in addition to any data protection requirements. You will need to design administrative procedures that address the following issues:

● accepting applications by phone/walk in/electronically
● sending forms/information
● acknowledgement of applications received.

In deciding on the appropriate administrative procedures you will need to address questions about what you want to achieve, but also the question of cost. There is a public relations element in every recruitment exercise, as your organisation will have contact with many people who will not become employees, but who may be potential customers and will certainly relate to others how you treated them. You will want to create a good impression with every applicant, but the desire to do this must be tempered by the question of cost. Many organisations are now alerting potential applicants that they will not receive an acknowledgement of receipt of their application form due to rising postal costs and the number of applications expected (IRS, 2003a). A sample letter can be found in Appendix 6.1, but one alternative is to include a statement on the application form.

Global issues in recruitment

The first point to make about global recruitment issues is that the recruitment and retention of personnel, particularly in crucial leadership positions, is currently reported as one of the key issues in people management, not only on a national but also on a global basis (Ready and Conger, 2007; Wooldridge, 2006). Ready and Conger (2007) write about the talent management strategies employed by two major companies to address this challenge. For one of them, Procter and Gamble, the company's HRIS provides rapid access to 'a global database of talent profiles' (p. 70) which means that positions can readily be filled by internal talent. The system is also designed to report on the achievement of diversity goals.

Organisations recruiting for international operations can make choices about where they wish to focus their recruitment efforts. The four approaches identified by Perlmutter and Heenan (1974) are ethnocentric, polycentric, regiocentric or geocentric or indeed a combination of these.

An ethnocentric approach means that senior, and perhaps other managerial positions in overseas locations will be filled by parent country nationals. The assumption underlying such decisions is that the knowledge and expertise needed to make decisions at that level reside only in the parent country. The parent company may also wish to impose its organisational culture on overseas branches.

Polycentrism implies that people local to the particular location would be chosen to occupy managerial as well as operational positions. Regiocentrism means that the best person suited to any job at any level would be selected from within a wider geographical region, e.g. the EU, whereas geocentrism entails recruitment of talent from anywhere in the world.

Each of these approaches will have an impact on the way people in locations around the world are managed on a day-to-day basis, but ethnocentrism in particular might have an inhibiting effect in terms of freeing up the potential of diversity in the workforce. Although the contingency approach to analysing aspects of business life has been emphasised elsewhere in this text, i.e. a belief that there is normally no one interpretation that can be universally applied to business situations, Perlmutter and Heenan (1974) identify ethnocentrism as being problematic in general and something to be avoided. A polycentric approach also does not encourage the benefits of diversity as the emphasis is on local knowledge, expertise and culture. Regiocentric and geocentric approaches obviously encourage greater diversity, but this then needs to be managed in order to gain the maximum benefits.

Conclusion

This chapter has discussed the aims of recruitment and the range of policies and procedures involved in effective recruitment which is a crucial element of talent management. We have emphasised the need for a methodical approach, using job descriptions, person specifications/competency profiles and well-designed advertisements and application forms to support the process. The next two chapters will examine the processes and techniques involved in making a selection from the applications you receive.

REVIEW QUESTIONS

You will find brief answers to review questions 2 and 4 on pages 473–474.

1 Choose five current advertisements for job vacancies from different sources. Comment on the structure, content and placement of the adverts, evaluate their effectiveness and suggest improvements.

2 Describe the uses of the job description and person specification/competency profile in the recruitment process.

3 Interview someone about his or her job. Draft a job description, person specification and advertisement for the post.

4 Comment on the approaches to recruitment an employer can adopt in order to create and project a positive public image.

SELF-CHECK QUESTIONS

Answer the following multiple-choice and short-answer questions. The correct responses or page references are given on page 474 for you to check your understanding of this chapter.

1 List three things you would consider when deciding whether or not a vacancy exists.

2 Name three standard methods of advertising vacant posts.

3 List the major components you would include in a job advert.

4 Does targeted recruitment mean that members of under-represented groups will be selected in preference to other candidates? YES or NO

5 Everyone involved in selecting candidates should see the equal opportunities monitoring form. TRUE or FALSE?

HR IN THE NEWS FT

Computer says: 'You're hired'

By Jessica Twentyman

Edgars Consolidated Stores (Edcon) is something of a national institution in South Africa. Since 1929, the chain of department stores has supplied generations of South Africans with clothing and footwear, from school shoes to funeral suits.

Naturally, keeping a network of more than 1,000 stores in South Africa, Botswana, Namibia, Swaziland and Lesotho fully staffed is a big challenge for the company's human resources department, which oversees a workforce of 20,000 people – especially in the busy run-up to Christmas, when its headcount doubles.

Widespread unemployment in South Africa, meanwhile, means that for every position the company advertises, it receives approximately 100 applications, according to executive HR manager, Andrea Wiehahin.

'We're very aware of the need to handle those applications sensitively,' she says. 'Our job applicants are our customers as well, and even unsuccessful candidates need to be treated with respect, so that they go away from the experience with a positive feeling about the Edcon brand.'

To compound the issue, she adds, economic and political transformation in South Africa means that the company needs to demonstrate compliance with a complex web of government-mandated employment equity policies.

That is a big challenge, but Edcon is evidently handling it well. In a 2005 survey conducted by management consultancy Deloitte, it was named one of the 15 best companies to work for in South Africa and the best company to work for in the retail market.

Edcon makes sure it has the internet on its side. When a store manager has a vacancy to fill, they enter the details of the position on the company's new Softscape Apex HR system. It is automatically forwarded to the relevant senior manager for approval, and from there, it is posted on the career section of the company's website (www.edcon.co.za), as well as online job boards, such as Career Junction (www.careerjunction.co.za).

The e-recruitment process does not end there. Job seekers submit their applications over the internet via the website, and those applications are subsequently held and managed in the Softscape system. Around three-quarters of all applications Edcon receives are now made over the internet, says Leon Vermaak, Edcon's business integration manager.

The system's talent acquisition tools, meanwhile, enable managers to search applications, retrieve details for prospective employees, contact them and organise interviews, explains Alex Bartfeld, Softscape's director for the EMEA region.

Not only that, the system also holds a wealth of information about the company's recruitment processes, adds Ms Wiehahin, enabling the HR team to report on metrics relating to ethnic diversity in the workforce, as well as calculating the time and cost involved in bringing new hires on board.

Like Edcon, organisations around the world are finding that the internet provides the perfect platform for attracting recruits and streamlining their applications. In fact, it is critical in a world where the job of finding, attracting, selecting and securing top talent has never been more important, according to Peter Cheese, managing partner of management consultancy firm Accenture's 3,500-strong Human Performance practice.

'The thing that's driving attention on recruitment is a general shortfall of skills,' he says. 'The demographics of developed countries are against us, and that's put a great deal of pressure on how companies attract and retain talent,' he says.

Certainly, things have come a long way from the days when job seekers would frequently find that the careers section of a company's website offered no more information than a generic e-mail address for the HR department. 'A whole host of developments are fuelling e-recruitment right now: internet-enabled HR systems, e-mail, online job boards, social networking sites, virtual worlds, and so on. As a term, e-recruitment covers a huge array of tools, but they have one thing in common: the internet,' says Mr Cheese.

Take KPMG, the management consultancy, for example, or the Royal Bank of Scotland, or data storage giant EMC – all three have held careers fairs in Second Life, the online 'virtual world'. And in a recent survey of IT recruiters by the Association of Technology Staffing Companies (ATSCo), 58 per cent said that social networking sites such as LinkedIn, Facebook and MySpace are more useful for recruitment than print advertisements. Eighty-three per cent, meanwhile, said they used those sites to trawl for potential job candidates.

'Sites such as LinkedIn are an incredibly powerful form of recruitment, as it puts the power in both parties' hands – the recruiter in identifying the right candidate and the individual in deciding whether or not to engage in an offer,' says Dan Nye, CEO of LinkedIn.

'Some people are connected to hundreds of professionals across industries and borders, which in turn are connected to thousands more. This immediately places a well-connected recruiter in touch with a large number of possible candidates.'

But it is those organisations that have tightly integrated their e-recruitment tools with their back-end HR systems that have achieved the most notable successes – and that is true whether those back-end systems are hosted in-house or by a third party specialist, under the software-as-a-service (Saas) model, according to Colin Tenwick, chief executive of hosted talent management software specialist Stepstone, a company that offers both options.

'An all-encompassing e-recruitment tool won't just post vacancies to a website and capture applications,' he says. 'It will provide a robust framework for all the processes that surround bringing new recruits on board, and then managing their performance for as long as they work for you,' he says.

Such systems need to be capable of doing some pretty heavy lifting. Mobile services operator Orange, for example, uses Stepstone's i-Grasp system to process about 80 per cent of the 5,000 applications it receives each year and currently holds 50,000 CVs, says David Roberts, Orange's employer brand manager.

I-Grasp enables Orange's 200-strong HR team to promote the company culture to applicants from the first contact, he says, primarily using the company's careers portal, www.orange.co.uk/jobs, as well as a number of retail recruitment microsites.

It also helps to ensure that applicants are kept informed of the progress of their application, via e-mail and text message – and that was certainly welcome to Elly Hallwood, who joined Orange's in-house legal team as senior counsel in August this year, after applying for the job via the portal.

'I was kept informed all the way down the line,' she says. 'Moving from a law firm to an in-house legal department can be quite a transition, but the amount of information that I received from Orange regarding my application made the whole process much less stressful.'

The biggest benefits of effective e-recruitment, however, are encapsulated in two key metrics: time to hire and cost to hire. At Hyatt Hotels, for example, a hosted talent management system from Taleo has cut the process of hiring a front desk employee from four weeks to five days, according to Randy Goldberg, Hyatt's executive director of recruiting. And hotels that have moved both managerial and hourly positions online have reported a 50 per cent reduction in recruitment advertising spending.

But above all, it is quality of candidates that really counts, says Michael Gregoire, CEO of Taleo. 'If e-recruitment means you get people on board quickly and at a lower cost, then that's great, but what companies really need to know is whether they're hiring the kinds of people that have a material positive impact on their organisation,' he says.

That kind of insight, he adds, can only be achieved with a robust set of HR tools that enable companies to manage their ongoing performance in attracting and retaining talent.

Or as Mr Bartfeld of Softscape puts it: 'The story doesn't end when you click on the "hire" button.'

(FT.com, 7 November 2007, © Jessica Twentyman. Reproduced with permission)

Question

List the ways that e-recruitment can be used to improve the recruitment process.

WHAT NEXT?

Now that you have mastered the introductory level of information presented in this chapter, you may wish to take your studies to a higher level. The article cited below is an American publication, reviewing the major current issues in recruitment and selection, so it is relevant to the next two chapters in this textbook as well as this one. Ployhart describes the key issues concisely, but the great joy in reading this article is that he identifies a large number of potential research questions. For example, under the heading 'What We Know,' he states that 'Employer brand image is an effective means to differentiate the firm from competitors' (p. 877). Under the heading 'What We Need to Know,' he identifies gaps in our knowledge with questions such as 'How do organizations best acquire a brand image, present it, and manage it?' and 'How do organizations that lack a familiar brand image compete?' (p. 877).

This article can take you forward on several levels. It gives you an American perspective while reviewing concepts that are also well established in the UK. It stimulates thoughts for those who are interested in conducting research on recruitment and selection or who are maybe seeking a topic for an undergraduate or postgraduate dissertation.

Ployhart, R.E. (2006) Staffing in the 21st century: new challenges and strategic opportunities, *Journal of Management*, 32, 868–97.

References

Advisory, Conciliation and Arbitration Service (2005a) *Religion or Belief and the Workplace: A Guide for Employers and Employees*, ACAS.

Advisory, Conciliation and Arbitration Service (2005b) *Sexual Orientation and the Workplace: A Guide for Employers and Employees*, ACAS.

Chartered Institute of Personnel and Development (2006a) *HR and Technology: Beyond Delivery. Change Agenda*, CIPD.

Chartered Institute of Personnel and Development (2006b) *Online Recruitment*, CIPD (factsheet available at www.cipd.co.uk; accessed 26.10.06).

Chartered Institute of Personnel and Development (2006c) *Recruitment*, CIPD (factsheet available at www.cipd.co.uk; accessed 26.10.06).

Chartered Institute of Personnel and Development (2006d) *Recruitment, Retention and Turnover. Annual Survey Report 2006*, CIPD.

Chartered Institute of Personnel and Development (2007a) *Recruitment, Retention and Turnover. Annual Survey Report 2007*, CIPD.

Chartered Institute of Personnel and Development (2007b) *Talent Management: Research Insight*, CIPD.

Chartered Institute of Personnel and Development (2007c) *The Changing HR Function: Survey Report September 2007*, CIPD.

Employers Forum on Age (2006) *Age Neutral Policies*, EFA (available at www.efa.org.uk; accessed 17.07.07).

Fraser, J.M. (1978) *Employment Interviewing*, 5th edition, Macdonald and Evans.

Henkes, M. (2007) *E-recruitment – Sorting the Wheat from the Chaff*, HR Zone (available at www.hrzone.co.uk; accessed 22.01.07).

HR Zone (2007) *Video CVs: Is this the Future of Recruitment?* HR Zone (available at www.hrzone.co.uk; accessed 31.05.07).

Incomes Data Services (2001) *IDS Study 706: Competency Frameworks*, April, IDS.

Industrial Relations Services (IRS) (2003a) Labour saving devices, *IRS Employment Review* 774, 18 April, 34–40.

Industrial Relations Services (IRS) (2003b) Setting the tone: job descriptions and person specifications, *IRS Employment Review 776*, 23 May, 42–48.

Industrial Relations Services (IRS) (2006) Using competencies in selection and recruitment, *IRS Employment Review 853,* 18/8 (available at www.xperthr.co.uk; accessed 27.06.07).

Industrial Relations Services (IRS) (2007a) Job applications, *Employment Law Reference Manual,* 30/4 (available at www.xperthr.co.uk; accessed 27.06.07).

Industrial Relations Services (IRS) (2007b) Outsourcing the recruitment process: quality gains over quantity, *IRS Employment Review 863,* 19/1 (available at www.xperthr.co.uk; accessed 27.06.07).

Information Commissioner's Office (2005) *Employment Practices Code,* ICO.

Paddison, L. (1990) The targeted approach to recruitment, *Personnel Management,* November, 54–58.

Pearn, M. and R. Kandola (1993) *Job Analysis: A Manager's Guide,* 2nd edition, IPD.

People Management (2006) Recruiting by text, *People Management,* 26 October (available at www.peoplemanagement.co.uk; accessed 02.11.06).

Perlmutter, H.V. and D.A. Heenan (1974) How multinational should your top managers be? *Harvard Business Review,* November–December, 121–131.

Ready, D.A. and J.A. Conger (2007) Make your company a talent factory, *Harvard Business Review,* June, 69–77.

Rodger, A. (1952) *The Seven Point Plan,* National Institute of Industrial Psychology.

Smethurst, S. (2004) The allure of online, *People Management,* 29 July, 38–40.

The Sunday Times (2007) Recruiting: how technology is shaping the future, 1 July (special supplement distributed with *The Sunday Times*).

Torrington, D., L. Hall and S. Taylor (2005) *Human Resource Management,* 6th edition, Financial Times Prentice Hall.

Tulip, S. (2003) A flying start, *People Management,* 7 August, 38–43.

Whiddett, S. and S. Hollyforde (1999) *The Competencies Handbook,* CIPD.

Wooldridge, A. (2006) A survey of talent, *The Economist,* 7 October, 3–20.

Books

Advisory, Conciliation and Arbitration Service (2006) *Recruitment and Induction,* ACAS. One of the advisory booklets that provide succinct advice on good practice. Available at www.acas.org.uk; accessed 09.09.07.

Chartered Institute of Personnel and Development (2007) *Recruitment, Retention and Turnover. Annual Survey Report 2007,* CIPD. The annual surveys for several years can be downloaded from the CIPD website so it is possible to analyse developments over time. The CIPD surveys a large number of employers to report on recruitment and selection practices, and comments on trends and key issues.

Incomes Data Services (2003) *IDS Studies: Recruitment Practices,* No. 751, June, IDS. A concise overview of the basic range of both recruitment and selection practices with case studies of six employers, including Surrey Police and 3, a mobile telecommunications company.

The Guide to Recruitment Consultancies, April 2007.

The Guide to Recruitment Marketing, June 2007. These guides were distributed with *People Management,* and they appear on a regular basis. They offer the latest insights into various aspects of recruitment from specialists in the field.

Articles

Industrial Relations Services (2003) Labour saving devices, *IRS Employment Review 774,* 18 April, 34–40. An overview of what employers are doing to make their recruitment processes cost-effective.

Industrial Relations Services (IRS) (2007) Determining the needs of the job, *Employment Law Reference Manual,* 31/3. Briefly addresses factors that should be considered when drawing up a job description and person specification, followed by detailed guidance on how to handle genuine occupational qualifications and requirements.

Jackson, R. and N. Osmond (2003) How to recruit and retain older staff, *People Management,* 15 May, 46–47.

Wilkinson, A. (2004) How to use recruitment advertising agencies, *People Management*, 15 January, 44–45. The 'How to . . .' series provides concise and practical information about topics of current interest in HR.

Internet

Many recruitment agencies are now using the Internet and many newspapers also have pages on it. Interesting sources of information on the Internet that we have checked include the following:

Age Posi+ive   **www.agepositive.gov.uk**
A website dedicated to 'tackling age discrimination and promoting age diversity in employment'.

BBC World of Opportunity   **www.bbc.co.uk/jobs**
The BBC is one example of a large corporation that regularly advertises job vacancies on its company website.

Chartered Institute of Personnel and Development   **www.cipd.co.uk**
The CIPD website contains a wealth of information on various aspects of recruitment, equality and the law.

Equality and Human Rights Commission   **www.equalityhumanrights.com**
Contains the information previously found on the websites of the three former commissions dealing with sex, race and disability discrimination. Equality information relevant to recruitment can be found here.

Monster Board   **www.monster.co.uk**
A worldwide professional employment and job search agency.

Total Jobs   **www.totaljobs.com** and **www.jobability.com**
The main site acts as a recruitment agency, but also has interesting profiles of a number of organisations (NHS, Carlsberg-Tetley, easyJet) and their use of the Internet. The company has also developed a site at 'jobability' specialising in information for the disabled applicant.

Sample letter to accompany application form

XYZ Company
1 Company Lane
Companytown
XY1 1YZ

Mr D White
3 Candidate's Close
Everytown
EF3 4GH

March 18, 2009

Dear Mr White

Thank you for your query about the post of Marketing Assistant. Please complete the enclosed application form and return it to us by April 8, 2009.

We regret that we are unable to acknowledge receipt of applications. However, if you wish to enclose a self-addressed and stamped postcard or envelope, we would be pleased to return this to you to indicate that your application has been received.

The selection committee will complete its review of all applications within three weeks of the closing date, and selected candidates will then be notified of an interview date. We intend to hold interviews in the week of May 11, 2009.

If you have not heard from us before May 5, 2009, you should assume that you have not been successful on this occasion.

Yours sincerely

N Barkley

Human Resource Manager

CHAPTER 7

Selection: shortlisting and interviews

Objectives

When you have studied this chapter you will be able to:

- explain the aims of the selection process
- name and describe the steps that can be taken in the selection process
- identify typical interviewer errors and explain how to avoid them
- plan an interview process and formulate appropriate questions
- conduct an interview, assess the candidates and record your evaluation
- justify your decision and provide feedback to unsuccessful candidates.

A successful recruitment campaign will have resulted in a good number of applications from people who are suitably qualified for your vacancy, and the next task is to select the most suitable person from this number. Employers must consider who should be involved in this task and provide support in terms of policies, procedures and training. This chapter will examine these factors as well as discussing the expertise needed to participate successfully in the selection process.

As with all other aspects of people management, organisations can adopt a strategic approach towards selection. Effective selection processes, aligned to the organisation's strategic goals, add value by ensuring the necessary human resources are in place for the achievement of these goals. It is advisable, therefore, to see selection processes within this wider context.

Aims and objectives of the selection process

The ultimate goal of selection is usually expressed as 'to choose the best person for the job'. Selectors attempt to match candidates to the job requirements, predicting how well they will perform if offered the position, but they also need to ensure that the candidates fully understand all major aspects of the job so that new recruits are not likely to become disillusioned and leave within a short period of time. The objectives of the selection process, which will lead to the fulfilment of the main goal, are as follows:

- gather as much relevant information as possible
- organise and evaluate the information
- assess each candidate

in order to:

- forecast performance on the job

and

- give information to applicants

so that

- they can judge whether or not they wish to accept an offer of employment.

Collecting information

Gathering and evaluating information in order to make the selection decision can be done in a number of stages. According to the CIPD (2007a and c), the most well-established methods used include:

- shortlisting from information on application forms and CVs
- interviews of various kinds
- tests
- assessment centre
- references.

This chapter will deal with shortlisting and interviewing as these two processes tend to be used in almost all cases. Alternative or supplementary methods of gathering information for the selection decision and methods of providing information will be discussed in Chapter 8.

Policy and procedures

It is amazing how many managers still claim to be good judges of character and ability based on very short acquaintance. These managers will tell you that within a few minutes they can tell whether they are going to get on with someone, and whether that person will do well in the job. This kind of overconfidence is a major contributing factor to the low validity of interviews as a selection method. The concept of validity will be discussed in more detail later in the chapter, but it can be stated here that the strategic HRM approach would suggest that employees are too valuable a resource to be selected or rejected in such a subjective and uninformed manner.

Every effort should be made to design a methodical and objective system for selecting employees. Personal factors and perceptions cannot be totally eliminated, but having objective policies and procedures in place can help to obviate any potentially harmful effects of individual persuasions. Good selection policies and procedures provide guidance and support to line managers and others involved in the selection process to carry out this duty successfully, confident that they are following the tenets of best practice.

Selection policies, like recruitment policies, are a statement of an organisation's intentions and should normally address such issues as equality of opportunity, maybe giving information about targeted groups. A selection policy might read as follows:

> The objective of the selection process is to obtain employees who will be productive and committed members of staff, working and developing to their full potential. This organisation will select employees on the basis of merit only. Internal and disabled applicants who have the required knowledge and skills are guaranteed an interview.

Selection procedures should address the following issues:

- the stages and techniques that should be used
- who is to be involved in assessing candidates
- administrative processes.

Several factors would be decided on for each of these issues, and relevant guidelines provided. The procedures documentation might, for example, indicate that a shortlist must be prepared and interviews conducted for each vacancy; guidelines might be given on who is to prepare the shortlist and conduct the interviews, and what methods should be used to accomplish these tasks. Further issues to be addressed in selection procedures include: guidelines on non-discriminatory questioning; the appropriateness of testing; whether references should be taken up and when. All these issues will be addressed in this and the following chapter.

Shortlisting

As mentioned earlier, most employers will wish to interview a number of applicants before offering a position. In many instances, however, a successful recruitment campaign will attract more applicants than it would be possible to interview. The first step is therefore to reduce the applications to a manageable number, a process known as shortlisting. The shortlisting of applicants is, then, a selection procedure that may be performed purely on the basis of the written information that applicants have supplied or which may involve the acquisition of additional information about candidates, for example by conducting a telephone interview.

Screening written applications

Often candidates for a post give information in their applications which is not required for making a selection decision, and which could lead to accusations of unfair discrimination if it were taken into consideration. For example, candidates might describe their family situation in order to explain a gap in their employment record. Applicants also, obviously, have to give their name so that the organisation can communicate with them. A name, however, can reveal information that is not apropos to the selection process, such as gender and racial origin. A useful technique to avoid being influenced by such information is to assess the application and make notes that refer only to relevant selection criteria. Furthermore, if these notes refer to the candidates only by their initials, any information that might indicate gender or racial origin is eliminated. If the persons shortlisting refer to these notes instead of the original applications when drawing up the shortlist, they will be greatly assisted in eliminating any unconscious biases.

As well as avoiding criteria that have been designated as unlawfully discriminatory, selectors should take care to avoid considering any other criteria that are not strictly related to the candidate's ability to do the job.

Pause for thought 7.1 Before you read on about poor practices in selection, can you suggest a methodical approach to shortlisting that would be fair and effective? That is, how would you decide on the 'relevant selection criteria' referred to above?

Selectors have been known to introduce a wide range of criteria that reflect their own preconceived ideas about people's circumstances and how people are likely to act in those circumstances. This is a matter of imposing one's own assumptions on other people. Some examples of this are selectors who exclude applicants who do not live locally, assuming they will frequently be late for work or will not wish to re-locate; selectors who exclude applicants who are currently earning more than the vacancy offers; selectors who exclude people who are currently unemployed. You should even think twice before rejecting an application simply because the writing is difficult to read. Medical practitioners notoriously have poor handwriting (although this is a stereotypical image and as such should be questioned), yet they hold responsible, professional jobs.

So what is the right way to shortlist applicants? If you have read the chapter on recruitment (Chapter 6), you will remember that certain documents should be available to support the whole of the recruitment and selection process. The person specification or competency profile, in particular, plays an important role throughout the selection process. Applications should be assessed against the skills and knowledge requirements listed on the person specification, and where possible against the personal qualities, although it may be more practical to assess the latter at the interview stage. Selectors should note where candidates meet the requirements of the person specification/competency profile and where they lack the required skills and knowledge. Each application could be scored with a series of + and − signs or with numerical grades if you wish to weight the criteria you have selected. To provide you with an example, the CV that appears later in this chapter, in Activity 7.3, has been assessed in relation to the receptionist person specification in Chapter 6 (see Table 7.1).

Table 7.1 Assessment of CV with reference to person specification for a receptionist

Post: Receptionist

Attributes	Essential	Desirable
Knowledge	Knowledge of clerical systems +	Knowledge of the company −
Skills	Experience of clerical work + Experience in handling queries in person and over the telephone ? Ability to extract information from a computerised database −	Supervisory experience −
Personal qualities	Polite manner ? Ability to work under pressure ?	

Why do you think some of the skills and personal qualities listed in the person specification in Table 7.1 have been marked with a question mark?

A preliminary evaluation of most of the skills of the applicant can be made at the shortlisting stage, but in this particular instance it is not possible to judge the applicant's personal qualities, for instance, based on the information contained in the curriculum vitae. Assessment of these elements will have to be made later in the selection process, and the question marks merely indicate that no assessment can be made at present.

If possible, at least two people should undertake to shortlist from the applications received, and they should do this independently of one another. After the initial selection they can then compare their evaluations of applicants, discuss any discrepancies in their judgements and justify the decisions they have made. If the two short-listers are following the same objective process, there should be a fair amount of agreement about suitable candidates, but the involvement of two people increases the objectivity of the process and helps to eliminate the effects of individual biases. The shortlisters should end up with a ranked list of candidates using the number of pluses and minuses given to each candidate. Typically they will try to obtain six suitable candidates to be invited for interview for a single vacancy, but this number will vary according to circumstances.

Welch (1998) reported that some organisations were beginning to use the Internet in their shortlisting process for graduates in the late 1990s. By getting students to complete online career and personality questionnaires which were matched against identified competencies, it was claimed that organisations could filter out as many as 90 per cent of applications at a very early stage in the selection procedure. With more experience of this approach, however, it has been recognised that, while electronic techniques can be useful in eliminating a number of unsuitable candidates (CIPD, 2007b), some candidates may potentially also be rejected simply because they did not use the precise terminology that the IT system is set up to search for (CIPD, 2006). This type of shortlisting software must therefore be used with caution.

A shortlisting checklist

- At least two people to shortlist applications independently.
- Note where applications meet and fall short of the person specification/ competency profile.
- Separate all applications according to agreed criteria: suitable/possible/ unsuitable.
- Rank the suitable applications.
- Shortlisters to confer on person specification/competency criteria only and select suitable number to call for interview.
- Use IT systems with caution.

Telephone interviewing

The CIPD (2004) pointed out that telephone interviewing as an initial part of the recruitment and selection process was becoming more popular, particularly with the growth of call centres. For these employers, telephone skills will be an essential requirement for many jobs, and the telephone interview can be used as a legitimate method of testing the telephone manner of applicants. The Institute cautions, however, that telephone interviews should be just as structured and focused as face-to-face interviews and not be allowed to degenerate into 'just a chat over the phone'.

The IRS (2007b) state that employers may use telephone interviews as a means of reducing the costs of the selection process. They can be used to provide an initial sifting from a large number of applications or to ensure that applicants satisfy some of the basic criteria for selection before using other selection techniques which might involve more expense.

> ### Did you know?
>
> The CIPD survey of recruitment, retention and turnover (2007a) revealed that 61 per cent of employers surveyed used telephone interviews in some way during the selection process.

Face-to face interviews

Almost every employer includes a face-to-face interview as part of the selection process. The initial selection interview might be delegated to a recruitment agency or a local job centre or might be conducted over the telephone, but most employers would be reluctant to take on new employees without having met them first in person. The face-to-face interview continues to be the most popular and frequently used method of selection, even though research studies have found interviews to be poor predictors of future performance in a job (Makin and Robertson, 1986) depending, of course, on how they are conducted. Poorly conducted interviews can lead to decisions with low validity, which means that they do not test what they purport to test, i.e. ability to perform a job well. As the CIPD (2007c) points out, these limitations on the validity of the interview mainly stem from the behaviours of inexpert interviewers. A number of interviewer errors contribute to the low validity of interviews, and awareness of these is one step towards eliminating them or at least reducing their impact.

Interviewer errors

Interviewer errors arise because of the perceptual process we all use to deal with the world around us. From myriad stimuli that surround us, we select those to which we will pay attention. This process is known as perceptual selection, and what we select is determined by our own experience, personality and motivation. This means that we focus on certain aspects of our environment and ignore others. Our own experience might lead us into focusing on inappropriate stimuli in some circumstances and ignoring information that is in fact apposite. A number of such perceptual errors have been identified, and those most relevant to the selection process are described here.

The halo effect

Some candidates for interview make a very strong impression on the interviewers as soon as they enter the room. They may be well dressed and attractive, have a firm handshake and a very confident manner. Research has shown that if interviewers form an initial good impression of a candidate, this has two effects. First, this good impression tends to influence positively their interpretation of everything else that happens in the interview. Second, the interviewers will seek more positive informa-tion to confirm their initial judgement. This is known as the halo effect, but it can also happen with an initial negative impression. This is sometimes referred to as the horns effect and can be detected when interviewers start to seek negative information to confirm their first impressions.

Making snap decisions

It is often said of interviewers that they make up their minds about a candidate in the first five minutes and then do not change their assessment of that person's suitability. In terms of the perceptual process this means that interviewers are responding to a limited range of stimuli and not taking the opportunity to elicit a wide range of information.

Hiring people like oneself

There is an innate human tendency to identify with people who are like us and share several of our characteristics. An outgoing person may feel more comfortable with other extroverts and the opposite is true for a more reserved person. These character-istics do not, however, necessarily equate with the ability to perform a job, and it is probably detrimental to an organisation to have only like-minded people on its staff. If interviewers fall prey to this tendency, they are said to be hiring in their own image.

Stereotyping

Allowing one's stereotyped images of people to influence selection decisions is prob-ably the most dangerous of the perceptual errors, and could very often equate to some form of unlawful discrimination. Stereotyping occurs when a person is identi-fied primarily with some group that he or she belongs to and then is assumed to have a range of characteristics that are thought to be common to all members of that group. Some examples of stereotypes are: that Scots are frugal; that all students are irresponsible and lazy; that Americans are brash and loud. It is not possible for all members of a group to have the same characteristics, and we should all guard against forming biases of this nature.

Making assumptions

The halo effect, making snap decisions and stereotyping are all specific forms of as-sumptions based on limited information, but making assumptions can also be a more generalised fault. There are many instances where inexpert interviewers might tend to impose their own personal view of how they would act in particular circum-stances, instead of ascertaining how the interviewee would act. One example of this is assuming that women will bear the major responsibility for child care, or that women are less likely to move their families to take up a new post.

Gathering insufficient or irrelevant information

Again, all the specific perceptual errors discussed in this section could be attributed to gathering insufficient or irrelevant information. Interviewers obviously need to be aware of this as a general fault and make sure they use proper techniques to counteract it.

The contrast effect

Imagine yourself in the following scenario. You are a final year student and you have been asked by one of your lecturers to judge presentations being made by students in the first year of your course. You are using a scale of 1–5, with 1 being poor and 5 being excellent. You watch one presentation and the student makes a really poor job of it. The presentation is boring, too long and the student uses no visual aids. You rate this presentation as poor and give it a score of 1. The next student gives a presentation which is somewhat better, and it is a relief to you that this presentation is not as boring. The contrast between the two presentations is likely to have an effect on your judgement, and you will probably rate the second presentation higher than you would have done on some objective measure. If the presentation actually merits a 3, you may rate it as a 4 because of the contrast with the preceding poor presentation. This is known as the contrast effect. It means that candidates at interview may be rated more highly than they merit by interviewers because they were preceded by a poor candidate, and by contrast they appear to be better than they are in reality.

Interviewer errors: summary

- Making snap decisions.
- Gathering negative/positive information to support first impressions.
- Hiring in one's own image.
- Stereotyping.
- Making assumptions; imposing one's personal view of how one would act in other people's personal circumstances.
- Gathering insufficient/irrelevant information.
- Contrast effect.

Eliminating interviewer errors

As stated earlier, the very fact that you are aware of interviewer errors can help you to eliminate them if you wish to do so and if you make a conscious effort while you are interviewing. There are also some techniques that you can deliberately employ to diminish the effects of interviewer errors.

Gather sufficient information

This is a general rule that will help to eliminate most interviewer errors. The interviewer should not decide early in the interview that a candidate is unsuitable and then fail to pursue the whole range of information necessary to make a proper decision. Interviewers who persist in gathering information even when a candidate has initially made a poor impression are achieving several goals that may contribute to better decisions:

- They are resisting the halo/horns effect.
- They are making an effort to gather the full range of information.
- They are giving candidates every opportunity to present themselves fully.

Structured interviews

Conducting interviews in a structured fashion will also contribute to the aim of gathering sufficient information on all candidates. Structured interviews involve the following steps:

- Design a set of questions to elicit information relevant to the selection decision.
- Provide all candidates with an opportunity to answer this complete set of questions.

Pause for thought 7.3 How would you go about designing a relevant set of questions? Why should you ask all of the questions of each candidate?

The way to design the basic set of questions for a structured interview is, of course, to refer to the person specification/competency profile and the job description, and to create questions related to the tasks, knowledge, skills and personal qualities listed there. The quality of the information gained will be influenced by the types of question asked, and this is dealt with later in this chapter.

Asking all candidates the same questions means that you will have a similar profile for each candidate which you can compare and use to assess each candidate against the others. Notice that the structured interview gives you a basic set of comparable details; you may wish to supplement this with individualised information on each candidate, clarifying particular details of their experience, etc. In other words, the structured interview guarantees that you will collect certain information, but it is not a straitjacket that restricts you to that information. The CIPD (2007c) refers to this as semi-structured interviewing which allows for the gathering of a wider range of relevant information and which may make candidates feel more comfortable. As well as preparing and using the questions for the structured interview, the interviewer must be adept at using probing questions, as described later.

Giving all candidates an opportunity to respond to a set of questions can also help to diminish the halo effect and gives a nervous candidate time to relax and do better as the interview proceeds. Preparing a set of questions in advance also means that interviewers:

- can relax during the interview and concentrate on the candidates' responses, rather than be thinking about what to ask next
- are less likely to inadvertently ask questions that may be construed as discriminating illegally.

More than one interviewer

In general, the one-on-one interview is not regarded as best practice for selection purposes. The IRS (2007a) identified that 98.7 per cent of employers in their study on selection processes involve at least two interviewers for some of their posts. One reason for this is to do with equal opportunities; the interviewer errors that arise because of individual perceptions are less likely to occur if more than one person is involved in interviewing.

The people involved in the selection process will vary from one organisation to another depending on factors such as size, management philosophy and organisational culture. The IRS (2007a) has, however, identified an increasing trend of devolution of selection responsibilities to line managers. Obviously, line managers know most about the work that needs to be done and are well-placed to judge whether candidates have the appropriate knowledge, skills and personal qualities. However, as the IRS (2007a) also points out, selection interviewing demands particular skills, so most employers recognise the need for training for line managers and others to be able to carry out this duty successfully.

Since human resource management specialists often hold responsibilities for an organisation's equal opportunities programmes, they often have some input into the interviewing process even if increased devolution of responsibilities to line managers means that there is not always an HR presence at the interview itself.

Consideration can also be given to involving others affected by the post, such as co-workers or members of other departments. Acceptance of the new employee can be increased if others are involved in the selection process, but this must be balanced against unwieldiness and, of course, everyone involved in interviewing must be trained.

Only trained people involved in interviews

Although the people involved in interviews may have different interests, they should all be working towards the same outcome, i.e. to select the best person for the post in a fair and objective manner. Training for interviewers usually includes an awareness of equal opportunity issues and development of questioning skills.

Allow sufficient time for interviews

In 1995 the BBC broadcast a series of programmes showing the recruitment processes followed by a number of organisations; one of the managers who took part in these programmes commented on the length of a courtship that precedes the decision to marry compared with the length of a selection interview on which one will base the decision about someone one may be working with on a daily basis for many years. He expressed a great sense of unease about the need to make such an important decision on such short acquaintance. Given what we have said in this chapter about the need to gather full information from candidates through careful questioning, it is self-evident that sufficient time must be allocated to the interview for this to occur.

Eliminating interview errors: summary

- Gather sufficient information.
- Allow adequate time.
- Structured interviews: gather the same, job-related information from all candidates.
- More than one interviewer.
- Only trained people involved in interviews.

CASE STUDY 7.1 Selection

George, the HR Manager, and Ruth, one of the HR assistants, were both conducting preliminary interviews of candidates for the post of PR assistant in the busy public relations department of a large organisation. The PR assistant would have to deal directly with the general public, sometimes with extremely irate people, and would also have to communicate with the press. George and Ruth had decided to interview the candidates separately and then get together to compare their impressions. Ruth was rather inexperienced at interviewing as she was new to the HR office. She was a quiet person who liked to approach work in a calm, methodical manner.

Ruth particularly liked one of the candidates, Jane Marsden. Jane seemed somewhat tense at the beginning of the interview, and Ruth empathised with this as she had recently gone through a number of interviews herself before she got her current job. Ruth got Jane to relax by talking about her interests, and her feeling that Jane was an interesting person was confirmed by the discovery that they shared interests in learning languages and travelling abroad. Ruth went on to tell Jane a little about the job, and Jane said she thought it sounded very interesting. Ruth also confirmed that Jane had actually dealt with customer complaints in previous positions.

Ruth noted the following points in her assessment of Jane:

- turned up for the interview well dressed and looking professional
- showed enthusiasm for the job
- has relevant experience.

She also wrote: 'Jane makes a good impression. I'm sure she'll be good at the job.' Ruth reflected that the other two candidates she'd seen that morning hadn't seemed as enthusiastic as Jane, weren't as smart in appearance and hadn't been very expansive about their experience.

When they got together to discuss the candidates afterwards, Ruth recommended Jane to George, but George responded by saying: 'Well, when I asked her to describe her experience of dealing with an irate customer, she told me that she had always worked in offices dealing only with correspondence. I think some of the other candidates have more suitable experience.'

Questions

1 Identify the perceptual errors that may have occurred in this case.

2 Suggest what George might do to help Ruth to avoid such errors in the future.

Look at the companion website at www.pearsoned.co/foothook for some suggested answers to these case study questions.

Interviewer skills

In addition to the techniques you may wish to employ to avoid common interviewer errors, there is a range of skills you can develop to ensure your effectiveness as an interviewer. Since we have established that both HRM specialists and line managers should be involved in selection interviews, these skills are important to both. The skills are presented below, followed by a more detailed discussion:

- Carry out thorough planning and preparation for the interview.
- Put candidates at their ease.

- Keep body language and tone of voice neutral.
- Ask a range of relevant questions.
- Encourage the candidate to talk.
- Record the information.
- Invite and respond to candidates' questions.
- Close the interview.
- Evaluate information and reach a decision.
- Record and justify the decisions.

Planning and preparation

The list of interview skills could almost double as a list of interview stages, and indeed the planning stage entails thinking through and planning the whole process, especially if you are responsible for coordinating it. This includes:

- arranging for the reception of candidates
- ensuring you have a private room available where you will not be interrupted
- reviewing the application forms so that you are properly informed about candidates
- reviewing the job description and person specification/competency profile so you are properly informed about the requirements of the position
- preparing the interview questions
- designing an assessment scheme in order to evaluate the candidates
- ensuring everyone knows what role he or she is to play in the process.

Put candidates at ease

It is widely acknowledged that most job applicants feel nervous about interviews, and this anxiety may be increased if the candidate is faced by a panel of interviewers or a series of interviews with different people. In some cases, interviewers deliberately subject candidates to stress, arguing that they wish to test the person's ability to handle stress in the job (see Figure 7.1).

A counter-argument to this is that the interview situation is stressful enough anyway, so there is no need to induce stress artificially. If one of the main objectives is to acquire as much information as possible from candidates, it is probably better on balance to try to get candidates to relax and talk freely. It is also worth remembering that for every candidate who eventually joins your organisation, there may be five or more for whom the interview is their only contact with you. It is better for an organisation's public image if these five leave the interview feeling they were treated properly.

Pause for thought 7.4   Make a list of three things you could do to help put interviewees at ease.

The techniques you might use to help put candidates at ease include:

- making introductions and explaining the interview process so that candidates have a chance to settle in before they have to respond to questions
- engaging in small-talk about the traffic difficulties, how the candidate travelled to your location, etc.
- starting the interview with easy questions that entail straightforward description rather than opinion or interpretation, for example: 'What are your major duties in your current post?' rather than 'How do your current duties make you qualified for this position?'

Figure 7.1 How not to put candidates at ease

Keep body language and tone of voice neutral

While interviewers should encourage applicants to open up and divulge relevant information, it is important that they do not overly influence candidates during interviews by indicating whether or not the candidate is doing well. This is especially so if a candidate starts out with weak responses, as any sign of impatience or boredom on the part of the interviewer will no doubt make the candidate more nervous, contributing to the horns effect.

Questioning techniques

In addition to using a variety of types of question, there is another component of effective information gathering that is probably just as important as asking the right questions. That is *listening*.

It is difficult to concentrate for prolonged periods of time, and often recruiters will find themselves involved in a series of interviews stretching over many hours or even a number of days. Interviewers need to become practised in the techniques of active listening (Rogers and Farson, 1976) to ensure that they maintain their concentration and gather as much information from the interviewee as possible. In general, active listening refers to the development of listening skills to promote better communication. It includes the use of reflective responses to develop and check understanding, but also involves a range of techniques to reassure the partner in conversation that he or she is being listened to. Reflective responses are used when the interviewer is trying to gain a better understanding of an interviewee, using a variety of techniques to encourage the interviewee to talk. Reflective responses include silence, non-committal conversational sounds, paraphrasing and asking questions to seek clarification of what an interviewee has said.

Silence; conversational sounds; non-verbal cues

These techniques are meant to encourage the other person to continue talking so he or she may go on to give you additional relevant information. Silence must be used judiciously, since a prolonged silence could lead to embarrassment and would inhibit communication rather than promoting it. Using silences merely means not jumping in too quickly to fill a pause; allow the other person to gather his or her thoughts. The term 'conversational sounds' refers to those companionable sounds we make to reassure someone who is talking that we are in fact listening. We use phrases such as: 'Yes, I see', 'Mmm', 'Oh, right', often accompanied by a nod of the head, a questioning frown or a smile. Consciously practising these techniques also ensures that you do not do too much of the talking.

Paraphrasing and asking for clarification

Paraphrasing what a person has said demonstrates active listening because you have to have listened carefully in order to do it. Summarising back to a person what you understand them to have said may at times also lead to further clarification as the person confirms or amends your understanding in response. Asking for clarification of a specific point again confirms that you were listening attentively and elicits more information.

Further techniques

As mentioned before, body language is important and can influence the proceedings. Maintaining good, but appropriate, eye contact with the interviewee, looking interested and not yawning or looking bored are all components of active listening.

Actively practising these techniques will help the interviewer to stay alert and concentrate on what the interviewee is saying. A further effect of active listening is that the interviewee is constantly reassured of your attention, which makes him or her more comfortable with the process.

Types of question

There are a number of ways of phrasing a question, and each will have an effect on the likely response. In choosing which type of question to ask, you should consider what the purpose of the question is. What type of information do you wish to elicit from the candidate?

The three basic forms of question are the closed question, the leading question and the open question. The closed question invites a response of 'yes' or 'no'; the leading question indicates to the interviewee what kind of response is expected; the open question is phrased in such a way that the interviewee is encouraged to speak freely and give information about himself or herself. Here are some examples of each type of question, together with a comment on what sort of response might be expected.

Closed questions

- Did you work with a computer at XYZ Ltd?
- Have you had sales experience?

Comment

Each of these questions could be answered by a simple response 'yes' or 'no'. If the interviewer is trying to elicit as much information as possible, these questions are not very useful. Closed questions can, however, be useful for checking the correctness of information. An example might be: 'Did you use Excel on the computer at XYZ Ltd?'

Pause for thought 7.5 Before you go on to read about leading questions and open questions, stop to rephrase the two closed questions in the example above as open questions. That is, how would you put these questions so that an interviewee would be encouraged to speak more freely?

Leading questions

- You do enjoy working with the computer, don't you?
- You have had sales experience, haven't you?

Comment

The phrasing of these questions implies that an affirmative response is expected of the candidate. At the very least this will destroy the confidence of a candidate who answers in the negative. It could also induce a nervous candidate to give false information on the spur of the moment. It is so easy just to answer 'yes' to questions like those above.

Open questions

- What experience have you had of working with a computer?
- Tell me about your experience working with a computer.
- What did you like about working in sales?
- How did you decide to take up a career in personnel management?

Comment

None of these questions can be answered with a one-word answer, neither do they indicate what the questioner expects to hear. Open questions usually start with words like what, why or how. Alternatively, the interviewee can simply be asked to talk about something: 'Tell me about . . .'

It should be obvious that the majority of the questions in an interview should be phrased as open questions, with relatively few closed questions to check facts. Leading questions are not very useful and should be avoided.

Did you know?

According to the CIPD survey of recruitment and selection processes published in 2003, there was a marked increase in the number of employers using competency-based interviews to improve their selection decisions. The percentage of respondents using these rose from 25.8 per cent in 2002 to 58.7 per cent in 2003 (CIPD, 2003). More recently, the IRS (2007b) has reported that 69.7 per cent of employers are using competency-based questions in their employment interviews. This is good evidence that employers recognise the value of this type of questioning.

Situational and behavioural questions

It is a fairly straightforward task to gather information about qualifications and skills by careful questioning and listening and by using a variety of tests. Assessing attitudes and interpersonal skills is more difficult. Situational and behavioural questions are suitable for this purpose, as well as for assessing skills and how these would be translated into behaviour in the workplace. Research has long since indicated that the use of these two types of question improves both the reliability and the validity of selection interviews (Latham *et al.*, 1980; Weekley and Gier, 1987).

More recently, the IRS (2003) reported on employers' attempts to improve the effectiveness of their selection processes by using competency-based questions, and further to that, the IRS (2007b) report that they are increasingly in common usage. These are essentially behavioural or situational questions based on a competency framework where such a framework is in place.

Both types of question require an analysis of critical incidents in the job. Interviewers can ascertain what would be critical incidents in the post using methods like those used to draw up a job description or to develop criteria on which to appraise a person's performance or evaluate a post. You will be able to read about the last two issues in Chapters 10 and 11. For the purposes of selection, you will need to design questions that will get candidates to talk about their performance in these areas and the competencies they would call upon (situational) or have demonstrated in the past (behavioural).

Situational interview questions

The interviewee is presented with a situation that represents a typical incident in the job for which he or she is being interviewed, and is then asked to describe what he or she would do in this situation.

The responses to a situational interview question need to be assessed carefully in order to achieve increased reliability between interviewers. There should be prior agreement on what constitutes a poor, an acceptable and a good answer to the question. A model of each type of answer should be designed, and points can be assigned to each level of response. Each interviewer then grades the actual answers of interviewees accordingly.

Latham *et al.* (1980) describe a fairly complex manner of designing the graded responses to situational questions, involving knowledge of what was said by previous candidates who turned out to be poor, average or good performers. For most interview situations in practice it is probably adequate for managers to suggest the type of behaviour that they would regard as poor, average and good performance.

An example of a situational question and graded answers for the receptionist post described in Chapter 6 is shown in Figure 7.2.

Behavioural interview questions

Behavioural questions are normally phrased in a standard way. They are similar to situational questions in that the interviewee is presented with a situation that represents a typical incident in the job for which he or she is being interviewed. The interviewee is then asked to recount what he or she did in a similar situation in a past position. Candidates may also be informed that competency in a particular area is required, and asked to recount the circumstances in which they have demonstrated that competency. Although this is a very useful approach, there are disadvantages compared to situational interview questions:

● Candidates who do not have any previous experience of the specific incidents will be at a disadvantage. Candidates may also not have had the opportunity to demonstrate a particular skill and yet may well be capable of developing it, given the chance. Interviewers will have to decide whether it is the previous experience that is important or the way people would behave in a given situation.

Figure 7.2 Example of a situational question with graded answers

---

Critical incident

Dealing with several customer enquiries simultaneously, maintaining a customer-centred approach and a friendly manner.

Situational question

One of the assistant receptionists has just gone to the cafeteria for his 15-minute coffee break and the other one is working in a nearby office on some invoices that have to be cleared this morning. You have just answered the phone and the caller has a query to which you don't know the answer. Suddenly a number of people come to the reception desk at the same time, so you have a queue of people wanting assistance. How would you handle this situation?

Ranked answers

3 (poor performance)
- Ask the caller to call back in the afternoon.
- Deal with the people at the reception desk.
- Find out the answer to the phone query.

4 (average performance)
- Ask the caller to hold.
- Deal with the people at the reception desk.
- Find out the answer to the phone query and deal with the phone caller.

5 (good performance)
- Explain the need to find out data to the phone caller, and offer to call back.
- Apologise for the delay to the people at the reception desk, and recall the assistant receptionist to the reception area. Deal with the customers together.
- Find out the answer to the phone query and call the customer back.

- It is not possible to design and rank expected answers, as candidates may respond with reference to a wide range of examples of when they encountered similar situations. It should be possible, however, to identify the range of skills and competencies you would expect candidates to allude to in their answers.

An example of a behavioural question for the receptionist post is: 'Tell us about an incident when you had to deal with several things at the same time.'

ACTIVITY 7.1

1 Choose a job and design a situational and a behavioural question for it. The job could be one you have experience of or know something about, or one for which you have found an advert in the press or online.
2 Try out your questions on members of your class. Judge the usefulness of the responses in terms of making a selection decision.

ACTIVITY 7.2

For a more complex exercise in designing behavioural questions, go to the student materials for Chapter 7 on the companion website at **www.pearsoned.co.uk/ foothook**, and find the additional activity there based on a *People Management* article about employee engagement and how to phrase questions to elicit information about underlying attitudes which may demonstrate the likelihood of an applicant becoming an engaged employee (McGee, 2006). The concept of employee engagement was dealt with in Chapter 3, so it may help to read that chapter again before embarking on this exercise.

Probing questions

Interviewers need to get over their inhibitions about pursuing information, and practised interviewers often go back to clarify what candidates have said before. The interview is essentially a one-time-only opportunity for both the interviewer and the candidate, and if candidates seem evasive, they may legitimately not realise what you want to know. It is fairer to do all you can to gather relevant information than to superimpose your own assumptions; you should find some polite but insistent way of doing it. It is better to reject someone for something you know than for an assumption made because information was missing.

Within this context it should be noted that interviewers will have to ask individualised questions to obtain clarification related to individual applicants. The set of questions designed for the structured interview is not meant to inhibit the collection of relevant information.

Questions to be avoided

In spite of what we have said about relating interview questions to the job description and person specification for the post, you will still no doubt encounter many interviewers who ask questions that do not seem to have been designed in this way. Some very general questions have almost become standard fare in interviews, such as:

- What are your strengths and weaknesses?
- Where do you see yourself in five years' time?
- Tell me about yourself.

Such questions might elicit relevant information, but they are vague, and given the time constraints of the interview process, it is better for the interviewer to focus more narrowly on essential information.

There are other questions that do not overtly contribute much to the selection process, apart perhaps from attempting to relax a nervous candidate by asking easy questions. These include questions like 'What were your favourite subjects at school?' or 'What do you do in your spare time?' In the limited time available for an interview, there are job-related questions that can be answered in a straightforward fashion which can be used to help candidates relax and which will contribute more to the proceedings. Such a question might be: 'Tell me what you do on a typical day at work.'

It should also be borne in mind that questions about what an applicant does outside of work may be regarded as an infringement of a person's right to respect for their private and family life under the Human Rights Act 1998. Candidates may also feel pressured by such questions into giving information that could potentially be perceived as unlawfully discriminatory, for example if a person is heavily involved in a religious group in his or her spare time or participates in gay rights campaigns. The widening scope of equality legislation reinforces the fact that employment interviews should focus on work issues and not personal matters. Indeed, the ACAS guidelines on how to implement the sexual orientation regulations recommend the avoidance of questions on a person's social life and the guidelines on the religion and belief regulations recommend the avoidance of questions on communal involvement (ACAS, 2005a and 2005b).

A third variety of questions of dubious merit consists of those that seem intended to put candidates on the defensive, including statements such as, 'You seem to think very highly of your interpersonal skills.'

All these questions should be judged against what they are meant to achieve. Better results are achieved by interviewers who concentrate on formulating questions related to the job and the skills, knowledge and qualities needed to perform well in the post. It bears repeating here that your questions should be linked to the job description and person specification/competency profile, that you should be able to demonstrate that this is the case and that you should be able to justify why every question is being asked.

Discriminatory questions

If you conduct structured interviews with a planned set of questions that have been designed on the basis of a properly constructed person specification, you are unlikely to ask any questions that are discriminatory in terms of the SDA, the RRA or any of the other equality regulations. The implication behind your questions is that if you ask the question, you intend to use the information to make your decision. Avoid any question that would result in your acquiring information on things the legislation or your policies have said would constitute unfair discrimination, for example marital status, race, age of dependants.

One procedure that is often recommended to avoid accusations of unfair discrimination under the SDA is to ask the same questions of all candidates, both male and female. This will supposedly preclude any suspicion of an intention to discriminate against female applicants. However, in today's society there is still generally an expectation that women bear more responsibility for child care than men. If a young woman said she had two children under the age of five, and a young man said the same thing, most people would draw different conclusions about the relative impact of this.

These assumptions are based on each individual's experiences and are not necessarily true for other people. It is best practice, therefore, simply to avoid questions about personal circumstances unless there is some specific element of the job, such as the ability to undertake shift work, where personal circumstances are in fact relevant. Even then, candidates can be asked whether something like shift work will cause them any problems, rather than the interviewer's imposing his or her own view of whether or not the applicant should undertake such work. The Equal Opportunities Commission provided further advice on discriminatory questions on its website, and this can now be found on the website of the Equality and Human Rights Commission (**www.equalityhumanrights.com.uk**; accessed 12.10.07).

Questions for candidates with little or no work experience

We have firmly established that it is best practice to acquire work-related and job-specific information from applicants to make good selection decisions. However, we must concede that a modified approach may be necessary when dealing with individuals who have no work experience, little work experience or no recent work experience. Typical examples we can identify include:

● school leavers
● students graduating from college and university
● the long-term unemployed.

Pause for thought 7.6   Review what we have said about questioning techniques, and consider how you might have to adapt your approach if you were interviewing an applicant in this category.

Asking open questions about work experience related to the tasks involved in the vacancy would obviously not be very productive with this group of applicants. However, it should still be possible to ask about relevant transferable skills. The interviewer might need to give fuller explanations about the requirements of the organisation before asking about the applicant's related knowledge and abilities. You should have identified that situational questions are suitable for people with little experience, so it would make sense to develop such questions in this case rather than behavioural questions. In addition, interviewers faced with people who are not currently accustomed to the working environment might recognise the potential for increased nervousness, and therefore decide to spend more time at the commencement of the interview on putting the applicant at ease.

Before we leave this discussion of the interviewer's questions, we should once again emphasise that it is more important for the candidate to talk than the interviewer. Interview questions are designed as keys to unlock information, and sometimes a pause to allow the candidate time to reflect can be more effective than jumping in with a new question.

Encourage candidates to talk

Proper formulation of questions should ensure that the candidate does most of the talking and not the interviewers. However, it is worth repeating that allowing candidates to talk to obtain the information you need is the objective of the interview, and interviewers should practise due restraint.

For all questions, you should decide in advance what it is you are trying to find out with the question; you can then rephrase and probe if the candidate does not respond with the expected information.

Record the information

You could simply note how each candidate scored on the criteria you are using to assess applicants, but it is much more helpful to have a record of what the candidate actually said. This means that it is necessary for someone to take notes during the interview. It is difficult to take notes, pay attention to what the candidate is saying and keep a normal flow of conversation going, but interviewers develop this skill with experience. Alternatively, roles/tasks can be shared among a panel of interviewers by pre-arrangement. It is also best to explain to candidates what you are doing and why someone is taking notes.

ACTIVITY 7.3

As Office Services Manager, you have received the CV shown in Figure 7.3 for the position of receptionist described in Chapter 6. The HR trainee has prepared three sets of questions, and asked you which set you would like to use in the interviews.

1 Review the following sets of questions and choose the one that you feel would get the best results. Give reasons for your choice and state why you rejected the other two sets.

2 Develop any further questions you would like to ask.

3 Use the chosen, revised set of questions as a basis for mock interviews with members of your class, using the data on the applicant's CV as the interviewee's background. Evaluate whether or not you have obtained sufficient information to make a selection.

Interview questions

Set 1

1 I see you've been with Marvel Appliances for a year. Do you like working there?
2 How do you think your past work experience has prepared you for this job?
3 Can you tell us of a time when you had to deal with several things at the same time?
4 One of our assistant receptionists is male and he's older than you. Do you think you'd have any problems being his supervisor?
5 What do you think contributes to good customer care?

Set 2

1 I see you've been with Marvel Appliances for a year. Can you tell me a little about what you do there on a typical day?
2 How do you think your past work experience has prepared you for this job?
3 I'd like to describe a typical situation you might encounter in this post, then ask you how you would respond to it.

   One of the junior receptionists has just gone to the cafeteria for his 15-minute coffee break and the other one is working in a nearby office on some invoices that have to be cleared this morning. You have just answered the phone and the caller has a query to which you don't know the answer. Suddenly a number of people come to the reception desk at the same time, so you have a queue of people wanting assistance. How would you handle this situation?
4 Can you describe any supervisory experience you have had?
5 What do you think contributes to good customer care?

Set 3

1 I see you've been with Marvel Appliances for a year. Why do you want to leave?
2 How do you think your past work experience has prepared you for this job?
3 Can you tell us of a time when you had to deal with several things at the same time?
4 What kinds of hobbies do you have?
5 If we employed you, how long do you think you would stay with us? What about your personal plans for the future?

Go to the student materials for Chapter 7 on the companion website at www.pearsoned.co.uk/foothook to find our comments on these sets of questions.

Figure 7.3   Example of a curriculum vitae

CURRICULUM VITAE

Joan Reives

Address:	23 Burns Street
	Dorton
	Manchester
	M16 9BF

Telephone: 0161 000 000 (home)   0161 000 000 (work)
0777 66 000 000 (mobile)

Education:

2005	Stalybridge High School	6 GCSEs incl English and Maths
2007	Stalybridge College	3 A-levels (Business Studies, English and History)

Employment:

July 2007–present   Assistant Receptionist, Marvel Appliances
My duties include welcoming visitors to the company, and calling the person they wish to see to the reception area.
I operate the switchboard and transfer calls to other employees. I perform clerical and administrative tasks for all departments when reception duties allow.

July–Sept 2006   Sales Assistant, Allgood's Department Store
I assisted customers to choose purchases and completed cash or credit card transactions.

Personal statement:
I have lots of experience as an assistant receptionist and working with customers. I am ambitious and hardworking and I know I could do a good job as a receptionist. I think I am ready for a promotion.

References available on request.

Candidates' questions

It is good practice in an interview, usually at the end, to allow candidates an opportunity to ask questions about the post. Remember that both parties can benefit from the interview being a two-way process; it is important that prospective employees find out about the job and the organisation so that they can make an informed decision if offered the post. This may help to avoid the situation where someone is hired, only to decide after a short while that he or she is not suited to the job. As well as responding to candidates' questions, organisations can employ other techniques to supply information to applicants. Some of these, such as supplying job descriptions and organisational literature, are relevant to the recruitment process, and others, such as realistic job previews, usually take place during the selection process. Realistic job previews are discussed more fully in the next chapter. Company web pages are also an excellent source of information for candidates.

Close the interview

To close the interview, the interviewer should thank the interviewee for attending and inform him or her of what to expect next. This may include a second stage of interviews for selected candidates, a variety of tests, the time frame for the decision and details about how candidates will be informed about the outcome.

Evaluate information

Even if the interview has been carefully structured, with the involvement of several interviewers and the use of a range of well-designed questions, there is still a temptation at this stage to revert to making a decision based on gut feeling or the overall impression that candidates have made. In order to achieve a more objective evaluation of the mass of information that has now been gathered, it is possible to devise a scoring system, either for the answers to interview questions or for the elements of the person specification. Marks can be allocated to each question and questions can be weighted according to their relative importance. It would also be possible to stipulate that a candidate should achieve a pass mark on a question of particular significance in order to be considered further. For example, candidates for an HR position might be rejected for giving an unacceptable answer on a sex or race discrimination issue, no matter how well they performed in the rest of the interview.

A numerical score for each candidate will allow the interviewers to create a ranked order of candidates following an agreed method. Another system that could be used is quite simply to mark the person specification/competency profile for each candidate, + for the criteria that have been met, and − for those that have not. The use of essential and preferred categories implies some weighting of elements.

Record and justify decision

The methodical approach described in the previous section means that it should be easy for the selection panel to justify why they have selected the chosen candidate and why the others have been rejected. All reasons for the decisions reached should be expressed in terms of where candidates did or did not meet the criteria stipulated in the person specification/competency profile.

It is important to keep a written record of these factors for several reasons:

- To be able to present evidence of a proper and fair procedure should a candidate decide to pursue a case under any aspect of the equality legislation.
- To be able to provide feedback to candidates who request it. Increasingly, applicants for posts do this in their quest to make a good impression and to improve their chances of finally securing a post. As you will read in the next chapter, there is an obligation to provide information to candidates who have completed psychometric tests, but it is part of an organisation's good image to be able to respond to requests of this nature from rejected applicants in any case.
- To ensure that interviewers follow a rigorous and methodical process.

Monitoring for equal opportunities purposes

On a longer-term basis, it is important for the human resource management department to monitor the selection process in order to ensure that no unlawful or unfair discrimination is taking place, to keep managers informed of the organisation's performance in terms of equal opportunity and to initiate appropriate programmes should any issues need to be addressed. Monitoring involves analysis of the information gathered on the equality monitoring section of the application form, and would normally relate to different stages of the recruitment and selection process:

● who applied for the position
● who was called for interview
● who was selected after the interview, either to be hired or to proceed to further stages.

Monitoring during the selection process, then, continues the monitoring process that should commence during the earlier recruitment stages, as described in earlier chapters. Monitoring for equality is regarded as good practice in general, but it is actually a legal requirement of public sector organisations with regard to racial, gender and disability equality. It may also provide relevant information and documentation, should an employer need to respond to an accusation of discrimination in an employment tribunal, as described in Chapter 5 in the section on the burden of proof.

Administrative procedures

The interview may represent the end of your recruitment and selection process. If so, you would proceed at this stage to offer the post to the successful candidate and to inform those who had not been successful. However, you may decide to incorporate additional stages in your selection process, such as a number of tests. These are discussed in the next chapter, and you will find more information about closing the selection process at the end of that chapter.

CASE STUDY 7.2 Recruitment and selection

The Fabric Brothers' recruitment drive

Thomas and Edward Fabric founded a small clothing manufacturing company in the early 1960s in the north of England. Over the years the company has grown and recently the Fabric brothers won a new contract to manufacture dresses for a catalogue company. This has necessitated their taking on 10 new sewing machine operators.

Edward's son, John, has taken care of recruitment since he joined the family enterprise in 1978 when he was 20 years old. The company had functioned very much as a small, family-owned business for many years, and John developed a paternalistic attitude which has never been challenged. He let the 'girls' in the sewing room know that he was looking for some additional employees, and he posted a notice on the factory gates, advertising the vacancies as a good opportunity for, as he put it, 'ladies looking to make some extra money while your children are in school'.

→

John interviewed a few people who dropped in to ask about the job, and he was able to fill his 10 vacancies with no bother. He was very surprised a few weeks later to get a letter from the Equality and Human Rights Commission stating that two Asian women, who had applied for the post and been interviewed but not selected, felt that they had been discriminated against on the basis of race. Talking it over with his father, John said: 'Well, I did ask them questions about how long they had been in England and whether they felt their English was good enough for the job, but surely that's not racial discrimination?'

John was actually quite upset because he did not think of himself as a racist. Of course, all the girls in the sewing room were white, but that's just the way things had worked out. Imagine his surprise, then, when a few days later he received another letter from the Commission stating that a man he had rejected had complained that he had been rejected on the basis of sex. This man had once worked as a tailor, so he felt he could not have been rejected on the grounds of competence.

John knows that you have some background in HR issues, so he has turned to you to explain to him how all this could have happened and to give him some advice about what to do both now in response to these complaints, and in handling recruitment and selection in the future.

Go to the student materials for Chapter 7 on the companion website at **www.pearsoned.co.uk/foothook** to find our comments on this case study.

REVIEW QUESTIONS

You will find brief answers to these review questions on pages 474–475.

1 Describe the aims of the selection process and comment on a methodical approach that can be used to achieve these aims.

2 Explain the terms 'validity' and 'reliability' with reference to employment interviews.

3 What factors contribute to the low validity of employment interviews and how can this be overcome?

4 Critically assess the value of different types of questioning in employment interviews.

SELF-CHECK QUESTIONS

Answer the following multiple-choice and short-answer questions. The correct responses are given on page 475 for you to check your understanding of this chapter.

1 Which of the following questions is an open question?
   (a) Did you get here by train?
   (b) Don't you enjoy working with computerised files?
   (c) What experience have you had in dealing with after-sales support services?
   (d) So you worked with your last employer for three years?

2 Is the following statement true or false? Of all the selection methods available to employers, interviews have been found to have the highest validity.

3 Which of the following is the best definition of validity?
   (a) A method of assessment that gives the same results when it is applied by a number of different people.

(b) A method of assessment that measures what it sets out to measure.

(c) A method of assessment that uses a wide range of techniques.

(d) Interviews conducted by more than one person.

4 An interviewer is very impressed by the smart appearance and confident manner of a candidate. The interviewer tends to seek positive information from this candidate and readily overlooks any negative information. This is known as:

(a) stereotyping

(b) the contrast effect

(c) closed questioning

(d) the halo effect.

5 The validity of an interview can be increased by:

(a) being aware of potential interviewer errors

(b) structuring interviews to obtain the same information from all candidates

(c) having interviews conducted by more than one interviewer

(d) all the above

(e) none of the above.

6 Which of the following is the best definition of (i) a situational interview question, (ii) a behavioural interview question?

(a) The interviewee is asked to describe a situation in which he or she has performed well.

(b) The interviewee is presented with a situation that represents a typical incident in the job for which he or she is being interviewed. The interviewee is asked to recount what he or she did in a similar situation in a past position.

(c) The interviewee is presented with a situation that represents a typical incident in the job for which he or she is being interviewed. The interviewee is asked to describe what he or she would do in this situation.

(d) The interviewee is presented with a situation that represents a typical incident in the job for which he or she is being interviewed. The interviewee is asked to describe what the ideal behaviour would be in this circumstance.

7 Which of the following best defines how to assess the responses to a situational interview to achieve increased reliability?

(a) Decide in advance what could be regarded as a good, an adequate and a poor response. Assign points to each level of response. Each interviewer grades answers accordingly.

(b) Each interviewer reviews responses from all candidates after the interviews. Each interviewer ranks the responses according to acceptability and compares the results with the other interviewers.

(c) The interviewers as a group review the responses from all candidates after the interviews. The interviewers as a group rank the responses according to acceptability.

(d) Decide in advance what could be regarded as a good, an adequate and a poor response. Assign points to each level of response. Interviewers as a group grade responses accordingly.

8 Is the following question a situational question or a behavioural question? 'Can you tell us about a situation where someone approached you with a problem that was affecting his or her work?'

9 What is the term that is used for analysing recruitment and selection data to ensure that no unfair or unlawful discrimination is taking place?

HR IN THE NEWS

FT

Call to raise job interview standards

By John Willman, Business Editor

A third of job applicants come away from their interview with a bad impression of the business, having faced questions unrelated to the job, poor interview preparation, sexism and bad personal hygiene, a survey has found.

In some cases applicants complained of racist questions and interviewers who were drunk.

Kevin Moran, a 29-year-old IT worker who went for a job in the City, said he had been surprised to find it was held in a bar.

'I had to shout over the noise, and one of the interviewers kept going to the bar when I was still speaking, butting in rudely and talking about things that were completely unrelated,' Mr Moran said. 'The other interviewer asked if I was "out of my league".'

The survey of more than 2,000 people, by Ipsos Mori for T-Mobile, found that applicants judged a potential employer on their impressions of the working environment and the people employed. They expected intelligent questions related to the job, and a clear career progression plan.

However, 40 per cent of those who judged their interview experience as bad said the questions asked were nothing to do with the job, while a third said the interviewer was unprepared.

More than 31 per cent of those finding the encounter disappointing had never heard from the company again.

Among the complaints about interviewers' behaviour by those who rated their encounter a bad experience were lateness (18 per cent), sexism (16 per cent) and bad personal hygiene (7.5 per cent).

Another complaint was that the interviewer ate during the process (5.2 per cent), while 11 of the 662 disappointed applicants said the interviewer was drunk.

Almost 30 per cent complained they had not been offered any refreshments, while 10 per cent said the building was dirty.

As a result, almost half those who had experienced a bad interview turned down the job when it was offered.

'Interviewees are always under pressure to create a good first impression, but it seems that businesses need to feel a bit of that pressure as well,' said Mark Martin, human resources director at T-Mobile UK.

'Candidates are beginning to place a company's culture and values at the top of their agenda, so businesses need to think about how these are expressed in an interview situation – or their reputation and brand could be on the line.'

(FT.com, 4 October 2007. Reproduced with permission.)

Questions

1 List the examples of poor interview practice addressed in this article, and link them, where possible, to the concepts covered in your textbook.

2 List the things that candidates expect of an interview, and link them, where possible, to the concepts covered in your textbook.

WHAT NEXT?

We have referred in this chapter to two Industrial Relations Services articles which appeared in 2007 on the subject of employment interviews. Based on their research of employer practices, the IRS have in fact provided a fairly comprehensive guide to various aspects of selection interviews. They cover telephone interviewing, scoring systems and record-keeping as well as other issues. The article cited here gives an overview of what is included in the multi-part guide, and also offers a number of links to other interesting documents such as guidelines for line managers on how to conduct employment interviews. Read this set of articles and follow up the links to expand and consolidate your understanding of selection interviews.

Industrial Relations Services (2007) Job interviewing: an overview of IRS's research, *IRS Employment Review 875*, 18/06 (available at www.xperthr.co.uk).

References

Advisory, Conciliation and Arbitration Service (2005a) *Religion or Belief and the Workplace: A Guide for Employers and Employees,* ACAS.

Advisory, Conciliation and Arbitration Service (2005b) *Sexual Orientation and the Workplace: A Guide for Employers and Employees,* ACAS.

Chartered Institute of Personnel and Development (2003) *Recruitment and Retention 2003: Survey Report,* CIPD.

Chartered Institute of Personnel and Development (2004) *Telephone Interviewing,* CIPD (www.cipd.co.uk; accessed 28.09.04; no longer available as a separate document).

Chartered Institute of Personnel and Development (2006) *Online Recruitment,* CIPD (www.cipd.co.uk; accessed 26.10.06).

Chartered Institute of Personnel and Development (2007a) *Recruitment, Retention and Turnover: Annual Survey Report 2007,* CIPD.

Chartered Institute of Personnel and Development (2007b) *Selecting Candidates,* CIPD (www.cipd.co.uk; accessed 08.03.07).

Chartered Institute of Personnel and Development (2007c) *Selection Interviewing,* CIPD (www.cipd.co.uk; accessed 08.03.07).

Industrial Relations Services (IRS) (2003) Sharpening up recruitment and selection with competencies, *IRS Employment Review 782,* 15 August, 42–48.

Industrial Relations Services (IRS) (2007a) Interviewers' roles, responsibilities and training, *IRS Employment Review 875,* 18/06 (www.xperthr.co.uk; accessed 27.06.07).

Industrial Relations Services (IRS) (2007b) Question styles and formats of job interviewing, *IRS Employment Review 875,* 18/06 (www.xperthr.co.uk; accessed 27.06.07).

Latham, G.P., L.M. Saari, E.D. Pursell and M.A. Campion (1980) The situational interview, *Journal of Applied Psychology,* Vol. 65, No. 4, 422–427.

Makin, P. and I. Robertson (1986) Selecting the best selection techniques, *Personnel Management,* November, 38–40.

McGee, L. (2006) How to interview for engagement, *People Management,* 27 July, 40–41.

Rogers, C.R. and R.E. Farson (1976) *Active Listening,* Industrial Relations Center of the University of Chicago.

Weekley, J.A. and J.A. Gier (1987) Reliability and validity of the situational interview for a sales position, *Journal of Applied Psychology,* Vol. 72, 484–487.

Welch, J. (1998) Graduate recruitment, *People Management,* 28 May, 14.

www.equalityhumanrights.com; accessed 12.10.07.

Further study

Books

Black, J.S., H.B. Gregersen, M.E. Mendenhall and L.K. Stroh (1999) *Globalizing People through International Assignments,* Addison Wesley. Although its focus is specifically on HR aspects of dealing with international employees, this book contains some interesting information about recruitment and selection which could have wider applications, including some good examples of open and behavioural questions on the competency areas of perseverance and delegation.

Chartered Institute of Personnel and Development (2007) *Recruitment, Retention and Turnover: Annual Survey Report 2007,* CIPD. An overview of what employers are currently doing in recruitment and selection, based on survey evidence. Highlights what employers consider to be the main issues affecting the sourcing and retention of employees.

Cook, M. (2004) *Personnel Selection: Adding Value through People,* Wiley. A thorough review of selection methods and issues, including interviews, tests, assessment centres and validity.

Incomes Data Services (2003) *IDS Studies: Recruitment Practices,* No. 751, June, IDS. A concise overview of the basic range of both recruitment and selection practices with case studies of six employers, including an NHS trust and Loop Customer Management.

Roberts, G. (1997) *Recruitment and Selection*: *A Competency Approach,* IPD. A general introduction to various aspects of HRM including chapters on screening and interviewing.

Smith, M. and I.T. Robertson (1993) *The Theory and Practice of Systematic Personnel Selection,* 2nd edition, Macmillan. A thorough discussion of all the stages involved in selection, and of issues such as ethical considerations, discrimination and validity of selection methods.

Articles

Industrial Relations Services (2007) Job interviewing: an overview of IRS's research, *IRS Employment Review 875,* 18/06 (www.xperthr.co.uk; accessed 27.06.07). Lists a number of articles that constitute the 2007 IRS studies on selection interviewing, and provides a further list of useful sources of information on this topic.

Jenks, J.M. and L.P. Zevnik (1989) ABCs of job interviewing, *Harvard Business Review,* July–August, 38–42. This article discusses how to formulate questions and gives practical guidelines.

Latham, G.P., L.M. Saari, E.D. Pursell and M.A. Campion (1980) The situational interview, *Journal of Applied Psychology,* Vol. 65, No. 4, 422–427. This article describes research into the validity of situational interviewing, and provides an example of a question used for manual employees.

Weekley, J.A. and J.A. Gier (1987) Reliability and validity of the situational interview for a sales position. *Journal of Applied Psychology,* Vol. 72, 484–487. This article describes research into the reliability and validity of interviews, particularly interviews using situational questions. A sample question is provided, together with suggestions on how to assess responses.

Internet

The Chartered Institute of Personnel and Development   **www.cipd.co.uk**
Browse the CIPD's website to find information related to recruitment and selection.

Equality and Human Rights Commission   **www.equalityhumanrights.com**
Provides a checklist specifically designed for line managers on handling situations that might arise during the shortlisting and interview processes, produced by the Equal Opportunities Commission. Go to the main site and search for the equality checklists.

CHAPTER **8**

Selection: supplementing the interview

Objectives

When you have studied this chapter you will be able to:

- name and describe selection methods that can be used to supplement the interview
- suggest a range of work sample exercises and design them
- assess the suitability of selection methods designed to supplement the interview
- decide how to integrate a range of techniques into the selection process
- describe the steps to be taken to complete the selection process.

In Chapter 7, we discussed interviewing techniques in great depth, and this is justified because of the predominance of interviewing as a method of selection. However, there are some strong arguments for developing a broader perspective on the selection process, and these are mainly to do with the validity of the interview as an assessment tool and with the importance of the selection process, as part of talent management, to the achievement of the strategic goals of the organisation.

Selection as a strategic activity

We established in Chapters 1 and 2 that employee selection contributes to the achievement of strategic goals and so is too important an activity to be conducted on the basis of what is familiar or expedient. Organisations may, therefore, depending on the circumstances, need to engage in a broader array of activities rather than simply interviewing alone. Sophisticated selection has been identified as part of the best practice associated with the HRM approach (Marchington and Wilkinson, 2005) and thus a necessary part of a strategic approach dedicated to obtaining the competitive edge that comes from having a superior workforce. The importance of getting the selection decision right is confirmed by the growing emphasis on the crucial contribution to organisations of their talent management processes. As Ready and Conger (2007, p. 68) proclaim: 'Stop losing out on lucrative business opportunities because you don't have the talent to develop them'. Supplementary techniques may not be needed for every vacancy, but at least the process should be examined and the appropriate action chosen for each contingency.

Interview validity

Many questions have been raised about the predictive validity of interviews, i.e. do interviews result in good decisions; do the people who are selected for posts actually perform well on the job? Another question which is rarely addressed but ought to be of concern is whether those who are rejected really are unsuitable for the post; in other words, is the selection process rigorous enough to ensure that good candidates are not inadvertently eliminated?

Most writers on selection methods refer to the fact that research has not been able to show that interviewing has high predictive validity as a selection technique (Armstrong, 2006; Smith and Robertson, 1993). The major reasons for this have to do with interviewer bias and the fallibility of human judgement. The problem of the low validity of interviews is compounded by evidence about poor interviewer reliability, i.e. that two interviewers may form very different opinions about the same candidate. Structured interviews and the use of situational and behavioural questioning go some way to correcting these interview faults, but it is worth considering whether there are some other methods of improving the validity and reliability of the selection process.

Pause for thought 8.1	If the results of interviews are not always reliable or valid, what can be done to improve the selection process? Write down three things employers could do to supplement the interview process.

In trying to think of some methods of supplementing the information gained during interviews, you may have focused on improving reliability or validity and decided that it would be a good idea to obtain some objective information, such as test results that can be scored objectively and are not subject to individual interpretation. This would help to counteract any interviewer bias present in the process.

Alternatively you may have focused on simply acquiring additional information from a range of sources, including other people's opinion of the candidates, for example by soliciting references, or even by conducting a second stage of interviews. A further issue you may have considered is the timing of these supplementary activities: should they occur before the interviews to facilitate the process of shortlisting or to reduce the number of interviewees, or after the interviews to assess further those who have passed the interview as the first hurdle? There is no hard and fast rule about this; it is a matter of judgement and depends on what you want to achieve in a particular circumstance. As you read this chapter, you will find examples of employers who have used a variety of methods at different points in the selection process.

You may also have remembered that the interview is not meant to be a one-way process and that it is important for candidates to be given adequate information so that they too can make an informed decision about the suitability of the post for them. Ways of giving this information may be included in your list. One of these is known as the realistic job preview, which is described later in this chapter.

Your list may include some of the following activities:

- psychological tests
  - ability
  - intelligence
  - interests
  - motivation
  - personality
- work sample
- role play; demonstration
- observation at work
- assessment centres
- references
- medical examination
- criminal record check
- drug use check
- lie detector test
- graphology
- phrenology
- astrology
- realistic job preview
- company tour
- opportunity to meet prospective colleagues.

Some of these are obviously *not* to be recommended, so the rest of this chapter will review some of the available selection methods and conclude with an overview of the activities that need to be undertaken to complete the selection process.

Supplementary selection techniques

Did you know?

A controversial example of an exercise conducted during a recruitment campaign occurred when the manager at a branch of B&Q was reported to have asked candidates to join in a dance routine during an interview day. The manager claimed that the purpose of the dance was to make candidates feel more relaxed, and the CIPD made a statement supporting the legitimacy of this approach. The authors of this textbook are rather more doubtful about the acceptability of this as part of the selection process for shop-floor staff and find it highly questionable in terms of face validity. What do you think? Reported in *Personnel Today*, 12 January 2007.

Note that we are using the term 'supplementary' and not 'alternative'. In spite of reservations about the effectiveness of interviewing, interviews are not likely to be replaced as a selection method. You will need to choose which methods to use to complement the information gained from interviews, and integrate these additional measures into your selection and decision-making processes. The description of supplementary techniques in this chapter should enable you to do this.

The essential criterion in choosing supplementary methods is that they should provide information that is directly related to performance on the job. This should be the guiding principle both in choosing off-the-shelf tests and in designing exercises tailor-made for a particular workplace. In their review of assessment centres, the IRS (2007) stress that tests and exercises used to assess candidates must relate closely to the competencies required in the job they have applied for. In addition to the employer gaining relevant information, a related issue is that candidates can easily see the point of a test that requires them to do something they know will be done on the job. This increases the face validity of the test, making it more acceptable to the candidates, which may in turn affect their willingness to take the test seriously and their motivation to perform the task to the best of their ability. Face validity is therefore something that should be taken into consideration when choosing or designing a test.

Psychological testing

Psychological testing is sometimes referred to as psychometric testing, and is a method of acquiring objective information about a range of individual abilities and traits. Psychological tests are defined as having the following characteristics:

- They are professionally developed and checked for reliability and validity.
- They are administered and scored in a standardised manner.
- They test maximum performance and habitual performance.
- They result in scores that can be compared to norms for relevant populations.

These characteristics will be explained more fully as we examine the various issues surrounding the uses of psychological tests.

The characteristics of psychological tests listed above indicate that their inclusion in the selection process will:

- add an element of objectivity
- increase the predictive validity of selection decisions
- measure some factors that cannot be assessed through the application form and interview.

The standardised administration of tests means that all applicants answer the same test questions in the same conditions, and objective scoring means that the scores are not open to individual interpretation as is the case with interview responses. There is a vast amount of research that underpins the development of commercially produced tests, including proofs of their reliability and validity. If this is properly documented, the user of the tests can rest assured that the tests will improve the validity of the selection process.

Because psychological tests are such complex instruments, they should be used only by people who have had specific training in how to administer them and how to interpret the results, and in fact reputable test providers will only supply commercially developed tests to properly accredited persons with appropriate training. The British Psychological Society (BPS) has approved the standards of training needed to administer and interpret tests at various levels and to give feedback to test-takers, and this training is available from various sources, including the suppliers of tests, who also provide additional training in the use of their own products. The basic level of training is level A, which qualifies persons to use ability and aptitude tests. This training takes approximately five days. Further training of approximately five days with a follow-up day some time after the initial training is necessary to be able to use personality questionnaires (level B). There is a cost implication in this for employers, but the cost of training staff and of staff time for administering tests may be offset by the improved validity of selection decisions. An alternative to having a trained member of staff is to use the services of an occupational psychologist on a consultancy basis when the use of psychological testing seems to be appropriate.

An issue that attracted attention in 2001 (*People Management*), and was regarded at the time as being somewhat controversial, was the use of the Internet to conduct psychological tests. This continued for a time to be an issue where pros and cons needed to be closely examined (Pickard, 2004), but the use of online testing is becoming more firmly established, mainly, it seems, to eliminate unsuitable applications early in the process, especially if a large number of applications are expected (HR Zone, 2006; Sloane, 2007). Although the CIPD's survey of recruitment, retention and turnover (2007c) still only reports 30 per cent of employers as using online tests for selection purposes, this is nonetheless an increasing trend. The figure for 2006 was 25 per cent and only 5 per cent in 2005 (CIPD, 2006a).

The CIPD factsheet on psychological testing (2007b) outlines what to consider when deciding whether to use a test. Their recommendations include, first, that the test should be directly relevant to requirements specified in the personnel specification/competency profile and should be capable of obtaining additional, pertinent information. There is a very wide selection of tests to choose from, and test suppliers provide brochures outlining the sort of information each test will provide and what types of job each test might be appropriate for. Tests are designed with different groups of people in mind, and test suppliers offer advice about who the tests are suitable for. Some examples of designated groups for whom tests are available are middle to senior managers, administrative/supervisory employees, skilled operatives and staff who have direct customer contact. Second, test suppliers should provide evidence that the test is reliable, valid and free of any bias against any particular group of people. Third, organisations should consider issues around the standard of competence required to administer and interpret the test appropriately. Further indicators of when to use psychometric tests and questionnaires are:

- when a faulty hiring decision would be extremely costly, for example for very senior positions or when employee errors could render employers liable for high financial outlay
- when the selection ratio (the ratio of applicants to the number of positions to be filled) is high and additional information is needed so that the number of candidates can be reduced.

Psychological tests cover a range of human characteristics and may assess:

- intelligence
- ability
- interest
- motivation
- personality.

Intelligence tests

General intelligence tests assess ability in a range of skills such as verbal, arithmetical and diagrammatical reasoning, producing an overall score.

Ability tests

Ability tests focus on specific mental abilities and produce separate scores for the different skills. Sometimes a distinction is made between tests of attainment and tests of aptitude, but in fact it is not always easy to distinguish between the two. Attainment tests assess skills and knowledge that have been acquired through experience and learning, and aptitude tests measure individuals' potential to develop ability. The results of an attainment test, say after learning a foreign language, might also be an indicator of aptitude for learning that language. Since both kinds of tests examine verbal, arithmetical and diagrammatical skills, it is probably more helpful to think of them under the general heading of ability tests.

Work sample tests or school exams are examples of attainment tests, and the use of these would not require the special training outlined above. There are aptitude tests for specific occupations such as word processing, and test batteries that produce a profile of the candidate over a range of abilities.

Tests of interest and motivation

The relationship between interests and motivation and successful performance is not a straightforward one. For this reason these tests are not used for selection (Smith and Robertson, 1993), but interest tests can be used for career guidance and counselling, and motivation tests can be used for decisions about how best to manage people and enhance their performance by responding to what motivates them.

Personality questionnaires

The expression 'personality questionnaire' has been used in preference to 'personality test', because in terms of measuring personality characteristics there are no right and wrong answers as would be the case in questions of verbal or arithmetical reasoning. Ability tests are examples of tests of maximum performance, meaning that they reflect the best performance an individual is capable of at that point in time in the skill being tested. Personality questionnaires are indicators of habitual performance, meaning that they reflect stable traits that are likely to be revealed in typical behaviour. Of all the assessments that are carried out in the workplace, personality questionnaires are probably the most contentious, especially with regard to acceptance by candidates. For this reason, it is particularly important to explain to applicants how the test is related to performance on the job concerned and to provide feedback on the results. Test users should also monitor results to ensure that tests do not discriminate unfairly.

Personality questionnaires examine aspects of personality that have been shown through research to correlate with performance at work. Murphy and Davidshofer (2001) refer to evidence that some personality characteristics are related to job performance in general, including agreeableness, conscientiousness and openness to experience. Together with extraversion and neuroticism (actually a measure of emotional stability), these traits are known as 'the Big Five', which are the focus of much interest in current psychological research (Robertson, 2001; Mol et al., 2005).

Most personality questionnaires are of the self-report variety, where applicants are asked to record how they see themselves on a range of characteristics or traits. Some items may be open-ended questions asking about preferred activities, and some items may be a choice from a number of statements, asking applicants to choose which statement most resembles them or is most unlike them. These measures usually result in a profile of the person on a range of personality dimensions. One of the most well known of these instruments is Cattell's 16 Personality Factor test (16PF). The 16PF test is based on Cattell's work in isolating a range of 16 elements which he believed could be used to describe the whole spectrum of an individual's personality. Cattell's personality dimensions include reserved–outgoing, tough minded–sensitive, conservative–experimenting and relaxed–tense.

Other established tests include the Saville and Holdsworth Occupational Personality Questionnaire and the Myers-Briggs Type Indicator. The Myers-Briggs test is most often used within the framework of training to identify personality types and examine their impact on personal interactions. There are also questionnaires that measure characteristics that predict success in specific occupations.

One of the reasons why personality tests are sometimes regarded with some scepticism is that in self-reporting, candidates may try to give the answers they think are expected. It is also recognised that the situation can affect the responses that people make, so personality test results are not always reliable.

This leads to a very important point with regard to the use of psychological tests in general: they should never be the sole means of assessing candidates, but should always be used as part of a wider process. Information about suppliers of psychological tests is available from the CIPD to its members and Toplis *et al.* (2004) provide a brief description of the whole range of available tests.

Work sample tests

As the term suggests, a work sample test consists of getting a candidate to perform some task or element of a task that forms part of the job. You can gain a better understanding of work sample tests by working through the design process using a familiar example.

How to design a work sample test

Let us take an example of a job with which you are all familiar, that of a university or college lecturer. If you were invited to design a work sample test to be used in hiring a new lecturer in human resource management, what preliminary issues would you consider? How would you approach the task?

The first consideration is that a work sample test makes sense only if it demonstrates abilities that are a major and integral part of the job. A critical incident analysis and selection of a critical task are therefore the first step in designing a work sample test. If you think back to the job analysis techniques discussed in Chapter 6, you will realise that you could perform a simplified critical incident analysis by interviewing a number of lecturers and heads of department, and asking them what they consider to be the most important activities that contribute to success in the job. Without doubt most lecturers would identify the ability to conduct a seminar as a critical task.

A second consideration ought to be how the performance of the work sample will be assessed, as this will affect the way the exercise is designed, and it may influence the instructions that are given to candidates.

Pause for thought 8.2   List the criteria on which you would assess a candidate's performance in delivering a seminar.

In deciding on your assessment criteria, you will no doubt have identified the lecturers you regard as being excellent in their seminar delivery, and then you will have identified the competencies and techniques that are part of that excellence. If you have worked with a group of colleagues you may have discussed what each of you considers to be important and agreed on a list. Your criteria will include some of the following:

- choice and relevance of topic
- knowledge of subject; integration of current material
- style of delivery
- use of materials
  - content
  - variety
  - visual aids
- ability to stimulate participation/discussion
- adequacy of preparation
- ability to handle questions.

For some of these criteria, you may also have outlined how each would be judged. Adequacy of preparation, for instance, might be judged by the absence of hesitation, well-ordered notes and materials, observable structure, control of physical equipment.

Some work samples, such as typing tests, can be assessed on an objective basis using a mathematical formula, but assessment of activities like delivering a seminar will still be subjective. It is important to have assessment guidelines to provide some level of standardisation and consequently to improve reliability among the assessors. Assessment criteria should obviously be related to what is regarded as superior performance on the job. This being the case, documentation relating to performance appraisal should be a good source of material to be used when designing work sample tests.

ACTIVITY 8.1

Make a list of the factors on which you would judge the criterion 'style of delivery'. Discuss your list with a group of fellow students and devise a set of assessment criteria for this performance criterion.

Since acceptability of the test to the candidate is an important factor, it may improve the face validity of the test to inform candidates how they will be assessed. You should consider incorporating this into the instructions to be given to candidates. For example, the instructions on conducting a seminar might be phrased as follows:

As part of the selection process you are requested to conduct a seminar in your subject area. The seminar should last one hour and be appropriate for a foundation-level course. Your performance will be judged in terms of the appropriateness of your material, the style of delivery and your ability to stimulate participation.

Assessing performance in the work sample exercise

The assessment criteria will already have been established in the process of designing the work sample. What remains is to ensure that all the assessors involved are fully cognisant of the criteria, and that there is some agreement on what represents acceptable standards of performance. This goal can be facilitated in two ways:

- the involvement of line managers both in the design of the work sample test and in the selection process
- the use of a scoring sheet listing the assessment criteria.

An example of a scoring sheet for the lecturer's work sample test is given in Figure 8.1.

We can now summarise the steps you have just worked through to design a work sample exercise:

- Identify key critical factors of performance.
- Choose factors that can be tested appropriately by a work sample.
- Identify assessment criteria.
- Design the work sample exercise.
- Write instructions for the candidate.
- Design the assessment form.
- Train the assessors.

Figure 8.1 Work sample assessment record

Post: Lecturer in HRM; delivery of a seminar				
Assess each of the following criteria on a scale of 1–5, where 1 = poor performance, 3 = acceptable performance, 5 = outstanding performance. An indication of factors you might consider is given for some of the criteria.				
	Candidate 1	**Candidate 2**	**Candidate 3**	**Candidate 4**
Choice and relevance of topic				
Knowledge of subject: up-to-date issues included				
Style of delivery: ability to attract and keep attention; natural, conversational tone; use of humour; movement about room				
Use of materials: content; variety; visual aids				
Ability to stimulate participation/discussion				
Adequacy of preparation: absence of hesitation; well-ordered notes and materials; observable structure; control of physical equipment				
Ability to handle questions				
Total				

Integration of work sample tests into the selection process

Work sample tests can easily be included in a selection process to provide additional information without necessarily developing a fully fledged assessment centre approach as described in the next section. A written work sample can, for example, be requested along with submission of the application form. This is especially useful if you are expecting a large number of applications for a particular post. Many senior posts with local and central government require the ability to absorb complex information and compile a written report for dissemination to a wide audience, integrating aspects of new legislation or policy for example.

By asking applicants to submit a written report along with their application form, such employers can potentially gain a vast amount of additional evidence about applicants' capabilities beyond what they would be able to glean from the application form alone. This would include evidence of:

● knowledge – more so than the assumption of knowledge because of academic qualifications and related experience
● report-writing skills
● ability to deliver work under the pressure of deadlines
● attitudes and abilities reflected in the content of the report.

If these factors were included in the job specification, this information would greatly assist the employer in its shortlisting task. The exercise no doubt also brings the additional advantage of discouraging any applicants who were not seriously interested in the post or not willing to make the effort to complete the assignment. Such tests can be designed to incorporate the critical requirements of various posts in any organisation.

ACTIVITY 8.2

Think of three occupations and decide on a job sample test that could be used prior to shortlisting or that could be run within the context of an interview day. Describe the test and explain how it would provide information that could be used to assess a person's suitability for the job.

When you have compiled your own list of three jobs, get together with two other students to compare your lists. Select the best three examples and present these to the rest of the class.

You can also visit the student materials on the companion website to this text at www.pearsoned.co/foothook to review our suggested answers for this activity.

Assessment centres

As Woodruffe (2000) points out, an assessment centre is a method rather than a place, although some employers, particularly large organisations, might have premises dedicated to assessment, especially if they use them for both selection and development purposes. Since an assessment centre is a method, it can be used flexibly by all employers. Each organisation can decide how many or how few of the assessment methods to use, but a range of techniques would have to be used to classify a selection event as an assessment centre. The IRS (2007) report that most assessment centres take place over one day, which means that they are an intense experience for candidates and assessors alike.

Basically, an assessment centre approach means that a number of people are assessed together by a number of assessors, using a variety of selection techniques. This enables the collection of a range of information and observation and evaluation of how individuals interact with other people. The basic assumption underlying the validity of assessment centres is that the behaviours displayed will be carried over into the workplace. Incomes Data Services (2002) point out that assessment centres are likely to lead to better results if they are designed around competencies that are used right through the recruitment and selection process. Also, the more the assessment exercises reflect aspects of what people would actually be doing in the job, the better the results are likely to be. In this way, assessment centres can also deliver a sort of realistic job preview to the candidates.

The range of activities that can make up an assessment centre include:

- work simulations
  - work samples
  - in-tray exercises
  - role plays
- group exercises and discussions
- psychological tests
- interviews
- peer assessment and self-assessment.

Makin and Robertson (1986) identified group discussion as the kind of exercise most used in assessment centres and the IDS (2002) state that all six of the companies in their study use some form of group exercise, often involving group discussion.

Work simulations

As the phrase suggests, work simulations entail engaging candidates in performing tasks that would actually be done on the job. These exercises can be performed by individuals, as in the in-tray and role-play exercises described below, or in groups if, for example, one of the tasks is to contribute to interdepartmental meetings. One issue to keep in mind when deciding what kinds of exercise to use is that individual exercises such as role plays are more demanding in terms of assessor time, since one assessor will have to be assigned to one individual rather than a group.

Work sample tests are an example of simulation, and have already been discussed in detail. In-tray exercises and role plays should be developed in the same way as we outlined for work samples in terms of isolating critical tasks, setting the assessment criteria, designing the exercise and assessing it. A typical in-tray exercise is to present a candidate for a managerial post with a number of different tasks that a manager would encounter at the beginning of the day, with instructions to prioritise the issues, respond to emails, write memos, make phone calls, etc. The IRS (2007), however, report a decline in the popularity of in-tray exercises. A role play could be used in situations where the employee would have to deal with customer complaints, and it would be usual for someone already employed with the company to take on the role of the customer.

Group exercises

A variety of tailor-made tests or exercises have been devised by various employers to assess leadership qualities that cannot easily be judged from application forms or straightforward questioning. These tests may be used in designated assessment centre days, but some of them can also be integrated into interview days if a number of candidates are called together. The following are some examples of the kinds of exercises that are used, together with some examples of employers that are known to have used them:

- A group of applicants sit around a table; four or five assessors sit around the room behind the applicants. The lead assessor explains that he or she has four or five job-related topics (depending on the number of candidates), which will be read out one at a time. When a topic has been announced, one candidate must volunteer to take that topic and conduct a discussion on it. Five minutes will be allowed for the discussion, and the discussion leader will be alerted when four minutes have elapsed. No further information is given to the candidates regarding what is expected of them. (A metropolitan police force; civilian post.)
- Round table interview. The participants are candidates who have passed a preliminary interview. Candidates introduce themselves, and contribute to a discussion of what a manager's job entails. This is followed by a team exercise with instructions to devise an employment strategy for a new store. (A retail outlet selling toys; trainee manager.)
- Candidates engage in teamwork to get equipment across a stream with limited physical resources, sometimes with a designated leader, sometimes as a leaderless group. (The Army; officer.)

As with work sample tests, candidate performance can only be judged fairly if assessors have agreed in advance which competencies and job-related behaviours they are looking for.

Pause for thought 8.3   Look again at the exercise used by the metropolitan police force. What competencies and qualities do you think they were trying to assess?

The assessors would be looking for evidence of negative and positive behaviours: domination of the discussion, assertiveness, who has good ideas, ability to get people discussing a range of ideas, sensitivity to conflicting ideas, ability to incorporate conflicting views.

ACTIVITY 8.3

Think of a number of occupations and come up with four or five topics that could be raised for discussion in a similar selection test.

You can visit the student materials on the companion website to this text at www.pearsoned.co/foothook to review our suggestions.

Issues

Woodruffe (2000) identifies a number of issues that must be considered when deciding to use the assessment centre technique, in designing it, running it, and assessing its effectiveness. Some of the major issues will now be discussed briefly.

As with any other selection technique, all the exercises used in the assessment centre must be designed to identify and measure specific competencies needed in the vacant post. There is a need to involve managers and others such as current postholders in identifying what the critical competencies are. The activities involved in designing assessment centre exercises should be directly linked with the information collated in the context of job analysis that you read about in Chapter 6.

Since assessment centres are very demanding in terms of time and effort, the need for acceptance of the centre by all parties becomes crucial. Line managers are being asked to give their time to the development and the assessment of exercises and to accept that the use of assessment centres will lead to better selection. Line manager acceptance is increased if they are involved at all stages. There is also a need for candidates to feel that the assessment methods used represent a relevant process, especially as the assessment centre is more demanding in terms of their time and energy than a simple interview would be. This can be achieved partly by proper design of the exercises and partly by providing feedback.

We should also briefly consider the pros and cons of assessment centres. Certainly there are identifiable costs associated with assessment centres. These include: the training of a number of assessors; the design of exercises and line manager time devoted to this; arrangements for facilities; the time needed to organise the events and coordinate group activities with individual activities, particularly when one assessor is needed per candidate as in role-play exercises; time spent giving feedback. The argument for assessment centres is that these costs are balanced by the acquisition of additional information, the opportunity to evaluate several candidates together and the increased validity of selection decisions. The importance of talent management, as discussed in this textbook, could serve as a justification for these expenses. The IRS (2007) also argue that assessment centres are not an unreasonable expense, given the importance of selecting the right people, and that organisations can often use a number of assessment exercises for several posts. An example of this would be if an organisation had core competencies such as communication or customer service, core meaning that an element of these competencies is required in all positions in that organisation.

Whenever a number of assessment techniques are used, there is a need to assign a weight to each technique. This is addressed later in this chapter after all assessment methods have been considered.

References

References are another method of gathering information on applicants, and a number of surveys indicate that the popularity of references as part of the selection process comes second only to the interview (Makin and Robertson, 1986; Newell and Shackleton, 1991). This is so in spite of the reference's poor showing in the validity league table. In their analysis of the accuracy of selection methods, Anderson and Shackleton (1994) found that references rated a correlation coefficient of only 0.13 (0 being equivalent to chance and 1.0 being the equivalent of perfect prediction). These facts seem to suggest that you will find the acquisition of references to be a part of most selection processes you will be involved in, but that great care is needed in their interpretation.

Pause for thought 8.4	At what stage in the selection process should a reference be solicited? Which candidates would you solicit a reference for?

There are no hard and fast rules that provide an answer to these questions, except that it is usual to solicit a reference only for a selection of applicants. There are various circumstances to consider, and this is another area where policy should be formulated to provide guidance to managers.

Most employers recognise that there are costs to providing references, so they would not wish to impose an unnecessary burden on other employers. This means restricting requests for references to an essential minimum. This would imply asking for references at a late stage in the process, after candidates have been assessed using a variety of other techniques. A further argument in support of this approach is that candidates on the whole prefer their current employer not to be approached unless there is a serious possibility that the candidate will be offered the post. The disadvantage of this view is, of course, that some time may elapse before a reference is received and the prospective employer will not want to delay in making the hiring decision.

Some organisations use all their other assessment techniques and make a job offer subject to receipt of a supportive reference. It must be remembered, however, that references are given in confidence, and in this instance, if a job offer is retracted, then the applicant will know it is because of his or her reference. This may have an impact on the extent to which referees are prepared to be truthful. Every organisation needs to think through these implications, design a policy, and stick to it.

In addition to the questions of when to secure a reference and for whom, there are considerations about what information to request, how to interpret the information supplied, and indeed what information to supply to those requesting a reference from you.

Part of the reason for the low validity of references lies in the perceptions and skill of the person writing them or in hidden agendas that may influence what is or is not said. The effects of perceptions that may occur here are similar to the interviewer errors that were discussed in Chapter 7 in that our opinions of people, even when we have known them for some time, are influenced by our own perceptual set. Lukewarm descriptions of people's abilities may also be due to inadequate powers of expression or reserve on the part of the writer.

Because of the low validity of references, employers are sometimes advised to use them to check factual information only, but references may indicate some serious problem that should be pursued for further clarification or some discrepancy in factual information such as dates of employment which should also be pursued. References should obviously, therefore, be used with caution, and human resource specialists should find ways to improve the quality of the information their organisation receives in response to requests for references.

Requesting a reference

What could you do to improve the quality of references you have solicited?

Referees are able to respond better if you indicate what areas you would like feedback on, such as skills and personal qualities. Since you are seeking information on these as they relate to performance on the job, it would be useful to provide a job description or a brief outline of critical tasks. You might also consider supplying a referee with documents and checklists you will be using to evaluate candidates, such as the person specification or checklists of competencies and behaviours.

Some employers provide a questionnaire to guide the referee and help him or her to save time when composing a reference. This, together with a covering letter explaining your request, shows courtesy to referees and may contribute to the probability of your receiving a useful response.

Supplying references

Although you are not involved in making the selection decision when you provide a reference, it is worth considering the responsibility of the referee at this stage. In giving a reference to a potential employer, referees owe a duty of care to the receiving organisation. That is, referees would render themselves culpable if they knowingly deceived another organisation and misled it into hiring a person whom they knew to be unsuitable. In the case of *Spring* v. *Guardian Royal Exchange* (1994), the House of Lords also ruled that an employer has a duty to the employee to provide a reference composed with due care and may be held liable for losses due to negligent misstatement.

The laws and regulations on discrimination also apply to actions that might be taken subsequent to employment, for example the provision of references. It is, therefore, unlawful to make discriminatory statements in references, for example with regard to a person's sexual orientation or beliefs as covered in the relevant regulations (ACAS, 2005a and 2005b).

Criminal record checks

You may remember that the Rehabilitation of Offenders Act was mentioned in Chapter 5. Essentially this Act outlines the concept of offences that are spent and protects offenders from having to reveal these spent offences. There are, however, some offences that are never spent, and some positions for which those guilty of particular offences will not be suitable. For example, any person who has been found guilty of assaulting a child would not be considered suitable for a position working in a school where unsupervised contact with children might occur. Such positions are excepted from the Rehabilitation of Offenders Act, and there are arrangements for organisations such as local authorities to obtain a check of criminal records for individuals applying for posts such as these.

Criminal Records Bureau

The Criminal Records Bureau (CRB) was set up under Part V of the Police Act 1997 and it currently supplies two levels of information relevant to individuals' suitability for certain types of employment or volunteer activities. The levels of certificate available are standard and enhanced. The main characteristics of each, as described on the CRB website **www.crb.gov.uk**, are:

Standard

- All convictions and cautions including spent convictions.
- Available when people apply for work or volunteer activities with children or vulnerable adults.
- Available only for positions excepted under the Rehabilitation of Offenders Act 1974 (Exceptions) Order 1975.
- The individual's application form is countersigned by the representative of a registered body.
- Certificate is sent to the individual applicant and a copy to the registered body.

Enhanced

- All convictions and cautions including spent convictions as for the standard certificate, but with additional information on non-conviction incidents recorded in local police records.
- Available where people will have substantial, unsupervised access to children and vulnerable adults.
- Available only for positions excepted under the Rehabilitation of Offenders Act 1974 (Exceptions) Order 1975.
- The individual's application form is countersigned by the representative of a registered body.
- Certificate is sent to the individual applicant and a copy to the registered body.

Standard and enhanced certificates also include information from lists of people barred from working in schools or deemed unsuitable for work with children or vulnerable adults by the responsible government authorities. There are charges for organisations which wish to register with the Bureau and for the issue of certificates.

Employer access to records

The reason for the establishment of the CRB was to provide a safer environment for vulnerable groups such as children, the elderly, sick and the disabled, and to set up a system for handling the growing number of requests for information on those wishing to work with these groups. It should be noted that employers requiring a certificate that reveals spent convictions, i.e. a standard or enhanced certificate, must register with the Bureau, supplying it with evidence that such requests are for a legitimate purpose. In essence, this means employers referred to in the Rehabilitation of Offenders Act 1974 (Exceptions) Order 1975.

A source of potential difficulty lies with other employers enquiring and making decisions based on a person's past offences. Employers are entitled to ask potential employees the question: 'Do you have a criminal record?' Ex-offenders are protected by the Rehabilitation of Offenders Act 1974 from having to reveal *spent* convictions, but, as the CIPD (2007a) highlights, they may experience a dilemma when faced with having to declare *unspent* convictions to a potential employer. It is an accepted fact that obtaining employment is a major factor in rehabilitation and preventing recidivism, so it is socially desirable that every opportunity to secure suitable employment should be obtainable for ex-offenders. The CIPD therefore urges employers to ask questions about criminal records only where it is relevant to the job, and to handle any information provided with sensitivity. The CIPD provides several documents examining good practice with regard to selection decisions about ex-offenders, and promotes a risk assessment approach for organisations (**www.cipd.co.uk/ research_offenders**).

Graphology, phrenology, astrology, lie detector tests

These tests have been grouped together because of their somewhat dubious predictive validity, and none of them is used to any great extent in the UK, if at all. Graphology refers to the analysis of handwriting, phrenology to the examination of bumps on the head and astrology to the influence of the stars. Lie detector or polygraph tests involve the measurement of physical reactions that supposedly reveal whether a person is lying or telling the truth when answering a set of questions. Polygraph tests are known to identify correctly people who are lying, but they also sometimes give false positives and identify as lying people who are telling the truth.

Health checks

Most positions require only general good health, and the completion of a routine questionnaire should suffice to judge a candidate's suitability. Information about absence records can also be specifically requested as part of the reference from former employers. If medical evidence is required from an applicant's general practitioner, the applicant's consent must be obtained first.

Making the final selection

In the two chapters on selection we have described a number of techniques for your consideration. An important issue to identify and emphasise at this stage is the need to use *all* the information that has been gathered.

There is a tendency to focus on the last stage of the process one has engaged in and to forget prior information, or at least to attribute undue weight and importance to the last stage. For instance, it will often happen that a person who is well qualified on paper but has poor interview skills is eliminated. Is the possession of polished interview skills really a critical success factor for the post in question? Is it wise to allow the interview to be so influential, given the evidence on the reliability and validity of interviews? If you are using a variety of selection techniques, you must decide in advance what each method is going to contribute to the overall assessment. Some things will carry more weight than others, and this should be decided in advance and each component appropriately weighted. Some things will be designated as essential prerequisites, and the lack of other things may be balanced by the presence of something else. For a post managing an accounting unit, for example, good writing skills may be allowed to balance a lack of polished presentation skills, but mathematical ability will be essential. You must decide what to do if there is conflicting evidence, for example if someone performs well in the interview but not in the ability tests or vice versa.

Scoring and ranking

It is, then, important to find some methodical approach to evaluating the information you have gathered, enabling you to rank the candidates in order of preference. There are several approaches to this and a variety of issues to consider:

- Decide on the cut-off percentage score a candidate must achieve in order to be considered.
- Decide which criteria must be met and which can be traded off against each other.
- Use ticks and crosses to record the assessment of candidates.

Figure 8.2 Sample candidate assessment form

Key for individual scores: 5 = excellent, 3 = good, 1 = acceptable Minimum acceptable scores Job knowledge: 38.4/64 (60%) Total score: 74.5/149 (50%)	POST: _____ ASSESSOR: _____			
	Job knowledge Weight factor: 0.8	**Organisational ability** Weight factor: 0.6	**Experience** Weight factor: 0.5	**Ability to persuade** Weight factor: 0.6
Application form Weight factor: 4	3×4 12		4×4 16	
Interview Weight factor: 6	4×6 24		3×6 18	3×6 18
Work sample test Weight factor: 6	4×6 24	5×6 30		
Ability test Weight factor: 4		3×4 12		
Personality questionnaire Weight factor: 4				4×4 16
Weighted criterion totals	48	25.2	17	20.4

Candidate total score: 110.6
Candidate ranked against others: 2nd of 6

Explanatory notes

The form indicates weightings that would be agreed on some justifiable basis. In this case, job knowledge is weighted higher than the other criteria, and more weight is given to the interview and work sample test than the other assessment methods.

The line under the scores would appear on the blank form to indicate which factors are to be scored under each assessment method.

Any score that fell below the agreed minimum could be ringed on the form to draw attention to the fact that the candidate is no longer to be considered.

● Decide on the relative weight of each assessment criterion and assign points accordingly to each factor, amalgamating scores from the various assessment methods. Calculate a total score for each candidate.

Figure 8.2 is a sample form to record and tabulate results.

After all the selection activities have been completed, all the selectors should compare their rankings of the candidates and decide on the best candidate. If there are discrepancies in the ratings, these discrepancies can form the basis of discussion and, if necessary, of further information seeking.

● Providing information

It is often forgotten that applicants for a post also have a decision to make about whether or not they wish to accept the offer of employment. It is risky to assume that merely applying for a job means the applicant will ultimately want the post. If new employees leave shortly after being hired, this can hardly be considered to be successful selection. Just as the selectors gather information on which to base their decision, so the applicants should gather or be given information so that they too will make the right decision.

One obvious way of giving applicants information is to encourage them to ask questions during the interview. In this way you know that you have clarified any points that are important to individual applicants, and these may of course differ from one person to the next. Also, if your interview questions and work sample tests are properly constructed to obtain job-related information from applicants, these questions and tests will have imparted a wealth of information to the interviewee, albeit obliquely. Applicants may, however, still be unaware of certain aspects of the job, and it is incumbent on the selectors to make sure that applicants know about any factors that might influence their decision, and in particular the likelihood of their remaining with the organisation for a reasonable length of time if they do accept an offer of employment.

Very often the factors that cause rapid turnover among new employees are to do with unpleasant working conditions. If recruitment and selection were just about getting people to accept employment with your organisation, it would make sense to hide information about the negative aspects of your workplace. Many organisations have realised, however, that there is a greater likelihood of retaining new recruits if they are open and honest about the less pleasant aspects of their work environment. Offering interviewees information of this nature is known as a realistic job preview. Realistic job previews can take the form of oral information given by interviewers either to individual interviewees or in a group session before the interviews, or written documentation provided to candidates, for example statements about the working conditions included in job descriptions. There are, however, some more innovative ways of providing this kind of information.

In 1995 students in the Transport and Logistics department at the University of Huddersfield created a short video film for a distribution company that wanted to alert applicants to the fact that the jobs in its warehouse involved cold, uncongenial working conditions, as most of the work took place in refrigerated areas. This film was made available in job centres so that people who did not wish to work in such conditions would not even apply in the first instance. Realistic job previews can, then, be provided at any stage in the recruitment and selection process, but they are probably most useful at the interview stage, when there is an opportunity to discuss and clarify details.

Additional activities that could be undertaken with the specific purpose of giving information to candidates include a tour of the organisation's premises, which gives applicants a first-hand look at the environment they would be working in and an opportunity to meet prospective colleagues. Letting applicants chat unattended with prospective colleagues means that managers have no control over the kinds of information that will be exchanged; it is rather akin to using the 'sitting at Nellie's knee' method of training you will read about in Chapter 9. However, the exercise would make additional information available to potential employees, and it is worth considering the inclusion of such an opportunity in your selection process.

Administrative procedures

Once you have completed your selection process and made a decision about the successful candidate, there are a number of things you need to do to close the process:

- The successful candidate
  - offer the position to the successful candidate
  - secure his or her acceptance of the position
  - agree the details of the appointment
  - confirm the details in writing
  - check essential qualifications
  - initiate new employee processes.
- The unsuccessful candidates
  - inform the candidates of the outcome
  - provide feedback if appropriate.
- Prepare adequate records.
- Monitor the process.

Offer the position and agree details of appointment

Many employers prefer the personal touch of using the telephone to speak directly to the person they hope will be joining their organisation. Some organisations still prefer to make the initial offer in writing. Important details that need to be agreed at this stage include the start date, the starting salary and details about salary progression.

Confirm details in writing

Although an oral agreement can be regarded as a contract, most employers and employees feel more secure about the arrangement if it is put in writing. Usually the employer will write to the candidate to confirm the appointment and in turn require written confirmation of acceptance from the candidate. There is also a legal obligation to give a statement of terms and conditions to most employees, as we discussed in more detail in Chapter 4.

Check essential documents

If specific qualifications are required for the post, for example, a degree, a driving licence or professional certification, the selected candidate should be required to present the documentation as proof that he or she does in fact possess the relevant qualifications.

A further, general requirement that applies to all employees is, of course, that they are legally entitled to work in the UK. The Asylum and Immigration Act 1996 reinforced the employer's responsibility for ascertaining that every new employee has the appropriate status. If employers selectively check only those applicants who, because of their appearance or a foreign-sounding name, arouse doubts about their citizenship status, such action could be deemed to be unlawful racial discrimination. To avoid this and at the same time fulfil the section 8 requirement to check employees' status, employers need to audit the documentation of all new employees at some stage in the selection process. A record of documented evidence of a person's national insurance number, such as a pay slip issued by a former employer, was originally deemed to be adequate proof of the fact that an employer had carried out this duty, but this was changed with effect from 1 May 2004 with regard to all persons hired from that date on. Section 8 now requires that employers check and copy either one document from a given list or a specified combination of two documents from a second list. An example from the first list (one document only required) is a document showing that the holder is a national of a European Economic Area country or Switzerland. This must be a national passport or identity card (**www.homeoffice.gov.uk**; accessed 13/08/07). Employers may also hire asylum seekers, but only if they have an application registration card issued by the Home Office, specifically giving permission to work in the UK. A letter from the Home Office is not sufficient. This example demonstrates how complex the issues can be, so it always advisable for employers to check on the Home Office website where they will find a lot of helpful and detailed information and guidance. The website also gives information about documents that are not acceptable, such as a UK driving licence or a utility bill.

Initiate new employee processes

In addition to the appointment letter and check of credentials, there are a number of administrative details that need to be attended to for each employee. These include such things as acquiring details on pension arrangements, ascertaining preferences with regard to benefits (if a cafeteria system of benefits is in place, and employees can choose some benefits in preference to others), acquiring personal details such as bank account data for payroll purposes, and determining whether the person wishes union dues to be deducted from salary if a check-off system is in place. These administrative details will vary from one workplace to another, and it is sufficient here to note that they need to be planned and administered.

Inform the unsuccessful candidates of the outcome

Unsuccessful candidates should be treated with courtesy and informed as soon as possible of the outcome of the selection process, usually as soon as the preferred candidate has accepted the post. We have mentioned before that there is a public relations element in the way that recruitment and selection are performed. It is probably one of the few times that outsiders are invited into your organisation and are able to observe at first hand how you treat people. You will usually reject more people than you hire, and these people could be customers or even still potential employees whom you would not wish to alienate. Most candidates who have made it through the interview stage are serious about wanting the post, and inevitably will be disappointed that they have not succeeded. The rejection message needs, therefore, to be delivered with some sensitivity and, if possible, to avoid implying that these candidates have failed or are of inferior calibre.

ACTIVITY 8.4

Compose a standard letter that could be used for informing applicants that they have not been selected for a position. A model letter is given in Appendix 8.6 for you to compare with your proposed letter.

● Feedback to candidates

Usually employers do not take the initiative in offering feedback to rejected candidates unless psychological tests have been used, in which case it is considered to be good practice to do so. However, some candidates are aware that asking for feedback can make a good impression with potential employers and that honest feedback might assist them in their further job search. Proper assessment of candidates should enable employers to be ready to give feedback to candidates in a sensitive manner.

● Record keeping

The assessment record can form part of the recorded justification of why candidates were selected or rejected. In addition, preparing a summary statement of the reasons for the decisions, i.e. a statement of why the selected candidate was the preferred candidate and why the unsuccessful candidates were rejected, adds some rigour to the process. It is also necessary to keep such records to be able to provide evidence of good practice in case any applicant feels he or she has been subjected to unlawful discrimination and takes a complaint to an employment tribunal. The burden of proof, which means that employers, when challenged at a tribunal, must provide positive evidence of non-discrimination, is described in more detail in Chapter 5. Since the time limit for presenting a claim of discrimination to an employment tribunal is three months, it would seem sensible to keep detailed records of selection decisions for at least that period of time, and indeed the CIPD (2006b) recommends keeping them for one year.

● Monitor the process

The selection process should be monitored for several purposes:

- to ensure that selection is being conducted within the framework of the organisation's policies and equality legislation
- to examine the validity of selection decisions
- to ensure there is an acceptable level of reliability among assessors and interviewers.

A statistical analysis of the candidates who proceed through the various stages of selection will identify trends and provide feedback about how various groups fare throughout the selection process. The data could be analysed in terms of groupings of internal vs. external candidates, male vs. female, age profiles, racial groups and the disabled, etc. Remember that public sector employers are obliged by law to carry out monitoring of their recruitment and selection processes with regard to racial, gender and disability equality. Monitoring by private sector employers is not prescribed by legislation but is regarded as good practice and may be helpful if decisions are challenged in an employment tribunal.

Another important consideration is whether the selection process results in the acquisition of high-performing employees. Data from performance appraisals and information about promotions could be cross-referenced with the ratings awarded to candidates in the various selection exercises to show whether assessment during the selection process correlates with performance on the job.

The ratings arrived at by individual interviewers and assessors can be compared and the reasons for discrepancies investigated. This information can be used to identify the training needs of those involved in selection.

International issues in selection

It was established in Chapter 6 that recruitment for international operations could be ethnocentric, polycentric, regiocentric or geocentric or indeed a combination of these. Our main focus in this section, because the wider picture is so complex and beyond the scope of this textbook, will be on geocentric expatriate assignments.

It is well established that the success of overseas assignments is regarded as being crucial for organisations as much expense is involved in organising them and settling the employee and potentially his or her family abroad (IRS, 2000). This is especially so if the assignment is for a considerable length of time (2–5 years), usually referred to as an expatriate assignment. Working as an expatriate also means calling on a wider range of competencies than working in the home country environment. Workers posted overseas will need all of the competencies required of a domestic employee in their line of work with additional competencies to cope with working in a foreign environment. A number of researchers have identified a range of these competencies, including flexibility and adaptability, higher levels of communication skills, resilience and intercultural awareness (Joynt and Morton, 1999; Edwards and Rees, 2006).

The contribution of selection processes to organisations has been established in this textbook, and given the crucial need for expatriate assignments to succeed, it is obvious that careful selection of employees for these assignments must play an essential role in their success. A sophisticated approach involving psychological tests *could* be the answer, but Lucas *et al.* (2006) note that many multinational enterprises will select internal candidates whose competencies they already know well for overseas assignments. They also maintain, however, that increasingly organisations will need to select from a global, external labour market. In the latter case, sophisticated assessment methods will become more important.

Transnational companies draw their employees from all over the world, a geocentric approach, so tests must be capable of measuring the required competencies without ethnic bias. Pickard (2004) has written about the search for psychometric tests which an organisation could use all over the world, and the issue about the transferability of tests across different countries is raised by Brewster *et al.* (2007). It is an issue identified by these writers as needing further development. A further matter for concern which acquires greater significance in an international context is the use and integrity of Internet-based tests (Lucas *et al.*, 2006).

Conclusion

Now that you have reviewed the approaches you can adopt to find a person who is going to be a productive colleague, you must turn your thoughts to what you can do to help integrate this person into your organisation as quickly and smoothly as possible. You will find a discussion of induction activities in Chapter 9. You should find the case study at the end of this chapter a useful exercise in putting together and applying all you have learned about recruitment and selection in this chapter and in Chapters 5, 6 and 7.

SELF-CHECK QUESTIONS

Answer the following multiple-choice and short-answer questions. The correct responses are given on page 475 for you to check your understanding of this chapter.

1 What kind of exercise did Makin and Robertson identify as being used most in assessment centres?
   (a) handwriting tests
   (b) group discussion
   (c) work sample
   (d) information technology skills.

2 A good selection technique predicts success on the job. Is this validity or reliability?

3 Interviews, according to Makin and Robertson, are used more than psychological tests. Is this because they have a higher validity? YES or NO

4 Psychological tests are most useful when the selection ratio is high. TRUE or FALSE?

5 Which of the following tests is regarded in the UK as being the least acceptable?
   (a) personality questionnaires
   (b) leaderless group test
   (c) graphology
   (d) attainment test.

6 Applicants for teaching posts may be asked to teach a class in their subject as part of the selection process. This is an example of:
   (a) a leaderless group exercise
   (b) a job sample test
   (c) a personality test
   (d) an attainment test.

7 Is the following statement true or false? The benefit of a realistic job preview is that it persuades people to join the organisation by presenting positive information about the job.

8 Which of the following statements best describes an assessment centre?
   (a) An assessment centre is a location where groups of candidates can be assessed by a number of assessors using a range of tests and exercises.
   (b) An assessment centre is a method of collecting information where groups of candidates are assessed by a number of assessors using a range of tests and exercises.

9 References are one of the most valid techniques of acquiring information about candidates. TRUE or FALSE?

10 When an activity has face validity, it means that it:
   (a) tests what it purports to test
   (b) resembles the activity it is testing for
   (c) includes a one-on-one interview together with written tests.

CASE STUDY 8.1 Recruitment and selection

Background information

You are the head of personnel management at the headquarters of the Recovery Insurance Group. The group has 40 branch offices based in the north of England. The Regional Head Office is in Leeds, and this is where you are based. You determine company personnel policy for the region. You normally have three personnel assistants who report to you, but there is a vacancy in one of these posts which you hope to fill soon. Each personnel assistant is responsible for the day-to-day personnel activities in a group of about a dozen branch offices which are generally between 15 and 20 miles apart from each other, but some of these are located 100 miles or so away from Leeds. Because the responsibility for some of the branches requires more travelling than others, the custom has been to rotate the allocation of branches among the personnel assistants on an annual basis.

You have been with the Recovery Group for just over 3 months, so you are still getting up to speed yourself on some of the people management issues that Recovery needs to focus on. You are professionally qualified yourself. You undertook a BA in Business Management before getting your first job as an administrative assistant in a personnel department in a bank. While you worked there, you studied part time for your CIPD qualifications and progressed to being one of the personnel officers for the bank. Since then you have worked for a further two years for another insurance company in the south of England before taking up your present post as head of personnel at Recovery.

The company operates a performance appraisal scheme and at present has a manual system for keeping personnel records. You have been particularly concerned by the fact that the system seems unable to provide information about employee time-keeping and absences. However, the senior managers in the company have decided to introduce a computerised personnel and payroll system in the future, and as soon as you started with them you were given the responsibility for leading a team which has chosen and recommended the purchase of a system called PersPay. Now one of your major responsibilities will be to ensure the successful implementation of this system.

You have persuaded the senior managers of Recovery to upgrade the vacant personnel assistant post, as you will need to have someone to help with the development of the computerised operations. This person will have to work closely with members of the payroll office as some parts of the system will be linked, for example, the entry of salary figures, and start and termination dates. Relations between the payroll and personnel offices have been good, but each department is facing increasing workload demands with no possibility of acquiring extra staff, so there may be some difficulty in agreeing the assignment of duties between the two departments.

→

A further matter you are working on is the development of a new application form for Recovery as their current version has become outdated in the face of the growth of equality legislation over the last few years. Because of this, you have decided to accept CVs for all vacancies until the new form is designed.

Incidentally, you have also secured the agreement of the senior managers that you may rename your department and call it the Department of Human Resource Management to reflect the change in approach you wish to bring to the management of employees at Recovery.

Your tasks

1 One of the first things you want to do is fill the vacancy for the personnel assistant. You find a job description on file (see Appendix 8.1), but you feel it could be better written and needs to be updated. Produce the new job description.

2 Produce a person specification to accompany the job description.

3 Design an advertisement, and say where you will place it and why.

4 Outline the selection process you intend to follow, including any techniques you will use to supplement the interview.

5 Prepare a set of questions to be asked at interview. Write a brief rationale for these questions.

6 Among the CVs you receive from applicants for the post are four included here as Appendices 8.2, 8.3, 8.4 and 8.5. Evaluate these four applicants, and explain whom you would invite for interview, giving your rationale for reaching these decisions.

7 After reviewing Chapters 5 and 6, and conducting any further research necessary, design an application form for this post, paying due attention to the implications of equality legislation. Write some brief notes explaining the structure and content of your application form.

HR IN THE NEWS
FT

Psychometric tests: why it pays to practice

By Richard Donkin

The prospect of negotiating yet another series of hoops either before or after university 'finals' is rarely welcomed among graduates.

But psychometric testing has become so ubiquitous in candidate sifting and assessment that some occupational psychologists believe that job applicants can benefit by familiarising themselves with the most popular selection methods.

'I think graduates today are accepting that psychometric testing is part of the deal and many of them will have practised tests before they go for a job,' says Penny Moyle, head of research and product development at OPP, the business psychology consultancy. 'There's a degree of comfort in doing so.'

The testing market has benefited in the past few years from the accumulation of information that has become available through greater use of online testing and better data collection.

The broader availability of tests, particularly online, means that it is difficult for test publishers to produce material that job applicants have not encountered before. Specific questions can be changed but the nature of questioning in many tests is becoming increasingly familiar to job applicants.

So anyone trying a psychometric test for the first time could be placing themselves at a disadvantage.

The most widely used tests are those examining abilities such as verbal and calculating skills and problem solving. Some look for a specific skill such as understanding graphs and diagrams.

There is also a growing market for personality questionnaires seeking to tease out the sort of social situations in which a candidate feels most comfortable. Some selling roles, for example, may look for evidence of an extrovert nature.

Yet more questionnaires – and these are not strictly tests – are looking for evidence of certain competencies – a combination of skills and traits that define how people approach their work.

In a recent study, Hobsons, the graduate information business, included within its summer survey of 26,000 UK graduates a set of questions prepared by SHL, the human resources group.

The questions focused on graduates' perceptions of their own skills, abilities and behaviours, covering what SHL calls the 'great eight' competencies in workplace performance: leading, supporting, presenting, analysing, creating, organising, adapting and enterprising.

Since these were not job applications where candidates might have been tempted to second-guess the qualities being sought, the students could be frank in their self-assessments.

The survey found that very few graduates were what it called 'all singing and all dancing'. Students among the Russell Group of 19 leading universities demonstrated strong decision-making, analysing and organisational skills, as might be expected.

But the same students did not rate themselves highly when it came to team-working roles that require support and co-operation – the very kind of working practices expected in most large organisations.

The results may say more about an examination-driven education system than student behaviour. Students are graded individually from school to university in a system that fosters competition among individuals, often at the expense of co-operation. In written tests schoolchildren are not encouraged to share their thinking.

Recruiters are looking for evidence in job applications that graduates can overcome such institutional insularity. Team-working and good communication skills tend to be sought after in many of the competency-based questionnaires.

'Companies are looking for the underlying competencies that make people good management and leadership material and they are trying to identify that at the point of entry,' says Ms Moyle.

She recommends that graduates familiarise themselves with the sort of questions they will face in ability tests but believes there is 'no point' in practising personality tests. 'They are hard to second guess and even if you did you are probably not doing yourself much of a service if you end up a square peg in a round hole,' she says.

Job applicants are not always in a position to question the selection process but where tests are being used it is reasonable to expect feedback, says Ms Moyle. She believes occupational psychologists should be closely involved in the interpretation of test results, particularly when selectors are using personality tests.

'There are still vast swathes that we know very little about so it's important that we do not oversell the promise of these tests,' she says.

(FT.com, 13 October 2006. Reproduced with permission.)

Questions

1 Why should graduates prepare themselves for psychometric tests?

2 Which competencies are normally assessed in psychometric tests?

WHAT NEXT?

Now that you have mastered the introductory level of information about supplementary selection techniques presented in this chapter, you may wish to take your studies to a higher level. The IRS article cited below is a 20-page review of current practice with regard to assessment centres. Read the article and make notes of what employers see as the important issues. You might also want to follow the links given in the article to acquire more practical knowledge about how to run assessment centres, for instance by reading the guidelines produced by the British Psychological Society.

> Industrial Relations Services (2007) Assessment centres: the IRS report, *IRS Employment Review 877*, 16/7 (available at www.xperthr.co.uk; accessed 20/07/2007).

Another article looks at the Big Five characteristics discussed in this chapter, and reviews research to determine the relevance of these characteristics for predicted performance in the expatriate context compared with their use in domestic recruitment and selection. The article provides an interesting review of the factors that are important in selecting employees for long-term overseas postings.

> Mol, S.T., M.P. H. Born, M.E. Willemsen and H.T. van der Molen (2005) Predicting expatriate job performance for selection purposes: A quantitative review, *Journal of Cross-Cultural Psychology,* Vol. 36, No. 5, September, 590–620.

References

Advisory, Conciliation and Arbitration Service (2005a) *Religion or Belief and the Workplace: A Guide for Employers and Employees,* ACAS.

Advisory, Conciliation and Arbitration Service (2005b) *Sexual Orientation and the Workplace: A Guide for Employers and Employees,* ACAS.

Anderson, N. and V. Shackleton (1994) Informed choices, *Personnel Today,* 8 November, 33–34.

Armstrong, M. (2006) *A Handbook of Human Resource Management Practice,* 10th edition, Kogan Page.

Brewster, C., P. Sparrow and G. Vernon (2007) *International Human Resource Management,* 2nd edition, CIPD.

Chartered Institute of Personnel and Development (2006a) *Recruitment, Retention and Turnover: Annual Survey Report 2006,* CIPD.

Chartered Institute of Personnel and Development (2006b) *Retention of Personnel and Other Related Records* (www.cipd.co.uk; accessed 17.08.07).

Chartered Institute of Personnel and Development (2007a) *Employing People With Criminal Records* (www.cipd.co.uk; accessed 06.03.07).

Chartered Institute of Personnel and Development (2007b) *Psychological Testing* (www.cipd.co.uk; accessed 06.03.07).

Chartered Institute of Personnel and Development (2007c) *Recruitment, Retention and Turnover: Annual Survey Report 2007,* CIPD.

Edwards, T. and C. Rees (2006) *International Human Resource Management,* Financial Times Prentice Hall.

HR Zone (2006) *Over 200,000 Royal Mail Candidates to be Assessed Online* (www.hrzone.co.uk; accessed 20.06.06).

Incomes Data Services (2002) *IDS Studies 735: Assessment Centres,* September, IDS.

Industrial Relations Services (2000) Working all over the world, *IRS Employment Trends 699,* March, 3–11.

Industrial Relations Services (2007) Assessment centres: the IRS report, *IRS Employment Review 877,* 16/7 (available at www.xperthr.co.uk; accessed 20.07.07).

Joynt P. and B. Morton (eds.) *The Global HR Manager,* IPD.

Lucas, R., B. Lupton and H. Mathieson (2006) *Human Resource Management in an International Context,* CIPD.

Makin, P. and I. Robertson (1986) Selecting the best selection techniques, *Personnel Management,* November, 38–40.

Marchington, M. and A. Wilkinson (2005) *Human Resource Management at Work: People Management and Development,* 3rd edition, CIPD.

Mol, S.T., M.P. H. Born, M.E. Willemsen and H.T. van der Molen (2005) Predicting expatriate job performance for selection purposes: A quantitative review, *Journal of Cross-Cultural Psychology,* Vol. 36 No. 5, September, 590–620.

Murphy, K.R. and C.O. Davidshofer (2001) *Psychological Testing: Principles and Applications,* 5th edition, Prentice Hall.

Newell, S. and V. Shackleton (1991) Management selection: a comparative survey of methods used in top British and French companies, *Journal of Occupational Psychology,* Vol. 94, 23–36.

People Management (2001) Frames of mind, 14 June, 26–37.

Pickard, J. (2004) Testing times, *People Management,* 29 January, 43–44.

Ready, D.A. and J.A. Conger (2007) Make your company a talent factory, *Harvard Business Review,* June, 68–77.

Robertson, I. (2001) Undue diligence, *People Management,* 22 November, 42–43.

Sloane, W. (2007) Online probes to the parts others don't reach, *The Sunday Times: Recruiting* (insert).

Smith, M. and I.T. Robertson (1993) *The Theory and Practice of Systematic Personnel Selection,* 2nd edition, Macmillan.

Toplis, J., V. Dulewicz and C. Fletcher (2004) *Psychological Testing,* 4th edition, Chartered Institute of Personnel and Development.

Woodruffe, C. (2000) *Development and Assessment Centres: Identifying and Developing Competence,* 3rd edition, CIPD.

www.homeoffice.gov.uk; accessed 15.08.07.

Further study

Books

Advisory, Conciliation and Arbitration Service (2006) *Recruitment and Induction,* ACAS. A concise overview of good practice in recruitment and selection, available at www.acas.org.uk.

Ballantyne, I. and N. Povah (2004) *Assessment and Development Centres,* 2nd edition, Gower/ Personnel Today Management Resources. A practically orientated overview of the various aspects of assessment centres with detailed chapters on their design and implementation.

Chartered Institute of Personnel and Development (2007) *Psychological Testing.* A factsheet available at www.cipd.co.uk. A concise guide to the issues involved in choosing to use psychological tests and advice on how to use them in a professional manner.

Cook, M. (2004) *Personnel Selection: Adding Value through People,* Wiley. A thorough review of selection methods and issues, including interviews, tests, assessment centres and validity.

Incomes Data Services (2000) *IDS Study Plus: Psychological Tests,* IDS. Good information on psychological testing in a concise format.

Incomes Data Services (2003) *IDS Studies: Recruitment Practices,* No. 751, June, IDS. A concise overview of the basic range of both recruitment and selection practices with case studies of six employers, including B&Q and Marks & Spencer.

Roberts, G. (1997) *Recruitment and Selection: A Competency Approach,* IPD. A readable overview of all aspects of the recruitment and selection processes.

Toplis, J., V. Dulewicz and C. Fletcher (2004) *Psychological Testing,* 4th edition, Chartered Institute of Personnel and Development. Provides an excellent overview of everything managers need to know about psychological testing in the workplace in order to be able to make informed decisions.

Articles

Anderson, N. and V. Shackleton (1994) Informed choices, *Personnel Today,* 8 November, 33–34. A brief overview of the popularity and accuracy of various selection methods and a comment on patterned behaviour description and situational interviews.

Drury, B. (2001) How to assess criminal convictions, *People Management,* 22 March, 52–3. A succinct summary of the law and the system for accessing criminal records, and recommendations for good employment practice.

Fowler, A. (1998) How to create effective job simulations, *People Management,* 11 June, 52–5. The 'How to . . .' series provides very useful summaries of the major considerations in a range of human resource management activities. See also McHenry (2003), below.

Industrial Relations Services (2001) Checking out new recruits, *Employee Development Bulletin 135,* March, 11–16. Reviews the reasons for pursuing references, their usefulness, the legal position, and advice on how to structure reference requests.

Lynch, B. (1985) Graphology: towards a hand-picked workforce, *Personnel Management,* March, 14–17. A review of some personal responses of various individuals to an analysis of their handwriting.

McHenry, R. (2003) How to make use of psychometrics, *People Management,* 17 April, 52–3.

Internet

British Psychological Society   **www.psychtesting.org.uk**
Offers information about psychological tests to test-takers and test-users, as well as general information and pages on current issues. Check out the interesting frequently asked questions and the links to companies which offer practice tests. Look also for the Guidelines and Information section where a number of useful documents on psychological testing, assessment centres and international tests can be downloaded.

Chartered Institute of Personnel and Development   **www.cipd.co.uk**
The CIPD site provides useful information on psychological testing and other aspects of recruitment and selection.

Criminal Records Bureau   **www.crb.gov.uk**
Describes the work of the CRB and provides recommendations on good practice.

Equal Opportunities Commission   **www.eoc.org.uk**
Provides a checklist specifically designed for line managers on handling situations that might arise during the selection process, including the use of tests. Go to the main site and search for the equality checklists.

HR Zone   **www.hrzone.co.uk**
Over several weeks in 2006, HR Zone presented concise reviews of a number of psychological tests under the heading 'Psychometrics Spotlight', including comment on their usefulness in the workplace. The 16PF Personality Questionnaire, the FIRO-BTM personality questionnaire, the ABLE exercises and the Innovation Potential Indicator are all described as being useful during the selection process as well as for other HR applications.

Immigration and Nationality Directorate   **www.homeoffice.gov.uk**
This site will give you very detailed information about employers' responsibilities with regard to the Asylum and Immigration Act 1996.

Appendix 8.1

Recovery Insurance Group

JOB DESCRIPTION

Job title: personnel assistant

Responsible to: personnel manager

Responsible for: no one reports to this position directly, but can request work from the word-processing pool and personnel records clerks

Main purpose: to provide a day-to-day advisory service to branch managers on personnel policy and procedures

Duties: to monitor application for employment forms submitted by branch managers for candidates selected by them

to agree salary details (in accordance with company pay scales) with branch managers

to pass rejected applications to word-processing for standard rejection letters and check and sign those letters

to enter agreed salary, contract, job title and joining details on selected applications and pass to word-processing for documentation

to sign joining documentation on behalf of company

to advise branch managers on the interpretation and implementation of the company's disciplinary procedure

to advise branch managers on the interpretation and implementation of the company's sick pay scheme

to advise branch managers on the interpretation and implementation of relevant legislation – including Employment Protection, Race Relations, Rehabilitation of Offenders, Disabled Persons, and Health and Safety at Work

to pursue references, by letter and telephone, for selected applicants

to provide references, by letter and telephone, for past employees

to advise branch managers on current employees' salary entitlement, according to company incremental scales

to advise branch managers on the purpose and use of the company's performance appraisal scheme

to visit branches to advise on problems in any of the above areas, as necessary

General circumstances: Recovery Insurance Group has divided its business into four areas for administrative purposes, each containing about 12 branches. The branch managers are all experts in insurance, not necessarily in staff matters. As all are at different locations in the north of England, much of the communication with the personnel department is by telephone, although about one day per month is normally spent visiting branch offices.

Appendix 8.2

CURRICULUM VITAE

Jenni Paulson

Address:	9 Queen's Way Harrogate HA4 5SC
Telephone:	01423 000 000 0776 65 000 000 (mobile)

Employment history:

1999–2003   Personnel Coordinator, Hartley Building Society

Responsible for overseeing all personnel operations for the SW region of the building society. This included recruitment and selection, advice on policy and procedure to managers, and coordination of training. (Final salary: £25,000 per annum)

1996–1999   Assistant Personnel Manager, Hart, Fleet and Bunthorne Legal Group Recruitment of office staff, induction and training.

Professional membership: Chartered MCIPD

Education:

1996	University of Nottingham	MA (Industrial Relations)
1994	University of London	BA (Hons) 2.1 (English Language and Literature)
1989–1991	Hillingdon Girls School	9 GCSEs; A level English, German, Maths

Personal statement:

I have 7 years' experience in responsible personnel management positions and excellent academic qualifications. I have experience in all of the areas listed in your job description and feel sure I would enjoy the work at Recovery and make an excellent contribution as an employee.

During my career break since 2003, I have organised a mother and toddler group and I have been active at my local church.

References

Mr Peter White	Reverend Mark Acton
Director of Personnel	St Nicholas Church Vicarage
Hartley Building Society	Parkes Road
Regents Road	Harrogate
Cheltenham	HA4 9VP
Glocs	
CH4 9TS	
Tel: 01242 000 000	Tel: 01423 000 000

Appendix 8.3

Amanda Walters
43 Jackland Road
Newcross
Huddersfield
HD9 5CK
Tel: 01484 000 000

PERSONAL DETAILS

Date of Birth:	25 August 1962
Marital Status:	Divorced with one adult son

QUALIFICATIONS

1983 Secretarial Course. Typing 80 w.p.m
Shorthand 120 w.p.m

Short courses in word processing, databases and spreadsheets, including software for Windows.

Short courses in health and safety, supervisory skills, equal opportunities, and presentation skills.

EMPLOYMENT

1983–1995	Secretary to General Manager, Dyason's Cleaning Products.
1995–1997	Office Manager, Dywell Clothing Company.
1997–2000	Personal Assistant to the Director of Personnel, Dywell Clothing Company.
2000–2007	Assistant Personnel Officer, Dywell Clothing Company.
2008	Temporary jobs for Ace Recruitment Agency.

REASONS FOR APPLYING FOR THIS POST

I have worked for ten years in a personnel department and I have a wide range of experience including recruitment and selection, administration of personnel records, and running short courses in health and safety and supervisory skills. I am a trained secretary and have kept up my typing skills as well as updating my skills in office software. I feel that with my experience and background in personnel I have a lot to offer in a personnel position.

INTERESTS

I enjoy travelling abroad in the holidays, walking my two dogs, and I am also a member of the operatic society. I have taken part in several productions in recent years.

FURTHER INFORMATION

I was made redundant when Dywell was taken over by another company in 2007, and I have been working in temporary posts since then.

Appendix 8.4

Karim Hamid
5 Merton Road
Coldfield
Leeds
LS14 3BD

Telephone: 0113 000 000 (home) 0113 000 000 (work)
0777 88 000 000 (mobile)

CURRICULUM VITAE

Education:

1997–2004	Leeds High School	5 GCSEs A levels in History and Business Studies
2006–2007	Metropolitan University of Leeds	Professional Management Foundation Course (1st stage of CIPD PDS)

Student member of CIPD

Employment:

Oct 2004–Feb 2006   Meltham Office Supplies
Worked as a wages clerk. Recorded hours worked by part-time staff and calculated wages.

March 2006–present   Meltham Office Supplies
Personnel Assistant. I create personal files for all new starters and keep the files up to date. I send all details about new starters to the payroll office. I place adverts for all positions and organise the applications and interviews for the managers.

Personal statement:

I am very interested in developing my career in personnel. I feel I can expand on the skills I am learning at Meltham Office Supplies. I have successfully completed stage one of the CIPD qualification, and I hope to continue with this in the near future.

References available on request.

CURRICULUM VITAE

NAME   Arthur Jackson

ADDRESS   19 Craigley Road
                    Eastleigh
                    Hants.

TELEPHONE   Eastleigh 000000

EDUCATION

1983–1988   Eastleigh Comprehensive School, Eastleigh.
                    Obtained 4 GCSEs.

WORK EXPERIENCE

1991–1997   Office Clerk, Bilton Insurance Company, Eastleigh.
1997–1999   Assistant Supervisor, Bilton Insurance Company.
1999–2000   Assistant Training Officer, Bilton Insurance Company.
2000–2001   Temporary Office Worker, Eastleigh Council.
2001–2005   Insurance Salesman, Staywell Insurance, Portsmouth.
2005–2007   Personnel records clerk, Staywell Insurance.
2007–2008   Personnel Assistant, Stay well Insurance.

I would like this job because all my jobs have been in insurance companies
and i have lots of experience in personnel and training.

Appendix 8.6

Company name and logo
Company address
Town
PC1 1XX

Ms C Candidate
1 Named Street
Candidtown
PC1 1XX

1 June 2008

Dear Ms Candidate

I regret to inform you that the selection panel has selected another candidate for the position of Human Resource Assistant. I would like to thank you for the time and effort you put into your application for this post and for your participation in our selection process. The panel was impressed with the calibre of the candidates and had a difficult decision to make.

Please do not hesitate to apply again for any suitable position with Company Name.

Yours sincerely

A Barker
Director of Human Resources

CHAPTER **9**

Performance management and appraisal

Objectives

By the end of this chapter you will be able to:

- state what is meant by the term 'performance management'
- give examples of techniques used in the management of performance at work
- design a simple performance appraisal system
- discuss some of the key issues of performance management in international organisations.

It is always important for managers and supervisors to get the best performance from their workforce in terms of levels of production and quality of output. Performance management is concerned to get the best performance from the individual, but goes further in that it also aims to get the best performance from the team and from the organisation as a whole. It aims to improve performance in the workplace in order to achieve the organisation's strategic objectives.

Definitions of performance management

Armstrong and Baron (2005) define performance management as a process which:

> contributes to the effective management of individuals and teams in order to achieve high levels of organisational performance. As such, it establishes shared understanding about what is to be achieved and an approach to leading and developing people which will ensure it is achieved.

They endorse the definition produced by the IPM in 1992 that performance management is:

> a strategy which relates to every activity of the organisation set in the context of its human resource policies, culture, style and communication systems. The nature of the strategy depends on the organisational context and can vary from organisation to organisation.

Models of performance

Figure 9.1 shows what we regard as some of the key features of the performance management process but these will vary depending on the strategic objectives and culture of the organisation.

The organisation's strategic objectives need to be expressed in a way that everyone within the organisation understands, in effect by clearly communicating the organisation's vision for the future, or their Big Idea. While the strategic objectives will be primarily formulated by senior management this should be part of a two-way process and the strategic objectives should be agreed after extensive discussion. Involvement and clear communication should mean that everyone in the workforce feels engaged and that they can contribute to the achievement of the organisation's goals or big ideas either individually or as part of a team. The right-hand side of Figure 9.1 lists some of the tools and techniques that can be used as part of the performance management process for individuals, teams and the organisation itself.

While the tools and techniques used in performance management for the individual, the team and the organisation differ slightly, the performance management process itself is very similar for each and can be shown as a cyclical process. Figure 9.2 shows the performance management implementation process in this form. It does not matter whether the focus is on the individual, the team or the organisation as for each the performance management implementation process involves evaluating current levels of performance and assessing them against the desired levels. The aim is to improve performance, add value and contribute to meeting objectives at whatever level. Different techniques will be used in the evaluation and assessment of current levels of performance. The individual may be assessed against their objectives by using personal development reviews, performance appraisal interviews, or perhaps reports of errors or complaints. For teams or departments the information needed may involve a comparison with team or departmental targets or a summary of faults and complaints for that department. On an organisation-wide basis a great deal of data would need to be collected to indicate the extent to which the whole organisation was meeting objectives and cumulative feedback may be compiled using information from performance appraisals throughout the organisation, or from customer satisfaction surveys. Organisations need individuals to feel engaged in the process and may also conduct surveys to establish the extent to which the workforce feel motivated by various aspects of the performance management process such as the pay and incentives or the learning and development opportunities offered.

In each case the aim is to evaluate the current levels of performance and compare this with the assessment of the performance levels required. The levels of performance required will depend on the organisation's objectives which in turn feeds into departmental objectives, team objectives and individual objectives. In each case it will be necessary to decide whether the aim is to achieve a satisfactory level of performance, or whether it is to achieve higher performance levels to add more value to the organisation, or whether the objective is to transform performance levels by encouraging and enabling increasingly new or innovative ways of working.

Once a comparison has been made between desired performance levels and existing performance levels, choices have to be made about how these can be achieved for individuals, teams, departments or organisation-wide. Some of the techniques listed in Figure 9.1 may be chosen for each category and these then need

Figure 9.1 Performance management: a dynamic approach

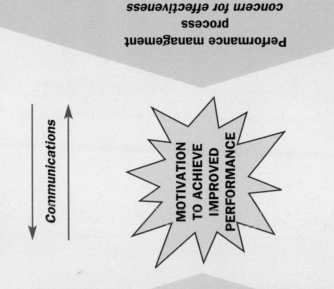

HRM approach

Mission statement
The Big Idea

Organisation's
strategic
objectives and
performance standards

Organisational
strategy

MOTIVATION
TO ACHIEVE
IMPROVED
PERFORMANCE

Communications

Involvement

Performance management
process
concern for effectiveness

Individual
Objective performance
appraisal and assessment
360° feedback
Performance and development reviews
Clear links to job descriptions
Measurement
Individual development plans
Performance-related pay
Competencies assessed
Learning and development
Coaching
Performance problem solving

Team
Objective ongoing assessment
Measurement
Annual/6-monthly team reviews
using performance indicators
Team building
Quality circles
Team incentives
Learning and development
Coaching
Performance problem solving

Organisation
Measurement
TQM
Organisation-wide incentives
Ongoing assessment of
organisation's objectives
Quality of working life
The learning organisation
ISO 9000
Investors in People
The balanced scorecard
Ways of getting line manager commitment
Learning and development
Coaching
Performance problem solving

Figure 9.2 The performance management implementation process

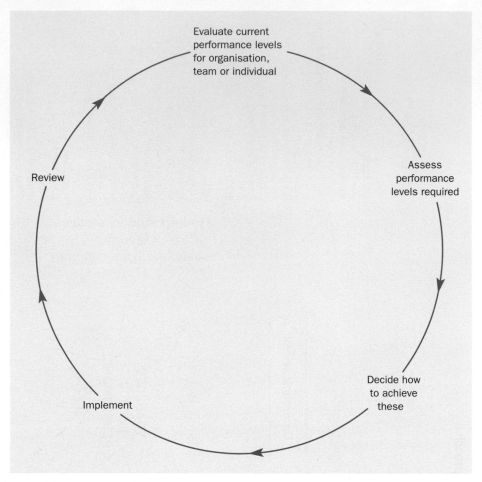

to be implemented. The process on an organisation-wide basis is likely to take a substantial amount of time.

Whatever techniques are chosen as part of the performance management process there should be a review to establish whether or not they have succeeded in meeting the objectives set and this continues into evaluating current performance levels against those required as new objectives are set to meet strategic objectives.

As far as the individual is concerned the performance management process could be viewed as starting at the selection stage as individuals are selected because of their skills, knowledge and competencies in order to make a contribution to the achievement of the strategic objectives. When the individual joins the organisation the induction into that organisation will be a way of communicating the organisation's strategic objectives, perhaps in a simpler form of one Big Idea that encapsulates the objectives. It also reinforces the organisation's culture and values. As they find out more about their job they should also discover how they can make a contribution to the performance of the organisation and the achievement of its strategic objectives. Figure 9.3 shows a model of the performance management process for the individual employee.

The induction should also be used as an opportunity to evaluate the individual's skills, knowledge and competencies using a personal development review and to

Figure 9.3 A model of the performance management process: the individual employee

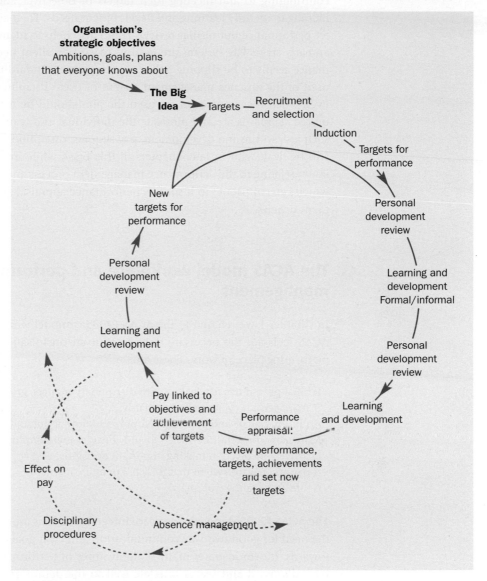

compare these with the organisation's or team's needs. Even though the person has been selected to carry out a specific job they may lack some of the skills, knowledge or competencies needed to work in that job or team. Plans should be made to meet any gaps between the individual's skills, knowledge and competencies and the organisation's or team's requirements for these. Decisions need to be made about the appropriate ways to fill any gaps between the two and this may involve using formal and informal learning and development methods. Individual goals and objectives will be set and the contribution expected by the individual to team or departmental goals and objectives will also need to be discussed. (The topics of induction and learning and development will be dealt with in more detail in the next chapter but they do contribute to the process of performance management.)

In a performance management system there will be regular performance development reviews throughout the year and also formal appraisal interviews at regular intervals. Each aims to monitor performance and see how individuals or teams are contributing to and meeting their targets or objectives and they are important in helping to identify learning and development needs. Their aim is to motivate for better performance but regular reviews could also help to identify poor performance at an early stage. Pay systems are used to reward excellent performance and if performance seems to be slipping below an acceptable standard then counselling may be used or the absence management system or even disciplinary system may be used. Even when these processes are used the aim should be to make clear what the required standards are and motivate the individual and team to achieve them. Topics such as learning and development, pay systems, discipline and absence management will be dealt with in later chapters of this book while in this chapter we focus on issues relating to the performance management process and some specific techniques which can contribute to it such as performance appraisal and performance development reviews.

● The ACAS model workplace and performance management

In Chapter 1 we referred to the ACAS (2005a) model workplace and outlined what ACAS feels are the necessary steps to turn an organisation into an effective high-performing place of work. These are:

> Formal procedures for dealing with disciplinary matters, grievances and disputes that managers know about and use fairly.
> Ambitions, goals and plans that employees know about and understand.
> Managers who genuinely listen to and consider their employees' views so everyone is actively involved in making important decisions.
> A pay and reward system that is clear, fair and consistent.
> A safe and healthy workplace.

The ACAS (2005a) model workplace integrates various aspects of HR and emphasises the need for good two-way communication and clear goals that employees can work towards. It demonstrates many of the features of performance management that we have discussed and seems to relate well to the definition given at the start of this chapter that stated performance management is a 'strategy which relates to every activity of the organisation set in the context of its human resource policies, culture, style and communication system' (IPM, 1992). We have advocated throughout this book the need for policies and procedures so that everyone knows and shares a common understanding of what is supposed to be done and this is clearly a key aspect of performance management. ACAS (2005a) says that this is a good start, but that the way things are done is also important. This is an approach we also emphasise throughout this book, as the way organisations manage performance can impact on most of the areas listed in the ACAS (2005a) model workplace and consequently can impact on workplace effectiveness.

Did you know?

The term performance management is used in a rather different way in a few organisations when they refer to 'performance managing someone out of an organisation' or putting someone on 'performance management'.

Have you heard the term used like this?
What do you think of this approach to performance management?

Performance management should be about trying to get improvements in performance but, as we showed in Figure 9.3, processes like attendance monitoring or disciplinary procedures are likely to form part of a performance management system. However, organisations that use the term performance management as almost a synonym for disciplining someone have not got the right idea about managing performance and motivating people. Performance management should be about motivating individuals, teams and organisations to make a contribution to the organisation's strategic objectives and should have much more focus on incentives and positive aspects of motivation rather than just focusing on a negative approach to people management as is the case when an organisation thinks that performance management is about 'performance managing someone out of the organisation'. Such a negative approach to performance management is certainly not an approach that we advocate.

The people and performance model

In Chapter 1 we also referred to the research carried out by Professor John Purcell and his team at the School of Management at the University of Bath (Purcell *et al.*, 2003). Their people and performance model also showed the interrelationship of different HR policies. However, while traditional HR policies and procedures were important in this, the other area that they said really made a difference in organisations was 'the way people work together to be productive and flexible enough to meet new challenges'. They found in the organisations they studied that the organisation first had to have strong values and an inclusive culture and, second, have sufficient numbers of skilled line managers to be able to bring the HR policies and practices to life. Both elements fit well with the view of performance management shown in the definition we used earlier from Armstrong and Baron (2004) that performance management is a process for sharing an understanding about what needs to be achieved and then managing and developing people in a way that enables such shared objectives to be achieved.

Purcell and his team found that in the organisations that were most successful at managing performance, everyone did share common values. There was generally what the researchers called 'a Big Idea' that was meaningful to everyone in the organisation (Purcell *et al.*, 2003). This could be about the importance of customers to the organisation or the pursuit of quality, but in all cases it was an idea that everyone could relate to. Whatever it was, they all shared the idea and then managed the performance of people accordingly.

The people and performance model indicates that it is not just the people management policies and practices that create value to an organisation but that they help form part of the process by creating the blocks that form the basis of achieving increased performance which Purcell calls ability, motivation and opportunity (AMO) (CIPD, 2007a). This assumes that people have the **ability** to learn new skills and will want to work in organisations where their abilities and skills are recognised and can be developed further. **Motivation** assumes that the organisation will be successful in motivating them to use their abilities in a way that is useful to the organisation in achieving its strategic objectives, while **opportunity** makes the assumption that people will use opportunities to do high-quality work and participate in team activities or problem-solving initiatives if the organisation provides them with opportunities to do this. A successful performance management system should certainly help to identify **ability, motivate** both individuals and teams and also provide them with **opportunities** to use their skills and abilities.

The role of line managers in performance management

Another important strand in Purcell's effective performance model is line managers. Some traditional appraisal schemes have been accused of being run for the benefit of HR managers or top managers, with many other people in the organisation not really understanding or appreciating what the performance appraisal scheme was trying to achieve. This may be true of some poorly designed schemes, but is a rather harsh judgement on many excellent appraisal schemes and HR managers and on the contribution they make to their organisations' effectiveness. In order to ensure that performance management does not make the same mistake, there is an increased emphasis on the role of the line manager and on gaining involvement of teams and individuals.

A definition of performance management taken from Michael Armstrong (1994) defines performance management as 'a process which is designed to improve organisational, team and individual performance and which is owned and driven by line managers.' It is certainly true that line managers have started to take increased responsibility for many areas in relation to managing their staff, but it is disappointing to note that in some organisations they do not always see the necessity for performance management, or that it is a key aspect of their job.

In a CIPD performance management survey involving over 500 participants, it was claimed that in only 16 per cent of the organisations sampled was there complete buy-in from line managers, with them becoming actively involved in the performance management process (CIPD, 2005). However, on a more positive note, it was also discovered that line managers in 62 per cent of the organisations surveyed found performance management to be useful, while 22 per cent of the line managers were totally indifferent to the process and 1 per cent were actively hostile. This shows that there is still some way to go in terms of getting all line managers actively involved.

This reluctance to get involved in performance management may not be entirely the fault of line managers as they may not have been adequately trained and the relevance of performance management to them and to the organisation's strategic objectives may not have been made clear. In order to make the performance management process as effective as possible it is vital that line managers are trained properly and that they have been trained thoroughly in skills such as coaching (Cunneen, 2006). They have to understand the relevance of performance management to the performance of their team and that it can make a difference to meeting their targets and improving their team performance. It should not be perceived by them to be just an exercise completed once a year where they tick boxes to satisfy the whims of the HR department but as a continuous process involving coaching and feedback which will make a difference to improving performance and developing talent in their team. If line managers are to use this process to maximum effect to achieve both their team's and the organisation's strategic objectives then top management also have responsibilities to ensure that they clearly demonstrate the importance and relevance of performance management and that they provide adequate resources and training to support this (Cunneen, 2006).

Performance management as an integrated and strategic process

As you can see from Figure 9.1, performance management is a process that involves many aspects of people management and each of the topics covered in this book makes a contribution towards it. But simply initiating a new performance management scheme or introducing new HR practices or policies as part of the process will not in itself bring about the desired motivation of workers. These schemes need to be part of a wider process that is undertaken within the organisation and in the CIPD (2005) survey 95 per cent of the respondents agreed that performance management will only be successful if it forms part of an integrated approach to people management. HR policies and procedures should therefore all be integrated with and contribute to strategic objectives.

Performance management should be a shared process between managers, individuals and teams in which objectives are agreed and jointly reviewed and in which corporate, individual and team objectives are integrated. All should feel ownership of the process and share a complete understanding of the system.

Because it should also be strategic in nature it should be clearly linked to broad issues and establishing long-term goals. In order to achieve these things managers must ensure that the people or teams they manage:

- know and understand what is expected of them
- have the skills necessary to deliver on these expectations
- are supported by the organisation to develop the capacity to meet these expectations
- are given feedback on performance
- have the opportunity to discuss and contribute to individual and team aims and objectives (Armstrong and Baron, 2005).

According to Cannell (2007), the tools typically used in performance management include the following:

- performance and development reviews
- learning and development
- coaching
- objectives and performance standards
- competences and competencies
- pay
- teams
- 360° feedback
- performance problem solving.

These are all tools used as part of the strategic performance management process. Some of these such as learning and development, coaching and pay will be discussed in detail later in this book, so we shall not discuss these here. Instead we shall focus on some of the other tactical tools such as performance appraisal and performance development reviews which can be used as part of the performance management process, or which may be used alone in their own right.

Performance appraisal

A good system of performance appraisal is important as part of the performance management process but many organisations who have not yet developed a strategic viewpoint also use performance management on its own. Performance appraisal systems were developed as a tactical approach to developing people before the more strategic idea of performance management had been thought of. Performance management as an approach is widely held to have grown out of performance appraisal, and also to have absorbed some of the newer techniques used in performance appraisal such as emphasis on setting objective standards of performance and competence-based appraisals. However, while most performance management systems do use performance appraisal as a central tactical activity in the good management of employees there are still many other organisations which use performance appraisal as a standalone activity so it is important to consider performance appraisal both as a tool in performance management and as a procedure in its own right.

Performance appraisal is one way of giving employees feedback about their performance at work. According to ACAS (2006):

> Appraisals regularly record an assessment of an employee's performance, potential and development needs. The appraisal is an opportunity to take an overall view of work content, loads and volume, to look back on what has been achieved during the reporting period and agree objectives for the next.

This definition clearly shows that the employee does get feedback about his or her past performance, but indicates that in performance appraisal there is the opportunity to assess or judge various aspects of an employee's work performance by looking back at how they have performed in the past and then by looking forward to agree future objectives or workload.

Fletcher and Williams (1985) went further than this in their definition of appraisal, saying that the assessment of people is not the only thing that we do when we appraise a person's work performance. They feel that there are in fact two conflicting roles involved in appraisal – those of judge and helper. We shall consider each of these facets of appraisal in turn.

First, we all act as judges when we make informal judgements about the way people talk, what they wear and how they behave. These informal judgements may be objective or subjective and we may not even be aware that we are making them. They may not have much effect on people in everyday life, as we don't normally have any right to try to change these things in others, and we don't usually have any power to influence the way people behave. If we start to judge people in a work situation in this informal way with regard, for example, to the way they dress, we are likely to be accused of being too subjective and we might, quite rightly, be accused of treating people unfairly according to our own whims and prejudices. This sort of appraisal is not likely to encourage people to feel motivated about work. In this sense the term 'appraisal' means judging the worth, qualities or value of something, and in a work situation especially it is important that any judgements are fair and are based on objective job-related criteria.

Second, the term 'appraisal' is also used in another way, as Fletcher and Williams (1985) have indicated. When we appraise people in the work situation, we not only judge them but we usually also try to help them to improve aspects of their performance. We may suggest alternative ways of behaving, or suggest training courses or provide developmental opportunities in order to help employees improve their performance and assess their own developmental needs.

Performance appraisal is therefore about giving feedback to the employee, but also involves the appraiser in being both judge and helper to an individual employee. The performance appraisal interview represents the organisation's provision of a formal opportunity in which to give feedback and be both judge and helper to that employee.

Performance appraisal schemes may be used for a wide range of reasons, some of which may conflict with each other, but the main reasons are likely to include the following:

- to improve current performance
- to provide feedback
- to increase motivation
- to identify potential
- to identify training needs
- to aid career development
- to award salary increases
- to solve job problems
- to let individuals know what is expected of them
- to clarify job objectives
- to provide information about the effectiveness of the selection process
- to aid in career planning and development
- to provide information for human resource planning
- to provide for rewards
- to assess competencies.

Randell *et al.* (1984) suggest that for most employers there are three main uses for appraisal reviews: **performance, potential** and **reward.** That is to say that organisations want to assess an individual's past performance; they may also want to identify their potential for future roles in the organisation and any development necessary to achieve this and they may want to use the appraisal interview as a means of allocating rewards for good or excellent performance. All the reasons listed above fall into one of these three categories but there could be conflicts between the various approaches. For example, if the organisation uses performance appraisal as a means of allocating rewards then it is likely that individuals will be much less likely to discuss any developmental needs in case this prevents them getting a bonus. Many organisations try to get too much from one appraisal scheme, and try to use one scheme to fulfil all three purposes. This is unlikely to work, and usually results in the scheme falling into disrepute.

Consequently organisations that use performance appraisal as part of a performance management system will usually conduct the performance appraisal on an annual or biannual basis but will separate these from the personal development reviews which they will organise at various times throughout the year. In this instance the development reviews would be used to discuss development issues while the performance appraisal might be used as part of the process for identifying reward for excellent work.

Personal development review

Personal development reviews are often used alongside performance appraisals, either as standalone tools or as part of the strategic performance management process. In some organisations they are referred to as 'one-to-ones' as they provide an opportunity for the line manager to have a one-to-one discussion at regular intervals with individual members of their teams. Performance appraisal interviews usually happen just once or twice a year but personal development reviews are likely to happen much more frequently than this and to start during the induction period when the line manager is able to have a one-to-one discussion with the individual team member to identify any gaps in knowledge and skills that they have which need to be developed in order for them to become an effective team member. Cannell (2007) emphasises the constructive nature of personal developmental reviews and the need to use a variety of techniques to encourage the individual to participate fully and to do most of the talking as the point of the review is to discuss their development.

Regular personal development reviews will result in each individual having an individual development plan designed to give detailed goals and provide for activities to enable that individual to achieve his or her goals. This should start at induction although some aspects of the individual development plan may have been identified as early as the selection stage and then this continues throughout their career. The plan is jointly designed by the manager and the employee, and the manager will provide support and coaching to help the employee to meet his or her goals.

Objectives or competencies

There are basically two different approaches that can be used by employers when assessing performance. The first is concerned with outputs from the employee: it uses objectives and sets targets for the employee to work towards. The alternative approach is to examine the input that the employee makes to the organisation and determine the level of competence that the employee must achieve in their job.

In organisations where job descriptions based on competence are used, and where staff are used to working towards the achievement of NVQs, the second approach is likely to be favoured. Whichever approach is used there will still be a need to develop a method of assessing the employee's performance using some form of rating scale.

If the first of these approaches using objectives is to work well, then clearly the organisation needs to have 'ambitious goals and plans that employees know about and understand' – point 1 of the ACAS (2005a) model workplace. They also need 'managers who genuinely listen to and consider their employees' views' – point 3 of the ACAS (2005a) model workplace. The management by objectives approach to performance appraisal interviews, discussed later in this chapter, is likely to be preferred in this type of organisation.

If the focus is on the employee's level of competence, then 'people will need to feel valued so they can talk confidently about their work and learn from both successes and failures' – point 6 in the ACAS (2005a) model workplace. Competency concerns the behaviour that a worker must have or gain in order to be able to contribute to the achievement of high levels of performance. Competence on the other hand relates to a system of occupational standards with specified levels of achievement. The CIPD (2004) says:

> Competences describe what people need to be able to do to perform a job well (the descriptions in National Vocational Qualifications are examples of competences). Competencies (more helpfully 'behavioural competencies') are defined as dimensions of behaviour that lie behind competent performance.

However, Hogg (2007) discusses the use of these terms and claims that although in the past HR practitioners have distinguished between the two terms, nowadays they are used interchangeably.

Employees need to be able to operate in a competent way and to possess behavioural competencies that reinforce their technical skills. Competency frameworks have increased in popularity and the CIPD (2007b) survey of learning and development found 60 per cent of organisations in their sample had competency frameworks in place. They also found that most popular use, by 56 per cent of their sample organisations, was as part of performance reviews and appraisals. When an organisation adopts this approach then competence will be measured and this gives a useful way of comparing actual levels of competence with required levels. This can obviously provide a useful tool for measurement of performance and consequently for the performance management process and it is not surprising that it has grown in popularity.

● Problems

A number of problems may prevent the appraisal schemes from being as effective as they should be as not all organisations follow the ACAS model and some try to create an appraisal scheme that does not fit with the normal culture of their organisation. These problems include:

- the organisation not being clear about the purpose of the appraisal system and consequently trying to use the appraisal scheme to fulfil too many different purposes
- links with pay preventing open discussion of problems or of areas where improvement could be made
- keeping information secret from the employee
- the appraiser attacking the appraisee's character
- being too subjective in judgements
- using appraisal as part of the disciplinary process.

Did you know?

It is often suggested that as many as two-thirds of all appraisal schemes are abandoned or altered substantially within two years of their creation. This, to a very large extent, is due to organisations not being aware of, or not paying enough attention to, a range of problems that can be avoided with sufficient forethought and planning, and to trying to make one scheme serve too many incompatible purposes.

Lack of clarity

We have already shown that most appraisal schemes fall into one of three categories, i.e. they are concerned with performance, potential or reward. An organisation should not attempt to use one appraisal scheme to fulfil all three categories. The particular objectives of an appraisal scheme should be clarified before the scheme is designed in detail, and should have been discussed with employees and other workers, trade unions and managers in order to take account of their views and to gain their commitment to the new appraisal scheme. Everyone should then be clear what the particular scheme is trying to achieve. Any scheme, however good the design, is unlikely to succeed if the managers and the workforce are suspicious of the reasons for its introduction and are opposed to making it work effectively.

While there are good reasons why employers should seek to appraise performance potential or give rewards to good employees, problems can also occur if employers try to achieve too much from their performance appraisal scheme. It is difficult, if not impossible, to devise a scheme that will appraise successfully all three areas, and there is a grave danger that the performance appraisal scheme will be rejected if it fails to live up to all that is claimed for it. This can easily happen if the scheme is poorly designed or if the managers show a reluctance to impart critical assessments, or if people are not trained properly in the appraisal process.

Linking appraisal with pay

It is quite common for appraisal-related pay to be part of the performance management process and if done well this can be effective and of benefit to both employers and employees. It is generally introduced in order to emphasise a clear link between achieving high standards of performance in jobs and increased pay and is used as a motivational tool (ACAS, 2005). However, there are also problems associated with its introduction: in particular, it is difficult to imagine that a person being appraised is likely to admit to any developmental need, or be willing to accept any help in their performance, if their salary increase depends on a good appraisal. It is therefore recommended that employers should in general try to keep reward considerations separate from the other areas of performance review.

In spite of this advice and research evidence which suggests that performance-related pay (PRP) does not always motivate everyone in a workforce, many employers think that the offer of an incentive or reward is the only way to motivate employees to work harder, and this is often their main reason for introducing performance appraisal. The motivational aspects of pay will be discussed in more detail in Chapter 11, but the important point is that great care needs to be taken if appraisal systems are linked to pay. It will be especially important to ensure that the criteria being appraised are objective and free of unfair bias, and that there are genuine opportunities for all employees to be rewarded for their efforts. Some employees may be motivated by other things such as increased holiday or more flexible benefits so appraisal-related pay may not motivate them to work harder.

In many organisations financial constraints mean that the number of people who are awarded PRP is severely restricted and there is a serious danger that if the vast majority of the workforce does not feel they have any opportunity to receive a reward, they may feel much more demotivated than they did before the appraisal scheme was introduced. Only the select few who receive the reward will then feel positive about the experience and about the organisation, and even they will not necessarily be motivated to work harder.

When appraisal-related pay is introduced as a part of the performance management system there will be also be other regular development reviews or performance reviews which provide opportunities for discussion of both good and bad performance. These reviews are normally kept separate from the review at which pay is discussed. Consequently they do not provide such an immediate deterrent to discussion of any weaknesses or aspects of poorer performance since their focus should be on past and future performance and the development needs of the individual. However, although this approach does weaken any direct link between pay and performance and learning, it would be foolish to think that it breaks the connection entirely. Employees may still feel reluctant to fully discuss their development needs unless they feel confident it will not affect their pay, even if that review is held at a different time of year. On the other hand, they may take the view that discussion of areas of their performance in which they have done less well are worthwhile if this means that they gain access to more learning and development opportunities which may ultimately result in them getting more pay or being more employable.

Keeping information secret from the employee

Appraisal involves, as we have already said, being both a judge and helper for an individual employee. In order that we can help the individual it is also important that they know about the judgements that have been made about them and that they receive feedback about these. Therefore, if people are to be helped to develop, there must be discussion about problem areas, and any judgements made about employees should not be kept secret from them. Obviously the appraisal interview and reports of it do need to be confidential from other employees, but not so confidential that they are a secret from the employee concerned.

Subjectivity or attacks on the appraisee's character

If the person doing the appraising feels insecure about his or her own performance, there could be a tendency to try to ensure that the employee being appraised doesn't become a threat to them by focusing solely on the aspects of the job that have not been handled well and failing to show recognition for jobs that have been done well. In some cases, subjective judgements may be made because there are no clear criteria on which to appraise the employee, and the appraiser may resort to attacking aspects of the person's character that the person cannot do anything about. In the past many appraisal schemes were based on assessing personality traits that were thought to be important to a particular job, but that in fact were very broad categories that could only be judged subjectively. These included personality traits such as enthusiasm, application, intelligence and resourcefulness.

Pause for thought 9.1 How would you feel if one of your tutors said that you lacked integrity or that your intelligence was inadequate?

We imagine that you would not feel very happy with comments about your lack of integrity or poor level of intelligence, and would want to know on what criteria these comments were based.

If appraisal schemes are to be credible to employees, great care must be taken that judgements made are objective and have some basis that can be discussed with the employee. Integrity is likely to mean slightly different things to different people, and judgement of a person's integrity is likely to be fairly subjective. Rather than focusing on subjective topics such as this or on aspects of an individual's personality which they cannot alter, it is better to examine aspects of the job that the person actually does, and make an objective judgement about the person's effectiveness at carrying out each aspect of the job or their success in meeting their objectives.

Appraisers should also concentrate on seeking to help to bring about an improvement in areas of the employee's work where the appraisee can do something to make an improvement. Criticising someone for not being intelligent enough is similar to criticising them for being too short. There is really not much that they can do about it, so it is pointless to judge them on it and impossible to help them to change.

The relationship between appraisal and the disciplinary process

We have already said that appraisal is partly about making judgements about an employee's performance, and that areas where performance is not as effective as it should be need to be discussed. However, this does not mean that disciplinary matters should be saved for several months to be dealt with at the appraisal interview. If a disciplinary offence occurs, then it should be dealt with immediately and not saved for discussion at the time of the appraisal interview. The appraisal interview should be about seeking to motivate employees, not an opportunity to discipline them although, as we shall show later, dealing with poor performance should be part of the performance management process.

The role of the line managers in performance appraisal

We have already emphasised the role of the line manager in performance management and traditionally the people who are most likely to be involved at the tactical level in the appraisal process are the person who is to be appraised and his or her immediate manager. This has the advantage that the managers or supervisors should know their subordinates and should also know about each subordinate's job and the way in which the subordinate carries out his or her duties. Managers and their subordinates will see each other every day but may be too busy to discuss performance. The performance appraisal interview provides the time for the individual and the manager to sit down together to discuss the individual's progress. This should enable the manager to feel that he or she is helping the career of one of the staff, and prove to be a motivating experience for the employee, who has the undivided attention of the manager listening to his or her views and focusing attention on his or her development.

There can, however, be some disadvantages in having the employee's immediate manager carry out the appraisal, especially if there is a conflict of personalities or if the manager perceives the employee to be a threat and is therefore unwilling to look for positive aspects of the employee's performance. If the appraisal scheme allows a high degree of subjectivity in comments made by the manager, then there is a danger that more will be learnt about the manager's attitudes to work and managing employees than about the employee's performance. Training in performance appraisal techniques is obviously extremely important here.

While it is always important that the line manager is involved in the process of performance management there are others who could be involved in performance appraisal.

ACTIVITY 9.1

The appraisee's immediate supervisor or manager is usually the person most in-volved in the appraisal process, although in some organisations other people may be involved. Using Table 9.1, write a list of people who you think might be involved in the appraisal process. For each of them, list the advantages and the disadvantages of their involvement.

Table 9.1 People involved in the performance appraisal process

People who may be involved in the appraisal process	Advantages	Disadvantages

Although, as we said earlier, line managers are the most frequent group to be involved in conducting appraisal interviews, they do not always relish this part of their job or see its importance. A list of the others who could be involved in performance appraisal is given in Table 9.2 at the end of this chapter.

The main problem with line manager involvement according to Gillen (2001) is that managers see appraisal as a low priority for two reasons and that it is necessary to understand their viewpoint on this in order to be able to convince them of the relevance of appraisal to them and to their department. According to Gillen (2001), the first reason why it can be difficult to get managers to conduct performance appraisal interviews is because they prefer to spend their time doing things rather than managing things or managing and leading people. Gillen (2001) says that generally most managers went into their jobs not to manage, but to do things, for example to build things, to teach things or to sell things. They did not specifically go into the job to manage either things or people and often consider that these parts of their job are difficult and mean they spend less time on what they enjoy. They therefore tend to put off doing them because they do not see the immediate relevance to them or to their department of initiatives such as performance appraisal.

According to Gillen (2001), the second reason is because managers perceive some specific problems related to appraisal. These will vary from organisation to organisation but are likely to result in line managers saying or feeling some of the following:

1 I've got enough to do without also having to fill in forms for Personnel.
2 The appraisal process is 'divorced' from the realities of my 'business cycle'.
3 Appraisal is inherently unfair.
4 Appraisal is amazingly time-consuming.
5 Giving staff feedback on their performance during an appraisal interview is uncomfortable (Gillen, 2001).

Some of these statements are undoubtedly true. As we said, it can be difficult to give staff feedback on their performance and sometimes managers struggle to remember their employee's key achievements, particularly those that occurred some months earlier. Appraisal can seem quite time-consuming and may appear to be organised to suit someone else's time schedule.

Some of the other statements are less easy to justify and may result from the line manager's false perception of the situation. If an organisation has established a performance appraisal scheme in the ways we will describe, then it should certainly not be perceived as 'inherently unfair' and managers who feel that the appraisal process is undertaken just to please the personnel or HR department have not had the process properly explained to them.

Whatever the reasons for these negative perceptions of performance appraisal, they do need to be overcome if the scheme is to be successful. Gillen (2001) suggests various ways to erase these misconceptions and to help line managers appreciate the benefits of appraisal. One useful idea he suggests is that line managers should be made aware of the three main elements to their job: doing things, managing things, and managing and leading people, and that they should be involved in a discussion about which of these they enjoy most. After a discussion in which he establishes that performance requirements in a job are generally getting harder and that people do not want to work even longer to achieve them, he then draws a parallel with lifting a heavy load using a lever and explains that this becomes easier if one uses a longer lever. He says that for managers, using performance appraisal and working on the managing and leading element of their job is the equivalent of using a longer lever. It is about working smarter and not harder.

CASE STUDY 9.1 Performance appraisal

Joan Bywell is a busy manager in an insurance company, heading the life insurance division. She has worked with the company for six years and has always enjoyed organising the work to reach targets and implementing new ideas to improve sales and streamline the processing of policies.

The company has now introduced a performance appraisal system so that managers can formally evaluate their staff on a regular basis. Angela Jones, the HR manager, sees this partly as a preliminary step to introducing performance-related pay for administrative staff within the next five years. Angela has devised a form for managers to use to evaluate their staff, and she has distributed these to managers with instructions to complete the evaluation within four weeks and return the forms to the personnel office, to be held on the employees' personal files.

Joan is reluctant to waste valuable managerial time on this process, but she duly fills in the forms for her administrative staff. She decides not to waste more time on endless discussions with her staff, so she gives each employee the completed form and asks them to sign it to confirm they have seen the evaluation and return it to her the next day. She suggests that if they wish to discuss any points, they should make an appointment to speak to her.

George has been with the company for three years. He feels that he works hard and he is hoping he will be considered for a supervisory post when one of the unit supervisors retires next year. George is incensed when he looks at his evaluation and sees that his performance has been graded as 'satisfactory' on a number of criteria such as 'initiative', 'reliability', and 'amount of work completed'. He would have expected a grading of very good or excellent.

George storms into Joan's office and says: 'I know you said we could talk to you if we had any queries about this so-called performance appraisal, but if this is what you think of me, I do not see any point. I think my best plan is to look for a job with a company that will appreciate hard work'.

Joan actually thinks quite highly of George and is perturbed at this turn of events.

Question

1 Comment on what is wrong with this performance appraisal system and make suggestions for improvement.

Discussion of case study 9.1

This disastrous appraisal nearly ended with the loss of George, a good worker, and is the result of several factors. First, the HR manager Angela Jones has not actually consulted with or involved anyone in the organisation in the design of the appraisal forms or in conducting the appraisal interview and no one has received any training in how to use them. Consequently managers such as Joan are not aware of how important an issue performance appraisal is for motivating her team and improving her team's performance.

Joan is also typical of many of the supervisors described earlier who are very good at the aspects of the job which they see as important, such as achieving targets. However, she does not realise that managing people is an equally important part of her job. If Angela Jones had explained how the performance appraisal process could help Joan achieve her targets and had given her training to this effect then she would have viewed the process in a much more positive light and would have spent time on it.

The performance appraisal form is designed badly so that employees and their supervisors are being asked to rate the individual against criteria which may have nothing to do with their jobs. The amount of work is probably much less important than the quality of the work done and this should be broken down to consider various aspects of the job or to specific objectives or competencies needed. Initiative could be difficult to assess and may not be particularly useful in a job where perhaps there is very limited scope to exercise initiative. Reliability is also a rather vague term as it does not describe the circumstances in which reliability is needed. Angela Jones needs to consult more widely about the criteria that would work on a performance appraisal form and needs to tailor the forms to objectives, job descriptions or competencies required. She then needs to provide training for both managers and subordinates so that everyone is clear about the purpose of the performance appraisal scheme before it is introduced into the organisation. The next section discusses the design of the documentation and Table 9.2 gives an example of documentation using objectives.

Design of documentation

In most appraisal systems it is necessary to have some type of documentation to record what has been agreed. At its simplest this could just be blank sheets of paper for both the appraiser and appraisee, on which they both assess the performance of the appraisee. This provides a means for jotting down ideas and views on performance which can then be used as a basis for discussion at the time of the performance appraisal interview. The disadvantage of this system is that there may be little basis for agreement about the topics to be discussed.

In order to provide for a systematic and consistent approach to performance appraisal, many organisations design an appraisal form. In this case, the manager and the person being appraised both complete a form prior to the appraisal interview. They then exchange forms and at the interview use both the forms as a basis for discussion. This has the advantage of both parties having focused on similar topics and saves time at the interview, as both should have already done quite a bit of preparation for the interview. When designing such a form, there should be clear guidelines explaining what is meant by each section, and the points already discussed in the section on problems must be borne in mind. The criteria to be appraised should not be subjective and should be fair. They should relate to things that employees could improve, and there should be opportunities for the employee to see the appraiser's comments and a section in which to respond to those comments. There should also be a right of appeal. The guidelines should indicate what should then happen to the appraisal forms. Where will they be kept? Who will ensure that action is taken on key points?

The actual content of such a form will be influenced by the type of appraisal scheme adopted by the organisation. This will now be discussed.

Types of performance appraisal

Management by objectives (MBO)

We have already said that appraisal schemes are most likely to succeed if the criteria to be appraised can be assessed objectively rather than subjectively, and that the appraisal of aspects of a person's personality should be avoided. One way of achieving this is to set clear objectives for the employee to achieve before the next appraisal, and then to focus the discussion at the appraisal interview on the extent to which these objectives have been achieved. An appraisal interview also provides an opportunity to look forward, so the next stage would be to set and agree objectives for the next review period.

One way in which to achieve this would be to look first at the job description and then agree specific objectives for each of the main tasks. This has the additional advantage that the objectives can be linked very clearly to the organisation's strategic goals, so that the individual can see exactly what to do to help the organisation meet its objectives. A sample form for this type of performance appraisal is shown in Figure 9.4.

In this example there is an opportunity to look at past objectives and consider the extent to which they have been achieved, and also a chance to look forward and agree future objectives. Here the appraisee has an opportunity to write comments, as do the manager and countersigning manager. This type of appraisal can also link with overall organisational objectives, and is often used as part of a performance management system, as we shall show later.

Rating scales

This is another form of performance appraisal scheme that seeks to encourage objectivity by focusing on aspects of the employee's job and then indicating by graded statements how successfully the employee has fulfilled each of the main duties listed in his or her job description. The statements would be linked to the job description, and the team of writers would provide a series of statements for each category of the job description, indicating levels of performance or level of competence required in that duty, ranging from excellent to poor. The appraiser would discuss the person's performance using these scales during the appraisal interview, and would then tick the statement that he or she and the appraisee agreed best summed up the appraisee's performance or which matched their level of competence.

Figure 9.4 Sample form for performance appraisal using management by objectives

NAME . . . .   JOB TITLE . . . .

DATE OF APPRAISAL . . . .   DEPARTMENT/SECTION . . . .

JOB DESCRIPTION (To be agreed with employee)

REVIEW PERIOD . . . .

1. Objectives agreed for this last review period. (This should include special tasks, personal training and development.)

2. To what extent have these objectives been achieved?

3. Were there any other major achievements?

4. Were there any obstacles which prevented achievement of agreed objectives?

5. What steps need to be taken to overcome these obstacles?

6. What training, development and education were undertaken during the review period?

NEXT REVIEW PERIOD . . . .

1. What specific objectives have been agreed for the next review period?

2. What training, development and education should be undertaken during the next review period?

3. What follow-up action is needed?

COMMENTS OF APPRAISER

Signed . . . . (Appraiser)

COMMENTS OF APPRAISEE

Signed . . . . (Appraisee)

COMMENTS OF COUNTERSIGNING MANAGER

ACTIVITY 9.2

Do you remember the job description which we gave in Chapter 6? The main duties for this are listed in Figure 9.5. For each of these duties, write a series of statements to indicate the possible degrees of success of someone who is working in this job. It is intended that these statements will form the basic information with which the individual's performance in that job is compared by the appraiser. We have started this for you by suggesting some graded statements for the first row.

Figure 9.5 Job rating

Name of job holder: . . . .

Job title: Receptionist

Date of appraisal: . . . .

Main duties	Appraiser's comments	A (Well ahead of standard performance)	B (More than satisfactory, slightly above job requirements)	C (Less than satisfactory, needs slight improvement)	D (Requires constant supervision)
Greet walk-in visitors and ascertain purpose of their visit. Handle or redirect queries as appropriate		Always quick to greet visitors and ascertain purpose of visit, dealing with queries extremely rapidly and effectively so visitors are always highly satisfied	Greets visitors, ascertains purpose of visit and deals effectively with queries	Normally greets visitors promptly and ascertains purpose of their visit; sometimes slow to redirect queries	Slow to notice walk-in visitors, does not always greet them promptly, and is not always able to deal with queries or redirect them to the appropriate place
Answer phone queries as above					
Answer all initial queries about receipt of payments using the online payment receipts system					

→

Figure 9.5 Continued

Main duties	Appraiser's comments	A (Well ahead of standard performance)	B (More than satisfactory, slightly above job requirements)	C (Less than satisfactory, needs slight improvement)	D (Requires constant supervision)
Open and sort incoming post by department. Organise delivery of post by assistant receptionist					
Perform clerical tasks assigned by department in agreement with the Office Services Manager					
Supervise assistant receptionists and delegate work as appropriate					
Perform other duties as assigned by the Office Services Manager or other authorised manager					

Comments of appraiser

Signature . . . . (Appraiser)

Comments of appraisee

Signature . . . . (Appraisee)

Comments of countersigning manager

Signature . . . . **(Manager)**

Discussion of Activity 9.2

This gives a simple way of rating the employee's behaviour in the job that is clear and easy to use, as the appraiser simply ticks the box containing the comment that most nearly reflects the actual performance of the employee. It also means that there is a common standard which all appraisers would use when appraising a person doing that job. In this case, examples of four types of behaviour had to be provided for each aspect of the main duties listed in the job description. This was because many appraisers tend to rate employees as average just to avoid upsetting people or to avoid giving too much praise: by not allowing a middle category, they are encouraged to be more decisive. There may still be a tendency to go for the middle two boxes (and for many employees this will be highly appropriate), but appraisers must be encouraged by training to use the full range of categories if and when this is needed.

In this Activity you were the only person to choose the descriptions for the criteria to be rated, so there could still be some degree of subjectivity involved, as you may have described the performance of each duty in a different way to other people. It would be more usual to involve a team of people to provide the descriptors for each main duty and to get consensus about the descriptors to be used.

Behaviourally anchored rating scales (BARS)

If this appraisal system were to be introduced in a large organisation, it would not rely on just one person's ideas of a suitable range of categories. In the first section of the ratings exercise we have used the following terms as descriptors of the first of the major duties listed in the job description:

- Always quick to greet visitors and ascertain purpose of visit, dealing with queries extremely rapidly and effectively so visitors are always highly satisfied.
- Greets visitors, ascertains purpose of visit and deals effectively with queries.
- Normally greets visitors promptly and ascertains purpose of their visit; sometimes slow to redirect queries.
- Slow to notice walk-in visitors, does not always greet them promptly, and is not always able to deal with queries or redirect them to the appropriate place.

These were purely our own subjective choices, and we had not checked whether or not other people would describe this aspect of the job in the same way. You could find other descriptors that may be more effective than these. We may have chosen terms to describe each level of performance that are different from the way in which other people would describe the same task.

One way to try to get round the subjectivity of having just one person writing the descriptions of behaviour is to use a newer technique, known as behaviourally anchored rating scales. In this case a group of other raters would also be asked to suggest descriptions for a range of behaviour for each aspect of the main duties, so that a wide range of behavioural examples could be collected.

These descriptions are then collated and returned to the sample raters, but this time there is no indication of the scale point for which they were suggested. The sample raters are asked to indicate a scale point from A to D, where A represents excellence and D represents bad work, to which they think each descriptor most aptly relates. The descriptors that are consistently located at the same point of the scale are then used in the final version of the behaviourally anchored scale. This is intended to remove the subjectivity inherent in the simpler rating method and ensure that descriptions used are likely to mean the same thing to most people.

ACTIVITY 9.3

What do you see as the main advantages and disadvantages of this system of behaviourally anchored rating scales? Make a list.

Discussion of Activity 9.3

Compare your list of advantages and disadvantages with the following list.

Advantages
- Objective rating of each of the main duties listed in job description.
- Agreement over suitable descriptors for each category of behaviour.
- Easy to use.
- Useful if lots of people have the same job descriptions so that the amount of time involved in designing the system will be repaid.

Disadvantages
- Time-consuming, as it takes a long time to get agreement on descriptors for each job.
- Only takes account of existing job performance; does not allow for discussion of future potential.

Behavioural observation scales (BOS)

These form another way of rating performance in a job. These scales are also developed as a result of lengthy procedures, and indicate a number of dimensions of performance with behavioural examples for each. Job analysis is used to identify the key determinants of performance and the performance dimensions are once again related to the job description, but in this case the appraiser is asked to indicate a point on a scale by a numerical value.

An example of such a scale in relation to selected aspects of a lecturer's job is given below. The appraisers simply circle the number that they think relates most closely to the usual behaviour of the appraisee.

ACTIVITY 9.4

You can try this for yourself by selecting a lecturer you know well and assessing him or her on this scale. Circle the number that most closely relates to the lecturer's normal behaviour.

1 Provides clearly structured lecture that is easy to follow

| Almost never | 5 | 4 | 3 | 2 | 1 | Almost always |

2 Provides up-to-date and interesting material in lectures/tutorials

| Almost never | 5 | 4 | 3 | 2 | 1 | Almost always |

3 Explains to students exactly what is expected of them when they complete written work

Almost never	5	4	3	2	1	Almost always

4 Is willing to give advice and guidance

Almost never	5	4	3	2	1	Almost always

5 Gives detailed and helpful feedback concerning written work that students have completed

Almost never	5	4	3	2	1	Almost always

Discussion of Activity 9.4

We hope that you were fair in your assessment and were not influenced by personality or past grades given to you! In this case you were assessing the lecturer from the position of a student, and you are likely to have a very different view of his or her work performance to the lecturer's manager or the human resource manager. You may not, however, be able to assess all aspects of the lecturer's job such as his or her ability to carry out research, or an individual's administrative capabilities, but this exercise is similar to assessment by a person's subordinates which we mentioned earlier. It has the same type of limitations that we discussed then, but it gives you some idea of the way in which different points of view can be important and shows that if this were combined with appraisal from other perspectives, as in a system such as 360 degree appraisal, it could contribute to developing a full picture of a person's effectiveness and provide valuable feedback.

Critical incidents

This involves keeping a record of positive and negative behaviour during a specified period of time. This record of critical incidents is the basis for the appraisal interview although the appraiser would normally be expected to also give feedback on both positive and negative critical incidents as and when they happened. This method does have some benefits as it does not just rely on annual reporting and has the benefit of giving immediate feedback but according to ACAS (2006) the main disadvantage is that it is also very time-consuming.

Narrative report

Using this method the appraiser describes the behaviour of the individual being appraised in their own words in either an essay or report style, as preferred, but without the use of any form for a prompt or for structure. For a narrative report one could start with just a blank sheet of paper as this form of recording is a flexible format which can be adapted to varying circumstances. However, for some appraisers this lack of structure and choice of approach will be too vague and they may have difficulty choosing which aspects of performance to focus on. It also requires the appraiser to have good writing skills and the subjectivity of this format also makes it very difficult to compare levels of performance. There could be accusations of too much subjectivity particularly if there is any link to pay involved.

The appraisal interview

Interviews have already been discussed in some detail in Chapters 4 and 5, and the points made there with regard to selection interviews also apply to appraisal interviews. Preparation, privacy and confidentiality, good questioning technique, avoidance of bias, good records and attention to the style of interview will also be important in the appraisal interview.

Preparation

There is a need, as we explained in Chapter 7, for careful preparation before any interview and employees should be given adequate notice of the date of the appraisal interview to allow them time to prepare. In the appraisal interview this is also likely to mean that care needs to be taken with the layout of the room, so that the person being appraised will not be intimidated by a formal set-up with barriers such as a big desk, and so that he or she feels comfortable and at ease. There is also a need to avoid interruptions and to ensure that telephone messages are taken elsewhere and that there are no unnecessary distractions.

If the person has been appraised in the past, then the last appraisal record will need to be read to check what objectives, if any, were agreed for the current appraisal period. The individual's job description will also need to be checked and the training and development records examined to discover what training and development has occurred since the last interview. In some cases, if the person who is to be appraised works for several people, it may also be necessary to obtain information from other managers, or in the case of other types of performance appraisal, from subordinates or peers.

It is also useful for both parties in the appraisal to prepare for the meeting, and both the appraiser and appraisee need to have received training so that they know what to expect in order that they can both skilfully handle what is potentially a difficult interaction. A constructive approach used by many organisations is to give both the appraiser and appraisee a form to complete prior to the appraisal interview. In some organisations these are then exchanged, and this has the advantage of focusing the attention of appraiser and appraisee on common issues. In other organisations these forms are simply used as an aide-memoire for the individuals concerned, but if they are exchanged prior to the interview, they can help to clearly identify areas where there is broad agreement so that more time can be allowed to discuss other topics where there are differences of opinion.

Privacy and confidentiality

We have already indicated that the appraisal is an important way of giving feedback to the employee about his or her work performance. In the past some organisations did not allow the appraisee to see the records of their appraisal, but we feel that this misses a valuable opportunity for providing feedback from which the employee could learn. On the other hand, the appraisal form and interview have to be kept confidential from other people as there will probably be very personal information on the form, and no one who feels that half the department can hear every word of the conversation is likely to feel willing to discuss his or her performance openly.

Good questioning technique

The appraisal interview has, as we have already said, much in common with all other types of interviews. Once again the type of questions asked will be important. As this is an opportunity to provide feedback to the employee there will perhaps be slightly more opportunity for the interviewer to do more talking than in some other forms of interview, but this should be treated with caution. It is certainly not the time for the appraiser to do all the talking.

There should be an introductory phase where the interviewer tries to put the person being appraised at ease. It is generally better to follow this with a discussion of the employee's strong points and then try to get information, especially about any areas of perceived weakness, from the employee by asking open questions and teasing out the information. Areas of weakness need to be raised and discussed fully, and open questions are important here. If the interviewer uses closed questions that merely need yes or no answers, he or she will end up doing most of the talking. Leading questions, which put words in the appraisee's mouth or indicate what the appraiser wants him or her to say, should also be avoided.

Appraisers should also take great care not to be unduly influenced by a high assessment in one particular area, and should not allow this to cloud their judgement so that they rate all other areas of the employee's performance highly, even though these may not deserve such a high rating. This is known as the 'halo' effect. Similarly, care should be taken to avoid being unduly influenced by one very poor assessment. This is known as the 'horns' effect.

The contingency approach to interviews

While it is fair to say that the style of interview that is generally recommended for appraisal interviewing is a joint problem-solving approach which involves the appraiser and appraisee equally, it is also possible that some other styles of interview may be appropriate in certain circumstances. For example, if the person being appraised is new to the department they may have less to say than someone who has been there longer and so it may be appropriate for the appraiser to do a little more of the talking. If, on the other hand, the person being appraised is very experienced and has worked for the organisation for many years then they may hold many views about their own performance and have clear ideas for improving it. In this case it is possible that the person being appraised might be allowed to do slightly more of the talking. The contingency approach means that the most appropriate style of interview will depend on the circumstances at the time: the approach will be contingent on the circumstances.

The choice of style depends on factors such as the manager's own style, the organisation's culture and the behaviour of the appraisee themselves. In an autocratic organisation where people are not used to having their views considered, there may be a high degree of suspicion if at the time of the appraisal interview the manager suddenly adopts a joint problem-solving approach and actually asks for the views of the employees. This can be a problem for many organisations, because if the organisation normally conducts its affairs in such a way that the employees don't trust the managers to treat them fairly, then it is going to be extremely difficult, if not impossible, for the employees suddenly to start trusting the person who is conducting their appraisal, and to talk in an open and honest way to them. This shows that appraisals should not be used just as an isolated technique to try and motivate the workforce. They need to be an integral part of the way the organisation treats people, and fundamental issues such as the culture of the organisation and its normal style of management also need to be addressed.

Information technology and performance management

Increasingly organisations are using information technology as a part of their performance appraisal or performance management system. This is not just about record-keeping although some organisations do use their intranet site for this and also to explain procedures and for online training for appraiser and appraisee. Some organisations even complete the initial stages of the performance appraisal system online and both appraisee and appraiser can complete online forms and exchange these prior to meeting for a face-to-face interview where they discuss the contents, focusing particularly on differences in their views of performance. In *People Management* journals there are increasing numbers of IT systems which claim to help with performance appraisal and Google UK lists over one and a half million online providers for 360 degree feedback so this is clearly an area where IT is providing a great deal of support (Coomber, 2006).

The opportunity to complete performance appraisal questionnaires online is particularly useful when 360 degree appraisal is used. Getting forms completed using pen and paper from several sources is arduous and collecting and collating the information from a range of sources manually can be very time-consuming. Using online resources has made the use of 360 degree appraisal much easier and may be partially responsible for the increase in its popularity. Online forms can also benefit from being interactive so that the appraisee can even elect to receive feedback on specific aspects of their competence or performance. According to Coomber (2006), other benefits of online collection of appraisal information include improvements in confidentiality and accuracy. It is also much easier and requires much less administration to collate the information from several appraisers into an easily accessible format using graphs and charts.

International issues in performance management and performance appraisal

Performance management and performance appraisal can be difficult to get right but when organisations succeed in this they do create a motivating experience for workers and help to improve performance. In a global organisation operating across many countries and several cultures this is especially difficult to achieve. In some cultures it is difficult to introduce 360 degree appraisal as subordinates may feel reluctant to criticise their immediate manager, because in that culture it is unthinkable to criticise one's superior. In other cultures it may also be difficult for the appraiser to make any comments that would improve the work of someone who was older in years than themselves. Some cultures prefer openness and transparency in the performance management process so individuals know who is responsible for comments about their performance, while in other cultures individuals would be unwilling to comment on performance if they thought the appraisee would know the source of comment.

Organisations have to make choices about the extent to which they take account of different cultures and decide whether to operate different performance management systems in each country or whether they try to get something that will be acceptable to all by adapting the host country's performance management scheme as standard.

One organisation which faced this problem was Kimberley-Clark, probably best known for its Andrex toilet paper, the Andrex puppy and for Kleenex tissues. They operate in 68 countries but did not have a standard approach across all. Their competencies approach was interpreted in differing ways in different countries, resulting in problems when moving staff from one part of the organisation to another, or from one country to another. While their sales and share price were doing badly the performance ratings of their employees still seemed very high as individuals were reluctant to give a below average rating to anyone, even for a below average performance.

In 2003, Tom Falk, the chief executive of Kimberly-Clark, launched a global business plan designed to increase the emphasis on talent management and development of a high-performance culture. The performance management system was a key part of this and in order to get global buy-in from everyone an international project team was appointed representing all regions so that regional and cultural issues were addressed. A system of 360 degree feedback was agreed upon but because of the concerns expressed by workers in some parts of the world, particularly Korea, South America and Asia, it was decided that this feedback had to be anonymous and, while this didn't entirely suit all Western countries, this was the approach adopted. The performance management scheme was web-based but was also translated into the languages of all the countries where the group was based and training was also given in the languages of each country. This meant that each part of the organisation in each country felt increased ownership for the scheme and the amount of effort put into consultation, translation and training seemed to be worthwhile, as in a survey conducted by the company a year after the launch of the new performance management system, 95 per cent of the workforce said that they were confident about its use (Arkin, 2007).

Conclusion

Performance management derives from the human resource management approach as a strategic and integrated approach to the management and development of people. It emphasises the important role of line managers to take responsibility for the management of the performance of the people in their department. With its emphasis on the need for continuous performance review, performance management also relates clearly to the ideas of continuing development and learning. It uses the techniques of performance appraisal but prefers to use the more objective types, such as setting objectives. It does, however, go further than performance appraisal as what is appraised is clearly derived from the strategic plan and both individuals and teams are involved in setting objectives for themselves and in evaluating their success in achieving these objectives.

Line managers play an important part in reviewing the performance of individuals and teams and have responsibility to review progress and development throughout the year, not just at the time of the annual appraisal interview. Both individual and team objectives are clearly derived from the corporate strategic objectives, and everyone is aware that management of performance is the concern of all in the organisation, and not just HR management or the senior management team. Performance management is, above all, a process for sharing an understanding about what needs to be achieved, and then managing and developing people in a way which will facilitate this so that excellent communications, in all directions, are achieved, particularly in global organisations – and employee involvement and engagement are also extremely important.

Improvements in online performance appraisal schemes are helping to increase the use of 360 degree appraisal and can also be particularly useful in international organisations where it may be very time-consuming to collect information from participants who work in different parts of the world. Performance appraisal and performance management are important tools that can contribute not only to an organisation's effectiveness, but they can also help ensure that it becomes a high-performance workplace.

REVIEW QUESTIONS

You will find brief answers to these review questions on pages 475–476.

1 Discuss the reasons for line managers' apparent reluctance to get involved in performance management and suggest ways to convince them of the value of this process to them.

2 What are the main advantages and disadvantages of using 360 degree appraisal?

3 Performance appraisals are intended to motivate employees towards greater productivity and improve communication/relations between managers and their team members. Explain why performance appraisals often fail to achieve this goal, and comment on the skills that managers need to make performance appraisal work.

4 Performance management is described by Armstrong and Baron (2005) as a process which 'contributes to the effective management of individuals and teams in order to achieve high levels of organizational performance.'
    (a) Describe the key stages in the performance management implementation process.
    (b) List the different HR techniques that could be used as part of performance management in relation to the organisation, the team and the individual.

5 Describe three different approaches to performance appraisal and comment critically on the benefits to be gained from these systems.

SELF-CHECK QUESTIONS

Answer the following multiple-choice and short-answer questions. The correct responses are given on page 476 for you to check your understanding of this chapter.

1 Which of the following is stated in this chapter as being least likely to contribute to an organisation becoming an effective workplace?
   (a) Policies and procedures that everyone knows about and understands.
   (b) Effective health and safety policies and procedures.
   (c) Line managers who perceive performance appraisal as totally separate from the realities of their business cycle and their business objectives.
   (d) Line managers who perceive performance appraisal as an important aspect of their job that they need to spend time on so they develop their staff and then meet their business objectives.
   (e) An organisation with a 'Big Idea' that everyone knows about and understands.

2 Which of the following acronyms is used in Purcell's (2003) People and Performance Model?
   (a) AMO
   (b) AMP
   (c) IMP
   (d) AMA
   (e) IMO

3 In this chapter we said that when we appraise someone there are three key, but sometimes contradictory, roles. Which of the following are the three roles to which we referred?
   (a) Giving feedback and being friend and helper.
   (b) Giving feedback and being judge and source of discipline.
   (c) Giving feedback and being judge and helper.
   (d) Giving a subjective assessment of performance and being judge and helper.
   (e) Giving feedback and being judge and critic.

4 Which of the following is a good reason for organisations to introduce a performance appraisal scheme?
   (a) to improve current performance
   (b) to provide a check on their staff's integrity
   (c) to check on the honesty of their employees
   (d) to clarify the employee's contract
   (e) to discipline individuals.

5 Appraisal schemes may not be as effective as they should be because of a number of problems. Which of the following is not one of the problems associated with the introduction of performance appraisal schemes?
   (a) The organisation is not clear about the purpose of its appraisal scheme.
   (b) The performance appraisal scheme is too objective in the judgements made.
   (c) Information is kept secret from the employee.
   (d) The performance appraisal scheme is too subjective in the judgements made.
   (e) Appraisal is used as part of the disciplinary process.

6 Which of the following best describes what is meant by the term 'performance management'?
   (a) A process which contributes to the effective management of individuals and teams in order to achieve high levels of organisational performance.

→

(b) A process which contributes to the effective management of the HR department in order to achieve high levels of departmental performance.

(c) A process which contributes to the effective management of teams in order to achieve high levels of team performance.

(d) A process which contributes to the effective management of individuals in order to achieve high levels of individual performance.

(e) A process which contributes to the effective management of individuals and teams in order to improve the personnel department's performance.

HR IN THE NEWS

FT

FT Report – Digital Business 2007: Tools help staff see the effects of effort

By Sam Hiser

Securing the services of the best available candidates is at the heart of e-recruitment systems. But once the new recruits are on board, technology now plays a big part in helping to monitor, incentivise and manage them.

Performance management software tools are maturing, taking advantage of the internet and replacing custom-grown solutions to help managers more effectively monitor and offer incentives to staff.

Also known as business intelligence (BI) or business performance management (BPM), e-performance management is a growing field.

Oracle, through its Peoplesoft and Hyperion acquisitions, SAP, Cognos and Business Objects are some of the big software providers helping managers collect, organise and massage data coming in from across finance, back office, manufacturing, production, sales and compensation business processes.

A growing list of smaller players, too, provides targeted services in a variety of niches. In the sales performance management (SPM) arena, for example, sales personnel and managers need a clear view of objectives and sales plan rules. They also need real-time visibility on their compensation statements and incentive goal sheets as well as performance comparisons versus prior periods.

A dashboard screen on a desktop, laptop or smartphone allows them to absorb this information by showing up-to-the minute sales and compensation statistics and integrates incentive plan information.

In any sales organisation where the compensation plan drives the business, there is a need for everybody to be connected to central goals and respond quickly.

'You want to turn the business rules into compensation. With a centralised book, you can cascade strategic changes in the call plan,' says Leslie Stretch, senior vice-president of global sales, marketing and on-demand business at Callidus Software. The implications penetrate to the bottom line.

Mr Stretch says integrated software permits incentive compensation to be awarded faster and targeted with precision, while slowness and inaccuracy can demoralise a sales force.

Callidus, for example, is establishing a de facto standard for sales performance it calls the 'true performance index', that a professional can use to monitor the effects of their efforts. They can take this statistic with them – possibly to different employers. For heavily unionised customers, such as telecoms companies, Mr Stretch reports fewer disputes, due partly, he claims, to trust in the Callidus data.

E-performance management tools are making a difference in operations management, too. A UK software and consulting group, eg Solutions, offers straightforward technology and advice which seeks to identify processes and tasks, assign roles, groups, teams and skills, and match desired outcomes with human activity. The business-intelligence gathering mechanism is embedded in the process, which means data input is not segregated from the work itself.

Elizabeth Gooch, eg's chief executive, says: 'It's like driving a car, first in manual and then in automatic.' The key is to make people autonomous optimisers by showing them the results of what they do.

Employees are said to appreciate sharper e-performance management tools and thrive because they feel a greater sense of accomplishment when their efforts are connected with results.

(*Financial Times*, 7 November 2007, © Sam Hiser. Reproduced with permission.)

Questions

1 What do you think are the main advantages of using performance management software?

2 What in your view are the disadvantages?

Now that you have read this introductory chapter on performance appraisal and performance management, and have completed all the exercises, you may feel ready to progress further. If you would like more opportunities to test your own learning on this subject then you can go to the student website that accompanies this book: **www.pearsoned.co.uk/foothook**.

WHAT NEXT?

If you feel ready to examine this subject in more depth then there have been several research studies that could help you to further your understanding of how organisations achieve improvements in performance. Some of the CIPD-sponsored studies were referred to at the end of Chapter 1 and include:

Chartered Institute of Personnel and Development (2003) *People and Performance in Knowledge-intensive Firms,* CIPD.

A bulletin summarising this study is also available from the CIPD:

Chartered Institute of Personnel and Development (2004) *People and Performance in Knowledge-intensive Firms: An Emerging Model of People Management Practices,* CIPD (www.cipd.co.uk; accessed 2.10.07).

A further study from the research team at the University of Bath examines case study organisations and how they achieve success when times are difficult:

Hutchinson, S., N. Kinnie, J. Purcell, J. Swart, B. Rayton (2003) *Understanding the People Performance Link: Unlocking the Black Box,* CIPD.

A summary of research in this area is also available from the CIPD:

Chartered Institute of Personnel and Development (2002) *Sustaining Success in Difficult Times: Research Summary,* CIPD (www.cipd.co.uk; accessed 2.10.07).

References

Advisory, Conciliation and Arbitration Service (2005a) *The ACAS Model Workplace,* ACAS (www.acas.org.co.uk; accessed 17.09.07).

Advisory, Conciliation and Arbitration Service (2005b) *Appraisal-Related Pay,* ACAS.

Advisory, Conciliation and Arbitration Service (2006) *Employee Appraisal,* ACAS.

Armstrong, M. (1994) *Performance management,* Kogan Page.

Armstrong, M. and A. Baron (2005) *Managing performance: Performance management in action,* CIPD.

Cannell, M. (2007) *Performance management: An overview,* February, CIPD.

Chartered Institute of Personnel and Development (2005) *Performance management: Survey report September 2005,* CIPD.

Chartered Institute of Personnel and Development (2007a) *The people and performance link,* May, CIPD.

Chartered Institute of Personnel and Development (2007b) *Learning and development: Annual survey report 2007,* CIPD.

Coomber, J. (2006) *360 feedback,* CIPD.

Cunneen, P. (2006) How to improve performance management, *People Management,* 12 January, Vol. 12, No. 1, 42–43.

Fletcher, C. and R. Williams (1985) *Performance Appraisal and Career Development,* Hutchinson.

Gillen, T. (2001) *Appraisal: Getting managers' buy-in,* CIPD (www.cipd.co.uk; accessed 17.9.07).

Hogg, C. (2007) *Competency and competency frameworks,* April, CIPD (www.cipd.co.uk; accessed 17.09.07).

Institute of Personnel Management (1992) *Performance management in the UK: An analysis of the issues,* IPM.

Kaplan, R.S. and D.P. Norton (1992) The balanced scorecard – measures that drive performance, *Harvard Business Review,* January–February, 71–79.

Kaplan, R.S. and D.P. Norton (1996) *The Balanced Scorecard: Translating Strategy into Action,* Harvard Business School Press.

Kubicek, M. (2004) Turning appraisals around, *Training Magazine* produced by *Personnel Today,* September, 20–22.

Purcell, J., N. Rinnie and S. Hutchinson (2003) Open minded, *People Management*, Vol. 9, No. 10, 31–33.

Randell, G.A., P.M.A. Packard, R.L. Shaw and A.J.P. Slater (1984) *Staff Appraisal,* IPM.

Further study

Books

Advisory, Conciliation and Arbitration Service (2005) *Appraisal-Related Pay,* ACAS. Another excellent guide, this time to the complex task of linking performance appraisal to pay.

Advisory, Conciliation and Arbitration Service (2006) *Employee Appraisal,* ACAS. An excellent, clear guide to performance appraisal.

Armstrong, M. and A. Baron (2004) *Managing performance: Performance management in action,* CIPD. This has become a classic text on the subject of performance management.

Articles

Arkin, A. (2007) From soft to strong, *People Management,* 6 September, Vol. 13, No. 18, 30–33. An overview of how Kimberly-Clark, a multinational, introduced performance management into its companies across the world.

Cunneen, P. (2006) How to improve performance management, *People Management,* 12 January, Vol. 12, No. 1, 42–3. A short article that makes suggestions about getting the best from a performance management system.

Fielder, R. (2006) How to unlock discretionary behaviour, *People Management,* 12 October, Vol. 12, No. 20, 44–5. Another brief article that explains how to energise and motivate staff to work at peak performance.

Table 9.2 People involved in the performance appraisal process

People who may be involved in the appraisal process	Advantages	Disadvantages
The appraisee's manager's immediate manager	Often used as well as the appraisee's manager to check that the manager is being fair. When used as sole appraiser there is the possible advantage of being more objective about employee's work and of not being directly threatened by their success.	Not likely to know the appraisee well and likely to have to obtain information about the individual's performance from their immediate manager.
The HR manager	Often used as a check that the manager is being fair and as a monitor of consistency of approach throughout the organisation. HR managers are sometimes used as sole appraiser for reasons of fairness and consistency and because they are not perceived to be a threat to the manager.	Not likely to know the appraisee well and likely to have to obtain information about the individual's performance from their immediate manager.
Colleagues	This can be especially useful where teamwork is important or in an enterprise with a matrix organisation structure where the individual may report to more than one manager. The main advantage is that colleagues are likely to have a clear idea of how effective the individual is at working with them and the views of several people are likely to provide a balanced perspective.	The colleagues concerned may not know about all aspects of the individual's job. They may be reluctant to express an honest opinion about a colleague, and may be influenced by whether they have a good or poor relationship with that person, or by jealousy or rivalry.
Subordinates	People who work for the individual who is being appraised will certainly have a different view of that individual's abilities and performance and can therefore provide valuable information about the person's performance.	They may be too frightened to express their real opinion if they feel that their manager might hold this against them at some future date. The person being appraised may be reluctant to accept the views of his or her subordinates.
Self-appraisal	Often used as part of the appraisal process, as in many systems the appraisers and the appraisee complete forms independently of each other and then use them as the basis of discussion. The individual will have more detailed knowledge of the standard of their own work performance than their manager. Since individuals should be encouraged to take a great deal of responsibility for their own development, this increased self-awareness will be useful.	Some people may find it difficult to analyse their own work performance and may have unrealistic views of how well they have actually done. They may not be willing to admit to weaknesses, although in many cases the opposite is true, and people are more critical of themselves than their manager would be.
360° appraisal (not actually a person, but gathers information from all the people mentioned so far)	This form of appraisal gathers information from all the above sources to gain an all-round view of the person's performance. This is extremely thorough and will provide information on different aspects of the individual's performance so that it is possible to compile a total picture of the person's job performance. This may also include those outside the organisation, such as clients or customers who may be able to provide very valuable insights into how an individual is performing.	It can be very time-consuming to collect information from so many people, and may not always be cost-effective. It is also subject to all the disadvantages listed above. If it uses customers or clients it may prove particularly difficult to organise as customers or clients may not wish to spend time participating in questionnaires and cannot be coerced into doing so. Many employers will also be hesitant to use this approach as they may not wish to give their clients or customers any cause to think that they, or any of their employees, might ever provide a less than perfect service or product.

Table 9.2 Continued

People who may be involved in the appraisal process	Advantages	Disadvantages
Assessment centres (not actually a person, so you may not have included assessment centres in this list, but we include them as they form yet another important way of assessing performance)	Individuals undertake a battery of tests to measure: aspects of personality; verbal, numerical and reasoning skills; and ability to lead and work in a team. This provides an all-round view of the person's talents and abilities. Particularly useful when assessing future potential and in the appraisal of potential supervisors or managers.	Expensive and time-consuming to carry out for all employees.

CHAPTER **10**

Learning and development

Objectives

By the end of this chapter you will be able to:

- explain why learning and development is important both to organisations and individuals
- describe a systematic approach to strategic learning and development
- identify when to use a variety of learning and development techniques
- explain what is meant by experiential learning
- describe the roles of HR, L&D and line managers in learning and development
- demonstrate the importance of induction training
- outline key issues in international learning and development.

Why is learning and development important?

Most organisations want to improve performance, meet their strategic objectives or become high-performance organisations and they generally want to increase profits for shareholders, increase their market share or provide better services for customers. In order to achieve these things they need to recruit, select, develop, motivate and retain the most talented people. Learning and development is one of the key aspects in performance management which can help them achieve these things and it is also a key factor in managing talent.

Some individuals also want to improve their performance in their jobs or learn new skills, perhaps to get a pay increase or promotion or maybe to move to a better job. Learning and development can help achieve these aims for individuals too. It can also help attract individuals to an organisation and can then engage their commitment so the organisation benefits by keeping their talent within and this in turn helps the organisation to achieve its current and future strategic objectives. Learning and development has a positive role to play in talent management and according to Geoff Armstrong (2007), Director General of the Chartered Institute of Personnel and Development, there are huge benefits to be gained by organisations that get talent management right, particularly where the market for talented people is very competitive. Adopting positive approaches to learning and development will help in this.

Governments too are concerned that their countries are economically viable and that they can provide good level of services and standards of living for individuals; once again learning and development can play a key role in achieving this. Although there are huge benefits to be gained for organisations, individuals and countries, there has sometimes been reluctance by some employers in the UK to spend money on training or promoting learning and development so successive governments have started various initiatives such as NVQs, apprenticeships, New Deal, Train to Gain and Investors in People to encourage employers to improve the skills of their workforce. The Leitch Report in 2006 called for the UK to spend much more money on boosting skills for everyone at every level in order to avoid the UK losing competitiveness because of lack of skills. The report also called for the creation of a new Commission for Employment and Skills and to give employers more say in the way skills were developed (Kingston, 2006).

This chapter is about the contribution that learning and development can make to organisations and individuals in terms of improving their performance and helping each to achieve their particular objectives. It is also about what organisations and the people in them need to do to ensure that learning and development makes this positive contribution to performance.

What do we mean by learning and development and how does this differ from training?

We have chosen to use the phrase **learning and development** in the title of this chapter rather than the word **training.** What exactly do we mean by these terms and does this choice of terminology make a difference?

The term learning and development has gained in popularity in recent years as organisations increasingly recognise that in order to stay competitive they must utilise and develop the knowledge of their workers as fully as possible, and as a result the focus of their activities has switched from training to learning. This is because we have moved from a largely manufacturing economy, where it was appropriate to train people to carry out clearly specified tasks and where a top-down instructor-led approach was suitable, to a much more flexible service and knowledge-based society where good workers become a source of competitive advantage to an organisation and where it is more appropriate to focus on individual learning and encouraging people to learn how to learn. This puts the process of learning very clearly under the individual's ownership and training as something organised by the employer to meet specific needs.

The word **development** also implies something that is ongoing and that progress is made over time and this fits also with the emphasis nowadays on lifelong learning. As people work longer they need to continue to develop to improve their skills, knowledge or competencies.

People do learn in all sorts of ways, some of them planned and some totally unplanned. Organisations still have a role to play to create suitable environments in which learning can occur and it is important that they do this as they can clearly benefit from the learning and knowledge of their workforce.

The concept of individualised learning and development implies that this occurs in all sorts of situations, not just in the more traditional, formal training opportunities, although we hope that learning will occur here too. Learning and development includes other less formal, more learner-centred approaches to learning such as coaching, mentoring, work shadowing and job swapping. Changes in technology also play a part, enabling the completion of learning and development packages wherever individual workers are in the world, whether at home or at work, as long as they have access to a computer or telephone.

A move from training to learning also needs different roles to be adopted by line managers, human resource managers and learning and development specialists who have to become increasingly flexible, often adopting a facilitator role rather than always appearing to be the expert as the traditional trainer might have been. However, although this change in emphasis is undoubtedly occurring, you will still find other terms such as training being used as different organisations will be at different stages in changing the emphasis from training to learning.

Creating a learning culture

If an organisation is to encourage learning to occur, then it must develop a culture which recognises that people learn in different ways and must provide a range of experiences from which they may learn. Human resource managers and learning and development specialists have an important role to play in ensuring that the organisation develops in a way which facilitates the learning that the organisation wants to occur, and that a suitable environment is created in which continuous improvement is actively encouraged. They themselves need to understand the learning process and the key stages in the provision of learning and development activities to ensure that this happens. Line managers also need to be involved in understanding and encouraging learning to occur, and the organisation should try to minimise barriers and encourage individuals to seek learning opportunities for themselves. The training or learning and development opportunities that occur should clearly link with the objectives of the organisation, and its efficiency and effectiveness should be regularly evaluated.

Sometimes organisations aspire to calling themselves a learning organisation. In some ways the term is confusing, since people actually do the learning, but it is good that people have started to see learning within organisations as being of importance. According to Jones and Hendry (1992), the term at its simplest means an organisation where there are 'a lot of people learning' and according to Pedler *et al.* (1988) it means 'an organisation which facilitates the learning of all its members and continuously transforms itself'. In today's fast changing world it is necessary for organisations constantly to try to keep ahead of the competition and in order to achieve this increasingly many organisations are creating a coaching culture to facilitate in a cost efficient way the learning of all in their organisation.

Not all organisations have been as proactive about encouraging learning and development as those that aspire to become learning organisations and governments have also developed many initiatives to encourage organisations to promote learning so that the skills of the country improve. The UK Government has had many initiatives such as National Vocational Qualifications (NVQs), New Deal and apprenticeships. One initiative that seems to have been instrumental in encouraging many organisations in the UK to become more proactive about learning and development and to link their learning and development initiatives to their organisation's strategic objectives is the Investors in People award which is available to those organisations deemed to have met the standards, giving them the IiP Kitemark of quality.

The Investors in People award (IiP)

This initiative aims to improve the quality of British training and development practices by setting national standards for good practice and by linking these to the achievement of business goals. Since training and development is closely linked to the organisation's objectives it will result in people being trained and developed in ways which exactly suit the organisation's requirements and this should enable the value of these activities to be clearly demonstrated.

The national standard was originally developed during the 1990s but has subsequently been revised every three years in order to ensure the award is accessible and relevant to a range of organisations, particularly small organisations which might not have an HR expert. It aims to provide a national framework which will help to improve business performance and competitiveness and which will add real value to an organisation, doing this by providing a planned approach to establishing and communicating the business objectives of an organisation and achieving these by developing the people within that organisation. Once again, learning and development activities are perceived to be vital in making an organisation competitive.

The Investors in People Standard was last revised in 2005. According to the CIPD (2007a) the three key principles of IiP are:

- *Developing strategies to improve the performance of an organisation* – an Investor in People develops effective strategies to improve the performance of the organisation through its people.
- *Taking action to improve the performance of an organisation* – an Investor in People takes effective action to improve the performance of the organisation through its people.
- *Evaluating the impact on the performance of the organisation* – an Investor in People can demonstrate the impact of its investment in people on the performance of the organisation.

The standards have been simplified and these three principles now form the basis of the IiP cycle and are in turn broken down into ten indicators. Any organisation wanting recognition as an Investor in People will now be assessed against these three principles and ten indicators.

The earlier version of the Investors in People standard had focused on gaining commitment from the top to learning and development, and making clear the strategic links so learning and development clearly supported the organisation's strategic objectives. IiP seems to have been largely successful in achieving this. The focus of the new standards has shifted and is now on employee involvement and engagement, a topic we covered in more detail in Chapter 3, and on maximising worker potential to achieve high-performance working. Organisations are further encouraged to engage their employees in decisions about learning and development initiatives.

The new revised standards recognise that all managers, at whatever level, have a vital role to play in the development of their workers. As we said earlier in this chapter, it has often been difficult to get the commitment of line managers to spending time and money on the learning and development of their workers. These new standards emphasise this vital role and are likely to have quite an impact in this area. Achieving the IiP award is not the final stage as the organisation will then need to continue to encourage continuous improvement in order to get even better at developing its people and in order to meet the requirements of the standard again in future years.

Many organisations have demonstrated commercial benefits from achieving the standards and there are benefits for their workforce too, not only in being part of a thriving organisation but also in improvements in their own training and development.

Designing learning and development

The Investors in People standard provides a framework for organisations to follow to ensuring that they utilise key principles when designing learning and development initiatives. However, not all organisations work towards the achievement of these standards and it is still important for those organisations and their managers to take account of certain key issues when designing learning and development initiatives. It is important that when you become managers that you are aware of these principles as well.

It is not enough just to choose the techniques to be used and hope that these will develop into a programme. When you are designing a learning programme you should have in mind clear objectives for it. What do you want the learners to be able to do and what do you want them to know by the end of the course?

Our approach to the design of learning opportunities is derived from the systematic approaches to training and learning such as the systematic training cycle. The systematic training cycle is shown in Figure 10.1. Most recent models of the learning and

Figure 10.1 The training cycle

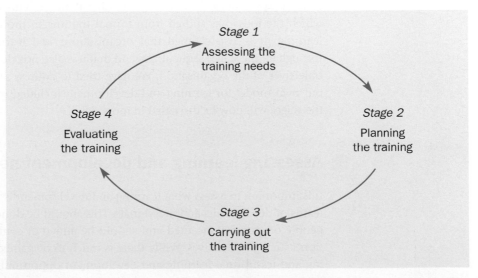

Figure 10.2 Model for learning and development

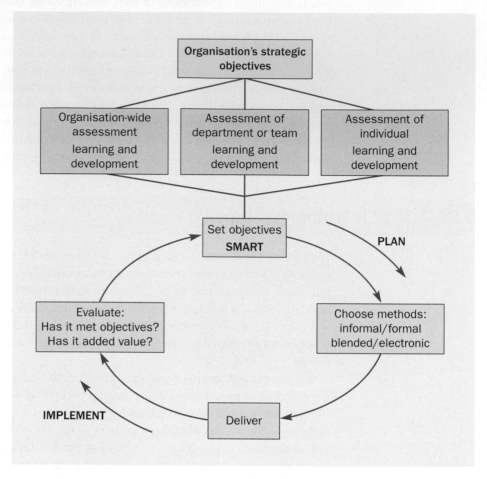

development process, including our own, have used it as a starting point. There are of course many valid criticisms of the systematic training cycle which relate to the fact that its focus is in on training rather than individualised learning and that it is more suited to a stable work environment rather than a rapidly changing environment in which the focus has shifted from formal training to more informal approaches to learning. It is also claimed that organisations and learners do not always work through all the stages sequentially and that it is also not clearly linked to the strategic objectives of the organisation. We have tried to address some of these criticisms in our own model for learning and development included in Figure 10.2 and each of the stages will now be discussed in more detail.

Assessing learning and development needs

It is important to assess what learning and development is needed for organisations, teams or departments and individuals. This should be done in conjunction with the people or groups concerned and should be aimed at contributing to the organisation's strategic objectives. While there is much to be gained from both formal training and less formal learning and development opportunities in terms of improved skills and productivity for the workforce, they are nevertheless costly activities, so it is important to provide learning opportunities of the right type for the people or groups who need them.

This stage of the cycle is referred to as assessing learning and development needs and this is frequently done for individuals using the performance appraisal process or personal development review. Learning and development needs can be assessed in many ways, but one of the easiest ways is to examine the job that has to be done and the knowledge, skills or competencies that the organisation needs the job holder to have, and then to examine the knowledge, skills and competencies of the person in that job and assess whether there is any gap between the two.

This type of assessment can be completed for a whole organisation, a team or department or for an individual. If there is a gap then a learning and development initiative may help the individual, team or indeed the whole organisation to progress to the required standard, but if the gap is caused by some other factor such as poor recruitment, then it may be a waste of money to use learning and development to try to bridge this gap. However, individuals do not always want the same learning and development opportunities as their organisation wants and may want to try to develop their careers by identifying their own gaps in their skills in comparison with the direction in which they wish to develop. Although no organisation has a limitless budget for learning and development some organisations are able to cope better with the differences between individual learners' aspirations than others. Organisations that are flexible in their approach and that budget for a certain amount of money to be spent on each individual's learning, whether or not it contributes directly to the strategic objectives, are likely to benefit from this approach as they are creating a positive feeling about learning which should result in the individual being more positive about the organisation resulting in turn in them being successful in learning in other ways that will benefit the organisation.

Job analysis needs to be undertaken to establish what is involved in the job. Refer back to Chapter 2 to refresh your memory of the ways in which to carry out this job. The usual result of job analysis is a job description, and a training specification can be written from this. In many organisations, where employees are encouraged to work towards National Vocational Qualifications (NVQs), there will already be a national standard for the employee to work towards.

Learning and development needs can also be assessed by asking the person or people concerned about their learning and development needs, by using questionnaires, or by an analysis of mistakes (faults analysis). If there are any gaps where they do not meet the standards then there is a possible need for learning and development to help to close the gaps, and so a need has been identified.

Setting objectives

To do this the person organising the L&D event or process needs to be clear about what the individual, team or organisation needs to know, or be able to do, or the competencies they need to have acquired after the learning and development has taken place. It is important to establish clear objectives for the learning or development event since without them there is a danger that the event will become unfocused and will not achieve its objectives. It also provides a basis for one way of evaluating the L&D by establishing whether or not the objectives of the event have been met. 'SMART' objectives are recommended: the acronym can stand for a variety of things but generally refers to the objectives being specific, measurable, achievable, realistic and timely or time-bound.

Planning the learning or development initiative

Once you have decided your objectives for the learning and development event, you are then able to plan a programme that uses a variety or blend of techniques in order to achieve this aim in the most effective way.

If the learning and development is to be effective it cannot be left to chance and a great deal of planning needs to happen first in terms of basic preparation of materials and administration, such as notification to all participants and organisation of the event itself. You need to ensure that everyone is aware in advance of what will be involved in the learning and development event and its timing and location in plenty of time. Letters should have gone to the learners, the people involved in running the event, and the supervisors and managers of those who will be involved so that there is time to arrange cover for their absence from work, if necessary.

Once a learning or development need has been identified, there are a number of choices to be made about how it should be met. First, should it be carried out in the organisation (in-house) or by an external organisation such as a college or other training provider? Second, the line manager or learning and development specialist needs to consider which techniques should actually be used. Should formal instructor-led traditional training be used or would the need be met better by less formal individualised learning such as e-learning, coaching, mentoring or the use of learning logs? Once this has been established a specific learning and development programme needs to be identified or designed.

Internal or external learning and development

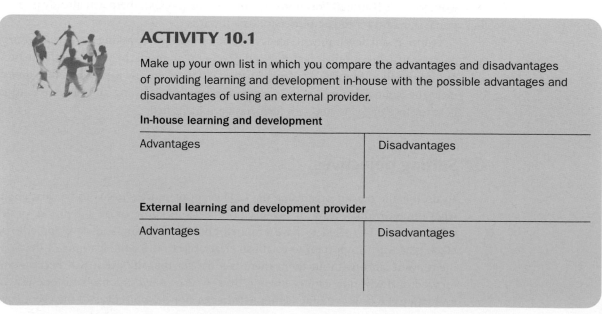

ACTIVITY 10.1

Make up your own list in which you compare the advantages and disadvantages of providing learning and development in-house with the possible advantages and disadvantages of using an external provider.

In-house learning and development

Advantages	Disadvantages

External learning and development provider

Advantages	Disadvantages

Discussion of Activity 10.1

Your lists are likely to contain several advantages and disadvantages for both approaches. Among the points you should have considered are the cost and resources available to carry out the initiative. It is likely that in-house learning and development will be cheaper and will be tailored perfectly to meet your organisation's needs. However, if the particular need identified is very specialised and is required for only one or two people, or if there is no one with suitable qualifications or experience available to conduct or facilitate the initiative, then it may be better and more cost-effective for them to join a course run by an external provider. This, although it may not be tailored to meet the organisation's specific needs, will have the advantage of providing a wider experience and opportunities to find out how other organisations do things.

In the past, when people were trained in traditional ways they were often just made to sit next to someone and told to do what they did. This is often referred to as 'sitting by Nellie', and the effectiveness of the training depended on how good Nellie was at her job. If she was good at it, and a naturally good instructor, then it could work well, but there was always a danger that the trainee would learn faults as well as good practice. This was one of the main disadvantages of using 'on-the-job' training. In more recent times the emphasis in a great many organisations has switched back to on-the-job training with the introduction of NVQs. This time, however, the person who does the training and assesses what has been learnt is trained themselves, and there are national standards to work towards, so there should be much greater consistency in approach. This aims to harness the benefits of on-the-job training, in terms of low cost and relevance to the organisation, while ensuring that standards are high and consistent. In this case using on-the-job training could be beneficial, as the training has been planned, there is a trainer who knows how to train, and a qualified person will test whether the individual is competent in that job. According to the CIPD's annual survey on learning and development (2007b), 'the most frequently used learning and development activities are on-the-job training (81%) and in-house development programmes (60%)' while 'a significant proportion of respondents (73%) expect their use of coaching by line managers to increase in the next few years.'

Learning and development techniques

We stated earlier that once the decision has been made about where the learning and development activity is to take place, it is also important to decide on the most appropriate techniques to use. Will formal trainer-centred approaches work best or will more informal learner-centred approaches be better? How much technology should be used? The method used must be chosen to be appropriate for the particular need that has been identified for that person or group and it must fit with the culture and resources of the organisation. Table 10.1 lists some of the available methods, with suggestions as to training situations in which they might be suitable. Some of the methods listed are traditional trainer-led methods while others are much more learner-centred.

E-learning

As well as the more traditional approaches to learning, trainers and individual learners now have a choice of using e-learning techniques. There is some confusion about what exactly constitutes e-learning but it can include computer-based training and

Table 10.1 Learning techniques and their suitability

Training technique	Formal trainer-centred or informal learner-centred approaches	Suitability
Lecture	Formal trainer-centred	This is suitable when a large amount of information needs to be given to a large number of people at the same time. The information can be prepared in advance but a disadvantage is the lack of participation from the audience.
Role play		Here a small group of people have the chance to act as if they were in a real work situation. They have a problem or situation to deal with which would be similar to a situation that they might experience at work. They can practise their responses and receive help and support from the trainer and from the others in the group. This can help in developing awareness of interpersonal skills and can give confidence, as there is an opportunity to practise skills in a protected environment where it does not matter if mistakes are made. There can sometimes be a problem if the role play is not taken seriously or if trainees are too nervous or embarrassed to perform their roles.
Group discussion		This can lead to a free exchange of knowledge, ideas and opinions on a particular subject among the trainees and the trainer with the opportunity to air various viewpoints. It can be useful when there are varying opinions about an issue, or a range of ways in which a situation could be handled. There is a danger that the trainees may wander too far from the subject if it is not handled skilfully by the trainer, and that important points may not be discussed.
Video or film		These can be used to show a real situation and differing ways of handling that situation, or to give information to several people at once. They can show examples of good and bad use of interpersonal skills to a large number of people at once and be used as the basis for a group discussion. They do not demand much involvement from the audience, although the trainer could add to this by use of discussion or questions after each showing.
Project		Normally a task is set by the trainer which will give an individual or group general guidelines to work to, but will also leave a great deal of scope for them to show creativity or initiative. This is a good way of stimulating creativity or initiative but, in order to do so, the project has to be about something that will interest the trainee.
Case study		A case study is a history of some event or situation in which relevant details are supplied for the trainee to get an overall picture of the situation or organisation. Trainees are then asked to diagnose the problems or suggest solutions. A case study provides the opportunity to examine a situation in detail yet be removed from the pressure of the real work situation. This allows for discussion and provides opportunities to exchange ideas and consider different options. Since a case study can limit the number of factors or issues that should be discussed, it may sometimes seem too easy and trainees may not fully appreciate that in the real-life situation there may be other more complex issues to take into account.
Computer-based training		This allows the trainee to work at their own pace through a series of questions or exercises using a computerised training program. The trainees get immediate feedback from the computer program and can cover a range of work in a short space of time, going back over exercises if necessary and learning at a time that is convenient for them. Trainees may be nervous of the technology or may experience difficulties so it is normally useful to have easy access to help or advice at least via a telephone.

Table 10.1 Continued

Training technique	Formal trainer-centred or informal learner-centred approaches	Suitability
Guided reading		A series of recommended reading is provided on a topic, perhaps graded according to difficulty. The trainee is able to work at their own pace through this. Since the reading has been selected by someone else to highlight points on that subject, this can save the trainee time, since they know that the materials will be relevant to the subject. It does not encourage the trainee to research further around the subject or seek materials for themselves.
In-tray exercise		Trainees are given a series of files, memos and letters similar to those that they might have to deal with in a real work situation. They need to decide on the appropriate action to take and the priority for action. This gives an opportunity for trainees to experience the sort of issues that can arise, but it is important that the contents of the in-tray are realistic.
Online discussion groups		
Audio or video conferencing		
Podcasts		

learning, technology-based training and learning and web-based training and learning. It may be integrated alongside traditional learning as a support mechanism, or be used separately as part of a distance learning or open learning course. Some university degrees, post-graduate qualifications and training packages are delivered totally by e-learning methods and this makes them easily accessible to people in any part of the world at any time.

One major advantage is that individuals, so long as they have access to the technology, should be able to choose when, where and what they learn and this should increase opportunities for learning. Support can be provided by chat rooms, discussion groups and online tutoring with everyone involved able to respond at a time that is convenient. Alternatively, approaches such as virtual classrooms, audio-visual conferencing and two-way live satellite broadcasts provide immediate feedback so learning and development managers and learners can interact with each other almost as quickly as they would in a more traditional classroom situation.

With the current concern for environmental issues and our carbon footprints it will be interesting to see whether these approaches will become more popular and replace some of the travel by students and their lecturers.

ACTIVITY 10.2

How do you feel about e-learning as an approach to learning? Is it a method you enjoy or is it an approach you dislike?

You can experience some aspects of e-learning for yourself by using the support materials for this book at www.pearsoned.co.uk/foothook. Go there now and complete exercise 10.2.

Other learning and development techniques

Many other techniques could also be used and we have summarised the suitability of some of these in Table 10.1. Complete the second column for yourself to identify whether in your opinion the particular type of learning and development activity is led more by the learning and development specialist, the learner or equally by both. From your reading in this chapter so far, use the blank spaces in the table to assess the suitability of online discussion groups and audio or video conferencing and the use of podcasts. Spaces have also been left at the end of Table 10.1 for you to add your own suggestions for different training techniques.

Some of these learning and development methods are much more participative than others, and it is a good idea to use a variety of techniques to avoid the trainee becoming bored and also to give opportunities to practise skills if a skill is being taught. This will also mean that if you are working with a group of people and you utilise a variety of techniques, you are likely to use the preferred learning styles of different individuals at various times. Learning is an active process, and even if it is a list of facts that needs to be learnt, most people learn more effectively when they test themselves, or rewrite information in their own words. This also improves their recall of the information.

Did you know?

It is often claimed that the average rate of retention when learning new material is as follows:

- 10% of what is read
- 20% of what is heard
- 30% of what is seen
- 50% of what is seen and heard
- 70% of what the trainee says
- 90% of what the trainee says and does.

These points emphasise the importance of providing some opportunities for the learner to practise what they are supposed to be learning, and underline the value for you of completing the exercises as you go through this book so that you continue to learn effectively.

Delivering the required learning or development event

Although specialist learning and development managers will be trained in learning techniques it is also important that line managers and any other members of staff involved in facilitating or running learning and development events should also be trained appropriately. This is still important if informal learner-centred approaches are being used, since mentors, coaches or group facilitators also need training.

Even if the people involved are trained well they will still find that delivering specific learning events will seem different each time as the process also involves interaction with learners who may have different learning styles as well as differing personalities. Some degree of flexibility is therefore necessary to take account of these differences.

Evaluating the learning

This is an extremely important stage in the learning and development cycle, and one that is often neglected by organisations. According to Findlay (2004), it is still true to say that 'many learning and development specialists do not evaluate the outcomes of their work – beyond handing out "happy sheets" at the end of courses. These provide feedback on whether the learners have enjoyed a course or other learning interventions but do little to measure its impact.' If no evaluation of learning and development is carried out at all then the organisation does not know whether it has been enjoyed or been successful, or even whether the learning and development objectives have been met, so it may have wasted money and resources on events that were not very effective and which did not help the organisation meet its strategic objectives.

Very little has actually changed in the way training or learning and development is evaluated. Donald Kirkpatrick set out the general principles in 1956 in an article 'How to start an objective evaluation of training' (see Findlay, 2004) and, although there have been criticisms of his work, his ideas have lasted well. He basically argued that there should be four levels of evaluation. First, at the end of the learning and development event, the participants should be asked their views on the effectiveness of the learning experience. This could be done by means of a simple questionnaire to the event or course participants and this will at least give clear views as to whether the people concerned liked the learning or developmental experience, what they felt would be useful and what they felt was less useful. Consequently it should yield a great deal of valuable material, which the manager responsible for the design of the learning event should be able to incorporate usefully in the next course.

According to Kirkpatrick's levels of evaluation, the happy sheets equate to level one evaluation. However, this only establishes what the participants say they feel about the course or learning event and it is also important to establish what they have actually learnt so both knowledge and skills also need to be tested. One very effective way to achieve this is to test these both at the start of the learning event and at the end of it. This achieves Kirkpatrick's level two evaluation as it should show how much the person has learnt during the learning and development event.

If the learning is going to have an effect on the department and on the organisation and contribute to its strategic objectives it is also vital to find out what effect the learning and development event has had when the person actually gets back to work. Sometimes people may do well in a learning situation but when they return to their normal work area they revert to their usual behaviour and they seem to forget or not use the learning that has occurred. From the perspective of their line manager and from the organisation's point of view this is a waste so it is important to find out whether transfer of learning to the work situation has occurred. This can be done by questionnaires or with interviews with participants and their line manager a few weeks later, or by a review of the person's work and the effect that the learning or development opportunity has had on him or her. Kirkpatrick's level three evaluation aims to test whether the learning that has occurred has successfully transferred to the workplace and essentially this level of evaluation aims to measure changes in job behaviour.

Kirkpatrick's fourth level of evaluation relates to whether the learning and development activity has made a difference to the bottom line in an organisation. Has it succeeded in making a difference to the organisation or added value? According to Martin Sloman (2004), 'If you focus your training on the organisation's learning requirements, you won't need to get hung up on assessment.' To achieve this level of evaluation it may be necessary to examine organisational statistics to see, for example, whether sales targets have been met or whether levels of customer satisfaction have improved.

According to Ian Thomson (2004), 'Evaluating training is a way of combining the assessment of the impact of training and development, while raising the profile and influence of HR and training functions.' Therefore it is in the interest of these departments to evaluate at all levels, not only to ensure that the learning objectives have been met, but also to demonstrate to the rest of the organisation that they have been successful in adding value to the organisation by making a difference in key strategic areas.

One of the things that have changed since Kirkpatrick's day is the emphasis that is nowadays placed on the reason for the evaluation. If you understand why you are evaluating something it is easier to select an appropriate method of evaluation. CIPD (2007c) state that there are four key reasons why learning and development should be evaluated. These are to:

1 prove the value of the training
2 improve quality of the training offered
3 evaluate as a contribution to the learning process
4 evaluate as a control over the training.

Various methods that can be used for evaluation of learning and development or training including the following:

- questionnaires completed at the end of a course by course participants
- interviews of learners asking their opinion of the value of the learning
- calculation of the return on the investment in training
- assessments by tests of what the person has learned or is able to do
- self-review by participants of what they had learned
- discussion with the learner's immediate superior of the improvement in performance
- cost analysis of the learning and development.

ACTIVITY 10.3

For each of the main purposes listed in Table 10.2 write next to it which forms of evaluation are likely to be most useful and in the third column write for whom that form of evaluation would be particularly useful.

Table 10.2 Forms that evaluation can take and those who would find them useful

The purpose of the evaluation	The main forms that the evaluation could take	The people or groups who would benefit most from the evaluation
1 Prove the value of the training		
2 Improve quality of the training offered		
3 Evaluate as a contribution to the learning process		
4 Evaluate as a control over the training		

Suggested answers will be found at www.pearsoned.co.uk/foothook.

We have gone through the key principles involved in designing learning and development activities but the choices made will depend on the organisation's strategic objectives, what the specific learning and development is aiming to achieve, the organisation's culture and the resources and skills available. We shall now examine some of the ways these could be undertaken in one specific form of training called induction.

Induction training

Anyone who leaves one organisation and goes to work in another will appreciate that things are done differently in different organisations, and people sometimes suffer a feeling of culture shock if behaviour that had been acceptable in their previous organisation is not viewed in the same way in the new one. This feeling of culture shock is likely to be even greater if the individual has moved from another country to work or to study. The new person picks up clues from the behaviour of others as to what is acceptable and what is not. Supervisors and managers will be seen to praise certain types of behaviour but will frown on others. At its simplest they are learning about the common view within that organisation of 'the way we do things around here' – the organisation culture.

Although employees will learn a great deal in this informal way, it is also a good idea for organisations to try to ensure that they have the opportunity to learn things that will enable them to perform to their best ability. This will mean that the organisation will need to:

- assess what it thinks people need to learn in order both to do their jobs and to contribute effectively to the organisation's strategic objectives
- plan opportunities to facilitate learning experiences
- evaluate what has worked well, and what has been less successful.

CASE STUDY 10.1 Induction

Read the following story about a student, Ros, who hoped to improve her language skills and earn some money for university by working as a waitress in a hotel in France for the summer. She has just started work as a trainee and is telephoning her mother a few days after her arrival.

Read the story and answer the questions at the end of it.

Ros   Hello, Mum. I got here in the end and I've survived the first day, but it has been quite difficult. I'm not sure how long I will stay.

Mum   Oh dear! What has happened? Was the journey OK? Were you met by someone with a car from the hotel, as they had arranged?

Ros   No, the hotel car didn't turn up. I had to get a taxi and it was miles from the airport, so it cost a fortune. The human resource manager took me to my accommodation, but no one else seemed to be expecting me. I'm living in an apartment with about another eight people, but they were just going out when I arrived and no one had told them that I was also going to be joining them in their accommodation. They were really nice but had trouble finding a bed for me and the only spare bed is in the kitchen and it's broken.

Mum   Well, I expect you felt better when you found out what your job was and got your uniform.

Ros   Well, I'm still not sure what is happening. I got up early yesterday morning, because no one had told me when to start work, but when I got to the office I was told that I was not on duty until today so I'm still not sure what hours I'm actually working. I thought I would only be working for 35 hours a week in France, but some of the others told me that this can be averaged over a few weeks, so it may be more.

I haven't got a uniform yet either, as the only one the HR manager had left was extra large, so was much too big for me. He suggested I wore a black skirt and white blouse until they can get a uniform in a small size for me. I spent the day on the beach with some of the other trainees, so at least that was good, but I had to borrow some clothes for work as the airline has lost my luggage.

| Mum | Oh dear! Have you reported it? I hope your luggage will turn up soon. You'll feel a lot more positive when you have your own things. |
| Ros | Yes, I reported it at the airport and it will be sent here when they find it, but I wonder if I'll still be here by then. Everything is different to what I expected. |

The HR manager told me that I would be joining the receptionists rather than the waitresses. Then when I turned up for work again this morning, I was placed in the marketing department. Another girl, who had been working there, has been moved to help at another hotel this week, because the Tour de France is going through the town. Consequently that hotel is full, so a lot of the temporary staff have been moved there to help for the week.

Mum	You should get plenty of opportunities to improve your French working in marketing.
Ros	My boss in marketing is really nice and I have been phoning French and English hotels to check on competitors' prices and I'm going to be helping to do a customer satisfaction survey in both French and English. Mind you, they really need a staff satisfaction survey!
Mum	Well, at least the job sounds interesting.
Ros	Yes, my boss says she wants to keep me in the marketing department, as she has plenty of work for me to do, even when the other trainee returns. The HR manager was talking about me helping to clean chalets next week, so I'm still very confused about the job I'll be doing. I want to come home.
Mum	You're bound to feel unsettled for the first few days, but I'm sure you'll feel better when you get a bit more established and when you have your luggage. Have the meals been good? At least you get your board and lodging provided on top of your wage.
Ros	I hope I'll feel better soon, but today I missed meals so I've only had a baguette.
Mum	Oh dear! Why was that? I thought free meals were part of your payment and in France you would expect them to be good, even for the staff.
Ros	The office staff have breaks at a different time to the people working in the restaurant and the hotel, so there was no food left when I arrived. I'll have to buy something later. I thought I was being paid weekly in cash, as it said in the letter that I was sent. The others say we get paid at the end of the month and that I'll need to set up a French bank account for myself as we get paid by cheque. I hope my euros will last until I get paid. It is proving much more difficult than I thought. All the information I was sent has been wrong.

Questions

1 Comment on what happened.

2 What information should she have received before she left England?

3 How could her first few days have been made easier?

ACTIVITY 10.4

Imagine that you are the learning and development manager at the hotel in France where Ros had her summer job.

Design an induction course for Ros and the other students at this hotel.

- What will be your objectives for the induction programme?
- What would you want Ros to know at the end of the programme?
- What do you want her to be able to do by the end of her induction programme?

Induction

New employees are each likely to have their own individual learning needs and establishing what these are during the induction process is important. Starting individual personal development reviews during the induction period and setting times for individual interviews to review progress regularly is important. However, they all have to learn certain things about the organisation and its culture. This could be even more important if the person is working in another country or using a second language, and intervention to help awareness of cross-cultural differences or in language skill may also be needed as part of the induction. New employees need to learn a great deal of information when they join an organisation. This can be learned informally, but this may take a long time and the employee may learn the wrong things.

Induction is the process of helping a new employee to settle quickly into their job so that they soon become an efficient and productive employee. It also helps create a favourable image of the organisation in the mind of the new employee, and is therefore also a valuable public relations exercise. Part of the induction process starts at the time of interview, with the information and impression of the organisation that is given at that stage. Any letters or booklets given after this also form an important part of the induction process. Some of the induction may be completed online with materials provided on the company intranet site and tests of knowledge of material carried out online.

When new employees actually start work, they will need also to get to know people with whom they will be working, become familiar with their surroundings, learn about their new job and learn about the organisation in which they will be working. Although there is a great deal of information to impart to the new employee, not all of it is needed immediately and in fact there is a danger of overloading the individual with information if it is all given at once. If formal induction courses are run for all new starters then these could be spread over parts of several days, imparting first the most urgent information, such as the geography of the building, canteen arrangements and introductions to supervisors and work colleagues. It may be that the formal courses do not even need to start on the first day, especially if recruitment is sporadic. Small groups of employees may be gathered, perhaps once a month, for the formal induction course, providing of course that their immediate induction needs such as information on safety rules have been adequately covered.

A formal induction course is useful, as several new starters can be given information at the same time. However, the new employees are likely to be starting different jobs in various departments, so that there is still an important role for their line managers to play in their induction, particularly in carrying out personal development reviews and then tailoring individual learning and development initiatives to meet the specific learning and development needs of the individual in that department. A checklist indicating which topics will be covered, when they will be covered and who will cover them is also extremely useful. This can be signed by the employee when he or she has gone through all the topics and then stored with his or her training records. It also provides a useful reminder to all of the need to cover these topics.

Table 10.3 gives an indication of the type of things that need to be covered during an induction period. It is useful to indicate who is responsible for dealing with each topic and when it should be covered. A section for the trainee to sign to say that she or he has completed each topic would also be useful.

Some of the information will need to be given in a written form, perhaps in a handbook, although increasingly nowadays organisations will keep much of this information also on their intranet system. Although much of this information may also have been given verbally in the formal induction course, it is useful to have a source of reference for things such as who to notify when you are ill. This might not

Table 10.3 Sample induction checklist

Topic	Person responsible for covering this topic	Day 1	First week	First month
Reception	Human Resource Manager	★		
Documentation and introduction to manager	Human Resource Manager	★		
Hours, clocking on, flexitime, lunch breaks, overtime	Human Resource Manager	★		
Layout of department, outline of function and introduction to staff	Supervisor	★		
Tour of main work areas, staff restaurant, toilets, fire exits	'Buddy' or person delegated by the supervisor to look after and befriend the new starter	★		
Health and safety rules	Supervisor	★		
The organisation – products, services, the organisation's handbook	Learning and Development Officer or on company intranet			★
Rules and procedures – discipline and grievance	Human Resource Manager		★	
Payment, holiday pay and sickness pay	Human Resource Manager Support materials on intranet system		★	
Communication and consultation	Learning and Development Officer			★
Training and development	Learning and Development Officer			★
Performance appraisal and set-up of personal development plan and reviews	Learning and Development Officer Additional materials on the intranet system			★
Pensions	Learning and Development Officer Additional materials on the intranet system			★
The trade union and trade union appointed learning representatives	Shop Steward			★

have seemed particularly relevant to a new starter, and indeed may not be needed for a year or two, by which time it may have been largely forgotten unless there is a handbook to refer to and an intranet site where the information is also easily accessible.

Since it is important not to give too much information, as the new starter may feel overwhelmed, it is better to spread the information over a period of time and alternate with periods where the person is introduced to his or her new job and given a chance to settle into this. After all, that is the reason they have joined the organisation. In some organisations new recruits are asked to arrive later than the rest of the workforce on their first day, so that those who will be involved in their induction can get things organised and deal with any crises that may occur, and then have time to spend on the new recruit.

If the new employee comes from another country, or if the work is in an international organisation where workers come from many different countries, there is also likely to be a need to deal with cross-cultural issues to encourage greater understanding and increase tolerance of different ways of working. The induction period would provide a useful foundation for this and progress could be reviewed during subsequent personal development reviews.

How do people learn?

Did you know?

Henry Ford said, 'Anyone who stops learning is old, whether at 20 or 80. Anyone who keeps learning stays young. The greatest thing in life is to stay young.'

In a knowledge-based economy, where there is constant change and where people are regularly required to develop new knowledge and skills, perhaps the most useful skill of all is knowing how you and others learn, as well as understanding the key principles involved in designing learning and development programmes.

In this section a range of learning and development and training techniques will be discussed which may also help you to learn more efficiently as well as preparing you to help others to learn.

Henry Ford's statement, above, is becoming even more relevant today, not just so that we all stay young but so that as retirement ages increase we can continue to lead productive and enjoyable lives as we continue to update our skills, knowledge and learning, whether for work purposes or for leisure. According to Age Positive (2007), a team working on strategies and policies to support people making decisions about working and retirement for the Department of Work and Pensions, 'Employees of all ages are benefiting from training and development' and organisations are benefiting too as 'employees of all ages have a variety of skills which make the organisations more effective.'

Factors affecting learning and development

In view of the change of focus to individual learning a good place to start is to consider your own approach to learning which you can do by completing Activity 10.5.

ACTIVITY 10.5

Make a list of a range of situations where you feel that you have learnt something.

- In each case consider what was your drive, or motivation, to learn.
- Was there a stimulus to increase your drive to learn? What was this?
- Was there any form of reinforcement of your learning? What was this?

Discussion of Activity 10.5

People are motivated to learn by a variety of things, so you may have listed quite a few drives to learn. These may take the form of incentives, encouragement or rewards. Some people may be motivated by the need to do well in an examination or they may perhaps be motivated to learn a new skill because it may provide an improved opportunity for getting a better job or more pay. In other cases the motivation may be the pleasure of learning something new for its own sake or for the respect that other people may feel towards you when you have learnt something impressive. Other people may be motivated to learn by a sense of curiosity or by anxiety or fear of failure and your motivation may change at different stages of your life as you continue with life-long learning.

The tests and exercises in this book and on the associated web pages at **www. pearsoned.co.uk/foothook** should help you to prove to yourself that you are learning. They are one way in which you can show your response to learning.

Learning theories

Psychologists have always been interested in how people learn and there are far too many theories of learning to discuss them all here. Besides, you will undoubtedly study some of these theories of learning in other subjects such as organisational behaviour. However, it is important to consider some of the common issues that occur in these theories as they may give us insights into how we learn and how we can help those in our organisations to learn so that we create high-performing organisations or nations. In particular, drives and motivation and knowledge of results or feedback are important.

The drive and motivation to learn

Behavioural psychologists such as Pavlov and Skinner referred to the instinctive need that led to learning as 'the drive'. In animals this was normally provided by a desire for food, but in people the drive or motivation might be to pass an exam or just to achieve the satisfaction derived from mastering something new. This aspect of their work points to the importance of considering people's motivation to learn. If we can find out what makes people want to learn we should then be able to tailor our instruction better and be more likely to create better performance at work. In Activity 10.5 you identified your own drives and motivation to learn but if you compare them with those of your friends you may find that they are motivated by different factors.

Organisations also need to be aware of what will motivate their worker to learn as part of their approach to performance management and need to ensure that other HR policies such as that for reward clearly support their approach.

Behaviourist concepts

Although work with pigeons and dogs may not appear at first sight to be very relevant to learning that occurs within organisations, this work does, in fact, raise a great many important issues, of which those specialising in learning and development should be aware.

Early in the last century Pavlov (1927) trained dogs to salivate when he rang a bell. He noticed that dogs salivated naturally as a reflex response when food was put in front of them. For his experiment he rang a bell every time the dogs were fed; after a time, the dogs would salivate when the bell was rung, whether there was food or not (Figure 10.3). He deduced that the dogs had learnt to salivate by associating the bell with the food, and came to see the learning process as the development of responses to the new stimuli given by the world. He called them conditioned responses, as opposed to the unconditioned or natural responses that came before. His term for the process of learning was 'conditioning'.

Later, Skinner (1953) took the theory further. The limitation of Pavlov's work was that it showed that animals (or people) could learn to apply instinctive responses to new sets of circumstances, but it did not show how totally new responses could be learnt. Skinner in fact succeeded in teaching pigeons to play ping-pong by a process

Figure 10.3 Pavlov's dogs

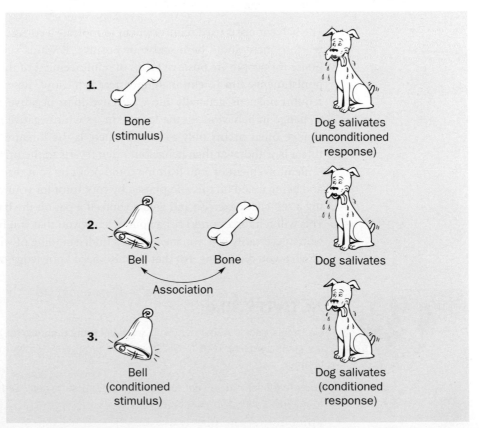

1. Bone (stimulus) — Dog salivates (unconditioned response)

2. Bell — Bone (Association) — Dog salivates

3. Bell (conditioned stimulus) — Dog salivates (conditioned response)

that he called operant conditioning. In this process, the pigeons were watched for any patterns of behaviour that might be useful when playing ping-pong, and whenever they performed they were rewarded with food. Not surprisingly, the birds soon learnt to do certain movements, and they retained their learning better if the reward was repeated regularly, a process Skinner called 'reinforcement'. In human learning, Skinner believed, reinforcement mainly took the form of feedback – information telling the learner whether he or she is getting the task right.

Skinner believed that all learning took place in this associative manner, and that all complex patterns of behaviour, such as learning ping-pong or learning to speak, could be broken down into small steps that could be taught one by one in a simple fashion. He applied this theory both to training workers and to the education of his own children, and his work is still very influential. It obviously makes sense to break down routine tasks into their component parts, and to provide methodical training to cover them. In addition, his emphasis on the visible or objective side of learning led to the practice of setting learning objectives or statements of what a learner had to achieve in terms of action.

On the other hand, you might be wondering whether Skinner's account of the pigeons' learning process was complete. Did insight play no part in their grasp of the rules of the game? In human learning insight often seems to enable people to cut the corners on the road to knowledge, and experience of behaviouristic attempts to teach complex matters suggests that they can lead to a slow, mechanical set of activities. Many psychologists have challenged Skinner's view, particularly with regard to the learning of complex behaviour such as speech.

Reinforcement and feedback of learning

The behaviourists used reinforcement to indicate a correct behavioural response. The reinforcement could be negative or positive. Rewards such as food for animals or praise for people are positive forms of reinforcement of the desired behaviour, while punishments aim to eliminate incorrect behaviour. Research suggests that positive reinforcement is generally more effective than negative reinforcement in gaining a change in behaviour in the long term, as with negative reinforcement the desired change often occurs only as long as there is the threat of punishment. When this threat is withdrawn then behaviour often reverts to the original behaviour.

Reinforcement of your learning could occur by your reading or viewing something and being tested on this and praised by your tutor for your efforts, or by you completing a self-check exercise and giving yourself a pat on the back if you have done well. This will reinforce correct behaviour or show you that you have the right answers, but won't necessarily give you any detailed understanding of what you have done well or of what you did wrong. For that you also need knowledge of results or feedback.

ACTIVITY 10.6

Go to this book's website, now at **www.pearsoned.co.uk/foothook**, and complete exercise 10.6 to check and reinforce your own learning in this chapter.

What feedback did you get for this? Was it of use to you? Did this help you to reinforce your own learning?

Knowledge of results or feedback is important if we are to learn effectively. In a training situation this could be by the trainer giving comments on the person's progress, or perhaps by a manager appraising the work of one of their staff as part of the performance management process.

When giving constructive feedback one should start with the positive, and focus first on the behaviour that has been done well before giving feedback about behaviour that has been done less well. Feedback about incorrect behaviour, if given skilfully, is extremely important; it doesn't have to be destructive, and here it is important to focus on specific aspects of behaviour that can be changed. General statements such as 'that was awful' are much too vague to be helpful in changing behaviour. It would be easy for the person receiving the feedback to feel that they are just being criticised unless the person who is giving the feedback also suggests alternative ways of behaving. For example, you might say, 'The fact that you seemed pre-occupied with your paperwork when Rosalind walked into the room, and took some time before you greeted her, seemed a very unwelcoming start to an interview. I think that if you had acknowledged her presence immediately and got up and walked towards her to greet her, it would have been a much more welcoming start to the interview, and would have been likely to have made Rosalind feel much more at ease.'

Feedback is a very important part of the learning process. The saying 'Practice makes perfect' could well be modified to 'Practice with appropriate feedback makes perfect', since without the feedback the person could just carry on with the same inappropriate behaviour over and over again.

Experiential learning

Experiential learning, or learning from experience is particularly useful for learning and development in the workplace situation. It is derived from the work of Kolb *et al.* (1974) in America, and of Honey and Mumford (1992) in Britain. Honey and Mumford's approach to experiential learning can be illustrated by the learning cycle shown in Figure 10.4. Their theory also suggests that different people may have

Figure 10.4 The learning cycle

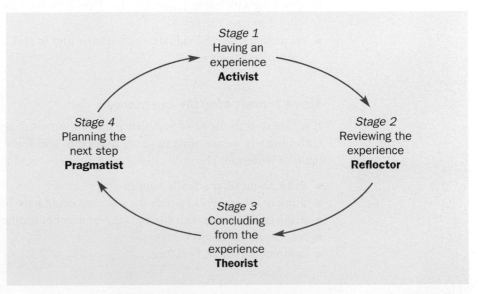

different preferred styles of learning and this is an important factor to consider if we want people to learn effectively.

The learning cycle

People learn in a variety of ways, and over the years may develop certain learning habits which enable them to benefit from certain types of experience more than other types. Students in college and people learning in the workplace are both likely to meet a range of different learning opportunities. Most full-time students nowadays will also work to supplement their student loan and will themselves have a range of work experiences from which they can learn. Some will be mature students who have already worked for a number of years, some will be part-time students combining study with a career, and yet others will be on sandwich course degrees where they have the opportunity of gaining work experience in a placement for a period of time. Knowing about your own learning preferences may help you to understand and you may become more efficient in learning from these experiences.

Stage 1: Having an experience

Most people have plenty of experiences from which they could learn, but age does not necessarily mean that people have learnt more. Some people do not use the experiences that they have. One way of learning is to let experiences come to you (reactive), and the other is to deliberately seek out new experiences (proactive). Anyone who provides learning development opportunities whether as a specialist or a line manager needs to provide suitable experiences from which people can learn (in the form, for example, of case studies, role plays and other simulations), but learners also need to appreciate the need to be proactive and seek for themselves suitable experiences from which to learn. The use of suitable individuals who are willing to act as mentors, or forming a supportive study group of friends, can assist in this process by:

- helping to identify suitable experiences from which to learn
- reviewing with individuals what they have actually done and helping to draw out what they have learnt
- encouraging the individual to be proactive and to seek for themselves suitable learning experiences.

Stage 2: Reviewing the experience

If we are to learn from an experience it is important to review what has happened. Unfortunately we are often too busy to do this, and some people never develop the habit of reflection. The individual should be encouraged to:

- think about what actually happened
- think of other ways in which the situation could have been handled
- make comparisons with what happened in other similar situations
- read about the subject
- compare theory and practice.

Stage 3: Concluding from the experience

There would be little point in reviewing the experiences unless we then drew some conclusions from them. This involves scanning the raw material for lessons to be learned and reaching some conclusions. The individual should be asking:

- What have I learnt from this?
- What could I have done differently?

Stage 4: Planning the next stage

Having reached a conclusion, it is important to try to do things better next time. To be able to do this we need to be able to plan, and this involves translating at least some of the conclusions into a basis for appropriate action next time. The individual should be encouraged to:

- state what they would actually do next time
- draw a plan of action for handling such a situation again.

The four stages in the process of learning using experiences are mutually dependent. The whole process is summarised in the learning cycle (Figure 10.4).

Learning styles

Honey and Mumford have developed a questionnaire so that individuals can establish their preferred learning style. They developed this approach as a result of their work with managers, as they became concerned to discover why one person will learn from a particular experience but another does not appear to learn anything from the same experience. Further details of their approach are given in the recommended reading. Most people only use one or two learning styles although these are not fixed and can change over time. They say that there are four differing learning styles that clearly link with the four stages of the learning cycle: activists, reflectors, theorists and pragmatists. These will now be discussed in turn.

Activists

Activists like to get fully involved in whatever is happening. They seek out new experiences and tend to be enthusiastic about new ideas and new techniques. They tend to be open minded and not sceptical, and are often enthusiastic about novelty. They tend to act first and then consider the consequences later. Their days are filled with activity and they often tackle problems by brainstorming.

Reflectors

Reflectors prefer to stand back and observe experiences from different perspectives. The thorough collection and analysis of data are important to them, so they try to avoid reaching definite conclusions for as long as possible. They would rather take a back seat in meetings and discussions and get the drift of the discussion before making their own points. When they act it is as part of a larger picture which includes the past as well as the present and takes into account other people's observations as well as their own.

Theorists

Theorists tend to adapt and integrate observations into complex but logically sound theories. They think problems through in a vertical, step-by-step, logical way. They assimilate disparate facts into coherent theories, and tend to be perfectionists who will not rest easy until things are tidy and fit into a rational scheme. They value rationality and logic.

Pragmatists

Pragmatists are keen to try out new ideas, theories and techniques to see if they work in practice. They positively search for new ideas and take the first opportunities to experiment with applications. They are the type of people who return from a training course full of ideas that they want to try out immediately. They like to get on with things and act quickly and confidently on ideas. They hate long ruminating discussions.

ACTIVITY 10.7

1   Read the description of the four learning styles again or go to http://www. campaign-for-learning.org.uk/aboutyourlearning/whatlearning.htm (accessed 29.09.07). This site provides some clear diagrams and additional explanations about Honey and Mumford's learning styles as well as hints on how to make learning more effective for each style of learner. It also provides lots of useful information about ways to learn more effectively.

2   From the descriptions given, which learning style do you think you use most frequently?

3   Try to discover your learning style. You could do this by testing whether how you think you learn matches an analysis of your learning style by using Honey and Mumford's online questionnaire at http://www.peterhoney.com/content/ LearningStylesQuestionnaire.html (there is a charge for this which at the time of writing was £10.00). Alternatively you could use a shorter online version which claims to provide similar results in a rough and ready learning styles questionnaire: http://www.brainboxx.co.uk/A2_LEARNSTYLES/pages/learningstyles.htm.

4   Reflect on your findings. Examine the theory by rereading the description of the styles outlined earlier and on these websites.

Discussion of Activity 10.7

You may have discovered that you are equally at home learning in each of these styles. Two per cent of the population use all four styles. The majority of the population – 70 per cent – tend to prefer to use just one or two learning styles. You can use the understanding that you have gained about your learning styles in various ways. You might choose to seek out opportunities to use the learning styles that you generally use less often, and in this way you may become a more rounded learner who is able to make use of a wider range of learning opportunities.

You might, on the other hand, choose to make use of the learning styles that you know you prefer to use, so that if learning opportunities are presented to you in ways that you don't like, you may look for alternative ways to learn about the topic which are more in line with your learning style preferences.

Did you know?

It is generally believed that the two sides of the brain are used for different things. The left side of the brain is used mainly for analysis, words, planning and dealing with things in a logical, rational way. The right side of the brain is better at the synthesis of ideas, presenting information in pictorial form, spatial competencies, and creativity and the generation of new ideas.

● Other approaches to learning styles and methods

There are many different ways of analysing approaches to learning. We have already mentioned the Honey and Mumford learning styles inventory and that of David Kolb *et al.*

However, other approaches are used. For example, are you a visual, auditory or kinaesthetic learner? This is sometimes referred to as VAK.

ACTIVITY 10.8

You can check whether you are a visual, auditory or kinaesthetic learner (VAK) at **www.businessballs.com/vaklearningstylestest.htm**.

If you like to visualise, seeing things in colour and using pictures such as mind maps, then you are probably a visual learner. If you prefer to listen to the sounds of things then you are probably an auditory learner, and if you like to move around while learning and link learning with movement then you could be a kinaesthetic learner. Do you associate other senses such as smell with particular things you have learned? Are you more of a left-brain (logical) or right-brain (intuitive) learner?

● Practical issues relating to individual learning

Whenever we are designing training for individuals or groups, we need to consider learning theory and build into the learning experience as many conditions as we can to ensure effective learning. Not only is it important when learning from experiences for the individual learner to be aware of their preferred learning style, it is also important that the L&D specialist or the line manager should be aware of differing learning styles and cultural preferences in order to provide a learning experience which will be congruent with the way in which each individual learns best.

● Recent approaches to learning and development

Mind mapping techniques

Psychologists are finding out more about the ways in which we think and learn and psychologists now say that our minds work in patterns and that several ideas can be developing at once. The brain then goes through a process of integrating ideas, but this doesn't necessarily happen in a linear order.

Tony Buzan (1982) developed the idea of mind maps to allow people to express themselves freely and encourage creativity, without being necessarily governed by the linear form. Many people, when presenting information in the form of a mind map, show a very detailed grasp of the subject which they were not be able to demonstrate in a traditional written form. The mind maps (some examples are used as chapter summaries in this book) start with the central subject, which can be presented pictorially. Lines then lead from this subject to other connected topics. This gives more freedom for ideas to appear without worrying at first about the connections, and it allows for several links to be made between related parts of a topic.

The mind map shown in Figure 10.5 illustrates our view of the key points with which this chapter has been concerned so far. Mind maps encourage creativity, and if they are to be used in a way that helps someone to remember and learn effectively then they should be very visual. The central topic should be written clearly, preferably in capital letters, and underlined. A pictorial representation of that topic is also useful, as it encourages easier recall. Lines should then be drawn from this key word, and the main areas relating to the subject area should be drawn.

Further diagrams or pictures can be useful to make the mind map of the topic memorable. Further lines and words should branch from each of these, and the pattern is then developed. Groups of ideas can be linked by the use of different colours. Links can be made easily, by using arrows or lines, between related topics. Relationships and links with other subjects can also be made and identified at the edges of the mind map.

Figure 10.5   Partial mind map of learning and development chapter

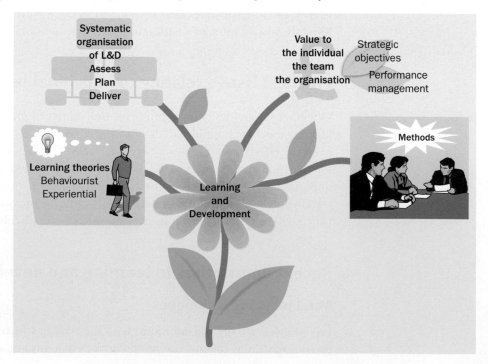

ACTIVITY 10.9

The mind map in Figure 10.5 is incomplete, since it is being used part-way through this chapter. When you have read the rest of this chapter, complete the remainder of the mind map in a way that will make it memorable for you. Draw links with other subjects or topics around the edge of the mind map.

Discussion of Activity 10.9

After reading the whole chapter you may want to include more things that you consider relevant such as e-learning, bite-sized learning and blended learning, roles of specialists and line managers and international learning and development so you can continue to build your mind map and add further topics to make it relevant to you. In order for it to be useful and memorable you should try to make your mind map as visually attractive as possible.

ACTIVITY 10.10

Consider each of the learning techniques listed in Table 10.1. Make four new lists as shown below, naming the learning and development techniques you think will suit activists, reflectors, theorists and pragmatists. (Some of the techniques may suit more than one style of learning.)

Learning and development techniques to suit people who prefer each of the four learning styles

Activist	Reflector	Theorist	Pragmatist

Discussion of Activity 10.10

Your list is likely to include a variety of different learning techniques, some of which we listed earlier and some that you have added for yourselves. We will consider in turn each of the preferred learning styles.

Activist

The techniques that allow activists to participate fully in the learning experience will be the ones that appeal most to them. These could include: role play, group discussion, project work, case studies, computer-based learning and in-tray exercises. The role play is especially likely to appeal to the activist, as it provides plenty of opportunity for them to become involved in a leading role. Activists are likely to be bored by the lack of involvement required from them in techniques such as lectures, videos or films.

Reflector

Reflectors are likely to appreciate learning techniques where they are presented with information that they can then think about, so lectures, films, videos and guided reading are likely to appeal to them. They will probably also appreciate to some extent group discussions and case studies, as long as they do not have to take too active a part and have plenty of time for reflection afterwards. Computer-based training courses, in which they can progress at their own speed and go back to examine again points that they want to look at in more detail, may also prove popular.

Theorist

Theorists welcome opportunities to examine new theories and compare them with other points of view. Lectures and guided reading are likely to appeal most to them as training techniques. Lectures with a fairly academic content are preferred, so that ideas gained can be compared with other ideas and theories. If the guided reading covers a suitable range of material this could also be useful to a theorist, although if the material is not extensive or theoretical enough for them, they are likely to want to delve further into other areas.

Pragmatist

The pragmatist wants to know how things will really work in practice, so they are likely to find training techniques that are close to reality useful. Case studies, role plays and in-tray exercises will appeal to them if they think that they are realistic and of immediate use to them at work.

Bite-sized learning

Some of you may have experienced bite-sized learning for yourselves as the BBC's revision programmes for GCSE use this approach. Octavius Black, managing director of the Mind Gym (2004), says that:

> People often thought that the more time they spent on learning, the better their knowledge would be. In fact, they could learn equally effectively – if not more so – in short bursts. Research shows that we remember and apply much more knowledge when we learn little and often than when we learn lots in one go.

This fits very well with what we said earlier about remembering information. You are likely to be more successful in remembering information if you are frequently spending small amounts of time going over what you have learned.

According to Crofts (2004), one of the most common barriers to learning cited by CIPD members is the amount of time it takes and as workers in the UK work increasingly long hours, bite-sized training certainly fits a need. However, trainers are likely to need to develop different skills to deliver material in a fast-paced way, with exercises taking only a few minutes to complete.

Blended learning

Another type of learning and development that is currently proving popular is the concept of blended learning. According to Allison Rossett and Felicia Douglas (2004):

> A blend is an integrated strategy for delivering on promises about learning and performance. It involves a planned combination of approaches as varied as coaching by a supervisor, participating in on-line class, self-assessments, and in on-line attendance in workshops and in on-line discussions.

We have already advocated that there should be a mix of learning and development methods to suit the needs of the learners, and blended learning involves planning this into the learning in ways that will suit the needs of particular groups.

In many instances, online learning forms part of the blend and cuts down the need for time spent on classroom-based learning, but every organisation has to reach its own blend of learning and development ingredients to suit the needs of the organisation and the participants in the learning and development programme.

Mentors

Rather than just leaving learning experiences to chance, many organisations now use mentors to help individuals to learn. Mentors need to be prepared to guide and suggest suitable learning experiences for their protégé. They may encourage reflection on these learning experiences by asking for reports, and may suggest books to read on the subject. They may also sometimes provide opportunities for the individual to demonstrate what he or she has learnt by, for example, reviewing a presentation before the learner makes it to the target audience. While their main aim is to encourage individuals to learn, mentors are also likely to learn a great deal themselves by their involvement in this learning experience. In effect, mentors will be encouraging the individual to learn in different ways according to their development needs and to practise using different learning styles and different stages of the learning cycle.

Coaching

Coaches help individuals or groups to perform better, rather like a sports coach. They could be external to an organisation or internal although, according to the CIPD's (2007b) survey of learning and development, 'the majority of coaching is being carried out by either internal coaches (coaching those who do not report to them) or by line managers (coaching those who report to them).' This is another approach to learning and development that as we mentioned earlier has been gaining in popularity although the CIPD's 2007 survey found there had been an unexpected drop in the number of organisations actually involved in coaching activities from 79 per cent in 2006 to 63 per cent in 2007. However, in the same survey 73 per cent of respondents indicated that they still expected that the amount of coaching carried out by line managers would increase.

According to Sol Davidson (2002), there are three types of coaching: traditional, transitional and transformational:

- Traditional coaching is closely related to training and involves a coach who is an expert in a subject helping to improve the skills and knowledge of an individual or group.
- Transitional coaching is useful where large changes are about to be made in an organisation. Here the coach does not necessarily know all the answers, but will help the group to find successful new ways of working.
- Transformational coaching is targeted at senior management but is aimed at helping the whole organisation move to new ways of working. It could be appropriate when an organisation is faced with a great deal of change.

Pause for thought 10.1 Which of these forms of coaching are most likely to be carried out by internal coaches who are not the person's line manager? Which are most likely to be conducted by line managers and which by external coaches?

Learning logs

Another way in which individuals may be encouraged to learn from their experiences is by the use of a learning log. A learning log is a way of keeping track of a person's development, with emphasis on unstructured, informal activities. This is likely to involve individuals in describing events that they feel are important for their own development process. They would then need to comment on what they had learnt from the experience and how, if a similar situation were to arise again, they would handle that situation. The idea is that because individuals have to write up their learning experiences, they will be likely to do things better in the future. Learning also ceases to be a haphazard process, as it becomes conscious and increasingly learner centred. This means that the individual will have used several of the stages of the learning cycle.

Keeping a learning log should encourage activists to be more reflective and encourage reflectors/theorists to take action and to do things after reflecting on them. This could be undertaken with a mentor or as a totally self-directed method of gaining insights into your own learning processes. This method is very subjective but tends to encourage an analytical approach to problems. It can also be helpful to get a problem sorted out on paper, with clear targets for how you would handle a similar situation in the future.

Nowadays the pace of change is rapid and people who studied 20 years ago, or even a couple of years ago, may find that their skills and knowledge are outdated. In order to update their members, many professional groups have introduced the concept of continuing professional development (CPD) and they often use learning logs as one way of recording the learning that has occurred and for planning for future learning.

The roles of people involved in learning and development

Learning and development specialists

Learning and development activities should be linked to the organisation's strategic level so that it can be clearly seen that they are making a difference and adding value to the organisation. When there is someone appointed at a very high level within the organisation it is likely that this will happen. Ulrich and Brockbank (2005) identified four key roles in HR which were the employee advocate, functional expert, human capital developer and strategic partner. Of these both the human capital developer and strategic partner are likely to operate at a senior level where they can make a difference by ensuring that learning and development activities are integrated with the strategic objectives of the organisation. The functional expert may also sometimes operate at this level and many functional experts are likely to be specialists in learning and development.

As line managers take on more of the responsibility for the learning and development in their teams it is likely that the roles of the specialist will also change. According to Harrison (2005) the future roles may become professional adviser, knowledge architect, brand manager, commercial lead, learning specialist or administrator. She envisages the professional adviser role being a type of business partner who produces learning and development solutions to address specific strategic aims for organisations and who plays a large part in helping prepare organisations for change.

The knowledge architect will also operate at a strategic level and will be concerned with knowledge creation and ways of sharing knowledge so that this adds value to the organisation. The brand manager will create a consistent brand image for all learning and development activity and will ensure engagement and motivation of those using the services of the L&D department. They will be involved in marketing learning and development so that everyone understands what it can do for the organisation and for the team. The commercial lead will have another role to play in terms of creating revenue from learning and development by selling their services to internal and external customers.

Harrison (2005) still visualises the need for learning specialists whose job is to design, deliver and evaluate learning and development activities and that there will also be administrators to support the learning and development specialists at all levels. However, in her future-oriented typology of learning and development roles she envisages L&D specialists developing into the new roles of professional adviser, knowledge architect, brand manager and commercial lead as more line managers get involved in the provision of learning and development activities for their own teams and departments. They will still need some learning and development experts to advise and perhaps change them but devolving more to line managers does free learning and development specialists to develop in other more strategic directions.

The roles of line managers in learning and development

In the UK and around the world not only are line managers likely to be involved in learning and development for their own staff and to be trained and encouraged to seek a range of suitable developmental opportunities, but the staff themselves will also be encouraged to actively seek opportunities for their own development. In organisations where there is often little room for promotion, and where the future of the organisation itself is insecure, it is in workers' own interests to keep themselves as up to date as possible and to seek out new opportunities for developing new skills or new knowledge. Hutchinson and Purcell (2007) see the role of line managers as vital to organisations as they move from traditional training to learning. They say this is in part a result of the growth in team work as working in teams helps individuals to learn their job. The line manager has a key role here as by ensuring that their team works effectively they are also encouraging learning. They also have an additional role in coaching and guiding their teams.

Getting line managers involved in learning and development is essential. There is a great deal of research evidence nowadays that suggests that learning and development makes a huge difference to the profitability of organisations, but it can be difficult to get line managers to see how it will make a difference to them and how it will enable them to contribute to the organisation's strategic objectives. One barrier is terminology. While it is important for students of this subject to be aware of the changing emphasis in the move towards learning and development, it is not always helpful to use these terms with managers. They are not usually interested in the subtle distinctions between different terms. What they want is something that will work for them. Ian Cunningham (2001) says that 'Mentioning learning, training or any other related term can put off busy managers. Rather than becoming instant converts to the latest idea they can become averse to the attempts at selling from trainers and HRD professionals.'

Cunningham (2001) offers additional tips for getting managers interested:

- not overselling the training and development
- not always accepting someone else's view of what needs to be done without exploring further
- accepting that managers make decisions on their own terms
- spotting the best moment to involve them in learning and development; only introducing a maximum of four concepts at any one time
- tackling only what should be potentially achievable problems
- structuring presentations to make the business case
- linking the learning to the business.

In this way Cunningham (2001) argues that line managers will want to be involved in the learning and development activities as they will be able to see the benefits both for themselves and for the organisation. Dalziel and Strange (2007) offer further tips for engaging line managers in various aspects of HR. They also emphasise the need to avoid jargon and suggest one uses the term 'people management' rather than 'HR' when talking to line managers and that the specialist also needs to help the line managers to see how they can add value to the organisation.

Learning and development should help the managers find solutions to problems they have, meet their targets, add value and in turn contribute to the achievement of the organisation's strategic objectives, so using various techniques to engage line managers in this process is important.

Trade union learning representatives

As part of the shift from training to learning, and in order to promote learning at all levels and within all organisations, the Employment Act 2002 established a new group known as learning representatives. These learning representatives are appointed by trade unions and have several statutory rights. These include the right to time off work in certain circumstances in order to:

- analyse learning and training needs
- provide information or advice relating to any learning or training issues

- organise specific learning or training
- consult with the employer about learning and training issues
- participate themselves in training for their role as a learning representative.

The ACAS (2003) *Code of Practice on Time off for Union Duties and Activities* gives further details of these rights. Union members also have the right to time off to discuss issues or attend learning activities organised by trade union-appointed learning representatives, although they do not have to be paid for this.

Pause for thought 10.2 Compare the role of the union learning representative with the role of the learning and development specialists within an organisation. To what extent do the roles differ? To what extent do the roles overlap?

Both the L&D specialists and the trade union learning representatives are concerned to promote learning so to that extent their roles do overlap but their focus will be different. The specialists, according to Harrison (2005), will be concerned that learning and development adds value to the organisation and to make the link between learning and development and the organisation's strategic objectives. They will be concerned to operate at a strategic level and may take on roles such as promoting L&D, managing knowledge, or generating income from L&D activities: there will still be many other L&D specialists involved in running specific learning and development activities and in training managers to do this.

Learning representatives will also be concerned to promote learning but they are operating at a different level as they try to encourage more of the workforce to become involved in learning. As they are a part of the workforce their role is to reach and inform workers who might not normally get involved in learning and development activities to do so: to encourage and discuss options with workers who might have been put off by having to discuss their learning needs with management. If lifelong learning is to become a reality then their role should help to kick-start some learning and development activities for all workers.

The learning representatives have a role to play in fostering a positive attitude towards learning and development and increasing motivation to learn. It has also been claimed that large numbers of workers lack basic skills in numeracy and literacy but have successfully hidden this from their employers for many years. In many organisations L&D specialists are now working with learning representatives to reach groups of workers who have not traditionally participated in learning and development and who may have poor basic skills which could be holding back their career progression so the roles of the L&D specialist and the union learning representative are in many ways complementary to each other.

International differences in learning and development

Cross-cultural issues will be of importance to many HRM or HRD practitioners, particularly if they work in multinational organisations or come to study HRM away from their home country. Therefore, it is important to consider to what extent there is a cultural dimension to learning. Hofstede's work does enable us to gain some insights into cultural effects on learning and these cultural differences do need to be taken into account when learning or designing learning materials for others. These cultural differences may influence individual learning styles since in countries where it is normal for the learning to be very tutor/trainer-centred and for the learner just to absorb knowledge without questioning, individual learners are less likely to have opportunities to develop an activist or pragmatist approach to their learning. It is likely that trainers will have to adjust their approach for learners who are used to being less participative and hold more formal training sessions than would be necessary in countries and cultures that have moved to being more learner-centred.

The roles of learning and development specialists in international organisations

While there may be differences in styles of learning, according to Sloman (2007) 'It seems that the issues faced by learning, training and development professionals are pretty much universal – whether they are in Britain, Bulgaria or further afield.' The CIPD carried out a survey of the changing role of the trainer involving 300 trainers and assembling '50 case studies from 19 different countries, and investigated how trainers in the United States, "old Europe", new emerging Europe, China, India and South Africa saw their roles.' They concluded that 'overall we found more similarities across the world than we thought we would.' There was no single approach that illustrated best practice but lots of approaches were found that showed good practice where trainers and learning and development practitioners were adapting learning approaches to the context of the country they were working in and to the learning styles of the learners in that country. The approaches identified in the CIPD (2007b) survey as good practice were:

- showing a clear understanding of the business drivers in their organisation;
- helping their organisation add value and move up the value chain;
- establishing a clear vision and strategy for people development;
- involving others and engaging shareholders in a transparent and open way;
- having both a good overview of what is needed to advance in the long-term and also of the short-term priorities;
- using processes and techniques appropriately – without being overcommitted to any one method of delivery;
- applying metrics to demonstrate value, and above all
- understanding the legacy that learners bring with them and adjusting their interventions accordingly.

The factors identified here in an international context by the CIPD survey fit well with our model of the learning and development cycle described earlier in this chapter with the emphasis on adding value and contributing to the strategic objectives. It also clearly emphasises the importance of adopting techniques to the learning styles and culture of the people being trained as we discussed earlier. Other areas highlighted by this survey were the move from the more directive forms of training towards less directive

Did you know?

'Toy workers are killed in factory fires in the Far East, children work for a pittance in India unprotected from damaging chemicals.'

(*Source*: Roger Cowe, 1998)

Many big-name manufacturers have excellent policies, procedures, training and quality standards for their staff in Western countries, but have still been exposed for profiteering from the exploitation of workers in developing countries.

more learner-focused approaches such as coaching, action learning and off-the-job training.

Conclusion

In this chapter we have provided an introduction to learning and development and have emphasised the need for a systematic approach which helps the organisation to achieve its strategic objectives. We have also shown that people learn in a variety of ways and that specialist L&D managers and line managers will need to adapt the learning experiences they provide to suit individuals and groups. However, while individuals often use only one or two preferred learning styles these are not fixed but will vary over time and will be affected by the culture within an organisation or indeed a country. While the concept of the learning organisation may still be aspirational, organisations wishing to improve learning do adopt a wide range of approaches. These include some formal training programmes such as apprenticeships, or the training element within New Deal and less formal more learner-centred approaches such as mentoring or coaching. There is an emphasis throughout such organisations on all aspects of learning and development and of identifying and agreeing the learning needs with the people concerned. All programmes also emphasise the difference that learning and development can make to an organisation by adding value to that organisation.

REVIEW QUESTIONS

You will find brief answers to these review questions on page 476.

1 To what extent do you agree with Harrison's (2005) predictions that the future roles of learning and development specialists will be: professional adviser, knowledge architect, brand manager, learning specialist or administrator? What evidence do you have for your assertions?

2 Use the Internet, Government publications or your local Learning Skills Council to find out more about one of the following topics: Investors in People, apprenticeships, New Deal. Using this information, describe how you would persuade a sceptical line manager of the benefits to be gained from introducing the chosen initiative into an organisation of your choice.

3 Interview a manager about his or her organisation's strategic plans and objectives and try to assess the extent to which learning and development in that organisation contributes to the achievement of those strategic plans.

4 Many organisations do not provide an adequate induction programme for new employees. Comment critically on the benefits to be gained from implementing a good induction programme, and outline what should be contained in that programme.

5 Evaluate the relative effectiveness of on-the-job training and off-the-job training.

SELF-CHECK QUESTIONS

Answer the following multiple-choice questions. The correct responses are given on page 477 for you to check your understanding of this chapter.

1 Which of the following is not one of the HR roles described by Ulrich and Brockbank (2005)?
   (a) Mentor
   (b) Functional expert
   (c) Human capital developer
   (d) Strategic partner

2 The illustration in Figure 10.6 shows what happens when Caroline makes a cup of tea. She often chooses to feed the cats at the same time as putting the kettle on. Thus the kettle and the tin of cat food being opened are linked in the cats' minds. Sometimes she puts the kettle on but she doesn't open a tin of cat food. However, the cats now appear when they hear the sound of the kettle.
   (a) What is this effect known as?
   (b) According to Pavlov, how should we label the cat food at point 1 in Figure 10.6?
   (c) According to Pavlov, what is the link between the kettle and the cat food known as? Label point 2 in Figure 10.6.
   (d) According to Pavlov, what should the kettle be labelled as at point 3 in Figure 10.6?

Figure 10.6 Caroline's cats

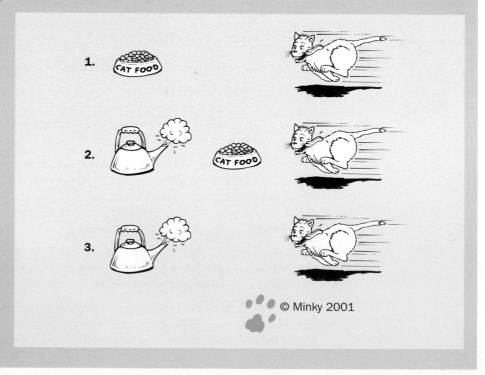

© Minky 2001

3 When there are very few new recruits to an organisation, should induction be left for several months until there are sufficient to form a group? YES or NO

4 Which of the following is not a coaching technique advocated by Sol Davidson (2002)?
(a) traditional coaching
(b) disciplinary coaching
(c) transitional coaching
(d) transformational coaching

5 Are mentors always training managers? YES or NO

6 Which of the following is true, according to Honey and Mumford?
(a) Learning has occurred when knowledge has been acquired by study.
(b) Learning has occurred when a person knows something that they did not know earlier and can show it, or is able to do something that they were not able to do before.
(c) Learning has occurred when a person knows something that they did not know earlier but can't show it, or is able to do something that they were not able to do before.
(d) Learning is shown by a change in behaviour that occurs just as a result of experience.

7 According to Honey and Mumford, a pragmatist is someone who:
(a) seeks out new experiences and is open-minded, not sceptical, and who is enthusiastic about anything new
(b) integrates and adapts observations into logically sound theories
(c) is keen to try new ideas, theories and techniques to see if they work in practice
(d) collects data in a very thorough way and then analyses it

8 Which of the following is not one of the stages in the systematic training cycle?
(a) assessing learning and development needs
(b) having an experience
(c) planning the learning and development activities
(d) evaluating the learning and development

9 Does CPD stand for continuing professional development? YES or NO

10 Which of the following learning and development methods, according to the CIPD, was found to be increasing in popularity?
(a) sitting by Nellie
(b) e-learning
(c) traditional off-the-job training
(d) coaching

HR IN THE NEWS

FT

FT Report – Professional Development 2007: Keeping managers sane and ahead of the game

By Rod Newing

Training courses and promotions are only part of the management development toolkit. Experience is an important factor and managers must be helped to improve their performance by stretching them as they work. Approaches include coaching and mentoring, but organisations are finding innovative new ways to develop management skills.

The importance of experience is shown by a comparative study of the capability of managers in Germany, Norway, Spain and the UK carried out by the Institute for Employment Studies for the Sector Skills Development Agency. It showed that innate ability and job experience are considered the most important factors in the creation of a good manager.

Similarly, a survey by Investors in People, a public body given the task of improving productivity and performance, identified that the most popular type of manager is someone who delegates, highlighting employees' eagerness to take on activities and responsibilities that provide them with the opportunity to develop their skills and experience.

An increasingly popular means of stretching employees in their current roles is coaching. The Learning and Development Survey 2007, by the Chartered Institute of Personnel and Development (CIPD), estimates that more than 60 per cent of organisations are involved in some form of coaching activity.

External coaches improve performance, particularly at senior levels, by helping the individual to set goals, develop strategies, explore outcomes, understand their motivations and management style and identify barriers.

Gladeana McMahon, co-founder of the Association for Coaching, explains that it typically involves six 90-minute sessions in the workplace, with assignments between sessions. The cost can vary from £3,000 for addressing a specific weakness in a middle manager to £15,000 for bringing a chief executive up to a new level of performance.

'Coaching for excellence has become a badge of honour in a lot of organisations,' she says.

'Given the global war for talent, organisations will often position a coach as an added perk. We help managers to hone their skills and stay "sane and ahead of the game".'

External coaches can bring in both perspective and skills, says the CIPD, but anybody can call themselves a coach and the body advises choosing someone with experience and knowledge of the organisation or the sort of situation the manager wants to address.

However, external coaches are not always necessary and Ms McMahon points out that good leadership is almost synonymous with good coaching skills.

Leaders need to understand their team and motivate them to deliver their strategy efficiently and effectively. Very successful leaders use coaching skills to help people grow in their role and achieve the objectives.

Mentoring is another formalised method of improving performance. It involves linking inexperienced staff with more experienced senior staff. The main problem is the senior managers' time commitment.

Another mechanism for stretching managers is to give them responsibility for managing a project, which can be in addition to their current role. As well as growing project management skills, it gives experience of working across functions and influencing managers.

Joanna Causon, director of corporate affairs at the Chartered Management Institute, points out that it can also give those in staff positions experience of managing people.

Fiona Lander, managing director of consultancy Lander Associates, says: 'Cross-functional working helps the manager to get the full picture of how things work and how they can do their job better. It also engenders empathy and teamwork.'

Toshiba has a stable organisation with a flat structure and high retention, so opportunities to move upwards can be rare. It therefore looks to develop skills through horizontal advancement and secondments to different departments.

'It is extremely useful in sharing best practice and developing employees' knowledge,' says Susan Stevens, its head of human resources.

Another way of stretching a manager is to give them experience of a more responsible role on a temporary basis. They can fill a more senior position while the incumbent is temporarily absent on a sabbatical, maternity leave, sickness, secondment or managing a project full-time.

Another way of stretching employees is to bring specific problems along to the traditional two- or three-week residential development course.

A key part of the annual talent academy for BT, the telecommunications company, for its high-potential people is 'challenge projects', where participants are put into groups and given three months to design, develop and implement revenue-generating projects. This gives people a chance to experience what it feels like to be an entrepreneur.

Consultancy Capita Symonds operates an inverted organisation, where its most experienced people are client-facing.

'We take someone relatively young and inexperienced, but extremely bright, and get them to run a smallish section of the business with people who would normally be more senior to them,' says Jonathan Goring, its managing director.

'This gives them very early exposure to serious management responsibility by running a business at a very young age.'

(*Financial Times*, 12 November 2007, Rod Newing. Reproduced with permission.)

Questions

1 Why is coaching such a popular method of developing managers in the countries mentioned in this article?

2 What other approaches to management development are discussed here?

3 What are the advantages and disadvantages of these methods?

WHAT NEXT?

1 ACAS provides some excellent opportunities for you to experience e-learning on its website at **www.acas.org.uk** (accessed 17.09.07). It is developing a range of e-learning resources and you can undertake short e-learning courses and test your understanding of several topics covered in this book, such as discipline and grievance, informing and consulting, and absence management and redundancy.

2 Listen to the following podcasts from the Chartered Institute of Personnel and Development to examine some of the current issues in learning and development at **www.cipd.co.uk/podcasts**:

The value of learning – episode 12. This examines the contribution that learning and development makes to an organisation and links with a key theme of this chapter.

Learning and development – episode 7. This discusses the findings of the Chartered Institute of Personnel and Development's 2007 survey of learning and development issues.

References

Advisory Conciliation and Arbitration Service (2003) *The Code of Practice on Time Off for Union Duties and Activities,* ACAS (www.acas.org.uk; accessed 31.08.04).

Age Posi+ive (2007) *Training and development,* Department for Work and Pensions (www.agepositive.gov.uk/good_practices/training.asp; accessed 04.04.07).

Armstrong, G. (2007) Taking care of talent is critical, *The Guardian: HR focus,* 15.09.2007.

Black, O. (2004) The future's bite, *People Management,* Vol. 10, No. 8, 25.

Chartered Institute of Personnel and Development (2003) *The Change Agenda: Focus on the Learner,* CIPD (www.cipd.co.uk; accessed 31.0.04).

Chartered Institute of Personnel and Development (2007a) *Fact Sheet: Investors in People.* CIPD (www.cipd.co.uk; accessed 14.9.07).

Chartered Institute of Personnel and Development (2007b) *Learning and development: annual survey 2007,* CIPD.

Chartered Institute of Personnel and Development (2007c) *Fact sheet: evaluation of training,* CIPD.

Cowe, R. (1998) Code breaks the ethics ploys, *The Guardian,* 13 June, 30.

Crofts, P. (2004) Support key to success, *People Management,* Vol. 10, No. 11, 55.

Cunningham, I. (2001) How to get managers' support for learning, CIPD (www.cipd.co.uk; accessed 19.9.07).

Davidson, S. (2002) How to choose the right coach, *People Management,* Vol. 8, No. 10, 54–55.

Dalziel, S. and J. Strange (2007) How to engage line managers, *People Management,* Vol. 13, No. 19, 56–57.

Findlay, J. (2004) Evaluation is no white elephant, *People Management,* Vol. 10, No. 6, 50.

Harrison, R. (2000) *Employee Development,* 2nd edition, CIPD.

Harrison, R. (2005) *Learning and Development,* 4th edition, CIPD.

Hofstede, G. (2006) *Cultural Dimensions,* www.geert-hofstede_kingsom.shtml (accessed 14.9.07).

Hutchinson, S. and J. Purcell (2007) *Learning and the line: The role of line managers in training, learning and development,* Change Agenda, CIPD.

Jones, A.M. and C. Hendry (1992) *The Learning Organisation: A Review of Literature and Practice,* HRD Partnership.

Kingston, P. (2006) Boost investment to solve skills crisis, Leitch report urges, *The Guardian: Education Guardian,* 5 December (http://education.guardian.co.uk; accessed 22.09.07).

Megginson, D. and V. Whittaker (2004) *Continuing Professional Development,* CIPD.

Pavlov, I. (1927) *Conditioned reflexes,* Oxford University Press.

Pedler, M., J. Burgoyne and T. Boydell (1988) *The Learning Company Project,* Training Agency.

Reid, M., H. Barrington and M. Brown (2004) *Human Resource Development,* 7th edition, CIPD.

Rossett, A. and F. Douglas (2004) The house blend, *People Management,* Vol. 10, No. 8, 36.

Skinner, B.F. (1953) *Science and human behaviour,* Macmillan.

Sloman, M. (2004) Evaluation and evolution, *People Management,* Vol. 10, No. 14, 50.

Sloman, M. (2007) World Standard, *People Management,* 22 March, Vol. 13, No. 6, 38–40.

Thomson, I. (2004) The power and the impact, *People Management,* Vol. 10, No. 8, 15.

Ulrich, D. and W. Brockbank (2005) Role call, *People Management,* 16 June, Vol. 11, No. 12, 24–28.

Further study

Books

Advisory, Conciliation and Arbitration Service (2006) *Recruitment and Induction,* ACAS. A very useful guide to this subject.

Harrison, R. (2005) *Learning and Development,* CIPD. An excellent textbook for those who wish to study the subject of learning and development in more depth.

Reid, M., H. Barrington and M. Brown. *Human resource development,* 7th edition, CIPD. Another excellent textbook that covers various aspects of learning and development.

Articles

There are many specialist journals covering the subject of learning and development including the following:

Human Resource Development International
Human Resource Development Quarterly
Human Resource Development Review
Learning and Training Innovations

Internet

Apprenticeships (England and Wales)	www.realworkrealpay.info
Apprenticeships (Scotland)	www.scottish-enterprise.com/modernapprenticeships
Chartered Institute of Personnel and Development	www.cipd.co.uk
Department for Children, Schools and Families (formerly the Department for Education and Skills)	www.dfes.gov.uk
The Information Network on Education in Europe	www.eurydice.org
Investors in People UK	www.iipuk.co.uk
Learn Direct	www.learndirect.co.uk
Learn Direct Scotland	www.learndirectscotland.com
The Learning and Skills Council	www.lsc.gov.uk
The National Academic Recognition Information Centre for the UK	www.naric.org.uk
New Deal	www.newdeal.gov.uk
Qualifications and Curriculum Authority	www.qca.org.uk

CHAPTER **11**

Payment systems

Objectives

By the end of this chapter you will be able to:

- explain the main factors that influence the choice of a particular payment system and the advantages and disadvantages of different types of payment systems
- explain the importance of developing a reward strategy for an organisation
- explain the process of job evaluation and how to use particular job evaluation systems
- identify issues relating to equal pay in organisations
- identify issues relating to payment systems in international organisations
- identify potential ethical and environmental issues about pay.

We have indicated in previous chapters that human resource management is concerned that people should work as effectively as possible for the organisation, and that one of the ways in which the organisation attempts to achieve this is by using an appropriate system of payment to encourage and reward them. The payment system that is adopted must, as stated in Chapter 2, be in line with and support the key elements of the strategic plan and organisations should develop a reward strategy that suits their particular organisation. This will be discussed later in the chapter.

In this chapter we shall be examining a variety of payment systems and discussing the philosophies on which they are based, and the links with motivation theory, as well as the circumstances in which particular payment systems may prove appropriate.

Definitions

Before we proceed, it will be useful to define some of the words we shall use throughout this chapter. Several words are commonly used to refer to the payment made to people at work, and these include the terms 'reward', 'pay', 'wages' and 'salaries'. We shall also explain other terms used in connection with payments, such as 'harmonisation' and 'job evaluation' before examining the different types of payment system that are available for an employer to use.

Reward is frequently used nowadays to refer to payment systems, especially since many payment systems try to motivate people to work harder and then reward them for their extra effort. The word 'reward' is useful in this sense, and could apply to either a monetary or non-monetary award, but it also implies that something special is being rewarded. While it is true that many payment schemes do seek to reward extra effort, this is normally only one part of the payment system. The term 'reward' also seems to have theory X overtones, as it implies that it is always necessary to dangle a carrot in order to get good work from an employee.

Payment is the more straightforward term, and seems to us to be the most appropriate term to use as it *can* include monetary or non-monetary payment. This is therefore the term we shall use in general throughout this chapter. We include under this heading various types of both monetary and non-monetary payment, as well as sickness pay, maternity pay and pension arrangements.

Although distinctions between wages and salaries are decreasing as many organisations move towards harmonisation of terms and conditions for different groups of workers, it is also useful to define the differences that do still exist.

Wages tend to be paid weekly and may be based on an hourly rate of pay, with possible deductions for lateness or absence, and this hourly rate is often the rate that is referred to in negotiations. Wage-earners are often still paid in cash and are less likely to have fringe benefits such as luncheon vouchers, company cars or expenses. Organisations paying wages have traditionally expected short-term thinking from their employees, and incentives for wage-earners are also usually quick and precise. There has traditionally been less job security for wage-earners than for salaried employees (although this has changed to some extent in recent years) and the emphasis is on a short-term relationship with the employing organisation. The peak of wage-earners' earning capacity is comparatively early, perhaps while they are still in their twenties.

Salaries tend to be paid monthly, and these monthly payments are normally expressed as an annual salary, this being the figure that is normally referred to in negotiations on salary. Those who are salaried normally have their salaries paid directly into a bank or building society and they are also likely to have several fringe benefits, such as company cars, extra payments for additional qualifications, or luncheon vouchers. Some salaried workers get immediate incentives added to their incomes, but generally the most widely held incentive is supposed to be a much longer-term consideration, that of good prospects. Salaried employees either are in managerial posts or tend to identify very closely with management, and they perceive themselves to be on a lengthy career progression with the peak of their earning power achieved relatively late in life. In addition, until fairly recently they have expected to have long-term job security.

● Harmonisation

There are differences in organisations' attitudes towards those paid wages and those paid salaries, but as mentioned earlier, many organisations have tried to get away from the problems that this sometimes causes, and have moved towards a common system of payment with the harmonisation of terms and conditions of employment for both groups of workers. This means that there is an expectation that all employees can be treated in the same way and will expect the same benefits. In these organisations, everyone is paid a monthly salary rather than a weekly or hourly rate of pay, and everyone gets the same sick pay and redundancy arrangements, works the same hours and eats in the same canteen.

Nowadays there is also much less job security, and career progression for salaried employees and promotion or even job security cannot be regarded as automatic, as many organisations in which salaried jobs were normally secure have removed whole strata of managers. The growing trend towards the acquisition of a flexible workforce with increasing numbers of part-timers and contract workers has also led to a blurring of distinctions between the two groups.

The term may also be used to refer to the harmonisation of wages and conditions of employment in different countries. Since 2002, when countries within the euro zone adopted the euro as their common currency, workers in these countries have been able to compare their wages with workers doing a similar job in different countries. This increased level of transparency may result in wages and conditions of employment in different countries becoming increasingly similar, or harmonised.

● Job evaluation

A further term that is relevant to payment systems and will be discussed fully later in this chapter is 'job evaluation'. ACAS (2003) defines job evaluation in the following way:

> The aim of job evaluation is to provide a systematic and consistent approach to defining the relative worth of jobs within a workplace, single plant or multiple site organisation. It is a process whereby jobs are placed in a rank order according to overall demands placed upon the job holder. It therefore provides a basis for a fair and orderly grading structure. Job evaluation does not determine actual pay. That is a separate operation, normally the subject of negotiation between management and employees or their trade union representatives. Only the job is evaluated, not the person doing it.

As you can see here, job evaluation does not actually determine rates of pay that any individual employee should receive, but it can be used as a systematic basis for determining differences in jobs and subsequently the different pay levels for those jobs. As such it seems to us to be an appropriate topic to discuss in this chapter.

The main influences on payment systems

What the organisation decides to pay staff will depend on many factors, some of which are under the control of the organisation and relate to its strategic plan and some of which are external.

ACTIVITY 11.1

We have provided you with a selection of job titles and you have to decide how much to pay these staff. You are to consider who you think ought to be paid the most rather than considering what actually happens in reality.

(a) Put the jobs listed below in order of importance, i.e. with number 1 being the job that you judge should be paid the most.

(b) List the factors that will influence how much you will pay these staff.

Waiter or waitress	_____
Nurse	_____
Sales assistant (clothes shop)	_____
Car park attendant	_____
Office cleaner	_____
Accountant	_____
Police officer	_____
Receptionist	_____
Teller (bank)	_____
Warehouse supervisor	_____
University lecturer	_____
Truck driver	_____
Secretary	_____
Traffic warden	_____
Security guard	_____
Safety officer (manufacturing company)	_____
Warehouse picker	_____
Doctor	_____
Human resource manager	_____
Church minister	_____
Fruit picker	_____
Ambulance driver (paramedical)	_____
Transport manager	_____
Computer services officer	_____
Lawyer	_____
Undertaker	_____
Professional football player	_____
IT consultant	_____

(c) Compare your order with others and try to reach agreement about a list of factors that should be taken into account when you are making these decisions.

Discussion of Activity 11.1

The relative worth of these jobs is likely to vary according to the type of organisation, and your ranking is likely to vary compared with that of your colleagues because you have been highly subjective. You should think about what influenced your choice of each job's worth. Did you have knowledge of some jobs? Did you most value strength, skill, level of responsibility or a caring response, or were you influenced by people you know who do some of these jobs, or by your own career aspirations? There will be many highly subjective influences on your decision.

Many other factors may influence the relative worth of jobs. Your list is likely to include at least some of the following:

- what the organisation can afford to pay
- what other organisations in the area are paying for similar jobs
- national or international rates of pay within the organisation
- legislation and the minimum wage
- trade union or employee demands
- Government initiatives
- the scarcity of particular skills
- the state of the economy
- the introduction of new technology
- the relative worth of jobs as rated by a job evaluation exercise
- the actual performance of the person in the job.

As you can see from this list, an organisation does not have a completely free hand when it decides how to pay someone. Many factors influence the decision of how and what to pay, and we shall discuss these more fully in turn.

What the organisation can afford to pay

Obviously, no organisation can afford to put itself out of business by paying more than it can afford, so this has to be one of the first factors that influence how much an organisation will pay.

What other organisations in the area are paying for similar jobs

Most organisations will at least take account of the rates that other local organisations are paying. The organisation may refer to published pay surveys or do its own survey of the local area to establish rates that others are paying for similar jobs. If it can afford to, and if it wants to be able to select the best employees, it may choose to pay slightly more than the going rate. This can cause a spiral of wage increases as other employers retaliate by increasing their wages. When labour is scarce this is one way in which many employers will behave.

Even when employing people on a small scale, the rate of payment can have quite an effect locally. Sometimes people from London, or perhaps those moving to or buying second homes in countries such as France or Spain, may have an effect on local wages when they employ a local gardener or cleaner and pay much more than the local rate. Those with second homes will probably be able to afford to pay good wages, particularly if they are used to paying for similar services in a more expensive area such as London. When they pay these same rates to local cleaners they obviously attract good staff, but are then accused by other locals of poaching their cleaners and of setting rates that the locals cannot afford to match. In this situation the second home owners get excellent cleaners but may not make many friends.

National or international rates of pay within the organisation

If the organisation is part of a larger organisation, there may be national or international agreements that will affect what is actually paid, and the human resource manager also needs to assess these rates.

Nowadays as travel to other countries is easier and quicker than in the past, pay rates often have global implications. In recent years poor pay for nurses in Britain, and the subsequent staff shortages, meant hospitals and NHS trusts increasingly had to search further afield for qualified nurses. Many carried out recruitment drives which attracted nurses from countries such as the Philippines to Britain. Poor pay and working conditions for teachers have also resulted in many education authorities conducting recruitment drives in countries such as Russia and South Africa.

What is considered poor pay in one country may seem a fortune to an individual coming from a poorer country. Individually they gain an opportunity to travel and broaden their own experience and may even be able to save money to send home to their families. This may in turn create skills shortages for those countries losing people and consequently some governments have requested that Britain does not carry out recruitment drives in their country.

There may be other ethical and legal issues where companies employ large numbers of low-skill migrant workers who come to this country in search of jobs and better pay than that found in their home country. While they are recruited to fill skills gaps and work in jobs which many UK worker are unwilling to do, in some cases they have been exploited. There have been claims that they are treated badly and are not even paid the legal minimum wage. In 2007 administrators were called into Bomfords, a company which supplied more than 50 per cent of large UK supermarkets with vegetables such as spring onions, beans and peas. According to Felicity Lawrence (2007), 'the company which has a turnover of £150m a year and employs more than 2,000 people at the height of the season – the majority migrants who pick and pack its vegetables – was recruiting its temporary staff through seven agencies. Each of those agencies was found to be breaking the law and had its licence revoked. Some of the Poles employed by one of the agencies were in such fear that the GLA revoked its gangmaster's licence on the spot.' Lawrence (2007) claimed 'Bomford's offered gangmasters an hourly rate for workers that made it all but certain that these gangmasters would be breaking the law.'

Did you know?

The Gangmasters Licensing Authority (GLA) was set up in April 2005 to end the exploitation of workers in agricultural, horticultural, shellfish-gathering and associated processing and packaging activities. In April 2006 the GLA began operating a licensing scheme for providers (gangmasters) supplying workers into these industries.

(Source: HSE (2007) The Gangmasters Licensing Authority)

The global effects of pay rates are not all in one direction. In the 1960s and 1970s there was talk of a 'brain drain' from Britain and more recently similar problems have arisen as some senior academics and particularly scientists go to America in search of better pay and working conditions and for better research facilities. Multinational organisations also have a range of other issues to consider in relation to achieving equity and fairness in their payment systems and these aspects of international payment will be discussed later in the chapter.

● Legislation

All organisations are affected by the law of the country in which they operate, even if they are bringing in migrant workers. In Britain they will also be affected by European Union legislation. The legislation that will have most effect on payment or reward systems is:

- The Equal Pay Act 1970
- The Equal Pay Amendment (Regulations) 1983
- The Employment Rights Act 1996
- National Minimum Wage Act 1998
- The Employment Equality (Age) Regulations 2006
- The Equality Act 2006

The Equal Pay Act 1970

The Equal Pay Act 1970 actually came into effect in December 1975, at the same time as the Sex Discrimination Act 1975, which is discussed in Chapter 3. It was part of a two-pronged attack on inequality and specifically aimed to ensure that men and women who were doing the same job, or jobs that were broadly similar in nature, would receive the same pay. Consequently it is now illegal to pay men and women doing the same or broadly similar jobs different amounts of pay.

Under the Equal Pay Act 1970 it is also illegal to pay different rates to men and women who do different jobs, but whose jobs have been rated the same under a job evaluation scheme. The whole topic of job evaluation and problems of fairness and equality within job evaluation will be discussed later in this chapter.

The Equal Pay Amendment (Regulations) 1983

This legislation added a further category to the Equal Pay Act 1970, that of equal value. It is therefore possible for men and women who are doing totally different jobs and who are paid differently to bring a case against their employer if they feel that their job is of the same value to the organisation as the job done by the higher paid group. The legislation is complex, and most who have brought cases have been supported by their trade union or the Equal Opportunities Commission. Criteria such as the level of qualifications required, the level of effort or skill involved, and the amount of responsibility and decision making involved in each of the jobs are factors that are likely to be taken into account. In a tribunal hearing of this type, the person of the opposite sex with whom the claimant wishes to compare himself or herself must first be identified. Finding a comparator of the opposite sex within the organisation can often be a problem. Both the Equal Opportunities Commission and the TUC have suggested the use of hypothetical comparators so that women or men who worked in highly segregated industries would find it easier to bring a case if there was no suitable comparator of the opposite sex within their organisation. The Government is committed to introducing a Single Equality Bill for Great Britain and in 2007 it issued a consultation document which is seeking views on various aspects of equal pay including the issue of comparators. The topics for consultation include:

- that we should bring equal pay provision within a Single Equality Act but retain the current differences between claims relating to contractual and non-contractual issues;
- whether the legislation should include settled principles of equal pay law which have come out of judgments in legal cases;
- how else we can simplify equal pay legislation or make it easier to work in practice; and
- that we should continue with the current approach to comparators, which requires an actual comparator. (Department of Communities and Local Government, 2007)

Pause for thought 11.1 Consider the last bullet point.

1 Do you think a real comparator should be used in equal value cases or should there be the option of using a hypothetical comparator if there is no suitable comparator of the opposite sex within the organisation?

2 The Government proposes to introduce a Single Equality Bill after the publication of this textbook. Check the current state of legislation and find out what the Government actually decided on these issues. (There will be an update on our website at www.pearsoned.co.uk/foothook.)

Did you know?

'More than thirty years after the Equal Pay Act 1970 (EPA) came into force UK employers are having to reconsider their approach to equal pay issues following some much needed clarification by the European and UK courts and an increasingly high profile for equal pay issues . . . The issues have been particularly brought into focus for public sector employers and voluntary and private sector organisations that carry out public functions which, since April 2007, must meet the requirements of the new gender equality duty.'

(*Source:* (Walter, C. and J. Geler (2007))

One of the causes for the differences in pay is segregation of jobs:

'Three-quarters of women work in sectors described by the EOC as the "five Cs" – cleaning, catering, caring, cashiering and clerical jobs.'

(*Source:* Welfare, S. (2007))

So at the time of writing the comparator used must be of the opposite sex although multiple comparators can also be used. If the tribunal then decides that there are reasonable grounds for determining that the work is of equal value, a report will be commissioned by an independent expert as to the relative worth of each of the jobs. The tribunal will then convene once again after receiving the report of the independent expert, and will make a decision.

The Employment Rights Act 1996

The Employment Rights Act 1996 is a consolidation Act which consolidates previous legislation relating to employment rights. Under the Employment Rights Act 1996 an employer is not allowed to make deductions from an employee's wages except in the following circumstances:

- When deductions are authorised by law, such as tax or national insurance contributions or orders such as a court order relating to the provision of maintenance.
- When there is a statement in the employee's written contract which specifies that certain deductions may be made from wages and when the worker has already given consent in writing to the deduction, e.g. to pay membership fees for a sports or social club or when deductions are agreed for lateness or poor work.
- Accidental overpayment of wages, or of expenses, even though this is likely to be the fault of the employer.

- When the employee has been absent from work due to strike or other industrial action it is permissible for the employer to deduct money from the employee's wages.
- In retail organisations, employers may also deduct money from wages to make good any cash deficiency in the till or any shortfall in stock. This deduction should not exceed 10 per cent of the wages due to the employee concerned on a particular day and the deduction must also be made within 12 months from the date that the discrepancy or shortfall in stock was discovered.

The National Minimum Wage Act 1998

The National Minimum Wage Act 1998 established a single national minimum rate with no variation for regions, jobs, size of organisation or industrial sector. Differences in the minimum wage rate will be allowed, however, based on age and this has not changed in spite of the changes to the legislation relating to age. The national minimum wage provides a degree of protection for some of the lowest paid groups of workers as it applies not just to full and part-time employees but also to workers paid by piecework, to homeworkers, agency workers, commission workers and casual workers. So the migrant workers involved in fruit picking who were discussed earlier in the chapter are among those covered by it. Although the minimum wage legislation does apply to all employers regardless of their size, the type of business or the region in which they are based there are still certain groups who are exempt from its provisions. The main groups which do not qualify for the minimum wage are:

- The self-employed
- Volunteers
- Apprentices aged under 19 or who are still within the first twelve months of their apprenticeship
- Students working as part of their undergraduate or postgraduate degree programme
- Workers on specified training schemes
- Residents of some religious communities
- Prisoners
- The armed forces

From 1 October 2007 the adult national minimum wage rate for workers aged 22 and over is £5.52 per hour while the development rate for workers aged 18–21 inclusive is £4.60 per hour. The rate for 16- and 17-year-old workers is £3.40 per hour.

These rates are subject to the continuation of favourable economic conditions and usually they are updated each year. Employers have to keep records for national minimum wage purposes and employees should have access to these records with a right to complain to an employment tribunal if the employer fails to give them the required access to the records.

The Employment Equality (Age) Regulations 2006

Payment can involve money or other benefits and the Employment Equality (Age) Regulations 2006 affects all benefits which could be based on seniority or length of service and experience. Employers need to take care when designing their payment and benefit systems not to either directly or indirectly discriminate on the grounds of age. Some employers have for example provided long-service employees with additional annual holidays. Since it is likely that in general it will be the older workers who are likely to have longer service, the provision of any benefit such as additional holidays linked to longer service could be potentially discriminatory. However, there are some exceptions and exemptions for employment benefits which are linked to length of service of less than five years. If the employer is able to demonstrate that benefits that involve employment of more than five years is not age related but is actually rewarding factors such as loyalty to the company, increased experience or as part of a motivational package then these too could be exempt.

The Equality Act 2006

The Equality Act 2006 amended some parts of the Sex Discrimination Act 1975 and in April 2007 introduced a new legal obligation for public bodies called the gender equality duty. This new duty places a legal obligation on all public bodies such as government departments, colleges and universities, schools, NHS Trusts, local authorities and police to actually promote equality between women and men as well as eliminating any unlawful harassment or sex discrimination. Public sector organisations therefore have to develop policies and design and implement employment practices with the differing needs of men and women in mind. Public bodies have to conduct a gender impact assessment to discover how the services provided impact on each sex. The Equality Act does not specifically say that an equal pay review needs to be carried out but any discrimination in payment systems must be eliminated so one way to establish this is by conducting an equal pay review and once that has been done by monitoring the pay systems regularly. The ways to do this will be discussed in more detail later in the chapter.

Trade union and employee demands

Under the last Conservative Government a framework of legislation was introduced to curb the power of the unions and ensure that they were a less powerful force in bargaining on wages. Although under the Labour Government some of this legislation has been relaxed a little, it is not the pay of mainstream workers which is rising most, but that of their senior managers and chief executives. Nevertheless it is important to consider the views of both trade unions and employees in general, and any payment system that an organisation may design needs to be introduced after full discussion and consultation with employees and trade unions. The most effective payment systems will have been selected to meet the needs of both the organisation and the workforce, will have the commitment of all groups and will have been developed, introduced and updated with the participation of employee representatives, whether or not they are members of a trade union.

> **Did you know?**
>
> According to the Equal Opportunities Commission (2005), women students can expect to be earning 15 per cent less than men within five years of leaving college.
>
> Equal pay is an important issue for all students, not just the women. An employer who can demonstrate they value their women employees is likely to be a good employer to work for in other respects. If you go to work for a company which short changes women, what else might you find?

Government initiatives

The Government can have an effect on the supply of labour as it introduces various training initiatives for adults or young people who are facing unemployment. This should have the effect of providing people with relevant skills that employers need, but it also has an effect on wage expectations, since if people are used to receiving a very low training allowance they are likely to feel pleased if they get a job that pays more than this, even if it is still a comparatively low wage.

The scarcity of particular skills

Even in years where there has been high unemployment, there has also been a scarcity in some industries of particular types of skilled workers. This may be due to failure in the past to train people adequately, but it appears that there is often a mismatch between the skills that employers require and the skills that those who are without jobs can offer. In a situation such as this, the relatively small number of people who do have the necessary skills can command high wages or salaries and may move from one organisation to another as different employers try to outbid each other for their scarce skills.

The state of the economy

We have already mentioned that the availability of labour and the scarcity of particular skills will have an effect on the wages paid. Other economic factors such as inflation will also have an effect, as in times of high levels of inflation there will be increasing pressure from workers to increase salaries to keep pace with, or get ahead of, inflation.

New technology

The relative pay levels of people in different jobs can change over time, for example, when new skills have to be learnt with the introduction of new technology, so that a particular group of workers change from being of low skill level to needing a high level of technical expertise. This change in skill level is likely to be reflected in a demand for higher wages.

The relative worth of each job as rated by a job evaluation exercise

Job evaluation is a way of rating the value to the organisation of the jobs that people do. It does not in itself decide what pay should be awarded to each job, but it is a systematic way of comparing different jobs so that this can be used as the basis for a payment system. The various ways in which job evaluation can be carried out and the different types of scheme will be discussed later in this chapter.

The performance of the individual employee in the job

In many organisations it will also be important to assess the effectiveness of the person doing the job. Whether this happens will depend on the type of payment system used and the organisation's views on collectivism or individualism with regard to payments. Organisations that favour collectivism will want to minimise differences in pay between employees as this may avoid costly or time-wasting disputes, while other organisations will want to pay everyone individual rates as far as possible in order to reward each person for his or her efforts, and these two perspectives will result in a variety of differing types of payment system.

It is clear that the last two factors are of great importance to payment systems, so we shall now go on to discuss each in detail.

Job evaluation schemes

Very few organisations will pay all the people who work for them exactly the same regardless of the job they do or how well they do that job. Most organisations therefore seek to find ways to compare the worth of different jobs to the organisation, as well as a person's performance in each job. We considered in the previous chapter the ways in which individual performance may be assessed, but here we shall concentrate on ways of comparing the relative worth of different jobs. If organisations were to base decisions about the relative worth of different jobs on managerial whims, they would be accused, quite rightly, of being unfair. That is why many organisations use a system for assessing the worth of different jobs based on job evaluation.

Job evaluation does not determine the correct payment level for a job, but rather provides a possible ranking of a job relative to other jobs. This has the merit of being systematic and of appearing objective, although in reality there is normally some degree of subjectivity in all job evaluation schemes. There are normally three stages involved when an organisation is deciding how much to pay for each job:

- evaluate the jobs in the organisation and get a ranking for them
- decide which jobs are similar in terms of the job evaluation exercise and group them together
- decide what pay to attach to these jobs, partially on the basis of market value.

There are a variety of job evaluation schemes in existence, and discussion of these could occupy a full chapter in its own right. We shall seek to give a brief outline of some of the more commonly used types of job evaluation scheme. They can be divided into non-analytical and analytical schemes, and we shall consider each of these groups in turn.

Non-analytical schemes or analytical schemes

Non-analytical job evaluation schemes compare whole jobs rather than analysing the components of each job and assessing them factor by factor. There are three main types of non-analytical scheme:

- whole job ranking
- paired comparisons
- job classification.

Analytical schemes break the jobs down and try to compare skills or competencies needed in each job. The main analytical schemes are:

- points rating
- proprietary schemes.

In order to understand the basics of each of these approaches, you should read the following case study and complete Activities 11.2, 11.3, 11.4 and 11.5.

CASE STUDY 11.1 Job evaluation

The Hookworth Department Store is concerned that its payment system does not accurately reflect the true value of different jobs to the organisation. The management is trying to decide on a form of job evaluation to use as part of a review of the jobs for the whole organisation. They have provided you with three job descriptions to use as a way of identifying the most suitable form of job evaluation to use. You need to consider the job descriptions provided and imagine that you have to evaluate the jobs as part of a job evaluation exercise which will ultimately be used as the basis of the organisation's payment system. You are being asked to evaluate only three jobs, whereas in reality there would be far more jobs than this in a full job evaluation exercise in most organisations.

Read the following three job descriptions and complete Activities 11.2, 11.3 and 11.4. When you have completed these you should be in a good position to decide on an appropriate form of job evaluation to adapt for the whole organisation as requested in Activity 11.5.

Job description A

Job title:	**Office Receptionist**
Reports to:	Office Services Manager
Responsible for:	Assistant Receptionists (2)
Purpose of post:	To ensure that visitors to the company are received in a welcoming fashion, answer routine queries and ensure that all other queries are handled expeditiously by the appropriate staff member. To ensure that all telephone queries are handled in the same manner.
	As the first point of contact for the company, the receptionist must maintain high standards of customer care.
Contacts:	All customers and other visitors, to deal with initial and routine queries. All members of staff, to pass on queries as appropriate.

Major duties:

- Greet walk-in visitors and ascertain purpose of their visit. Handle or redirect queries as appropriate.
- Answer phone queries as above.
- Answer all initial queries about receipt of payments using the online payment receipts system.
- Open and sort incoming post by department. Organise delivery of post by assistant receptionists.
- Perform clerical tasks assigned by departments in agreement with the Office Services Manager.
- Supervise assistant receptionists and delegate work as appropriate.
- Perform other duties as assigned by the Office Services Manager or other authorised manager.

Job description B

Job title:	**Human Resource Assistant**
Reports to:	Human Resource Manager
Responsible for:	No one

Purpose of post:	To provide a day-to-day advisory service for the managers in the company on matters of human resource management policy and procedures, and to monitor and implement procedures.
Contacts:	Managers from head office and throughout the branches. Employees, to deal with initial and routine queries. Prospective employees, to deal with initial enquiries regarding job vacancies. Outside organisations such as employment agencies, training organisations and newspapers.

Major duties:

- Greet visitors and ascertain purpose of their visit. Handle or redirect queries as appropriate.
- Answer phone queries as above.
- Answer all initial queries about applications for employment.
- Pass all rejected applications to typist for standard rejection letters and check and sign these letters.
- Monitor application for employment forms submitted by line managers on behalf of candidates selected by them.
- Agree salary details, in accordance with company pay scales, with line manager.
- Enter agreed salary, contract, job title and joining details on successful applications and pass to typist for documentation.
- Sign joining documentation on behalf of the company.
- Advise line managers on the interpretation of the organisation's human resource policies and procedures.
- Advise line managers on the interpretation and implementation of the organisation's sickness pay and pension schemes.
- Advise line managers on the interpretation of relevant employment legislation.
- Advise line managers on employees' salary entitlements.
- Ensure that the human resource management records are kept up to date on the computerised information system, and that there is no unauthorised access to these and any manually produced records.
- Provide up-to-date reports or data for use by managers.

Job description C

Job title:	**Sales Assistant**
Reports to:	Buyer of China Department
Responsible for:	No one
Purpose of post:	To sell china goods and assist customers with their purchases and with any queries or problems that they might have.
Contacts:	All customers and other visitors to make sales of china and deal with routine queries.

Major duties:

- Sell china goods to customers.
- Provide expert advice about the various products on sale.
- Provide a high standard of service and customer care.
- Unpack with care valuable merchandise and pack customers' purchases carefully, including packing them for export.
- Display products attractively to encourage sales and promote certain special offers.
- Perform clerical duties associated with the work of the department, e.g. completion of orders, forms for returns or breakages.
- Handle accurately and honestly cash and credit transactions.
- Total cash and credit transactions and deliver money to Cash Control Office.

Non-analytical job evaluation schemes

The first two activities ask you to consider the non-analytical approach to job evaluation.

Whole job ranking

ACTIVITY 11.2

(a) Consider each of the three job descriptions given in case study 11.1 and decide which job you feel is worth most to the organisation, which is the next in value and which is of least value to the organisation. Rank the jobs in order with the job you feel is worth most to the organisation being ranked as number 1.

1 _____

2 _____

3 _____

(b) What are the advantages and disadvantages of this approach which is known as whole job ranking?

Discussion of Activity 11.2

This is the simplest form of job evaluation exercise and we have ranked the three jobs in the following order: 1. Human Resource Assistant 2. Sales Assistant in China Department; 3. Receptionist. You may have reached a different rank order to us or to other students. This is because this is a very subjective way of ranking the jobs, and the criteria we took into account may be different to those that you have used. There is nothing in this method to indicate what criteria have been chosen. We have asked you to make decisions about only three jobs, and it would be more difficult to use the whole job ranking system in a large organisation where there were many different jobs to rank. In that case, the jobs would probably have to be grouped into categories first for ease of comparison and so that the appropriate criteria were used, e.g. for clerical jobs, as it could be a problem to identify suitable criteria if the jobs were very dissimilar.

We could make this system slightly more objective by agreeing the criteria to be considered in advance of the exercise, but even this would not help us to identify the extent of difference in the value of the different jobs to the organisation, so we would still have difficulty deciding how much more to pay the job that was ranked first compared to the job that was ranked second. In reality, job evaluation schemes should not depend on the subjective judgements of just one person. It would be better to involve more people in an exercise such as this and then get a consensus view from this job evaluation panel about the ranking of each job.

Advantages of whole job ranking

● simple
● cheap to operate
● easy to understand.

Disadvantages of whole job ranking

- subjective
- no analysis of jobs to explain reason for ranked order
- difficult to use with large number of jobs.

Paired comparisons

ACTIVITY 11.3

(a) Refer to the three job descriptions given in case study 11.1, but this time compare pairs of jobs and decide which you feel is worth more to the organisation, so that each job is compared with the other jobs in turn. Use the following points system to work through this exercise.

- If you feel that a job is worth more than the job it is being compared with, give it 2 points.
- If you feel it is worth the same as the job it is compared with, give them both 1 point.
- If you feel it is worth less than the other job, give it zero points.

Enter the values that you give each job in the chart below, and then add the scores for each job. The job with the highest value will be the one that you decide to pay the most, followed by the job with the next highest value and the job with the lowest value.

We'll start by examining Job A, the job of the receptionist, and will compare our view of its value to the organisation with the value of the other two jobs to the organisation. Place all your scores for Job A in the vertical column below the heading Job A so that at the end of the exercise you can add up all the points for this job.

For example, if you think that Job A, the office receptionist's job, is of more value to the organisation than Job B, the Human Resources Assistant's job, then on the chart below you should write '2' in the vertical column below Job A and on the horizontal line next to Job B.

Now compare Job A with Job C and, for example, if you decide that Job A is perhaps of less value to the organisation than Job C, you should write '0' in the next space down in column A, on the horizontal line next to Job C. Then add the total points in this column to gain a total score for Job A. Now complete this exercise for yourself and add up the total score in each column for each of the jobs in turn.

	JOB A	JOB B	JOB C
JOB A	No score in this section as Job A cannot be compared with itself		
JOB B		No score in this section as Job B cannot be compared with itself	
JOB C			No score in this section as Job C cannot be compared with itself
TOTAL SCORES FOR EACH JOB			

→

Total points for each job A =   B =   C =

1st job _____

2nd job _____

3rd job _____

(b) Did you rank the jobs in the same order as before? What are the advantages and disadvantages of this approach?

Discussion of Activity 11.3

This is also a simple method of job evaluation, but it is slightly more systematic than whole job ranking. It still does not analyse particular jobs in detail and, although the numerical values attached to each job create an impression of objectivity, this is really not the case as again there is nothing to indicate what the criteria used might be. A large number of calculations may need to be made – for an organisation that intends to analyse 50 or more jobs, 1,225 calculations would need to be made. There are, however, computerised systems that work on this basis and solve this particular problem. Once again, an improvement to this approach would be to involve a job evaluation panel, drawn from various sections of the workforce, and then try to get agreement about the rating of various jobs.

Advantages of paired comparisons

- simple
- easy to understand
- slightly more systematic than whole job ranking
- it is easy to fit new jobs into this system.

Disadvantages of paired comparisons

- subjective
- no analysis of jobs to explain reason for ranked order
- the need for an enormous number of calculations if it is to be used with a large number of jobs.

Job classification

The exercises you have just completed indicate in a very simple way the main stages and the main problems with two forms of non-analytical job evaluation. The third non-analytical form of job evaluation is known as job classification. It is similar to job ranking but uses a different approach. In this case the number of groups of jobs, or pay grades, is decided first and a general job description is then produced for all the jobs in each of these groups. An individual job that is considered to typify this group of jobs is then used as a benchmark. Each job is compared with the benchmark jobs and the general job description, and placed in an appropriate grade.

Advantages of job classification

- simple to operate
- easy to understand
- it is easy to fit new jobs into job classification structure.

Disadvantages of job classification

- difficult to use with a wide range of jobs
- not analytical.

Analytical methods of job evaluation

Now consider an approach to job evaluation which is described as analytical by completing Activity 11.4.

Points rating

ACTIVITY 11.4

In this approach you will work with a job evaluation committee who have specified that the following criteria should be used in evaluating jobs:

- skill
- responsibility for people, e.g. in a job caring for children
- responsibility for equipment and materials
- responsibility for other employees
- mental effort
- physical effort
- working conditions.

Rate the three jobs, as described in their job descriptions in case study 11.1, according to these criteria. You can give up to 10 points for each of these factors for each job:

10 exceptional
7–9 high
4–6 medium
1–3 low
0 negligible

Then add the total scores for Job A, Job B and Job C.

For example, if you feel that a medium level of skill is required by an Office Receptionist as described in job description A you will give that job between 4 and 6 points in that category. If you feel that Job B, the Human Resource Assistant, shows a high level of responsibility for people, you will give it between 7 and 9 points. Remember that in job evaluation it is the job you are evaluating, not the person, so you do not need to know how effective a person actually is in that job.

Discussion of Activity 11.4

The points rating approach is probably the most commonly used type of job evaluation scheme, and is regarded as analytical because instead of comparing whole jobs, the jobs are broken down into a number of factors such as skills, responsibility, physical requirements, mental requirements and working conditions. Each of the factors is awarded points based on a predetermined scale, and the total points determine the position of that job in the rank order. A weighting is often attached to the particular importance of each attribute to the organisation.

Although this scheme is analytical, there is, as we said earlier, an element of subjectivity in all job evaluation schemes, as subjective decisions are made about which factors will be weighted most highly to show their importance to the organisation.

Care should be taken to avoid sex bias in the choice of factors for high weighting. Many older schemes based on this system were biased against women as characteristics such as physical strength, normally associated more with male employees, were given higher weighting than factors such as dexterity, which is more often associated with women.

Points rating schemes are easy to understand and are more objective than the non-analytical schemes. Because they are analytical, they can be used to explain the extent of differences between jobs and hence to justify subsequent differences in pay. They can, however, be time-consuming and costly to develop as a panel of people is likely to be involved.

Proprietary schemes

Faced with the time and costs involved in designing and validating their own job evaluation scheme and checking that it is free of unfair bias, many organisations decide to buy a proprietary scheme or employ a consultant to design a scheme specifically for them. A scheme designed specifically for one organisation is obviously a good idea and is likely to have a great deal of credibility with the workforce, but buying a proprietary scheme has the advantage of giving access to extensive comparative data on job markets and rates of pay which designers of proprietary schemes also collect. This can provide much more comprehensive data on which to base decisions about payment levels to relate to jobs than any one organisation could collect.

ACTIVITY 11.5

Compare your evaluation of the three jobs using this points rating method with your earlier evaluations of the same jobs completed using the whole job ranking method and then the paired comparison method.

Were your rankings of the jobs the same or different in all three cases? Why was this? Which of these methods would you recommend to the senior management at the Hookworth Department Store for use in their full job evaluation for the whole store? Why was this?

Discussion of Activity 11.5

Having completed activities to establish the ways that two non-analytical approaches to job evaluation work, and Activity 11.4 to see how one analytical scheme, the points rating method, works, you should now be in a position to make a recommendation to the management of the Hookworth Department Store as to the most suitable form of job evaluation for them to use.

Since only the analytical forms of job evaluation would stand up to examination in an equal pay case at an employment tribunal we hope that you have selected the points rating method, or a proprietary scheme based on a system of points rating, to recommend to the management of the Hookworth Department Store.

Different types of payment system

There are, as we have shown, many factors that affect what the organisation pays its workforce, but whatever payment system is chosen will give a different message to the workforce about the issues and values that the organisation feels are important. In this section we shall consider some of the different payment systems that the organisation might choose. There are many variations in systems of payment: some of the more common types will be considered here.

- time rates
- individual payment by results (piecework)
- group incentives
- profit sharing
- performance-related pay or merit rating
- non-monetary awards
- cafeteria-style payments or flexible pay
- total reward.

Time rates

This is the simplest of all payment systems: as the name implies, people are paid according to the time they spend at work. This may be based on an hourly rate, a weekly rate or an annual salary. In spite of all the talk of incentive schemes and movement towards a human resource management approach with performance-related pay systems, this is still an extremely popular way for many organisations to pay people. This is largely because it is a simple system that is easy to understand and does not result in a great many industrial relations disputes. On the other hand, organisations that have moved away from this system of payment have done so because it provides little incentive to improve productivity or efficiency.

As we said earlier, employers vary in their beliefs about what motivates employees. Those who say that employees can be motivated by the satisfaction gained from the job itself will be concerned to provide a reasonably competitive level of pay for all employees and won't want to pay bonuses or divide the workforce by performance-related pay systems, so that time rates and harmonisation of terms and conditions of employment are likely to appeal to them. The basic rate paid must be sufficiently high that it is adequate for most people's needs. If the rate of pay falls behind this level then the workforce are likely to be demotivated.

Pause for thought 11.2 What do you think about this philosophy? Does it link with anything you have studied on other modules about motivation theory?

The idea that pay is necessary at a certain level to provide for an employee's basic needs, but that to increase pay beyond this is not likely to result in increased performance at work, links very clearly with the work of another motivation theorist, Frederick Herzberg (1966), whose ideas you may have studied, and with his motivation/hygiene theories. Herzberg said that certain things, such as pay and good conditions at work, which he referred to as hygiene factors, were necessary to prevent employees from becoming dissatisfied with work, but that an improvement in these things would not necessarily motivate employees to work harder although it would remove the dissatisfaction. He said that these were the sort of things that people moan about, but that when the dissatisfaction had been removed and the pay or working conditions improved, these people would still not be actually motivated to work harder. The motivators, according to Herzberg, were factors such as making the job more interesting or giving the employee more responsibility.

Payments on time rates, as we have said, don't normally vary from week to week and people are paid for going to work, regardless of how hard they actually work when they are there. In the next Activity we would like you to consider a particular example of a time rate payment system, where there are some variations in the payments people receive.

ACTIVITY 11.6

Imagine that you are a branch manager in a large building society. You are talking to one of your staff, a graduate who is regarded as being bright and a hard worker and who should have an excellent future with the organisation. You ask how things are going and are rather dismayed when she replies, 'OK, but I'm getting a bit disillusioned. I seem to work hard and yet it will take me at least six years to get to the top of the pay scale. Most people around here seem to be at or near to the top of the pay scale already and they seem to take life easy and don't work nearly as hard as I do. I'm thinking seriously about looking for another job.'

1 What is this type of pay scale supposed to achieve for the organisation?
2 What are the advantages and disadvantages of this type of payment system?
3 How does this payment system relate to what you know about motivation theory?

Discussion of Activity 11.6

1 An incremental pay scale is a form of time rate payment system, as people are still paid for the time that they spend at work regardless of the amount of effort they put into their work. In this case they are also paid an extra amount or increment for each year that they work for the employer. This is supposed to encourage employees to stay with the same employer for a long period of time, and so result in a stable workforce. There is also an implication that people will become more knowledgeable and effective in their job as they work for more years and gain more experience. This is not necessarily true, and although some people do learn from experience and will become more valuable employees the longer they are employed, you may be able to think of people that you know who have done the same job for years and who seem to have stopped learning from experience, and who do not appear to be any more effective in their job than they were on the day they started. Care needs to be taken with this type of payment scheme to ensure that it meets the requirements of the Employment Equality (Age) Regulations 2006.

2 Advantages of incremental payment schemes:
   ● simple
   ● easy to calculate wages

- rewards experience
- leads to a stable workforce.

Disadvantages of incremental payment schemes:

- no incentive to work harder
- slow progress for high fliers
- needs to be used with great care to avoid accusations of age discrimination
- no incentive at top of the scale.

3 This approach tends, like other forms of time rates, to reflect a collectivist view that everyone should be treated the same and that to pay people differently would be divisive. With incremental pay scales such as this, differences that are taken into account are usually about non-contentious things such as length of service. Everyone can see that people are treated fairly and that they will get the same treatment. This approach tends to be favoured in relatively large, impersonal, bureaucratic organisations, which place emphasis in determining pay on the jobs rather than the people. This form of payment system will also work best where the pace of change is slow and where there is little scope for individual initiative. An incremental pay system doesn't tend to work well in a fast-moving organisation where it is likely to stifle initiative and innovation.

We shall now examine a group of payment systems that reflect a more individualised approach, where individuals are rewarded for their contribution. We shall consider both individual payment by results and performance-related pay.

Individual payment by results (piecework)

This approach, based on individualism, reflects the view that since some people work harder than others they should be paid different amounts to reflect the differences in effort that they have made. In this system the amount that people are paid depends on how much they produce, so there are very clear criteria and a strong link between earnings and effort. This system is most common in types of manufacturing environment where it is easy to identify the products that each individual has made, or to identify clearly an individual's contribution to a manufactured product.

The main advantages to the employer of payment by results can be summarised as follows:

- there is a strong incentive to increase effort, as there is a very clear link with earnings
- if an increased number of tasks are completed in the same amount of time, using the same equipment, the costs per unit of output will be lower.

Like all payment systems, there are disadvantages as well as advantages. The main disadvantages are that:

- it can be expensive to install and maintain
- it can result in many disagreements about standards or levels of production
- production may increase at the expense of quality
- the emphasis on personal performance can cause friction between employees.

This payment system is expensive to install and maintain, as there needs to be a fair system for assessing the norm for levels of production so that production over and above this level can be paid. Work study engineers are often employed to find the most efficient method of carrying out a task, and managers and trade union officials may spend a great deal of time timing different stages in the production process. There is an emphasis in the payment by results system on providing an incentive, but also on control and measurement. Even with controls in place there can be problems, as Activity 11.7 shows.

ACTIVITY 11.7

Imagine that you are the human resource manager in a knitwear manufacturing company. You are about to negotiate with the trade union on the current round of pay talks. The sewing machinists are paid on a piecework system but there is a great deal of absenteeism, particularly on Fridays. It seems to you that many workers increase their levels of production on the other days of the week so that they can have Fridays off. The company wants to ensure regular high levels of production on every day of the week in order to meet its full order books.

1 What is the underlying message that a piecework system, such as this one, intends to give to the employees?
2 Why is this system not working as well as the organisation wants?
3 How does the situation within this organisation link with motivation theories?

Discussion of Activity 11.7

1 The underlying message that a piecework system is intended to give is that a person will be rewarded for working hard, and the more they produce, the more they will be paid.

2 The system is not working as well as management had hoped because management have assumed that the workforce are only motivated to work harder for money, and that they will continue to work harder and harder for more and more money. Remember the factors that Herzberg (1966), for example, suggested as motivating factors.

3 This situation relates to the view that people may be motivated by a variety of things. In this case the workers wanted a high level of income, but they also wanted some time to relax and spend that income. Some people may be motivated by the opportunity of earning more money, especially if they are saving for some large expenditure. However, not everyone will attach the same degree of importance to financial rewards all the time, and the organisation needs to find out what its employees will value. The employees here seem to be sending a message that leisure is something they value, but other people might be motivated by promotion, a company car, increased responsibility or the increased respect of colleagues.

Individual payment by results is not always particularly appropriate, as we have seen in Activity 11.7. This payment system is most appropriate where:

● it is possible to measure work
● it is easy to attribute it to individuals
● the pace of work is under the employee's control
● management can provide a steady flow of work for the employee to do
● the work is not subject to constant changes in method, materials or equipment.

There are a variety of payment by results schemes. These include:

- group incentives
- individual time saving
- measured day work.

Group incentives

These are based on the same principles as the individual payment by results system, but are used when the individualistic approach is not wanted by the organisation. For example, in order to try to encourage teamworking or to take into account support workers who contribute to overall output, but whose contribution may be difficult to assess, some organisations introduce a system of group payment by results.

The size of the group may vary from small teams or work units to the whole plant or enterprise.

ACTIVITY 11.8

Make a list of the advantages and disadvantages of plant- and enterprise-wide payment by results schemes.

Discussion of Activity 11.8

You may have suggested some of the following advantages and disadvantages.

Advantages
- Employees see how they contribute to the whole organisation's effectiveness.
- Employees are usually encouraged to find ways to improve performance and productivity.
- Employees become interested in how the organisation is managed.
- It is cheaper to install plant- or enterprise-wide payment by results schemes than individual payment by results schemes.
- There is usually a need to discuss financial information with employee representatives and this can result in an improved understanding of how the organisation is run.

Disadvantages
- There is a weaker link in employees' minds between the bonus and the level of their effort, so it may not be a strong incentive.
- Schemes can be difficult to understand.
- Bonus payments could be affected by factors such as inflation which the workforce can do nothing about.

Measured day work

Measured day work is another individualised payment scheme. In this case pay rates are agreed at a higher rate than would normally have been paid for a time worker doing the same job, but there is an agreement that the workers will work at a speci-fied level of performance. These levels of performance are agreed using work study techniques and then management carefully monitors the actual level of performance. A further variation of this is the stepped measured day work system, where a number of levels of performance are specified and workers can choose at which level to work. If their work improves they can progress to higher levels and increased pay. These systems have the advantage that the employees' pay will not fluctuate wildly on a daily or weekly basis, and so they provide for stability, but they do not allow individ-ual workers as much flexibility as to how hard they want to work each day.

Profit sharing

This is a form of payment scheme where the focus is on the group rather than the individual. Employees all receive a bonus, and its size depends on the profits made by the organisation that year. Once again there is little direct incentive for individuals to work harder, as it is difficult to see how their contribution actually relates to the profit made, but many profit-sharing schemes encourage employees to get involved with how the scheme is run. Sometimes, bonus payments are made in shares rather than cash. This is also intended to give employees an interest in the enterprise, but can result in a risk to both shares and job if the organisation does not do as well in the future. It is difficult to see this as a strong motivational force.

Performance-related pay or merit rating

Performance-related pay, which is sometimes referred to as merit rating, is also a way of linking an individual's pay progression to his or her level of performance or to a rating of competence. It is once again an individualistic approach which favours re-warding people differently according to level of performance or competence, and it aims to motivate all employees and give clear indications of what the organisation expects from employees. Performance-related pay differs from payment by results as it doesn't relate just to the quantity of a product that is produced, and may apply to workers even where there is no end product to measure.

Initially, performance-related pay was used as a motivational tool primarily for non-manual employees, but in recent years it has been extended to shop floor workers and has been discussed as a tool for use in the health service and in educa-tion. It is increasing in popularity, and is often introduced even when organisations are aware of the fact that money is not necessarily a motivator to all employees in all circumstances, as it is felt to be fair to pay people according to the contribution that they make to the organisation.

Performance-related pay is often regarded as a key feature of performance management, as outlined in the previous chapter, and although some performance management schemes do not operate performance-related pay, most do use it. While the motivational theorists cast doubt on the value of money as a motivator, many managers instinctively feel that money will motivate employees. Some organi-sations, even if they do not feel that it will have a strong motivational effect, intro-duce performance-related pay as a way of being fair and rewarding high performers' past performance, and so argue that equity is the rationale for the introduction of such a scheme. The fact that performance is considered at all can also have positive effects, in that it helps to create a culture in which performance is valued and recognition of good performance can be a reward in itself. It is important once again to emphasise that performance-related pay needs to be based on what can be seen to be a fair and just system of allocation, with clear objective criteria being used.

ACTIVITY 11.9

Imagine that you work in an organisation where performance-related pay has recently been introduced. You are appraising one of your subordinates, a man in his fifties who has been with the organisation for about 15 years. You have discussed most of the rating criteria, which have all been satisfactory. You say, 'Your work has been good but are there any areas where you feel there could be improvements?' He replies, 'I'm happy in the job but I don't really see much point in working a great deal harder. The mortgage is paid off now, the children have finished their education and if I earn more money I will only have to pay more tax on it. I want to take life a bit easier now and spend more time at home or away in the caravan. I don't always want to be taking work home with me.'

1 What are the advantages and disadvantages of performance-related pay?
2 How does the situation here link with what you know about theories of motivation?
3 Suggest alternative ways of motivating this employee to work to his full potential.

Discussion of Activity 11.9

1 *Advantages* of performance-related pay:

- Rewards the individual by linking systematic assessment of their performance to their level of pay or to a bonus.
- The factors taken into account may be weighted to reflect their relative importance to the organisation.
- It can be used where an incentive is needed but the actual work rate is difficult to measure.
- It can reward factors not easily taken into account in other payment systems.

Disadvantages of performance-related pay:

- There may be disagreements about the performance factors to be assessed, and if great care is not taken in the choice of the factors there may be claims that they are too subjective or even of sex bias.
- Bonus payments may be too infrequent to provide a direct incentive.

2 This is another example of the view that individuals will be motivated by different things and that we value different things. This would link with Maslow's (1954) hierarchy of needs mentioned in Chapter 12 on health, safety and welfare.

3 The situation described reflects the view that there needs to be a range of different forms of incentive so that individuals can choose what will motivate them. In this case the employee might well be motivated if he was offered the opportunity to work for increased holidays.

Performance-related pay can be paid in several ways, and may even involve non-financial rewards. The most commonly used financial rewards are:

- salary increases within the normal salary scale
- salary increases above the maximum point of the normal pay scale
- where each employee is paid on an individual fixed rate, with good performers getting something above the normal rate
- lump sum payments that are not included in salary.

Salary increases within the normal salary scale

This is a commonly used form of performance-related pay, and gives a clear message that although there is a fixed scale for the job and everyone's pay depends on performance, exceptional performers can progress through this scale more rapidly than others.

Salary increases above the maximum point of the normal pay scale

This is sometimes used when the organisation wants to maintain its existing incremental pay scales but also wants to reward excellent performance. In this case high performers benefit as everyone else progresses along the normal scale until they reach the maximum, but it is of no benefit to average employees who have reached the top of the scale because of the length of their employment.

Each employee is paid on an individual fixed rate, with good performers getting something above the normal rate

In this case the individual is paid on a particular rate, but there is no automatic annual salary increase. The organisation budgets for a percentage increase each year, but then allocates this money according to assessments of employee performance, with excellent performers receiving most, good performers getting some allocation of award and poor performers receiving nothing at all. This gives a very clear message to all concerned, and may result in those who are assessed as being poor performers leaving the organisation.

Lump sum payments that are not included in salary

This can be added to most payment systems, and it can be argued that a lump sum payment will have more impact than if the same amount were included in normal salary. This provides the opportunity to draw attention to the organisation's policy for rewarding excellence, especially if the opportunity is used for a special presentation ceremony.

Non-monetary awards

As shown in Activity 11.9, people may be motivated by a range of different factors and may not always be motivated by being paid more money directly in their pay, especially if they lose a great deal in tax. Although we are all pleased to get more money, there is no public recognition of a job well done in that approach. This view is recognised in many organisations, which now seek to provide both monetary and non-monetary awards. Some of the non-financial awards we have selected will also have a monetary value. We have included them as non-monetary awards as the fact of an award being special, in recognition of a job well done or special effort made, may have a motivating effect larger than purely monetary value. Saying 'thank you' is a much overlooked form of non-monetary award in many organisations. The most commonly used non-financial rewards are:

- commendation
- overseas travel
- gifts
- gift vouchers
- green/environmental rewards.

Commendation

The opportunity to commend someone for the efforts that they have made can be extremely important as a way of rewarding and motivating them, whether this is done through the normal performance appraisal interview or at a public ceremony at which a letter or certificate of commendation is presented. The latter situation, with the attendant publicity, will serve as a reinforcement of the values that the organisation wishes to encourage and may also motivate others to improve their work performance.

Overseas travel

This type of reward used to be used primarily to reward sales staff for improvements in sales, but in recent years it has become an incentive on offer to many other individuals. Sometimes overseas travel is used as an incentive for team effort, with the whole team being rewarded with a trip abroad.

This type of reward can be in the form of overseas holidays or the opportunity to attend a high-profile training course held at an exotic destination.

Gifts

Other gifts awarded to people who have made significant improvements in their performance include consumer items such as cameras, household luxuries or jewellery. Once again there is the problem of choosing an appropriate range of gifts, as individuals are not likely to be motivated by the opportunity to acquire a new microwave oven, for example, if they already own one.

Gift vouchers

Gift vouchers are perhaps the most flexible form of incentive payment and are also very popular with individuals, as they offer real choice. Many high street stores promote the use of their gift vouchers to organisations that are thinking of establishing this type of scheme.

Green/environmental rewards

This is a new type of award which recognises workers' concerns about environmental issues or about individuals' carbon footprints and which aims to provide rewards which address in a positive way their environmental concerns. Clive Wright (2007) said that a recent CIPD meeting discussion about the forms these awards could take included the following:

> company discounts for solar panels or wind turbines; home efficiency consultancy as another option in a flexible benefits programme; extra volunteer days for green projects . . . discounts or preferential loans for public transport or access to discounts on recycled products.

Pause for thought 11.3 What do you feel about green awards as a motivational tool? Which potential green or environmental reward would motivate you to work harder?

Cafeteria-style payments or flexible pay

An even more flexible approach to pay is sometimes referred to as the 'cafeteria approach' or 'flex pay', because employees can choose their own preferred reward or combination of rewards. It gives an opportunity for employers to find a pay package that will suit a diverse range of staff, whether male or female, full time or part time, and who come from a wide age range. This can prove attractive for recruiting and retaining labour. In the cafeteria approach the workforce are told what rewards or benefits they can choose from each year. This could mean that they select from gift vouchers, gifts or holidays or they may prefer to choose from other benefits such as improved healthcare options, health or life insurance, an improved pension scheme, longer holidays or even additional cash. Companies that have introduced flexible schemes such as this have done so not to cut costs but to tailor their benefits to the needs of their workforce, and they have found that younger staff prefer cash or a second car, older staff often prefer to improve their pensions or health cover, while staff with young families may prefer longer holidays.

In order for a flexible system to work there has to be an excellent system established for administration, and improvements in computer technology help here. There must also be an appropriate culture within the organisation and excellent communication with members of the workforce and their representatives. Not all organisations have moved towards a complete menu of options: some have felt that staff might be confused by too much choice and have gone for schemes that offer core benefits to all staff with some additional choice over certain options.

Total reward

Total reward, like that of flexible pay, recognises that pay is not the only motivating force for people but it goes even further to include other aspects of employment in the total reward package. Total reward is a newer concept than flexible pay that some organisations are developing although according to the CIPD (2007a) their reward management survey found 'that only around four in 10 employers have adopted this approach so far.' Total reward schemes normally do offer flexible benefits but also include aspects of work such as career and personal development, flexitime, a challenging job at work, opportunities for individual growth and development and recognition for achievements. Sometimes they even allow for individual preferences for type of office layout, space and equipment as well as for administrative support. Total reward schemes aim to align employers' HR and business strategies with employees needs in order to ultimately achieve improved performance. According to the CIPD (2007a) total reward 'goes beyond standard remuneration by embracing the company culture, and is aimed at giving all employees a voice in the operation, with the employer in return receiving an engaged employee performance.'

Total reward is a new idea that employers are experimenting with, but many experts say it should only be tried once flexible pay and benefits have been successfully implemented and established. At the moment there are not many employers that have reached this stage and there is much debate about whether issues such as choice of office workspace or computer are actually suitable choices for individuals to make or whether they should remain purely business decisions. It is an interesting new concept but could be difficult to apply in practice within an organisation.

Reward strategy

We have shown some of the influences that exist on the way that pay is determined within an organisation and the messages that each payment system gives to workers. Because the payment system is important for motivating and giving clear messages about what is considered by the organisation to be important it should be related to the organisation's strategic objectives. However, according to the CIPD (2007b) the results of their 2007 annual reward survey show that 'Thirty-five percent of respondents report having a reward strategy. Another 40% plan to create one in 2007.' This seems a relatively low number for such an important issue but employers in that survey are clearly aware that they should have a reward strategy and hopefully most of the 40 per cent that intend to develop a reward strategy will go some way to doing so in 2007. In a CIPD podcast about reward (2007c) Charles Cotton says, 'Our research still shows that most organisations are kind of adopting a tactical approach to reward. It tends to be knee-jerk, short-term, reactive, rather than actually going out there and saying, well actually, what as an organisation do we need or want to achieve to be successful? What do we need from our employees in terms of values, attitudes and behaviours to be successful and, actually, how are we then going to reward and recognise them for when they actually show and exhibit those values?'

Pause for thought 11.4 Consider the quotation from Charles Cotton taken from the CIPD (2007c) podcast. Which of the views expressed here is most typical of the performance management approach to managing people?

The Equal Opportunities Commission Revised Code of Practice on Equal Pay

The Equal Opportunities Commission's (EOC's) Revised Code of Practice on Equal Pay (2003a) came into force in December 2003. Like other codes of practice, such as that for discipline and grievance (discussed in Chapter 14) an employment tribunal may take into account any failure by the employer to act on its provisions. This code is admissible in evidence in any cases relating to the Sex Discrimination Act 1975 and to the Equal Pay Act 1970 (each as amended) so is very important and it aims to provide practical guidance on ways of achieving equal pay without sex discrimination.

Regular, transparent equal pay reviews are recommended as a key means of ensuring that equal pay is achieved. Other recommendations include the establishment of a clear, transparent pay system that is regularly monitored to ensure it achieves what it sets out to achieve and regular consultation with the workforce or their representatives.

The Equal Opportunities Commission (2003b) says that the foundations of a good review are:

- to compare the pay of men and women doing equal work and that employers must examine like work, work that has been rated as equivalent under a job evaluation scheme and work which is of equal value
- to identify any pay gaps
- to eliminate any pay gaps that cannot be explained on grounds other than sex.

Although there is no legal compulsion for employers to conduct an equal pay review, the EOC says that this is the most appropriate way of delivering equal pay that is free of sex bias. It further outlines a five-step model to achieve this. The five stages in the EOC's pay review model are:

Step 1: Deciding the scope of the review and identifying the data required.
Step 2: Determining where men and women are doing equal work.
Step 3: Collecting and comparing pay data to identify any significant pay gaps.
Step 4: Establishing the causes of any significant pay gaps and deciding whether these are free from discrimination.
Step 5: Developing an equal pay action plan and/or reviewing and monitoring. (EOC, 2003c)

Some of the issues can be very difficult as it is necessary both to have a transparent review so workers can see that everything is being treated in a fair manner and at the same time to be aware of the need to keep personal data confidential, as is required under the Data Protection Act 1998. Each of the stages in the EOC pay review model is discussed below.

1 Deciding the scope of the review and identifying the data required

This involves making decisions about who should be included in the review and also the type of information about pay that needs to be included. There will need to be an analysis of the workforce according to criteria such as gender, hours worked and qualifications. All aspects of pay and benefits such as pensions will also need to be examined.

Another crucial question is: Who will actually conduct the review and how much involvement should the workforce have? Certainly there are many people with specialised information, such as payroll managers or HR specialists, that are likely to be involved at different stages and in some instances it may be necessary to call on independent expert help. However, there seems to have been little interest by employers in the private sector in conducting this type of review and in the *Inland Revenue Service Employment Review* authored by Welfare (2006), Terry Lippiatt, an ACAS national conciliator, is quoted as saying, 'In the private sector, there are not many great signs of activity on pay reviews, and companies tend to see the issue as something to be avoided rather than something to be planned for strategically.' The same survey said, 'As many as 82% of employers in the most recent EOC research on the extent of pay review activity said that they had neither completed an equal pay review nor planned to do one, leading the researchers to suggest: "the issue seems to be falling off HR departments' agendas".'

> **Pause for thought 11.5** While it is disappointing that so few private sector employers are conducting equal pay reviews the situation should be different in public sector organisations. Why might this be? Refer back to the section on pay legislation if you cannot remember.

2 Identifying where men and women are doing equal work

This will involve examining whether men and women are doing work that may be considered to be 'like work' or 'work that has been rated as equivalent under a job evaluation scheme' or even whether men and women are doing work which is of 'equal value' to the organisation. This can be difficult to establish.

Analytical job evaluation schemes, discussed earlier in this chapter, will be very useful in establishing whether men and women are doing equal work. Of course, as we stated earlier, such schemes should have been designed to ensure that they contain no unfair bias so they do not discriminate on the grounds of sex. The Equal Opportunities Commission has produced the EOC Pay Review Kit to help organisations with this.

3 Collecting and comparing pay data to identify pay gaps

The third stage in the equal pay review should be to gather data relating to actual pay rates of men and women doing equal work. Information is needed relating to the average basic pay and total earnings of men and women, and this should also include an analysis of the component parts of the pay package.

Any gaps should then be identified and reviewed to establish whether they are significant enough to merit further investigation and whether or not they seem to be based on gender. The EOC recommends that records are kept of all significant gaps even if they do not seem to be gender based.

4 Establishing the causes of any significant pay gaps and deciding whether these are free from discrimination

Once any gaps have been identified, employers need to establish whether they are due to some genuine reason, other than the sex of the jobholders, and then they should examine their pay systems to try to discover which pay policies or practices are contributing to pay gaps based on gender.

5 Developing an equal pay action plan or reviewing and monitoring

If differences based on gender are discovered within the pay system then the employer must tackle this, for both the existing and future workforce. An action plan to tackle things in stages may be needed, and a system for monitoring and reviewing whether the changes have worked would also be necessary.

Even when the employer has established that there are no problems, it should continue to review and monitor its pay systems at regular intervals.

Developing an equal pay policy

It is obviously in everyone's interests that employees do not end up being dissatisfied with their pay, for whatever reason, as organisations normally want to motivate people to work well. One way to try to ensure this does not happen is for employers to think about the issues and develop an equal pay policy that clearly states what they are doing to tackle this issue and how they are going about it and monitoring it.

Possible penalties

If employees are unhappy with their pay because they feel they have been discriminated against on the grounds of their sex, they may bring a case before an employment tribunal, and any failure to take into account the EOC's Revised Code of Practice on Equal Pay is likely to count against the employer.

Employment tribunals can make awards to remedy any gender-based inequality in pay, if someone is still employed by the organisation. They may also award compensation for arrears of pay and/or damages. In England, five years' worth of back pay can be awarded while in Scotland it can amount to up to six years' back pay for a person who succeeds in proving they have been underpaid for many years and that this was based on their sex. In addition, the employment tribunal may award interest on the award of compensation, and this alone could be a substantial amount.

Equal Pay 1970 (Amendment) Regulations 2004

This amendment to the Equal Pay Act increases a tribunal's powers when dealing with equal value cases. The amendment creates a strong presumption that where a job evaluation exercise has been conducted and has attributed different values to the work of the applicant and the comparator jobs, then these jobs are not of equal value. A tribunal can only decide that the jobs are of equal value if it establishes that the job evaluation exercise itself was flawed in some way or that the job evaluation exercise itself discriminated unfairly on sex discrimination grounds.

International issues in managing pay

Anyone who is concerned with HR in a multinational organisation will appreciate the added complexities of establishing a fair and equitable payment system which operates successfully across many countries. Some of the factors that determine payment systems will be the same as those we have discussed earlier in this chapter when determining pay rates in organisations in the UK but added to these will be issues such as fluctuating currency exchange rates and varying costs of living. There may also be additional payments relating to the need to provide for security and safety for the workforce and to pay people at a substantially higher rate if they are working in a dangerous area. Issues relating to family, accommodation, schooling, healthcare and regular flights home may also form part of an international payment package.

The euro

Although Britain has no commitment at present to join the single European currency and has to hold a referendum before any decision is made, the fact that other European countries are using the euro does have an impact. UK organisations need to consider the strategic implications as there is increased competition and greater transparency on pricing and easier comparison of wages and benefits between those countries within the euro zone. The introduction of the euro in these countries brings both opportunities and threats which organisations should examine.

Wages and pensions departments have had to review their practices if their workforce covers several European countries. Data relating to pay in those countries using the euro are easier to compare but historical data on pay may also need to be converted to ease comparisons. For ex-pats working abroad, life is easier if both their home country and host country are in the euro zone, as there will be no exchange rate fluctuations to alter the value of their salaries.

The adoption of the single currency is supposed to result in increasing levels of movement of workers between countries within the euro zone as people find it easier to compare wages and conditions. This is also a help for trade unions when negotiating pay deals for workers in several countries and can lead to a greater harmonisation of not only wages but also terms and conditions. Pension plans, share option schemes and profit-related pay schemes are also affected. However, the fact that Britain has not adopted the single currency does not seem to have deterred many European workers from seeking jobs in Britain. While in some areas of France jobs for French graduates continue to be difficult to find there is a thriving community of French graduates living and working in London and in many other large British cities. Having a good command of the language, a high degree of education and desirable skills and competencies means that these workers are able to take up opportunities in Britain which may not be available to them at the moment in France.

HR departments have a very important role to play in examining the strategic implications of the euro for their organisation and may need to develop, in some cases, into a Europe-wide function. In multinational organisations, particularly where some of the workforce work in euros but others are outside the zone, communications and training will be particularly important. The HR department may also need to review their organisation's payment systems, pensions scheme, expatriate programmes and procedures for union negotiations and consider the cultural implications of the single currency and possible need for harmonisation of pay and conditions. They will also be involved in any practical issues relating to actual payments to some workers in euros.

Ethical issues

When considering what to pay people there are many ethical issues to consider in terms of what society values and is willing to pay people in differing jobs and professions. While the law does provide some guidance to employers in terms of equal pay or ensuring the minimum wage is paid there are still some groups such as migrant workers who, as we have seen, are sometimes exploited by unscrupulous employers and who have not even received this minimum level of protection. While people in the UK continue to expect clothes and food at cheap prices this is often also achieved at the expense of overseas workers who may be working long hours in poor conditions for less than a living wage. According to McVeigh (2007a), 'Charities campaigning for workers' rights accuse retailers of maximizing profits in demanding rock bottom prices from suppliers in the developing world.' As a result of allegations in the *Guardian* newspaper about the exploitation of workers in Bangladesh, MPs called for action to protect overseas workers. 'Lynne Featherstone, the Liberal Democrat international spokeswoman, said legislation should guarantee that pay and conditions of overseas workers met international standards: "It's obscene that [UK shoppers] can earn more through their club card points than the people who produce the goods they are buying"' (McVeigh 2007b).

Pause for thought 11.6 What do you think? Should there be stronger legislation in place to protect overseas workers? Would you be willing to pay more for goods you buy if it meant that overseas workers received a living wage?

Conclusion

We have examined some of the types of payment systems that are available to employers and related them briefly to motivation theory. No scheme is perfect for all organisations, and all schemes have advantages and disadvantages. Each scheme gives a clear message about the values of the organisation and should be a reflection of its mission statement. The choice of payment scheme will depend on the wishes of the workforce as well as the culture of the organisation, and these should be taken into account before any scheme is introduced. The workforce should be involved in discussion, design, implementation and review of whatever payment scheme is introduced. With the increasingly diverse workforce at the start of the twenty-first century, and moves towards a flexible workforce, many organisations have introduced flexible approaches to the pay and benefits that they provide for employees, using their payment systems as one mechanism for achieving their strategic goals whether these are national or international.

Particular care should be taken to ensure that the basis for the chosen payment system is transparent and understood by the workforce; full consultation with the workforce has occurred; and the selected pay system does not lead to unfair discrimination based on gender. This is still as necessary today as it was more than 30 years ago when the Equal Pay Act 1970 was first introduced. All organisations should review the basis of their pay systems in light of the Equal Opportunities Commission's Revised Code of Practice on Equal Pay to ensure that they are rewarding and motivating all members of their workforce, regardless of their sex, in a fair way. A modern workforce has to be based on fair reward.

REVIEW QUESTIONS

You will find brief answers to these review questions on pages 477–478.

1 The minimum wage alters each year. Find out how much the minimum wage actually is at the present time. How much is the rate for adults aged over 21?
How much is the rate for those aged 18–21?
What are the rates being paid to those who are on Government training schemes such as apprenticeships or New Deal?

2 Interview managers or employees from three organisations of your choice from different industrial sectors to establish what effect, if any, the introduction of the national minimum wage has had on that organisation/industrial sector.

3 Explain the process of job evaluation and comment on how a points rating job evaluation scheme can contribute to perceptions of fairness from the point of view of employees.

4 Fairness in pay is an objective of both employers and employees. Describe briefly the issues that need to be considered with reference to fairness, and evaluate critically the approaches that employers could adopt to achieve fairness.

5 Imagine that you are a consultant employed to select a job evaluation scheme for an organisation that employs 500 employees in a large range of clerical jobs. Write a report to the human resource manager in which you outline the advantages and disadvantages of the various types of job evaluation scheme and recommend what you consider to be a suitable job evaluation scheme for this organisation.

SELF-CHECK QUESTIONS

Answer the following short-answer questions. The correct responses are given on page 478 for you to check your understanding of this chapter.

(a) Does harmonisation of wages and conditions of employment mean that managers and other employees and workers in the same organisation in different countries get different payment systems and conditions of employment to each other? YES or NO

(b) Does job evaluation determine the amount of pay for a person doing a particular job? YES or NO

(c) Are the following all types of non-analytical job evaluation schemes: whole job ranking, paired comparisons, points rating? YES or NO

(d) Are all of the following advantages of the whole job ranking method of job evaluation: it is simple, cheap to operate and easy to understand? YES or NO

(e) Is the points rating system of job evaluation an analytical method of job evaluation? YES or NO

(f) Does job evaluation take account of the individual's performance in the job? YES or NO

(g) Does an incremental pay scheme provide an incentive for people to work harder? YES or NO

→

(h) Does a payment system based on time rates reflect an individualistic approach to the way people are paid? YES or NO

(i) Is piecework another name for individual payment by results? YES or NO

(j) Is performance-related pay a way of linking an individual's pay progression to their length of employment with the organisation? YES or NO

WHAT NEXT?

1 This chapter aimed to introduce you to the topic of payment systems and by this stage you should be able to meet the objectives stated at the beginning. You may now want to go further with the subject and the resources listed in the references and further study sections will help you to do this. There are lots more activities for you to check your understanding of Chapter 11 on our student website at **www.pearsoned.co.uk/foothook**.

2 Go to **www.cipd.uk/podcasts** and listen to or print the transcript for *Reward– episode 5*. This explores differing views of the ways organisations are tackling payment systems and also discusses the benefits of additional pay as a motivational tool compared with other forms of benefits. Which of the views expressed in this podcast do you agree with?

HR IN THE NEWS   FT

FT Report – Recruitment:
Executives should pay the price of failure

By Richard Donkin

You chair the board of a company and you need to fill the role of chief executive.

The headhunters have done their job, you are down to a shortlist of one and there is not much left to do other than settle the package with the candidate's lawyers. Is there an argument, at this stage, for considering the consequences of failure?

This hardly ever happens. By the time a headhunted individual has reached the finishing straight for the role of chief executive in a big company, the psychological state of the recruiting board has shifted.

This is the stage that the prospective chief executive's lawyers can ask for the Earth. One of the first things they do is attempt to secure a lucrative exit package because, even if the recruiting board is naïve enough to ignore the possibility of failure, the contract lawyers would be in dereliction of their duty in making the same omission.

When corporate horizons are as short as they are, clauses dealing with 'tomorrow money' are easily inserted. The chairman, indeed, may be looking to retirement just a year or two down the line. Besides, few of those present within the recruiting company will want to present themselves as killjoys or doom-mongers. Companies rarely welcome pessimism.

It is only when the unthinkable happens that those cleverly-inserted severance clauses will come back to haunt a company. These are the sort of arrangements that allowed Bob Nardelli to leave his chief executive job at Home Depot in January – after failing to live up to shareholder expectations – with a pay-off worth $210m.

More recently we have witnessed the departure of Stan O'Neal as head of Merrill Lynch, after the bank lost nearly $8bn in mortgage-related losses. Merrill Lynch provided Mr O'Neal with a leaving package of $160m, dressing up his removal as a retirement. In doing so the company avoided a legal tussle over his severance entitlements.

It might be right, when the stakes are so high for those taking top jobs, that there should be some compensation for failure, but should there be limits on such pay-outs?

I raised the issue last week with Mark Hoble, a specialist in senior executive pay at Mercer, the human resources consultants. Mr Hoble was speaking at Mercer's European member conference in Lisbon.

He suggested it might not be a bad thing to contemplate the downside at recruitment. 'In reality, people don't want to think about the possibility of failure at that stage. But the lawyers do,' he said.

One possibility may be for companies to look at introducing private-equity style arrangements. The packages in these ventures are often weighted heavily towards share options that can bring big rewards if value is added for a profitable sale two or three years later. An executive who grows the equity value is rewarded by sharing the winnings with other investors.

Some of these packages, said Mr Hoble, require a co-investment in equity by the appointed executive to encourage owner-like behaviour with the accompanying downside risk.

My own feeling is that the potential of high rewards should be accompanied by some element of risk. Too many executive packages in the past have resembled a one-way bet.

It is almost as if elevation to the senior executive cadre is the equivalent to winning the game of life, after which you gain membership to an exclusive club where failure constitutes bad luck and success is a reflection of your talents – rather than good luck.

The media are sometimes criticised for highlighting so-called 'fat cat' pay deals enjoyed by some top executives. Often, however, such headlines are in response to complaints from shareholders and, in some of the most recent cases, they have been generated by concerns over what appeared to be rewards for failure.

The pay and retirement package prepared for Hank McKinnell, chairman and chief executive of Pfizer, for example, came under shareholder scrutiny ahead of his premature departure in July 2006. Some shareholders thought the package – worth about $6.5m a year for life – did not reflect the company's unspectacular performance under his stewardship.

Whatever the sentiments of the shareholders, complaining after the horse has bolted – or is half-way to the knacker's yard – is not going to alter a tightly-worded executive pay contract. The only way to exert any realistic pressure is to make representations ahead of the next appointment and it is difficult to do so when you are not a party to the arrangements.

The board of Chrysler, however, does appear to have been alert to the possibility of failure in its appointment of Mr Nardelli as chief executive and chairman in August. It set his base pay at $1. Mr Nardelli – who hardly needs the cash – would not disclose details, except to say that his success was 'rooted in the success of the company'.

This points to a package that is wholly incentive-led, where Mr Nardelli has bet his talents on raising the fortunes of the company and its share price.

It's difficult to quibble with this. Even though his pay-off at Home Depot might have been interpreted by the company's shareholders as a reward for failure, in that case the company's investors did seem to have an unrealistic view of the company's growth prospects.

A period of consolidation for Home Depot seemed prudent – but prudence does not count for much among investors accustomed to double-digit annual growth. Neither did it count for much among those banks that allowed themselves to become heavily exposed to sub-prime mortgage lending.

But prudence might well be a quality worth nurturing in boardroom recruitment. It will not rid the market of compensation for failure, but it might bring some transparency to the long-term risks.

Football clubs live with this all the time. Managers are hired in the knowledge that their tenure might be cut short by poor results. The sensible ones have the cushion of a lucrative contract and a good prospect of another job in an industry that takes a realistic view of failure. It happens to some of the best of them.

→

Another thing mentioned during the Mercer conference that could be worth considering is the role of corporate governance guidelines in shaping executive pay arrangements. Just as governance codes influenced the length of executive contracts, perhaps they could be brought to influence the size of severance packages for those who have presided over a corporate debacle.

I could be accused of old fashioned thinking here, but shouldn't losers lose?

(*Financial Times,* 15 November 2007. Reproduced with permission.)

Question

Do you think that chief executives should still receive an enormous bonus even if the organisation that they have led has performed badly? List the arguments for and against this.

References

Advisory, Conciliation and Arbitration Service (2003) *Job Evaluation: An Introduction,* ACAS (available at www.acas.org.uk; accessed 23.6.03).

Chartered Institute of Personnel and Development (2004) *Reward Management 2004: A Survey of Policy and Practice,* CIPD (www.cipd.co.uk/surveys; accessed 28.6.04).

Chartered Institute of Personnel and Development (2007a) *Total Reward,* CIPD (www.cipd.co.uk; accessed 07.08.07).

Chartered Institute of Personnel and Development (2007b) *Reward management: annual survey report 2007,* CIPD (www.cipd.co.uk; accessed 29.08.07).

Chartered Institute of Personnel and Development (2007c) *Podcast: Reward – episode 5,* CIPD, 06.03.2007 (www.cipd.co.uk accessed 29.08.07).

Department of Communities and Local Government (2007) *Discrimination Law Review – A Framework for Fairness: Consultation Proposals for a Single Equality Bill for Great Britain.*

Equal Opportunities Commission (2003a) *Code of Practice on Equal Pay,* EOC (www.eoc.org.uk; accessed 10.09.07).

Equal Opportunities Commission (2003b) *Campaign: 15% Off – Why are Women Workers still Going Cheap?* EOC (http://www.eoc.org.uk/EOCeng/dynpages/camp_pay.asp; accessed 10.09.07).

Equal Opportunities Commission (2003c) *Conducting an Equal Pay Review in Accordance with Data Protection Principles,* EOC (www.eoc.org.uk; accessed 08.08.07).

Equal Opportunities Commission Hong Kong (2003) Eliminating discrimination: systems and policy reviews, equal pay for work of equal value, *Equal Opportunities Commission Hong Kong Annual Report 2001–2,* HKEOC (www.eoc.org.hk//EOC/GraphicsFolder/Inforcenter/Annual/default.aspx?year=2001; accessed 24.6.04).

Health and Safety Executive (2007) *The Gangmaster's Licencing Authority,* HSE (www.hse.gov.uk/agriculture; accessed 08.08.07).

Herzberg, F. (1966) *Work and the Nature of Man,* Staples Press.

Income Data Services (2003) *Editorial, Brief 739,* IDS (www.idsbrief.co.uk; accessed 28.6.04).

Lawrence, F. (2007) The miracle of cheap fresh food depends on illegality, *The Guardian,* 17 July, 28.

Maslow, A. (1954) *Motivation and Personality,* Harper & Row.

McGregor, D. (1960) *The Human Side of Enterprise,* McGraw-Hill.

McVeigh, K. (2007a) Asda, Primark and Tesco are accused over clothing factories, *The Guardian,* 16 July, 1.

McVeigh, K. (2007b) MPs want UK to pay living wage to overseas staff, *The Guardian,* 17 July, 9.

Walter, C. and J. Geler (2007) Equal Pay: follow the US leader, *Employers' Law,* 1 July, (www.xperthr.co.uk; accessed 07.08.07).

Welfare, S. (2006) Equal pay at a crossroads, *IRS Employment Review,* Issue 843, 24.03.06 (www.xperthr.co.uk; accessed 08.08.07).

Wright, C. (2007) Letter from the chair, *Reward Review,* CIPD, Spring/Summer 2007.

Further study

Books

ACAS Advisory Booklets, particularly those on payment systems, job evaluation and appraisal-related pay.

Perkins, Stephen J. (2006) *International Reward and Recognition,* CIPD. This is a clear guide to the difficult area of managing international reward.

Perkins, Stephen J. and G. White (2008) *Employee Reward,* CIPD. This provides an in-depth coverage of all aspects of employee reward.

Articles

People Management (2007) The Guide to Reward, *People Management*, 5 April, Vol. 13, No. 7.

Tatton, S., and S. Glenn (2007) How to Get the Most out of Salary Surveys, *People Management*, 17 May, Vol. 13, No. 10, 40–41.

Internet

The Advisory, Conciliation and Arbitration Service   **www.acas.org.uk**
This site has guidance on various aspects of pay and texts of leaflets that can be downloaded directly or ordered.

Department of Communities and Local Government   **www.communities.gov.uk**

Department for Business, Enterprise and Regulatory Reform   **www.berr.gov.uk**
Up-to-date information about the minimum wage at this site.

Incomes Data Services (IDS)   **www.incomesdata.co.uk**
Abstracts from articles in the section on pay and labour market data.

CHAPTER **12**

Health, safety and welfare

Objectives

By the end of this chapter you will be able to:

- explain what is meant by the terms 'safety', 'hazard', 'risk', 'welfare' and 'health'
- explain the key points in the main legislation relating to health, safety and welfare at work
- explain the reasons for managing employee health, safety and well-being
- explain the role of various people and groups in health and safety and welfare at work
- describe the Health and Safety Executive's approach to stress management
- explain the main health and safety issues in an international context.

In Chapter 1 we traced the history of people management and considered several approaches to welfare. Some people who adopted the 'hard' human resource management approach tried originally to distance themselves from all these welfare approaches, as they felt that these approaches showed a lack of business awareness. However, reducing accidents and improving occupational ill-health is important for organisations today and many organisations are taking an increasing interest in areas such as managing absenteeism. Health in particular is also coming under government scrutiny as they want to improve the productivity of the workforce. According to the CIPD (2007a), 'a comprehensive review of the nation's health is to be launched by the Department of Work and Pensions, in an attempt to identify improvements that could help the working population.' In the same document, John Hutton, who was Minister for Work and Pensions, is quoted as saying, 'The UK has one of the best health and safety records anywhere in the world . . . but 30 million working days are still lost every year due to occupational ill-health and injury, leading to lower quality of life and economic prospects for many people and reducing the productivity of the workforce.'

Many organisations have already realised the importance to their success of a healthy and productive workforce and are increasingly seeking to adopt a more proactive approach. Health, safety and welfare have also come under the spotlight as a result of recent legislation banning smoking in public places, including the workplace, and also because increased penalties have been introduced for breaches in safety that result in death under the Corporate Manslaughter and Homicide Act 2007. There is clearly a case to be made for organisations to have some interest in the health, safety and welfare of their workforces.

Definitions

Safety

We define safety as absence from danger and avoidance of injury.

According to this definition, we should expect employers to do everything in their power to keep employees away from danger and free of injury while at work. This does not sound like a great deal to expect from an employer, but there is often a conflict in the employer's mind between increased production, which sometimes may involve some risk taking, and the necessity to keep employees safe and uninjured, which may cost money. Legislation has developed over a number of years to protect workers, and was initially designed to protect those who were weak and particularly vulnerable to exploitation from any employers who, tempted by the lure of increased production, might put their employees at risk of injury. Nowadays, with increasingly flexible patterns of work being available, many employees may work from home, or even from their car, for all or part of their working week, so employers will also have to consider the health and safety issues arising from this.

Hazard

A hazard is something that could cause harm to someone. Employers who are being proactive about health and safety therefore have to try to identify potential hazards before they actually do cause any harm. Stranks (2007) says that a hazard can further be defined in three areas as follows:

- exposure to harm
- something with the potential to do harm – this can include substances or machines, methods of work and other aspects of work organisation
- the result of departure from the normal situation, which has the potential to cause death, injury, damage or loss.

Risk

The term risk relates to the chances of the hazard actually resulting in harm being done to someone. Once the employer has identified a potential hazard then they have to estimate the chances or risk of someone being harmed by it.

We shall discuss the idea of risk assessment later in this chapter. The emphasis in health and safety today is on the prevention of accidents if possible by eliminating anything that could be a hazard and by predicting the level of risk in various situations. It is not, of course, always possible to eliminate all hazards or minimise all risks in a workplace, but employers are expected to predict potentially dangerous situations and then do something about them to ensure they become less dangerous.

The emphasis in modern health and safety is to encourage those who own, manage or work in organisations to take responsibility for health and safety in them. For this to happen, both the workforce and safety representatives also need to be involved, risks need to be assessed and action needs to be taken to reduce these where possible.

Welfare

Welfare can be defined as 'well-being', and health and safety are both aspects of welfare as they are both important to the employee's well-being. In the past many employers merely reacted to issues about health and safety without appreciating the benefits that adopting a more proactive approach could bring them. Many still operate in this way. However, some more progressive employers are adopting a much more proactive approach to health and safety and welfare to prevent problems arising in the first place.

Health

Did you know?

In 2004 a senior pilot was forced to resign and two senior cabin crew were dismissed by Ryanair after the two off-duty crew members travelled on a full plane from Gerona to Dublin. Since there were no seats available for them, they sat in the rear toilets of the plane for both take-off and landing. The captain had allowed them to do this even though it contravened aviation regulations and was obviously potentially hazardous.

Here the concern is for good health. We define good health as being physically and mentally well with body and mind in excellent working order.

This goes further than safety in that the employer is no longer just expected not to do anything to injure his or her employees, but should seek to promote activities that encourage the good health of the employees. We shall return to a discussion of health promotion activities later in this chapter.

Safety

According to the Health and Safety Executive's (HSE's) *Health and Safety Executive Statistics* (HSC, 2006a) there were 212 workers fatally injured at work during 2005–6, which is a 5 per cent decrease compared with 2004–5 when the final figure was 223. Accidents that required people to be absent from work for three or more days rose slightly to 146,076 and a further 328,000 accidents at work were reported. In all, 30 million working days were lost at work which averaged to 1.3 days per worker. According to the HSE (2006a), 24 million of these were due to work-related ill-health and 6 million were lost because of injuries at work.

ACTIVITY 12.1

Sometimes employers are reluctant to spend money on safety improvements as they don't feel this is justified. There are, however, costs associated with accidents. What are the possible costs to the employer of accidents at work?

Discussion of Activity 12.1

Obviously, depending on the severity of the injury, there are costs to the injured person in terms of pain and suffering, and possible loss of earnings. There are also costs to the employer, and your list is likely to include at least some of the following:

- cost of lost time and production due to absence caused by injury
- cost of lost time and production due to dealing with the injury
- cost of replacement worker or of training the replacement
- cost of replacing broken machinery or unsafe machinery or equipment
- cost of compensation to injured employee
- higher insurance premiums if the organisation's accident record is not good
- cost involved in carrying out a full investigation into the causes of the accident
- cost of paying fines or even facing imprisonment if the employer was to blame for the accident
- cost of poor morale within the workforce
- cost of people not being willing to work for the organisation because of its poor reputation for safety.

You may have found some other costs involved in accidents as well. Employers should be aware of the hidden costs of accidents; if they carried out a cost–benefit analysis they would probably be amazed at how much accidents were costing them and be more prepared to spend money on accident prevention. In their studies of accidents, the Health and Safety Executive (1995) identified one organisation where the costs of accidents amounted to as much as 37 per cent of profits. This organisation did not have a particularly bad record on health and safety, nor had it suffered any major disasters, fatalities or prosecutions.

We believe that health and safety is an important area of concern for all HRM practitioners, since it is in the organisation's interest to pursue any initiatives that will provide benefits and services which the employees will want and value but that will also fit with the strategic needs of the organisation by enhancing levels of employee performance.

Employers can check for themselves the actual costs both of accidents and work-related incidents in their organisations by using the accident and incident calculators provided by the Health and Safety Executive. They allow employers the choice of two different ways to calculate the annual costs of accidents in their organisation and also of using an interactive tool to calculate costs of other work-related incidents. Now there is really no excuse for employer ignorance of the cost of accidents or work-related incidents in their organisations.

If you would like to see how easy it is for employers to calculate the costs of accidents and work-based incidents by examining these tools for yourself, go to **www.hse.gov.uk/costs/accidentcost_calc/accident_costs_intro.asp** (accessed 20.04.07).

Legislation

Much of the early development of legislation to protect employees at work was closely linked to the historical development of people management. The more enlightened employers were concerned to improve working conditions for their employees and appointed industrial welfare workers to help with this. Less enlightened employers were compelled to pay some attention to the protection of selected groups of employees, and as early as 1840 legislation designed to limit the hours that children worked was passed. In more recent times several new Acts have been passed and regulations issued to protect employees.

The Health and Safety at Work Act 1974 (HASAWA)

In Great Britain the foundation for the system of regulating health and safety at work was introduced by the Health and Safety at Work Act 1974. Although this was a long time ago, HASAWA is still very important today and forms the foundation for much of the later legislation. According to XpertHR (2004) one of the fundamental principles underpinning the Health and Safety at Work Act is that 'those who create risk from work activity are responsible for protecting workers and the public from its consequences.'

Before HASAWA, the legislation that could be used to protect employees at work was patchy and applied to vulnerable groups such as women or children, or to particular industries where there were thought to be high risks. The vast majority of the working population before 1974 were not actually protected by any health or safety legislation. The Health and Safety at Work Act 1974 set up some new bodies and reinforced the power of others. The roles of the following will be discussed later in this chapter:

- the Health and Safety Commission (HSC)
- the Health and Safety Executive (HSE)
- the enforcing authorities.

HASAWA was the first piece of legislation designed to protect everyone at work, and also to protect others who were not at work, such as customers or even passers-by. It is estimated that it brought an extra 3 million people under the scope of protective safety legislation for the first time.

The main aim of the Act was to provide a comprehensive system of law which would raise standards of safety and health for all persons at work and also protect members of the public who might be affected by their actions.

More than 30 years after the Health and Safety at Work Act 1974 became law it still forms the foundation of health and safety legislation in the UK, so it is important to understand some of the fundamental principles that underpin this important piece of legislation.

ACTIVITY 12.2

Both employers and employees have responsibilities under HASAWA. List what you would expect to be the duties of employers and employees with regard to health and safety.

Duties of employers	Duties of employees

Compare your lists with the following duties summarised from the Health and Safety at Work Act 1974.

Discussion of Activity 12.2

Your list probably included some indication that employers were to take responsibility for having a safe workplace with safe equipment that would not injure anyone, and you also probably thought that employees too should take care not to harm anyone at work. There are no specific rules about lighting or temperature in the way that there are in the earlier Acts. Instead the Act is trying to involve people and make everyone take some responsibility for his or her actions. This approach is therefore moving towards a human resource management approach, and health and safety is not just in the domain of the human resource specialist but is shared with others. Sometimes the human resource specialist does have some aspects of health and safety included in his or her job description, and he or she may, for example, be expected to chair the safety committee if there is one.

The responsibilities of employers under the Health and Safety at Work Act

Employers have a basic duty of care to their employees to ensure their health, safety and welfare. As well as this rather general duty, they have five other duties. These are:

- to ensure that the workplace itself is safe; that equipment has been maintained correctly and work is safely organised
- that accidents do not occur because of incorrect handling, storage or transportation within the workplace
- that there is training, supervision and information relating to health and safety
- that the workplace itself is maintained adequately and that there are safe ways to get into and out of the buildings
- that welfare provisions are adequate.

All of these duties are expressed in quite general terms and there is nothing in the Act to specify, for example, how much training or information should be given. The words 'so far as is reasonably practicable' are used frequently within HASAWA. The exact meaning of this phrase will be discussed later in this chapter. The employer also has a further specific duty to produce a safety policy statement and we shall also discuss later in the chapter what this involves.

As we said earlier, HASAWA was designed to gain involvement in health and safety from as many sources as possible, so the responsibility was not just one way. Employees also have responsibilities.

The responsibilities of employees under the Health and Safety at Work Act

As you might expect, there are fewer responsibilities for the employees than for the employers. They have three main areas of responsibility under HASAWA in relation to health and safety. These are:

● to take responsibility for their own health and safety, and for any health and safety problems which might be caused to colleagues by their actions or in some cases their failure to act
● not to recklessly interfere with or misuse any machinery, equipment or processes
● to cooperate with employers about health and safety initiatives.

Although they may not seem very onerous responsibilities, they are important since employees who do not follow these guidelines could be disciplined or even face prosecution themselves if an accident occurred for which they were responsible. They should cooperate about health and safety issues, such as wearing protective clothing, if the employer provides it. Since they must take responsibility for their own health and safety and that of others, they must also not do anything to interfere with safety guards, as this could result in injuries to themselves or to other people.

Pause for thought 12.1 The phrase 'as far as is reasonably practicable' is used several times in HASAWA. What factors do you think should be considered in determining whether or not something is 'reasonably practicable'?

This phrase means that circumstances, risks and cost need to be considered when an employer is endeavouring to make the workplace safe for employees. It would be very difficult to make anywhere completely safe and eliminate all accidents. Accidents are by definition something that you cannot predict; nevertheless, many situations do occur where it is possible to predict that someone could be injured if improvements are not made, and employers should try to anticipate the likelihood of these types of accident and take steps to prevent them from occurring. 'Reasonably practicable' means that a calculation must be made in which the risk is compared with the sacrifices, cost and level of effort needed to avert that risk. If there is a very slim chance that a comparatively minor accident might occur, but this chance could be eliminated by spending thousands of pounds on new equipment and also by disrupting the workforce, it might not be considered to be reasonably practicable to do so. If, however, the risk was of a serious injury or possibly death, then it would be reasonable to take every step and spend any amount of money to eliminate this risk. The term 'as far as is reasonably practicable' therefore means that the employer should do as much as they can to try to eliminate risks but that they need to review the balance between the risk and the amount of effort required to eliminate that risk.

Control of Substances Hazardous to Health Regulations (COSHH) 1988

This is another far-reaching piece of legislation comprising 19 regulations and 4 approved codes of practice which came into effect on 1 October 1989 and which have subsequently been revised in 1999, 2002 and 2003. Apart from some minor changes to tidy up the 1999 regulations, as these amendments relate to fairly specialised areas they do not alter the main thrust of this legislation and are too detailed to include in an introductory HRM textbook.

COSHH is designed to protect anyone who works with substances that could be hazardous to health. The regulations apply to all workplaces and include all substances with the exception of asbestos, lead, materials that produce ionising radiations and substances underground, which all have their own separate legislation. The legislation basically applies to any other substances that can cause harm by being inhaled, ingested, coming into contact with the skin, or being injected or introduced into the body, so they do cover a very wide range of substances.

COSHH regulations require all employers to carry out an assessment of risks to their employees from substances that are identified in the workplace as being potentially hazardous to either their employees or others who might be affected. Any risks that are identified must then be controlled. This emphasis on assessing risk and then doing something about it is a very different approach to that of HASAWA.

While it would be easy to assume that these regulations would not have much effect on ordinary workplaces, this is not in fact the case, as many of the substances identified as potentially hazardous will be found in any workplace – e.g. fluid for photocopiers or cleaning products – so in reality all workplaces are affected. The main areas that employers should focus on are:

- assessing the risk of substances used and identifying the required precautions
- introducing appropriate measures to control or prevent the risk
- ensuring the correct use of the control measures, and that equipment is regularly maintained
- conducting health surveillance to monitor health of employees where there is a known identifiable risk
- informing and training employees about risks that may arise from their work, and informing them of the necessary precautions to take.

The Framework Directive

The European Union Framework Directive has broad objectives which were implemented in EU member states by 31 December 1992. This established in general terms the European Commission's approach to health and safety. The main objectives of the directive were to introduce measures to encourage improvements in safety and health of workers at work. In order to do this it contains general principles concerning the prevention of occupational risks, the protection of health and safety, the elimination of risk and accident factors, as well as informing, consultation and providing balanced participation in accordance with national laws.

The British response to the EU directive was made in the Management of Health and Safety at Work Regulations 1992, which were accompanied by an approved Code of Practice which came into effect on 1 January 1993. Five further sets of regulations were also implemented in Britain on 1 January 1993 and all these have become known as the 'six-pack'. The 'six-pack' comprised:

- Management of Health and Safety at Work Regulations 1992
- Workplace (Health, Safety and Welfare) Regulations 1992
- Provision and Use of Work Equipment Regulations 1992

- Personal Protective Equipment at Work Regulations 1992
- Health and Safety (Display Screen Equipment) Regulations 1992
- Manual Handling Operations Regulations 1992.

Legislation becomes out of date and does not always meet the requirements of modern organisations, so amendments are often necessary. All of the original 'six-pack' regulations have recently been amended and updated so the new dates and any significant changes will be included with the regulations as they are discussed. The Provision and Use of Work Equipment was amended in 1998 and the Management of Health and Safety at Work Regulations in 1999. The remaining four regulations were also amended later under the Health and Safety (Miscellaneous Amendments) Regulations 2002.

The Management of Health and Safety at Work Regulations 1999 (MHSWR)

This is the law in the UK that implemented the Framework Directive. The HASAWA covered some parts of the directive but there were also new things that employers needed to do, such as carrying out certain detailed procedures, assessing risks, implementing certain safety measures and communicating with staff on health and safety. According to Stranks (2007), 'these regulations do not stand alone – all other modern health and safety legislation such as the Workplace (Health, Safety and Welfare) Regulations 1992 and the Provision and Use of Work Equipment Regulations 1998, must be read in conjunction with the general duties under the MHSWR.' This is therefore a very important piece of legislation which has the following key features.

It states that employers shall:

- carry out assessment of health and safety risks to both employees and the public (this may be done in writing or on computer)
- monitor and review protective and preventive measures
- appoint a competent person or persons to be responsible for protective and preventive measures
- establish emergency procedures
- give comprehensible and relevant information and training to employees (the training can be provided by a suitable training provider other than the employer)
- cooperate with any other employers who may share the same work site.

Also, employees shall:

- use equipment in the way in which they have been trained to use it
- report any dangerous situations or any problem areas that they spot in the arrangements that the employer has made for health and safety.

These regulations are intended for use in cases of criminal action against an employer, and may not be used in any civil cases as evidence of negligence.

Pause for thought 12.2 To what extent do you feel that the Management of Health and Safety at Work Regulations 1999 differ from the HASAWA 1974?

These regulations are more forceful than HASAWA and specify that employers 'shall' do certain things, whereas HASAWA only expected employers to carry out its provisions 'so far as it is reasonably practicable' to do so.

The new regulations also mean that employers have a legal duty to predict what could go wrong, before it actually happens, and to take preventive action to avoid it happening. They must record the preventive action that they have taken. This is referred to as risk assessment and is the same principle as under COSHH, but it is now applied more widely. This will be discussed more fully later in the chapter.

The new regulations require employers to be proactive and actively manage activities aimed at protecting the health and safety of their employees. This is more in line than previous legislative measures with the human resource approach of being proactive and actively managing human resources.

Workplace (Health, Safety and Welfare) Regulations 1992, amended by the Health and Safety (Miscellaneous Amendments) Regulations 2002

This law is intended to rationalise older pieces of legislation and provide clearer ruling as to exactly what facilities the employer should provide for the employee. As stated earlier it is important that it is read in conjunction with the Management of Health and Safety at Work Regulations (MHSWR) 1999.

Employers shall:

- provide a good working environment with appropriate temperature, ventilation and level of lighting
- carry out maintenance and be responsible for keeping the workplace clean.

The 2002 amendments include further guidance for employers about achieving this, primarily in relation to rest rooms and rest areas. The amendments specify that there should be sufficient seats (with backs) and tables for the number of people likely to use them at any one time.

The 2002 amendment regulations state that employers must ensure they meet the needs of any disabled workers by also providing suitable rest areas for them. Other equipment and facilities, such as workstations, passageways, doors, and washroom facilities, should also be designed to meet the specific needs of disabled workers.

Provision and Use of Work Equipment Regulations 1998, amended by the Health and Safety (Miscellaneous Amendments) Regulations 2002

This law aims to bring together many older laws governing equipment used at work.

Employers shall:

- consider when they purchase new equipment the working condition of the equipment and risks that it may pose to employees
- ensure the provision of appropriate levels of lighting and warnings about the safe use of the equipment
- ensure that the equipment is suitable for the use to which it will be put

369

- provide adequate information and training
- provide adequate protection from any potentially dangerous parts of the equipment or machinery.

Personal Protective Equipment at Work Regulations 1992, amended by the Health and Safety (Miscellaneous Amendments) Regulations 2002

These regulations replace part of more than 20 old pieces of legislation which were concerned with provision of protective equipment for employees. They aim to ensure suitable provision of protective equipment such as head protection, high visibility clothing or safety harnesses. Employers must ensure the equipment is appropriate for the likely type of risks, the specific working conditions in the workplace and the duration for which it is likely to be worn. In addition, they should consider the ergonomic requirements of the job, state of health of the person employed and any particular characteristics of their workstation that might affect the use of the personal protective equipment. Particular attention should also be paid to ensuring that the equipment provided is hygienic and compatible with any additional personal protective equipment that the worker may need to wear simultaneously.

Employers shall:

- ensure that equipment used is suitable for the job to be done
- adequately maintain, clean and replace equipment as necessary
- store it safely when it is not in use
- ensure correct use of the equipment
- inform and train employees in the correct use of the equipment.

Health and Safety (Display Screen Equipment) Regulations 1992, amended by the Health and Safety (Miscellaneous Amendments) Regulations 2002

This law implements the EU's Visual Display Unit Directive and specifies minimum levels of health and safety for people who spend a large part of their time at work working in front of computer screens or who are about to become employed in that capacity. It is primarily aimed at the prevention of damage to their upper limbs, and to prevent eye strain, fatigue and stress.

Employers shall:

- assess the risks and reduce any that are found
- ensure that workstations meet at least the minimum requirements
- ensure that the work is planned to include breaks and changes of activity
- arrange for employees to have their eyes tested regularly at time limits designated by the optician appointed by the employer and provide spectacles if necessary
- provide appropriate training for users or those about to become users of visual display units.

Eyesight tests should be completed as soon as possible after any request, or in the case of someone who is about to start work, before he or she becomes a computer user.

Manual Handling Operations Regulations 1992, amended by the Health and Safety (Miscellaneous Amendments) Regulations 2002

This aims to reduce the levels of injury and ill-health associated with manual handling of loads at work.

Employers shall:

- ensure, as far as is practicable, that employees do not need to use risky techniques when handling loads
- assess whether any risks are inherent in the manual handling that has to be done
- take necessary steps to reduce risks by introducing mechanical help, ensuring loads are lighter and assessing the capabilities of the individual
- ensure the provision of information to all employees
- if employees sometimes work on another employer's premises, liaise closely with the other employer.

When trying to determine whether each specific manual handling activity involves any risk, employers should pay particular attention to the following:

- the physical suitability of the employee for safely completing the particular form of manual handling required
- what the person is wearing and its suitability for the job
- the amount of knowledge and training that the person has received
- the results of any risk assessments that have already been completed that relate to the job
- whether the employee has been identified as being one of a group of employees who are particularly at risk
- the results of any health surveillance that has been undertaken.

This legislation is far reaching in its scope although its effects will vary from one organisation to another, depending on the nature of the work undertaken.

Reporting of Injuries, Diseases and Dangerous Occurrences Regulations (RIDDOR) 1995

RIDDOR requires employers to report certain work-related accidents, diseases and dangerous occurrences to the enforcing authorities so that they can identify risks and investigate serious accidents. The following briefly describes some of the circumstances in which reporting should occur:

- The death or major injury of an employee, or of a self-employed person working in the organisation, or of a member of the public must all be reported to the enforcing authorities immediately and this must be followed within 10 days by a completed accident report. Reportable major injuries include fractures, amputation, dislocation, loss of sight.
- If an employee or self-employed person working on your premises suffers an accident or injury which requires that person to be absent from work for at least three days, then a completed accident form must be sent to the enforcing authorities.

- Some work-related diseases, such as occupational dermatitis, skin cancer or occupational asthma have also to be reported on a disease report form to the enforcing authority, as do infections such as hepatitis, tetanus or tuberculosis.
- There may be instances where something occurs which does not actually result in a reportable injury but which could have done. For example, the collapse of a lift or an explosion in a closed vessel are likely to constitute a dangerous occurrence, even if no one is injured. Any dangerous occurrence has to be reported immediately by telephone to the enforcing authorities. An accident report form should also be completed within 10 days of the dangerous occurrence. (Details of where to find more information are given in 'Further study' at the end of the chapter.)

The enforcing authority will be the environmental health department of the local authority if the type of the business is an office, retail or wholesale, warehousing, hotel or catering, sports or leisure, a residential home or place of worship. Accidents or dangerous occurrences which happen in any other type of business will need to be reported to the area office of the Health and Safety Executive. Nowadays accidents and dangerous occurrences can even be reported using the Internet. Have a look at the websites at the end of this chapter for more details of how to do this.

The Working Time Regulations 1998

We discussed the Working Time Regulations 1998 briefly in Chapter 4, but have also included them here, since the hours people work can have a big impact on both their health and safety in the workplace.

It is often claimed that the UK is the 'long hours capital' of Europe and that working such long hours adversely affects workers' health. In some organisations there is a culture of 'presenteeism', where people are expected to arrive early for work and leave late, forgoing home and social life. While some workers thrive in a long hours culture and live to work, such a culture is likely to hide a great deal of inefficiency and result in increased levels of stress and ill-health for many other workers. These regulations attempt to control the hours worked and control the way the hours are organised. They also establish minimum holiday levels for employees in the UK, although it is frequently claimed that a large number of UK employees actually fail to take all the holiday they are entitled to, either because they are too busy or are too frightened to be away from work for their whole holiday entitlement.

Although the regulations emanate from the Working Time Directive, adopted by the EU Council of Ministers in 1993, and therefore apply to all EU countries, there is some flexibility available for countries to implement European directives in their own way. Other European countries, for example France with its 35-hour working week, have implemented the directive differently. The main features for adult workers in the UK were outlined in Chapter 4.

Although the 48-hour working week means workers in the UK still work much longer hours than their counterparts in France, it is nevertheless considerably better than the

Did you know?

Death from overwork is so common in Japan that they even have a special word for it, *Karoshi*. The first documented case of Karoshi occurred in Japan in 1969 but there have been many cases since. In Japan the spouses of those who have died from Karoshi have won claims for compensation from the companies concerned and each year between 20 and 60 claims for compensation are brought. This is still probably a gross underestimate of the real number of cases of Karoshi in Japan.

(*Source*: Nishiyama and Johnson, 1977)

expectation in countries such as Japan. In Japan it has been documented that many workers regularly work for over 100 hours per week, for many weeks, or even years at a time and that this frequently leads, not surprisingly, to ill-health or even death. Since we work increasingly in a global economy, where people are constantly accessible via mobile phones or email, these long-hour work practices are spreading to the USA and the UK.

Statutory holiday entitlement in the UK increased to 4.8 weeks from 1 October 2007 and from 1 October 2009 to 5.6 weeks. This right applies to all workers and not just employees. (The distinction between workers and employees will be discussed in Chapter 13.) Having rights to increased holiday is not of much use if workers do not take it. According to XpertHR (2006), 'As the Working Time Regulations are essentially a health and safety measure, [employers] should take steps to ensure that workers take the holidays to which they are entitled.' Here there is a role for both HR managers and line managers to ensure that good management practices are carried out and that a culture is built that should discourage a culture of presenteeism.

Legislation about smoking

Four related pieces of legislation have been introduced in Scotland, Wales, Northern Ireland and England prohibiting smoking in public places, including workplaces, and similar legislation has been introduced throughout the rest of Europe.

The Smoking, Health and Social Care (Scotland) Act 2005 was the first to come into effect and resulted in a ban on smoking in public places, including workplaces from March 2006. A similar ban on smoking in public places came into effect in Wales from 2 April 2007, in Northern Ireland from 30 April 2007 and in England from 1 July 2007. These related pieces of legislation are designed to protect workers who may previously have been affected by passive smoking and also to promote positive health improvements by encouraging smokers to stop.

The Corporate Manslaughter and Corporate Homicide Act 2007

The Corporate Manslaughter and Corporate Homicide Act 2007 makes corporate manslaughter a criminal offence from April 2008. This has also increased the interest in health safety and welfare as companies found guilty could face an unlimited fine if they are found to have caused death through gross negligence or failures in their safety systems. People working for some organisations such as Crown bodies, previously exempt from prosecution, will now be covered by this legislation. While this is to be welcomed, Richard Jones (2007) argues that it does not go far enough and that there are still too many exemptions. He goes on to say that 'HR needs to actively engage workers in helping keep workplaces safe, and should regularly consult them on health and safety issues.' Safety should certainly be of concern to all managers including HR managers and line managers.

Most of the legislation discussed here, with the exception of the anti-smoking legislation, has focused primarily on safety although clearly health and welfare are also closely linked to this.

The people and organisations involved in health, safety and welfare

We have already discussed at length the roles of employers and employees and have mentioned briefly others such as the Health and Safety Executive. But there are other health, safety and welfare roles currently undertaken by the Health and Safety Commission and local authorities. What do these organisations actually do? How are they organised?

● The Health and Safety Commission (HSC)

The Commission was set up under the Health and Safety at Work Act 1974 and is a quango responsible for carrying out the policy of the Act and for providing advice to local authorities and others about how to implement the provisions of the Act. It is largely independent and acts on behalf of the Crown, but reports to Parliament primarily through the Secretary of State for Work and Pensions. It has a chairman and nine other members drawn from bodies representing employers, employees and local authorities, who are appointed by the Secretary of State for Transport, Local Government and the Regions.

In 1999 John Prescott, who was the Deputy Prime Minister at that time, announced a new impetus for health and safety called Revitalising Health and Safety. He said that the Health and Safety at Work Act 1974 had done its job as evidenced by the fact that the 'number of deaths at work today is a quarter of the 1971 level'. However, he wanted a strategic appraisal of the health and safety framework in order to build on the work of the previous 25 years and to establish a new agenda for the first 25 years of the new century (Prescott, 2000).

The HSC, after consulting widely about ways of revitalising health and safety produced targets for health and safety in Great Britain and a Strategy Statement and Action Plan. The HSC (2000) said that targets for health and safety in Great Britain are needed because:

> Health and safety is central to sustainable development and securing a better quality of life for all.
>
> ● Raising workplace standards will promote better public health and *social progress which recognises the needs of everyone.*
> ● Reducing the £18 billion bill for health and safety failures will contribute to *maintaining high and stable levels of economic growth and employment.*
> ● Controlling harmful substances in the workplace will help to *protect our environment.*

● The Health and Safety Executive (HSE)

The Health and Safety Executive (HSE) consists of three people who advise and assist the HSC. The executive also has a staff of approximately 4,000 to help carry out all its responsibilities in relation to its day-to-day functions. The HSE consists of policy advisers, inspectors and experts in medicine, science and technology. They are responsible for making provision for enforcing the legislation, for dealing with daily administration and conducting research, and for identifying the range of information necessary to enable the HSC to remain properly informed.

Guidance

This fulfils three main purposes:

1 To help people to understand the law by explaining it in a clear way.
2 To ensure they then comply with the law.
3 To provide rather more specialist advice.

Approved codes of practice

These give examples of good practice and help employers and workers understand what they should do to comply with the legislation. Failure to comply with a code of practice would not in itself mean that the individual or organisation would be prosecuted but, in any legal proceeding brought against them, failure to comply with an approved code of practice would be used as part of the evidence against them.

Regulations

Regulations can be made under HASAWA 1974 to identify specific risks in specific situations and the actions that need to be taken.

As well as enforcing health and safety legislation the, HSC and HSE have also been given the following tasks by the Government:

● Modernise and simplify the regulatory framework.
● Provide appropriate information and advice.
● Promote risk assessment and technical knowledge.
● Operate statutory schemes. (HSC, 2001)

Local authorities (LA)

Local authorities also have responsibility for enforcement of health and safety in approximately 194,000 workplaces. Under HASAWA, the Secretary of State for Work and Pensions (DWP) can make regulations for local authorities to take on responsibility for certain activities and to ensure that there is no duplication of effort between them and the Health and Safety Executive. The local authority inspectors, normally known as environmental health officers, are responsible for health and safety mainly in the services sector, while the HSE tends to concentrate on the more hazard-prone industries. There is a liaison committee which ensures consistency of approach between the HSE and local authorities. The HSE publishes a wide range of material each year explaining its role and the practical implications of legislation. The Health and Safety Executive can provide guidance, approved codes of practice and regulations.

The Gangmasters Licensing Authority (GLA)

Not all workers are lucky enough to work in well organised and regulated workplaces even in the UK. The death of 18 Chinese cockle pickers in Morecambe Bay, Lancashire, in 2004 drew attention to the world of unscrupulous operators who employ migrant workers, sometimes illegally, to work in low-skilled jobs. The Gangmasters Licensing Authority was formed to license genuine workforce organisers and providers of migrant workers and has the power to revoke licences where poor practice has occurred. Initially legislation targeted the agricultural sector where gangmasters and migrant workers primarily worked. However, it is claimed by MPs and trade unions that 'legislation to regulate gangmasters in the agricultural sector could be pushing unscrupulous operators into providing workers for care homes instead' (CIPD, 2007c). The Labour MP Jim Sheridan who was responsible for legislation creating the GLA has been pushing for a new bill to extend the GLA's scope to other sectors. Sheridan said, 'We believe the GLA's remit could be rolled out universally sector by sector. There are really important health and safety issues here. We don't want workers to be abused or intimidated, but we don't want them in skilled jobs either if they are not qualified' (CIPD, 2007c).

Changes to the organisations involved in health and safety

In 2004 Bill Callaghan, chair of the HSE, in the foreword to *A strategy for workplace health and safety in Great Britain to 2010 and beyond* (HSE, 2004) said, 'This strategy is to promote our vision, which is to see health and safety as a cornerstone of a civilized society and with that, to achieve a record of workplace health and safety that leads the world. This strategy builds on success and takes forward the Revitalising Health and Safety Statement of 2000.'

The HSC and HSE's continuing aims (2007) are to:

- Protect people by providing information and advice, promoting and assisting a goal-setting system of regulation, undertaking and encouraging research and enforcing the law where necessary.
- Influence organisations to embrace high standards of health and safety and to recognise the social and economic benefits.
- Work with business to prevent catastrophic failures in major hazard industry.
- Seek to optimise the use of resources to deliver our mission and vision.

HSC and HSE's new aims are to:

- Develop new ways to establish and maintain an effective health and safety culture in a changing economy, so that all employers take their responsibilities seriously, the workforce is fully involved and risks are properly managed.
- Do more to address the new and emerging health issues.
- Achieve higher levels of recognition and respect for health and safety as an integral part of a modern, competitive business and public sector and as a contribution to social justice and inclusion.
- Exemplify best public sector practice in managing our resources.

The world of work has changed dramatically over the years and there is now a much more diverse workforce working in increasingly flexible ways. These new aims are intended to address this. New health and safety issues arise as people work from home, or while on the move and the risks to their health and safety also need to be assessed. There are also fewer large organisations and more small ones. According to the HSE (2007), '90% of the 3.5 million or so businesses employ fewer than 10 people but nearly half of the workforce are employed in large organisations.'

There are still rather too many bodies involved in health and safety and this in itself can be confusing as there can be an overlap of responsibilities. To make sure that *A strategy for workplace health and safety in Great Britain to 2010 and beyond* is achieved the main factor that needs to change according to the HSE is the way that the organisations concerned with health and safety work together. HSE feel there is 'a perception that there is no coherent direction to the overall health and safety system. HSC, HSE and LA cannot/should not do it all. There is agreement that boundaries need to be set.' A consultation document written in 2007 sets out proposals for a new organisation where all three former organisations work together and where boundaries are removed.

The enforcing authorities

We shall now discuss how the current inspection of workplaces and investigation of accidents is shared between HSE inspectors and local authority enforcement officers. Basically the HSE inspectors cover work conducted primarily in factories, building sites, mines, fairgrounds, quarries, railways, chemical plants, offshore and nuclear installations, schools or hospitals. The local authority enforcement officers cover retailing, some warehouses, most offices, hotels, catering, consumer services, sports and leisure activities and places of worship. Both have similar powers of enforcement. These include a right to:

- enter employers' premises
- carry out inspections/investigations
- take equipment or materials on to premises
- take measurements, photographs or recordings
- carry out tests on articles or substances
- examine books and documents
- issue improvement notices
- issue prohibition notices.

The last two points are very important and we shall consider each in turn. However, sometimes when an enforcing inspector finds a breach of the law which is relatively minor he or she may feel that improvement notices and prohibition notices are not appropriate.

Informal methods

In the case of a minor breach in legislation the inspector may choose to use informal methods and may simply give the employer or contractor advice about what they should do to comply with the law, and explain the reasons.

Improvement notices

If the inspector feels that an organisation is contravening one of the relevant provisions of legislation then he or she can issue an improvement notice which will specify that improvements must be made within a specified time limit to bring the equipment or process up to the required standard of safety.

Prohibition notices

If when the inspector visits he or she feels that there is serious danger or risk of injury to employees, he or she can issue a prohibition notice which will stop work activity immediately until the risk has been dealt with. In some circumstances a deferred prohibition order may be issued: this would occur, for example, if it would be difficult to stop a process in mid-cycle or if there was no immediate risk of injury. The Health and Safety Commission's Enforcement Policy Statement (2002) states the approach which both the Health and Safety Executive and local authorities should take in relation to law enforcement. The overall aims of the HSC are to protect the health, safety and welfare of employees and to safeguard others such as members of the public who may be exposed to risk from the workplace or activity.

> **Did you know?**
>
> In 2005/06 1,012 offences resulted in prosecution by the HSE and the local authorities prosecuted 332 offences. (See **www.hse.gov.uk/statistics** for latest figures.)

Normally in England and Wales most prosecutions would go to a magistrates' court but more serious cases are referred to the Crown Courts. Under the Scottish judicial system the majority of cases go to a sheriff court or before a jury. Organisations and individuals can face prosecution, and prison sentences and unlimited fines can also be given by the Crown Courts.

Any accidents at work that result in death are treated as manslaughter. The police are involved in these cases and have overall responsibility for them. However, there had been general dissatisfaction that the system was not tough enough and that employers were on occasions shirking their responsibilities with regard to health and safety and frequently escaping prosecution even when an employee had died as a result of the company's actions or inactions. The Corporate Manslaughter and Corporate Homicide Act (2007) is intended to create a criminal offence of corporate manslaughter for the first time. According to Baker (2007), 'The law is likely to lead to more prosecutions for deaths resulting from an organisation's acts or omissions, and may lead to higher fines. It will certainly lead to greater scrutiny by the courts of the way in which companies organise themselves internally in terms of health and safety.' This should make it easier to examine the conduct of senior managers, and a company can be found guilty of corporate manslaughter if it can be proved that the way they managed and organised their activities led to a death and that this amounted to a gross breach of its duty of care to the employee.

In 2002 the HSC (HSC, 2002) revised its Enforcement Policy Statement and set out the criteria for whether or not particular incidents or complaints should be investigated. This Policy Statement stresses four main things:

1 *The principle of proportionality.* This means that the severity of the action taken should be in proportion to the level of risk and the seriousness of the breach of law.
2 *Targeting.* The people/organisations who cause the most serious risks or who have failed to control hazards in the workplace adequately should be the ones to be targeted by the inspectors.
3 *Consistent.* For people to have faith in the system and the inspectors they need to feel that they will be treated in a consistently fair way.

4 *Transparent.* Every action taken should be clear, with explanations given for any action that is taken.

Prosecution

If the case is very serious then the inspector may also need to initiate a prosecution. Any decision about whether or not to prosecute will be taken after considering the HSC's Enforcement Policy Statement.

Safety representatives

As we said earlier, there is a duty for employers to consult with and involve safety representatives in the workplace. In October 1978 the Safety Representatives and Safety Committees Regulations came into effect. These regulations form part of the Health and Safety at Work Act, and within a year over 100,000 safety representatives were in post. The regulations provide that any recognised trade union can appoint safety representatives, and they recommend that in general the people who are appointed should have worked for that employer for at least two years so that they have a reasonable range of experience from which to draw. In some trade unions the shop stewards take on the role of safety representatives, while in others the safety representative is a separate post. The people to fill these positions are, however, selected by the trade union, not by the management. Organisations where there are no recognised trade unions can still appoint safety representatives, and they are normally elected by the workforce.

The safety representative's main function is to represent the employee in consultation with the employer on issues relating to health and safety in the workplace, and they can investigate hazards or potential hazards as well as carrying out inspections of the workplace. They are entitled to paid time off to perform their duties and for training to enable them to carry out their duties effectively, and they may also require some facilities such as the use of a telephone, a filing cabinet and a room to conduct interviews. If two or more safety representatives make a written request to management for a safety committee to be established, then the employer is legally obliged to do so.

The Management of Health and Safety at Work Regulations 1992 (MHSWR) as amended in 1999 add to the Safety Representatives and Safety Committees Regulations 1977 and specify that every employer shall consult safety representatives in good time with regard to:

- the introduction of any measure at the workplace which may substantially affect health or safety of the workforce
- arrangements for appointing or nominating a 'competent person' who is able to assist the employer to carry out risk assessment exercises and help him or her in carrying out duties in relation to health and safety
- the health and safety information that the employer is supposed to provide to employees
- the planning and organisation of health and safety training
- the health and safety consequences of the introduction of new technology at work.

There are, as you can see, a wide range of duties performed by safety representatives. Safety representatives usually receive excellent training from trades unions for this demanding role and those who take on these roles can also choose to take the training further and use it as part of a professional qualification in health and safety.

Safety officer or safety adviser

None of the legislation actually specifies the need for a safety officer but, as the law has grown in complexity, many organisations have felt that it is necessary to appoint a person to specialise in this area of work. This is a management appointment and must not be confused with the trade union/employee-appointed safety representative. Safety officers are sometimes appointed to advise senior management without being part of any other department and report directly to the board, but in many organisations they form part of the human resource management department. Smaller organisations may not wish to appoint a full-time safety officer and may instead call on the expertise provided by independent consultants to act as safety advisers. It is important that anyone appointed as safety officer or safety adviser has the status and level of competence to provide authoritative advice to management and the workforce on aspects of health and safety.

A competent person

This has a specific meaning in terms of health and safety as the Framework Directive (Article 7), which is discussed later, says that employers must designate 'a competent person' who has practical and theoretical knowledge of particular equipment and who is able to identify any problems that may occur with it. The provision of this directive is reflected in Regulation 6 of the Management of Health and Safety at Work Regulations 1992 and clearly refers to a management nominee, although not necessarily to the safety officer but to someone who because of his or her knowledge and experience of particular machinery, plant or equipment is able to identify problems or defects in it. That person needs to be competent not just to do the job but to carry out risk assessment for health and safety for employees and the public, and must monitor and review protective and preventive measures. A safety officer may fulfil this role but is not likely to be the only designated competent person, as she or he is unlikely to have the required level of knowledge or experience for all machinery.

Safety committees

Safety committees have to be established, as we said earlier, if two or more safety representatives request the organisation to do so, but many organisations do not wait for this request, and it is good practice to set up a safety committee in any case. The main objective of a safety committee is to promote cooperation between employers and employees in instigating, developing and carrying out measures to ensure the health and safety at work of employees. They are likely to provide some or all of the following functions:

- study figures and trends for accidents and notifiable diseases
- examine safety audit reports
- consider reports and factual information provided by inspectors
- consider the reports of safety representatives
- assist in development of safety rules and safe systems of work

- monitor the effectiveness of safety training in the workplace
- monitor the effectiveness of the safety and health communication in the workplace
- encourage publicity for health and safety programmes in the workplace
- provide a link with the appropriate inspectorates.

Membership of the health and safety committee

The membership of the committee should be agreed between management and the employees. The committee should normally include equal numbers of people from management and the workforce and should have representation from different areas of the workforce and different grades of management. People such as the organisation's doctor, nurse or safety officer should also be invited to attend as ex officio members. It is a good idea for the person who chairs the committee to have sufficient status within the organisation that they can authorise money to be spent on necessary aspects of health and safety without having to refer all such decisions to higher authority. A senior member of the management team would fulfil this role well, although in many organisations the chair of the safety committee may also alternate between management and the workforce.

Health and safety arrangements

Safety policy statement

You will remember that under HASAWA one of the duties of an employer is to provide a safety policy statement to show each person's responsibilities and the arrangements they have made to carry out the policy. The safety policy applies to all organisations that employ more than five employees. This is supposed to be a document that can be used to show in a practical way how the arrangements for health and safety are to be carried out in the workplace, and it should be designed to have a genuine effect on health and safety working practices. This means that it should be clearly written and should be easily available to any employee, and a copy should preferably be given to each employee. It does not mean that it is a secret document, as some organisations in our experience seem to think, kept locked in a filing cabinet well away from the gaze of employees. In order to encourage awareness of health and safety and produce an effective safety policy document, it is also advisable that a range of people should be involved in its design and that key decision makers have been involved fully in these discussions. In some organisations a person will be chosen to champion the policy and targets for improvements in specific areas of health and safety may also be set. Arrangements should also be made to review the health and safety policy regularly, at least annually, since what is important is whether the policy is having an effect on health and safety in the workplace, rather than how well written it is.

The HSE recommends that the following two issues should be addressed in a safety policy statement.

- Who has responsibility for health and safety?
- What are the arrangements made for health and safety?

● Responsibility for health and safety

The safety policy should show management's approach to health and safety and who is actually responsible for specific tasks. The safety policy is basically concerned with people, their duties and their accountability. It should include a management chart showing the chain of command in respect of health and safety, with a clear statement that the ultimate responsibility for health and safety rests with the board or chief executive or equivalent. The safety policy document should carry at the end the signature of the person with the ultimate responsibility for health and safety at work. There should be a clearly defined role for the safety adviser, if such a position exists, and clear explanation of his/her relationship to senior management and line management. This part of the document should also indicate the role of those appointed as 'competent persons' to assist the employer in implementing the safety policy.

According to David Morris (2001), Head of the HSE's Strategy and Management Branch:

> In principle, small firms will have much the same policy statements as larger firms, and their risk assessments will cover much the same ground. But there are differences. The policy statement is likely to show that there is less scope for delegation in a small firm, where many responsibilities are exercised directly by the owner. Equally, small firms may have relatively few, or simple, hazards, meaning that risk assessment will be less complex.

● The practical arrangements

This section should establish systems and procedures and the practical arrangements for their implementation. It should also show the system for monitoring safety and for publishing results. The section of the safety policy covering arrangements should be a practical section that is regularly reviewed and updated.

The HSE (2003), in a booklet, *Stating Your Business,* suggests that small organisations organise their arrangements for managing health and safety under the sections listed below.

- health and safety risks arising from our work activities
- consultation with employees
- safe plant and equipment
- safe handling and use of substances
- information, instruction and supervision
- competency for tasks and training
- accidents, first aid and work-related ill-health
- monitoring
- emergency procedures – fire and evacuation
- key areas of risk.

Health and safety risks arising from work activities

This means that the arrangements for carrying out risk assessments, the results of the risk assessments and the actions taken will all need to be shown, although the findings and resulting actions will need to be shown in a separate document. Risk assessments will be discussed in more detail later in the chapter.

Consultation with employees

We have already discussed the fact that if there is a recognised trade union which has appointed safety representatives then by law they must be consulted about any changes likely to affect the health and safety of their members. If there is not a recognised trade union then the employers must consult their employees directly or through a works council.

Safe plant and equipment

This requirement is taken directly from HASAWA and means that employers must keep vehicles, machinery and equipment in good working order. In the safety policy, the names of people responsible for this should be stated, as should arrangements to deal with problems. Those responsible for checking that new machinery and equipment meets the required standards should also be listed here. Records of maintenance and service history of vehicles should be kept, perhaps separately in a log book.

Safe handling and use of substances

This section relates to those responsible for identifying substances that need a COSHH assessment. Once again the names of people with responsibilities should be listed here. This includes the names of those carrying out the assessments, those responsible for ensuring that any actions needed are taken, those who have to tell employees about the results of the assessments as well as the names of those people who have responsibility for checking the safety of new substances prior to purchase. There should also be an indication as to the frequency of assessments.

Information, instruction and supervision

This should show where health and safety law posters are displayed or where leaflets relating to health and safety are kept. It should also detail where health and safety advice can be obtained and the names of those responsible for supervising the work of trainees or young employees.

Competency for tasks and training

The names of people who provide induction training and job-specific training should be listed here. Some jobs may pose particular risks, for example the risk of back injury to workers involved in the manual handling of heavy or awkwardly shaped goods. Both the jobs and the training needed should also be identified. Training records should be kept for all health and safety training as well as other training and the safety policy should indicate where the records are stored and by whom.

Accidents, first aid and work-related ill-health

In this section any health surveillance required for certain jobs, such as work with flour, asbestos or some chemicals, needs to be identified. This should mean any problems in a worker's health caused by the job will be identified at an early stage so that action can be taken to prevent their health becoming worse. It shows who is responsible for health surveillance and where records are kept.

The locations of first aid boxes need to be shown and first aiders should be listed. Records of all accidents, however trivial, and instances of work-related ill-health should be recorded in the accident book and the location of this book should also be given in the health and safety policy.

Monitoring

It is very important that the policy is used and that good practices are checked regularly. Those who have responsibility for checking that working conditions are safe and that safe practices are being followed should be listed here, as should those who are responsible for carrying out investigations of accidents or investigating work-related causes of sickness absence.

Emergency procedures – fire and evacuation

Obviously it is important that there are adequate safety procedures in place in case there is a need to evacuate the building in an emergency. In this section it is important to state who checks the escape routes and the frequency of these checks. Safety equipment such as fire extinguishers have to be maintained and checked, alarms need to be tested, emergency evacuation drills need to be carried out and records of these must be kept.

Key areas of risk

These will vary depending on the organisation and the type of work undertaken, but might include risks relating to particularly dangerous substances such as asbestos, or to stress or potential violence to staff from members of the public. Each organisation will need to carry out its own risk assessments relating to the areas of risk which are identified.

People need to be aware of their responsibilities as, if something goes wrong and a serious accident occurs, the relevant enforcement officers will want to know who was responsible. These enforcement officers would carry out a full investigation and would also want to examine the safety policy document. If a supervisor did not know that he or she was responsible for checking that a protective guard was in place, then the employer would have to be able to prove that he or she had informed the supervisor of his or her responsibilities and had also trained him or her adequately in the fulfilment of these responsibilities. Many tasks will of course be delegated to different levels of management and employees do, as we have seen, have some responsibility for their own actions. Senior management cannot, however, abdicate their ultimate responsibility for overall safety within the organisation, and must try to ensure the health and safety of their employees and others affected by their employees' actions. Those who carry the ultimate responsibility for this, such as the board of directors, could face prosecution and possibly a large fine or even a spell in prison for individual directors if their organisation is found to be at fault. Similarly, others with specific responsibilities such as safety officers, human resource managers, line managers or training officers could be charged and convicted of an offence.

First consider the following case study and identify the health, safety and welfare issues that you think occur here then complete Activity 12.3.

CASE STUDY 12.1 Health and safety

The Sheffley Company employs nearly 330 employees and specialises in the production of steel castings. The organisation has a director, Mr Jones, whose great-grandfather founded the business. There is a new production manager, Mr Tandy; an import and export manager, Ms Jeffries; and an administration manager, Mrs Groves. Mr Tandy has eight line managers reporting to him, who have a total of 280 employees working for them. Mrs Groves has a payroll manager, a canteen manager and a personnel officer reporting to her and Ms Jeffries runs the purchasing, goods inward and goods outward departments, and the warehouse and export sections.

The work involved in the production of steel castings is hazardous and the company has not had a good record with regard to health and safety. It is not only in the production areas that there have been problems – the offices also have suffered rather a large number of accidents which have required employees to have more than three days off work to recover. The office staff are expected to regularly work long hours and work whatever hours are necessary to complete the job. Several are absent with serious long-term illnesses including the payroll manager and of course this puts additional pressure on those who remain. Mrs Groves is beginning to show signs of the strain from doing her own job and that of the absent payroll officer and is suffering from regular headaches and feelings of anxiety.

The new production manager decides that something must be done about the record on health, safety and welfare. He decides a punitive approach will work best and in the weekly meeting with the production supervisors he informs them that from next week any employee who does not wear the protective equipment provided will be dismissed. The safety equipment comprises safety boots, safety goggles and overalls.

During the lead-up to the introduction of the safety equipment, notices are put up to explain the disciplinary penalty for non-compliance with the regulation, but information about the use and location of some of the equipment is not provided. Neither the safety representatives nor the safety committee have the opportunity to inspect the new protective equipment or to advise employees on its suitability.

The employees prove to be reluctant to wear the protective goggles which, they complain, pinch their skin and impair their vision. The production manager realises that the enforcement of safety is going to be problematic, and at the next week's meeting informs the supervisors that they do not have to be too rigid in their enforcement of the rules.

Two serious accidents occur just a month later in the production area and a further serious accident occurs in the offices. In the first incident molten metal splashes on to the foot of an employee, causing serious burns. In a separate accident a few days later an employee slips, splashing molten metal close to his eyes. Luckily his sight is saved, but he suffers severe burns and scarring. The accident record in the offices is also unsatisfactory, and one employee is injured when chemicals used in the photocopier spill on her leg, causing a severe itchy rash to develop. She has been having problems at home but has felt she must keep working although her mind has not been on her work all the time. Other employees in the wages office complain of backaches and headaches which they say are caused by poor lighting, uncomfortable chairs and badly adjusted screens on their visual display units.

You should be able to identify some of the many issues raised here about health, safety and the welfare of the employees such as the exact nature of the employer and employee responsibilities. The employer in this case, and indeed anyone involved in this area of work, also needs to comply with legislation, so, based on your reading of the chapter so far, you should also be able to identify the key legislation infringed by both the employer and the employees. A full discussion of this case study can be found if you go to our website at **www.pearsoned.co.uk/foothook**.

ACTIVITY 12.3

Design a safety policy statement for Sheffley Company. Remember that this should be a practical document that can be used by people in the organisation. Use the sections and main headings that we have given earlier (see pages 382–384).

Risk assessment

The idea of assessing and controlling risks was introduced to Britain with the Control of Substances Hazardous to Health Regulations 1988, when employers had to assess the risk of harm to people from certain substances being used at work. This was developed further in the 'six-pack' regulations in 1992. The 1992 Code of Practice for the Management of Health and Safety at Work made it a legal duty for employers to assess and record health and safety risks, and to appoint a 'competent person', i.e. a person who has been suitably trained, and who is allowed adequate time and facilities, to perform this role and assist in this and other safety tasks.

Every organisation has to carry out its own risk assessment, and strategies for this should be devised by management after consultation with all interested groups in the workforce.

According to the HSE in the booklet *Five Steps to Risk Assessment* (2006), the five main steps involved in assessing risks and hazards in the workplace are:

1 Identify the hazards.
2 Decide who might be harmed and how.
3 Evaluate the risks and decide on precautions.
4 Record your findings and implement them.
5 Review your assessment and update if necessary.

Assessments do not have to be carried out by health and safety experts and small organisations may choose to undertake the initial assessment of risk by themselves: alternatively, they may prefer to employ a consultant.

Steps 1 and 2 Identify the hazards and decide who may be harmed by them

Most organisations should be able to carry out the first two steps quite easily and identify sources of risk and then identify those who may be harmed by the risks. Many of the risks will probably be well known to you already such as the risk of slipping in areas where the floor may sometimes be wet, but sometimes even obvious hazards such as this are ignored. Identifying hazards involves looking and talking to people in the area being assessed. It also involves identifying which groups of workers are likely to suffer harm and the type of injury that they are likely to suffer.

Step 3 Evaluate the risks and decide on precautions

Once you have identified the hazards and those likely to be affected by them then you must do something about them. Remember under the Health and Safety at Work Act 1974 you have to do everything that is 'reasonably practicable' to protect people from harm.

Pause for thought 12.3 If the floor is sometimes wet due to cleaning or spillages, what could you do as a precaution?

It is best to try to get rid of the risk if it is possible but if not then ways to minimise the risk should be tried. What could you do to prevent accidents in the case of a wet floor that was slippery in your college/university or workplace?

Your answers should follow the following order if possible. Complete them in the grid below.

Order for trying to control risks	Your response to each of these where there is a wet and slippery floor
1 Try to find a way of doing the job that carries less risk 2 Ensure people don't come into contact with the hazard 3 Minimise exposure to the hazard 4 Issue personal protective clothing 5 Provide adequate facilities to deal properly with people who have suffered in some way because they come into contact with the problem	

Go to **www.pearsoned.uk/foothook** now to check your answers to this exercise.

Step 4 Record your findings and implement them

Small organisations with five employees or fewer do not have to record their findings but it would be good practice to do so anyway. Workers need to know what is happening as far as minimising risks is concerned and it also helps to involve them more in health and safety. According to the HSE (2006b) employers need to show that:

- a proper check was made;
- you asked who might be affected;
- you dealt with all significant hazards, taking into account the number of people who could be involved;
- the precautions are reasonable, and the remaining risk low; and
- you involved your staff or their representatives in the process.

Although it would be excellent if you could tackle all hazards immediately this will probably not be practicable so you need to plan an order of priority. Which are the most dangerous hazards? Which are quick and easy to solve? Are there any temporary solutions that could be used while a longer term solution is being organised? How will you monitor your solutions are working? Who is due to take action on each point and by when?

Step 5 Review your risk assessment and update if necessary

All workplaces are subject to constant change so something that works well at first may, due to changing circumstances or work patterns, no longer be so effective. Therefore the risk assessment needs to be monitored on a regular basis. For some organisations where there is a great deal of change this may involve reviewing risk assessments on a monthly or perhaps even weekly basis, while for other organisations an annual review may be more appropriate unless some unexpected change makes it more urgent to review risks.

Welfare

As described in Chapter 1, the main focus of people management has changed over the years. One of the earliest roles for HR specialists included that of the welfare officer (Fowler, 1994). The focus of this role was on the well-being of employees and it sometimes meant taking a paternalistic viewpoint, i.e. adopting a moral stance and telling people what was best for them. The modern HR function has changed and become more complex, adopting a more strategic and integrated approach to human resource management, a theme taken up in a number of chapters. Individual well-being, however, is still a factor which has an obvious impact on employees' ability to function at high levels and add value to their organisation. Employees who cannot concentrate at work or who may even stay away from work because of physical or psychological health problems obviously cannot contribute to their full potential, which has a negative impact on the goal of high-performance working (Income Data Services, 2002). In this context, the Engineering Employers' Federation (EEF, 2001) identifies effective stress management as 'a key part of a positive, proactive human resources policy'.

There is evidence then that a concern for employee welfare is nowadays an important aspect of human resource management. Even if the aforementioned paternalistic elements are not acceptable in our modern culture, employers are expected to care about their employees, and responsibility for this may be held by line managers as well as human resource and other specialists. There is a range of business and legal reasons for saying that an employer has not just an obligation but also a right to be involved in employee welfare.

The Health and Safety Executive (HSE) has also been focusing on ways to draw all employers' attention to the benefits to be gained from a more proactive approach. It has launched a series of initiatives called Revitalising Health and Safety because organisations are increasingly operating in new ways with increasingly flexible ways of working. The HSE has been consulting with and involving employers to demonstrate the business case for improved health and safety measures.

The role of the employer in employee well-being

One area of debate on the subject of welfare is whether this is a personal and private matter. We have already said that there is a business case for employer involvement in the health and safety of their workforce but should an employer also have a right to enquire into other aspects of the well-being of employees that involve their private lives? If so how far should this go?

Pause for thought 12.4 Before you read on, take a few minutes to think about your position on this issue. Make a list of arguments for saying that employers should be concerned about the personal welfare of their employees, and a list of reasons why they should not.

Go to our website at **www.pearsoned.co.uk/foothook** for further discussion and to check your arguments with ours.

Did you know?

In November 1994, John Walker, a senior social worker with Northumberland County Council, won his case in a high court, claiming that the employer had been negligent in its handling of this employee's stress. Mr Walker had returned to work after suffering a nervous breakdown. After his return to work the employer failed to make adjustments in his workload, and Mr Walker was dismissed on ill-health grounds after he had a second nervous breakdown. The fact that Mr Walker had suffered a first nervous breakdown meant that it could reasonably have been foreseen that the workload was a potential hazard for this employee. Mr Walker received an out of court settlement of £175,000.

(*Source:* Midgley, 1997, p. 36)

If an employee's personal problems result in falling standards at work, or even in an event that could be construed as misconduct, this could result in formal disciplinary action. On the whole, managers prefer to handle such issues in an informal manner to preserve good working relationships, and regard formal discipline as an action to be taken if the informal approach fails. This approach is encouraged by the ACAS guidelines on discipline (2004). You will find a fuller discussion of this in Chapter 13. It should suffice to make the point here that the proper use of counselling may obviate the need to embark on formal disciplinary action. According to the Inland Revenue Service (2007) at least one in five employers do provide employee assistance programmes (EAPs) though most are actually funded by the employer and are provided on their behalf by external suppliers. Typically about 10 per cent of the workforce use the EAP in any year but the popularity of EAPs has increased with employers after a legal case in 2002, when it was argued that just having an EAP provided sufficient defence for an employer against stress compensation claims. This was subsequently modified in a 2007 case so that it is not now possible just to rely on this as a defence in stress management cases. Typically the EAP service provided involves help with counselling, often by providing access to telephone helplines and to specialist advisers. Since corporate manslaughter is now a criminal offence employers should certainly be diligent in their responsibilities regarding any health, safety or welfare issues that could result in death and should of course take their responsibilities for all health, safety and welfare issues equally seriously.

Finally, we can justify an employer's interest in the well-being of employees with reference to the basic need to develop good working relationships, on the part of individual employees, individual managers, and from a corporate point of view. Abraham Maslow (1954) was one of the first writers to describe motivation in terms of human needs, and these concepts have often been applied to the workplace. One of the needs that Maslow identified is the social need for relationships, and indeed the importance of relationships has been reinforced by the inclusion of this factor in the HSE's list of aspects of stress management. A number of surveys on motivation have identified the importance of good relationships at work, and specifically the relationship between supervisor and subordinate. It is not inappropriate to care about the people we work with. Much has also been written about corporate image, and many employers wish to be recognised as 'good employers', especially since corporate image can affect an organisation's ability to attract and retain good employees and can therefore have a major impact on the success of the organisation.

The reasons for employers to be involved with employees' problems can be summarised as follows:

● to address problems with productivity, standards of work, attendance and turnover
● to meet legal obligations to ensure the health, safety and welfare of employees
● to avoid the development of disciplinary problems
● to maintain good employee relations.

Types of problem and their sources

There can be an infinite range of personal problems faced by workers which could affect their work. Many will arise from sources outside the organisation, such as family breakdown, alcoholism, drug abuse, care duties or bereavement, while others might be the result of bullying, working conditions, excessive workload or some form of discrimination in the workplace. The HR department needs to be clear about each of these issues and have policies and procedures in place to deal with issues such as alcoholism or drug abuse and should certainly also have effective policies to prevent unfair discrimination or bullying within work. It is not within the scope of this textbook to deal with all these specific issues but one area which has caused a lot of concern recently is the area of stress, which we shall focus on next. As you saw in the case of *Walker* v. *Northumberland County Council*, there can be serious repercussions for both the employee and the organisation if an employer fails to deal with stress in an appropriate way.

Stress and stress management

Stress is one major area of concern, and can be regarded as an umbrella term for a range of problems. Stress is manifested when people are dealing with so many pressures that their normal behaviour patterns become affected. Hans Selye (1956 and 1974), a noted writer on stress, used the terms 'eustress' and 'distress' to explain that stress is not always a negative concept. Sometimes people are stimulated by having to deal with a number of issues; this can be exciting and motivating. When it becomes too much and one cannot cope and at the same time continue to behave within the range of one's normal behaviour patterns, this is what Selye refers to as distress. This is what we normally mean when we refer to stress these days (Le Fevre *et al.*, 2003).

What are the causes of stress? There are a wide range of factors that cause stress both in personal relationships and in work relationships (see Figure 12.1); these factors are referred to as stressors. Holmes and Rahe (1967) identified a number of life events as being sources of stress. Ranked at number one as a source of stress was the death of one's spouse, and other factors identified included divorce, taking on a high mortgage and taking a holiday.

Figure 12.1 Some causes of stress

It is also recognised that circumstances at work such as poor relationships, especially with one's manager or supervisor, and overwork or underemployment can contribute to stress. The case of John Walker mentioned earlier is an example of too high a work-load combined with the demanding nature of the work contributing to stress.

The symptoms of stress include the behavioural changes we previously identified that might alert you to the fact that a colleague is under pressure. If not dealt with, the end result can be physical or mental illness leading to mental breakdown.

The Health and Safety Executive (HSE) has played a major role in the develop-ment of guidelines for employers on various aspects of stress management. The duty of care addressed in the Health and Safety at Work Act 1974 applies to employees' physical and mental well-being, and since these can be affected by stress caused by workplace factors, the duty of care constitutes an obvious legal obligation to pay attention to stress management. The Management of Health and Safety at Work Reg-ulations 1999 also impose a duty on employers to conduct a risk audit on potential hazards in the workplace, which also applies in this area as the effects of stress can be regarded as a hazard.

The main focus of the Health and Safety Executive has been on the development of standards for employers to achieve in terms of stress management, and after a series of consultation and pilot exercises, the HSE (2005) launched an official set of standards.

Organisations can use these standards to measure their achievements in terms of stress management. The stress management standards are not legally enforce-able on organisations, but the HSE may use them as evidence that an organisation is not fulfilling its duty with regard to stress management. The HSE has already issued an improvement order against one organisation for failing to manage stress

Did you know?

According to the Health and Safety Executive (2005):

- About one in five people say that they find work either very or extremely stressful.
- Over half a million people report experiencing work-related stress at a level that they believe has actually made them ill.
- Each case of stress-related illness leads to an average of 29 working days lost. A total of 13.4 million working days were lost to stress, depression and anxiety in 2001.

adequately: West Dorset Hospitals NHS Trust in 2003 (reported by Hayden-Smith and Simms, 2003), though Income Data Services (2004) report that the Trust has since remedied the situation with suitable interventions.

The standards address six areas of work that should be audited. These are laid out with a brief description of what each entails in Table 12.1. The basic idea is to ascertain what percentages of staff feel that they are able to cope with any work situations in these six areas. According to the International Stress Management Organisation (2004), 'the target is for all organisations to match the performance of the top 20% of employers that are successfully minimalising work-related stress.' Organisations must also be able to show that they have systems in place locally to respond to any individual concerns and should be carrying out risk assessments for stress. As Quinn (2004) points out, the identification of stress factors

Table 12.1 HSE stress management standards

Area of work	The standard	Desirable outcomes that organisations should be working towards
Demands This is about demands caused by the workload, work pattern or the work environment.	Employees should be able to indicate that they can cope with the demands of their job. There should also be systems in place to help deal with individual concerns.	The organisation should ensure hours of work are reasonable and that demands made on the workers are not excessive. There should be a matching of people's skills to their jobs. There should be systems set up to address concerns that workers may have so that these can be resolved.
Control This is about how much influence an individual has about their job.	Employees should be able to indicate that they get a say in the way they do their work. There should also be systems in place to respond to individual concerns.	Individuals should have control over their pace of work wherever possible. They should get opportunities to use their skills and initiative in their work. They should be encouraged to develop new skills so they can undertake new or more challenging work. The employees should also have a say about when breaks should be taken and be consulted about their work patterns.
Support This concerns the support mechanisms, or lack of them, from colleagues, line managers, and others such as HR staff. It is also about levels of employee awareness about support.	Employees should be able to indicate that they receive adequate support and information from colleagues and superiors. There should also be evidence of systems in place to adequately address employee concerns.	There should be policies and procedures in place to adequately support staff and there should also be systems in place to enable and encourage managers to support staff. Since support is also sometimes provided by colleagues there should be systems in place to encourage employees to support others. Employees should know how to access resources necessary to do their job and should also get regular and constructive feedback.

Table 12.1   Continued

Area of work	The standard	Desirable outcomes that organisations should be working towards
Relationships This is about encouraging positive behaviour so that conflict is avoided and about creating ways to deal with unacceptable behaviour.	Employees should be able to indicate that they are not subjected to unacceptable behaviour at work such as bullying or harassment and that there are systems in place to deal with these issues.	The organisation should promote positive behaviour to ensure fairness and avoid conflict and employees share information about their work. The organisation should have policies in place to prevent or resolve unacceptable behaviour and employees should be able to report unacceptable behaviour.
Role This concerns the extent to which people understand their role and whether the organisation ensures the individual does not have conflicting roles.	Employees should be able to indicate that they understand their role and responsibilities and there should be systems in place to address individual concerns.	The organisation should try to ensure as far as possible that the different requirements it places on employees are compatible and clear and that the individual understands them. If they have concerns about role conflict or about their role then they should be able to raise them.
Change How much change are employees expected to cope with, and how well prepared are they when they do have to deal with change? Are the arrangements for information sharing and consultation adequate?	Employees should be able to show that the organisation consults with them frequently when undergoing organisational change and that there are systems in place to respond to any concerns they may have.	The organisation should be consulting adequately and providing opportunities for individuals to contribute to and influence the changes. This information needs to be timely and sufficient for employees to understand the reasons for the changes and the likely impact on their jobs. Employees also need to be aware of the timetable for changes and have suitable access to support during the change period.

Source: Adapted from HSE (2005) *Tackling Stress – The Management Standards Approach*.

through such an audit makes the eventuality of stress foreseeable, so employers would be obligated to take some action in such an instance.

Pause for thought 12.5   Consider any organisation in which you have worked. To what extent to you think that organisation has considered each of the stress management standards?

What is your evidence for this?

How does this compare with the views of others in your class about organisations in which they have worked? Did job roles seem clear and unambiguous? Were you made aware of structures to support you?

As you can see from these standards there are a great many implications for HR departments to ensure that they have not only policies in place but also that they have designed jobs well to ensure there is no role incompatibility or work overload, that individuals understand their roles through induction and subsequent training and that there are support systems in place for those who may be experiencing problems. Management also need training to ensure they respond in an appropriate way to those suffering from stress. This means that they need to recognise that just increasing workloads and hoping that the person can cope is not a satisfactory way to manage but that there is a need for proper analyses of the job and the workload, and to match these to the person's capabilities.

An additional factor to do with employer obligations is that employment tribunals hearing cases of unfair dismissal would expect employers to have conducted a full investigation of the circumstances surrounding an incident of alleged misconduct or incompetence. The investigation should have shown whether this may have arisen as a result of personal problems or stress, particularly in the case of a person who previously had a good work record. Employers would be expected to take any such extenuating circumstances into consideration. You can read more about this in Chapter 14. The point about legal obligations could be summarised in the statement that employers have a duty of care.

The Chartered Institute of Personnel and Development in conjunction with the HSE (2007b) have sponsored a research project to develop a competencies framework for stress management. This aims to identify and develop the behaviour needed by managers for reducing and preventing stress at work and this is part of ongoing research in this area.

Organisational policy and procedures

Policy statements and procedures provide guidelines for all employees. They let managers know how to handle problems, and inform everyone about the help, assistance and support they can expect to receive including the things in the stress management standards. There is a dual role for policies as far as situations requiring counselling are concerned. First, there is a need for policies relating directly to the provision of counselling and, second, an organisation should have policies dealing with workplace behaviour or events that have been identified as causing distress. For instance, in a *Guardian* Careers Section article, Professor Cary Cooper was quoted as saying that bullying probably accounted for a third to a half of all stress-related illness (Venning, 1995).

Did you know?

Some occupational groups and industry groups are more prone to stress than others. According to the HSE, groups that suffer particularly high levels of stress include teachers and nurses, professional and managerial groups, particularly those in the public sector.

(*Source*: HSE, 2007)

Policies on bullying and sexual/racial harassment can help to eliminate these unwanted behaviours and promote a less stressful working environment. Many organisations such as banks and retail outlets, where staff handle cash and at the same time have direct contact with the public, have recognised that specialised counselling is necessary to deal with the trauma their employees can suffer after an episode involving violence or a threat of violence. This is true when they have either been directly threatened or witnessed an incident. Employers will obviously have to decide which issues are most important for their organisations, and this may involve surveying employees to discover which issues are of concern to them, and which solutions the employees would most like to take advantage of. The package of welfare policies, procedures and benefits an employer offers to employees is often referred to as an 'employee assistance programme'.

Policies should also address the following issues:

- who will be involved in providing counselling, and what are the parameters of their roles
- what type of services will be offered
- issues of confidentiality. (Seenan, 2004)

Health promotion

So far, we have focused primarily on approaches to safety and welfare in response to legal requirements and as a way for employers to ensure that they motivate their workers. Recent legislation does encourage employers to be proactive about safety and to carry out risk assessments and then take action to reduce or eliminate risks identified. Many good employers take this a stage further and not only promote measures to promote improvements in safety and welfare but also encourage developments to ensure good health among their workforces.

The high cost of absenteeism is a strong financial reason for taking measures to promote and improve health. Many employers have provided health screening services and membership of private health insurance schemes for their managers, and some are extending this provision to the workforce as a whole. Increasingly, organisations are actively trying to promote a healthier lifestyle among their employees. Among the measures that have been tried are:

- help for smokers to quit, with support/self-help groups and psychologists giving advice and support
- a healthy diet, with a wider choice of health foods on the menu at work
- membership of a health club or purchase of multi-gym exercise equipment for employees to use to get fitter
- stress management programmes
- policies and education programmes on HIV/Aids
- policies and education on substance abuse.

In organisations where these programmes have been made available to all the workforce on a long-term basis, there have been benefits to employees' health, with weight reduction and improvements in blood cholesterol and blood pressure levels, and also improvements in absenteeism rates. It is claimed that the cost of the introduction of this type of programme is more than offset by the savings from lower rates of absenteeism. The CIPD (2004) stated that 'a survey of 97 organisations showed that employees who were participating in "wellness" programmes each incurred between £1,335 and £2,910 less per year in healthcare and absenteeism costs than colleagues who were not participating.'

Absence management

While prevention is always better than cure one of the areas that many HR departments are also becoming increasingly interested in, and which can be used in a complementary way to a wellness programme, is absence management. Westminster City Council 'introduced improved absence management procedures which have reduced its absence rate by more than two days per person per annum and saved it £800,000 annually' (Inland Revenue Service, 2007b). They achieved this by using a mixture of approaches such as the introduction of an employee assistance programme and a new absence management programme which involved return to work interviews and earlier and more positive use of the occupational health department and trigger points. This meant that 'once an employee had more than seven cumulative days' sickness absence in any rolling period, then an enhanced sickness management procedure kicks in. And if sickness absence exceeds 20 days in any one episode, then long-term sickness management procedure applies. Further, when more than eight days of sickness have been recorded over the rolling 365-day period the employee's manager will refer the employee to the council's in-house occupational health service.'

The occupational health strategy

While the numbers of accidents in the workplace has dropped steadily, there is now a focus on achieving the same effect for work-related illness. In 2000 one of the priorities of the HSE was to improve this situation and an Occupational Health Strategy was devised to:

1 Stop people from becoming ill because of work.
2 Help those who are absent due to long-term illness to get back into work.
3 Improve work opportunities for those who are not currently in employment because of their ill-health or disability.
4 Use the workplace to encourage people to maintain or improve their health.

This approach is based once again on the idea of partnership between Government, the HSE and employers, workers and trade unions. Targets were set to inspire action and five key programmes were started to complement other Government initiatives, such as the Welfare to Work schemes. The five programmes of work which were established were about:

1 compliance
2 continuous improvement
3 knowledge
4 skills
5 support.

Targets were also set and it is hoped that all interested parties will be involved in working towards their achievement. It is hoped that by 2010 the following targets will be achieved:

● A 20 per cent reduction in the incidence of work-related ill-health.
● A 20 per cent reduction in the ill-health of members of the public that has been caused by work activity.
● A 30 per cent reduction in the numbers of days absence caused by work-related ill-health.
● All who are employed but who are unable to work because of their ill-health or disability should be made aware of opportunities for speedy rehabilitation back into work.
● Everyone who is not employed because of their ill-health or disability should be offered opportunities to prepare for and find work.

It has been estimated that if just three of these targets are achieved, the value to the UK could be huge and worth somewhere between £8.6 and £21.8 billion, although it is obviously very difficult to calculate such figures with any degree of accuracy.

A Partnership Board was established, not only to oversee the implementation and delivery of the strategy but also as a way of drawing on ideas from a range of interested parties. The roles of the Partnership Board are to:

● be strategic
● act as a champion
● use contacts to network and solve problems
● review progress overall
● make sure that sound management practices, such as evaluation, are fully used
● provide regular reports on progress to the HSC.

> **Did you know?**
>
> A casino worker, Michael Dunn, received £50,000 in an out-of-court settlement after he developed asthma as a result of passive smoking at work.
>
> (*Source:* Cacanas, Z., 2004)

Failure to take steps to reduce risks in the workplace is likely in the future to lead to higher insurance payments for organisations as insurance companies start to link premiums to the way that organisations manage risks of accidents and ill-health. Smokers generally suffer worse health than non-smokers and the charity Action on Smoking and Health (ASH) claims that 34 million working days are lost in Britain each year, just because of smoking. Some employers are becoming more proactive about their employees' health and are introducing measures such as bonuses to encourage smokers to quit. These can, however, prove controversial as non-smokers may then also want to benefit from bonuses.

International issues in health and safety

Although British health and safety legislation does not apply to workers based outside Britain, employers still have a duty of care towards their employees, no matter where they work. Employees who operate in a global scene need additional knowledge relating to the particular country in which they are working, and this also applies to health and safety. The HR departments in those organisations need to check on health and safety legislation in the countries concerned, and should also carry out a risk assessment of not only the job but also the country, and should evaluate the employee's health. This would help ensure, for example, that they are not sending an asthmatic employee into a very dusty desert environment that would probably make the employee's health worse.

There are also social and ethical responsibilities that large organisations need to take into account when some of their products such as clothing or food is being produced in third world countries for them. Although they produce goods at cheap prices for those in the developed world, this is often at the expense of the workers in that country, by paying people poorly and by allowing them to work in poor health or safety conditions that would not be tolerated in the UK.

Even within Europe we have seen that individual countries can interpret European directives in different ways so the actual health and safety legislation in countries may vary. Attitudes to safety can be different and vary from one culture to another. In cultures where people tend to sue for damages, such as America, people are used to having lots of rules even when they are relaxing, away from work, so on beaches they only swim in the designated areas and obey the lifeguards. In the Greek islands, tourists would seek their own sheltered cove and swim from their own secluded beach so would have to take more responsibility for their own safety. Such differences in cultural expectations do shape attitudes to health and safety, so it is important to take into account the culture of the country and consider this in relation to health and safety. When Disney first opened in Paris some of the instructions on rides such as the requirement 'to exit the ride using your left foot first' jarred a little with Europeans who were used to making such decisions for themselves!

Some employees are sent to work in countries which may be regarded as high risk and where dangers such as kidnapping could occur. Staff need to be briefed as to precautions to take in these countries, as do the local staff, who may actually be more at risk than the ex-pat staff, who probably live in a secure compound and have a driver to transport them safely. Some groups such as humanitarian aid workers are also likely to be at risk, since the nature of their jobs ensure that they are likely to be working in high-risk areas. However, they should still not be exposed to unnecessary risks.

HR departments who have staff working in potentially high-risk countries should carry out risk assessments, relating both to the dangers to health and to potential threats to safety, and should devise suitable emergency plans which can be put in place quickly. They should also devise suitable training programmes, perhaps drawing on local knowledge and expertise, for people undertaking these jobs. The workforce could even be involved in analysing the hazards and designing their own security plans for the compounds in which they live. Training in potential high-risk countries is likely to cover specific issues such as personal safety, office security, compound security, threats to convoys, risk analysis, first aid and emergency evacuation plans.

If this is done the workers are likely to feel and be safer and since health and safety will be perceived as being important, it is likely that they will take more care themselves. Measures such as these can do a great deal to eliminate unnecessary risks, although it is impossible to eliminate all risks completely.

Did you know?

In response to the killings of three UN workers in West Timor on 6 September 2000, humanitarian workers from around the world marched in protest for better protection. They sent a petition to the UN headquarters demanding 'greater pressure from the UN on national governments to guarantee the safety of humanitarian workers, together with internal measures addressing management accountability, risk assessment and more funding for security provision'.

(*Source*: Hammond, D., 2001)

Conclusion

We said at the beginning of this chapter that it is not enough for employers just to be concerned about preventing accidents in order to comply with legislation, although that in itself is a good start. We have shown in this chapter that there has been a change of approach within the law, from mere compliance with minimum legal requirements in the legislation prior to HASAWA to the encouragement of increased involvement of all, and from compliance with legal requirements 'so far as it is reasonably practicable' under HASAWA to placing the duty on managers that they must introduce management systems, implement these systems and monitor the effectiveness of them.

Although the newer legislation is more forceful and hence more prescriptive, in some respects it is more in tune with the human resource management approach, since there is an emphasis on the need for managers to manage, on the development of strategies, procedures and systems for improving health and safety, as well as on a need for monitoring the implementation of these systems. This approach to health and safety should link with the overall business objectives of maximising efficiency and effectiveness by improving morale and reducing costs, and also allows for some scope for individuality and flexibility in how this is to be achieved. It is the approach to health and safety that we would advocate, and it is a very different approach to the purely legalistic one of just being concerned with not breaking the law. This approach to health and safety involves the following features:

- The need to create a culture in which health and safety are seen to be important to the organisation. The safety policy statement will contribute to this if it is effectively written, known about and acted upon. The legal requirements must be complied with and risk assessments carried out, as well as gathering information about health and safety and carrying out a cost–benefit analysis. If there is to be a culture of health and safety awareness, there also need to be campaigns and publicity, and involvement of top management, individuals and teams. There needs to be regular communications and discussion of health and safety and the contribution that improvements will make to the organisation's overall effectiveness, so that all members of the organisation realise that health and safety are important to the way it operates.
- Commitment from the top to the achievement of progressively higher standards as expressed in the mission statement and safety policy. Top management must not only sign the policy documents but also set a good example in relation to health and safety, and emphasise that it is an area of importance to them and to the future of the organisation by showing their interest and by setting up new systems and monitoring the effectiveness of these systems.
- Commitment throughout the organisation, with all parties clear about their own responsibilities for health and safety, the targets they have to meet and the contribution these make to the organisation's objectives. This should be considered as an aspect of performance management, as individuals and teams would be encouraged to take responsibility for their own actions and to agree and work towards targets when making improvements.
- Managers to demonstrate by their example their commitment to the importance of a safer and healthier work environment. They should also find ways to motivate everyone to make a contribution to health and safety improvements. Prizes and awards to individuals and teams can have an important effect.
- Policies and procedures designed to take account of the importance of a safer and healthier environment. There should also be effective systems to monitor their effectiveness.
- Policies to be backed by adequate resources for equipment and training. Provision of good health and safety costs money but the cost of not providing these can be higher, as any cost–benefit analysis is likely to prove.
- The setting of realistic and attainable targets for everyone in the organisation.
- Encouragement of all to take responsibility for their own actions and involvement of all in health and safety.

The approach of the HSE to revitalising health and safety also reinforces these points. They encourage employers to become aware of health and safety issues by emphasising the business case for health and safety. They also encourage managers to be proactive about managing both the health and safety of their workforce. National targets have been set as part of the process to reduce both the number of accidents and the number of days of sickness absence. Involvement and partnership are both approaches which are strongly encouraged and these methods are typical of the HRM approach.

REVIEW QUESTIONS

1 Interview people (friends, family or work colleagues from a range of organisations) about their own responsibilities in relation to health and safety and then about their perceptions of other people's roles in their particular organisation. Try to establish how the roles relating to health and safety differ for managers, other employees, human resource managers, safety officers, safety representatives and someone designated to be a 'competent person'. Are these roles the same in different types of organisation? How do they compare with what we said earlier in the chapter about these roles?

2 Obtain a copy of the safety policy for either your college or your workplace.
   (a) Use this to identify the roles of various people in the organisation in relation to health and safety.
   (b) Use the safety policy to assess whether health and safety are linked to the organisation's strategic objectives.

3 Design a checklist for carrying out a safety inspection in the workplace. Use your checklist to actually carry out an inspection of a designated area either at work or in your college. Write a report about your findings for the safety officer.

4 Write a short report in which you assess the impact of one piece of health and safety legislation on an organisation of your choice.

5 Prepare arguments and then debate the following statements in two teams. Try to persuade the members of the other team to your point of view.

   TEAM A: There is much too much legislation regarding health and safety at work and this is unnecessary as it is in the employers' interests to look after their employees. Legislation merely hinders employers in their ability to run their businesses effectively.
   TEAM B: Legislation is necessary to control employers who would otherwise ignore health and safety issues at the expense of their employees' health, safety and welfare.

SELF-CHECK QUESTIONS

Answer the following multiple-choice and short-answer questions. The correct responses are given on pages 478–479 for you to check your understanding of this chapter.

1 Which of the following was the first piece of legislation designed to protect every-one at work, and also to protect others who were not at work, such as customers or passers-by?
   (a) the Factories Act 1961
   (b) the Offices, Shops and Railways Premises Act 1963
   (c) the Fire Precautions Act 1971

(d) the Health and Safety at Work Act 1974

(e) the Control of Substances Hazardous to Health Regulations 1988.

2 Which of the following pieces of legislation established the Health and Safety Commission?

(a) the Factories Act 1961

(b) the Offices, Shops and Railways Premises Act 1963

(c) the Fire Precautions Act 1971

(d) the Health and Safety at Work Act 1974

(e) the Control of Substances Hazardous to Health Regulations 1988.

3 An improvement notice is issued when:

(a) something is found to be so dangerous that the factory inspectorate feels it necessary to stop work immediately

(b) improvements are required by the factory inspectorate but the employer can decide when these should take place

(c) improvements are required by the factory inspectorate within a specified period to bring the equipment or process up to the required standard

(d) the required improvement has been made by the employer

(e) improvements are required by the safety committee to be made within a specified period.

4 The term 'so far as it is reasonably practicable to do so' means:

(a) that employers must do everything in their power to make the workplace safe

(b) that employers may weigh up the costs of a safety improvement against the risks when deciding whether to make the improvement

(c) that employers must assess the risks of substances used and identify the required precautions to be taken

(d) that employers have a legal duty to predict what may go wrong before it happens

(e) that employers should be proactive and actively manage health and safety issues.

5 The Management of Health and Safety at Work Regulations contain the following legal requirement:

(a) that employers must do the best that they can to make the workplace safe

(b) that employers may weigh up the costs of a safety improvement against the risks when deciding whether to make a safety improvement

(c) that employers must assess the risks of any substances used by employees and identify the required precautions to be taken

(d) that employers should carry out an assessment of health and safety risks to both employees and the public

(e) that employers should carry out an assessment of health and safety risks for their employees only.

6 The term 'six-pack' refers to the following six pieces of legislation:

(a) the Factories Act 1961, the Offices Shops and Railways Premises Act 1963, the Fire Precautions Act 1971, the Health and Safety at Work Act 1974, the Control of Substances Hazardous to Health Regulations 1988, the Manual Handling Operations Regulations 1992

(b) the Factories Act 1961, the Offices Shops and Railways Premises Act 1963, the Fire Precautions Act 1971, the Health and Safety at Work Act 1974, the Control of Substances Hazardous to Health Regulations 1988, the Management of Health and Safety at Work Regulations 1992

→

(c) the Factories Act 1961, the Health and Safety at Work Act 1974, the Control of Substances Hazardous to Health Regulations 1988, the Management of Health and Safety at Work Regulations 1992, Workplace (Health, Safety and Welfare) Regulations 1992, Provision and Use of Work Equipment Regulations 1992

(d) Management of Health and Safety at Work Regulations 1992, Workplace (Health, Safety and Welfare) Regulations 1992, Provision and Use of Work Equipment Regulations 1992, Personal Protective Equipment at Work Regulations 1992, Health and Safety (Display Screen Equipment) Regulations 1992, Manual Handling Operations Regulations 1992

(e) the Health and Safety at Work Act 1974, the Control of Substances Hazardous to Health Regulations 1988, Management of Health and Safety at Work Regulations 1992, Workplace (Health, Safety and Welfare) Regulations 1992, Provision and Use of Work Equipment Regulations 1992, Personal Protective Equipment at Work Regulations 1992.

Refer back to Case study 12.1 (page 385) and answer the following questions.

7 Describe what the role of the safety committee should have been within the Sheffley Company.

8 Imagine that you are a consultant brought in to advise about health and safety at the Sheffley Company. Write a report to the director in which you outline the improvements that should be made in health and safety at Sheffley, and recommend how these improvements should be introduced.

HR IN THE NEWS

FT

Health and safety red tape

Government attempts to reduce the burden of health and safety legislation are having little effect, according to the Federation of Small Businesses.

Almost three-quarters of small companies surveyed by the FSB said the administrative requirements of health and safety legislation were more bureaucratic than five years ago.

A separate FSB report claimed that small companies on average spent seven hours a week dealing with red tape.

The study is part of a federation campaign to push the UK government and the European Commission to deliver on their promises to reduce the regulatory burden.

Tina Sommer, EU affairs chairman for the FSB, said: 'There is no doubt that the volume and complexity of red tape is excessive. Shorter, simpler regulations will enable businesses to follow the rules more easily as well as protect their existing employees.'

(*Financial Times*, 6 October 2007. Reproduced with permission.)

Union hits at labour safety stance

By Andrew Taylor

Failure to introduce tougher laws to punish company directors who do not follow safety rules has cost workers' lives, according to a union report that criticises the 'voluntary approach' adopted by the Health and Safety Executive.

The report by UCATT, the construction union, coincides with voluntary guidance notes for directors due to be published on Monday by the HSE and the Institute of Directors.

The safety body, which is due later this week to publish national injury figures, has reported an 11 per cent rise in the number of employees killed at work during the 12 months to the end of April.

Ministers rejected union calls to make directors personally liable for safety breaches when the corporate manslaughter and homicide bill was passed in July.

Monday's report, commissioned by UCATT from the Centre for Corporate Accountability, says the HSE had revealed that only 44 per cent of companies had appointed a director responsible for safety since it introduced its voluntary guidelines in 2001.

The union's report finds that accident levels fell by 25 per cent on average at companies that had taken 'positive action at director level regarding health and safety'.

Alan Ritchie, UCATT general secretary, said: 'This damning report demonstrates the government's failure to introduce statutory legal duties forcing directors to take responsibility for their companies' health and safety policies is literally costing workers their lives.'

The Health and Safety Commission, which oversees the HSE, reported earlier this summer that 241 lives had been lost at work during the 12 months to the end of April. This compared with a record low of 217 deaths the previous year.

UCATT said the results were particularly poor in the construction industry, where 347 workers had been killed between 2002–03 and 2006–07. Only 13 directors or senior managers had been prosecuted for health and safety breaches during that period, it added.

Judith Hackitt, of the Health and Safety Commission, recognised that some groups 'believe that the approach we are currently taking is by no means strong enough' but said the corporate manslaughter bill would 'make it easier to prosecute companies'.

Miles Templeman, director general of the IoD, said it was 'vital that board members should lead the approach of their organisation to health and safety'.

(FT.com, 29 October 2007. Reproduced with permission.)

Question

1 These two articles show very different attitudes to health and safety. To what extent do you agree with either of these articles? Do you think that there is too much red tape regarding health and safety or that there is too little protection for workers? List the arguments for and against your point of view.

WHAT NEXT?

Do you remember the balanced scorecard that we discussed in Chapter 1? Research conducted by Aberdeen University on 13 offshore oil installations applies the balanced scorecard to occupational health. The article also discusses the results of interviews with UK and Norwegian managers on health and safety performance indicators and the reasons for including occupational health and safety as one measure of performance within the balanced scorecard. What do you think about the idea that measures of occupational health should be included in an assessment of an organisation's performance?

Mearns, K. and J.I. Havold (2003) Occupational health and safety and the balanced scorecard, *The TQM Magazine,* Vol. 15, No. 6, 408–423.

References

Advisory, Conciliation and Arbitration Service (2004) Discipline and Grievances at Work, *The ACAS Advisory Handbook,* ACAS.

Baker, J. (2007) Net closes on corporate killing, *People Management,* Vol. 13, No. 5, 8 March, 22.

Cacanas, Z. (2004) *The Guardian,* 24 July.

Chartered Institute of Personnel and Development (2006) *Occupational Health and Organisational Effectiveness,* CIPD (available at www.cipd.co.uk; accessed 10.09.07).

Chartered Institute of Personnel and Development (2007a) *DWP work-health review launched,* CIPD (www.cipd.co.uk/news; accessed on 17.04.07).

Chartered Institute of Personnel and Development and Health and Safety Executive (2007b) *Managing stress at work: a competency framework for line managers,* CIPD (www.cipd.co.uk/subjects/health/stress/_lnstrwkcmptn.htm; accessed 10.09.07).

Chartered Institute of Personnel and Development (2007c) *Gangmaster legislation should be extended,* CIPD, 31 July (www.cipd.co.uk/news/_articles/gangmasterlegislationshouldbe extended.htm; accessed 10.09.07).

Department for the Environment, Transport and the Regions (2000) *Revitalising Health and Safety: Strategy Statement June 2000,* DETR (www.hse.gov.uk/revitalising/strategy.pdf; accessed 10.09.07).

Eagle, M. (2007) *Justice for Corporate Deaths: Royal Assent for Corporate Manslaughter and Corporate Homicide Act* (www.justice.gov.uk/news/newsrelease260707b.htm; accessed 10.09.07).

Engineering Employers' Federation (2001) *Managing Stress at Work,* EEF.

Fowler, A. (1994) Personnel's model army, *Personnel Management,* September, 34–3.

Hammond, D. (2001) Dangerous liaisons, *People Management,* 30 May, 26–7.

Hayden-Smith, J. and R. Simms (2003) Pressure points, *People Management,* 25 September, 17.

Health and Safety Commission (2000) *Revitalising Health and Safety: Strategy Statement,* HSE.

Health and Safety Commission (2001) *Strategic Plan 2001–4,* HSE (www.hse.gov.uk/aboutus/plans/hscplans/plan0104-07.htm; accessed 10.09.07).

Health and Safety Commission (2002) *Enforcement Policy Statement,* HSE (www.hse.gov.uk/pubns/hsc15.pdf; accessed 10.09.07).

Health and Safety Commission (2004a) *Accident Costs: Work Out Yours, Revitalising Health and Safety,* HSE (www.hse.gov.uk/costs/accidentcost_calc/accident_costs_intro.asp; accessed 10.09.07).

Health and Safety Executive (1995) *Be Safe: Save Money. The Costs of Accidents: A Guide for Small Firms,* HSE Books, 4.

Health and Safety Executive (2003) *Stating Your Business. Guidance on Preparing a Health and Safety Policy Document for Small Firms,* HSE, INDG 324 (available at www.hse.gov.uk; accessed 20.07.04).

Health and Safety Executive (2004) *A Strategy for Workplace Health and Safety in Great Britain to 2010 and Beyond,* HSE.

Health and Safety Executive (2005) *Tackling Stress: The Management Standards Approach* (available at www.hse.gov.uk/pubns/indg406.htm; accessed 10.09.07).

Health and Safety Executive (2006a) *HSE Statistics,* HSE (available at www.hse.gov.uk/statistics; accessed 10.09.07).

Health and Safety Executive (2006b) *Five Steps to Risk Assessment,* HSE, INDG 163 rev. 2 (available at www.hse.gov.uk/pubns/indg163.htm; accessed 10.09.07).

Health and Safety Executive (2006c) *HSE Statistic: Occupational Health Bulletin 2005/6,* HSE (available at www.hse.gov.uk/statistics/overall/ohsb0506.htm; accessed 10.09.07).

Health and Safety Executive (2007) *Statistics: Stress-related and psychological disorders,* HSE (available at www.hse.gov.uk/causdis/stress.htm; accessed 10.09.07).

Holmes, T.H. and R.H. Rahe (1967) The social readjustment rating scale, *Journal of Psychosomatic Research,* August, 216.

Incomes Data Services (2002) *IDS Studies Plus: Employee Assistance Programmes,* IDS.

Incomes Data Services (2004) *IDS HR Studies 775: Managing Stress,* IDS.

Inland Revenue Service Employment Review (2007a) *Employee assistance programmes: the IRS report,* IRS 874, 04.06.07.

Inland Revenue Service Employment Review (2007b) *Westminster City council's successful absence management procedure,* IRS 877, 16.07.07.

International Stress Management Association UK (2004) *Working together to reduce stress at work,* International Stress Management Association UK.

Johnson, R. (2001) Security counsel, *People Management,* Vol. 7, No. 11, 31 May.

Jones, R. (2007) Manslaughter Act doesn't go far enough, *Personnel Today,* 6 March.

Le Fevre, M., J. Matheny and G.S. Kolt (2003) Eustress, distress, and interpretation in occupational stress, *Journal of Managerial Psychology,* Vol. 18, No. 7, 726–744.

Maslow, A. (1954) *Motivation and Personality,* 2nd edition, Harper & Row.

Midgley, S. (1997) Pressure points, *People Management,* 10 July, 36–39.

Ministry of Justice (2007) Justice for Corporate Deaths: Royal Assent for Corporate Manslaughter and Corporate Homicide Act, Ministry of Justice (www.justice.gov.uk/news/newsrelease260707b.htm; accessed 12.09.07).

Morris, D. (2001) How to draw up a health and safety policy, *People Management,* Vol. 7, No. 10, 17 May.

Nishiyama, K. and J. Johnson (1997) *Karoshi – Death from Overwork: Occupational Health Consequences of the Japanese Production Management,* 6th Draft for International Journal of Health Services, 4 February (available at www.workhealth.org/whatsnew/lpkarosh.html; accessed 10.09.07).

Quinn, J. (2004) Dodging the draft, *People Management,* 30 June, 17.

Sample, I. (2007) Stressful Jobs Double the Risk of Depression for Young Workers, *The Guardian,* 2 August, 10.

Selye, H. (1956) *The Stress of Life,* McGraw-Hill.

Selye, H. (1974) *Stress without Distress,* Lippincott.

Seenan, G. (2004) No frills – and no travelling toilet class, *The Guardian,* 24 July.

Stranks, J. (2007) The Health and Safety Handbook: a practical guide to health and safety law, management policies and procedures, Kogan Page.

Venning, N. (1995) Taking the bull by the horns, *Guardian Careers Section,* 15 April, 2–3.

XpertHR (2004) *How to comply with general health and safety duties,* XpertHR, 03.09.2004 (www.xperthr.co.uk; accessed 29.07.07).

XpertHR (2006) *How to manage workers' statutory entitlement to paid holiday leave,* XpertHR, 16.03.2006 (www.xperthr.co.uk; accessed 29.07.07).

Further study

Books

Advisory, Conciliation and Arbitration Service (2003) *Health and Employment,* ACAS. This booklet focuses on measures that employers can take to help promote good health in their workforce.

Stranks, J. (2006) *The Health and Safety handbook,* Kogan Page. A book and a CD which give clear practical guidance for managers and others who are interested in health and safety.

Stranks, J. (2007) *Human factors and behavioural safety,* Butterworth-Heinemann. This book examines factors such as human behaviour and human error and their impact on safety.

Articles

HSE publications exist on a wide range of topics, too numerous to include here, from general books to detailed explanations of legislation. Some of its leaflets are also available on the web page listed at the end of this chapter.

Internet

Control Risks Group	**www.crg.com**
Employment Conditions Abroad	**www.eca-international.com**
The Health and Safety Executive	**www.hse.gov.uk**
The International Labour Organization's report on teleworking which includes	
health and safety issues	**www.ilo.org/safework/telework**
The Job Stress Network	**www.workhealth.org**

Site with articles about many work and health issues including stress and *karoshi.*

RIDDOR   **www.riddor.gov.uk**

The site gives information about RIDDOR and has forms which can be downloaded to report accidents and dangerous occurrences, or these can now be reported directly online.

XpertHR   **www.xperthr.co.uk**

An excellent source of articles from various publications.

CHAPTER **13**

Discipline and grievance

Objectives

By the end of this chapter you will be able to:

- understand the meaning of the terms 'discipline' and 'grievance'
- understand the role of human resource managers and line managers in discipline and grievance handling
- explain the importance of the ACAS Code of Practice on Disciplinary and Grievance Procedures (2003)
- describe the main stages in a disciplinary procedure and in a grievance procedure
- design a simple disciplinary and grievance procedure.

In any organisation, however good the management and however highly motivated the workforce, there will be occasions when problems or difficulties occur between management and employees. In order that employees are able to work to their optimum performance and that these problems do not turn into even bigger issues, suitable ways of dealing with them need to be devised before they occur. If the problem has arisen from something that management has done, this may result in the employee concerned having a grievance. If, however, it is a problem arising from the behaviour or attitude of an employee, then disciplinary action may be called for.

Human resource managers are concerned to get the best out of people, and although the human resource approach tends towards a dislike of rules and procedures, in favour of a more individualised approach, there are times when this is not possible because of the need to comply with legislation or codes of practice. This is the case where discipline and grievance are concerned. While discipline and grievances are individual issues, it would be unfair to treat each case in a totally different way, and to do so might result in a claim for unfair dismissal against the organisation, or dissatisfaction among the workforce. Human resource managers need to consider these issues and design suitable procedures in order to enhance both the performance management process within the organisation and to enable employees to contribute fully to the strategic objectives of the organisation.

The role of the human resource manager and the line manager

Discipline and grievances are sensitive issues requiring skilful handling, and in many organisations they have traditionally been an area that has been left to human resource managers. This has been partly due to the fact that the human resource managers were likely to be trained in skilful handling of sensitive interpersonal issues, but also many managers and supervisors were often unwilling to tackle something that might result in their unpopularity and cause difficulties in maintaining a suitable relationship with someone they had to work with on a daily basis. This attitude has changed considerably in recent years, as more and more of the human resource function has been devolved to line management; line managers in many organisations are nowadays expected to handle any discipline or grievance situations that arise in their section, at least in the early stages. Human resource managers still have several important roles to play, however:

- in devising the procedures
- in providing specialist advice
- in ensuring that everyone is aware of the procedures and acts consistently
- in ensuring that line managers are suitably trained
- in monitoring the effectiveness of the procedures.

The ACAS Code of Practice recommends that grievance and disciplinary machinery should be kept separate, although some organisations do provide for an appeal against a disciplinary action being handled through the general grievance procedure.

Discipline: introduction and definitions

The *Shorter Oxford English Dictionary* defines discipline in the following ways: 'To subject to discipline; in earlier use, to educate or train; later, to bring under control'. The term 'discipline', as we can see from this definition, can be used in various ways. It can refer to self-discipline, where an individual as a result of practice and training works in a ordered, self-controlled way, or is trained by others to work in a certain way, or it can be used to refer to the need to discipline someone by pointing out to them the error of their ways or by punishing them for mistakes that they have made. Human resource managers are concerned to motivate people to ensure they reach their maximum potential, and the adoption of a punitive approach is unlikely to facilitate much motivation.

Students dealing with case studies about disciplinary situations often tend to respond initially by enjoying the power to punish and often want to dismiss the alleged offenders. Sometimes new, inexperienced managers may adopt the same approach. In reality this approach is likely to prove counterproductive, as valuable staff who have been costly to recruit and train would be lost, and the motivation of everyone concerned would be low. Handling a disciplinary situation in an unfair way may result in the employee being dismissed, but this might also result in a case for unfair dismissal being brought against the organisation. This could be expensive if the organisation lost, and in any case would be expensive in terms of:

- the time needed to prepare for the tribunal
- the time lost

- disruption caused as witnesses are called
- the bad publicity for the organisation itself
- the poor employee relations likely to ensue because of unfair handling of a disciplinary situation.

In order to try to minimise these problems and to encourage employers to handle disciplinary offences in a fair and reasonable manner, the Advisory, Conciliation and Arbitration Service (ACAS) has published codes of practice since 1977 and the *Code of Practice on Disciplinary and Grievance Procedures* was most recently published in 2003 and came into effect in 2004.

Disciplinary procedures and practices

The ACAS Code of Practice on Disciplinary and Grievance Procedures

This aims to help all who may be concerned with this topic by providing practical advice about handling disciplinary and grievance procedures. A code of practice has an interesting status in law. An employer cannot have an unfair dismissal case brought against it in an employment tribunal just because it has not carried out a procedure as stated in the code of practice, but it would ignore the code of practice at its peril, as failure to comply with it is likely to be used as part of the evidence against it in an unfair dismissal case.

In the code, ACAS clearly states that although disciplinary rules are likely to be mainly designed by management, other groups such as trade unions, line managers, workers and employees should also have a part to play in formulating them. ACAS emphasises the fact that the main reason for having disciplinary rules is to promote fairness and set standards of conduct, and to provide a fair and consistent method of dealing with alleged offences. According to ACAS, one of the main reasons for having procedures is to ensure there are orderly employment relations so that everyone knows what is expected of them. If the rules have been designed solely by management without the involvement of other interested parties, employees and workers may be more cynical about management's motives and individuals may feel that when they are disciplined it is because of victimisation, or because their supervisor dislikes them. In order for the disciplinary procedure to be credible to employees and other workers, it is clearly in management's interests to involve them in its design. Good employers will certainly appreciate this need.

Other employers, however, may merely be motivated in their provision of a disciplinary procedure by the need to comply with the legislation. The Employment Rights Act 1996 requires employers who employ 20 or more employees to provide them with a copy of their disciplinary procedure within two months of the commencement of their employment or provide access for the workers to an accessible document, which gives appropriate information. Although smaller employers do not have same the legal compulsion as large employers to provide their employees with a copy of their discipline and grievance procedure, it is still clearly good practice for them to do so. Employment tribunals will take into account the size of the organisation and the administrative resources that are available to the organisation when they consider cases. Small organisations do need to ensure that everyone is aware of the procedures and if they are unable to provide everyone with their own individual copy then they must ensure that there are copies on noticeboards or in other easily accessible places such as on a company intranet site. It is good practice to go through such a procedure with all new employees and ensure that they understand it. It is vital that all employers, regardless of their size, do follow the minimum statutory dismissal and discipline procedures.

These factors should prove sufficient to motivate the employer to provide a disciplinary procedure but, if not, in the last resort some employers may be motivated by the fact that they may need evidence that they have acted fairly and followed a fair procedure in the event of an alleged unfair dismissal claim before an employment tribunal. For whatever reason, it is obviously important to adopt a clear disciplinary procedure so that both the employer and the workforce know what standards of conduct are expected and what may happen if these standards are not achieved.

Pause for thought 13.1 Consider for a moment the word 'worker' and the word 'employee'. What is the difference between the two?

'Worker' applies to all workers whether they are employed on a contract of employment or not. As such it is much broader term than 'employee' since it could apply also to workers who were employed by an agency or who worked as volunteers in a charity. In the ACAS Code of Practice on Disciplinary and Grievance Procedures both these words are used. Some of the provisions in this Code of Practice refer to just employees while others, in particular the right to be accompanied at disciplinary and grievance hearings, apply to all workers.

The essential features of a disciplinary procedure

The ACAS Code of Practice (2003) lists the following as essential features of a disciplinary procedure.

According to ACAS, good disciplinary procedures should:

1 be in writing;
2 specify to whom they apply;
3 be non-discriminatory;
4 ensure matters are dealt with without unnecessary delay;
5 allow for information about proceedings, witness statements and records to be kept confidential;
6 state the disciplinary actions which may be taken;
7 specify the levels of management which have the authority to take the various forms of disciplinary action;
8 provide for workers to be informed of complaints against them and where possible all relevant evidence before any hearing;
9 give workers an opportunity to state their case before a decision is reached;
10 provide for workers to be accompanied;

11 ensure that, except for gross misconduct, no worker is dismissed for a first breach of discipline;

12 ensure that disciplinary action is not taken until the case has been carefully investigated by management;

13 ensure that workers are given an explanation for any penalty imposed;

14 provide a right of appeal – normally to a more senior manager – and specify the procedure to be followed. (Code of Practice on Disciplinary and Grievance Procedures, ACAS, 2003)

It may seem obvious that rules should be in writing and should specify to whom they apply, and that disciplinary issues should be dealt with quickly. If they are not written down people will remember the rules differently, and varying approaches to discipline will occur. Many organisations nowadays will put disciplinary rules on their intranet sites, as well as in their organisational handbooks. Since the management must ensure that these rules are available to everyone, the rules may also need to be translated into other languages where English is not the first language of some of the workers. They should also be explained orally, perhaps for new workers during the induction period. This will be of help to those with a disability such as a visual impairment, who may also require a large print, Braille or an audio-tape version of the procedure, but will also ensure any workers who are unable to read will know of the rules. Employees may otherwise be uncertain as to what they may and may not do, and supervisors and managers may adopt different approaches to discipline between different departments, with some supervisors unsure of what action they have the power to take.

In some rare cases it may be legitimate to have different rules for different departments. A catering department is likely to have additional rules about hygiene that are not likely to be as relevant to a transport department. So the rules should specify to whom they apply.

It is necessary to indicate what disciplinary actions may be taken so that there is a level of consistency and employees know what misdemeanours are regarded as serious by management. In order to be fair, the worker should know of the case against them and have an opportunity to state their case and, if they want, have a trade union official or a friend accompany them.

Workers can make genuine mistakes, and as we have already shown it is extremely expensive to recruit and train staff. On these grounds alone it pays to be fair to workers and to avoid dismissing them wherever possible. In order to give workers a fair chance it is important not to dismiss anyone for a first breach of discipline, unless it is a case of gross misconduct. This ensures that the individual has a chance to learn from his or her mistake.

Management may also occasionally make mistakes, and the worker may not have committed a disciplinary offence at all. To prevent someone being disciplined for something they did not do, it is important to ensure that no disciplinary action is taken before a full investigation into the alleged offence has been carried out.

If workers are to learn from their mistakes, then they need to be very clear about what they did wrong, how to do it right and also to have a clear explanation of any penalties imposed. It is still possible that, in spite of all these precautions, occasionally management may make a mistake in disciplining a person. In order to remedy this and to ensure that people don't feel that they are being disciplined just because their supervisor doesn't like them, it is important to have an appeal procedure that is made known to them.

The Code of Practice also makes clear that, as well as the 14 features listed, a disciplinary procedure should follow what ACAS regards as core principles for reasonable behaviour by:

- using the procedures to help and encourage better standards of work rather than as a punishment
- ensuring that the worker knows of the case against them and has a chance to give their side of the story before any decision is made
- ensuring workers are accompanied by a colleague or trade union official at the hearing itself
- making sure that all the facts of the case are established before any disciplinary action is taken, and that whatever action results is reasonable in the unique circumstances of that case
- ensuring that no one is dismissed for a first offence, unless for a case of gross misconduct
- giving the worker a written explanation for whatever disciplinary action is taken and ensuring they know exactly what improvement is required from them
- providing an opportunity for appeal
- dealing with all issues as thoroughly and promptly as possible
- acting consistently.

It is also vital to follow the requirements of natural justice so employees should be given the chance to talk with someone who has not been, and will not be, involved at all in this issue. They should then be informed of allegations and the evidence against them prior to any meeting. Opportunities for them to challenge the allegations before decisions are reached should also be ensured and, as already mentioned, there should be a right of appeal.

Disciplinary offences

It would be impossible to itemise fully the range of behaviour that might result in disciplinary action being taken. Employers seem to regard the more common offences as being issues about absenteeism, timekeeping or poor performance at work. There may also be concern about a range of issues including failure to obey organisation rules, such as rules about health and safety, email abuse, use of social networking sites during work time, theft, sexism, racism, problems arising from fighting or threatening behaviour, and alcohol or drug abuse. Many employers divide offences into two categories depending on the seriousness with which they are viewed within that organisation. They list issues that they regard as disciplinary offences, and then itemise as gross misconduct further offences that they consider to be more serious. These offences may be handled in different ways, depending on the seriousness with which the organisation views them.

Pause for thought 13.2 Consider any organisation that you know reasonably well, perhaps one where you have worked yourself.

1 What disciplinary rules did the organisation have?
2 How were these disciplinary rules made known to you?

3 What were considered to be disciplinary offences?
4 Were there any offences that were regarded as particularly serious in this organisation and that constituted gross misconduct? List these.
5 Compare your list with the list made by someone who has experience in a different organisation. Can you find reasons for the differences and similarities?

It is probable that there were disciplinary rules in most organisations and these were made known to you, either informally by your supervisor telling you about them or, more likely, by you being given or shown a copy of them as part of your induction to your new job. It is likely that in most organisations there will also be a list of offences that might constitute gross misconduct. When you compare your list with that of a friend who has worked in a different organisation, you will probably have listed many of the same offences as ones that constituted gross misconduct. Theft, dishonesty, verbal or physical abuse are likely to be regarded as serious in most organisations. It is also probable that there will then be some variation in your lists as to what else constitutes an offence, depending on the attitudes in that particular organisation and the nature of the work done there.

Organisations involved in food preparation may be particularly concerned with hygiene, and may list offences concerning lack of personal hygiene as ones that could constitute gross misconduct. Organisations such as banks or building societies, where there is a need for a high degree of security, may be very concerned with email abuse and have extremely strict rules about what is acceptable for workers to both send and receive. Other organisations, such as universities, may be much more concerned with freedom of information and ensuring access to information, so may have very different rules. Offences also change with time, fashion and new technology. Many organisations now have specific policies regarding both email and appropriate use of the Internet at work and some have also had to introduce policies to control the use of mobile phones at work.

Pause for thought 13.3 Tim Hancock has worked for your organisation for nearly a year. He has in general been a good employee, but you have noticed that recently he has started to arrive about 10 minutes late for work each morning. You are his supervisor. Describe the action you would take.

The way in which you, as Tim's supervisor, choose to deal with this situation depends on a number of factors. First, there is your own attitude to this issue, but more importantly there is also the attitude of the organisation to issues of poor timekeeping to consider. You may have personal views about this but you need to act in a way that is consistent with the organisation's views. Personally you may not feel too concerned about this issue as long as the work gets done, or you may take the view that it is a form of dishonesty when an employee steals time from an employer. In some organisations this may not be viewed as a problem at all. Employees may have the opportunity to create their own flexitime system without management worrying unduly about this. However, the views of the organisation will be expressed in its disciplinary procedure, and it is likely that poor timekeeping will be an area of concern. If that is the case, you, as Tim's manager, have to do something about Tim's lateness. It is not as yet a particularly serious offence, but it has the potential to become more serious if left unchecked. There may of course be a perfectly good reason why Tim has suddenly started to arrive slightly late for work. The first thing that needs to be done is for you to have a chat with Tim about it and try to find out the reason for this change in behaviour. This can be informal. It gives Tim the opportunity to explain, and also lets him know that you are aware of his lateness and are concerned about it. If he has a good reason then you will have to consider your reaction. If there is illness at home, this is likely to be a temporary situation, and you may reach an arrangement with Tim about his time of arrival for a limited period of time which can be reviewed at a later date. If the problem is related to a change in a public transport timetable, you may have to consider whether you can be flexible or not.

> **Pause for thought 13.4** Jasmine has worked for your organisation for nearly five years. Her work has always been good, but recently you have received many complaints from customers about the goods that they have ordered being late or not being received at all. You check through the records and find that all these delays can be traced back to orders that Jasmine has dealt with. You are Jasmine's manager. How will you deal with this situation?

As Jasmine's manager you will have to take some action about her poor quality of work since it is causing problems to customers, and there have been complaints. However, you know that Jasmine has always been a good worker so you need to talk to her about the problem and try to find out what the cause is. Once again, you need to have an informal chat with her to find out the cause of the problem and then decide on the action to take. You may find that there is a perfectly good reason, such as a problem relating to home life, for the change in the standard of her work. If this is the case then a counselling interview is likely to be most appropriate. If, however, there doesn't appear to be a clear reason, an informal discussion which lets Jasmine know of your concerns and reaches agreement about expected improvements should suffice.

The disciplinary procedure

This will be set out in writing and needs to fulfil the criteria already discussed as essential features of a disciplinary procedure. The self-help guide produced by ACAS (2002) suggests that there should be several sections to the procedure itself. These will vary according to the size of the organisation, but are likely to include as a minimum the following. We have also added records to this list since we feel this is an area that is sometimes overlooked.

1 the purpose of the procedure
2 the principles that underlie the procedure
3 informal actions
4 formal actions
5 the nature of gross misconduct
6 the appeals procedure
7 records.

1 The purpose of the procedure

The disciplinary procedure is likely first of all to explain why a disciplinary procedure is needed. It will probably indicate that the aim of the procedure is to help all employees to achieve high standards of conduct, attendance and job performance. It will also indicate what action should be taken if there is a breach of disciplinary rules, and refer to the need for fairness and consistency for all. It would also be useful to emphasise here the fact that the formal disciplinary procedure should only be started if discussions under the informal procedure have failed to bring about the requisite change in behaviour.

2 The principles that underlie the procedure

This section is likely to include a list of several of the essential principles that ACAS gives for a disciplinary procedure. This may vary in detail according to the size and nature of the organisation concerned. For example, in a small organisation where a simple disciplinary procedure is required, the principles might be stated as follows:

1 The procedure is to investigate fully the offence, to deal consistently with any disciplinary issues that arise and to ensure that no action will be taken until this investigation has been completed.
2 At every stage, the individual will be advised of the type of complaint.
3 To ensure fairness, the employee concerned will have an opportunity to state his or her case and be represented by a trade union representative or friend if so desired.
4 For a first breach of discipline, then the individual should not be dismissed unless it is a serious case that counts as gross misconduct.
5 The employee will have a right of appeal at any stage against disciplinary action that may be taken.
6 The procedure may be started at any stage if the alleged misconduct justifies this.

3 Informal action

Informal action is normally the most appropriate way of dealing with alleged minor misconduct or unsatisfactory performance. This may just involve the supervisor or manager having a quiet word with the individual and can be a quick and easy way of sorting out a problem. This type of informal action was exactly what we recommended in both the situations in the 'Pause for thought' exercises 13.3 and 13.4 which you examined earlier in this chapter. However, if this doesn't work, or if the alleged offence is regarded as being rather more serious in nature, then it is time for the employer to show his or her dissatisfaction and to take some formal action.

Pause for thought 13.5 Consider once again Pause for thought 13.3. If after the informal chat or chats there was still no improvement in Tim's timekeeping, his manager would be likely to start the formal disciplinary process.

4 Formal action

Investigation

Once the informal action has been taken, if the misconduct reoccurs or the unsatisfactory performance fails to improve, it may be necessary for the employer to try a more formalised approach. The organisation needs to carry out a full investigation before this is decided upon. According to Kaye (2007), the Employment Appeal Tribunal has given guidance that indicates that 'employers should carry out an investigation, even if the employee is arrested and charged with a criminal offence. It may not be practical to wait for the outcome of criminal proceedings, because these may take several months.' A thorough investigation is important.

While workers have rights to be accompanied at disciplinary meetings, Cole (2007) says that we should 'Remember the right to be accompanied does not apply to a genuine investigatory/fact-finding meeting.' Therefore, it should be made clear exactly what the nature of the meeting is going to be and it should not be allowed to drift into a disciplinary hearing as at that stage the worker would have other rights such as the right to be accompanied. The investigatory meetings and potential disciplinary meetings should be kept separate. On this subject Cole (2007) says, 'Halt an investigatory meeting if it looks like turning into a disciplinary meeting and start formal disciplinary procedures.'

If after conducting a thorough investigation it appears that there may have been misconduct then under the statutory disputes procedure the next stages should involve a letter, a meeting and possibly an appeal. The actual procedure may vary depending on whether the potential disciplinary action involves misconduct or capability, but both will be similar.

Letter

After a thorough investigation has been conducted the first stage in the formal process is to inform the employee of the alleged misconduct in writing to ensure that the individual realises that there actually still is a problem. This letter should explain the nature of the alleged misconduct and the reasons that this not acceptable within the organisation. The letter must also inform the individual of the basis of the complaint against them and should also invite them to a meeting and inform them of their right to be accompanied at this meeting. Copies of documents such as witness statements that will be used at that meeting should be given to them.

Meeting

Setting up the meeting

The date, time and place of the meeting should, if possible, be agreed with the individual concerned and should also be timed to allow them sufficient time to prepare adequately for this meeting. The meeting should be held somewhere private where there will not be any interruptions.

At this meeting the employer should first explain the complaint and go through the evidence. Then the individual should go through his or her case and answer any allegations that have been made against them. They can also ask questions, call witnesses, present evidence and raise any points about witness information.

If there is a problem in holding this meeting at the agreed time due to a legitimate reason, e.g. employee illness or unavailability of their chosen companion on that date, then the employer can arrange another date. This should normally be within five working days but this can be extended by mutual agreement. However, if the individual simply fails to attend the meeting, without giving any good reason, then the employer could hold the meeting and even reach a decision in their absence.

After the meeting a decision should be made about whether disciplinary action is justified

(a) If it is decided that disciplinary action is not justified, or if no further action needs to be taken then the employer must notify the individual in writing of this fact so they no longer worry.

(b) If, however, disciplinary action is decided upon then the employer has to decide the form of the action, taking into account the individual's explanations, their past employment record and length of service, any actions that have been taken in similar cases in the past, and whether the proposed disciplinary action is reasonable in the circumstances. It is normally good practice to give all employees at least one chance to improve before issuing them with a final written warning.

Types of formal action that could be taken

Slightly different forms of action may be appropriate for cases of misconduct or for those involving unsatisfactory performance but basically after conducting a full investigation the steps are as follows.

The first forms of formal action in a case of alleged *misconduct* could include the following:

- *A written warning* stating the nature of the misconduct and stating what change in behaviour is required.
- The individual being told that this is part of a formal disciplinary process and the consequences if they fail to change their behaviour.
- The likely consequences, such as a final written warning which could ultimately lead to their dismissal or some other sanction, but that this would only happen after they had been given the chance to present their case at another formally convened meeting. (If the employer considers dismissal or an action other than a warning or suspension on full pay, then they need to take into account the statutory minimum procedure which will be discussed in Chapter 14 where we consider dismissals.)

The first forms of formal action in a case of alleged unsatisfactory performance may be slightly different but could include *a written improvement note* being given to any individual who is performing in an unsatisfactory way which states:

- the nature of the performance problem
- the required improvement
- the timescale within which the improvement should occur
- a review date and
- the support, if any, that the employer will provide to help the individual to reach the required level of performance
- notification that failure to improve, if this is what has been decided upon, could result in a final written warning and ultimately dismissal.

Final written warnings

When the requisite improvement in either performance or behaviour has not been made within the stated timescale, or if the alleged offence is sufficiently serious, the employee should normally be issued with a written warning. Once again, before this stage of the process they should be given the opportunity to present their case at a meeting.

Any final written warning that is issued should once again make the following clear to the individual:

- the grounds for the complaint
- that failure to make the required improvement within a specified time may result in dismissal or another penalty
- that there is a right of appeal.

Final written warnings should be disregarded once the specified time limit has elapsed. ACAS provide an excellent set of sample letters to be used in various circumstances. These can be accessed at **www.acas.org.uk**.

Dismissal or other penalty

The subject of dismissal will be considered in more detail in the next chapter. However, we shall mention it briefly here as it is sometimes the final stage in the disciplinary process. Any decision to dismiss must be taken by a manager who has the necessary authority. The employee must be told as soon as possible of the decision to dismiss them, the reasons for the dismissal, the date on which their employment contract will end and their notice period and right of appeal.

Some organisations may choose to use alternative forms of sanction against the individual rather than dismissal. These could include demotion to another job, loss of seniority or pay, or a disciplinary transfer. These types of sanction may only be used if the employee's contract specifies these as alternatives or if agreement is reached with the individual concerned to allow them to be used.

5 The nature of gross misconduct

As we said earlier, organisations will have different ideas as to what constitutes gross misconduct. The employee should be given some indication of this also in the disciplinary procedure. It is impossible to design a list that covers all possibilities, but the organisation should list some of them. For example, the procedure may say that the following constitute gross misconduct and if any employee, after a full investigation, is found guilty of any of these offences he or she will be dismissed, even for a first offence:

- theft
- deliberate damage to the organisation's property
- fraud
- incapacity to work because of the influence of illegal drugs or alcohol
- physical assault
- sexual harassment
- racial harassment
- serious infringement of health and safety rules.

These are examples of offences that normally constitute gross misconduct, but it is not an exhaustive list and other serious offences may also constitute gross misconduct and merit dismissal.

It is also a good idea to state the organisation's position on criminal offences committed outside employment. There should be a statement in the disciplinary procedure indicating that a criminal offence which occurs outside employment may be considered as gross misconduct and may result in dismissal. The word 'may' should be stressed here, as this is not an automatic reason for dismissal. The main considerations should be the nature of the offence and the type of work that the employee normally does, and whether the offence makes the employee unsuitable for his or her job.

In these cases, the employee concerned will normally be suspended from work on full pay while a full investigation is being carried out. Suspension on full pay does not imply any guilt.

In the case of **gross misconduct** a modified procedure may be used. However, failure to comply with the standard statutory procedure in this or any other dismissal case will mean that if an employee is eligible to apply for unfair dismissal then the employment tribunal will automatically find the dismissal unfair. Not only that but it will also increase the level of compensation awarded by between 10 per cent and 50 per cent.

Employers certainly need to heed this requirement. This will be discussed in more detail in Chapter 14.

6 The appeals procedure

The last section of the formal disciplinary procedure should indicate what the employee should do if he or she is not happy with the action taken against him or her. There should be a clear appeal procedure, with time limits for the submission of appeals stated. The appeal procedure should of course meet the requirements set in the standard statutory procedure. Once again there should be the opportunity for a meeting to discuss the appeal and the person once again has the right to choose to be accompanied at this meeting. The appeal should be heard by a senior manager who has not been involved in the original disciplinary meeting. Again the employer must inform the employee about the final appeal decision.

7 Records

It is extremely important that accurate records of the proceedings are kept. According to the CIPD (2007a), 'All records should be kept meticulously, as this will be vital should a case be pursued at an employment tribunal. Since the burden of proof is on the employer to show that the dismissal is not unfair or unreasonable, keeping records is vital. Types of records that should be kept by employers are minutes of meetings, email, attendance notes, notes of telephone calls, copies of correspondence etc.' While it is important to keep accurate records should the case become one of alleged unfair dismissal, it is also important at all stages of the disciplinary process to have an accurate record of what has happened so that the organisation is aware of the stage in the proceedings which has been reached.

All warning letters should also state that the warning will be recorded on the employee's file for a set period of time. The period of time will vary between organisations. It may perhaps be three months for a written warning and six months for a final written warning. Once that period of time has elapsed, if the worker's conduct or performance has improved to the employer's satisfaction, the letter and note of the offence should be removed from that person's record. If he or she later commits the same or a different breach of disciplinary procedure, then the procedure must be started again. So if the employee who has been given a warning for an infringement concerning timekeeping then commits a different infringement, for example, by carrying out poor quality work, the employer should not go to the next stage of the disciplinary procedure but should start with an informal talk and issue a separate warning if that proves necessary.

If the employer ignored the fact that the warning was out of date or was about a different type of disciplinary offence, then it could hardly expect to win its case if it eventually dismissed the worker and he or she later decided to go to an employment tribunal to claim unfair dismissal. Such actions would be regarded as procedurally incorrect.

If records of warnings are kept on a worker's file indefinitely, then this could prejudice the person reading the file at a later date against this employee. The employee may well have changed over the years and so an unfair impression of this person would be given. The employee has the right, under the Data Protection Act 1998, to check his or her records to ensure that erroneous or out-of-date information is not being held and possibly used against them. Refer to the section on data protection in Chapter 4 for more information.

Groups that may pose particular problems

The ACAS Code of Practice also advises that certain situations may require special consideration. They list as particularly difficult cases:

- workers to whom the full procedure is not available
- trade union officials
- criminal charges or convictions outside employment
- cases involving statutory registration authorities, e.g. in the case of doctors the General Medical Council or for solicitors the Law Society.

The mini case studies in Activities 13.1 and 13.2 serve to illustrate some of these areas of concern. How would you handle each of these cases?

ACTIVITY 13.1

Paul has worked for Shepley Computers for four years, and for the past six months has worked on the night shift. He has a blemish-free record and is a highly regarded member of the workforce. One hot night in summer he leaves work after signing in at nine o'clock and goes to the pub. He returns to work under the influence of alcohol, and his supervisor, who has noticed his absence, tells him that he is suspended and must go home immediately. Paul becomes abusive and threatens to punch his supervisor. He takes his supervisor by the shoulders and shakes him while all the time threatening to punch him. His supervisor tells him that he is dismissed and should collect all his money and documents at the end of the week.

1 Do you feel that Paul's supervisor acted correctly in this case?
2 If not, how would you have handled this situation?

Discussion of Activity 13.1

1 Offences that occur when the human resources department is not available to give advice, as in this case, need particular attention. Paul's supervisor, who works on the night shift, would not be likely to have the human resource manager to turn to for advice when a potential disciplinary situation such as this suddenly occurs, so he needs to be well trained to know how to handle a situation such as this. He needs to be very clear in his own mind exactly what powers are available to him. In this case the supervisor initially acted well in suspending the employee. Paul was drunk and abusive and was behaving in a threatening manner towards him. Suspension with pay is a useful technique when there needs to be an opportunity to calm the situation or when time is needed to complete an investigation into whether or not an offence has occurred. He then acted rather rashly in telling Paul that he had been dismissed. No one should be dismissed unless a proper investigation has been carried out. Taking away someone's livelihood is a serious matter which could result in an employment tribunal case for unfair dismissal being brought against the organisation. Even though some of Paul's actions, such as being drunk at work and acting in an abusive and threatening manner, could clearly be classified as gross misconduct, there still needs to be a full investigation with an opportunity for Paul and his superior to state their cases and for union representation, before a disciplinary decision is reached, so clearly Paul's supervisor has not acted in a correct manner.

2 Clearly in this situation the statutory discipline, dismissal and grievance procedure was not followed, so your answer about how you would have handled the situation should have followed this:

(a) Suspend Paul on pay.

(b) Investigate.

(c) Write a letter to inform Paul of the concerns and give him the opportunity to be represented by a colleague or trades union official.

(d) Hold a meeting with Paul and his representative.

(e) Make a decision and advise Paul of his right to appeal.

ACTIVITY 13.2

Jane has been employed by your organisation for 10 years. She works as the assistant manager in the wages office and has always been an excellent worker. You hear, on the grapevine, that she has been accused of stealing £100 from the funds of the local youth club, where she acts as treasurer.

Imagine that you are the manager of the wages office. What will you do when:

1 you first hear the rumours?

2 she is subsequently convicted but given a conditional discharge for this offence?

Discussion of Activity 13.2

1 This is perhaps one of the most difficult situations for a manager to deal with. If the offence had happened at work it would have been a clear case of theft from work and, after going through an investigation and the statutory procedure, may have been considered gross misconduct with the possibility of dismissal. As it is,

should the manager consider this to be a disciplinary issue or not? ACAS (2002) says that being charged with a criminal offence, and even being convicted of one, does not necessarily warrant disciplinary action being taken. Even if the employee is convicted of the offence and is absent from work because they are being remanded in custody, there is no automatic reason for disciplinary action or dismissal.

Initially when you, the manager, hear of the alleged theft from youth club funds you will need to establish the facts of the case as best you can. You are likely to need to talk to Jane as part of this process. The main question that you as an employer must decide is whether the matter is sufficiently serious to warrant starting the disciplinary procedure. The main consideration should be whether the offence, or the alleged offence, makes the employee unsuitable for the type of work they are currently doing. You then have three options:

(a) You could do nothing, if you are satisfied with Jane's explanation and decide that the matter is not sufficiently serious to be taken further within the disciplinary procedure.

(b) You might consider suspending her on full pay pending the result of the court case. This would remove her from the situation at work where there would be gossip and rumours, and would also ensure that if anything went missing from work she would not be automatically accused. In many ways this is an attractive option, but the manager would need to be aware that the organisation may be paying Jane for several months before her case is heard.

(c) You could consider moving her to another section where she would not deal with cash handling, although of course many wages offices do not necessarily deal with money anyway. This would have the same advantages as in (b), but she would be earning her wages. She still might be accused, however, every time anything went missing. You may of course not have any other suitable post to which she could transfer, and depending on her contract you may need her agreement to the transfer.

2 When she is found guilty, then there are once again a variety of appropriate responses. The main guidance is given in the ACAS Code of Practice, which states that offences which occur away from the workplace should not be treated as automatic reasons for dismissal. It goes on to say that the most important factor will be whether the nature of the offence makes the employee unsuitable for their particular job. The statutory disciplinary, dismissal and grievance procedure would still need to be followed. She should be written to and called to an interview with representation if she requires it. A decision then needs to be made. The right of appeal should also be explained.

In the case of Jane, it would be possible to say that since she was found guilty of theft, this would affect people's view of her in a position of trust and so she may be dismissed for gross misconduct. Most disciplinary procedures follow ACAS's guidelines and include a section which states that offences which occur outside work may constitute gross misconduct. Dismissal should not be automatic, however. Other options are available and it depends on the circumstances.

These two case studies, concerning potential disciplinary offences that occur away from the place of work or outside normal working hours, help to illustrate some of the more difficult cases that may arise and show how useful it is to refer to the ACAS Code of Practice on Disciplinary Procedures for guidance in these areas.

Absence control

Absences are often another area of particular concern to employers. Here what is important is to find out exactly what the reasons are for the absence. In many organisations an absence control procedure is used, and this may result in the disciplinary procedure being used less frequently. Absence control systems usually require the employee to telephone the supervisor on the first day of absence, and the supervisor will go through a checklist of points with him or her. If the supervisor is not available there will be a second or a third designated person with whom the absent person will have to speak. An interview will be held with the supervisor or other designated person when the absentee returns to work.

There will also be a system of visits for people who are absent on a long-term basis to ensure that the organisation stays up to date with their current situation and knows when to expect them to return to work. Supervisors and managers will be aware of the level of absenteeism in their sections and will encourage good attendance.

The aim of an absence control procedure is to minimise the need for the use of the disciplinary procedure, by creating a culture in which everyone is aware of the importance of good attendance and of their value to the organisation. The danger is that some employees may feel pressurised into returning to work before they are really fit, and this may prove to be counterproductive, resulting in their needing more time off later to recover fully.

If there is not a good reason for the absence then this is likely to be an issue considered to be misconduct. If a person has a record of short-term absences without suitable explanations or adequate medical evidence, then they can be dealt with under the organisation's normal disciplinary procedure. There is usually a specified level of absence, e.g. 10 days in three months, after which more formal controls will be introduced, leading to counselling or disciplinary action as appropriate.

Disciplinary procedures and ill-health

If employees are away on a long-term absence due to a genuine illness then the situation needs to be dealt with in an entirely different way. You cannot warn someone that there must be an improvement in their attendance if you know that this is impossible because of the nature of their illness. Instead, regular contact needs to be maintained with such employees to establish the likelihood of their return, and medical evidence needs to be sought. A company doctor's advice may be needed. In the end it may be that the person is unable to return to work in the foreseeable future, and it may be necessary to consider whether there are any other suitable jobs that they may be able to undertake, or whether their employment needs to be terminated. Other factors, such as whether they have exhausted the organisation's sickness pay scheme, the age of the person, whether the illness is as a result of a disability as defined by the Disability Discrimination Act 1995, and whether they could take early retirement under the organisation's pension scheme, will need to be considered here in order to find the best solution for both the employee and the organisation. There is also likely to be a need for employee counselling and advice, and this process, if handled with the sensitivity it deserves, is likely to be extremely lengthy.

Disciplinary hearings

The actual disciplinary hearing is similar in many ways to the interviews discussed in Chapter 7. The manager who is conducting the hearing will need to prepare thoroughly, have the relevant information to hand and arrange for a quiet room with no disturbances and with an appropriate layout in which to hold the hearing. The disciplinary hearing should be conducted in a systematic and fair way in order to ensure that all the relevant information is considered. The manager chairing it should explain clearly the purpose, who is present and why they are there, and the sequence.

Although there are many similarities between disciplinary hearings and interviews, and one would expect them to be conducted in a similar way, there are some specific legal definitions that apply to disciplinary hearings. It is important to consider these as there is a legal right for workers to be accompanied at a disciplinary hearing and this is not something that would normally apply at most other hearings, with the exception of the grievance hearing which will be discussed later in this chapter.

Disciplinary hearings are defined as all meetings where either disciplinary action or some other action could be taken against a worker. This includes any meeting that might result in actions such as a warning, final written warning, suspension without pay, demotion or dismissal being taken against the worker. It also applies to meetings to confirm warnings or other disciplinary action and to appeal hearings, even if they are held after the worker has left the employment concerned.

The right to be accompanied at a disciplinary interview

The Employment Relations Act 1999 gave workers the right to request a companion to accompany them at disciplinary or grievance hearings. This can be a fellow worker or a trade union official or even, in certain circumstances, a lay trade union official. The companion can address the hearing and advise workers, but is not supposed to answer questions on behalf of the worker. It is in order for a worker to request an alternative date for a hearing if the companion of their choice is unavailable on the designated date for the hearing.

The ACAS Code of Practice on Disciplinary and Grievance Procedures (2003) was written to take into account the statutory discipline and grievance procedures set out in the Employment Act 2002 and so gives practical guidance about workers being accompanied at disciplinary hearings. It explains that as well as the rights to be accompanied already mentioned, some workers may have other additional rights to be accompanied by different people specified in their contracts of employment. Employers should also consider sympathetically any specific needs raised by disabled workers or by a disabled companion.

Trade unions are supposed to ensure that there are suitable training and refresher courses for all their officials, so that they can confidently take on the role of companion if requested. However, ACAS explains that although workers can request a trade union official or a fellow worker to accompany them at any disciplinary hearing, the person selected for this role does not have to agree to do this and should not be pressurised to take on the role if they do not want to do it.

Before the hearing the worker should inform the employer of the name of their companion so that the companion can also be involved in discussions about choosing a convenient date and time for the hearing. The companion may carry out the following roles:

- state the worker's case for them
- summarise the worker's case
- respond on behalf of the worker to any views expressed at the hearing
- discuss points with the worker during the hearing
- ask witnesses questions.

However, the role of companion will depend on what the worker wants them to do and the worker may choose not to allow them to do some of these things.

If an employer fails to comply with a reasonable request for a worker to be accompanied at a disciplinary hearing then the worker may complain about this to an employment tribunal. If the worker's companion cannot attend the hearing on a specific date and the employer fails to rearrange a hearing to take account of this then this can also be the cause for a complaint to an employment tribunal. Two weeks' pay can be awarded by a tribunal in these cases and this could be increased if the tribunal also decides that the worker has been unfairly dismissed.

Grievance: introduction and definitions

The *Shorter Oxford English Dictionary* defines grievance as: 'The infliction of wrong or hardship on a person; injury, oppression; a cause or source of injury.' When referring to grievances it is useful to follow the approach of Pigors and Myers (1977) and identify the strength of the feeling about the behaviour or attitude of management that has resulted in injury, and how this is then expressed. Pigors and Myers distinguish between dissatisfaction, complaint and grievance:

- *Dissatisfaction*: anything that disturbs an employee, whether or not he expresses his unrest in words.
- *Complaint*: a spoken or written dissatisfaction, brought to the attention of the supervisor and/or shop steward.
- *Grievance*: a complaint which has been formally presented to a management representative or to a union official. (Pigors and Myers 1977, p. 229)

ACAS (2003) define grievances as 'concerns, problems or complaints that employees raise with their line managers.' We shall use the term 'grievance' in this way as a form of dissatisfaction about which the employee feels sufficiently strongly that he or she formally raises the issue with his or her management representative or shop steward.

The ACAS Code of Practice on Disciplinary and Grievance Procedures (2003) provides guidance on grievance handling. Grievances may arise for a multitude of reasons. An employee may become dissatisfied with his or her hours of work or working conditions, he or she may feel a supervisor shows unfair favouritism to others, or may feel dissatisfaction about pay or sexual harassment. Some grievances may appear trivial and others, such as alleged sexual harassment, may be very serious, but to the employee concerned they will all have been serious enough to raise formally. A survey of 147 organisations by the IRS Employment Review (2007) found that among this sample 'the most common cause of grievances were breakdowns in relationships between colleagues or between employees and their line managers.'

Anyone in an organisation could have a grievance, even a member of management. Some grievances may become a collective issue, with negotiations between management and a trade union arising over an issue such as a collective grievance about pay or working conditions. This chapter will focus solely on grievance as an individual issue.

Grievance procedures and practices

Reasons for having a grievance procedure

Employees need to know how they can raise a grievance and seek redress for any grievance that they might have. They need to feel confident that their grievance will be treated in a fair way and that they will get to know the result of raising this grievance within a short period of time. It is also important to settle the grievance quickly, to prevent it becoming a larger grievance that involves more people and takes longer to resolve.

It is regarded as good employment practice for employers to have a grievance procedure and the Government has also introduced statutory grievance procedures for all workers, not just employees.

If there were no procedure for raising and resolving grievances, it would be likely that employees would grumble to colleagues, and not only their work but the work of the department would be liable to suffer as a result. Therefore the main aim of the grievance procedure is to settle disputes fairly and as near to the source of grievance as possible. If there were a grievance over an issue such as safety or harassment, failure to provide a mechanism to deal with the grievance could result in serious repercussions, with perhaps accidents or a sexual or racial harassment case occurring. A grievance procedure in effect provides a safety mechanism to prevent issues from getting out of control. It also ensures that management have a channel to hear about issues that may be worrying their staff.

Discipline versus grievance

Disciplinary action is, as we have seen, normally initiated by management to express dissatisfaction with, and bring about changes in, employee behaviour; grievance, on the other hand, is normally initiated by employees for similar reasons, but in respect of management's, or perhaps co-workers', behaviour. There is a need for fairness and justice in both procedures although they are initiated by different parties. Because of this it is sometimes claimed that they are the opposites of each other, and should be viewed as complementary processes in industrial justice.

Pause for thought 13.6 Consider what you have just learned about grievance and discipline. In what ways do you consider discipline and grievance to be opposites? Are there any facts which make you think that they are not truly opposites?

As we have shown, discipline and grievance are both concerned with fairness and justice. They differ in that the people who initiate the action in each case differ. The management initiates disciplinary action against employees, and employees initiate grievances mainly against their supervisors and managers. In this way they may be considered to be opposite faces of industrial justice. However, this disregards the balance of power in these cases. To consider them to be true opposites would entail the assumption that when an employee initiates a grievance they have the same amount of power as management, which is clearly not the case. An employee who has a grievance will not be able to insist that action is taken against the person who has caused the grievance, and will have to rely on management's willingness to take action.

The informal grievance procedure

The Labour Research Department (1995) conducted a survey of the grievance procedures of 85 organisations. It found that the majority of complaints are resolved in an informal way, making it unnecessary to raise them as a formal grievance. Informal grievance procedures seem to be just as important in organisations as informal disciplinary procedures. However, a small number of complaints will not be resolved informally, and for these it is necessary to have a grievance procedure.

These findings are supported by Cully *et al.* (1999) in their study of Britain at Work as depicted by the *1998 Workplace Employee Relations Survey*. This showed that while 91 per cent of employees had access to grievance procedures in the organisations which were surveyed, in only 30 per cent of the organisations had the formal grievance procedure actually been used during that year. According to Cully *et al.* (1999), 'One reason for this might be that employees had nothing to complain about. Another might be that the procedure is not a particularly effective mechanism for resolving problems.'

We have already outlined the reasons for having a grievance procedure, and in the next section will consider the form that the grievance procedure should take and the main points to be considered when designing a grievance procedure, before considering the way in which the grievance interview should be handled.

The formal grievance procedure

In order that both workers and managers are clear about how to handle grievances and to ensure grievances are resolved quickly and fairly, a grievance procedure should be designed and issued to all employees and other workers. It is a good idea, once again, to involve various groups in the design of a procedure to suit a particular organisation. A suitable format for the grievance procedure might be to use similar headings to those used in the design of a disciplinary procedure. Suitable headings could be:

1 the purpose and scope of the grievance procedure
2 the principles that underlie the procedure
3 the stages in the grievance procedure
4 exceptional circumstances
5 the appeals procedure.

The purpose and scope of the procedure

This section is likely to indicate which employees are covered by this particular procedure if there are slightly different procedures for different groups. It should also state that the aim of the procedure is to settle any grievances in a fair manner and as near to the source of the grievance as possible. In order to minimise problems at work and ensure a happy and productive working environment, the procedure should be simple to use and rapid in operation.

The principles that underlie the procedure

This is likely to include some statements concerning the employer's views on fairness and justice and how these will be achieved, for example:

- All workers have a right to raise a grievance that they may feel with their supervisor or manager without fear of recrimination against themselves.
- Grievances will be investigated within specified time limits and the person with the grievance will be notified of the outcome.
- At each stage of the procedure they will have the right to be accompanied by a trade union representative or a friend.
- If the worker is not satisfied with the outcome of raising their grievance they will have a right of appeal.

The stages in the grievance procedure

The Labour Research Department (1995) found that 80 per cent of the grievance procedures that it reviewed had between three and six stages after the informal stage. ACAS (2003) in its code of practice says that: 'In most organisations it should be possible to have at least a two-stage procedure. However, where there is only one stage, for instance in very small firms where there is only a single owner/manager, it is especially important that the person dealing with the grievance acts impartially.' We do not feel that there is any advantage in having more levels than three in the procedure, even if there are more levels in the management hierarchy. We would suggest that three main levels should prove adequate for most organisations.

Outlined below are the possible main stages in the grievance procedure.

Stage 1

The worker should raise the grievance in writing, with the immediate supervisor, who will reply within a specified time, e.g. three days. If the grievance is about the supervisor, there needs to be an opportunity to bypass this stage and to raise the grievance with a manager at the next highest level. Once the formal grievance has been raised there should then be a meeting at which the grievance is discussed and then the manager should set out their decision with reasons.

The worker has, depending on the nature of the grievance, a statutory right to be accompanied at a grievance hearing and the manager should make him or her aware of this right. The statutory right applies if the grievance relates to something that concerns the performance of 'the duty of the employer in relation to a worker'. For example, this could apply in relation to a grievance raised about equal pay, because the employer has a clear duty to provide equal pay to all workers. Ultimately it will be the employment tribunals that will decide in which cases the worker should have been given the right to be accompanied at the grievance hearing, so it would be good practice to allow any worker raising a grievance to be accompanied, if they request it.

Stage 2

If it has not been resolved, the individual should request in writing an interview with a more senior manager. This manager should then arrange to hear the grievance within a specified time period, e.g. within five working days. The worker should once again be informed of their statutory right to be accompanied and a date set for them to present their case at a meeting. The manager should make a decision about the grievance within a specified time period and the worker should be informed of this. If there is likely to be a delay in reaching a decision then the worker should also be given a clear reason for this and told when he or she can expect a decision.

Stage 3

If it has not been resolved at stage 2, the individual should raise the grievance with the general manager or director or the next most senior person. Once again, the worker should be told of his or her statutory rights to be accompanied at a hearing at which they present their case. As in the earlier stages, an indication about the time it will take to reach a decision should be given to the worker, as should explanations about any unavoidable delay.

Time limits

You will have noted that fairly strict time limits were specified in the section on stages in the procedure. If there is not a satisfactory response to the grievance within a specified time limit, then the employee should be able to raise the grievance with the supervisor's immediate management. There should be a clear time limit for each stage of the grievance procedure, as without this there is a danger that, although a manager or supervisor may have good intentions to deal with a grievance, it will nevertheless be overlooked. According to Crail (2007), 'Formal grievance policies often recognize that not all disputes will be resolved entirely within the organisation. Sometimes there is an agreement that once all internal steps are exhausted, employment of experts from outside may be asked to conciliate between the parties.' The IRS Employment Review survey (2007) 'found that more than 1 in 4 (28.2%) panel organisations had provision for organisations such as ACAS to become involved in individual grievance procedures at some point. Of these one in three (32.5%) said that they had activated this during the past three years.'

Representation

At each stage in the formal grievance procedure the worker should be informed of their statutory right to be accompanied by a companion who is another employee or who is a trade union representative. This right, once again, applies to all workers and not just employees, so agency workers, home workers, the self-employed or those doing voluntary work could all raise grievances and have the right to be accompanied. As we said earlier in this chapter, the right applies specifically when there is a requirement to attend a grievance hearing which relates to legal or contractual commitments such as grievances relating to grading or promotion, if they arise out of a contract. Some other grievances may not relate to contractual or legal matters but it may be safer for employers to allow workers to be accompanied rather than finding themselves testing the interpretation of the law at an employment tribunal.

Exceptional circumstances and special considerations

In exceptional circumstances it may not be practicable to raise the grievance with the immediate manager. This may be because the grievance is caused by the manager or because the manager will not be available, perhaps because of illness, to deal with the grievance with the urgency that it deserves. In those exceptional circumstances the grievance may be taken to the next level of supervision.

Some organisations may also want to establish special additional procedures to deal with specific types of grievances relating, for example, to discrimination, harassment or bullying and may design policies specific to these issues. The organisation may feel the need to have separate procedures as these are all very difficult areas that may need extra-sensitive handling.

Appeals

A right of appeal should be specified for each stage, with time limits within which the appeal should be heard.

Records

Records of grievances raised and the responses made to them should be kept. They should, in accordance with the Data Protection Act 1998, be kept confidential but certain information or data should normally be available to the individual concerned on request.

Pause for thought 13.7 Shazia, the shop steward, asks you for time off to make a complaint to the general manager about something in your department. You are the manager of that department: what will you do?

Shazia, as the shop steward, is entitled to reasonable time off to carry out her trade union duties, so she is in order to request time off. However, as we said earlier, a grievance should be settled as near to the source of the problem as possible. You need to remind Shazia, who as a shop steward should certainly be aware of this, that if she has a grievance herself, or if she is acting on behalf of one of your department, then you are the person with whom the grievance should first be raised. You should point out that if you cannot deal with this satisfactorily within the specified time period then of course she may then raise the grievance, in line with the grievance procedure, with the general manager.

Although there is a need for grievances to be settled as near to the source of grievance as possible, this becomes difficult if the grievance is about the manager or supervisor concerned, so if the grievance is about you as the supervisor, Shazia may be unwilling to discuss it with you. Nevertheless, if it is about you, you will need to know about it sooner or later, so at least you should try to ascertain the nature of the grievance before allowing it to go further.

Grievance interviews

Many of the features of a grievance interview are the same as for other types of interview. There is a need for a quiet, private room arranged to facilitate ease of communication. The employee or his or her companion is likely to do most of the talking, since they are raising the grievance. There may be a need to call witnesses, and after hearing all the evidence from both sides the manager may wish to adjourn before reaching a decision. The manager must ensure a fair hearing and that everyone concerned is aware of the purpose of the meeting, who is to be called as witnesses, the time limits within which a decision will be reached, and the way in which the decision will be announced to the employee or worker concerned. If there is not a swift and fair resolution of grievances, the grievances may tend to build up and the work of the section is likely to suffer. At worst this could ultimately result in a high labour turnover or a high level of absenteeism as people remove themselves from a situation where they feel unhappy, or it might escalate into an industrial dispute.

Some organisations may, in addition to these procedures, decide to have a whistle-blowing procedure. This will then provide additional protection for workers who raise grievances about issues that involve some form of wrongdoing within the organisation, e.g. workplace hazards or fraud.

Changes to the statutory disciplinary and grievance procedures

The statutory disciplinary and grievance procedures introduced in 2004 have not proved popular with employers and have also failed to achieve one of their original aims that fewer cases should end at an employment tribunal for unfair dismissal. A review by Michael Gibbons in March 2007 recommended 'a major overhaul of these statutory procedures' even though they had only been introduced three years earlier (CIPD, 2007b). According to the CIPD (2007b), 'the Gibbons review has suggested that there should be non-prescriptive simple guidelines on grievance, discipline and dismissal for both employers and employees, together with the following:

● Financial and other incentives to comply with the new guideline
● Increased tribunals' discretion to take into account reasonable behaviour and procedure when making awards and cost orders

- A new, simple process to settle monetary disputes on issues such as wages
- Encouragement for all employer and employee organisations to commit implementing and promoting early dispute resolution through greater use of in-house mediation, early neutral evaluation, and provisions in contracts of employment
- Simplification of some aspects of employment law.'

There do seem to be extensive changes being planned but in the IRS Employment Review survey (2007) there is little enthusiasm shown by the employers in the sample for the proposals: 'While most want to see the 2004 Regulations repealed and replaced, almost half believe that current proposals will bring about little improvement in dispute resolution.' Any changes that occur will be likely to happen after the date of publication of this book in 2008 so any further information about changes will be posted on the student website at **www.pearsoned.co.uk/ foothook**.

As well as recommending changes to discipline and grievance procedures the Gibbons review also recommended changes to the employment tribunal procedure and these proposals will be discussed in the next chapter.

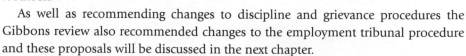

Conclusion

We have shown in this chapter the meaning and the importance of grievance and disciplinary procedures to the organisation. Both specialist human resource managers and line managers have an extremely important role to play in the design of procedures that are fair to all; it is also important that cases of grievance or discipline are dealt with in accordance with the organisation's procedures. Knowledge and understanding of the ACAS Code of Practice, and the ACAS self-help guide for producing discipline and grievance procedures are valuable aids to help ensure that fair procedures are designed and that disciplinary and grievance interviews are handled well. Good procedures and clear policies for dealing with both discipline and grievance issues should result in fewer of this type of problem for the organisation. Any issues that do arise are dealt with in a fair way that everyone understands. Organisations should at the design stage involve representatives from different levels and types of work to ensure policies and procedures really do meet the requirements of both the organisation and the workers. The chosen form of their policies and procedures should also be guided by advice in the ACAS Code of Practice (2003) and include the statutory right to be accompanied for workers at both discipline and grievance hearings. Organisations must also be clear about whether they are interpreting the right to be accompanied in its strict legal sense at specific types of discipline or grievance hearings, or whether they are extending this right to workers in any discipline or grievance situation. In the next chapter we examine the consequences of getting a disciplinary case wrong, and discuss unfair dismissal and redundancy.

The mind maps shown in Figures 13.1 and 13.2 summarise the key points covered in this chapter. When you have examined these, test your understanding of the chapter with the review questions and self-check questions.

Figure 13.1 Mind map: discipline

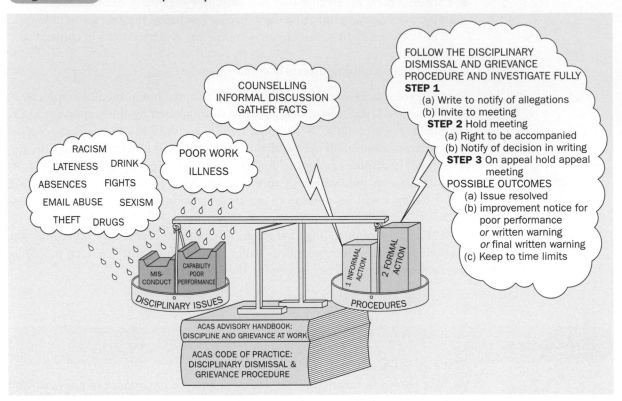

Figure 13.2 Mind map: grievance

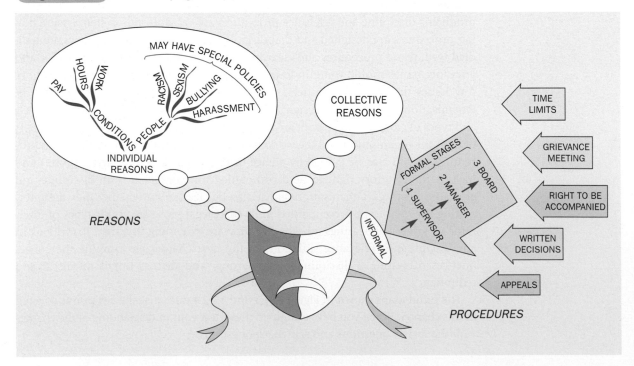

REVIEW QUESTIONS

Brief answers to review questions are provided on pages 479–480.

1 Interview both a line manager and a personnel manager and try to establish what roles they play in relation to grievance and discipline handling in the workplace. How do your findings compare with what we have said in this chapter?

2 Obtain a copy of an organisation's discipline or grievance procedure and compare it to our suggested outline for these. Identify and comment on the similarities and differences.

3 Obtain a copy of the ACAS Code of Practice on Disciplinary and Grievance Procedures (2003). Use this, and our suggestions in this chapter, to rewrite or modify either of the procedures you used for question 2, if you find that this is necessary.

4 You have joined an organisation which has expanded recently and now has 100 employees. This organisation started as a small undertaking with only 18 employees and has never had a formal grievance procedure. Write a report for the general manager outlining why it is important to have a formal grievance procedure and suggesting what the procedure should contain.

SELF-CHECK QUESTIONS

Answer the following multiple-choice questions. The correct responses are given on page 480 for you to check your understanding of this chapter.

1 According to ACAS, disciplinary procedures should be designed to:
   (a) provide a fair way to gather evidence against the offender
   (b) ensure that someone is caught for the offence
   (c) promote fairness and set standards of conduct
   (d) point out the mistake that has been made
   (e) provide fair methods of punishing the offender.

2 According to Pigors and Myers, a grievance is:
   (a) anything that disturbs an employee
   (b) anything that disturbs an employee and is discussed with the manager
   (c) a spoken dissatisfaction brought to the attention of the manager
   (d) a complaint that has been formally presented to a management representative or shop steward
   (e) anything that disturbs an employee and is expressed in words.

3 Which of the following are listed as essential features of a disciplinary procedure in the ACAS Code of Practice?
   (a) Be in writing, provide for fair punishment, specify to whom the rules should apply.
   (b) Be in writing, specify to whom the rules should apply, ensure that (except for cases of gross misconduct) no one is dismissed for a first disciplinary offence.
   (c) Provide for the matter to be dealt with quickly, provide for witnesses to give evidence, ensure that (except for cases of gross culpability), no one is dismissed for a first disciplinary offence.

→

    (d) Be in writing, provide for a fair system of punishment, specify all the offences that constitute gross misconduct.

    (e) Provide for the matter to be dealt with quickly, specify all the offences that constitute gross misconduct, ensure that except for gross misconduct no one is dismissed for a first offence.

4 The Employment Act 2002 states which of the following?

    (a) That only employees have the right to be accompanied at disciplinary hearings.

    (b) That only employees have the right to be accompanied at grievance hearings.

    (c) That workers have the right to be accompanied, in certain circumstances, at formal disciplinary or formal grievance hearings.

    (d) That workers have the right to be accompanied, in certain circumstances, at informal discussions or counselling relating to discipline.

    (e) That workers have the right to be accompanied, in certain circumstances, at informal discussions relating to grievances they raise.

5 Once the time limit for a written warning has elapsed:

    (a) the warning should still be kept on the employee's personal record file

    (b) the warning should be removed from the employee's personal record file and placed in a central file in which records of all disciplinary offences are kept

    (c) the warning should be removed from the employee's personal record file only if the data are stored on computer

    (d) the warning should be removed completely from the employee's personal record file

    (e) the warning should be removed from the employee's personal record file after a further three months has elapsed.

6 According to ACAS, if a serious criminal offence occurs outside employment:

    (a) this is automatically considered to be gross misconduct and dismissal is justifiable

    (b) this is automatically considered to be gross misconduct and dismissal may be justifiable

    (c) this should not be treated as an automatic reason for dismissal – the main consideration should be whether or not the offence makes the employee unsuitable for his or her type of work

    (d) this should not be treated as an automatic reason for dismissal – the main consideration is whether you think that the employee is likely to commit the offence again

    (e) this should not be treated as an automatic reason for dismissal – the main consideration should be the length of service the employee has had with your organisation.

7 The recommended first stage in a grievance procedure is:

    (a) to raise the grievance with the top management immediately

    (b) to grumble to your colleagues about your grievance

    (c) to raise the grievance with your supervisor's manager

    (d) to raise the grievance with the area manager

    (e) to raise the grievance with your immediate supervisor.

8 Which of the following is TRUE?

    (a) The statutory disciplinary and grievance procedure introduced in 2004 has not proved popular with employers.

(b) The statutory disciplinary and grievance procedure introduced in 2004 has proved to be very popular with employers.

(c) Only large organisations with over 500 employees need to be have a formal disciplinary procedure.

(d) Workers who are not employees of the organisation never have the right to be accompanied by a trade union official or colleague at a disciplinary hearing.

(e) Workers who are not employees of the organisation never have the right to be accompanied by a trade union official or colleague at a grievance hearing.

9 Nowadays the role of human resource managers in handling discipline and grievance situations is:

(a) always purely advisory

(b) non-existent, as line managers deal with these topics

(c) purely to check on line managers and ensure they handle things correctly

(d) only to design the procedures themselves

(e) a mixture of things, including advice and guidance.

10 The initials ACAS stand for:

(a) Advisory, Counselling and Aid Service

(b) Aid, Counselling and Arbitration Service

(c) Aid, Conciliation and Arbitration Service

(d) Advice, Conciliation and Arbitration Service

(e) Advisory, Conciliation and Arbitration Service.

HR IN THE NEWS

FT

FT Report – Recruitment:
Social networking and workplace discipline

By Richard Donkin

About six years ago I embarked with two collaborators on a book about the importance of networks in the future of work. I wrote an introduction and a chapter, then waited . . . and waited.

The collaboration died; a pity because we had some good material, including stories about early communications networks in Roman times, the road networks of the Incas and various intelligence networks, both ancient and modern.

The time seemed right. The initial internet-inspired investment euphoria had disappeared and there was not much sign of what would come to be known as Web 2.0 technology or any discussion of long-tail distribution graphs that were still confined to statistics textbooks.

Interest in networks was spreading, however, as work-related networking groups such as First Tuesday began to grow in popularity and books such as Malcolm Gladwell's *The Tipping Point* were beginning to investigate the workings of networks. The internet had stimulated a thirst for sharing information very similar to that during the Enlightenment when thinkers and scientists exchanged letters through European academies and societies.

I can trace my interest in networks back to a column in 1998 inspired by a meeting with Karen Stephenson, an anthropologist, who specialised in studying the social dynamics of communications and how they applied in the workplace.

→

She was fascinated by the way information was distributed among groups of people on what she called 'invisible lines of trust'. The most interesting people in these lines of communication she described as 'pulse-takers', what Gladwell called 'mavens'.

Mavens are the people in offices or pubs who seem to know everything. They are the ones with their ears to the ground. They are not usually the bosses (who might well know things but are bound by confidentiality obligations).

Mavens do not know all the answers, but they know where to find snippets of information and where they can go to test their theories. Sometimes their 'news' is no more than an educated guess but, for those who rely on them, they become a trusted source. People not only seek information from them but also pass on to them their own titbits.

I had seen the way this worked in a newsroom that had also benefited from an early electronic message system that allowed the creation of special-interest 'user groups'. In this way, long before the email, or social networking websites, journalists had been exchanging vital screen-based messages such as: 'Fancy a pint?'

So there is nothing really very new about social networking. Nor is there anything new in the fears that this kind of thing can be disruptive to the working environment. In the 1930s typing pool supervisors were constantly complaining about what they regarded as distracting levels of gossip among their workers.

Today the complaint is levelled at internet-based social networking. The worry is well founded. Various studies have been published recently arguing that internet-based social networking in offices is wasting business time. Whether or not you subscribe to the dodgy statistics presented in these studies, it's difficult to deny there must be a significant cost to business in lost hours.

A recruitment company head told me a week ago he had banned access to the Facebook website in his office. 'I noticed that the people who seemed to be on there all the time were the ones that were the least productive. The most productive people didn't go there much in work time,' he said.

In this respect I would say there are three categories of office workers: those who just get on with their work and don't take much interest in internet-based exchanges. Those who enjoy looking in to their web pages during breaks and slack periods and, finally, those who become addicted to the technology and can't help popping on to these sites at every possible opportunity.

The first two are not a great problem for managers. It is the third – usually people who find little intrinsic stimulation in office work – that poses the biggest problem. But this group has always existed. It exists in school classrooms, offices and on factory floors.

Ironically it's among such groups that you can sometimes find entrepreneurs, artists and dreamers. But that doesn't help when work consists of repetitive administrative tasks.

I'm not seeking to disparage this kind of work, or to defend the fickleness of dreamers.

There are individuals, however, who simply do not thrive in routines. Perhaps they should be sifted out by those who recruit for routine work. But the workplace would be pretty dull without them.

Depriving easily-distracted individuals of external stimulation may be the only way to suppress their mercurial instincts long enough to focus their talents on the job in hand.

But it cannot be a long-term solution. First, many people are learning to bypass attempts to block access to certain sites. My schoolboy son was explaining to me this weekend how he achieves this in his classroom. I didn't know whether to be angry or proud.

Second, social networking is a phenomenon that is not going away. As the initial excitement dies, its use will become routine. I noticed this week that newspaper accounts reporting the deaths of four firefighters, at the Atherston warehouse fire in Warwickshire, had drawn biographical details from Facebook entries. Photographs of the dead were being compiled on a Facebook group and friends were visiting the site of one of the firemen to pay condolences. Socially this is comparable with the in-memoriam columns in newspapers. Disseminating information in this way is important: the full disaster of the battle of the Somme in 1916 was not revealed by the government of the day but in the long columns of deaths recorded publicly by families in British newspapers.

Here is the real issue of social networking for business. Its potency has taken companies by surprise. Many bosses, initially dismissive of these sites, now feel threatened, partly because they worry their workplaces are being undermined and partly because they feel they must exclude themselves for fear that their presence in a network will be unwelcome. Not unreasonably they feel they must preserve distance from staff they may discipline, promote or make redundant.

Just as any social arena – the home, the workplace, the street – becomes a stage for human interaction, so does the internet network. Yes, there are threats but there are opportunities too. We all need to learn how to use this thing sensibly. Education and debate may prove a more positive route than censure.

(*Financial Times*, 8 November 2007. Reproduced with permission.)

Questions

1 Do you think that employers are justified in banning the use of social networking sites and treating their use during working time as a disciplinary offence?

2 List the advantages and disadvantages of including social networking sites as part of a disciplinary procedure.

WHAT NEXT?

Find some good examples of disciplinary and grievance letters and forms by going to the ACAS website: **www.acas.org.uk/index.aspx?articleid=389**.

Still on the ACAS website, test your knowledge and understanding of discipline and grievance issues by taking its online course. This is designed for managers but if you have studied this chapter and answered the questions as you have gone through it you should have a good basis for developing your knowledge and understanding further by using these online materials: **www.acas.org.uk/elearning**.

References

Advisory, Conciliation and Arbitration Service (2002) *Producing Disciplinary and Grievance Procedures: Self-Help Guide,* ACAS.

Advisory, Conciliation and Arbitration Service (2003) *Code of Practice on Disciplinary and Grievance Procedures*, ACAS.

Chartered Institute of Personnel and Development (2007a) *Discipline and grievances at work: fact sheet,* CIPD, originally issued May 2004, latest revision May 2007 (www.cipd.co.uk/subjects/emplaw/discipline/disciplingrievprocs.htm? accessed 12.09.07).

Chartered Institute of Personnel and Development (2007b) *Discipline and grievance procedures: member resource,* CIPD (www.cipd.co.uk/EmploymentLaw/FAQ/_Discipline/Discipline.htm? accessed 12.09.07).

Cole, K. (2007) Look beneath the labels, *People Management,* 25 January.

Cully, M., S. Woodland, A. O'Reilly and G. Dix (1999) *Britain at Work as Depicted by the 1998 Workplace Employee Relations Survey,* Routledge.

IRS Employment Review (2007) *Survey: dispute resolution, disciplinaries and grievances 2007,* IRS, 879, 20.08.07.

Kaye, M. (2007) Unspoken disciplinary requirements, *People Management,* 25 January.

Labour Research Department (1995) *Bargaining. Report 149,* Labour Research Department, April.

Pigors, P. and C.S. Myers (1977) *Personnel Administration,* 8th edition, McGraw-Hill.

Further study

Books

Advisory, Conciliation and Arbitration Service (2006) *Advisory Handbook: Discipline and Grievances at Work,* ACAS. This gives practical guidance about the ACAS Code of Practice on Disciplinary and Grievance Procedures.

Articles

Harding-Hill, R. (2005) More than the minimum, *People Management,* Vol. 11, No. 24, 19.

Hook, C., D. Rollinson, M. Foot and J. Handley (1996) Supervisor and manager styles in handling discipline and grievance. Part one – comparing styles in handling discipline and grievance, *Personnel Review,* Vol. 25, No. 3. An article about the ways managers deal with discipline and grievances.

Mordsley, B. and C. Aylott (2006) A grievance by any other name. *People Management,* Vol. 12, No. 14, 19. This discusses the way that employment tribunals have interpreted the definition of a grievance.

Nelson, N.C. (2006) Good grievances. *HR Magazine,* Vol. 51, No. 10, 113–4, 116. This provides a clear discussion about the way that managers should handle potential grievances in the workplace.

Rollinson, D., C. Hook, M. Foot and J. Handley (1996) Supervisor and manager styles in handling discipline and grievance. Part two – approaches to handling discipline and grievance, *Personnel Review,* Vol. 25, No. 4. An article that provides more detail on some of the research findings mentioned in the earlier article in this section by Hook, C., D. Rollinson, M. Foot and J. Handley (1996).

Internet

The Advisory, Conciliation and Arbitration Service   **www.acas.org.uk**
Another source of information for ACAS publications, some of which are published in full on this site.

The Department for Business, Enterprise and Regulatory Reform   **www.berr.gov.uk**
Many useful publications, discussion documents and some pieces of legislation can be found on this site.

The TUC   **www.tuc.org.uk**
This gives the TUC's views on many current issues and new legislation.

CHAPTER 14

Dismissal, redundancy and outplacement

Objectives

By the end of this chapter you will be able to:

- explain what is meant by the term 'fair dismissal'
- explain what is meant by 'redundancy'
- define the term 'outplacement'
- describe the services that an outplacement consultancy may provide.

In Chapter 13 we explained that there may be occasions when not everything in the relationship between employer and worker goes smoothly: the employee or worker may be dissatisfied with the employer and raise a grievance, or the employer may have to use a disciplinary procedure against an individual who is proving to be unsatisfactory. Human resource managers want to get the best from the people they employ: people are, as we have shown, very expensive to recruit and train, and HRM specialists will not wish to waste these resources. However, there will be occasions when it becomes inevitable that the organisation will have to end the employment of one or more employees, and line managers as well as human resource specialists will need to know something about this process.

This chapter will examine ways in which employment may be ended fairly. We shall then consider one particular type of dismissal – redundancy – and examine ways in which the effects of redundancy may be lessened by the provision of an outplacement service.

The chapter presents general guidance only, and is intended to provide not a complete or authoritative guide to employment law, but rather an appreciation of general principles with which students of HRM should be familiar and which they may use to guide them in dealing with people who are dismissed from an organisation.

It is important for a number of reasons that any dismissal should be fair. The workforce will be better able to trust and work effectively for a management that operates fair procedures and the reputation of the organisation in general will also benefit from this.

Fairness is both a moral and a legal issue, and sometimes organisations that have tried very hard to be fair in their procedures and practices will still be found in the eyes of the law to have acted unfairly. This may be because individual managers or supervisors have made errors in the way they handled an issue, or failed to document their actions adequately, or because of some legal technicality. HRM practitioners, therefore, need to be aware of the importance of legislation and must endeavour to have systems, procedures and training in place so that everyone involved in the dismissal process acts in a fair way. They also need to know where to find detailed guidance, as they cannot know in minute detail every aspect of the law: there are many specialist texts that can help with this. Although the HRM practitioner needs to be sufficiently aware of legislation and the need for fair procedures to be able to deal with issues that arise on a day-to-day basis, it may be that, faced with an unusual problem, he or she will also need the advice of the organisation's solicitor.

Legislation changes constantly, which means that you should be aware of general principles with regard to dismissal but you should always be prepared to check for the most recent legislation and the most recent interpretation of it, and not just rely on notes that you made years earlier. Textbooks become out of date, and you should always look for the most recent edition to guide you, although even this may not be enough to take account of the latest changes in law. As we said in the previous chapter, changes have been proposed for the statutory discipline, dismissal and grievance procedure which will also affect dismissal and employment tribunals. These are not due to happen until after the publication of this book so check our website at **www.pearsoned.co.uk/foothook** for an update on these proposals. We have also listed some useful sources of information at the end of the chapter.

People leave organisations for a host of reasons, and of course not all who leave are dismissed. Resignations and retirements do not normally cause any legal problems to the organisation, but employers need to take great care in the case of dismissals that they abide by the law, and ensure not only that they dismiss for a potentially fair reason, but that the way they handle the dismissal and the whole dismissal process is also fair. As we said in Chapter 13, this means that employers who are dismissing someone must also take into account the statutory discipline and grievance procedures that were introduced by the Employment Act 2002.

Organisations, in particular, which employ people abroad need also to ensure that they are fully aware of the legislation which applies within the countries in which they operate.

Dismissal

Usually both employers and employees understand when a dismissal has occurred as it results in a person's employment being ended. That person may have to work their notice period or the employer may prefer to pay them for this time, but terminate their employment immediately. This is often referred to as payment in lieu of notice. In circumstances where the dismissal has occurred because of the employee's gross misconduct, the employee is not entitled to any notice or payment in lieu of notice. There are, however, other circumstances in which dismissal may occur which may be less well known, such as the non-renewal of a fixed-term contract or constructive dismissal. We shall consider each of these in turn.

Fixed-term contract

This sounds straightforward enough, and occurs when there is a fixed-term contract for a particular period of employment. If the contract is not renewed, this technically counts as a dismissal although it is normally expected by both the employer and the employee. Sometimes in the past, organisations insisted that individuals whom they employed on fixed-term contracts gave up their rights to claim unfair dismissal by making them sign a waiver clause at the start of their employment. Waiver clauses in fixed-term contracts were abolished under the Employment Relations Act 1999 so an individual can no longer be made to sign away their right to claim for unfair dismissal.

Constructive dismissal

The second definition given here is a little more complicated, and is known as constructive dismissal. It is often hard to prove that the dismissal was unfair, as the person has normally resigned and given some other reason for leaving. It is later, when he or she realises that the resignation was because of the employer's conduct that he or she might decide to bring a case of constructive dismissal. For a case to succeed, the employer normally has to have done something so seriously wrong that the employee was justified in feeling that he or she could no longer work in that workplace, as the employer's action would be regarded as a significant breach of the employment contract. A possible example is an employer who bullied the employee so that his or her life was a total misery and the person felt obliged to leave. In this type of case the employer would not have followed the statutory discipline, dismissal and grievance procedure since they did not actually dismiss the employee. However, the employee should normally have followed the statutory grievance procedure before presenting a claim for constructive unfair dismissal.

Pause for thought 14.1 We said earlier that dismissal should be for a potentially fair reason and that a fair dismissal procedure should also be followed. What do you consider to be potentially fair reasons for dismissal?

Potentially fair reasons for dismissal

You have probably listed offences such as theft, poor attendance, assault, fraud, being under the influence of drugs or alcohol, sexual harassment or racial harassment, or perhaps a serious breach of a safety rule. If you refer back to Chapter 13, you will see that these are all examples of misconduct or of gross misconduct, although poor attendance, if it is due to ill-health, may be an example of lack of capability.

There are four other potentially valid reasons for dismissal besides misconduct and lack of capability, and each of these covers a wide range of situations. For a dismissal to be fair, an employer must first be able to prove it was for one of these six reasons:

- conduct
- capability
- a statutory requirement

- some other substantial reason
- redundancy
- retirement.

The need to act reasonably

Do you think that if an employee is guilty, for example, of misconduct or proves incapable of doing the job, this means that if the employer dismisses him or her it will automatically be fair? In Chapter 13 we said that it was important for an organisation to have a fair disciplinary procedure modelled on the ACAS Code of Practice. It is important, if an organisation is considering dismissing someone, that it not only has potentially fair grounds for dismissing them (i.e. it is dismissing them for one of the reasons listed earlier), but it also acts fairly in the way that it carries out this dismissal. The organisation needs to have a fair procedure for handling dismissals and should have followed its own procedure in a fair way. This also means, as we have already said, that the employer must have complied with the statutory discipline and dismissal procedures. This is what we mean by the condition that the dismissal also has to be actually fair. An employer should strive to be fair but may still face a claim for unfair dismissal, as dismissed employees may have a different perception of whether their treatment was fair.

Employment tribunals examine dismissal cases from two points of view. One is whether employers have acted reasonably in treating the grounds as sufficient reason to justify dismissal. The other is that they must satisfy the tribunal that they acted reasonably in the dismissal procedure. If an employee brings a claim for unfair dismissal, the tribunal will have to make a judgement about what happened after considering evidence from both parties; consequently it is important for employers to follow their own procedure and have clear records and documentary evidence.

ACTIVITY 14.1

Susan has been employed by your organisation for three years as a clerical assistant. During the past year there have been many problems with poor attendance and timekeeping. Susan's manager has tried to establish whether there is a problem underlying this poor attendance and timekeeping, but has found no clear explanation. Susan has been counselled about this situation and has gone through the disciplinary procedure. She was written to and invited to attend two disciplinary interviews to discuss her poor attendance and timekeeping and she has been issued in the presence of her trade union representative with a written warning after the first meeting and a final written warning after the second meeting. The organisation has done everything required under the statutory discipline and dismissal procedures. The final written warning was issued only three weeks ago, and yet since then Susan has already had one day absent from work and has been late twice. She has not provided any good explanation for this, but simply says that she overslept and then did not feel like coming to work.

Do you think that the employer has potentially fair reasons for dismissing Susan? Give reasons for your answer. Which category of dismissal would this fall into?

If the employer does decide to dismiss Susan, do you think that it is being fair in the way that it is handling this dismissal?

Discussion of Activity 14.1

From the evidence given, this case looks to be a potentially fair dismissal on the grounds of misconduct, as Susan does appear to have behaved badly and the employer does appear to have a valid reason for dismissal. In this case, the management appear to have a disciplinary procedure which they followed and seem, from the evidence given here, to have acted reasonably and fairly. A case such as this would probably not go to an employment tribunal, but there may be other circumstances not given here that might lead Susan to feel her dismissal was unfair and to pursue a tribunal case.

Conduct

Conduct is the most common reason for dismissal and results in the most claims of unfair dismissal at employment tribunals. Both serious acts of misconduct, such as gross misconduct, and more minor but frequently repeated acts of misconduct result in dismissals that fall into this category. In Activity 14.1 Susan's dismissal was for a series of minor but repeated lapses in her conduct.

Capability

Lack of capability could arise for several reasons. According to the CIPD (2007a), capability issues normally fall into one of the following three categories:

- qualifications – defined as 'any degee, diploma or other academic, technical or professional qualification relevant to the position' held by the employee
- incompetence or poor performance – occurs where, usually through no fault of their own, the employee is simply incapable of delivering work to the required standard. For example, a person who works in a dog kennels who frequently forgets to lock the kennels and feed the animals. (Obviously great care must be taken to ensure that the incompetence is not related to a disability.)
- illness – for example, where an employee's illness makes it impossible for them to perform their duties.

The first of these categories is reasonably straightforward and would cover situations where the employee did not have the qualifications that they claimed to possess. Lack of qualification is a potentially fair reason for dismissal. Although good selection procedures should mean that people who do not have the desired qualifications are not employed, there are many well-publicised examples of people who have lied about their qualifications and who have worked for an organisation for a number of years before being found out and dismissed. There have even been cases of doctors who have practised for many years without people realising that they did not have any medical qualification. In a case such as this there would be a potentially fair reason for dismissal.

In the second situation the employee simply may not be able to do the job, however hard they try. Some people may prove to be incapable of doing the job required because they lack the required level of skill or ability. This could be a reflection on the organisation's selection techniques or training, but if training and opportunities to improve have been given, it may be necessary to dismiss the person if he or she still proves to be incapable.

Problems relating to absenteeism, particularly relating to long-term illness, can be more difficult. We discussed some of the problems in the last chapter, and clearly not all absenteeism would fall into the category of misconduct as Susan's behaviour did. Many absentees are genuinely ill but the organisation, as we said in Chapter 14, may reluctantly, having exhausted all its procedures, have to consider whether or not to dismiss. This needs to be handled in a totally different way to a misconduct dismissal, and such a dismissal would be on the grounds of the person not being capable of doing the job. The employer needs to show that it believed in the employee's lack of capability and had made reasonable enquiries about these.

Particular attention, however, should be paid to the requirements of the Disability Discrimination Act (1995) before making any decision to dismiss on ill-health grounds. If many of the absences are directly attributable to a disability the employer may have to discount these from their calculations when considering whether or not the employee's attendance record is satisfactory. This was the case in *Cox* v. *the Post Office* (IT/1301162/97) where it was decided that the Post Office should have discounted Cox's absences due to asthma, since this is classed as a disability, from the figures for his attendance which they had used to justify his dismissal.

It is also important to note that if the illness itself leads to a disability the employer should first try to establish whether reasonable adjustments could be made to enable them to keep their job, before considering dismissal. According to Gill Sage, an employment law specialist, 'No decision to terminate an employee's contract on the grounds of ill-health or to subject someone to any other detriment should now be taken solely on the basis of absence from the workplace' (Sage, 1998, p. 24).

● A statutory requirement

This is a rarer reason for dismissal, which deals with the situation where the employer would be breaking the law if it continued to employ that person. Possible examples of this would be employing a person who did not have a work permit, or employing a person who was legally too young to work full time in that particular work environment, the results of police checks on people working with children or vulnerable adults, or possibly employing a driver who had lost his or her licence and was disqualified from driving.

● Some other substantial reason

This category is to cover eventualities not listed already, where there is a genuinely fair reason for dismissal that does not fit neatly into any of the listed categories. One example of this is where the contract is only temporary and is not renewed. Legally the person has been dismissed. They have not been dismissed because of their misconduct or because of lack of capability or lack of qualification, or even because of some legal requirement, so this form of dismissal would fall into the category of some other substantial reason.

● Redundancy

Many employers dislike discussing redundancies and invent other names for this type of dismissal. They refer to it as 'downsizing' or 'delayering', or even as being 'forced to let someone go'. It is certainly a very unpleasant form of dismissal for all concerned, as the person involved is not normally being dismissed because of anything that he or she has done wrong but as a result of the organisation's need to streamline its operations or cut back in some areas because of an unforeseen crisis, or perhaps through poor human resource planning. Many organisations are striving to be increasingly flexible in their deployment of people and often employ temporary or agency staff, with the result that redundancy affects more and more people in an increasingly wide range of jobs as these organisations move from traditional employment patterns to new ones.

Redundancy can occur because of three main circumstances:

- the whole business closes
- part of the business or a particular workplace closes
- there is less need for a particular type of work, which results in some employees being surplus to requirements.

We shall return to the topic of redundancy later in this chapter.

Retirement

From 1 October 2006, as a result of the Employment Equality (Age) Regulations 2006, retirement became the sixth potentially fair reason for dismissal. From this date employees who are aged over 65 have been able to claim unfair dismissal if a proper retirement process has not been followed by their employer. However, there is a distinction to be made here between planned retirements and unplanned retirements as not all retirements will result in potentially unfair dismissal cases.

Planned retirements

Generally, planned retirements of employees where the normal retirement age is 65 will be deemed to be fair but in order to be fair the employer must have notified the employee of the date of their retirement at least six months in advance of that date. The employer must also follow the procedure fairly.

There is also a further duty for an employer which is referred to as a 'duty to consider.' According to CIPD (2006a), 'Employers must consider a member of staff's request to stay beyond retirement.' As part of this procedure the employer must initially give between 12 and 6 months' notice of their intention to retire the employee and set a date for this. They also need to make the employee aware of their right to request to work beyond the retirement age. The employee must make a written request to work beyond the retirement age and if the employer agrees they need to set a mutually acceptable date. Once the request has been received by the employer the CIPD (2006) say that they must:

- consider the request, and
- notify the member of staff in writing of the decision
- allow the right to appeal.

If the 'duty to consider' provision has been followed by the employer, and if they decide not to grant the employee the right to work beyond 65, then there will be a presumption that the dismissal is fair. There is no obligation for the employer to grant the request.

Unplanned retirements

In the event that the employer does not follow the procedure fairly or does not give the employee at least six months' notice of their date of retirement then the retirement would be deemed to be unplanned and in that event an employee may be able to claim unfair dismissal.

Who can bring a case for unfair dismissal

It is obviously important that all dismissals should be fair, but the law normally provides the opportunity for only some employees (those who have one year of service), to bring a case claiming unfair dismissal before an employment tribunal, though for some forms of dismissal categorised as automatically unfair there is no service requirement at all: this will be discussed later. If you remember our discussion of equal opportunities issues in Chapter 5, you will recall that there was no mention of a qualification period for cases of sex discrimination, racial discrimination or discrimination on grounds of disability. This is because many cases of discrimination occur before people are actually employed at all. However, for most cases of unfair dismissal to be brought before a tribunal, employees do have to have been employed for a certain length of time, although the actual length of employment required has varied over the years. This means that some unscrupulous employers may be tempted to treat people who do not have sufficient length of service with them in an unfair way, as they know that a case for unfair dismissal cannot be brought against them. Clearly this is not good practice and employers should treat all workers in a fair way.

> ### Did you know?
>
> Between 1 April 2006 and 31 March 2007 there were 35,583 claims to employment tribunals made for unfair dismissal. Of these 13,320 were settled before reaching the tribunal and a further 11,510 were withdrawn. 8,738 went to an employment tribunal while a further 1,645 had some other outcome.
>
> (*Source*: Advisory, Conciliation and Arbitration Service, 2007)

How to bring a case for unfair dismissal

Any employee with the required one year of service who feels that they were dismissed unfairly can complete an application for the case to be decided by an employment tribunal. Forms are easy to obtain and available from Job Centres, Law Centres or Citizens Advice Bureaux, or the process can be started by applying online at **www.employmenttribunals.gov.uk**. The tribunal system was overhauled in October 2004 and one result of this is that a new user-friendly application form (ET1) was introduced from April 2005. Once the claimant has completed their application it should be sent to the relevant employment tribunal office or it can now be completed online.

For acceptance of unfair dismissal cases, and most other types of case, there is usually a time limit of three months from the date the employment ended. Employment tribunals do not usually accept cases outside the relevant time limit, but this does depend on the reason for the delay and in some exceptional circumstances late cases may still be considered. Tribunals will not consider claims unless they are assured that the organisation's grievance procedure has been exhausted.

The application form is allocated a case number by the tribunal office and a copy is sent to the respondent within five days of the tribunal receiving the application. (The respondent is the person the case is brought against. In most cases it will be the employer.) The respondent will be sent a response form (ET3) which they are asked to complete, indicating whether they agree with or are resisting the claim against them. They must complete this form within 28 days in order to be allowed to answer the claim against them. Usually copies of both forms are also sent to ACAS, the Advisory, Conciliation and Arbitration Service.

ACAS has been using conciliation for several years but the concept of a conciliation period was changed in October 2004 to encourage employees and employers to try to reach a settlement at an earlier stage. Conciliation by ACAS will now normally be concentrated into a short, fixed period of between 7 and 13 weeks, depending on the nature of the claim, and once this time has ended ACAS is no longer able to be involved. In its role as conciliator, ACAS may repeat information provided by one side to the other side to try to bring about a settlement, but this information is not normally repeated at the tribunal itself, unless all parties give their permission.

In most cases the tribunal does not know about any of the correspondence between the parties and ACAS, so the tribunal will review the case on the evidence presented to it in writing and by witnesses at the tribunal hearing.

Did you know?

The Advisory, Conciliation and Arbitration Service is nowadays not just concerned with employment issues in Great Britain. As is consistent with working in a global economy ACAS (2007) say, 'We have spread the word that good employment relations make good business sense far and wide this year – not just locally or nationally, but also internationally.' In 2006–7 ACAS made visits to Bucharest to run workshops and presentations on internal and external communications and received a visiting delegation from Bosnia to look at e-communications. An EU-funded Romania twinning project was successfully completed to assist Romania prepare for joining the EU in 2007. Training programmes were delivered in Bulgaria and one member of ACAS staff was seconded to work in Bulgaria. Work was conducted with the Government of Brazil on alternative means of conflict resolution. ACAS also 'welcomed delegations from China as well as visitors from Australia, Ethiopia, France, Hong Kong, Japan, Malaysia and South Korea.'

(*Source*: Advisory, Conciliation and Arbitration Service, 2007)

Since 2001 there has been an alternative way to resolve unfair dismissal disputes, in which the ACAS arbitration service operates as a voluntary alternative to employment tribunal hearings. People who choose this option have to agree to accept the decision of the arbitrator, who is able to make exactly the same awards as an employment tribunal. The aims of this scheme are to cut the number of expensive tribunal cases and to create a quicker and simpler system that is free of much legal jargon. However, this has not proved to be a very popular alternative to employment tribunals and since its inception in 2001 there have only been 58 cases which used this service. During 2006–07 only three cases used this service but ACAS (2007) say that 'while the number of cases received has not fulfilled expectation, the scheme provides a low-cost, informal alternative to employment tribunals.' ACAS (2007) also comment on the levels of settlement made among those that do use their arbitration service and say that 'in cases where dismissals have been found to be unfair, settlements have ranged from £256 to £18,000. This is broadly consistent with the range of awards by employment tribunals.'

● Employment tribunals

The tribunal itself normally comprises three people: the chair, who has to be legally qualified and have worked as either a solicitor or a barrister for at least seven years, and two wing members. One of the wing members will be chosen from a list of names submitted by employers' organisations and the other will be chosen from a similar list submitted by workers' organisations. All are there because of their knowledge and experience, in their different ways, of employment issues and work-related problems and their aim is to ensure a fair hearing for all concerned. They will probably ask questions to clarify any points they are unsure of during the course of the tribunal hearing. The Gibbons review also recommended an overhaul of the employment tribunal system and if this is acted upon it will also be likely to occur after the publication of this book in 2008. We shall update the student website at **www. pearsoned.co.uk/foothook** with later developments about this.

ACTIVITY 14.2

Find out how many cases of alleged unfair dismissal have been brought during the last year.

(a) How many of these cases have been heard at employment tribunals?

(b) How many of these cases have been taken to ACAS voluntary arbitration?

(c) What was the success rate in each category?

Automatically fair reasons for dismissal

There are a very small number of situations in which dismissal is likely to be viewed as automatically fair. These include situations where the reason or main reason for the dismissal involved the employee:

- in problems of national security
- taking part in an unofficial strike or some other type of unofficial action (this does not apply in all circumstances)
- taking part in an official strike or some other form of official action and where all the relevant employees who participated in the same action were also dismissed and not re-employed during the next three months.

National security is obviously a serious concern, so someone who endangered national security, perhaps by selling secrets, would obviously come into this category. Taking part in unofficial strikes and even official strikes can also be a very risky undertaking for the employee, even though these actions do not seem to be in quite the same category as endangering national security.

Automatically unfair reasons for dismissal

Some reasons for dismissal are likely to be automatically unfair, and in these cases an employment tribunal does not need to go through the process of establishing whether there was a fair reason for the dismissal before it assesses whether or not the employer acted reasonably. These include dismissal related to discrimination on grounds of sex, race, disability or a spent conviction, as these areas are covered by the Sex Discrimination Act 1975, the Race Relations Act 1976, the Disability Discrimination Act 1995 or the Rehabilitation of Offenders Act 1974, and in all of these there is no requirement for a length of service qualification for bringing a claim before an employment tribunal. Similarly, it is also automatically unfair to use any of these as the basis for selection for redundancy.

Some other examples of automatically unfair dismissal are given next but this is not an exhaustive list:

- trade union-related dismissals
- dismissal on maternity- or pregnancy-related grounds
- dismissal for taking, or proposing to take, some action on health and safety grounds
- dismissal for having sought in good faith to exercise a statutory employment right
- dismissal of a shop worker or betting shop worker for refusing, or proposing to refuse, to do shop work on Sundays
- acting or offering to act as a representative for consultation about redundancy, business transfer or occupational pension trusteeship matters
- dismissal of the employee because they try to make the employer pay them the minimum wage
- a statutory discipline and dismissal procedure has not been completed by the employer and this is due to the fault of the employer.

In cases where there are automatically unfair reasons for dismissal, the employment tribunal does not have to go through the two-stage process, first establishing that there was a fair reason for the dismissal, then investigating whether the employer acted reasonably. In these cases the employment tribunal has to find the dismissal fair or unfair solely with regard to the reasonableness of the actions of the employer and the reason for the dismissal.

Trade union-related dismissals

It is an automatically unfair reason for dismissal if the dismissal is for trade union membership or activities. This will apply whether the employee is dismissed because of expressing his or her intention to join a trade union or not to join a trade union, or for his or her actual membership or non-membership of a trade union. It also applies if someone is dismissed just because of their trade union activities, such as handing out leaflets or going to a trade union meeting.

Dismissal on maternity- or pregnancy-related grounds

The law relating to pregnancy is complex but it obviously does not make very good business sense to dismiss someone in whom an organisation has invested time and training just because she is pregnant. This is another automatically unfair reason for dismissal. An unfair dismissal of this type could also prove to be potentially very expensive for an employer as many claims of this type are also brought under sex discrimination legislation and there is no upper limit set on the amount of compensation that the woman could claim.

Dismissal on health and safety grounds

Once again the dismissal will be automatically unfair if the employer dismisses the employee or selects him or her for redundancy because he or she tried to bring health and safety issues to the attention of the employer. It would also be an automatically unfair dismissal if it was because the employee carried out or even just tried to carry out designated duties relating to health and safety or prevention of accidents at work, or because of his or her activities as a safety representative or on a safety committee.

Dismissal for wishing to exercise a statutory employment right

The dismissal will be automatically unfair if it occurs as a result of the employee bringing proceedings against the employer or alleging that an employer has infringed a statutory employment right such as a right to a minimum period of notice or the right of a trade union official for paid time off to carry out duties.

Dismissal of a shop worker for refusing to work on Sundays

Shop workers or betting office workers who are dismissed for refusal to work on a Sunday are also able to claim this as an automatically unfair reason for dismissal. When Sunday trading was introduced, some workers feared that they would be dismissed if they were unwilling to work on a Sunday so this is designed to afford them some protection.

Dismissal of a person because of his or her actions as a representative of the workforce for consultation about redundancy or business transfer

Another automatically unfair reason for dismissal occurs if the employer dismisses a person who was acting on behalf of the workforce, or who is proposing to act as their representative in connection with negotiations about redundancy or business transfer or occupational pension trusteeship. This is to prevent unscrupulous employers from effectively 'shooting the messenger' by dismissing unfairly those who try to help or act on behalf of the employees.

Dismissal of the employee because they try to make the employer pay the minimum wage

In this instance the employee may have been trying to ensure that the employer pays the minimum wage to him or herself or to other employees. If they have not been paid the minimum wage it is against the law, and if the employee who raises this issue is dismissed because they have raised it, then it will be an automatically unfair dismissal.

A statutory discipline, dismissal and grievance procedure has not been completed by the employer and this is due to the fault of the employer

Introduced in October 2004, this is a relatively new addition to the list of automatically unfair dismissals which reinforces the fact that the Government wants employers to take seriously the need to complete disciplinary procedures and dismissals in a fair way and to comply with the statutory procedure. If a statutory discipline, dismissal and grievance procedure has not been completed and the employer is to blame for this then 'in these cases there is also a power to increase/decrease the compensatory award between 10% and 50% still within the maximum amount' (CIPD, 2007a).

Wrongful dismissal

Wrongful dismissal is based on contract law and relates to instances when the employer has broken the contract. One of the most common examples of breach of contract is when the employee is dismissed without notice in circumstances where this is clearly not deserved because of any wrongdoing on the part of the employee, or where the employee is dismissed but with the incorrect period of notice. Unlike claims of unfair dismissal, there is no qualifying length of service required for eligibility to bring a case of wrongful dismissal. According to the CIPD (2006b), 'the most common example of a wrongful dismissal is failure to give the employee the correct length of contractual notice or statutory notice.'

Compensation for unfair dismissal

If a former employee wins his or her case for unfair dismissal at an employment tribunal the compensation awarded may take several forms.

Reinstatement

In this case the employment tribunal or ACAS arbitrator says that the employer must give the former employee their old job back on exactly the same terms and conditions as before and pay compensation for any loss of wages while not employed. Failure on the part of the employer to comply with this order is likely to result in additional financial awards, known as an additional or special award, being made to the employee.

Re-engagement

This means that the employment tribunal or ACAS arbitrator states that the employer must re-employ their former employee but it may be in a different job or on different terms and conditions of employment. For example, it may not be possible to give them back their old job as the vacancy may already have been filled by a new employee.

Compensation

This means financial compensation and is divided into the basic award and the compensatory award. The basic award is calculated in the same way as the statutory redundancy payment which is discussed later in this chapter. It is calculated by taking into account the age, number of years in that employer's service and amount of the average weekly wage. At February 2007 the weekly wage included in the calculation is subject to a weekly maximum of £310 per week and the maximum basic award that can be awarded is £9,300. The Department for Business, Enterprise and Regulatory Reform (formerly the DTI) publishes an easy table for calculating these figures but these amounts are index-linked and change each year in February.

In some circumstances there may be deductions taken from the amount awarded by the employment tribunal – for example, if the employment tribunal feels that the employee partially contributed to his or her own dismissal or if the employer offered to reinstate the employee and he or she refused unreasonably.

A compensatory award may also be made and this is to take account of factors such as loss of earnings, loss of pension rights or loss of benefits, such as company car or house. There are unlimited awards made, as mentioned earlier, in cases of dismissal related to sex, race or disability discrimination. An additional award may also be made if the dismissal was for trade unionism.

451

Redundancy

We discussed earlier the fact that redundancy can be a potentially fair reason for dismissal. However, great care must be taken in the selection of those who are to be made redundant, and a large number of employment tribunal cases are brought each year where employees feel that they have been unfairly selected for redundancy.

Any organisation should first choose to take various steps to try to preclude or minimise the need for redundancies. Good human resource planning should help to minimise this need, but however effective the human resource planning, there may still be a need for redundancies because of other problems, such as the unexpected loss of a large order or the failure of the business of a large debtor.

Consultation

Consultation is a very important stage in redundancies, both for legal reasons and in order to maintain morale. Morale is always likely to be low when there is a threat of redundancy, but rumour and uncertainty are only likely to make it worse. The law on redundancy in Britain is mainly derived from the Trade Union and Labour Relations (Consolidation) Act 1992, the Collective Redundancies and Transfer of Undertakings (Protection of Employment) Regulations 1995 and the Collective Redundancies and Transfer of Undertakings (Protection of Employment) (Amendment) Regulations 1999. This means that:

- If 20 or more employees at one establishment are to be made redundant, within a period of 90 days, consultation should start at least 30 days before the first dismissal.
- If 100 or more employees at one establishment are to be made redundant, within a period of 90 days, this consultation should start at least 90 days before the first dismissal is to occur.

In practice, in Britain, consultation frequently occurs at the same time as the notification of redundancies so that the redundant employees are often already working their notice when the consultation is supposed to be taking place. This has the effect of making it rather more difficult to achieve much by consultation in terms of avoiding dismissals or reducing the numbers since those to be made redundant have already been selected.

Groups to be consulted in collective redundancies

The following rules apply to those who should be consulted in collective redundancy situations. In this instance the definition of redundancy is slightly different to the one we used earlier for redundancy pay. Here it relates to a situation where an employer proposes to dismiss at least 20 employees at one establishment within a 90-day period. The dismissal is unrelated to the quality of work of the individual concerned as it could be due to the need for fewer employees to do a particular task or because of reorganisation or reallocation of work:

- Under the 1999 regulations, if there is a recognised independent trade union within the organisation, then the consultation must be with them.

- If there is no trade union recognition agreement in place then the employer has a choice and may consult either with a trade union or with employee representatives.
- Representatives of all employees affected should be consulted and not just those who are likely to be made redundant.
- Any organisation that has been obliged collectively to consult must also notify the Department for Business, Enterprise and Regulatory Reform (BERR).
- If those employees who are likely to be affected by the redundancies are not in a trade union, and there are no other suitable representatives for employees already in place in the organisation, then the employees must be given the opportunity to elect representatives. The employer should make arrangements to ensure the fairness of these elections and must also comply with the election rules set out by BERR.
- If the employees fail to elect representatives after being given opportunities to do so, then the employer will have to give the information direct to all relevant employees in order to fulfil its legal obligation to consult.

The information needed for consultation

The employee representatives will need sufficient information from the employer about its proposals to be able to participate fully in a meaningful way in the consultations. Certain information must be given to them in writing. This must be handed individually to each of them, sent by post to an address they have given the employer or, in the case of consultation with a trade union, sent to its head office.

The employer must provide the following information:

- the reasons for the proposed redundancies
- the numbers and types of jobs that are likely to be affected by the proposals
- the anticipated total number of employees who are likely to be affected in each job at the organisation
- the proposed selection methods for those to be made redundant
- the proposed method of actually dismissing people and the anticipated period over which dismissals will take place
- the proposed methods of calculating redundancy pay.

Worker consultation in Britain and in other European countries

The penalties for not consulting adequately may result in a fine for not notifying the Department for Business, Enterprise and Regulatory Reform (BERR). The trade union representatives, employees' representatives or the employees themselves can apply to an employment tribunal which can make a protective award of up to 13 weeks' pay for each employee. Employers can, in their defence, claim that there were special circumstances which made it impossible to comply with the legislation and in many cases the consultation seems to amount to announcing the redundancies. The 1995 and 1999 regulations are the UK's response to a European ruling in 1994 from the European Court of Justice. However, the Government was not willing to sign up to a European Directive for Information and Consultation Rights. In spite of the fact that the British Government refused to sign this directive, which would have given greater rights to consultation for the British worker, it still claimed to be furious about the lack of consultation from Corus, the steel producer giant, when the company announced redundancies in 2000.

In spite of the British Government's initial refusal to sign these documents, it did eventually agree and the possible implications of the Information and Consultation Directive 2002 will be discussed later in this chapter.

The rules regarding redundancy in the other European countries do not appear at first sight to be very different to those of the UK, but the duty to consult starts sooner in France, Germany and Spain and usually applies when smaller numbers of employees are involved. Also, the duty to consult cannot be undertaken retrospectively in those countries, so the consultation has to occur before those selected for redundancy are told of the decision. It is often claimed that the laxer laws relating to redundancy in the UK make us the easiest European country in which to make staff redundant.

Marks & Spencer found, to its cost, that expectations of the way redundancy should be handled are different in the rest of Europe, when in March 2001 it announced it was closing all its stores abroad. It probably felt it had consulted sufficiently, and possibly this would be true if British standards applied. However, it was undoubtedly surprised by the way its staff in France reacted with instant walk-outs in protest, TV and radio interviews with tearful staff and pictures in newspapers in France and Britain which depicted window displays in their Nice store in which a coffin appeared draped in black with mannequins dressed in mourning and bound in chains. Support from the Prime Minister, Lionel Jospin, followed and the Government in France supported the trade unions in court action against Marks & Spencer relating to lack of consultation, and Marks & Spencer was effectively stopped from making the redundancies, at least for a time.

In France, employers are obliged by law to establish a workers' council and the council must be consulted throughout any redundancy process with a view to finding suitable alternatives to the redundancies, rather than, as so often happens in Britain, the consultation process starting as the employees are given their notice. Moreover, in France, each individual employee must be spoken to personally before any public announcements are made and plans for training individuals should also be established. Decisions on redundancies should not be sent by fax or email, as was alleged to have happened to Marks & Spencer's French employees. Trade unions in France can apply to the courts to stop redundancies from occurring, as happened in this case. John Monks, TUC General Secretary, said of the Marks & Spencer case, 'This welcome decision underlines the better protection available to workers across the Channel – French workers have shown they will not put up with such high-handed behaviour.'

> It may be the fashion in Britain to announce job losses to the media whenever a company needs a short term boost to its share price. But as this decision shows, in France employers need to act responsibly, taking into account the needs of their workforce as well as their shareholders. This shows why people at work in the UK need European proposals for wider information and consultation rights to become law as soon as possible.
>
> (Monks, 2001)

As well as an order by the courts to prevent redundancies from taking place, there are also other penalties available in France for non-compliance with the law. This could, in theory at least, be prison for the directors of a company, although in reality this has never occurred. There is also a requirement in France, Germany and Spain for a social compensation plan and, according to the European Industrial Relations Observatory (2001), this is common in most other European countries as a way of promoting redeployment and negotiating termination of employment through early retirement, redeployment and voluntary redundancy. According to the EIRO, 'The tangible outcome of redundancy negotiation tends to be:

- a reduction in the planned number of redundancies, the withdrawal of announced redundancies or the provision of employment guarantees
- the guaranteed safeguarding of wage and working conditions by the new employer
- a commitment to avoid compulsory redundancies.' (European Industrial Relations Observatory online February 2001)

The EU Information and Consultation Directive 2002 can also apply to redundancy consultation. The directive established, as we said in Chapter 3, a very general framework for information and consultation and applies from 23 March 2008 to all organisations, even small businesses.

Many EU states, as we showed earlier in relation to redundancy, already have legislation in place regarding information and consultation so this is likely to have the greatest effect on the UK and Eire, since they do not.

From the appropriate times, according to the size of the organisation concerned, it will be necessary for organisations to negotiate voluntary agreements about consultation and information with workers and whatever is agreed will need to be put in writing. The types of issue to be addressed should include information about the probable activities of the organisation and its financial situation, the employment situation within the organisation, especially where there is any likely threat to employment, such as in a redundancy situation. However, there should be information and consultation about any potential changes to the work situation, even if these do not go as far as actual redundancies.

Steps to preclude the need for redundancies

While good employers should always be looking to the future and planning their manpower needs to suit their strategic objectives, there can also be changing economic situations caused by situations such as global events that are outside the employer's control and not easy to predict. Employers do need to be flexible and so have to develop a range of strategies to avoid or limit redundancies.

Even before the Information and Consultation Directive 2002 came into effect, organisations in the UK were supposed to consult in order to prevent or minimise the need for redundancies. It is foolish to contemplate making good employees redundant if a simpler solution is feasible, so a calm, objective review of the situation is called for and a consideration of all possible alternatives. The consultation must be undertaken with a view to reaching agreement with the appropriate representatives and should include the following:

- the actual numbers and job categories likely to be affected
- the reasons for the redundancies
- the criteria for selection

- the dismissal procedures and timescales during which the redundancies will occur
- the basis for the calculation of compensation if it is different from the statutory minimum.

According to the CIPD (2007b), consultation should also include:

- why and how the individuals have been selected
- possible ways of avoiding redundancy
- possible alternative work.

This sounds reasonable but, as stated earlier, there have been many occasions in the UK where consultation has only started after the redundancy period has been announced so although it is possible that dismissals may still be avoided, it seems less likely. Some bad employers also prefer to face the financial penalties rather than go through the process in the way in which it was intended.

The steps which can be taken to avoid redundancies will depend to some extent on the timescale available. Some employers are keen to look after their employees and to part company with them on as good terms as possible. Employers are supposed to consider alternatives to compulsory redundancy and, according to the CIPD (2007b), 'Organisations should always try to avoid redundancies. Ways of doing this include:

- natural wastage
- recruitment freeze
- stopping or reducing overtime
- offer early retirement to volunteers (subject to age discrimination issues)
- retraining and redeployment
- offering existing employees sabbaticals and secondments.'

The methods chosen will depend on the particular circumstances within the organisation. Natural wastage may work well if two organisations are combining and if there is sufficient time to allow for natural wastage to occur, but is unlikely to be the best solution if the organisation needs to reduce staff immediately and most solutions also carry some costs to the organisation.

Many organisations do already engage in meaningful negotiation with their employees and do take steps to minimise the need for redundancies. Some go much further and provide outplacement services and these will be discussed later.

Selection for redundancy

If the consultations or measures chosen as a result of them fail to work, the employer needs to decide how to select and implement the redundancies. Ideally there should be an agreed procedure for handling redundancies but if not, then criteria which are fair need to be chosen and the pool of workers from among whom the redundancies are to occur also needs to be identified.

Selection criteria for redundancy

Employers need to choose criteria for selection carefully.

CASE STUDY 14.1 Redundancy

Read the following case study and answer the questions that follow.

The Spartan Insurance Company has decided that it is overstaffed and that it must cut back on its office staff. The departmental manager for administration recommends that the post room and print room, which between them employ seven staff, should be amalgamated into one section. This will eliminate the need for three members of staff.

The post room is run by Mr Arshad Mohammed, who is aged 34, is extremely efficient and has been with the organisation for three years. There are three other members of staff in this section – Mrs Sarah Sergeant, Ms Sandra Smythe and Mr Terry Gibbs. Mrs Sarah Sergeant, a widow aged 55, has worked for Spartan Insurance for 20 years. She has always been an extremely reliable employee, but since the death of her husband 18 months ago she has suffered greatly from ill-health and has had a series of illnesses linked to depression.

Ms Sandra Smythe is a fairly recent recruit to the organisation. She is aged 25 and has been employed for six months. She has settled into the job well and is very efficient in everything she has to do, but is the first to admit that she still has a great deal to learn.

The most junior member of staff in this section is Terry Gibbs. He is only 20 and joined Spartan Insurance Company straight from school. He has been employed by the company for two years and seemed to have a few problems making the transition from school to work; Mr Mohammed has spoken to him informally once or twice about his attitude to work. More recently Mr Mohammed has had to warn him about his timekeeping, and he received a written warning about this. The written warning is still current and does not expire for a further month, but Terry has taken this warning extremely seriously and there has been a noticeable improvement in both his attitude and his timekeeping.

The print room has three staff – Mr George Brownlow, Mrs Rashida Ali and Ms Sally Wilson. Mr Brownlow, aged 44, is the supervisor of this section but in reality he does not actually perform any supervisory duties. Neither is he qualified to service any of the machines. He spends most of his time grumbling about the company and telling the other staff to get on with their work. He has been employed by the organisation for 10 years and it is generally thought that he was moved to his present job where he would be out of everyone's way, because of his generally uncooperative nature. It is believed that this situation was allowed to develop because he was a close personal friend of a former branch manager. This manager has long since left the organisation but Mr Brownlow is always clever enough not to do anything to warrant dismissal, and has not even received any warnings about his work. He is also a prominent local councillor and spends quite a bit of time attending council meetings.

Luckily for Mr Brownlow there are two very efficient employees who cover for his inefficiency and who do most of the work. Mrs Ali is 35 and has worked for Spartan Insurance for four years. She knows almost everything that there is to know about the machines and in effect runs the section. Sally Wilson is also extremely efficient; she is 17 years old and has been employed for a year, having started last summer straight from school.

Questions

1 What criteria would you propose for selection for redundancy here?
2 Which employees would you select for redundancy?

Discussion of Case Study 14.1

You might have chosen criteria based on length of employment or factors such as level of competence or attendance and timekeeping.

If you chose to use the last in first out principle then you would make the following people redundant: Ms Sandra Smythe (employed for 6 months), Mr Terry Gibbs (employed for 2 years) and Ms Sally Wilson (employed for 1 year). LIFO has often been the preferred choice by trade unions and it seems an objective method of selection, with those who have the shortest length of employment with the organisation being chosen for redundancy. This method also has the advantage of being easy to use and understand as well as being less costly in terms of redundancy pay. It may, however, as in this case, mean that those who are selected for redundancy are those who, although they have the shortest length of service, may be keen, enthusiastic employees who will have much to offer the organisation in the future. This might result in a stagnating, ageing workforce who lack the skills and versatility required for future business success. From an employer's point of view it is not a very satisfactory way of selecting redundant employees. Care also needs to be taken with this approach to avoid accusations of age discrimination as it is quite likely in many organisations that the last to join may also be the youngest.

If you chose criteria such as timekeeping and level of efficiency you are likely to have proposed the selection of Mr Brownlow, Mr Terry Gibbs and Mrs Sergeant.

Employers often choose to use other criteria so that they can retain efficient employees while making redundant others who may not have given such good service, even though they have been employed for a much longer period of time. Caution also has to be exercised in this case to ensure that the criteria chosen are objective and fair. Just saying that someone has, for example, 'a poor attitude to work' is not likely to prove adequate grounds for selection for redundancy, as this is rather vague and subjective. More objective criteria need to be used, and the ability to do this depends on whether the organisation has effective records of employee capability and competence. You would need to break job performance down into several areas such as level of skill, knowledge, experience, flexibility, productivity, appraisal records. If you selected Mr Brownlow for redundancy, you would need to have clear evidence about levels of efficiency and output. If, on the other hand, you chose Terry Gibbs for redundancy because of his poor attendance record, you would have to ensure that there are clear records for absence and that the pattern of absenteeism does not appear high because of an uncharacteristic level of ill-health just prior to the redundancy period. Criteria such as disciplinary warnings also need careful checks to ensure that they are still 'live'.

Some criteria may also make the redundancies potentially unlawful if, for example, they apply disproportionately to one sex, one ethnic group, one age group or to employees with disabilities. Whatever the selection criteria used, employers should take care to ensure that the criteria are neither directly nor indirectly discriminatory. Selection of part-time rather than full-time employees may, for instance, constitute indirect sex discrimination if the majority of part-time employees are women and the majority of full-time employees are men.

According to the CIPD (2007b), 'where there is a choice between employees, selection must be based on objective criteria which may include:

- length of service
- attendance records
- disciplinary records

- skills, competencies and qualifications
- work experience
- performance records.'

Tribunals generally look favourably on selection procedures based on a points system. However, the fairness may be suspect if only one person has made the selection and care should also be taken to avoid factors which may be discriminatory such that 'selecting part-timers in preference to full-timers could be discriminatory if a high proportion of women are affected' (CIPD, 2007b).

Rights of redundant employees

Consultation with individual employees

Employers should also consult with each individual employee who is to be affected by the redundancies, even if there has also been consultation with the unions or with employee representatives. This consultation should:

- explain why the redundancies are needed
- explain why the particular employee has been selected
- show any relevant documentation
- explain why no suitable alternative work is currently available
- explain any requirements during the notice period such as whether normal working or part-time working is required, whether payment will be made in lieu of notice, and explain what time off is allowed to seek alternative work or for training.

Suitable alternative employment

The employer should offer a suitable alternative job if there is one, rather than making the employee redundant. If the employee's job title is broad, there may be sufficient flexibility to make an offer easily. If this is not the case, the employer should not automatically assume that any alternative employment that involved less pay or status would necessarily be unsuitable to the employee; it should still be discussed. The employees should, however, be given sufficient information about any alternative job so that they can realistically reach a decision, and they should also be offered the chance of a trial period. This should be of four weeks' duration, and will give both the employer and the employee the chance to assess the job's suitability. It should start as the old contract finishes. If a longer trial period is required because of the need for retraining, this should be agreed in writing before the date of commencement of the trial period. If either party finds the new job to be unsuitable during this period then the redundancy situation will still apply, and the redundant employee will still be entitled to his or her redundancy pay.

If the offer of suitable alternative employment is refused by the employee, then the employer has the option of withholding redundancy pay. Any claim to an employment tribunal will have to assess the suitability of the offer and the reasonableness of the refusal.

Right to time off for job searching or retraining

Employees who have worked for two years for the employer and are about to be made redundant have a statutory entitlement to a reasonable amount of time off from work to look for other jobs or to retrain in order to be able to improve their employment prospects. Any employee who is not allowed a reasonable amount of time off for these purposes can make a complaint to an employment tribunal.

Redundancy pay

Employers are expected to compensate any employee who has been made redundant, and who has worked for them for at least two years in continuous employment by paying them an amount of redundancy pay. The actual amount that the employee may be entitled to if they are redundant is calculated according to age, length of service and weekly pay. There is an upper earnings limit for the amount of weekly pay that may be included in this calculation, and this amount alters each year. Currently the limit on the weekly rate is £310 (2007). Redundancy pay is tax free and does not affect the right to unemployment benefit. Furthermore, the amount that the employee receives is not affected even if she or he starts another job immediately. Although redundancy pay has been largely exempt form the provisons of the Age Discrimination Act there have been some alterations to the upper and lower limits. The calculation of redundancy is based on the actual age of the employee at the date of dismissal, and takes account of each year of service in the appropriate age band as follows:

> **Did you know?**
>
> The reason redundancy pay increases with age is to compensate, to some extent, for the increased difficulty that older workers may experience when faced with finding a new job. A survey carried out by the Career Management Association on its website found that people made redundant up to the age of 44 remained out of work for an average of 2.8 months. Those aged 45 or over had an average period of unemployment of 18.7 months. Robert Mackmurdo, the CMA secretary, said, 'Our survey highlights the urgency with which the next government needs to outlaw age discrimination in employment.'
>
> (*Source*: Jobs and Money, p. 24, *The Guardian*, 14 April 2001)

- for each complete year of employment in which the employee was below the age of 22, half a week's pay
- for each complete year of employment in which the employee was aged 22 or over but was below the age of 41, one week's pay
- for each complete year of employment in which the employee was aged 41 or over, one and a half weeks' pay.

ACTIVITY 14.3

Consider once again Case study 14.1 and the above information about the rates of pay of the individuals concerned. In order to simplify the calculation, imagine that each of the people concerned has worked for a whole number of years for the organisation.

Mr Brownlow: £350 per week
Mr Mohammed: £300 per week
Mrs Sergeant: £220 per week
Ms Smythe: £180 per week
Mr Gibbs: £130 per week
Mrs Ali: £210 per week
Ms Wilson: £120 per week

How much redundancy pay would each employee be entitled to?

Discussion of Activity 14.3

Mr Brownlow has worked for the organisation for 10 years and is aged 44. He has worked for 3 complete years since age 41, so is entitled to 3 × 1½ weeks' pay = 4½ weeks' pay for that period of time. He has also worked for 7 years between ages 22 and 40, so is entitled to 7 × 1 weeks' pay = 7 weeks' pay.

Therefore Mr Brownlow would be entitled to 11½ weeks' redundancy pay if he were selected for redundancy. His weekly earnings are above the maximum allowed in this calculation, so he would actually be entitled to 11½ × £310 = £3,565.

Mr Mohammed has worked for the organisation for only 3 years and he is aged 34. He would therefore be entitled to 3 × 1 week's pay. Thus he would receive 3 × £270.00 = £810.00.

Mrs Sergeant has worked for the organisation for 20 years and is aged 55. She has worked 14 years since the age of 41 and would be entitled to 14 × 1½ weeks' pay = 21 weeks' pay. She worked for a further 6 years before she was 41 and would be entitled to 6 × 1 weeks' pay = 6 weeks' pay.

The total number of weeks of redundancy pay she is due is therefore 27. Her weekly wage is £220 which is below the maximum entitlement. She would be entitled to 27 × £220 = £5,940.

Mr Gibbs is aged 20 and has worked for the organisation for 2 years. Since he is still under 22 he will only be entitled to 2 × ½ weeks' redundancy pay = 1 week's redundancy pay. His weekly wage is £130 and so he would be entitled only to £130 in redundancy pay.

Sally Wilson and Sandra Smythe would not be entitled to any redundancy pay as they have not worked for the required qualification period of two years.

Tables are provided in the Department for Business, Enterprise and Regulatory Reform's website (formerly the DTI) so their guide to redundancy payments can be used to make this calculation easier.

More favourable redundancy schemes

You will have noticed that the statutory levels for redundancy pay are not very high, especially if the person concerned is young, or has not been employed by the employer for very long. This seems to contradict the huge amounts of redundancy pay that some people are rumoured to receive. This is because some employers have decided to make a more generous provision than is required by law. They may do this in some of the following ways:

- calculating entitlements based on actual pay rather than applying the upper earnings limit
- reducing the length of qualifying period necessary to receive redundancy pay from, for example, two years to one
- adding amounts to the statutory scheme
- making a more generous calculation such as two or three weeks' pay for each year of service.

Outplacement

Employers may also be concerned to help their employees in other ways through this difficult period, and may provide an outplacement service. This is the international name given to the process that many employers use to assist redundant

Did you know?

In the last 10 years even communist and former communist countries which traditionally had enjoyed full employment and jobs for life have had to come to terms with redundancy. In many ways procedures are surprisingly similar to those in the West but there are often some quirky rules that HR managers would need to know. Even in Russia, according to Mike Madgewick, 'legislation is flexible enough to accommodate the enterprise that wishes to dispense with the services of one or a larger group of workers. As with so much in Russia paper rules: therefore the first and most important item is to issue a decree. Ideally one decree needs to be issued for each individual and a signed receipt obtained. The next task is to lodge a list of those affected with the local labour office. Timings are crucial and one must ensure that at least two months' notice is given before the actual terminations (under redundancy) are to be carried out.' According to Madgewick, when selecting for redundancy 'consistency is vital, the principal criteria being length of service, skills, performance and experience. In addition there are special category staff, ignored at one's peril! These include, but are not limited to, pregnant women, those already on maternity leave, single mothers and war veterans.' Two months is the statutory notice period which employees may elect to work. 'There is one small quirk that management needs to be aware of, that is the right to a third month's money if the person is still unemployed at the end of three months.'

(*Source*: Madgewick, M. (1999) Russian redundancy: no longer a contradiction in terms, *Worldlink*, World Federation of Personnel Management Associations, Vol. 9, No. 6, 4–5)

employees. Outplacement can be defined as the process whereby the employer actively helps the employee to come to terms with the redundancy and assists them in the process of finding a new job or developing a new career. It is a type of aftercare service for employees who are facing redundancy, though it is by no means standard practice for all employers to provide such a service. It has been defined by Alan Jones (1994) as 'the provision of support to candidates during the transitional phase between involuntary/voluntary job loss and resettlement'. This is a useful definition as, although much of outplacement is concerned with job search skills and the finding of a new job or career, there are other avenues to explore such as further training or part-time or voluntary work, or perhaps self-employment. This definition also states that support is provided to the candidate, and this makes it clear that the responsibility for the resettlement process still rests with the candidate himself or herself but that help and active support will be given by the outplacement provider.

The CIPD (2003) adopts a similar approach and defines outplacement as:

> Activities designed to enable individuals to develop awareness of their capacities, potential, skills and limitations, to help them to pursue the career opportunities open to them and to manage the transition through a career change or into re-employment following the loss of a job.

Once again the emphasis is on helping the individual during a difficult period but in many ways the fact that the employer provides an outplacement service also gives a very strong message to those who are still employed that they are working for a caring employer even though times may be hard. This is important as managing to keep morale high among the remaining employees can be a very difficult issue during a redundancy period.

While outplacement is generally provided by or for employers, on occasions individuals whose organisation has not provided this facility may buy this provision for themselves, and a similar service is offered in many areas by BERR.

The consultancy firm Penna, Sanders and Sidney published in April 2001 the results of a survey it had conducted called 'Redefining Redundancy'. This 'highlighted a widespread belief that employers have a responsibility to help with the aftermath of redundancy. Yet only a third of respondents said that their employer had helped them to find another job or offered counselling' (CIPD, 2001).

Pause for thought 14.2 What do you think are the main benefits to the employer of providing an outplacement service? Make a list before you read on.

The benefits of providing an outplacement service

Many human resource managers, when faced with making employees redundant, realise that it is important for the organisation to handle this difficult process as smoothly as possible, both for the sake of the individuals concerned and for the morale of the remaining employees, and in order to maintain or even enhance the good reputation of the organisation. In particular, the benefits to the organisation are likely to include:

- improved morale for remaining employees
- key staff are more likely to remain with the organisation if they see that other employees are treated well even in a redundancy situation
- good public relations with the local community will be less likely to be affected by the redundancies if they have been handled well
- there may be fewer problems with objections from trade unions if a good outplacement service is provided.

Individuals vary in the effect that redundancy has on them. For a few people it may provide a welcome opportunity to change direction in their careers, while others who have worked for a long time for an organisation may find redundancy a very traumatic experience with which they need help.

The outplacement process normally consists of provision of the following services:

- Counselling about the feelings brought about by the redundancy itself. This may sometimes involve also counselling the partner of the person who has been made redundant.
- Counselling about career or other options.
- Provision of facilities for conducting a job search.
- Provision of facilities for writing letters of application or curriculum vitae.
- Help with writing curriculum vitae and applications for jobs.
- Psychological tests to assist in career choice.
- Opportunities for practising interview skills.
- Possible direct contact with prospective employers.
- There may be provision of facilities in which interviews can be conducted.

An outplacement service can be provided either 'in-house', by the human resource department, or by external consultants.

ACTIVITY 14.4

List the advantages and the disadvantages of the provision of an in-house outplacement service and compare these with the advantages and disadvantages of external provision of an outplacement service.

Provision of in-house outplacement service

Advantages	Disadvantages

→

Provision of external outplacement service	
Advantages	Disadvantages

Discussion of Activity 14.4

Your list probably indicates that provision of an internal outplacement service is likely to be cheaper than using a consultancy. Since many redundancies occur as part of a cost-cutting exercise, employers will be loath to spend additional money and cost may be a major concern. However, an organisation may not have sufficient facilities or levels of expertise to provide the standard of service that is required. Not only that, but it may be difficult, or even impossible, for redundant employees who have recently been told of their redundancy by their line manager or by the human re-source manager to be helped by counselling from the same manager or any other manager within the organisation. Even identifying managers or others with suitable expertise may be a problem.

On the other hand, there may also be problems in finding a suitable consultancy with a high degree of expertise in this area. Anyone can establish themselves in busi-ness as an outplacement consultant, and they do not necessarily have to have any qualifications. This has been a cause for concern in recent years, with some people being charged high fees for an inadequate service, which resulted in the Chartered Institute of Personnel and Development issuing a *Code for Career and Outplacement Consultants* (2003). This is a voluntary code of practice but gives some indication of the type of service and qualifications that an outplacement service should provide. It indicates that outplacement consultants should normally be able to demonstrate competence in 'the provision of career and outplacement consultancy services by possessing at least one of the following:

- chartered membership of the CIPD (Chartered MCIPD, Chartered FCIPD, Chartered CCIPD)
- registration with the British Psychological Society as a chartered psychologist
- other qualifications in psychology, vocational guidance or counselling recognised by a professional body
- psychometric testing and feedback must be conducted only by holders of the British Psychological Society Level A Statement of Certificate of Competence in Psychological testing. Those conducting personality testing should also hold the British Psychological Society Level B Statement or Certificate in Competence or the equivalent additional training specified by the supplier. Administration of psychological tests can also be carried out by members of the British Psychologi-cal Society Test Administration Certificate.' (CIPD, 2003)

Ideally a firm of consultants would want people who had a range of qualifications in these areas. The CIPD (2003a) differentiates between 'sponsored services where the client is an organisation paying for services provided to an individual or group of individuals' and 'private services where services are provided to clients as individuals for the services they personally receive'. All providers of whatever type of service should let the client know in advance, in writing, about the fees and terms of payment before the signing of any contract. They should also provide a written breakdown detailing exactly the service they will provide.

Conclusion

A discussion of dismissal and redundancy may seem a rather depressing topic but they are not inevitable stages if earlier advice for good human resource practices and procedures is followed.

We have gone through the employment process in an almost chronological order, and examined the approaches of human resource practitioners to finding and selecting people by the use of human resource planning. We have also examined the employment relationship and how people should then be treated while they are working for the organisation, whether as employees or in some other capacity, how they should be trained and developed, and how they should be motivated and rewarded to achieve a high-performance organisation. We considered ways in which some problems may be prevented or, failing prevention, how they should be handled and we discussed this in relation to counselling and welfare, employee involvement, health and safety, and discipline and grievance handling. We have included dismissal and redundancy since it is likely that even with the best planning there will be occasional dismissals, as people operate from different standpoints and have different points of view, and will therefore not always act in the way in which the organisation hopes that they will act.

Dismissal and redundancy can be avoided to some extent by adopting good HRM techniques and programmes described in the rest of the text. Problems associated with redundancy and dismissal, both for employers and employees, will also be minimised by proper handling as described in this chapter.

Just like any other area of HRM, this area is also subject to change, so one needs to be constantly vigilant.

All who are involved in the management of people, whether they call themselves HRM managers, personnel managers or line managers, must be aware of the need for strategic planning and clear links between everyone's work and the aims of the business even though most of you will not initially have the opportunity to operate at a strategic level.

All who are involved in human resource management also need to be aware of the law, and although this may be dealt with in more detail in other specialist modules in your course, we have felt it necessary to include brief summaries of relevant legislation in appropriate chapters for those of you who do not have the opportunity to study employment law modules. As you will have discovered by now, the law is always changing and varies from one country to another, so it is very important to ensure that you know how to find information about the current state of legislation.

REVIEW QUESTIONS

Brief answers to the review questions are provided on page 480.

1 In June 1998, after rioting and damage was caused by football hooligans attending the World Cup matches in France, Tony Blair, the Prime Minister, urged employers to deal severely with those employees found guilty of football hooliganism. Many commentators interpreted this as meaning that such employees should be dismissed. What advice would you give to employers who found that one of their employees was guilty of football hooliganism?

2 Outline the circumstances that are considered to constitute fair dismissal and comment on the extent to which an organisation should be expected to avoid dismissing employees.

SELF-CHECK QUESTIONS

Answer the following multiple-choice questions. The answers are provided on page 480 for you to check your understanding of this chapter.

1 Constructive dismissal is said to occur in which of the following circumstances?
  (a) The employer constructs a false case against the employee in order to dismiss him or her.
  (b) A fixed-term contract expires and is not renewed.
  (c) The employee leaves, with or without giving notice, in circumstances such that he or she is entitled to go without notice by reason of the employer's conduct.
  (d) The employment is terminated by the employer, with or without notice.
  (e) The employee is encouraged to take early retirement.

2 Which of the following is not a potentially fair reason for dismissal?
  (a) misconduct
  (b) lack of capability
  (c) lack of a qualification
  (d) a statutory restriction placed on the employer or on the employee
  (e) the employee has only worked for the organisation for six months.

3 Which of the following is a good definition of outplacement?
  (a) The employee is placed temporarily in another organisation with a view to improving their job chances.
  (b) The employee is actively helped by the employer to come to terms with the redundancy and assisted in finding a new job or developing a new career.
  (c) A form of job share that is introduced to minimise the need for redundancies.
  (d) Another word for the redundancy process.
  (e) A service provided by consultants to employers to help them out when faced with redundancies.

4 Which of the following should *not* be one of the steps to take to minimise the need for redundancy?
  (a) Give people the option of early retirement packages.
  (b) Use natural wastage over a period of time instead of making employees redundant.

(c) Dismiss all employees who do not have the necessary length of employment to bring a case for unfair dismissal.

(d) Terminate the use of non-employees such as self-employed or agency staff.

(e) Ask for voluntary redundancies.

5 An employer must disclose certain information to the trade unions before making people redundant. Which of the following is not one of the things that the employer must disclose at this stage?

(a) the names of the people to be made redundant

(b) the reasons for the dismissals

(c) the proposed method of selection for redundancy

(d) the method of carrying out the redundancies

(e) the number and description of employees likely to be involved in redundancy.

HR IN THE NEWS

FT

Europe: OECD warns unfair dismissal lawsuits discouraging French job creation

By Martin Arnold

The odds seem stacked against French companies when they try to sack staff. Two out of three cases for unfair dismissal in France end with the plaintiff winning or being awarded an out-of-court settlement, according to a new report by the justice ministry, reports Martin Arnold in Paris.

The risk of being embroiled in a long and costly lawsuit was one of the reasons France's unemployment rate of 9.6 per cent was higher than that of most other industrialised countries, said Raymond Torres, head of employment analysis and policy at the Organisation for Economic Co-operation and Development (OECD).

Mr Torres said that in France unfair dismissal lawsuits took on average at least a year to settle, compared with four weeks in the UK and three to four months in Germany. This made employers reluctant to take on new staff.

He said the probability of losing lawsuits was a bigger brake on job creation than the cost of paying redundancy money to sacked workers – though this is also higher in France, where a worker with 20 years' service gets 16 to 18 months' compensation, compared with only eight months' pay in the UK.

France has one of the lowest employment rates in the OECD for people aged 15 to 24, with only 26.4 per cent of its young people in work. Mr Torres said high unemployment benefits and relatively low back-to-work bonuses did little to encourage people to seek jobs.

(*Financial Times*, 31 March 2006. Reproduced with permission.)

Questions

1 How does the unfair dismissal in France that is described in this article differ from the situation in the UK?

2 How does the redundancy situation in France differ from that of the UK?

3 Similar statements that legislation is to blame for UK employers being reluctant to employ new staff are also sometimes made in the press. To what extent do you agree or disagree that employment legislation discourages employers from taking on new staff? What is your evidence for or against this?

WHAT NEXT?

1 Go to **www.acas.org.uk** and view the short video about the role that ACAS conciliation officers play prior to a case going to an employment tribunal.

2 Visit an employment tribunal to hear a case of alleged unfair dismissal. Assess the merits of each side's case and decide whether or not you think the participants in the case followed the statutory disciplinary dismissal and grievance procedures. A list of employment tribunals and further guidance about bringing cases to employment tribunals can be found at: **www.employmenttribunals.gov.uk**.

3 The procedures for employment tribunals are due to be reviewed in 2008. Check on our website **www.pearsoned.co.uk/foothook** whether there has been any change to the procedures since this edition of the book was published.

References

Advisory, Conciliation and Arbitration Service (2007) *Annual Report 2006–2007,* ACAS.

Chartered Institute of Personnel and Development (2003) *Code for Career and Outplacement Consultants,* CIPD.

Chartered Institute of Personnel and Development (2006a) *Age discrimination and retirement: member resource,* CIPD (www.cipd.co.uk; accessed 03.08.07).

Chartered Institute of Personnel and Development (2006b) *Wrongful dismissal,* CIPD (www.cipd.co.uk; accessed 04.08.07).

Chartered Institute of Personnel and Development (2007a) *Unfair dismissal: member resource,* CIPD (www.cipd.co.uk/EmploymentLaw/FAQ/_Redundancy/Redundancy.htm; accessed 12.09.07).

Chartered Institute of Personnel and Development (2007b) *Redundancy Fact Sheet,* CIPD (www.cipd.co.uk/subjects/emplaw/redundancy/redundancy.htm; accessed 12.09.07).

Department of Trade and Industry (1998a) *Fairness at Work,* Cm, 3968, DTI, May, Chapter 3 (www.berr.gov.uk/files/file24436.pdf; accessed 12.09.07).

Department of Trade and Industry (1998b) *Redundancy Consultation: Current Practice and the Effects of the 1995 Regulations,* DTI (www.berr.gov.uk/files/file11490.pdf; accessed 12.09.07).

Department of Trade and Industry (2003) *High Performance Workplaces: Informing and Consulting Employees,* DTI (www.berr.gov.uk/files/file21267.pdf; accessed 12.09.07).

European Industrial Relations Observatory online (2001) Industrial relations aspects of mergers and takeovers, February (www.eurofound.europa.eu/eiro/2001/02/study/tn0102401s.html; accessed 12.09.07).

Jones, A. (1994) *Delivering In-House Outplacement. A Practical Guide for Trainers, Managers and Personnel Specialists,* McGraw-Hill.

Monks, J. (2001) TUC welcomes French decision, TUC press release, 9 April (www.tuc.org.uk/international/tuc-3030-f0.cfm; accessed 12.09.07).

Sage, G. (1998) Health warning, *People Management,* 16 April, Vol. 4, No. 8, 23.

Further study

Books

Advisory, Conciliation and Arbitration Service (2005 (print)/2006 (web)) Advisory booklet, *Redundancy Handling,* ACAS. An excellent, clear guide to good practice (available at www.acas.org.uk/index.aspx?articleid=747; accessed 12.09.07).

Advisory, Conciliation and Arbitration Service (2001) *The ACAS Arbitration Scheme for the Resolution of Unfair Dismissal Disputes – A Guide to the Scheme,* ACAS.

Articles

Chartered Institute of Personnel and Development (2007b) *Redundancy Fact Sheet,* CIPD. This provides a useful summary of the key issues affecting redundancy.

Chiumento, R. (2003) How to support the survivors of redundancy, *People Management,* Vol. 9, No. 3, 48–9. This discusses what to do to help motivate those who have not been made redundant.

Other sources

ACAS telephone advice service. There are ACAS offices in most large towns and you should be able to find them in the telephone book. Alternatively, Department for Business, Enterprise and Regulatory Reform offices such as Job Centres should be able to give you their telephone number, which is also listed in BERR booklets.

Internet

Advisory, Conciliation and Arbitration Service   **www.acas.org.uk**
A very useful source of information relating to dismissal and redundancy in Britain.

Department for Business, Enterprise and Regulatory Reform   **www.berr.gov.uk**
Many useful publications relating to redundancy and dismissal in Britain can be found on this site.

Employment tribunals   **www.employmenttribunals.gov.uk**
A useful site for everything to do with tribunals.

European Industrial Relations Observatory   **www.eiro.eurofound.ie**
This has up-to-date information about issues in industrial relations, including redundancy and dismissal, throughout the EU member states and Norway.

European Trade Union Confederation   **www.etuc.org**
This provides information from the unions' and workers' perspective but on a European dimension.

Trades Union Congress (TUC)   **www.tuc.org.uk**
Lots of information from the perspective of the unions and employees relating to redundancy and dismissal. This also has a useful section for students.

Worldlink   **www.wfpma.com/pubs.html**
A journal with articles on international aspects of managing people at work.

Answers to review and self-check questions

We have provided a skeleton guide to issues you might address in answering review questions. In an exam or for an assignment, you would be expected to develop the ideas more fully to show your understanding of the topic. You can also enhance your response by making references to further reading.

Chapter 1 Introducing human resource management

Answers to review questions

It is not possible to provide model answers to the review questions for Chapter 1 because you will all have arrived at very individual answers to the activities suggested.

Answers to self-check questions

1 (c). **2** (c). **3** (b). **4** (d). **5** (a).

Chapter 2 Human resource strategy and planning

Answers to review questions

1 ● The levels of strategy are corporate, business and functional.
   ● You might wish to review the generic strategies associated with the corporate level (growth; stability; retrenchment) and the business level (cost competitiveness; differentiation of products or services; focus on a niche in the market). In general, it is expected that business strategies will grow out of corporate strategies and functional strategies will grow out of business strategies. However, each level can provide useful information for the others. Human resource strategies will have a direct impact on all the other functional strategies, and conversely cannot be formulated without knowledge of what the other functional goals are.
2 ● Name the major stages and describe how each is carried out.
   ● Development of the corporate plan: issues and information to be considered.
   ● Estimate demand for human resources: techniques such as work study.
   ● Estimate the internal supply of human resources: skills inventory; effects of labour turnover.
   ● Gather and analyse information about the external labour market. Labour force issues.
   ● Formulate human resource action plans: describe the functional areas.
   ● Comment on the need for evaluation and feedback into the corporate objectives.

3 ● Comment on the decisions made throughout the human resource planning process: what the corporate objectives are to be; what skills are required to achieve these objectives; how the organisation decides whether it has these skills; what action is to be taken.

 ● Describe the sources of information for each of these areas: knowledge of product and market developments; the need for environmental scanning; managerial judgement; HRIS; statistical information about the labour force.

4 Skills shortages occur when employers have vacancies they have difficulty in filling. Skills gaps occur within the existing workforce.

 Skills shortages may mean that the desired competencies are not available in the labour market, but it may also be that people with those skills are not attracted to the particular employer or do not wish to take on that type of job for some reason. Employers have a number of options: provide training; review pay and terms and conditions; develop and promote their employer brand; recruit overseas; focus on diversity if this has previously limited their recruitment practices.

Answers to self-check questions

1 Growth; stability; retrenchment. 2 Cost leadership; differentation, focus. 3 50%. 4 80%. 5 Problems or success with keeping long-term employees. 6 Estimate the supply of human resources. 7 Operational. 8 UK; other countries in the EU; USA. You should be able to find more examples of countries with the same issue.

Chapter 3 High-performance working: employee engagement through involvement and participation

Answers to review questions

1 ● Outline the concepts of unitarism and pluralism.
 ● Outline the concepts of participation and involvement; state how they differ from each other; identify each concept correctly as a unitary or pluralist idea.

2 ● Define employee involvement and give examples of individual techniques such as quality circles.
 ● Define commitment as an attitude; explain how this attitude might motivate towards more productive behaviour.
 ● Explain that engagement is identified when employees in fact do deliver the sought-after discretionary effort.
 ● Link the involvement initiatives you have described with motivation concepts; e.g. quality circles provide employees with feelings of responsibility and achievement because they see they can contribute their ideas. This in turn should contribute to the development of a high-performance workplace.

3 You will have to read some of the references in order to gather more information for this question. Your answer should address developments on both a national and EU-wide scale.

4 You should have identified elements such as employment security, and information for employees and consultation with them to ensure an adequate channel for employee voice. Partnership recognises that employees are stakeholders in an organisation and have an interest in its success.

 The aim of partnership is to improve productivity and competitiveness by fully engaging the capabilities of employees.

Answers to self-check questions

1 (*c*). **2** False. **3** At least 1,000 employees within the member states and at least 150 employees in each of any two member states. **4** (*b*) and (*d*). **5** (*b*). **6** False. **7**. Save As You Earn. **8** Team briefing; employer and employee publications; company videos; electronic news systems; roadshows. **9** (*d*). **10** Communication and evidence that it is sincere; managers who promote EI and adopt an appropriate style.

Chapter 4 The employment relationship

Answers to review questions 1–3

1 It is not possible to forecast what you may discover when perusing recent articles or court cases because although some issues remain contentious for many years, there are always new issues arising too. However, you will probably notice that some new issues can be directly linked to new legislation which needs to be interpreted. The meaning of new employment legislation is often tested in employment tribunals and the appeal courts.

Through doing this exercise, you will have further developed your competence in finding information. We hope you will also reflect on your learning. If you have done so, you may have realised a few implications, including the following:

- New issues are constantly arising in the HRM field, and practitioners need to stay abreast of developments by engaging in activities similar to the one you have just completed.
- You can adapt this activity to other issues too, such as unlawful discrimination, unfair dismissal, redundancy.

2 Annual leave; paternity leave: number of days/weeks allowed; may pay during paternity leave; may give more notice of termination of employment; maternity pay provisions may be more generous than the statutory minimum.

3 Employers use flexible working arrangements to minimise the amount of time that employees are underemployed and yet being paid. Employers also benefit from being able to call on different people at different times if they approach diversity in a strategic fashion, and this may also lead to a good employer image and a more creative workforce with high levels of job satisfaction. Employees look for flexible working arrangements in order to achieve an acceptable balance between personal and work commitments.

Flexible working arrangements include part-time work, annualised hours, teleworking, job sharing and fixed-term contracts. Go back and review Chapter 4 to ensure you have a good grasp of the pros and cons of these arrangements. There are many possible arrangements that can be made, and we have referred you to some sources if you are interested in following this up.

Answers to self-check questions

1 (*c*). **2** Express terms are those that are addressed directly; implied terms are those that are not expressed directly but are taken as assumed. **3** Fidelity; obedience of lawful and reasonable orders; and working with due diligence and care. **4** Nine weeks. **5** One week. **6** Employment Rights Act. **7** 26 weeks. **8** False. **9** False. **10** Isolation of employees; difficulties with supervision.

Chapter 5 Equality and diversity

Answers to review questions

1 ● You should name and describe each relevant Act and Regulation, including: Sex Discrimination Act 1975; Race Relations Act 1976; Disability Discrimination Act 1995; Employment Equality (Sexual Orientation) Regulations 2003; Employment Equality (Religion or Belief) Regulations 2003; Employment Equality (Age) Regulations 2006; Rehabilitation of Offenders Act 1974; Equal Pay Act 1970.
  ● Can you give a good description of the protection that each of these Acts provides?
  ● Explain what is meant by direct discrimination, indirect discrimination, victimisation, and harassment.
  ● Discuss the need for equality policies, their integration into procedures, and the need for training and awareness throughout an organisation.
  ● You might also comment that some employers are looking to go beyond equality of opportunity by encouraging the active management of diversity in the workforce.

2 *Direct discrimination* occurs when someone is treated less favourably for a reason directly to do with his or her sex, marital status (i.e. being married), race or racial origin, etc.

Indirect discrimination occurs when someone is treated unfairly because of some provision, criterion or practice that would disproportionately exclude the particular group that person belongs to, and when the requirement cannot be objectively justified.

Victimisation occurs when someone is treated less favourably because that person has made a complaint or indicated an intention to make a complaint about sex or race discrimination.

Harassment is defined as unwanted conduct that intimidates or humiliates an individual, affecting their dignity or creating a hostile work environmont.

3 Diversity is about celebrating the differences between people, and using these to enhance creativity, problem-solving, productivity and responsiveness to customer needs. A well managed diverse group of people should experience greater job satisfaction and appreciate their employer for their commitment to equality. Managing a diverse group of people calls for managers to recognise the value of what each person can bring to the workplace and to adopt a style which will encourage every member of the workforce to reach their full potential. In order to obtain and retain a diverse workforce, organisations will have to develop flexible working arrangements to suit the needs of various workers.

Answers to self-check questions

1 (*c*). 2 (*b*). 3 (*b*). 4 (*b*). 5 (*b*).

Chapter 6 Recruitment

Answers to review questions 2 and 4

2 ● Explain how each section of these documents is part of a systematic approach to recruitment and can help in designing a job advertisement.
  ● Comment on the need to give information of this kind so prospective applicants can engage in an informed process of self-selection.

4
- Effects of an internal recruitment policy; the message that the employer rewards good performance.
- Adoption of, and commitment to, an equality policy.
- Treating people well and with respect in any telephone, written or personal contact.

Answers to self-check questions

1 Is the post necessary at all? Can the tasks be distributed among other employees? Can the post be filled as a job share position? **2** Local or national newspapers; professional journals; online. **3** Company name; job title; tasks expressed as opportunities; competencies required; how to apply and by when. **4** No. **5** False.

Chapter 7 Selection: shortlisting and interviews

Answers to review questions

1 The aim of selection is to 'choose the best person for the job'. Selectors gather and analyse information in an attempt to predict the performance of applicants in the job. This must be done as objectively as possible by matching evidence of the knowledge, skills and personal qualities of applicants with the requirements outlined in the person specification. The selection process must also be fair, avoiding any unlawful discrimination in terms of sex, race and disability etc.

Methodical approaches include:
- having a selection policy and procedure which define the steps that will be followed in filling any vacancy
- using the person specification as a checklist when shortlisting applicants
- devising a set of standard questions to cover all the requirements on the person specification
- gathering a full set of information from all candidates and using this information to assess their suitability for the post.

Making sure that candidates can assess their own suitability for a post is also part of effective selection. Employers should therefore ensure that there is adequate opportunity for applicants to gather information about the organisation and the post during the selection process.

2 Validity and reliability are terms used in statistics to report on the results of tests. If a test consistently produces similar results when used at different times and administered by different people, then it would score high in reliability. Thus if an applicant was interviewed for a particular post by Mr Smith on Monday morning, and the same applicant was interviewed for the same post by Mr Jones on Friday afternoon, we would expect the same result if we thought that the interview was a reliable test. Research has, however, shown that interviews can be low in reliability.

Validity is an indicator of how well the test measures what it purports to measure. How well do interviews predict good performance on the job? Again, research has indicated that interviews can be low in validity. It must, however, be noted that a structured approach to interviewing can raise the level of both the reliability and the validity of employment interviews.

3 Employment interviews run a particular risk of being low in validity if they are approached in an unstructured fashion with the interviewers not properly prepared, and simply asking whatever they think is relevant in an impromptu manner. In these circumstances, interviewers are more likely to fall prey to perceptual errors than if they were conducting a structured interview.

Perceptual errors include the halo effect, the contrast effect, hiring in one's own image, and quite simply not gathering sufficient and relevant data.

These perceptual errors can be avoided simply by being aware of them and making a conscious effort to resist them. If a structured interview is conducted using a set of questions which is designed to elicit full information related to the person specification, and an attempt is made to assess all candidates objectively against these criteria, then the validity of the interview process should also increase.

4 The different types of questions that can be asked include open, closed, leading, probing, situational, and behavioural (or competency-based) questions. Each kind of question will typically elicit a different sort of response from applicants, so interviewers should carefully design their questions to gain the specific information they are seeking.

Closed questions can be used to confirm information. However, the interview is an opportunity to gain as much information as possible, and open questions are more likely to encourage applicants to talk freely. Most questions used in an interview should therefore be open questions. Probing questions can also be used to clarify points or seek more in-depth information.

Leading questions, which indicate to the interviewee what the expected response is, are not useful.

Experienced interviewers can make good use of situational and behavioural (or competency-based) questions. These require applicants to address their own behaviour in incidents which are typical of the post. Behavioural questions assume that applicants have previous related experience, whereas situational questions address what an applicant *would do* if faced with a particular situation in the future.

Answers to self-check questions

1 (c). **2** False. **3** (b). **4** (d). **5** (d). **6**(i) (c). **6**(ii) (b). **7** (a). **8** Behavioural. **9** Equality monitoring.

Chapter 8 Selection: supplementing the interview

Answers to self-check questions

1 (b). **2** Validity. **3** No. **4** True. **5** (c). **6** (b). **7** False. **8** (b). **9** False. **10** (b).

Chapter 9 Performance management and appraisal

Answers to review questions

1 Outline how performance appraisal motivates employees and improves relations: provides better understanding of, and agreement on, goals; gives opportunities for praise/positive feedback; encourages agreement on training needs/use of appraisal for staff development; and results in improved communication. Performance appraisal should therefore help individuals and their team to contribute to the organisation's goals.

You will achieve an even better answer by linking these factors with concepts from motivation theories (growth, achievement, etc.).

Reasons for failure:

Lack of managerial skill and training. Explore typical managerial failures such as inability to give critical feedback. This could be in relation to lack of planning and preparation, poor interpersonal skills such as interview skills, poor communications skills, inability to build and develop teams and give feedback to individuals or team, etc. Also indicate that processes can be counterproductive, and comment on the need for managerial training and for commitment to the system.

Address the use of appraisal systems for conflicting purposes: development and pay decisions may conflict, and comment on the lack of employee involvement in the appraisal system.

2 You should identify and describe three different approaches to performance appraisal, e.g. individual appraisal done by supervisor/manager, peer appraisal and 360° appraisal.

The general benefits relate to improved performance, motivation, communication and relationships. The actual nature of these benefits will need to be discussed in relation to the particular approach used.

Other general benefits include the opportunity to focus on future developments and to achieve organisational goals.

You might also mention the pitfalls, such as problems if there is lack of clarity in the purpose of the appraisal, e.g. reward or development. You may also mention skills needed in giving feedback and discuss in relation to approaches used, e.g. in peer appraisal, would everyone have the required level of skills and not have personal vendettas to settle?

There is also, regardless of the approach chosen, a need to encourage ownership and participation.

Answers to self-check questions

1 (c). **2** (a). **3** (c). **4** (a). **5** (b). **6** (a).

Chapter 10 Learning and development

Answers to review questions

1 It is impossible once again to give answers to this question as your answer will be individual to you.

2 There is a huge amount of information on the Internet relating to these topics. Once you have chosen your topic and found information you will need to list all the key benefits from the introduction of that topic if you are to persuade a line manager about the topic. Consider the benefits to the organisation and the individual and particularly the potential benefits to the line manager, such as greater efficiency and higher productivity and an easier job with a more highly trained workforce.

3 If you interview someone from a large organisation you are likely to find that learning and development is tied in very clearly with the strategic plan and objectives of the organisation and there are likely to be clear objectives set for the learning and development department which clearly contribute to the overall objectives of the organisation. This is not the case in all organisations and some may still operate without making these links.

4 Answers should include comments on the cost involved in designing and running an induction programme, but should generally identify the benefits of easing a new employee into the workforce and how this is likely to result in a speedier route to full productivity, less labour turnover and fewer bad work habits being acquired. There should then be an outline of a suitable induction programme spread over some time.

5 Answers should define each concept and list the pros and cons of each, e.g. learning-by-doing in a realistic environment versus cost of errors and distractions. You should explain which technique you feel is the more successful overall.

Answers to self-check questions

1 (*a*). **2** (a) This effect is known as a *conditioned response*. (b) The cat food is the *stimulus* for Caroline's cats to make an appearance. (c) *Association.* The cats have started to associate the sound of the kettle with the cat food being put out. (d) In time the sound of the kettle becomes the *conditioned stimulus,* and the cats' response to it becomes the *conditioned response*. **3** No. **4** (*b*). **5** No. **6** (*b*). **7** (*c*). **8** (*b*). **9** Yes. **10** (*d*).

Chapter 11 Payment systems

Answers to review questions

1 and **2** provide you with the opportunity to practise skills and seek relevant, up-to-date information for yourself and as such it is impossible to provide guideline answers here. The 'Pay and benefits bulletin', contained in the *IRS Employment Review,* is published twice a month and is an extremely useful source of articles and up-to-date information about pay and benefits in various sectors and organisations. This may be of help in getting the latest information on the minimum wage or rates paid to people on apprenticeships or New Deal. Publications such as *People Management* or *Personnel Today* may also prove useful, as should quality newspapers.

3 Your answer should define job evaluation as a method of deciding on the value of a job and address the need for a methodical approach. The points rating method and its main benefits should then be outlined. Benefits of the points rating approach to job evaluation include the fact that all jobs are rated using the same method and that these must be perceived to be fair. It is comparatively simple to use and understand and is analytical in nature.

The second part of your answer should examine perceptions of fairness. Involvement of representatives of the workforce in the design and implementation of job evaluation is likely to improve employees' perceptions of whether or not the system is fair. The points rating method is an analytical approach to job evaluation and so does break each job into parts rather than analysing the whole job. This is generally regarded as being more objective and hence fairer than non-analytical schemes. It is also more likely that this system could be justified in a tribunal if an equal pay/value claim was brought against the organisation. In order to be fair the Revised Code of Practice on Equal Pay should also be followed.

4 Your answer will describe issues such as internal and external relativities and differentials. You will also include and take account of the issues raised by legislation such as the Equal Pay Act 1970 and the Equal Pay (Amendment) Regulations 1983. Systems of job evaluation which try to ensure that fair systems of pay are in place need to be discussed. Those based on analytical methods of job evaluation are likely to result in fairer systems and it will be easier to prove the fairness, if necessary. Involvement of representatives of the workforce in the design and implementation of job evaluation is likely to improve employees' perceptions of whether or not the system is fair.

Better answers will also comment on issues such as performance-related pay and how this may affect perceptions of fairness. They should also refer to the revised Code of Practice on Equal Pay, published by the Equal Opportunities Commission (2003), and to the Equal Pay (1970) (Amendment) Regulations 2004. The five stages of the EOC's pay review model should also be fully discussed.

5 Your answer should be in report form as if you are a consultant employed to advise this organisation. You need to describe various forms of both the analytical and non-analytical forms of job evaluation and outline the advantages and disadvantages of each. You should then decide on a scheme that you feel is most suitable for this organisation and make recommendations about its use. You are more likely to recommend an analytical form of job evaluation such as the points rating system. This would have benefits of being easy to justify but may be time-consuming to introduce. However, since we are making recommendations for a fairly small organisation, cost is also likely be an issue here and this form of analytical job evaluation will probably be cheaper to install than any designed or provided by a firm of consultants. Better answers would also refer to the need for fairness in whatever scheme is introduced and the need to involve members of the workforce in decisions about which scheme should be chosen. Reference should also be made to the need to take into account legislation, for example the Equal Pay (1970) (Amendment) Regulations 2004, and also the guidance provided in the EOC Code of Practice on Equal Pay (2003) and pay review model.

Answers to self-check questions

(a) No. **(b)** No. **(c)** No. **(d)** Yes. **(e)** Yes. **(f)** No. **(g)** No. **(h)** No. **(i)** Yes. **(j)** No.

Chapter 12 Health, safety and welfare

Answers to review questions

It is once again impossible to give ideal answers to the review questions here as your answers will depend on who you talk to or the organisations you analyse.

Answers to self-check questions

1 (*d*). **2** (*d*). **3** (*c*). **4** (*b*). **5** (*d*). **6** (*d*).

7 The safety committee should have been a means of ensuring cooperation between management and the workforce and also as a method of ensuring improvements in health and safety in the workplace. In particular, the committee should:

Study figures and trends for accidents and notifiable diseases so that they have raised the issue or are aware and involved in the decision to introduce new safety equipment to prevent accidents happening.

Examine safety audit reports so that they are aware of the main areas where accidents are occurring and can make recommendations for improvements and the introduction of new safety equipment.

Consider reports and factual information provided by inspectors. At this point there has not been any report from the inspectors for them to study.

Consider the reports of safety representatives. Once again, they should have been aware from the reports that the safety representatives had made of the need for improvements in health and safety and for the need for suitable safety equipment.

Assist in the development of safety rules and safe systems of work. On the basis of the evidence collected from the various sources already mentioned, they should be helping the management to formulate disciplinary rules and to choose appropriate safety equipment and assess its suitability for use in the workplace. They should also be involved in publicising the changes, assist in the provision of advice and help the management with training, if required to do so.

Monitor the effectiveness of safety training in the workplace. The safety committee should be concerned to make comparisons after new safety procedures are introduced, and they should compare accident rates. If the procedures are inadequate, as in this case, they should be pressing the management to obtain more appropriate safety equipment.

Monitor the effectiveness of the safety and health communication in the workplace. The safety committee should be checking to ensure that the communication about the new safety equipment is adequate and should assist the management in designing new materials if it is inadequate.

Encourage publicity for health and safety programmes in the workplace. Support the management's efforts and publicity and encourage competitions to publicise health and safety changes.

Provide a link with the appropriate inspectorates. In this case, the inspectorates have not yet become involved. The committee could get further information from them and if the management do not handle the situation in a reasonable manner, they could inform the inspectorates of the dangers in the workplace and ask for them to inspect.

8 Improvements that a consultant might advise should be introduced at the Sheffley Company are likely to include the following:

Improve training for the supervisors and management in health and safety.

Appoint a trained safety officer.

Improve communication methods.

Encourage managers and supervisors to set a good example to the workforce.

Encourage managers and supervisors to investigate all accidents fully and to examine the statistics to identify trends.

Involve groups from the workforce including safety representatives and members of the safety committee in the design of a safety policy.

Publicise the policy.

Carry out exercises to assess risks in various parts of the workplace.

Appoint a competent person besides the safety officer to assess risks.

Introduce control measures in order to eliminate or minimise risks, e.g. substitute safer equipment or materials, improve design, replan procedures, and use protective clothing.

Monitor systems that are introduced.

Chapter 13 Discipline and grievance

Answers to review questions

It is impossible to give model answers for questions **1–3** as these require you to conduct your own research, so you may all have slightly different findings.

4 Your answer should be in the form of a report addressed to the general manager. When the organisation only employed 18 staff there was no legal requirement for it to have a grievance procedure, although it would still have been good practice to have had one. Now, since there are 100 employees there is a legal requirement to produce a grievance procedure (Employment Rights Act 1996).

You should explain not only the importance of the legal situation to the general manager, but also make clear that grievance procedures provide a useful way for employees to express their grievances, rather than becoming dissatisfied and expressing the grievance by poor-quality work or by leaving the organisation altogether.

A model grievance procedure should be described in order to show what the grievance procedure should contain. This should be modelled on ACAS, *Producing Discipline and Grievance Procedures: Self-help Guide* (2002). Key features should include: an informal stage before the formal procedure is reached; grievances should be settled as near to the source of grievance as possible, at the lowest level; a number of stages involving different people; time limits for responding at each stage and a right of appeal at each stage. There should also be a right to be accompanied by a friend or trade union official.

Answers to self-check questions

1 (c). **2** (d). **3** (b). **4** (c). **5** (d). **6** (c). **7** (e). **8** (a). **9** (e). **10** (e).

Chapter 14 Dismissal, redundancy and outplacement

Answers to review questions

1 Remember that offences that occur outside work are not automatic reasons to dismiss an employee. ACAS advises that what is important is the nature of the offence and whether it destroys the employer's confidence in that employee. According to *The Guardian,* a CBI source described Mr Blair's comments as a legal minefield. Employers' organisations, civil servants and lawyers cautioned against the difficulties of sacking a worker for a conviction overseas, saying an employer would be open to legal challenge. The onus would be on proving that the organisation's reputation was being damaged and the statutory discipline, dismissal and grievance procedure would also have to be followed. Even dismissing someone because they are not able to do their job because they are in prison has been found by many organisations to not necessarily be a good enough reason for dismissal.

2 You should outline the 6 main grounds for potentially fair dismissal as: misconduct, lack of capability, redundancy, statutory bar, retirement or some other substantial reason. Better answers are likely to give examples of these types of potentially fair reasons for dismissal.

You should also explain that the process followed for dismissals is as important as the reason for the dismissal and that the employer must act reasonably. This means that they must carry out a full investigation and follow the statutory discipline, dismissal and grievance procedure. Better answers are also likely to mention that some forms of dismissal are considered to be automatically unfair and for these there is only a one-stage process undertaken by the employment tribunals. You should outline some of the automatically unfair reasons for dismissal and indicate why these are designated as such.

You should express some considered opinion about the extent to which you feel that employers should try to avoid dismissals of employees. This is likely to include comment about managers taking early action to avoid the development of problems; the use of counselling skills by managers; the use of HRM planning to help avoid the need for redundancies; planned retirements and following 'the duty to consider' a request to work beyond normal retirement; the training and development of employees if skills need change; a proper recruitment and selection process to help minimise numbers of dismissals. Following good HRM policies and procedures should help to minimise costs involved. Sometimes, however, it is still necessary to dismiss and then it must be for a fair reason and must be handled reasonably in accordance with the statutory discipline, dismissal and grievance procedure.

Answers to self-check questions

1 (c). **2** (e). **3** (b). **4** (c). **5** (a).

Author index

Subject index